MACROECONOMICS

MACROECONOMICS

TENTH

Richard G. Lipsey

Simon Fraser University

CANADIAN

Christopher T. S. Ragan

McGill University

EDITION

Addison
Wesley
Longman

Toronto

Canadian Cataloguing in Publication Data

Lipsey, Richard G., 1928-
    Macroeconomics

10th Canadian ed.
ISBN 0-201-66471-2

1. Macroeconomics. I. Ragan, Christopher. II. Title.

HB172.5.L733   2001   339   C00-930277-8

0-201-66471-2

Vice President, Editorial Director: Michael Young
Acquisitions Editor: Dave Ward
Marketing Manager: James Buchanan
Developmental Editor: Maurice Esses
Production Editor: Mary Ann McCutcheon
Copy Editor: Edie Franks
Production Coordinator: Deborah Starks
Page Layout: Carol Magee
Permissions and Photo Research: Susan Wallace-Cox
Art Director: Mary Opper
Interior Design: Anthony Leung
Cover Design: Artville LLC
Cover Image: Artville LLC

2 3 4 5   05 04 03 02 01

Printed and bound in the United States

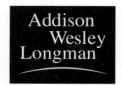

BRIEF CONTENTS

v

CONTENTS

LIST OF BOXES

Applying Economic Concepts

Extensions in Theory

Lessons from History

TO THE INSTRUCTOR

Economics is a living discipline, changing and evolving in response to developments in the world economy and in response to the research of many thousands of economists throughout the world. Through ten editions, *Macroeconomics* has evolved with the discipline. Our purpose in this edition, as in the previous nine, is to provide students with an introduction to the major issues facing the world's economies, to the methods that economists use to study those issues, and to the policy problems that those issues create. Our treatment is everywhere guided by three important principles:

1. Economics is *scientific,* in the sense that it progresses through the systematic confrontation of theory by evidence. Neither theory nor data alone can tell us much about the world, but combined they tell us a great deal.

2. Economics is *useful* and it should be seen by students to be so. An understanding of economic theory combined with knowledge about the economy produces many important insights about economic policy. Although we stress these insights, we are also careful to point out cases where too little is known to support strong statements about public policy. Appreciating what is not known is as important as learning what is known.

3. We strive always to be *honest* with our readers. Although we know that economics is not always easy, we do not approve of glossing over difficult bits of analysis without letting readers see what is happening and what has been assumed. We take whatever space is needed to explain why economists draw their conclusions, rather than just asserting the conclusions. We also take pains to avoid simplifying matters so much that students would have to unlearn what they have been taught if they continue their study beyond the introductory course. In short, we have tried to follow Albert Einstein's advice:

   Everything should be made as simple as possible, but not simpler.

Current Economic Issues

In writing the tenth edition of *Macroeconomics,* we have tried to reflect the major economic issues that we face as we begin the twenty-first century.

Globalization

Enormous changes have occurred throughout the world over the last few decades. Flows of trade and investment between countries have risen so dramatically that it is now common to speak of the "globalization" of the world economy. Today it is no longer possible to study any economy without taking into account developments in the rest of the world.

What is true for most countries is also true for Canada. Economic relations between Canada and the rest of the world have a significant impact on most of the major "domestic" issues in the news.

For example, some observers believe that the difficulties faced by Canadian farmers in recent years is caused partly by subsidies that U.S. and European governments provide to their farmers. Students should know how subsidies to foreign farmers affect farmers in Canada. They should also be able to discuss the overall costs and benefits to Canada from agricultural income-support policies, whether they are subsidies or supply-management schemes.

In recent years, many Canadians have begun worrying about a possible "brain drain" to the United States. The fear is that Canada's "best and brightest" are leaving in increasing numbers, in pursuit of greater employment prospects, lower income taxes, and higher living standards available south of the border. How mobile is labour across international borders? Does such labour mobility imply that Canada's policies cannot diverge significantly from those in other countries? We explore these issues at various points throughout the book.

Another example of the importance of globalization for domestic policy is related to the Asian economic crisis that began in the summer of 1997 and lasted into 1999. The Asian crisis represented both a negative demand shock and a positive supply shock for Canada. The importance of the open economy appears throughout the macroeconomics half of the book—we place a greater emphasis on the importance of exchange rates than we have in past editions.

The forces of globalization are with us to stay. In this tenth edition of *Macroeconomics,* we have done our best to ensure that students are made aware of the world outside Canada and of how events elsewhere in the world affect the Canadian economy.

Transition and Development

Over the past decade, the century-long ideological conflict between capitalism and communism has virtually ended. The most powerful communist economy in the world, the Soviet Union, has disappeared, both as a nation and as a planned economy. Mixed capitalism, the system of economic organization that has long prevailed in much of the industrialized world, now prevails in virtually all of it. Many of the developing economies are also moving in this direction. The reasons for the failure of the planned economies of Eastern Europe and the Soviet Union are discussed in Chapter 1 as a contrast to the reasons for the relative success of mixed capitalism.

Developing countries face many of the same problems being experienced by the transition economies of Eastern Europe and the former Soviet Union. Countries in the developing world have been trying—some for many years—to make the difficult transformation from agricultural-based economies to industrialized ones. In many cases, they lack the same institutions that the centrally planned economies had failed to develop. Thus the "development" challenges faced by these economies are very similar to the "transition" challenges faced by the formerly centrally planned economies. We discuss the challenges faced by the developing economies in Chapter 33, which builds on the more fundamental discussion of long-term economic growth in Chapter 32.

The Role of Government

The political winds appear to have shifted in Canada, the United States, and many other countries over the past two decades. Political parties that once advocated a greater role for government in the economy now argue the benefits of proscribed government. But has the fundamental role of government really changed? In order to understand the role of government in the economy, students must understand the benefits of free markets as well as the situations that cause markets to fail. They must also understand that governments often intervene in the economy for reasons related more to equity than to efficiency.

In this tenth edition of *Macroeconomics*, we continue to incorporate the discussion of government policy as often as possible. Here are but a few of the many examples that we explore:
- the effects of payroll taxes (in Chapter 4)
- fiscal policy (in Chapters 23 and 25)
- the importance of debt and deficits (in Chapter 31)

- monetary policy (in Chapters 27, 28, and 29)
- policies that affect the economy's long-run unemployment rate (in Chapter 30)
- policies related to the economy's long-run growth rate (in Chapters 32 and 33)
- trade policies (in Chapter 35)
- policies related to the exchange rate (in Chapter 36)

The Book

Globalization, growth and development, and the role of government are pressing issues of the day. Much of our study of economic principles and the Canadian economy has been shaped by these issues. In addition to specific coverage of growth and internationally oriented topics, growth and globalization appear naturally throughout the book in the treatment of many topics once thought to be entirely "domestic."

Most chapters of *Macroeconomics* contain some discussion of economic policy. We have two main goals in mind when we present these discussions:

1. We aim to give students practice in using economic theory, because applying theory is both a wonderfully effective teaching method and a reliable test of students' grasp of theory.

2. We want to introduce students to the major policy issues of the day and to let them discover that few policy debates are as "black and white" as they often appear in the press.

Both goals reflect our view that students should see economics as useful in helping us to understand and deal with the world around us.

Structure and Coverage

Our treatment of macroeconomics is divided into five parts: an introduction to macroeconomics; national income and fiscal policy; money, banking, and monetary policy; macroeconomic problems and policies; and international economics. The themes of internationalization and economic growth are interwoven throughout all five parts.

The first macro chapter, Chapter 19, identifies economic growth and the level of potential national income as the major determinants of a society's material standard of living. The discussion of national income accounting in Chapter 20 provides a thorough treatment of the distinction between real and nominal GDP, the distinction between GDP and GNP, and a discussion of what measures of national income *do not measure*. Chapter 21 presents a brief discussion of the important distinction between the short run and the long run in macroeconomics.

In Part 8, the core macro chapters (22–25) develop what has become the standard aggregate-demand-aggregate-supply approach. We start with a detailed exposition of the fixed-price (Keynesian cross) model of the determination of equilibrium income in Chapters 22 and 23. In Chapter 22 we consider a simplified economy, one with no international sector or government, in order to make the concepts of equilibrium income and the multiplier as teachable as possible. In Chapter 23 we add government and the international sector, thus opening our model economy to international trade at an early point.

In Chapter 24 we develop the aggregate demand (*AD*) curve and the short-run aggregate supply (*SRAS*) curve. Since we discuss the role of wealth in the consumption function in Chapter 22 and the international sector in Chapter 23, there is no mystery about why the *AD* curve slopes down—unlike other treatments where the *AD* curve is introduced prior to discussing these issues. Chapter 25 completes the core model by deriving the vertical long-run aggregate supply curve, which allows us to discuss the different effects of *AD* shifts in the short and long run. This leads directly to an introduction to fiscal policy and a discussion of business cycles in which both stabilization and growth are treated.

Part 9 focuses on the role of money and financial systems. Chapter 26 discusses the nature of money, various components of the money supply, the commercial banking system, and the Bank of Canada. In Chapter 27 we review the determinants of the demand for money. We then turn to a detailed discussion of the link between the money supply and other economic variables such as interest rates, the exchange rate, national income, and the price level. This chapter builds directly on the material in Chapters 24 and 25, with an emphasis on the distinction between short-run and long-run effects. In Chapter 28 we discuss the Bank of Canada's monetary policy. The chapter ends with a review of Canadian monetary policy over the past 20 years. This provides some important historical context for policy discussions in later parts, as well as an opportunity to draw some general conclusions about the operation of monetary policy.

Part 10 deals with some of today's most pressing macroeconomic policy issues. It contains separate chapters on inflation, unemployment, budget deficits, economic growth, and growth in the developing countries. Chapter 29 on inflation examines the central role of ex-

pectations in determining inflation, and the importance of credibility on the part of the central bank. Chapter 30 on unemployment examines the determinants of frictional and structural unemployment and discusses likely reasons for increases in the NAIRU over the past few decades. Chapter 31 on budget deficits stresses the effect of deficits on national saving and long-term economic growth. Chapter 32 provides a comprehensive summary of what is and is not currently known about the causes of economic growth. Although some of the discussion ties directly into the emphasis of previous chapters on national saving, much of it examines current research on induced technological innovation and technological diffusion. Our treatment of economic growth—which we regard as one of the most important macroeconomic issues facing Canada and the world today—goes beyond the coverage in most other introductory texts. Chapter 33 continues the growth theme by providing a summary of current views about economic growth in the developing countries.

Virtually every chapter contains at least some discussion of international issues. However, the final part of *Macroeconomics* focuses primarily on international economics. Chapter 34 gives the basic treatment of international trade, developing both the traditional theory of static comparative advantage and newer theories based on imperfect competition and dynamic comparative advantage. Chapter 35 discusses both the positive and normative aspects of trade policy, as well as the GATT and WTO and prospects for regional free-trade areas. There is also a detailed discussion of NAFTA and a box on Canada-U.S. trade disputes. Chapter 36 introduces the balance of payments and examines exchange-rate determination. Here we also discuss three "hot" policy issues: the desirability of current-account deficits or surpluses, whether there is a "right" value for the Canadian exchange rate, and the costs and benefits of Canada's adopting a fixed exchange rate.

We hope you find this menu both attractive and challenging; and we hope students find the material stimulating and enlightening. Many of the messages of economics are complex—if economic understanding were only a matter of common sense and simple observation, there would be no need for professional economists and no need for textbooks like this one. To understand economics, one must work hard. Working at this book should help readers gain a better understanding of the world around them and of the policy problems faced by all levels of government. Furthermore, in today's globalized world, the return to education is large. We like to think that we have contributed in some small part to the understanding that increased investment in human capital by the next generation is necessary to restore incomes to the rapid growth paths that so benefited our parents and our peers. Perhaps we may even contribute to some income-enhancing accumulation of human capital by some of our readers.

Substantive Changes to This Edition

We have done a major revision and update of the entire text with guidance from an extensive series of reviews and feedback from both users and nonusers of the previous editions of this book. As always, we have strived very hard to improve the teachability and readability of the book. We have shortened the overall length by two chapters (from 38 to 36) and by roughly 10 percent in terms of the number of words. There are two entirely new chapters, and several chapters have been completely rewritten. In the following subsections, we summarize the major changes that we have made for this edition. Later, in a separate section, we will describe the important new features that we have added in order to better accommodate the needs of both instructors and students.

Here is a brief description of the major changes in *Macroeconomics*.

Part 1   What Is Economics?

- Chapter 1 has been completely rewritten, incorporating some material from the previous Chapter 3 (which has been removed). The chapter now begins with a discussion about how market economies are self-organizing entities that coordinate the decisions of decentralized agents. This is not an analytical section, but rather an easy introductory discussion. The chapter then goes on to discuss resources, scarcity, opportunity cost, the economy's decision makers, specialization, the division of labour, money, and globalization.
- Chapter 2 is a new chapter that examines how economists think. We begin by discussing normative and positive advice. We then go on to describe theories and models. The section on graphing appears in the main text (rather than the appendix) and shows how economists think about data and how they test their theories. The result is a discussion of graphing that is livelier than in the previous edition.

Part 2   An Introduction to Demand and Supply

- Chapter 3, on demand and supply, has been streamlined but its basic structure is unchanged. In the section on price determination we have added an initial discussion on the concept of a market in which we provide a rough definition of competitive markets. We have added a brief discussion of the 1998 Quebec ice storm in a box. We have also added a new box discussing technical progress and falling computer chip prices.
- Chapter 4 on elasticity has been restructured. We have put the section on supply elasticity as the second section. After discussing supply elasticity, we then go straight into an examination of tax incidence as an important example of why elasticity matters. We have added a new box on the incidence of payroll taxes.

Part 7   An Introduction to Macroeconomics

- Chapter 19 offers the student an introduction to important macroeconomic variables and issues. There are no major changes in this chapter from the previous edition, though we have streamlined it, especially the section on inflation. We have also removed the final section "trends and cycles" from this chapter; this material now reappears in an entirely new Chapter 21.
- Chapter 20, on measuring GDP, is mostly unaltered. We have modified the discussion of the income approach to match the way Statistics Canada presents the data. We have replaced the discussion of "net domestic income" with one on "net national income at factor cost." The box on real and nominal GDP has been expanded to include a discussion of how the choice of the base year slightly affects the results, depending on relative price movements.
- Chapter 21 is a completely new chapter. The purpose is to provide some flexibility for those instructors who want to discuss some aspects of the long run before discussing the short run. But this chapter contains no formal modelling, and so can be covered whenever the instructor chooses. We begin with two interesting discussions of why the short run is different from the long run. We present a simple accounting identity that decomposes all changes in GDP into changes in factor supplies, factor utilization, and productivity. We then present Canadian data to show that factor supplies and productivity change considerably over the long run

but very little over the short run, whereas factor utilization changes a great deal over the short run but very little over the long run.

Part 8 National Income and Fiscal Policy

- Chapter 22 develops the simple income-expenditure model with a fixed price level and no government or foreign trade. We have tried to lighten what many instructors thought was a heavy chapter. We have added a new diagram explaining consumption smoothing. We have also added some data on investment volatility in Canada. In the discussion of the saving-investment approach to equilibrium, we have added some simple algebra to show that the difference between Y and AE is always equal to the difference between S and I.

- Chapter 23 adds government and foreign trade to the simple income-expenditure model. The saving-investment approach is now covered more efficiently. We have added some simple algebra to prove that the two approaches are equivalent. We have also rewritten the final section to highlight that the assumption of fixed prices is related to the assumption of demand-determined output.

- Chapter 24 introduces the *AD/AS* framework and is structurally the same as in the previous edition. We have completely removed the discussion of inside/outside assets and have rewritten the section describing the effect of a change in the price level on private-sector wealth. We have removed the subsection on "points off the *AD* curve." The old box on the shape of the *SRAS* curve has been eliminated, and the material on the *increasing* slope has been incorporated into the text. There is now greater emphasis on the role of aggregate supply shocks. In the final section we have added a discussion on why some economic events embody *both* demand and supply shocks. This leads to a new box on the Asian crisis and its effects on the Canadian economy.

- Chapter 25 takes the *AD/AS* model to the long run, with factor-price adjustment returning actual GDP to potential GDP. We now explicitly hold technology and productivity constant during the analysis. We have also brought the simple Phillips curve into this chapter (and stress that it describes the adjustment process from output gaps to factor-price changes). In the section on shocks, we have added a detailed discussion of aggregate supply shocks. The box on anticipated demand shocks has been removed. We have expanded the box on fiscal policy in the Great Depression by adding some data on GDP, prices and unemployment.

Part 9 Money, Banking, and Monetary Policy

- Chapter 26 is the first chapter on money. We now include an international scatter-plot on inflation and money growth so students can see the long-run relationship. The box on the globalization of financial markets now has a brief discussion of the recent drive for Canadian bank mergers. In the discussion of deposit creation, we have added a little algebra to clarify the point. We have also rewritten the discussion of cash drains.

- Chapter 27 puts money into the *AD/AS* model. We have streamlined the discussions of financial assets and of money demand. In the section on the transmission mechanism, we have emphasized the role of the exchange rate, thus eliminating a box that was difficult for many students. This new discussion ends with a diagram showing the open-economy transmission mechanism. We have removed the material on how increases in the money supply frustrate the adjustment process.

- Chapter 28 reviews the details of Canadian monetary policy. The basic structure of the chapter is unchanged, but there are many changes from the previous edition. The box on the bank rate has been updated, as has the discussion of negative and positive balances at the Bank of Canada. The open economy now figures more prominently in the chapter, both in the review of the transmission mechanism and in the review of recent policy. We have added a discussion and figure of how the need for a forward-looking monetary policy sometimes puts the Bank into awkward political situations, tightening monetary policy even though *current* inflation is low. The discussion of recent monetary history now begins with the 1981 recession. We have added brief discussions of the Asian crisis, the stock market, and the possible costs of low inflation as issues that the Bank had to face in the late 1990s. Finally, we have restored and rewritten the appendix on the stock market that existed in earlier editions of the book.

Part 10 Macroeconomic Problems and Policies

- Chapter 29 deals with inflation. We have reorganized this chapter somewhat, and have also shortened it and updated with some current debates. We have incorporated the box on constant inflation into the first section of the chapter. This way the student sees immediately how sustained inflation can be incorporated into the model. We then go on to the issue of demand and supply shocks. We have removed the discussion of "isolated versus repeated" shocks which many reviewers found confusing—in this section all shocks are one-time, permanent shocks. In the section on reducing inflation, we have now included a discussion and figure for the sacrifice ratio. In the final section on Canadian inflation policy we have added two current debates: Is inflation dead? Is inflation too low?

- Chapter 30 discusses unemployment. After the section discussing the New Classical and New Keynesian theories of cyclical unemployment, we have added a brief discussion of why these differences really only apply in the short run—both classes of models agree that the long-run effect of monetary policies are the same. We have added a new figure showing different unemployment rates by demographic group. In the final section we have added a new box on the Canada-U.S. unemployment gap.

- Chapter 31 deals with government deficits and debt. There is now more emphasis on surpluses since federal deficits appear to have been eliminated. The basic analysis of the effects of deficits is unchanged; but we have now added a final short section, which also acts as a review, in which we predict the effects of ongoing surpluses. The discussion of Ricardian equivalence has been reworked and we have also added a diagram to help the student visualize the lifetime effects on wealth from a tax reduction. The box on the "myths" of debt has been rewritten.

- Chapter 32 is on long-term economic growth. There are some noteworthy changes from the previous edition. We have shortened the introductory section and have added a figure to show the opportunity cost of growth. We have added some OECD data on cross-country investment and growth rates. In our discussion of technological change, we now go to a new box on whether workers should be afraid of technical change. We have added a discussion on measuring technical change in which we briefly discuss Solow's method of growth accounting. The section on new growth theories has been slightly streamlined, as has the final section on the limits to growth. The box on the Brundtland Commission has been removed.

- Chapter 33 addresses growth in the developing countries. It has been streamlined considerably. We have added some new data on the external debts of the Highly Indebted Poor Countries. We have also sharpened the discussion of the "new" view of development and the Washington Consensus. The box on South Korea has been removed.

Part 11   International Economics

- Chapter 34 examines the gains from trade. We have added a figure in the introduction showing the growth of trade relative to GDP. We have considerably shortened the first section on comparative and absolute advantage and have also added a figure to show the production possibilities boundary for two countries. We then go on to a section that formerly appeared in Chapter 6—showing the imports and exports of internationally traded goods with a simple demand-and-supply apparatus. This section should help students see that what is desirable as given by comparative advantage is also largely what happens with actual trade.

- Chapter 35 provides a discussion of trade policy. We have significantly shortened the theoretical discussion of strategic trade policy, but we have added a brief discussion of the Bombardier/Embraer dispute over subsidization. We have removed the section on nominal versus effective protection. The box on VERs has been removed, although the discussion in the text has been expanded slightly. There is a new discussion about the WTO and some of its recent political opposition. We have also added a new box on the Multilateral Agreement on Investment. In the discussion of NAFTA results, we have added a new box on Canadian wine as a surprising success story. We have also updated the box on "headline" Canada-U.S. trade disputes.

- Chapter 36 deals with exchange rates and the balance of payments. It has been entirely rewritten and brings in some material from the old Chapter 38 (which has now been removed). We have rewritten why the balance of payments must always balance. There is a new box showing an individual's balance of payments with the rest of the world. The section on the foreign-exchange market is roughly the same. The final section now examines three "hot" policy issues. The first is whether current account deficits are a problem. Here we bring in some of the material on "twin deficits" from the old Chapter 38. The second is whether there is a "right" value for the Canadian dollar. This gets us into the issue of PPP, revised from the previous edition. The final issue is whether Canada should adopt a fixed exchange rate. We explore flexible rates as shock absorbers and fixed rates as a means of reducing foreign-exchange risk. This naturally leads to a new box on the idea of optimal currency areas.

TO THE STUDENT

A good course in economics will give you insight into how an economy functions and into some currently debated policy issues. Like all rewarding subjects, economics will not be mastered without effort. A book on economics must be worked at. It cannot be read like a novel.

You must develop your own technique for studying, but the following suggestions may prove helpful. Begin by carefully considering the Learning Objectives at the beginning of a chapter. Read the chapter itself relatively quickly in order to get the general run of the argument. At this first reading, you may want to skip the boxes and any footnotes. Then, after reading the Chapter Summary and the Key Concepts (both at the end of each chapter), reread the chapter more slowly, making sure that you understand each step of the argument.

With respect to the figures and tables, be sure you understand how the conclusions that are stated in boldface at the beginning of each caption have been reached. You must not skip the captions. They provide the core of economic reasoning. You should be prepared to spend time on difficult sections; occasionally, you may spend an hour on only a few pages. Paper and pencil are indispensable equipment in your reading. It is best to follow a difficult argument by building your own diagram while the argument unfolds rather than by relying on the finished diagram as it appears in the book.

The end-of-chapter Study Exercises require you to practise using some of the concepts that you learned in the chapter. These will be excellent preparation for your exams. The Discussion Questions require you to apply what you have studied. We advise you to outline answers to some of the questions. In short, you should seek to understand economics, not to memorize it.

The bracketed boldface numbers in the text itself refer to a series of mathematical notes that are found starting on page M-1 at the end of the book. For those of you who like mathematics or prefer mathematical argument to verbal or geometric exposition, these may prove useful. Others may disregard them.

A time line, which runs from the mid 1600s to the mid 1900s, follows the mathematical notes. Along this time line we have placed brief descriptions of the life and works of some great economists, most of whom you will encounter in the textbook. So that you have a better appreciation of *when* these economists did their work, the time line also lists some major world events. We hope this will improve your sense of history and your sense of who these great economists are.

In this edition of the book, we have incorporated many elements to help you review material and prepare for examinations. Pay special attention to the learning objectives, the important concepts highlighted in red, the key terms that are boldfaced and restated in the margins, the captions that accompany the features and tables, the lists of key concepts, and the chapter summaries. A brief description of all the features in this book is given in the separate section that follows.

We strongly suggest you make use of the excellent *Study Guide* written expressly for this text. It will test and reinforce your understanding of the concepts and analytical techniques stressed in each chapter of the text and will help prepare you for your examinations. The ability to solve problems and to communicate and interpret your results are important goals in an introductory course in economics. The *Study Guide* can play an important role in your acquisition of these skills.

We hope you will find the book rewarding and stimulating. Students who used earlier editions made some of the most helpful suggestions for revision, and we hope that you will carry on the tradition. If you are moved to write to us (and we hope that you will be!), please do. You can send any comments or questions regarding the text (or any of the supplementary material, such as the *Study Guide*) to:

Christopher Ragan
Department of Economics
McGill University
855 Sherbrooke St. West
Montreal, Quebec
H3A 2T7

Or, if you prefer to communicate through e-mail, send your comments to:

ragan@leacock.lan.mcgill.ca

FEATURES OF THIS EDITION

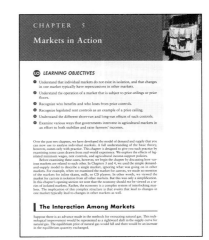

We have made a careful effort with this edition to incorporate features that will facilitate the teaching and learning of economics.

- **A new single-column design** has been created for the book, making it more accessible to today's reader.
- A new set of **Learning Objectives** at the beginning of each chapter clarify the skills and knowledge to be learned in each chapter. These same learning objectives are used in the chapter summaries, as well as in the *Test Item File* and the *Study Guide*.

- **Major ideas** are highlighted in red in the text.
- **Key terms** are boldfaced where they are defined in the body of the text and they are restated with their definitions in the margins. In the Index at the back of the book, each key term and the page reference to its definition are boldfaced.
- **Weblinks** to useful Internet addresses are given in the margins. Each weblink presents a URL address, along with a brief description of the material available there. Some links are to government home pages where much data can be obtained. Other links are to organizations such as OPEC, the UN, and the WTO. We have also included links to selected articles from *World Economic Affairs* that we have posted on the Companion Web Site for this textbook.
- **Study Guide** references in the margin direct students to appropriate questions in the *Study Guide* that reinforce the topic being discussed in the text.

- **Applying Economic Concepts** boxes demonstrate economics in action, providing examples of how theoretical material relates to issues of current interest.

xxiii

- **Lessons from History** boxes contain discussions of a particular policy debate or empirical finding that takes place in a historical context.

- **Extensions in Theory** boxes provide a deeper treatment of a theoretical topic that is discussed in the text.

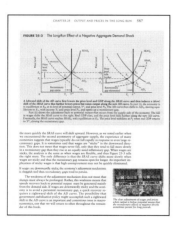

- **A caption for each Figure and Table** summarizes the underlying economic reasoning. Each caption begins with a boldfaced statement of the relevant economic conclusion.
- A **new colour scheme for Figures** has been established to make the use of colour in the graphs consistent. Curves of a particular type are now always presented in the same colour. For example, all demand curves are blue, whereas all supply curves are red.
- **Photographs with short captions** are now interspersed throughout the chapters to illustrate some of the arguments.

- **Chapter Summaries** are organized using the same main heading as found in the body of the chapter. And the relevant learning objectives (LO) numbers are given in red next to each heading in the chapter summary

- **Key Concepts** are listed near the end of each chapter.
- A new set of **Study Exercises** has been created for each chapter. These quantitative exercises require the student to analyze problems by means of computations or graphs.
- A set of **Discussion Questions** is also provided for each chapter. These questions require the student to synthesize and generalize. They are designed especially for discussion in class.

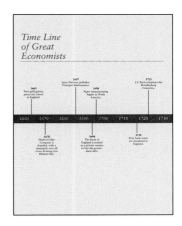

- A set of **Mathematical Notes** is presented in a separate section near the end of the book. Because mathematical notation and derivations are not necessary to understand the principles of economics but are more helpful in advanced work, this seems to be a sensible arrangement. References in the text to these mathematical notes are given by means of boldfaced numbers in square brackets.
- A **Time Line of Great Economists,** running from the mid seventeenth century to the mid twentieth century, is presented near the end of the book. Along this time line we have placed brief descriptions of the life and works of some great economists, most of whom the reader will encounter in the textbook. Along this time line we have also listed some major world events in order to give readers an appreciation for when these economists did their work.

SUPPLEMENTS

The following supplements have been carefully prepared to accompany the new edition:

- A **Study Guide**, written by E. Kenneth Grant and William J. Furlong, is designed for use either in the classroom or by students on their own. The *Study Guide* offers additional study support and reinforcement for each text chapter. It reuses the same learning objectives that appear in the textbook. For each chapter, it provides a prose Overview, a Chapter Review consisting of multiple-choice questions, Exercises, Extension Exercises, and a Practice Multiple-Choice Test.
- An **Instructor's Manual**, written by Christopher Ragan, provides for each text chapter an overview (with teaching suggestions), solutions to the Study Exercises, and suggested answers to the Discussion Questions.
- A **Test Item File**, written by Greg Flanagan and Mike Fellows, contains more than 3300 multiple-choice questions. For each question, the authors have identified the relevant learning objective from the textbook, and they have classified each question by difficulty type (i.e., definitions, using definitions, key concepts, and applying one or more concepts).
- A **Computerized Version of the Test Item File** will enable instructors to edit existing questions, create new questions, generate tests, and administer tests on line over a variety of networks. It also includes a powerful grading system that combines a powerful database with analytical capabilities so that instructors can generate a full set of statistics.
- **Transparency Masters** of all the Figures and Tables in the textbook are available to instructors.
- **Electronic Transparencies** of all the Figures and Tables in the textbook are also available to instructors.
- A special **Companion Web Site** has been created for this book at **www.pearsoned.ca/lipsey**. It includes, among other elements, self-test questions for students, CBC Video Cases, hotlinks to the home pages of governments and other organizations that provide much current data, and the posting of articles from *World Economic Affairs* that are cited in the text.

ACKNOWLEDGEMENTS

It would be impossible to acknowledge here by name all the teachers, colleagues, and students who contributed to the development and improvement of this book over its previous nine editions. Hundreds of users have written to us with specific suggestions, and much of the credit for the improvement of the book over the years belongs to them. We can no longer list them individually but we thank them all sincerely.

For the development of this tenth edition, we are grateful to the many people who offered informal suggestions. We would also like to thank the following instructors who provided us with formal reviews of the textbook:

- Panos C. Afxentiou (University of Calgary)
- Jeremiah Allen (University of Lethbridge)
- F. Michael Bradfield (Dalhousie University)
- Rosilyn G. Coulson (Douglas College)
- Melvin L. Cross (Dalhousie University)
- Martin Dooley (McMaster University)
- Paul Geddes (Columbia College)
- Jack Guthrie (Camosun College)
- Cheryl Jenkins (John Abbott College)
- Eric Kam (York University)
- Susan Kamp (University of Alberta)
- Nargess Kayhani (Mount Saint Vincent University)
- Robert R. Kerton (University of Waterloo)
- Ralph Kolinski (University of Windsor)
- Irwin Lipnowski (The University of Manitoba)
- Rocky M. Mirza (Langara College)
- Robin Neill (University of Prince Edward Island)
- Victor C. Olshevski (The University of Winnipeg)
- Dan Otchere (Concordia University)
- Ian Parker (Scarborough College, University of Toronto)
- Arne Paus-Jenssen (University of Saskatchewan)
- Laurie Craig Phipps (Camosun College)
- Don Reddick (Kwantlen College)
- Charlene Richter (British Columbia Institute of Technology)
- Gary E. Riser (Memorial University)
- James Sentance (University of Prince Edward Island)
- Larry Smith (University of Waterloo)
- Bertram A. Somers (John Abbott College)

In addition, we would like to thank the following instructors for providing formal reviews for some of the supplements that accompany this tenth edition;

- Peter R. Burrell (University of Windsor)
- David M. Cape (Ryerson Polytechnic University)
- Michael F. Charette (University of Windsor)
- Greg L. Flanagan (Saint Mary's University)
- Paul A. R. Hobson (Acadia University)
- Cheryl Jenkins (John Abbott College)
- Eva Lau (University of Waterloo)
- Charlene Richter (British Columbia Institute of Technology)
- Larry Smith (University of Waterloo)
- Donna J. Tibbett (University of Lethbridge)

We would like to acknowledge the work of David Gray (University of Ottawa), who performed a technical review of the textbook.

We would also like to express our thanks to the many people at Pearson Education Canada who spent long hours editing and producing this text.

Our special thanks go to Ingrid Kristjanson, who did a tremendous amount of editing and also carefully reviewed all changes made to this edition. Her comments led to many improvements. For her diligence and hard work we are especially grateful.

Photo Credits

Chapter 1 Canapress/Associated Press/Lionel Cironneau – 2, 6; Tony Stone Images/Daniel Bosler – 1, 9; PhotoDisc, Inc. – 15

Chapter 2 Tony Stone Images/Steven Peters – 28; Dick Hemingway – 1, 24, 31

Chapter 3 Tony Stone Images/Chris McCooey – 50; Saskatchewan Travel – 47, 48, 57; Canapress/Jacques Boissinot – 65

Chapter 4 Imperial Oil Limited – 47, 70, 77; Dick Hemingway – 87

Chapter 19 Marko Shark – 458; Canadian Pacific – 449, 450, 468

Chapter 20 Dick Hemingway – 477; Toyota Motor Manufacturing Canada Inc. – 484; FPG International LLC/Michael Goldman – 449, 475, 488

Chapter 21 Corbis Digital Stock Images – 449, 494, 496

Chapter 22 Dick Hemingway – 507, 508, 513; The Slide Farm/Al Harvey – 516

Chapter 23 Ontario Ministry of Tourism and Recreation – 507, 534, 548

Chapter 24 PhotoEdit/Myrleen Ferguson – 558; British Columbia Forest Service/Ray Wormald Photo – 507, 557, 565

Chapter 25 Dick Hemingway – 507, 579, 581; Impact Visuals Photos & Graphics Inc./Donna Binder – 587

Chapter 26 Corbis - 610; Tony Stone Images/Alan Klehr – 605, 606; Dick Hemingway – 624

Chapter 27 Leucar Photo – 605, 635, 636; Dick Hemingway – 636; Dick Hemingway – 640

Chapter 28 CP Archive Photo/Tom Hanson – 679; CP Archive Photo/Fred Chartrand – 605, 659

Chapter 29 CP Archive Photo/Ryan Remiorz – 691, 692, 701; PhotoDisc, Inc. – 715

Chapter 30 PhotoEdit/Spencer Grant – 691, 722, 734; Prentice Hall, Inc. – 737

Chapter 31 National Archives of Canada/Donald I. Grant/PA115568 – 754; PhotoDisc, Inc. – 691, 749, 765

Chapter 32 AP Wide World Photos – 691, 776, 780; PhotoDisc, Inc. – 784; PhotoDisc, Inc. – 793

Chapter 33 Hamilton Wright Organization Inc. – 805; United Nations Photo – 691, 800, 807

Chapter 34 PhotoDisc, Inc. – 827; British Columbia Forest Service/R.J. Challenger Photo – 821, 822, 831

Chapter 35 Superstock, Inc./Ping Amranand – 821, 841, 842; Agriculture Quebec – 856

Chapter 36 CP Archive Photo – 821, 864, 870; Tony Stone Images – 875

companion **Website...**

Your Internet companion to the most exciting, state-of-the-art educational tools on the Web!

The Pearson Education Canada Companion Website is easy to navigate and is organized to correspond to the chapters in this textbook. The Companion Website is comprised of four distinct, functional features:

1) **Customized Online Resources**

2) **Online Study Guide**

3) **Reference Material**

4) **Communication**

Explore the four areas in this Companion Website. Students and distance learners will discover resources for indepth study, research, and communication, empowering them in their quest for greater knowledge and maximizing their potential for success in the course.

A NEW WAY TO DELIVER EDUCATIONAL CONTENT

1) Customized Online Resources

Our Companion Websites provide instructors and students with a range of options to access, view, and exchange content.

- **Syllabus Builder** provides *instructors* with the option to create online classes and construct an online syllabus linked to specific modules in the Companion Website.

- **Mailing lists** enable *instructors* and *students* to receive customized promotional literature.

- **Preferences** enable *students* to customize the sending of results to various recipients, and also to customize how the material is sent, e.g., as html, text, or as an attachment.

- **Help** includes an evaluation of the user's system and a tune-up area that makes updating browsers and plug-ins easier. This new feature will enhance the user's experience with Companion Websites.

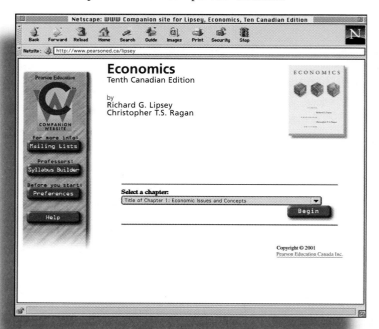

www.pearsoned.ca/lipsey

Pearson Education

COMPANION
WEBSITE

2) Online Study Guide

An Interactive Study Guide forms the core of the student learning experience in the Companion Website. Multiple Choice modules, organized by text chapter, provide students with the ability to send answers to our grader and receive instant feedback on their progress through our Results Reporter. Students can check suggested answers after submitting their problems.

3) Reference Material

Reference material broadens text coverage with up-to-date resources for learning. We have posted more than 35 journal articles from *World Economic Affairs*. Each article is cited by a special icon in the margin of the textbook. Special **CBC Video Case Studies** provide instructors and students with interesting video segments and stimulating cases for discussion. **Web Destinations** provides direct links to websites relevant to the subject matter in each chapter. **Net News (Internet Newsgroups)** are a fundamental source of information about a discipline, containing a wealth of brief, opinionated postings. **Net Search** simplifies key term search using Internet search engines.

4) Communication

Companion Websites contain the communication tools necessary to deliver courses in a **Distance Learning** environment. **Message Board** allows users to post messages and check back periodically for responses. **Live Chat** allows users to discuss course topics in real time, and enables professors to host online classes.

Communication facilities of Companion Websites provide a key element for distributed learning environments. There are two types of communication facilities currently in use in Companion Websites:

- **Message Board** – this module takes advantage of browser technology, providing the users of each Companion Website with a national newsgroup to post and reply to relevant course topics.

- **Live Chat** – enables instructor-led group activities in real time. Using our chat client, instructors can display Website content while students participate in the discussion.

Companion Websites are currently available for numerous Pearson Education Canada books, including

- Case, Fair, Strain, and Veall, *Principles of Microeconomics and Macroeconomics*, First Canadian Edition
- Miller and Clegg, *Economics Today*, First Canadian Edition
- Brown, Chambers, and Currie, *Personal Finance for Canadians*, Sixth Edition

Note: CW content will vary slightly from site to site depending on discipline requirements.

The Companion Website can be found at:

www.pearsoned.ca/lipsey

PEARSON EDUCATION CANADA

26 Prince Andrew Place
Don Mills, Ontario M3C 2T8

To order:
Call: 1-800-567-3800
Fax: 1-800-263-7733

For samples:
Call: 1-800-850-5813
Fax: (416) 447-2819
E-mail: phcinfo.pubcanada@pearsoned.com

PART ONE

What Is Economics?

Have you ever noticed that, when you go to a store to buy something, the product you seek is almost always available? Or, have you noticed that you rarely see either large numbers of people lined up waiting to buy goods or large amounts of unsold goods with nobody to buy them? What is it about a modern market economy that produces these remarkably coordinated outcomes in which the amount of something available is roughly equal to the amount that people want? What is the study of economics all about, and why will it help you to understand how today's economies function? How do economists do their job of analysing and explaining economic outcomes? What are economic models, and why are some models more sensible than others? Why is it that economists appear to disagree so much, or is this just an illusion? These are questions that you will be able to answer after reading the following two chapters.

Chapter 1 begins by talking about the self-organizing economy, and introduces Adam Smith's famous idea of an invisible hand. Here we see why markets made up of self-interested consumers and producers automatically produce the sort of coordination that we observe. We then examine the important concepts of scarcity, choice, and opportunity cost, three ideas that are central to all economic systems. We then introduce the various decision-makers in a typical market economy, including individual consumers, producers, and governments, and we see how their interactions can be represented by a circular flow of income and expenditure. Finally, we consider alternative economic systems, ranging from a pure market system to a centrally planned system in which a government planning authority makes all the decisions regarding who produces what and who consumes what. Canada, like all economies, is a mixed system, containing elements of both free markets and government intervention.

Chapter 2 discusses the study of economics itself. We consider the distinction between positive and normative statements, a distinction upon which the progress of economics as a social science is based. We then examine the role of theory in economics, and why economists—like physicists or chemists—build models to help them think about the complex world they are trying to understand. Finally, we will explain the way economists test their theories by confronting the predictions of their theories with the available evidence. Here we will also discuss graphing—a central tool for economists and one that is used extensively throughout this book—and you will see how different types of graphs can be used to present very different types of information.

CHAPTER 1

Economic Issues and Concepts

LEARNING OBJECTIVES

1. View the market economy as a self-organizing entity in which order emerges from a large number of decentralized decisions.

2. Understand the importance of scarcity, choice, and opportunity cost, and how all three concepts are illustrated by the production possibilities boundary.

3. Explain the circular flow of income and expenditure.

4. Recognize that there are several types of pure economic systems, but that all actual economies are mixed systems, having elements of free markets, tradition, and government intervention.

If you want a litre of milk, you go to your local grocery store and buy it. It probably does not occur to you that farmers may have stopped producing milk or that dairies may have stopped delivering it to stores. When the grocer needs more milk, he orders it from the distributor, who in turn gets it from the dairy, which in its turn gets it from the dairy farmer. The dairy farmer buys cattle feed and electric milking machines, and gets power to run all his equipment by putting a plug into a wall outlet where the electricity is supplied as he needs it. The milking machines are made from parts manufactured in several different places in Canada, the United States, and overseas. The parts themselves are made from materials mined and smelted in a dozen or more different countries.

As it is with the milk you drink, so it is with everything else that you buy. When you go to the appropriate store, what you want is normally on the shelf. Those who make these products find that all the required components and materials are available when they need them—even though these things typically come from many different parts of the world and are made by people who have no direct dealings with each other.

The Complexity of the Modern Economy

The sales and purchases in which you are involved are only a small part of the remarkably complex set of transactions that take place every day in a modern society. Shipments arrive daily at our ports, railway terminals, and airports. These shipments include raw materials, such as iron ore, logs and oil; parts, such as automobile engines, transistors, and circuit boards; tools, such as screwdrivers, lathes, and digging equipment; perishables, such as fresh flowers, coffee beans, and fruits; and all kinds of manufactured goods, such as washing machines, personal computers, and TV sets. Railways and trucking lines receive and dispatch these goods to thousands of different destinations within Canada. Some go directly to consumers. Others are used by local firms to manufacture their products—some of which will be sold domestically and some exported.

Most people who want to work can find work. They spend their working days engaging in the activities just described. In doing so, they earn incomes which they then spend on what they, and others like them, produce. Other people own firms that employ workers to assist in the many activities described above, such as importing, making, transporting, and selling things. They earn their incomes as profits from these enterprises.

The Self-Organizing Economy

Economics began when thoughtful observers asked themselves how such a complex set of dealings gets organized. Who coordinates the whole set of efforts? Who makes sure that all the activities fit together, providing jobs to produce the things that people want and delivering those things to where they are wanted? The answer is no one!

The great insight of the early economists was that an economy based on free-market transactions is *self-organizing*.

By following their own self-interest, doing what seems best and most profitable for themselves, and responding to the incentives of prices determined in open markets, people produce a spontaneous social order. In that order, literally thousands of millions of transactions and activities fit together to produce the things that people want within the constraints set by the resources that are available to the nation.

The great Scottish economist and political philosopher Adam Smith (1723-1790)[1], who was the first to develop this insight fully, put it this way:

> *It is not from the benevolence of the butcher, the brewer, or the baker, that we expect our dinner, but from their regard to their own interest. We address ourselves, not to their humanity but to their self-love, and never talk to them of our own necessities but of their advantages.*

Smith is not saying that benevolence is unimportant. Indeed, he praises it in many passages. He is saying, however, that the massive number of economic interactions that characterize a modern economy cannot all be motivated by benevolence. Although benevolence does motivate some of our actions, often the very dramatic ones, the vast majority of our everyday actions are motivated by self-interest. Self-interest, not benevolence, is therefore the foundation of economic order.

Efficient Organization

Another great insight, which was hinted at by Smith and fully developed over the next century and a half, was that this spontaneously generated social order is relatively *efficient*. Loosely speaking, efficiency means that the resources available to a nation are organized in such a way as to produce the maximum possible total output.

---

[1]Throughout this book we encounter many great economists from the past whose ideas shaped the discipline of economics. At the back of the book you will find a timeline, beginning in the 1600s, that contains brief discussions of many of these thinkers and places them in their historical context.

Smith said that a society whose economy is organized by free markets produces ordered behaviour that makes it appear as if people are guided by an *invisible hand*. He did not literally mean that a supernatural presence guides economic affairs. Instead, he referred to the amazing order that emerges out of so many independent decisions. The key to the explanation is that all individuals respond to the same set of prices, which are determined in markets that respond to overall conditions of national scarcity or plenty. Much of economics is devoted to a detailed elaboration of how this market order is generated.

A Planned Alternative

A century after Adam Smith, another great economist and political philosopher, Karl Marx (1818–1883), argued that although such a market system would produce high total output, it would distribute that output in such a way that, over time, the rich would get richer and the poor poorer. He went on to argue that when societies became rich enough, they should dispense with the spontaneous social order. They should then replace it by a consciously created system, called a *command economy*, or *communism*, in which the government plans all of the transactions we have just described and, in so doing, creates a more equal and socially just distribution of the total output.

Beginning with the Soviet Union in the early 1920s, many nations listened to Marx and established systems in which conscious government *central planning* largely replaced the spontaneous order of the free market. For much of the twentieth century two systems, the centrally planned and the market, competed with each other for the favour of undecided governments. Then, within the last two decades of the century, governments of one communist country after another abandoned their central planning apparatus. More and more economic transactions and activities were then left to be regulated by the self-organizing system of the market.

Lessons From History 1-1 elaborates on some of the reasons for the failure of the centrally planned economies. We hasten to add that Marx was right about many things, including the importance of technological change in raising living standards over the centuries (which is also a theme we discuss in this book). Where experience has shown him wrong, however, was in believing that central planning could successfully replace the market as a way of organizing all of a nation's economic activities.

In contrast to the failures of the command economies, the performance of the largely free-market economies is impressive. One theme of this book is *market success*—how the price system works to coordinate with relative efficiency the decentralized decisions made by private consumers and producers. However, doing things better does not necessarily mean doing things perfectly. Another theme of this book is *market failure*—how and why the unaided price system sometimes fails to produce efficient results and fails to take account of social values that cannot be expressed through the marketplace.

Today, as in the time of Adam Smith, economists seek to understand the self-organizing forces of a market economy, how well they function, and how governments may intervene to improve (but not to replace) their workings in specific situations.

Main Characteristics of Market Economies

What then are the main characteristics of market economies that produce this spontaneous self-ordering?

- Individuals pursue their own self-interest, buying and selling what seems best for themselves and their families.
- People respond to incentives. Other things being equal, sellers seek high prices and buyers seek low prices.
- Prices are determined in open markets in which would-be sellers compete to sell their wares to would-be buyers.
- People earn their incomes by selling their labour services, things they have produced, the services of the land, or buildings that they own to those who wish to buy them.
- All of these activities are governed by a set of institutions largely created by the state. The most important are private property and freedom of contract. The nature of private property and contractual obligations are defined by the legislature and enforced by the police and the courts.

Resources and Scarcity

All of the issues discussed so far would not matter much if we lived in an economy of such plenty that there was enough to satisfy all of everyone's wants. "Ask and you shall receive" would be the motto of such an imaginary world. In contrast, the motto of any real economy is closer to "Work for it and you may get at least some of it."

Why is the economy of plenty impossible? The short answer is "Because we live in a world of scarcity." Compared to the known desires of individuals for such products as better food, clothing, housing, education, holidays, health care, and entertainment, the existing supplies of resources are clearly inadequate. They are sufficient to produce only a small fraction of the goods and services that people desire. This gives rise to the basic economic problem of choice under conditions of scarcity. If we cannot have everything we want, we must choose what we will and will not have.

One definition of *economics* comes from the great economist Alfred Marshall (1842–1924), whom we will encounter at several points in this book: "Economics is a study of mankind in the ordinary business of life." A more penetrating definition is the following:

Economics is the study of the use of scarce resources to satisfy unlimited human wants.

Scarcity is inevitable and is central to economic problems. What are society's resources? Why is scarcity inevitable? What are the consequences of scarcity?

Resources

A society's resources consist of natural endowments such as land, forests, and minerals; human resources, both mental and physical; and manufactured aids to production such as tools, machinery, and buildings. Economists call such resources **factors of production** because they are used to produce the outputs that people desire. We divide these outputs into goods and services. **Goods** are tangible (e.g., cars and shoes), and **services** are intangible (e.g., haircuts and education).

People use goods and services to satisfy many of their wants. The act of making them is called **production**, and the act of using them to satisfy wants is called **consumption**. Goods are valued for the services they provide. An automobile, for example, helps to satisfy its owner's desires for transportation, mobility, and possibly status.

factors of production Resources used to produce goods and services; frequently divided into the basic categories of land, labour, and capital.

goods Tangible commodities, such as cars or shoes.

services Intangible commodities, such as haircuts or medical care.

production The act of making goods or services.

consumption The act of using goods or services to satisfy wants.

LESSONS FROM HISTORY 1-1
The Failure of Central Planning

In 1989, communism collapsed throughout Central and Eastern Europe, and the economic systems of formerly communist countries began the transition from centrally planned to market economies. Although political issues surely played a role in these events, the economic changes generally confirmed the superiority of a market-oriented price system over central planning as a method of organizing economic activity. The failure of central planning had many causes, but four were particularly significant.

The Failure of Coordination

In centrally planned economies, a body of planners tries to coordinate all the economic decisions about production, investment, trade, and consumption that are likely to be made by producers and consumers throughout the country. Without the use of prices to signal relative scarcity and abundance, central planning generally proved impossible to do with any reasonable degree of success. Bottlenecks in production, shortages of some goods, and gluts of others plagued the Soviet economy for decades. For example, for years there was an ample supply of black-and-white television sets but severe

shortages of toilet paper and soap. In 1989, much of a bumper harvest rotted because of shortages of storage and transportation facilities.

The fall of the Berlin Wall in November 1989 was the beginning of the end of the Soviet system of central planning.

Scarcity

For each of the world's six billion people, scarcity is real and ever present. As we said above, relative to people's desires, existing resources are inadequate; there are enough to produce only a fraction of the goods and services that are wanted.

But are not the advanced industrialized nations rich enough that scarcity is nearly banished? After all, they have been characterized as affluent societies. Whatever affluence may mean, however, it does not mean the end of the problem of scarcity. Most households that earn $100 000 per year (a princely amount by world standards) have no trouble spending it on things that seem useful to them and they would certainly have no trouble convincing you that their resources are scarce relative to their desires.

Choice

Because resources are scarce, all societies face the problem of deciding what to produce and how much each person will consume. Societies differ in who makes the choices and how they are made, but the need to choose is common to all. Just as scarcity implies the need for choice, so choice implies the existence of cost. A decision to have

Failure of Quality Control

Central planners can monitor the number of units produced by any factory and reward plants that exceed their production targets and punish ones that fall short. Factory managers operating under these conditions will meet their quotas by whatever means are available, and once the goods pass out of their factory, what happens to them is someone else's headache.

In market economies, poor quality is punished by low sales, and retailers soon give a signal to factory managers by shifting their purchases to other suppliers. The incentives that obviously flow from such private-sector purchasing discretion are generally absent from command economies, where purchases and sales are planned centrally and prices and profits are not used to signal customer satisfaction or dissatisfaction.

Misplaced Incentives

In market economies, relative wages and salaries provide incentives for labour to move from place to place, and the possibility of losing one's job provides an incentive to work diligently. This is a harsh mechanism that punishes losers with loss of income (although social programs provide floors to the amount of economic punishment that can be suffered). In planned economies, workers usually have complete job security. Industrial unemployment is rare, and even when it does occur, new jobs are usually found for all who lose theirs. Although the high level of security is attractive to many peo-

ple, it proved impossible to provide sufficient incentives for reasonably hard and efficient work under such conditions. In the words of Oxford historian Timothy Garton Ash, who wrote eyewitness chronicles of the developments in Eastern Europe from 1980 to 1990, the social contract between the workers and the government in the Eastern European countries was "We pretend to work, and you pretend to pay us."

Environmental Degradation

Fulfilling production plans became the all-embracing goal in planned economies, to the exclusion of most other considerations, including the environment. As a result, environmental degradation occurred in the Soviet Union and the countries of Eastern Europe on a scale unknown in advanced Western nations. A particularly disturbing example (only one of many) occurred in central Asia where high quotas for cotton output led to indiscriminate use of pesticides and irrigation. Birth defects are now found in nearly one child in three, and the vast Aral Sea has been half drained, causing major environmental effects.

This failure to protect the environment stemmed from the pressure to fulfill production plans and the absence of a "political marketplace" where citizens could express their preferences for the environment versus economic gain. Imperfect though the system may be in democratic market economies—and in some particular cases it has been quite poor—their record of environmental protection has been vastly better than that of the command economies.

more of something requires a decision to have less of something else. The less of "something else" can be thought of as the cost of having the more of "something."

Scarcity implies that choices must be made, and making choices implies the existence of costs.

Opportunity Cost

To see how choice implies cost, we look first at a trivial example and then at one that vitally affects all of us; both examples involve precisely the same fundamental principles.

Consider the choice that must be made by your little sister who has 50 cents to spend and who is determined to spend it all on candy. For your sister there are only two kinds of candy in the world: bubblegums, which sell for 5 cents each, and lollipops, which sell for 10 cents each. Your sister would like to buy 10 bubblegums and 10 lollipops but soon discovers that this is not possible: It is not an *attainable combination*, given her scarce resources. However, several combinations are attainable: 8 bubblegums and 1 lollipop, 4 bubblegums and 3 lollipops, 2 bubblegums and 4 lollipops, and so on. Some of these combinations leave money unspent, and she is not interested in them. Only six combinations, as shown in Figure 1-1, are both attainable and use the entire 50 cents.

FIGURE 1-1 A Choice Between Bubblegums and Lollipops

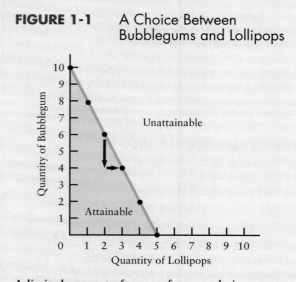

A limited amount of money forces a choice among alternatives. Six combinations of bubblegums and lollipops are attainable and use all of the child's money. The negatively sloped line provides a boundary between attainable and unattainable combinations. The arrows show that the opportunity cost of 1 more lollipop is 2 bubblegums.

After careful thought, your sister has almost decided to buy 6 bubblegums and 2 lollipops, but at the last moment she decides that she simply must have 3 lollipops. What will it cost to get this extra lollipop? One answer is 2 bubblegums. As seen in the figure, this is the number of bubblegums the child must forgo to get the extra lollipop. Economists describe the 2 bubblegums as the *opportunity cost* of the third lollipop.

Another answer is that the cost of the third lollipop is 10 cents. But this answer is less revealing than the first one. Though the real choice is one between more of this and more of that, the cost of "this" is usefully viewed in terms of what one cannot have of "that."

The idea of opportunity cost is one of the central insights of economics. Here is a precise definition. The **opportunity cost** of using resources for a certain purpose is defined to be *the benefit given up by not using them in the best alternative way.* That is, it is the cost measured in terms of other goods and services that could have been obtained instead. If, for example, resources that could have produced 20 km of road are best used instead to produce two small hospitals, the opportunity cost of a hospital is 10 km of road; looked at the other way round, the opportunity cost of 1 km of road is one-tenth of a hospital.

opportunity cost
The cost of using resources for a certain purpose, measured by the benefit given up by not using them in their best alternative use.

Every time a choice is made, opportunity costs are incurred.

See *Applying Economic Concepts 1-1* for an example of opportunity cost that should seem quite familiar to you—the opportunity cost of getting a university degree.

Production Possibilities

Although your sister's choice between bubblegums and lollipops may seem to be a trivial consumption decision, the essential nature of the decision is the same whatever the choice being made. Consider, for example, the choice that any country must face between producing military and civilian goods.

If resources are fully and efficiently employed, it is not possible to have more of both. However, as the government cuts defence expenditures, resources needed to produce civilian goods will be freed up. The opportunity cost of increased civilian goods is therefore the forgone military output. (Or, if we were considering an increase in military output, the opportunity cost of military output would be the forgone civilian goods.)

The choice is illustrated in Figure 1-2. Because resources are limited, some combinations—those that would require more than the total available supply of resources for their production—cannot be attained. The negatively sloped curve on the graph divides the combinations that can be attained from those that cannot. Points above and to the right of this curve cannot be attained because there are not enough resources; points below and to the left of the curve can be attained without using all of the available resources; and points on the curve can just be attained if all the available resources are used efficiently. The

APPLYING ECONOMIC CONCEPTS 1-1

The Opportunity Cost of Your University Degree

As discussed in the text, the opportunity cost of choosing one thing is what must be given up as the best alternative. Computing the opportunity cost of a college or university education is a good example to illustrate which factors are included (and which are excluded) from the computation of opportunity cost. You may also be surprised to learn how expensive your university degree really is!*

Suppose that a Bachelor's degree requires four years of study and that each year you spend $3500 for tuition fees—approximately the average at Canadian universities in 2000—and a further $1500 per year for books and materials. Does this mean that the cost of a university education is only $20 000? Unfortunately not; the true cost of a university degree is much higher.

The key point is that the opportunity cost of a university education does not just include the out-of-pocket expenses on tuition and books. You must also take into consideration *what you are forced to give up* by choosing to attend university. Of course, if you were not studying you could have been doing any one of a number of things, but the relevant one is *the one you would have chosen instead*—your best alternative to attending university.

Suppose that your best alternative to attending university was to get a job. In this case, the opportunity cost of your university degree must include the earnings that you would have received had you taken that job. Suppose that your (after-tax) annual earnings would have been $18 000 per year, for a total of $72 000 if you stayed at that job for four years. To the direct expenses of $20 000, we must therefore add $72 000 for the earnings that you gave up by not taking a job. This brings the true cost of your university degree—the opportunity cost—up to $92 000!

Notice that the cost of food, lodging, clothing, and other living expenses did not enter the calculation of the opportunity cost in this example. The living expenses must be incurred in either case—whether you attend uni-

versity or get a job. Of course, it is possible that your total living expenses as a student are different from what they would have been had you taken the job. In this case, the calculation of opportunity cost would need to be adjusted. For example, perhaps the job you would have taken *required* you to spend $3000 for clothes (over the 4 years) so that you could look presentable to customers. In contrast, you find that your university classmates and professors are pretty relaxed about fashion and that your old jeans are more than adequate. In this case, the opportunity cost of your university degree would be only $89 000 because by attending university you "saved" $3000 that you otherwise would have had to spend on clothes.

If the opportunity cost of a degree is so high, why do students choose to go to university? The simple answer is that they believe that they are better off by going to university than by not going (otherwise they would not go). Maybe the students simply enjoy learning, and thus are prepared to incur the high cost to be in the university environment. Or maybe they believe that a university degree will significantly increase their future earning potential. In this case, they are giving up four years of earnings at one salary so that they can invest in their own skills in the hopes of enjoying many more years in the future at a considerably higher salary.

Whatever the case, the recognition that a university degree is very expensive should convince students to make the best use of their time while they are there. Read on!

The opportunity cost to an individual completing a university degree in Canada is very large. It includes the direct cost of tuition and books as well as the earnings forgone while attending university.

---

* This box considers only the cost *to the student* of a university degree. For reasons that will be discussed in detail in Part 6 of this book, the government heavily subsidizes post-secondary education in Canada. Because of this subsidy, the cost *to society* of a university degree is generally much higher than the cost to an individual student.

production possibility boundary   A curve that shows which alternative combinations of commodities can just be attained if all available resources are used; it is thus the boundary between attainable and unattainable output combinations.

Practise with Study Guide Chapter 1, Exercise 2.

curve is called the **production possibility boundary** or *production possibility curve*. It has a negative slope because when all resources are being used efficiently, producing more of one kind of good requires producing less of the other kind.

A production possibility boundary illustrates three concepts: scarcity, choice, and opportunity cost. Scarcity is indicated by the unattainable combinations outside the boundary; choice, by the need to choose among the alternative attainable points along the boundary; and opportunity cost, by the negative slope of the boundary.

The shape of the production possibility boundary in Figure 1-2 implies that an increasing amount of civilian production must be given up to achieve equal successive increases in military production. This shape, referred to as *concave* to the origin, indicates that the opportunity cost of either good increases as we increase the amount of it that is produced. A straight-line boundary, as in Figure 1-1, indicates that the opportunity cost of one good in terms of the other stays constant, no matter how much of it is produced.

The concave shape in Figure 1-2 is the way that economists usually draw a country's production possiblities boundary. The shape occurs because each factor of production is not equally useful in producing all goods. To see why differences among factors of production are so important, suppose we begin at a point where all resources are devoted to the production of military goods, and then consider gradually shifting more and more resources toward the production of civilian goods. The first resources we shift might be, just to take an example, nutrient-rich land that is particularly well suited to growing wheat. This land may not be very useful for making military equipment, but it is very useful for making certain civilian goods (like bread). This shift of resources will therefore lead to a very small reduction in military ouptut but a substantial increase in civilian output. Thus the opportunity cost of producing the first unit of civilian goods, which is equal to the forgone military output, is very small. But as we shift more and more resources toward the production of civilian goods, we must shift more and more resources that are actually quite well suited to the production of military output, like aerospace engineers or the minerals needed to make gunpowder. As we produce more and more civilian goods (by having more and more resources devoted to producing them), the amount of military output that must be forgone to produce one *extra* unit of civilian goods rises. That is, the opportunity cost of producing one good rises as more of that good is produced.

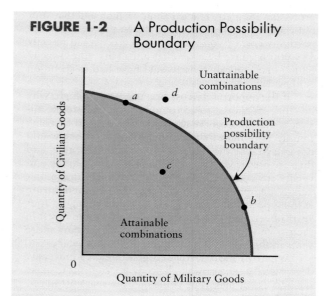

FIGURE 1-2   A Production Possibility Boundary

The negatively sloped boundary shows the combinations that are just attainable when all of the society's resources are efficiently employed. The production possibility boundary separates the attainable combinations of goods, such as *a*, *b*, and *c*, from unattainable combinations, such as *d*. Points *a* and *b* represent full and efficient use of society's resources. Point *c* represents either inefficient use of resources or failure to use all the available resources.

Four Key Economic Problems

Modern economies involve thousands of complex production and consumption activities. Although this complexity is important, many of the basic kinds of decisions that must be made are not very different from those made in primative economies in which people work with few tools and barter with their neighbours. Whatever the economic system, most problems studied by economists can be grouped under four main headings.

What Is Produced and How?

The allocation of scarce resources among alternative uses, called **resource allocation,** determines the quantities of various goods that are produced. What determines which goods get produced? Choosing to produce a particular combination of goods means choosing a particular allocation of resources among the industries or regions producing the goods.

Further, because resources are scarce, it is desirable that they be used efficiently. Hence it matters which of the available methods of production is used to produce each of the goods. What determines which methods of production get used and which ones do not?

In terms of Figure 1-2, these questions relate to where the economy will produce. Will the economy be inside the production possibility boundary because resources are used inefficiently? If resources are used efficiently, then at which point on the boundary will production take place?

resource allocation
The allocation of an economy's scarce resources of land, labour, and capital among alternative uses.

What Is Consumed and by Whom?

What is the relationship between an economy's production of goods and the consumption enjoyed by its citizens? Economists seek to understand what determines the distribution of a nation's total output among its people. Who gets a lot, who gets a little, and why?

If production takes place on the production possibility boundary, then how about consumption? Will the economy consume exactly the same goods that it produces? Or will the country's ability to trade with other countries permit the economy to consume a different combination of goods?

Questions relating to what is produced and how, and what is consumed and by whom, fall within the realm of microeconomics. Microeconomics is the study of the allocation of resources as it is affected by the workings of the price system and government policies that seek to influence it.

Why Are Resources Sometimes Idle?

When an economy is in a recession, many workers who would like to have jobs are unable to find employers to hire them. At the same time, the managers and owners of offices and factories would like to operate at a higher level of activity—that is, they would like to produce more goods and services. Similarly, during recessions raw materials are typically available in abundance. For some reason, however, these resources—labour, factories and equipment, and raw materials—are idle. Thus, in terms of Figure 1-2, the economy is operating within its production possibility boundary.

Why are resources sometimes idle? Should governments worry about such idle resources, or is there some reason to believe that such occassional idleness is appropriate in a well-functioning economy? Is there anything that the government can do to reduce such idleness?

Is Productive Capacity Growing?

The capacity to produce goods and services grows rapidly in some countries, expands slowly in others, and actually declines in others. Growth in productive capacity can be represented by an outward shift of the production possibility boundary, as shown in

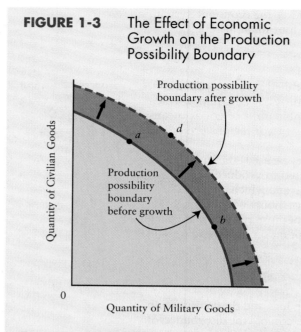

FIGURE 1-3   The Effect of Economic Growth on the Production Possibility Boundary

Economic growth shifts the boundary outward and makes it possible to produce more of all products. Before growth in productive capacity, points *a* and *b* were on the production possibility boundary and point *d* was an unattainable combination. After growth, as shown by the dark shaded band, point *d* and many other previously unattainable combinations are attainable.

Figure 1-3. If an economy's capacity to produce goods and services is growing, combinations that are unattainable today will become attainable tomorrow. Growth makes it possible to have more of all goods. What are the determinants of growth? Can governments do anything to increase economic growth?

Questions relating to the idleness of resources during recessions, and the growth of productive capacity, fall within the realm of macroeconomics. Macroeconomics is the study of the determination of economic aggregates such as total output, total employment, the price level, and the rate of economic growth.

Who Makes the Choices and How?

So choices have to be made, but who makes them and how are they made?

The Flow of Income and Expenditure

Figure 1-4 shows the basic decision makers and the flows of income and expenditure that they set up. Individuals own factors of production, including themselves. They sell the services of these factors to producers and receive payments in return. These are their incomes. Producers use the factor services that they buy to make goods and services for consumption. They sell these to individuals, receiving payments in return. These are the incomes of producers. These basic flows of income and expenditure pass through markets. Individuals sell the services of the factor that they own in what are collectively called *factor markets*. Producers sell their outputs of goods and services in what are collectively called *goods markets*.

The prices that are determined in these markets determine the incomes that are earned and the purchasing power of those incomes. People who get high prices for their factor services earn high incomes; those who get low prices earn low incomes. The income each person earns expressed as a fraction of all incomes that are earned in the nation shows the share of total income that each person can command. The *distribution of income* refers to how the nation's total production is distributed among its citizens. This is largely determined by the price that each type of factor service can command in factor markets.

Maximizing Decisions

The basic decision makers in a market economy are individual consumers and producers. To these two groups we will shortly add a third, the government. The most important thing about how these two groups make their decisions is that everyone tries to do as well as possible for themselves. In the jargon of economics, they are *maximizers*.

When individuals decide how many factor services to sell to producers and how many products to buy from them, they make choices designed to maximize their well-being, or *utility*. When producers decide how many factor services to buy from individuals and how many goods to produce and sell to them, they make choices designed to maximize their profits.

Marginal Decisions

The second key point about these choices is that they are all made *at the margin*. Let us see what this means. When you vote in a Canadian federal election, you have only one vote and you must support one party over the others. When you do, you vote for everything that party stands for, even though you may prefer to pick and choose elements from that party's political platform. You cannot say "I vote for the Liberals on issue A and for the Conservatives on issue B." You must make a total choice.

In contrast, when you spend your income, you do not have to decide which product to spend your entire income on. You can, and do, decide to spread your expenditure among many products. Furthermore, having decided to buy some CDs, you do not have to buy a large number or none at all. You can buy any number you wish and, as your circumstances change, you can vary the number you buy each month, raising it or lowering it a bit. These are *marginal* decisions—decisions to buy a bit more or a bit less.

Maximizing consumers and producers are constantly making marginal decisions, whether to buy or sell a bit more or less of each of the things that they buy and sell.

FIGURE 1-4 The Circular Flow of Income and Expenditure

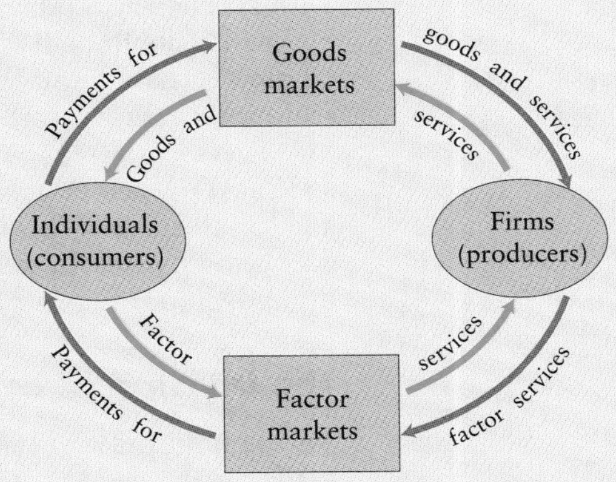

The green line shows the flows of goods and services while the blue line shows the payments made to purchase these. Factor services flow from individuals who own the factors (including their own labour) through factor markets to firms that use them to make goods and services. These goods and services then flow through goods markets to those who consume them. Money payments flow from firms to individuals through factor markets. These payments become the income of individuals. When they spend this income buying goods and services, money flows through goods markets back to producers.

Production Choices

Producers decide what to produce and how to produce it. Production is a very complex process in any modern economy. A typical car manufacturer assembles a product out of thousands of individual parts. It makes some of these parts itself. Most are subcontracted to parts manufacturers and many of the major parts manufacturers subcontract some of their work out to smaller firms. This kind of production displays two characteristics noted long ago by Adam Smith—*specialization* and the *division of labour*.

Specialization

In ancient hunter–gather societies, and in modern subsistence economies, most people make most of the things they need for themselves. However, from the time that people first engaged in settled agriculture and some of them began to live in towns, people have specialized in doing particular jobs. Artisans, soldiers, priests, and government officials were some of the earliest specialized occupations. Economists call this allocation of different jobs to different people the **specialization of labour**. There are two fundamental reasons why specialization is extraordinarily efficient compared with universal self-sufficiency.

specialization of labour The specialization of individual workers in the production of particular goods or services.

First, individual abilities differ, and specialization allows each person to do what he or she can do relatively well while leaving everything else to be done by others. Even when people's abilities are unaffected by the act of specializing, production is greater with specialization than with self-sufficiency. This is one of the most fundamental principles in economics. It is called the principle of *comparative advantage*. A much fuller discussion of comparative advantage is found in Chapter 34 where we discuss the gains from international trade.

The second reason concerns changes in people's abilities that occur *because* they specialize. A person who concentrates on one activity becomes better at it than could a jack-of-all-trades. This is called *learning by doing*. It was a factor much stressed by early economists. Modern research into what are called *learning curves* shows that learning by doing is important in many modern industries.

The Division of Labour

division of labour
The breaking up of a production process into a series of specialized tasks, each done by a different worker.

Throughout most of history each artisan who was specialized in making some product made the whole of that product. Over the last several hundred years many technical advances in production methods have made it efficient to organize agriculture and manufacturing into large-scale firms organized around what is called the **division of labour.** This term refers to specialization *within* the production process of a particular product.

Mass Production. In a mass-production factory work is divided into highly specialized tasks using specialized machinery. Each individual repeatedly does one small task that is a small fraction of those necessary to produce any one product. This is an extreme case of the division of labour.

Artisans and Flexible Manufacturing. Two very recent changes have significantly altered the degree of specialization found in many modern production processes. First, individual artisans have recently reappeared in some lines of production. They are responding to a revival in the demand for individually crafted, rather than mass-produced, products. Second, many manufacturing operations are being reorganized along new lines called "lean production" or "flexible manufacturing," which was pioneered by Japanese car manufacturers in the mid 1950s. It has led back to a more craft-based form of organization within the factory. In this technique employees work as a team; each employee is able to do every team member's job rather than one very specialized task at one point on the assembly line.

Globalization

Market economies constantly change, largely as a result of the development of new technologies. Many of the recent changes are referred to as *globalization*, a term often used very loosely to mean the increased importance of international trade. International trade, however, is an old phenomenon—just think of the ancient trading routes created largely by the spice trade. But the usual pattern over most of the last two hundred years was manufactured goods being sent from Europe and North America to the rest of the world, with raw materials and primary products being sent in return. What is new in the last few decades is the globalization of manufacturing.

Underlying the modern notion of globalization is the rapid reduction in transportation costs and the revolution in information technology that have occurred in the last half of the twentieth century. The cost of moving products around the world has fallen greatly in recent decades owing to containerization and the increasing size of ships. Our ability to transmit and to analyze data has been increasing even more dramatically, while the costs of doing so have been decreasing, equally dramatically. For example, today $2000 buys a computer that fits into a briefcase and has the same computing power as one that in 1970 cost $10 million and filled a large room. This revolution in information and communication technology (ICT) has made it possible to coordinate economic transactions around the world in ways that were difficult and costly fifty years ago and quite impossible a hundred years ago.

Fifty years ago, if a car was to be assembled in Oshawa, all the parts had to be made nearby. Today it is possible to make parts anywhere in the world and get them to Oshawa just as they are required. As a result, manufacturing, which was formerly concentrated in the advanced industrial countries of Europe and North America, now takes place all over the world. A typical CD player, TV set, or car contains components made in dozens of different countries. We still know where a product is assembled, but it is becoming increasingly difficult to say where it is *made*.

Globalization is as important for consumers as it is for producers. For example, as some tastes become universal to young people, spread by ever-increasing access to foreign television stations and global internet chat lines, we can see the same clothes and hear the same music in virtually all big cities. And as tastes become more universal, many *corporations* are globalizing, as they become what economists call **transnational corporations.** These are massive firms with a physical presence in many countries and an increasingly decentralized management structure. McDonald's restaurants are as visible in Moscow or Beijing as in London, New York, Vancouver, or Montreal. Many other brands are also known around the world, such as Calvin Klein, Nike, Coca Cola, Kelloggs, Heinz, Nestlé, Molson, Toyota, Rolls-Royce, Sony, and Mitsubishi.

The revolution in computer technology has drastically reduced communication and transportation costs. This reduction in costs lies at the heart of globalization.

Today no country can take an isolationist economic stance and hope to take part in the global economy where an increasing share of jobs and incomes are created.

transnational corporations (TNCs) Firms that have operations in more than one country. Also called *multinational enterprises (MNEs)*.

Markets and Money

People who specialize in doing only one thing, whether they are artisans, factory workers, or computer programmers, must satisfy most of their wants by consuming things made by other people. In early societies the exchange of goods and services took place by simple mutual agreement among neighbours. In the course of time, however, trading became centred on particular gathering places called *markets*. For example, the French markets or trade fairs of Champagne were well-known throughout Europe as early as the eleventh century AD. Even now, many small towns in Canada have regular market days. Today, however, the term *market* has a much broader meaning. We use the term *market economy* to refer to a society in which people specialize in productive activities and meet most of their material wants through exchanges voluntarily agreed upon by the contracting parties.

Specialization must be accompanied by trade. People who produce only one thing must trade most of it to obtain all of the other things they require.

barter   An economic system in which goods and services are traded directly for other goods and services instead of for money.

Early trading was by means of **barter,** the trading of goods directly for other goods. But barter is costly in terms of time spent searching out satisfactory exchanges. If a farmer has wheat but wants a hammer, he must find someone who has a hammer and wants wheat. A successful barter transaction thus requires what is called a *double co-incidence of wants*.

Money eliminates the cumbersome system of barter by separating the transactions involved in the exchange of products. If a farmer has wheat and wants a hammer, he does not have to find someone who has a hammer and wants wheat. He merely has to find someone who wants wheat. The farmer takes money in exchange. Then he finds a person who wishes to sell a hammer and gives up the money for the hammer.

Money greatly facilitates specialization and trade.

Is There an Alternative to the Market Economy?

The answer to the question in the above heading is no in one sense and yes in another. We answer no because the modern economy has no *practical* alternative to reliance on market determination. We answer yes because it is possible to identify other types of economic systems.

An economic system is a distinctive method of providing answers to the basic economic questions discussed above, such as who produces what, and who consumes what. All such systems are complex. They include producers of every sort—public and private, domestic and foreign. They include consumers of every sort—young and old, rich and poor, working and nonworking. They include laws—such as those relating to property rights—rules, regulations, taxes, subsidies, and everything else that governments use to influence what is produced, how it is produced, and who gets it. They also include customs of every conceivable kind and the entire range of contemporary mores and values.

Types of Economic Systems

Although every economy is in some ways unique, it is helpful to distinguish three pure types, called *traditional, command,* and *market* economies. These economies differ in the way in which economic decisions are coordinated. But no actual economy fits neatly into one of these three categories—all real economies contain some elements of each type.

Traditional Systems

traditional economy
An economy in which behaviour is based mostly on tradition, custom, and habit.

A **traditional economy** is one in which behaviour is based primarily on tradition, custom, and habit. Young men follow their fathers' occupations. Women do what their mothers did. There is little change in the pattern of goods produced from year to year, other than those imposed by the vagaries of nature. The techniques of production also follow traditional patterns, except when the effects of an occasional new invention are felt. Finally, production is allocated among the members according to long-established traditions. In short, the answers to the economic questions of what to produce, how to produce, and how to distribute are determined by traditions.

Such a system works best in an unchanging environment. Under such static conditions, a system that does not continually require people to make choices can prove effective in meeting economic and social needs.

Traditional systems were common in earlier times. The feudal system, under which most people in medieval Europe lived, was a largely traditional society. Peasants, artisans, and most others living in villages inherited their positions in that society. They also usually inherited their specific jobs, which they handled in traditional ways.

Command Systems

In command systems, economic behaviour is determined by some central authority, usually the government, which makes most of the necessary decisions on what to produce, how to produce it, and who gets it. Such economies are characterized by the *centralization* of decision making. Because centralized decision makers usually lay down elaborate and complex plans for the behaviour that they wish to impose, the terms **command economy** and *centrally planned economy* are usually used synonymously.

The sheer quantity of data required for central planning of an entire economy is enormous, and the task of analysing it to produce a fully integrated plan can hardly be exaggerated. Moreover, the plan must be continually changing to take account not only of current data but also of future trends in labour supplies, technological developments, and people's tastes for various goods and services. Doing so involves the planners in *forecasting*. This is a notoriously difficult exercise, not least because of the unavailability of all essential, accurate, and up-to-date information.

Fifteen years ago, more than one third of the world's population lived in countries that relied heavily on central planning to deal with the basic economic questions. Today, the number of such countries is small. Even in countries where planning is the proclaimed system, as in China or Cuba, increasing amounts of market determination are being quietly permitted.

command economy
An economy in which the decisions of a centralized planning authority exert the major influence over the allocation of resources.

Free-Market Systems

In the third type of economic system, the decisions about resource allocation are made without any central direction. Instead, they result from innumerable independent decisions made by individual producers and consumers. Such a system is known as a **free-market economy** or, more simply, a *market economy*. In such an economy, decisions relating to the basic economic issues are *decentralized*. Despite the absence of a central plan, these many decentralized decisions are nonetheless coordinated. The main coordinating device is the set of market-determined prices—which is why free-market systems are often called *price systems*.

In a pure market economy, all of these decisions, without exception, are made by buyers and sellers acting through unhindered markets. The state provides the background of defining property and protecting rights against foreign and domestic enemies but, beyond that, markets determine all resource allocation and income distribution.

free-market economy
An economy in which the decisions of individual households and firms exert the major influence over the allocation of resources.

Mixed Systems

Economies that are fully traditional or fully centrally planned or wholly free-market are pure types that are useful for studying basic principles. When we look in detail at any real economy, however, we discover that its economic behaviour is the result of some mixture of central control and market determination, with a certain amount of traditional behaviour as well.

mixed economy   An economy in which some decisions about the allocation of resources are made by firms and households and some by the government.

In practice, every economy is a **mixed economy** in the sense that it combines significant elements of all three systems in determining economic behaviour.

Furthermore, within any economy, the degree of the mix varies from sector to sector. For example, in some planned economies, the command principle was used more often to determine behaviour in heavy-goods industries, such as steel, than in agriculture. Farmers were often given substantial freedom to produce and sell what they wished in response to varying market prices.

When economists speak of a particular economy as being centrally planned, we mean only that the degree of the mix is weighted heavily toward the command principle. When we speak of one as being a market economy, we mean only that the degree of the mix is weighted heavily toward decentralized decision making in response to market signals. It is important to realize that such distinctions are always matters of degree and that almost every conceivable mix can be found across the spectrum of the world's economies.

Although no country offers an example of either system working alone, some economies, such as those of Canada, the United States, France, and Hong Kong, rely much more heavily on market decisions than others, such as the economies of China, North Korea, and Cuba. Yet even in Canada, the command principle has some sway. Crown corporations, legislated minimum wages, rules and regulations for environmental protection, quotas on some agricultural outputs, and restrictions on the import of some items are the obvious examples.

See Chapter 1 of www.pearsoned.ca/lipsey for an excellent discussion of Cuba's recent economic reforms: Archibald Ritter, "Is Cuba's Economic Reform Process Paralysed?" *World Economic Affairs.*

Ownership of Resources

We have seen that economies differ as to the principle used for coordinating their economic decisions. They also differ as to *who owns* their productive resources. Who owns a nation's farms and factories, its coal mines and forests? Who owns its railways, streams, and golf courses? Who owns its houses and hotels?

In a private-ownership economy, the basic raw materials, the productive assets of the society, and the goods produced in the economy are predominantly privately owned. By this standard, Canada has primarily a private-ownership economy. However, even in Canada, public ownership extends beyond the usual basic services such as schools and local transportation systems to include other activities such as housing projects, forest and range land, and electric power utilities.

In contrast, a public-ownership economy is one in which the productive assets are predominantly publicly owned. This was true of the former Soviet Union, and it is true to a significant extent in present-day China and in Cuba. In China, however, private ownership exists in many sectors, including the rapidly growing part of the manufacturing sector that is foreign owned, mainly by Japanese and by Chinese from Taiwan and Singapore.

Command Versus Market Determination

For over a century, a great debate raged on the relative merits of the command principle versus the market principle for coordinating economic decisions. The former Soviet Union, the countries of Eastern Europe, and China were command economies for much of this century. Canada, the United States, and most of the countries of Western Europe were, and still are, primarily market economies. The apparent successes of the Soviet Union and China in the early stages of industrialization suggested to many observers that the command principle was at least as good for organizing economic behaviour as the market principle, if not better. Over the long run, however, planned economies proved a failure of such disastrous proportions that they seriously depressed the living standards of their citizens. (Some of the reasons for this failure were examined in *Lessons from History 1-1*.)

Still Room for Disagreement

The failure of centrally planned economies suggests the superiority of decentralized markets over centrally planned ones as mechanisms for allocating an economy's scarce resources. Put another way, it demonstrates the superiority of mixed economies with substantial elements of market determination over fully planned command economies. However, it does *not* demonstrate, as some observers have asserted, the superiority of completely free-market economies over mixed economies.

There is no guarantee that completely free markets will, on their own, handle such urgent matters as controlling pollution or providing public goods (like national defence). Indeed, as we shall see in later chapters, much economic theory is devoted to explaining why free markets often fail to do these things. Mixed economies, with significant elements of government intervention, are needed to do these jobs.

Furthermore, acceptance of the free market over central planning does not provide an excuse to ignore a country's pressing social issues. Acceptance of the benefits of the free market still leaves plenty of scope to debate the kinds, amounts, and directions of government interventions into the workings of our market-based economy that will help to achieve social goals.

It follows that there is still considerable room for disagreement about the degree of the mix of market and government determination in any modern mixed economy—room enough to accommodate such divergent views as could be expressed by conservative, liberal, and modern social democratic parties. People can accept the free market as an efficient way of organizing economic affairs and still disagree about many things. A partial list includes: the optimal amount and types of government regulation of various parts of the economy; the types of measures needed to protect the environment; whether health care should be provided by the public or the private sector; and the optimal amount and design of social services and other policies intended to redistribute income from more to less fortunate citizens.

So, the first answer to the question posed at the outset of this section is no. There is no practical alternative to a mixed system with major reliance on markets but a substantial government presence in most aspects of the economy. The second answer is yes. Within the framework of a mixed economy there are substantial alternatives among many different and complex mixes of free-market and government determination of economic life.

Government in the Modern Mixed Economy

Market economies in today's advanced industrial countries are based primarily on voluntary transactions between individual buyers and sellers. Private individuals have the right to buy and sell what they wish, to accept or refuse work that is offered to them, and to move to where they want when they want.

Key institutions are private property and freedom of contract, both of which must be maintained by active government policies. The government creates laws of ownership and contract and then provides the institutions to enforce these laws.

In modern mixed economies governments go well beyond these important basic functions. They intervene in market transactions to correct what economists call *market failures*. These are well-defined situations in which free markets do not work well. Resources such as fishing grounds and common pastureland tend to be overexploited to the point of destruction under free-market conditions. Some products, called *public goods*, are not provided at all by markets because, once produced, no one can be prevented from using them. So their use cannot be restricted to those who are willing to pay for them. Defence and police protection are public goods. In other cases private transactors impose costs called *externalities* on those who have no say in the transaction. This is the case when factories pollute the air and rivers. The public is harmed but has no part in the producer's decisions about what to make and how to make it. These are some of the reasons why free markets sometimes fail to function as we would like them to. They explain why citizens wish governments to intervene and alter the allocation of resources that would otherwise result from leaving everything to the market.

Also, there are important equity issues that arise from letting free markets determine people's incomes. Some people lose their jobs because firms are reorganizing to become more efficient in the face of new technologies. Others keep their jobs, but the market places so little value on their services that they face economic deprivation. The old and the chronically ill may suffer if their past circumstances did not allow them to save enough to support themselves. For many reasons of this sort we accept government intervention to redistribute income by taking from the "haves" and giving to the "have-nots." Almost everyone supports some redistribution of incomes. Care must be taken, however, not to kill the goose that lays the golden egg. By taking too much from the haves, we risk eliminating their incentive to work hard and produce income, some of which is to be redistributed to the have-nots.

Governments also play a part in influencing the overall level of prices and in attempting to stabilize the economy against extreme fluctuations in income and employment. A stable price level and full employment are two major goals of the government's *macroeconomic* policy. These are dealt with in the second half of this book.

These are some of the reasons all modern economies are mixed economies. Throughout most of the twentieth century in advanced industrial societies the mix had been altering towards more and more government participation in decisions about the allocation of resources and the distribution of income. In the last two decades of the century, however, there has been a worldwide movement to reduce the degree of government participation. The details of this shift in the market/government mix, and the reasons for it, are some of the major issues that will be studied in this book.

S U M M A R Y

The Complexity of the Modern Economy   LO 1

- A market economy is self-organizing in the sense that when individual consumers and producers act independently to pursue their own self-interest, responding to prices determined in open markets, the collective outcome is coordinated and relatively efficient.

- An alternative economic system requires a central planning authority to make the decisions of who consumes and who produces which goods. The experience of those countries that adopted central planning was that such planning was extremely difficult and quite inefficient in allocating resources.

Resources and Scarcity ⓛⓞ❷

- Scarcity is a fundamental problem faced by all economies. Not enough resources are available to produce all the goods and services that people would like to consume. Scarcity makes it necessary to choose. All societies must have a mechanism for choosing what goods and services will be produced and in what quantities.
- The concept of opportunity cost emphasizes the problem of scarcity and choice by measuring the cost of obtaining a unit of one product in terms of the number of units of other products that could have been obtained instead.

- A production possibility boundary shows all of the combinations of goods that can be produced by an economy whose resources are fully and efficiently employed. Movement from one point to another along the boundary shows a shift in the amounts of goods being produced, which requires a reallocation of resources.
- Four basic questions must be answered in all economies: What is produced and how? What is consumed and by whom? Why are resources sometimes idle? Is productive capacity growing?

Who Makes the Choices and How? ⓛⓞ❸

- The interaction of consumers and producers through goods and factor markets is illustrated by the circular flow of income and expenditure. Individual consumers sell factor services to producers and, by doing so, earn their income. Similarly, producers earn their income by selling goods and services to individual consumers.
- Individual consumers make their decisions in an effort to maximize their well-being or utility. Producers' decisions are designed to maximize their profits.

- Modern economies are based on the specialization and division of labour, which necessitate the exchange (trade) of goods and services. Exchange takes place in markets and is facilitated by the use of money.
- Driven by the ongoing revolution in transportation and communications technology, the world economy is rapidly globalizing. National and regional boundaries are becoming less important with the rise of transnational corporations.

Is There an Alternative to the Market Economy? ⓛⓞ❹

- We can distinguish three pure types of economies: traditional, command, and free-market. In practice, all economies are mixed economies in that their economic behaviour responds to mixes of tradition, government command, and price incentives.
- In the late 1980s, events in Eastern Europe and the Soviet Union led to the general acceptance that the system of fully centrally planned economies had failed to produce minimally acceptable living standards for its citizens. All of these

countries are now moving toward greater market determination and less state command in their economies.
- Governments play an important role in modern mixed economies. They create and enforce important background institutions such as private property and freedom of contract. They intervene to correct situations where markets do not effectively perform their coordinating function. They also redistribute income and wealth in the interests of equity.

K E Y   C O N C E P T S

The self-organzing economy
Scarcity and the need for choice
Choice and opportunity cost
Production possibility boundary
Resource allocation

Growth in productive capacity
Specialization
Comparative advantange
The division of labour
Globalization

Traditional economies
Command economies
Pure market economies
Mixed economies

STUDY EXERCISES

For Questions 1-4, consider the following description of a mythical economy called Choiceland.

Choiceland has 250 workers and produces only two goods, X and Y. Labour is the only factor of production, but some workers are better suited to producing X than Y (and vice versa). The table below shows the maximum levels of output of each good possible from various levels of labour input.

Number of Workers Producing X	Annual Production of X	Number of Workers Producing Y	Annual Production of Y
0	0	250	1300
50	20	200	1200
100	45	150	900
150	60	100	600
200	70	50	350
250	75	0	0

1. Draw the production possibility boundary for Choiceland on a scale diagram.

2. Explain why the PPB is shaped concave to the origin.

3. Compute the opportunity cost of producing an extra 10 units of X if the economy is initially producing 60 units of X and 600 units of Y. How does this compare to the opportunity cost if the economy were initially producing 70 units of X?

4. Suppose now that the technology associated with producing good Y improves, so that the maximum level of Y that can be produced from any given level of labour input increases by 10 percent. Explain (or show in a diagram) what happens to the production possibilities curve.

5. Explain why a technological improvement in the production of one good means that a country can now produce more of *other* goods than it did previously.

6. Consider the decision you face when deciding whether to go skiing for the weekend. Suppose that transportation, lift tickets, and accommodation for the weekend costs $300. Suppose also that restaurant food for the weekend will cost $75. Finally, suppose that you have a weekend job that you will have to miss if you go skiing, a job that pays you $120 (after tax) for the one weekend day that you work. What is the opportunity cost of going skiing? Is there any other information that you need before computing the opportunity cost?

7. Suppose that you and a friend go wilderness camping for a week and must find your own food to survive. From past experience, you know that you and your friend have different abilities in fishing and hunting. If each of you were to work for one day either catching fish or trapping rabbits, the number of fish and rabbits that you could catch is given in the following table:

	Fish	Rabbits
You	6	3
Your friend	8	2

You and your friend decide that you should allocate the duties so that you get the most food for the least amount of work effort.

a. What is the opportunity cost for you to catch an additional rabbit? What is your friend's opportunity cost for catching an extra rabbit?

b. What is the allocation of tasks that maximizes total output for the least amount of work effort?

c. Suppose that you both decide to work for two days according to the allocation in part b. What is the total amount of output? What would it have been if you had decided the reverse allocation of tasks?

DISCUSSION QUESTIONS

1. What is the difference between scarcity and poverty? If everyone in the world had enough to eat, could we say that food was no longer scarce?

2. Evidence accumulates that the use of chemical fertilizers, which increases agricultural production greatly, damages water quality. Analyse the choice between more food and cleaner water involved in using such fertilizers. Use a production possibility curve with agricultural output on the vertical axis and water quality on the horizontal axis. In what ways does this production possibility curve reflect scarcity, choice, and opportunity cost? How would an improved fertilizer that increased agricultural output without further worsening water quality affect the curve? Suppose that a pollution-free fertilizer were developed; would this mean that there would no longer be any opportunity cost in using it?

3. Discuss the following statement by a leading U.S. economist: "One of the mysteries of semantics is why the government-managed economies ever came to be called planned and the market economies unplanned. It is the former that are in chronic chaos, in which buyers stand in line hoping to buy some toilet paper or soap. It is the latter that are in reasonable equilibrium—where if you want a cake of soap or a steak or a shirt or a car, you can go to the store and find that the item is magically there for you to buy. It is the liberal economies that reflect a highly sophisticated planning system, and the government-managed economies that are primitive and unplanned."

4. Consider the market for physicians' services. In what way has this market taken advantage of the specialization of labour?

5. "It is not from the benevolence of the butcher, the brewer, or the baker, that we expect our dinner, but from their regard to their own interest. We address ourselves, not to their humanity but to their self-love, and never talk to them of our own necessities but of their advantages." Do you agree with this quotation from Adam Smith's classic, *The Wealth of Nations*? How are "our dinner" and "their self-interest" related to the price system? What does Smith assume to be the motives of firms and households?

CHAPTER 2

How Economists Work

LO LEARNING OBJECTIVES

1 Recognize the difference between positive and normative statements.

2 Understand how theorizing and model-building help economists think about the economy.

3 Explain the interaction between economic theories and empirical observation.

4 Understand why testing theories about human behaviour usually requires studying large numbers of individuals.

5 Recognize several types of economic data, including index numbers, time-series and cross-section data, and scatter diagrams.

6 Understand that economic theories involve relations between variables and that such relations can be expressed in words, equations, or graphs.

7 Recognize that the slope of a relation between X and Y is interpreted as the marginal response in Y to a unit change in X.

In Chapter 1 we discussed the basic question whose answer gave rise to the study of economics. How do millions of producers and consumers, acting independently in their own self-interest, somehow become organized into a coherent system that delivers the goods and services where and when they are wanted and in the approximate quantities they are wanted? Economists study how this is done by the mixed market economies in which we live. Economists also identify situations in which markets fail to perform as well as they might. In such cases they ask whether specific markets may be able to perform more effectively. Usually this involves government intervention of one form or another. Economists then seek to evaluate the efficiency with which governments achieve their goals.

Having sought to understand what is happening in the mixed economy, the next step is often to give policy advice. Indeed, economists give advice on a wide variety of policy topics. If you read a newspaper, watch television, or listen to the radio you will often notice some economist's opinions being reported. Perhaps it is on unemployment, the exchange rate, or interest rates; on some new tax; on the case for privatization or regulation of an industry; or on the possible reforms to Canada's health-care system.

Economics is regarded as a social science. Unlike a training in chemsitry or physics, however, many economists would say that a training in economics provides the student more with a "way of thinking" than with a collection of facts. This does not mean that facts are unimportant to the economist—quite the contrary. It means only that facts are typically harder to establish in economics than in the "hard" sciences and often economists do not know which facts are important without first having a way to organize their thinking.

Central to the economist's way of thinking is the distinction between *positive statements* and *normative statements*. Also of crucial importance to the economist is the role of *theory* and, in particular, the use of economic *models* to provide a framework for thinking about complex issues. Such models can be used to generate *testable hypotheses*.

In this chapter, we explore what it means to be "scientific" in the study of human behaviour and to establish criteria for evaluating how well economics succeeds in meeting that goal.

Positive and Normative Advice

Economists give two broad types of advice, called *normative* and *positive*. They sometimes advise that the government ought to try harder to reduce unemployment or to preserve the environment. When they say such things they are giving normative advice. They may be using their expert knowledge to come to conclusions about the costs of various unemployment-reducing or environment-saving schemes. But when they say that the government *ought* to do something, they are making judgements about the value of the various things that the government could do with its limited resources. Advice that depends on a value judgement is normative—it tells others what they *ought* to do.

Another type of advice is illustrated by the statement "If the government wants to reduce unemployment, reducing unemployment-insurance benefits is an effective way of doing so." This is positive advice. It does not rely on a judgement about the value of reducing unemployment. Instead the expert is saying, "If this is what you want to do, here is a way to do it."

The distinction between positive and normative is fundamental to any rational inquiry. Much of the success of modern science depends on the ability of scientists to separate their views on *what does happen* in the world, from their views on *what they would like to happen*. For example, until the eighteenth century almost everyone believed that the Earth was only a few thousand years old. Evidence then began to accumulate that the Earth was billions of years old. This evidence was hard for most people to accept since it ran counter to a literal reading of many religious texts. Many did not want to believe the evidence. Nevertheless, scientists, many of whom were religious, continued their research because they refused to allow their feelings about what they wanted to believe to affect their scientific search for the truth. Eventually, all scientists came to accept that the Earth is about 4 billion years old.

Distinguishing what is true from what we would like to be, or what we feel ought to be, requires distinguishing between positive and normative statements.

Normative statements depend on value judgements. They involve issues of personal opinion, which cannot be settled by recourse to facts. In contrast, **positive statements** do not involve value judgements. They are statements about what is, was, or will be—that is, statements that are about matters of fact.

Examples of both types of statement are given in Table 2-1. All five positive statements in the table assert things about the nature of the world in which we live. In contrast, the five normative statements involve value judgements.

Notice two things about the positive/normative distinction. First, positive statements need not be true. Statement D is almost certainly false. Yet it is positive, not normative. Second, the inclusion of a value judgement in a statement does not necessarily make the statement normative. Statement E is about the value judgements that people

normative statement
A statement about what ought to be as opposed to what actually is.

positive statement
A statement about what actually is (was or will be), as opposed to what ought to be.

TABLE 2-1   Positive and Normative Statements

Positive		Normative	
A	Raising interest rates encourages people to save.	F	People should be encouraged to save.
B	High rates of income tax encourage people to evade paying taxes.	G	Governments should arrange taxes so that people cannot avoid paying them.
C	Raising wage rates causes people to work harder.	H	Firms should raise wage rates to provide a just reward for hard work.
D	Lowering the price of tobacco causes people to smoke less.	I	The government should raise the tax on tobacco to discourage people from smoking.
E	The majority of the population would prefer a policy that reduced unemployment to one that reduced inflation.	J	The government ought to be more concerned with reducing unemployment than inflation.

hold. We could, however, check to see if people really do prefer low unemployment to low inflation. We can ask them and we can observe how they vote. There is no need for the economist to introduce a value judgement in order to check the validity of the statement itself.

We leave you to analyse the remaining eight statements to decide precisely why each is either positive or normative. Remember to apply the two tests. First, is the statement only about actual or alleged facts? If so, it is a positive one. Second, are value judgements necessary to assess the truth of the statement? If so, it is normative.

Economic Theories and Models

Economists seek to understand the world by developing *theories* and *models* that explain some of the things that have been seen and to predict some of the things that will be seen. What is a theory and what is a model?

Theories

Theories are constructed to explain things. For example, what determines the number of eggs sold in Winnipeg in a particular week? As part of the answer to this question and ones like it, economists have developed theories of demand and supply—theories that we will study in detail in the next three chapters. Any theory is distinguished by its definitions, assumptions, and predictions.

Definitions

variable Any well-defined item, such as the price or quantity of a commodity, that can take on various specific values.

The basic elements of any theory are its variables. A **variable** is a magnitude that can take on different possible values.

In our theory of the egg market, the variable *quantity of eggs* might be defined as the number of cartons of 12 grade-A eggs. The variable *price of eggs* is the amount of money that must be given up to purchase each carton of eggs. The particular values taken on by those two variables might be 2000 cartons at a price of $1.80 on July 1, 1998; 1800 cartons at a price of $1.95 on July 1, 1999; and 1950 cartons at a price of $1.85 on July 1, 2000.

For a theory of the egg market we define the variable *demand* as the number of cartons of eggs consumers wish to purchase over a particular time-period. We define the variable *supply* as the number of cartons of eggs producers want to sell over the same time-period.

There are two broad categories of variables that are important in any theory. An **endogenous variable** is one whose value is determined within the theory. An **exogenous variable** influences the endogenous variables but is itself determined by factors outside the theory. To illustrate the difference, the quantity of eggs is an endogenous variable in our theory of the egg market—our theory is designed to explain it. The state of the weather, however, is an exogenous variable. It may well affect the number of eggs consumers demand or producers supply but we can safely assume that the state of the weather is not influenced by the market for eggs.[1]

Assumptions

A theory's assumptions concern motives, physical relations, directions of causation, and the conditions under which the theory is meant to apply.

Motives.   The theories we study in this book make the fundamental assumption that everyone pursues their own self-interest when making economic decisions. People are assumed to know what they want, and to know how to go about getting it within the constraints set by the resources at their command.

Physical Relations.   If egg producers buy more chicks and use more labour, land, and chicken feed, they will produce more eggs. This is an example of one of the most important physical relations in the theory of markets. It concerns assumptions about how the amount of output is related to the quantities of factors of production used to produce it. This relation is specified in what is called a *production function.*

Conditions of Application.   Assumptions are often used to specify the conditions under which a theory is meant to hold. For example, a theory that assumes there is "no government" usually does not mean literally the absence of government, but only that the theory is meant to apply when governments are not significantly affecting the situation being studied.

Direction of Causation.   When economists assume that one variable is related to another, they are assuming some causal link between the two. For example, when the amount of eggs that producers want to supply is assumed to increase when the cost of their chicken feed falls, the causation runs from the price of chicken feed to the supply of eggs. Producers supply more eggs because the price of chicken feed has fallen; they do not get cheaper chicken feed because of their decision to supply more eggs.

Although assumptions are an essential part of all theories, students are often concerned about those that seem unrealistic. An example will illustrate some of the issues involved. Much of the theory that we are going to study in this book uses the assumption that owners of firms attempt to maximize their profits. The assumption of profit maximization allows economists to make predictions about the behaviour of firms. They

endogenous variable
A variable that is explained within a theory. Sometimes called an *induced variable* or a *dependent variable.*

exogenous variable
A variable that influences endogenous variables but is itself determined by factors outside the theory. Sometimes called an *autonomous variable* or an *independent variable.*

---

[1]Other words are sometimes used to make the same distinction. One frequently used pair is *induced* for endogenous and *autonomous* for exogenous. Another pair is *dependent* for endogenous and *independent* for exogenous.

A key assumption in economics is that firms make decisions with the goal of maximizing their profits.

study how firms' profits are affected by the choices firms make. They then predict that the alternative that produces the most profits will be the one selected.

Profit maximization may seem like a rather crude assumption. Surely, for example, the managers of firms sometimes choose to protect the environment rather than pursue certain highly polluting but profitable opportunities. Does this not discredit the assumption of profit maximization by showing it to be unrealistic?

The answer is no; to make successful predictions, the theory does not require that managers be solely and unwaveringly motivated by the desire to maximize profits. All that is required is that profits be a sufficiently important consideration that a theory based on the assumption of profit maximization will lead to explanations and predictions that are substantially correct.

This illustration shows that it is not always appropriate to criticize a theory because its assumptions seem unrealistic.

All theory is an abstraction from reality. If it were not, it would merely duplicate the world in all its complexity and would add little to our understanding of it.

A good theory abstracts in a useful way; a poor theory does not. If a theory has ignored some genuinely important factors, its predictions will be contradicted by the evidence—at least where an ignored factor exerts an important influence on the outcome.

Predictions

A theory's predictions are the propositions that can be deduced from it. They are often called *hypotheses*. For example, a prediction from our theory of the demand and supply for eggs is that "if the price of chicken feed falls, producers will supply more eggs." A prediction concerning a different market, the market for labour services, is "if the hourly wage paid to workers increases, the amount of labour employed will fall."

Models

economic model
A term used in several related ways: sometimes as a synonym for theory, sometimes for a specific quantification of a general theory, sometimes for the application of a general theory to a specific context, and sometimes for an abstraction designed to illustrate some point but not meant as a full theory on its own.

Economists often proceed by constructing what they call **economic models**. This term has several different but related meanings.

Sometimes the term "model" is used as a synonym for a theory, as when economists speak of the model of the determination of national income. Sometimes it may refer to a particular subset of theories, such as the Keynesian model or the Neoclassical model of income determination.

More often, a model means a specific quantitative formulation of a theory. In this case, specific numbers are attached to the mathematical relationships defined by the theory, the numbers often being derived from observations of the economy. The specific form of the model can then be used to make precise predictions about, say, the behaviour of prices in the potato market, or the course of national income and total employment. Forecasting models used by the Bank of Canada and the International Monetary Fund (IMF) are of this type.

The term "model" is often used to refer to an application of a general theory in a specific context. So if we take the theory of consumer demand and apply it to the egg market in Winnipeg we might speak of a model of the Winnipeg egg market.

Finally, a model may be an illustrative abstraction, not meant to be elaborate enough to generate testable hypotheses. The circular flow of income and expenditure in Chapter 1 is a model of this sort. By illustrating how income and payments flow between consumers and producers, it helps us to understand how decisions of these two groups influence each other through factor markets and goods markets. However, the actual flows in any real economy are vastly more complex than the simple flows shown in the figure. The model helps us to understand what is going on without being detailed enough to yield specific testable predictions about real-world behaviour. In some ways, a model of this sort is like a political caricature. Its value is in the insights it provides that help us to understand key features of a complex world.

Testing Theories

Economists make much use of evidence or, as they usually call it, empirical observation. Such observations can be used to test a specific prediction of some theory and to provide observations to be explained by theories.

A theory is tested by confronting its predictions with evidence. Are events of the type contained in the theory followed by the consequences predicted by the theory? For example, is a decrease in the price of chicken feed followed by an increase in the amount of eggs producers want to sell? Generally, theories tend to be abandoned when they are no longer useful. A theory ceases to be useful when it cannot predict better than an alternative theory. When a theory consistently fails to predict better than an available alternative, it is either modified or replaced.

The old question, "Which came first: the chicken or the egg?", is often raised when discussing economic theories. In the first instance, it was observation that preceded economic theories. People were not born with economic theories embedded in their minds; instead, economic theories first arose when people observed the coordination of market behaviour and asked themselves how such coordination occurred. But, once economics was established, theories and evidence interacted with each other. It has now become impossible to say that one precedes the other. In some cases, empirical evidence may suggest inadequacies that require the development of better theories. In other cases, an inspired guess may lead to a theory that has little current empirical support but is subsequently found to explain many observations. This interaction between theory and empirical observation is illustrated in Figure 2-1.

Theories About Human Behaviour

So far we have talked about theories in general. But what about theories that purport to explain and predict human behaviour? A scientific study of human behaviour is only possible if humans respond in predictable ways to things that affect them. Is it reasonable to expect such predictability? After all, we humans have free will and can behave in capricious ways if the spirit moves us.

Think, however, of what the world would be like if human behaviour were really unpredictable. Neither law, nor justice, nor airline timetables would be more reliable than the outcome of a single spin of a roulette wheel. A kind remark could as easily provoke fury as sympathy. Your landlady might evict you tomorrow or let you off the rent. One cannot really imagine a society of human beings that could work like this. In fact, we live

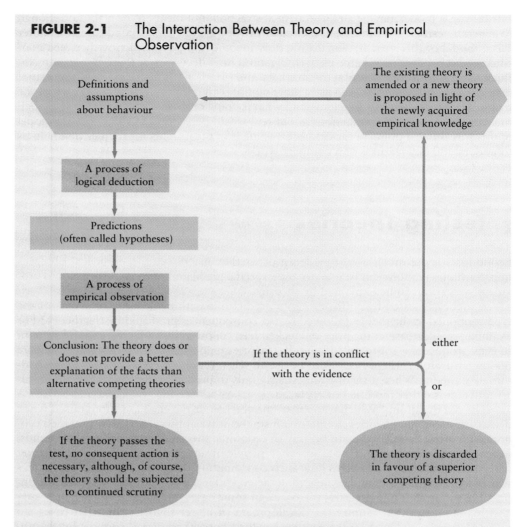

FIGURE 2-1   The Interaction Between Theory and Empirical Observation

Theory and observation are in continuous interaction. Starting (at the top left) with the assumptions of a theory and the definitions of relevant terms, the theorist deduces by logical analysis everything that is implied by the assumptions. These implications are the predictions or the hypotheses of the theory. The theory is then tested by confronting its predictions with evidence. If the theory is in conflict with facts, it will usually be amended to make it consistent with those facts (thereby making it a better theory); or it will be discarded, to be replaced by a superior alternative. The process then begins again: The new or amended theory is subjected first to logical analysis and then to empirical testing.

in a world that is a mixture of the predictable for "most of the people most of the time" with the haphazard or random.

How is it that human behaviour can show stable responses even though we can never be quite sure what one individual will do? Successful predictions about the behaviour of large groups are made possible by the statistical "law" of large numbers. Very roughly, this "law" asserts that random movements of a large number of items tend to offset one another.

For example, we might wonder if there is a relationship between highway speed limits and road accidents. When the speed limit is actually lowered, it will be almost impossible to predict in advance what changes will occur in any single individual's driving record. One individual whose record had been good may have a series of accidents after the speed limit is lowered because of deterioration in his physical or emotional health. Another person may have an improved accident record for reasons not associated with the change in the speed limit—for example, because she purchases a more reliable car. Yet others may have altered driving records for no reasons that we can discern—we may have to put it down to an exercise of unpredictable free will.

If we study only a few individuals, we will learn nothing about the effects of the altered speed limit, since we will not know the importance of all the other causes that are at work. But, if we observe 1,000 individuals, the effects of the change in the speed limit— if such effects do exist—will tend to show up in the *average* responses. If a reduced speed limit does discourage accidents, the group as a whole will have fewer accidents even though some individuals have more. Individuals may do peculiar things that, as far as we can see, are inexplicable, but the group's behaviour will nonetheless be predictable, precisely because the odd things that one individual does will tend to cancel out the odd things that some other individual does.

Testing theories about human behaviour requires studying large numbers of people—to take advantage of the "law" of large numbers.

Because the unusual behaviour of one individual often offsets the unusual behaviour of someone else, it is much easier to accurately predict the average behaviour in large groups of people.

Why Economists Disagree

When all their theories have been constructed and all their evidence has been collected, economists still disagree with each other on many issues. If you hear a discussion among economists on the evening news or if you read about their debates in the daily press or weekly magazines, you will find that economists frequently disagree with each other. What should we make of this disagreement? Here are five of the many possible sources of disagreement.

First, different economists may be using different benchmarks. For example, inflation may be up compared with last year but down compared with 1990. When this sort of thing happens the disagreement is more apparent than real, although it can be confusing to observers.

Second, economists often fail to make it clear to their audience whether they are talking about short-term or long-term consequences. For example, one economist may be noting that a tax cut will stimulate consumption at the cost of lowering saving in the short run while another is pointing out that it will stimulate investment and saving in the long run. Here, again, the disagreement is more apparent than real, since both these short-run and long-run effects command much agreement among economists.

Third, economists often fail to acknowledge the full extent of their ignorance. There are many things on which economists know little, and even more on which the evidence is far from conclusive. Informed judgements are then required before an economist takes a position on even a purely positive question. If two economists' judgements differ, the disagreement is real. Evidence is not sufficient, and different people can come to different conclusions on the basis of a given set of evidence. What a responsible economist will do in such cases is to make clear the extent to which informed judgement is involved in any position he or she is taking.

Fourth, different economists have different values, and these normative views play a large part in most public discussions of policy. Many economists stress the importance of individual responsibility, while others stress the need for collective action to deal with certain issues. Different policy advice may stem from such differences in value judgements about what is socially important. The responsible economist will make it clear which part of her advice is normative and which part is positive.

A fifth reason for disagreement lies in the desire of the media to cover both sides of any contentious issue. As a result the public will usually hear one or two economists on each side of a debate, regardless of whether the profession is divided right down the middle or is nearly unanimous in its support of one side. Thus, the public will not know that in one case a reporter could have chosen from dozens of economists to present each side, whereas in another case the reporter had to spend three days finding someone willing to take a particular side because nearly all the economists supported the other side. In their desire to show both sides of all cases, however, the media tend to present the public with the appearance of a profession equally split over all matters.

Anyone seeking to discredit some particular economist's advice by showing that there is disagreement among economists will have no trouble finding evidence of some disagreement. But those who wish to know if there is a majority view, or even a strong consensus, will find one on a surprisingly large number of issues.

Because the world is complex and because no issue can be settled beyond any doubt, economists are never in unanimous agreement on any issue. Nonetheless, the methods we have been discussing in this chapter have produced an impressive amount of agreement on many aspects of how the economy works and what happens when governments intervene to alter its workings. A survey published in the *American Economic Review*, perhaps the most influential economics journal, showed strong agreement among economists on many propositions, including "Rent control leads to a housing shortage" (85 percent yes), "tariffs usually reduce economic welfare" (93 percent yes), and "large government budget deficits have adverse effects on the economy" (83 percent yes). Other examples of these areas of agreement will be found in countless places throughout this book.

Economic Data

For data on the Canadian economy and many other aspects of Canadian life, see Statistics Canada's website: www.statcan.ca.

Economists seek to explain events that they see in the world. Why, for example, did the price of wheat rise last year even though the wheat crop increased? Explaining such observations typically requires an understanding of how the economy works, an understanding based in part on the insights economists derive from their models.

Economists also use real-world observations to test their theories. For example, did the amount that people saved last year rise—as the theory predicts it should have—when a large tax cut increased after-tax incomes? To test this prediction we need reliable data for people's incomes and their savings.

Political scientists, sociologists, anthropologists, and psychologists all tend to collect the data they use to formulate and test their theories. Economists are unusual among social scientists in mainly using data collected by others, often government statisticians. In economics there is a division of labour between collecting data and using it to generate and test theories. The advantage is that economists do not need to spend much of their scarce research time collecting the data they use. The disadvantage is that they are often not as well informed about the limitations of the data collected by others as they would be if they collected the data themselves.

Once data are collected they can be displayed in various ways, many of which we will see later in this chapter. They can be laid out in tables. They can be displayed in various types of graphs. And where we are interested in relative movements rather than absolute ones, the data can be expressed in index numbers. We begin with a discussion of index numbers.

Index Numbers

The top part of Table 2-2 shows how the prices of gold and silver varied over an eight-year period from 1992 to 1999. How do these two sets of prices compare in volatility? It is difficult to tell from the table because the two prices fluctuate around different levels. It is easier to compare the series if we concentrate on relative rather than absolute price changes. (The absolute change is the dollar value of the change in price; the relative change is the change in the price expressed in relation to some base price.)

Index Numbers as Relative Magnitudes

Comparisons of relative changes can be made by expressing each price series as a set of **index numbers**. To do this we take the price at some point of time as the base to which prices in other periods will be compared. We call this the base period. In the present example we choose 1992 as the base period for both series. The price in that year is given a value of 100. We then take the price of gold in each subsequent year, called the given year, and divide it by the price in the base year, and then multiply the result by 100. This gives us an index number of gold prices. We then do the same for silver. The details of the calculations for gold are shown in the middle part of Table 2-2.

The results, which are shown in the bottom part of Table 2-2, allow us to compare the relative fluctuations in the two series, even though their absolute values are quite different. It is apparent from the figures that silver prices have shown significantly more percentage variability than have gold prices.

The formula of any index number is:

$$\text{Value of index in given period} = \frac{\text{absolute value at given period}}{\text{absolute value in base period}} \times 100$$

An index number merely expresses the value of some series in any given period as a percentage of its value in the base period. Thus, the 1999 index of gold prices of 81.0 tells us that the 1999 price of gold was 81.0 percent of the 1992 price. By subtracting 100 from any index we get the change from the base to the given year, expressed as a percentage of the base year. So, in the above case, the price of gold in 1999 was 19.0 percent lower than in 1992. To take a second example, the silver index

index number   An average that measures change over time of such variables as the price level and industrial production; conventionally expressed as a percentage relative to a base period, which is assigned the value 100.

TABLE 2-2   Indexes for Gold and Silver Prices

Average January Price, US dollars per troy ounce

Year	Gold	Silver
1992	$354.83	$4.13
1993	329.78	3.68
1994	386.21	5.10
1995	378.81	4.78
1996	400.28	5.50
1997	351.01	4.78
1998	290.51	5.90
1999	287.41	5.16

Constructing an Index of Gold Prices (Base Year 1992)

Year	Procedure	Index
1992	(354.83/354.83) × 100	= 100.0
1993	(329.78/354.83) × 100	= 92.9
1994	(386.21/354.83) × 100	= 108.8
1995	(378.81/354.83) × 100	= 106.8
1996	(400.28/354.83) × 100	= 112.8
1997	(351.01/354.83) × 100	= 98.9
1998	(290.51/354.83) × 100	= 81.9
1999	(287.41/354.83) × 100	= 81.0

Index numbers are calculated by dividing the given price by the base-year price and multiplying the result by 100. For example, the given price of gold in 1998 of $290.51 is divided by the base-year price of $354.83 and multiplied by 100 to yield an index value for 1998 of 81.9.

Constructed Indexes of Gold and Silver Prices

Year	Gold	Silver
1992	100.0	100.0
1993	92.9	89.1
1994	108.8	123.5
1995	106.8	115.7
1996	112.8	133.2
1997	98.9	115.7
1998	81.9	142.9
1999	81.0	124.9

(*Source:* The BCA Research Group.)

of 124.9 in 1999 tells us that the 1999 price of silver was 124.9 percent of the 1992 price—or, the price had increased by 24.9 percent between those two years.

Practise with Study Guide Chapter 2, Exercise 3.

Index Numbers as Average Magnitudes

Index numbers are particularly useful if we wish to combine several different series into some average. Say, for example, that we want an index of precious metal prices and gold and silver are the only two commodities we need to worry about.

An Unweighted Index.   For any one year we could add the price indexes for gold and silver and average them. This would give us a precious metals index. But the index would give the two prices equal weight in determining the value of the overall index. Such an index is often called an unweighted index, but that name is misleading. Actually, it is an equal-weight index. It would be sheer luck if this were the appropriate thing to do.

A Proportional-Weights Index.   In practice, we need to weight each price by some measure of its relative importance, letting the more important prices have more weight than the less important prices in determining what happens to the overall index. In the present example, we take the value of the outputs of each metal as the appropriate weights. In the base year, gold and silver outputs were $25.4 billion and $2.6 billion respectively. In order to make the new index still have a value in the base period equal to 100, the weights are all expressed as decimal fractions that sum to 1. To do this we express each value as a fraction of the total value of $28.0 billion. This gives us weights of 0.907 for gold and 0.093 for silver. In other words, since the value of silver is only about one-tenth of the value of gold, silver prices will be given only one-tenth the influence of gold prices in determining the overall index of precious metal prices. To get our weighted index of precious metal prices, we multiply each index value in the bottom part of Table 2-2 by that metal's weight and sum the two to obtain the final index. The results are shown in Table 2-3. The quite different behaviour of the two indexes shows the importance of the choice of weights. When both prices are given equal weight, the index rises in 1998, reflecting the sharp rise in the price of silver that year. But when gold is weighted by its importance in production, the precious metals index falls in that year (because the price of gold fell in that year).

An index that averages changes in several series is the weighted average of the indexes for the separate series, where the weights should reflect the relative importance of each series.

Price Indexes.   Economists make frequent use of indexes of the price level which cover a broad group of prices across the whole economy. One of the most important of these is the consumer price index, CPI, which covers goods and services that individuals buy. This is described in detail in Chapter 19.

All price indexes are calculated using the same procedure. First, the relevant prices are collected. Then a base year is chosen. Then each price series is converted into index numbers, just as was done in Table 2-2. Finally, the index numbers are combined to create a weighted average index series where the weights indicate the relative im-

Table 2-3	Two Indexes of Precious Metals Prices	
	Equal Weights	Proportional Weights
1992	100.0	100.0
1993	91.0	92.6
1994	116.2	110.2
1995	111.3	107.6
1996	123.0	114.7
1997	107.3	100.5
1998	112.4	87.5
1999	103.0	85.1

Weights really matter! The equal-weight index is calculated for each year by adding the gold and silver price indexes from Table 2-2 and dividing by two (a simple average). The proportional-weights index is calculated for each year by taking a weighted average of the price indexes from Table 2-2, where the weights are .907 for gold and .093 for silver. These weights reflect the proportion of the total value of sales of gold and silver (in the base year) accounted for by each precious metal.

portance of each price series, as done in Table 2-3. For example, in any consumer price index the price of sardines would be given a much smaller weight than the price of living accommodation, because what happens to the price of accommodation is much more important to consumers, all of whom spend much more on accommodation than on sardines.

Graphing Economic Data

A single economic variable such as unemployment or GDP can come in two basic forms.

Cross-Section and Time-Series Data

The first is called **cross-sectional data**, which means a number of different observations on one variable all taken in different places at the same point in time. Figure 2-2 shows an example. The variable in the figure is unemployment as a percentage of the labour force. It is shown for each of the ten Canadian provinces in September 1999.

The second type of data is called **time-series data**. It refers to observations taken on one variable at successive points in time. The data in Figure 2-3 show the unemployment rate for Canada from 1978 to 1999. (Note that the Canadian unemployment

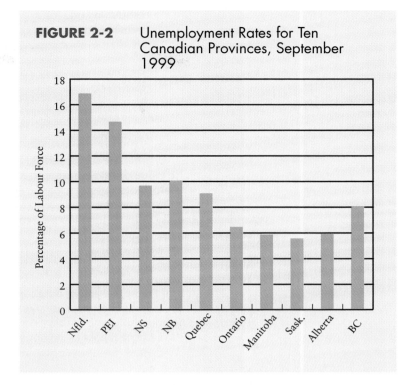

FIGURE 2-2   Unemployment Rates for Ten Canadian Provinces, September 1999

cross-sectional data A set of measurements or observations made at the same time across several different units (such as households, firms, or countries).

time-series data A set of measurements or observations made repeatedly at successive periods (or moments) of time.

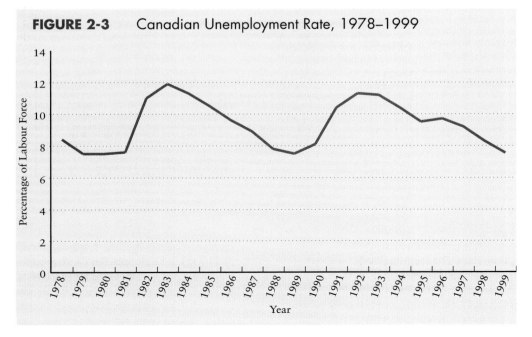

FIGURE 2-3   Canadian Unemployment Rate, 1978–1999

rate is simply a weighted average of the ten provincial unemployment rates, where the weight for each province is the size of that province's labour force expressed as a fraction of the total Canadian labour force.)

Scatter Diagrams

scatter diagram
A graph of statistical observations of paired values of two variables, one measured on the horizontal and the other on the vertical axis. Each point on the coordinate grid represents the values of the variables for a particular unit of observation.

Another way in which data can be presented is in a **scatter diagram**. This type of chart is more analytical than those above. It is designed to show the relation between two different variables, such as the price of eggs and the quantity of eggs purchased. To plot a scatter diagram, values of one variable are measured on the horizontal axis and values of the second variable are measured on the vertical axis. Any point on the diagram relates a specific value of one variable to a corresponding specific value of the other.

The data plotted on a scatter diagram may be either cross-sectional data or time-series data. An example of a cross-sectional scatter diagram is a scatter of the price of eggs and the quantity sold in July 1999 at two dozen different places in Canada. Each dot refers to a price–quantity combination observed in a different place at the same time. An example of a scatter diagram using time-series data is the price and quantity of eggs sold in Thunder Bay for each month over the last ten years. Each of the 120 dots refers to a price–quantity combination observed at the same place in one particular month.

The table in Figure 2-4 shows data for the income and the savings of ten households in one particular year and these data are plotted on a scatter diagram. Each point in the figure represents one household, showing its income and its saving. The positive relation between the two stands out. The higher is the household's income, the higher its saving tends to be.

Graphing Economic Theories

Theories are built on assumptions about relationships between variables. For example, the quantity of eggs demanded is assumed to fall as the price of eggs rises. Or, the total amount an individual saves is assumed to rise as his or her income rises. How can such re-

---

Figure 2-4   A Scatter Diagram of Income and Saving

Household	Annual Income	Annual Saving
1	$70 000	$10 000
2	30 000	2 500
3	100 000	12 000
4	60 000	3 000
5	80 000	8 000
6	10 000	500
7	20 000	2 000
8	50 000	2 000
9	40 000	4 200
10	90 000	8 000

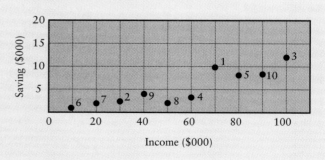

Saving tends to rise as income rises. The table shows the amount of income earned by ten selected households together with the amount they saved during the same year. The figure plots the income and saving for the ten households listed in the table. The number on each dot refers to the household in the corresponding row of the table. (Note that the scales are not the same on the two axes.)

lations be expressed? Here we introduce the concept of a *function* which is really just a special type of relation. When one variable, *X*, is related to another variable, *Y*, in such a way that to every value of *X* there is only one possible value of *Y*, we say that *Y* is a *function* of *X*.[2] When we write this relation down, we are expressing a *functional relation* between the two variables.

A functional relation can be expressed in words, in a numerical schedule, in mathematical equations, or in graphs.

To illustrate, we take a specific example of a relation between a family's annual income, which we denote by the symbol *Y*, and the total amount it spends on goods and services during that period, which we denote by the symbol *C*.

Verbal Statement.   When income is zero, the family will spend $800 a year (either by borrowing the money or by consuming past savings), and for every $1 of income that it obtains it will increase its expenditure by 80 cents.

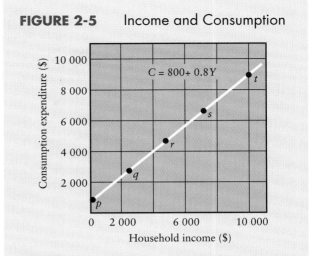

FIGURE 2-5   Income and Consumption

Consumption expenditure rises as income rises. The figure graphs the schedule and the equation for the consumption function discussed in the text.

Schedule.   This shows selected values of the family's income and the amount it spends on consumption.

Annual income	Consumption	Reference letter
$ 0	$ 800	*p*
2 500	2 800	*q*
5 000	4 800	*r*
7 500	6 800	*s*
10 000	8 800	*t*

Mathematical (Algebraic) Statement. $C = \$800 + 0.8Y$ is the equation of the relation just described in words. As a check, you can first see that when *Y* is zero, *C* is $800. Then you can substitute any two values of *Y* that differ by $1, multiply each by 0.80, and add 800, and see that the corresponding two values of consumption differ by $0.80.

Graphical Statement.   Figure 2-5 shows both the points from the preceding schedule and the line representing the equation given in the previous paragraph.

Comparison of the values on the graph with the values in the schedule, and with the values derived from the equation just stated, shows that these are alternative expressions of the same relation between *C* and *Y*. All four of these modes of expression refer to the same relation between total consumption expenditure and total income.

---

[2]For those who find this statement difficult to understand, here is a more detailed explanation. When a relationship between two variables, *X* and *Y*, is such that for any value of *X* there is one and only one value of the variable *Y*, then *Y* is said to be a function of *X*. For example, in the relation, $Y = a + bX + cX^2$, *Y* is a function of *X* because each value of *X* gives rise to one and only one value of *Y*. It is worth noting that *Y* being a function of *X* does not necessarily imply that *X* is a function of *Y*. For example, in the equation given in this footnote, *X* cannot be expressed as a *function* of *Y* because to many values of *Y* there correspond not one but two values of *X*. Though this distinction between relations and functions (a specific type of relation) is important in much of mathematics, it is not a distinction that will play a role in this book, where we confine ourselves to functions.

Functions

Let us look in a little more detail at the algebraic expression of this relation between income and consumption expenditure. To state the expression in general form, detached from the specific numerical example above, we use a symbol to express the dependence of one variable on another. Using "f" for this purpose, we write

$$C = f(Y) \qquad\qquad (2\text{-}1)$$

This is read, "C is a function of Y." Spelling this out more fully, we would say, "The amount of consumption expenditure depends upon the household's income."

The variable on the left-hand side is the dependent variable, since its value depends on the value of the variable on the right-hand side. The variable on the right-hand side is the independent variable, since it can take on any value. The letter "f" tells us that a functional relation is involved. This means that a knowledge of the value of the variable (or variables) within the parentheses on the right-hand side allows us to determine the value of the variable on the left-hand side. Although in this case we have used "f" (as a memory-aid for "function"), any convenient symbol can be used to denote the existence of a functional relation.

Functional notation can seem intimidating to those who are unfamiliar with it. But it is helpful. Since the functional concept is basic to all science, the notation is worth mastering.

Functional Forms

The equation $C = f(Y)$ states that C is related to Y. It says nothing about the *form* that this relation takes. The term *functional form* refers to the specific nature of the relation between the variables in the function. The example above gave one specific functional form for this relation:

$$C = \$800 + 0.8Y \qquad\qquad (2\text{-}2)$$

Equation 2-1 expresses the general assumption that consumption expenditure depends on the consumer's income. Equation 2-2 expresses the more specific assumption that C rises by 80 cents for every \$1 that Y rises. An alternative form for the function in Equation 2-1 would be $C = \$600 + 0.9Y$. You should be able to say in words the behaviour implied in this relation. There is no reason why either of these assumptions must be true; indeed, neither may be consistent with the facts. But that is a matter for testing. What we do have in each equation is a concise statement of a particular assumption.

Graphing Functional Relations

Different functional forms have different graphs, and we will meet many of these in subsequent chapters. Figure 2-5 is an example of a relation in which the two variables move together. When income goes up consumption goes up. In such a relation the two variables are *positively related* to each other.

Figure 2-6 gives an example of variables that move in opposite directions. As the amount spent on abating smoke pollution goes up, the amount of pollution goes down. In such a relation the two variables are *negatively related* to each other.

Both of these graphs are straight lines. In such cases the variables are *linearly related* to each other (either positively or negatively).

Practise with Study Guide Chapter 2, Exercise 4.

The Slope of a Straight Line

Slopes are important in economics. They show you how much one variable changes as the other changes. The slope is defined as the amount of change in the variable measured on the vertical or y-axis per unit change in the variable measured on the horizontal or x-axis. In the case of Figure 2-6 it tells us how many tons of smoke pollution, symbolized by P, are removed per dollar spent on pollution control, symbolized by E. As the figure shows, if we spend $2000 more we get 1000 tons less pollution. This is 0.5 tons per dollar spent. On the graph the extra $2000 is indicated by ΔE, the arrow indicating that E rises by 2000. The 1000 tons of pollution reduction is indicated by ΔP, the arrow showing that pollution falls by 1000. (The Greek uppercase letter delta, Δ, stands for a change in something.) To get the amount of abatement per dollar of expenditure we merely divide one by the other. In symbols this is $\Delta P/\Delta E$.

If we let X stand for whatever variable is measured on the horizontal axis and Y for whatever variable is measured on the vertical axis, the slope of a straight line is $\Delta Y/\Delta X$. [1][3]

In Figure 2-5 the two variables change in the same direction, so both changes will always be either positive or negative. As a result their ratio, which is the slope of this line, is positive. In Figure 2-6 the two variables change in opposite directions; when one increases the other decreases. So the two Δs will always be of opposite sign. As a result their ratio, which is the slope of the line, is always negative.

Notice also that straight lines have the same slope no matter where on the line you measure that slope. This tells us what inspection of the chart reveals: that the change in one variable in response to a unit change in the other is the same anywhere on the line. We get 0.5 tons of additional pollution abatement for every additional $1 that we spend on abatement no matter how much we are already spending.

Nonlinear Functions

Although it is sometimes convenient to simplify a real relation between two variables by assuming them to be linearly related, this is seldom the case over their whole range. Nonlinear relations are much more common than linear ones. In the case of pollution abatement

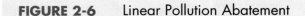

FIGURE 2-6   Linear Pollution Abatement

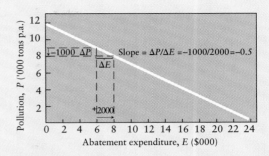

Pollution falls linearly as expenditure on abatement rises. The slope of the line indicates the marginal reduction in pollution for every increase of $1 of abatement expenditure. It is constant at -0.5, indicating that every extra $1 spent on abatement reduces pollution by half a ton.

FIGURE 2-7   Nonlinear Pollution Abatement

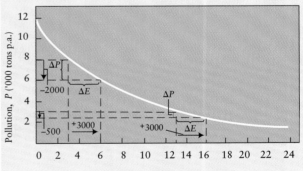

Pollution falls nonlinearly as abatement expenditure rises. When pollution is 8000 tons per year, an additional expenditure of $3000 reduces pollution by 2000 tons. The marginal return for $1 additional expenditure is $\Delta P/\Delta E$ or $-2000/3000$, which is two-thirds of a ton of pollution reduced per $1 spent on abatement. However, when pollution has already been reduced to 3000 tons, an extra $3000 spent on abatement reduces pollution by only 500 tons. The marginal return for $1 of additional expenditure, $\Delta P/\Delta E$, is now only $-500/3000$ or one-sixth of a ton of pollution reduced per $1 spent.

---

[3]Numbers in square brackets indicate mathematical notes that are found in a separate section at the back of the book.

FIGURE 2-8 Navigation Aids

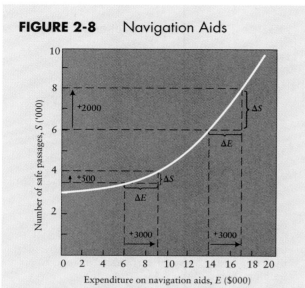

Number of safe passages, S ('000)

Expenditure on navigation aids, E ($000)

Safe passages increase at an increasing rate as navigation aids are increased. The figure shows the number of safe passages varying positively with the amount spent on navigation aids. Because of network externalities, the number of safe passages increases at an increasing rate as more is spent on navigation aids. An increase in expenditure on navigation aids by $3000 when expenditure is $6000 raises safe passages by 500 from 3500 to 4000. The marginal return to $1 extra spent on navigation aids is then 500/3000 or 0.167. In other words it takes $6 to get one more safe passage (3000/500). When $14 000 is already being spent, a further increase of $3000 increases safe passages by 2000 from 6000 to 8000. The marginal return from $1 spent on aids is now 2000/3000 or 0.667. In other words, it takes only $1.50 extra spending to get one more safe passage (3000/2000).

it is usually quite cheap to eliminate the first units of pollution. Then, as the smoke gets cleaner and cleaner, the cost of further abatement tends to increase because more and more sophisticated and expensive methods need to be used. As a result, the graph relating expenditure on abatement and amount of pollution usually looks more like Figure 2-7 than Figure 2-6. Inspection of Figure 2-7 shows that as more and more is spent, the benefit in terms of extra abatement for an additional $1 of abatement expenditure gets smaller and smaller. This is shown by the diminishing slope of the curve as we move rightward along it. As the figure shows, an extra $1 of expenditure yields two-thirds of a ton of pollution reduction when pollution is 8000 tons ($\Delta Y/\Delta X = -2000/3000$) but only one-sixth of a ton of pollution reduction when pollution is 3000 tons ($\Delta Y/\Delta X = -500/3000$).

Economists call the change in abatement when a bit more or a bit less is spent on abatement the *marginal* change. The figure shows that the slope of the curve at each point measures this marginal change. It also shows that, in the type of curve illustrated, the marginal return per dollar spent is diminishing as abatement proceeds. There is always a payoff to more expenditure over the range shown in the figure, but the return diminishes as more is spent. This relation can be described as *diminishing marginal response*. We will meet such relations many times in what follows, so we emphasize now that diminishing marginal response does not mean that the *total* response is diminishing. In the figure the total amount of pollution continues to fall as more and more is spent on abatement. But diminishing marginal response does mean that the amount of abatement obtained for each additional unit of expense is diminishing as more and more pollution is abated.

Figure 2-8 shows a graph where the marginal return is increasing. It relates expenditure on navigational aids to the number of safe passages. At low levels of expenditure the curve is nearly flat. An additional unit of expenditure does not yield much additional protection. But as more and more is spent, it becomes possible to employ more efficient navigation aids that work together as a whole system. Each extra unit of expenditure yields more additional protection than each previous unit. In this case we have what economists call increasing marginal response. The reason is that navigation aids encounter what are called *network externalities*. They are most effective not as single stand-alone bits, such as one lighthouse, but as an integrated whole. Each aid becomes more effective the more complex and interrelated is the whole system of which it is a part.

Functions with Maxima and Minima

So far, all the graphs we have shown have had either a positive or negative slope over their entire range. But many relations change direction as the independent variable increases. Figures 2-9 and 2-10 extend our navigation and pollution examples over a larger range of the independent variables. We find that as more and more is spent on navigation aids, not only does the marginal contribution of each additional $1 spent begin to decline, but eventually the *total* safety begins to decline. The reason is that the signals begin to interfere with each other and confuse rather than aid navigators. So, as expenditure on navigation aids increases, eventually the safety reaches a maximum and then begins to decline.

At the maximum point the curve is flat—it has a zero slope. Up to that point each $1 spent does increase safety—it has a positive marginal contribution. But after that point each additional $1 spent reduces safety—it has a negative marginal contribution. At the maximum point the marginal contribution is zero.

Now look at Figure 2-10, which extends the pollution abatement example. Here we see that each $1 spent on pollution control adds to abatement up to the amount E_1, but after that abatement begins to decline. The reason in this case may be that the regulations become so costly that firms find ways of evading them and total enforcement gets less effective. Pollution reaches a minimum when E_1 is spent but rises thereafter. Notice that up to E_1 the curve has a negative slope, indicating that more expenditure is associated with less pollution, but that after E_1 the curve has a positive slope, indicating that more expenditure is associated with more pollution. At the point of minimum pollution the tangent to the curve shown by the line T has a slope of zero.

These two cases illustrate an important point, which we will see over and over in what follows:

At either a minimum or a maximum value of a function, its marginal value is zero.

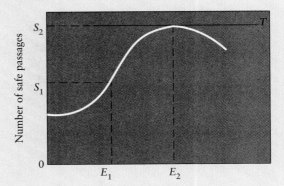

FIGURE 2-9   Aid Saturation

Increases in expenditure on navigation aids eventually serve to reduce the number of safe passages. Up to E_1, expenditure on navigation aids encounters increasing marginal returns. Each additional $1 of expenditure allows a larger increase in safe passages than each previous $1 of expenditure. As expenditure approaches E_2, it encounters decreasing marginal returns. Each additional $1 spent increases the number of safe passages by less than the previous $1 of expenditure. At E_2, safe passages reach a maximum of S_2. Further expenditure encounters negative marginal returns. Each additional $1 spent lowers the number of safe passages. At the maximum point the slope of the tangent T (the straight line that just touches the curve at that point) is zero. At that point the number of safe passages shows no response to small changes in expenditure on navigation aids.

A Final Word

We have done much in this chapter. We have discussed why economists use theory and how they build economic models. We have discussed how they test their theories and how there is a continual back-and-forth process between empirical testing of predictions and refining the theoretical model. Finally, we have devoted considerable time and space to exploring the many ways that data can be displayed in graphs and how economists use graphs to illustrate their theories.

FIGURE 2-10   Abatement Saturation

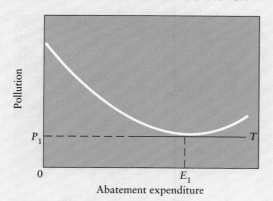

Beyond a certain point additional abatement expenditure increases pollution. Up to E_1, each additional \$1 of expenditure reduces pollution, but at a diminishing amount for each \$1. At expenditure E_1, pollution reaches a minimum of P_1. If further amounts are spent, pollution actually rises. At the minimum point the slope of the tangent line T is zero. At that point, pollution shows no response to small changes in abatement expenditure.

Many students find themselves intimidated when they are first confronted with all of the details about graphing. But try not to worry. You may not yet be a master of all the graphing techniques that we have discussed in this chapter, but you will be surprised at how quickly it all falls into place. And, as is true for most skills, there is no substitute for practice. In the next three chapters we will encounter many graphs. But we will start simply and then slowly attempt more complicated cases. We are confident that in the process of learning some basic economic theories you will get enough practice in graphing that you will very soon look back at this chapter and realize how straightforward it all is.

S U M M A R Y

Positive and Normative Advice

- A key to the success of scientific inquiry lies in separating positive questions about the way the world works from normative questions about how one would like the world to work.

Economic Theories and Models

- Theories are designed to explain and predict what we see. A theory consists of a set of definitions of the variables to be employed, a set of assumptions about how things behave, and the conditions under which the theory is meant to apply.
- A theory provides conditional predictions of the type "if one event occurs, then another event will also occur."

- The term "model" has a number of meanings, including (a) a synonym for theory, (b) a precise realization of a general theory, with a specific numerical relation in place of each general relation posited by the theory, (c) an application of a general theory to a specific case, and (d) a simplified set of relations designed to study one specific force in isolation.

Testing Theories

LO 3 4

- Theories are tested by checking their predictions against evidence. In some sciences, these tests can be conducted under laboratory conditions in which only one thing changes at a time. In economics, testing must be done using the data produced by the world of ordinary events.
- The fact that people sometimes act strangely, even capriciously, does not destroy the possibility of scientific study of group behaviour. The odd and inexplicable things that one person does will tend to cancel out the odd and inexplicable things that another person does. The law of large numbers thus means that group behaviour is often easier to predict than individual behaviour.
- The progress of any science lies in finding better explanations of events than are now available. Thus in any developing science, one must expect to discard some existing theories and replace them with demonstrably superior alternatives.

Economic Data

LO 5

- Index numbers express economic series in relative form. Values in each period are expressed in relation to the value in the base period, which is given a value of 100.
- Economic data may be graphed in three different ways. Cross-section graphs show observations taken at the same time. Time-series graphs show observations on one variable taken over time. Scatter diagrams show many points, each one of which refers to specific observations on two different variables.

Graphing Economic Theories

LO 6 7

- A functional relation can be expressed in words, in a schedule giving specific values, in a mathematical equation, or in a graph.
- A graph of two variables has a positive slope when they both increase or decrease together and a negative slope when they move in opposite directions.
- The marginal value of a variable gives the amount it changes in response to a change in a second variable. When the variable is measured on the vertical axis of a diagram, its marginal value at a specific point on the curve is measured by the slope of the line tangent to that point.

K E Y   C O N C E P T S

Positive and normative statements
Endogenous and exogenous variables
Theories and models
Variables, assumptions, and predictions

Economic data
Functional relations
Positive and negative relations between variables

Positive and negatively sloped curves
Marginal values
Maximum and minimum values

S T U D Y   E X E R C I S E S

1. Suppose that the relationship between the government's tax revenue (T) and national income (Y) is represented by the following equation: $T = 10 + 0.25Y$. Plot this relationship on a scale diagram, with Y on the horizontal axis and T on the vertical axis. Interpret the equation.

2. Consider the following three specific functional forms for a functional relation between X and Y:
   i) $Y = 50 + 2X$
   ii) $Y = 50 + 2X + 0.05X^2$
   iii) $Y = 50 + 2X - 0.05X^2$

a. For the values of X of 0, 10, 20, 30, 40 and 50, plot X and Y on a scale diagram for each specific functional form. Connect these points with a smooth line.

b. For each functional form, state whether the slope of the line is constant, increasing or decreasing as the value of X increases.

c. Describe for each functional form how the marginal change in Y depends on the value of X.

3. Suppose you want to create a price index for the price of pizza across several Canadian university campuses, as of March 1, 2000. The data are as follows:

University	Price per Pizza
Dalhousie	$6.50
Laval	5.95
McGill	6.00
Queen's	8.00
Waterloo	7.50
Manitoba	5.50
Saskatchewan	5.75
Calgary	6.25
UBC	7.25
Victoria	7.00

a. Using Calgary as the "base university," construct the Canadian university pizza price index.

b. At which university is pizza the most expensive, and by what percentage is the price higher than in Calgary?

c. At which university is pizza the least expensive, and by what percentage is the price lower than in Calgary?

d. Are the data listed above time-series or cross-section data? Explain why.

4. For each of the functional relations listed below, plot the relations on a scale diagram (with X on the horizontal axis and Y on the vertical axis) and compute the slope of the line.

i) $Y = 10 + 3X$
ii) $Y = 20 + 4X$
iii) $Y = 30 + 5X$
iv) $Y = 10 + 5X$

5. Suppose we divide Canada into three regions—the West, the Centre, and the East. Each region has an unemployment rate, defined as the number of people unemployed, expressed as a fraction of that region's labour force. The table that follows shows each region's unemployment rate and the size of its labour force.

Region	Unemployment Rate	Labour Force
West	5.5%	5.3 million
Centre	7.2%	8.4 million
East	12.5%	3.5 million

a. Compute an unemployment rate for Canada using a simple (equal weights) average of the rates in the three regions. Is this the "right" unemployment rate for Canada as a whole? Explain why or why not.

b. Now compute an unemployment rate for Canada using weights which reflect the size of that region's labour force as a proportion of the overall Canadian labour force. Explain the difference in this unemployment rate from the one in part **a**. Is this a "better" measure of Canadian unemployment? Explain why.

6. Draw three graphs in which the dependent variable increases at an increasing rate, at a constant rate, and at a diminishing rate. Then draw three graphs in which it decreases at an increasing, constant, and diminishing rate. For each of these graphs state a real relation that might be described by it—other than the ones given in the text of this chapter.

DISCUSSION QUESTIONS

1. What are some of the positive and normative issues that lie behind the disagreements in the following cases?

a. Economists disagree on whether the Government of Canada should try to stimulate the economy in the next six months.

b. European and North American negotiators disagree over the desirability of reducing European farm subsidies.

c. Economists argue about the merits of a voucher system that allows parents to choose the schools their children will attend.

d. Economists debate the use of a two-tier medical system in Canada (whereby health care continues to be publicly provided, but individuals are permitted to be treated by doctors who bill the patient directly—"extra billing").

2. Much recent public debate has centred on the pros and cons of permitting continued unrestricted sale of cigarettes. Proposals for the control of cigarettes range from increasing excise taxes to the mandatory use of plain packaging to an outright ban on their sale. Discuss the positive and normative assumptions that underlie the national mood to reduce the consumption of tobacco products.

3. Economists sometimes make each of the following assumptions when they construct models. Discuss some situations in which each of these assumptions might be a useful simplification in order to think about some aspect of the real world.

   a. The earth is flat.
   b. There are no differences between men and women.
   c. There is no tomorrow.
   d. There are only two periods—this year and next year.
   e. A country produces only two types of goods.
   f. People are wholly selfish.

4. What may at first appear to be untestable statements can often be reworded so that they can be tested by an appeal to evidence. How might you do this for each of the following assertions?

   a. Free-market economic systems are the best in the world.
   b. Unemployment insurance is eroding the work ethic and encouraging people to become wards of the state rather than productive workers.
   c. Robotics ought to be outlawed because it will destroy the future of working people.
   d. Laws requiring equal pay for work of equal value will make women better off.
   e. Free trade improves the welfare of a country's citizens.

5. There are hundreds of eyewitnesses to the existence of flying saucers and other UFOs. There are films and eyewitness accounts of Nessie, the Loch Ness monster. Are you convinced of their existence? If not, what would it take to persuade you? If so, what would it take to make you change your mind?

An Introduction to Demand and Supply

In January 1998, a massive ice storm hit Quebec and parts of Ontario and the northeastern United States, causing unprecedented stoppages in electric power. Did the ice storm cause the increase in price of portable electric generators that happened within a few days, or was this just a coincidence? In the summer of 1994, Brazil experienced a frost that severely damaged that country's coffee crop. Did it cause the large increase in the price of coffee that occurred almost immediately, or was that also a coincidence? Is the current housing shortage in Toronto related to the Ontario government's policy of rent controls, and if so, what is the connection? What determines the prices of specific products? What determines whether there will be a lot produced or only a little? These are the types of questions that you will be able to answer after reading the next three chapters.*

Chapter 3 introduces the basic concepts of demand and supply. We will see that the prices of goods in free markets are determined by the interaction of demand and supply. We will learn the meaning of equilibrium, and how equilibrium prices and quantities change in response to changes to either demand or supply. With this apparatus in place, we will look briefly at the 1998 ice storm and at Brazil's damaged coffee crop (the price increases were not coincidences!).

Chapter 4 then introduces the important idea of elasticity—the sensitivity of one variable to a change in some other variable. This concept is central to an understanding of whether a change in the demand or supply of some commodity primarily affects quantity or price. As an application of the concept of elasticity, we will examine the important policy issue of who bears the burden of commodity taxes. Do firms pay such taxes, or do consumers, or do both? How does elasticity affect the answer?

In Chapter 5 you get some practice in using what you learned in Chapters 3 and 4. We start with a discussion of how various markets interact with each other, so that events in one market lead not only to changes in that market but to changes in other markets as well. We then go on to explore two examples of government-controlled prices. The first is rent controls—you will see that the policy of rent controls produces some unusual outcomes in the rental-housing markets of Toronto, New York, and many other cities. The second is agricultural price-support policies—you will see what effects such policies have, both on farmers' incomes and on the allocation of resources.

---

*Chapter 5 does not appear in *Macroeconomics*.

CHAPTER 3

Demand, Supply, and Price

LO *LEARNING OBJECTIVES*

❶ Understand what determines "quantity demanded," the amount of some product that households want to purchase.

❷ Distinguish between a shift in a demand curve and a movement along a demand curve.

❸ Understand what determines "quantity supplied," the amount of some product that firms want to sell.

❹ Distinguish between a shift in a supply curve and a movement along a supply curve.

❺ Recognize the forces that drive market price to equilibrium.

❻ Understand the four "laws" of demand and supply.

How do individual markets work? We are now ready to study this important question. The answer leads us to what are called the laws of supply and demand. And though there is much more to economics than just demand and supply (as many following chapters will illustrate), this is an essential starting point for understanding how a market, and thus a market economy, functions.

As a first step, we need to understand what determines the demand for and the supply of particular products. Then we can see how demand and supply together determine the prices of products and the quantities that are bought and sold. Finally, we examine how the price system allows the economy to respond to the many changes that impinge on it. Demand and supply help us to understand the price system's successes and failures, and the consequences of many government policies.

This chapter deals with the basic elements of demand, supply and price. In the next two chapters we use the demand-and-supply apparatus to discuss such issues as cigarette taxes, legislated minimum wages, price controls on rental housing, the burden of payroll taxes, and agricultural income-support policies.

Demand

What determines the demand for any given product? How did Canadian consumers react to the large increases in fuel prices in the 1970s? How did they respond to the more recent declines in the prices of personal computers and cellular telephones? We start by developing a theory designed to explain the demand for some typical product.

What Is "Quantity Demanded"?

The total amount of any particular good or service that consumers wish to purchase in some time period is called the **quantity demanded** of that product. It is important to notice two things about this concept.

    First, quantity demanded is a *desired* quantity. It is the amount that consumers wish to purchase when faced with a particular price of the product, other prices, their incomes, their tastes, and everything else that might matter. It may be different from the amount that consumers actually succeed in purchasing. If sufficient quantities are not available, the amount that consumers wish to purchase may exceed the amount that they actually purchase. To distinguish these two concepts, the term *quantity demanded* is used to refer to desired purchases, and a phrase such as *quantity actually bought* or *quantity exchanged* is used to refer to actual purchases.

    Second, quantity demanded refers to a *flow* of purchases. It must therefore be expressed as so much per period of time: 1 million units per day, 7 million per week, or 365 million per year. For example, being told that the quantity of new television sets demanded (at current prices) in Canada is 50 000 means nothing unless you are also told the period of time involved. Fifty thousand TVs demanded per day would be an enormous rate of demand; 50 000 per year would be a very small rate. The important distinction between *stocks* and *flows* is discussed in *Extensions in Theory 3-1.*

    The amount of some product that consumers wish to buy in a given time period is influenced by the following important variables: [2]

- Product's own price
- Average household income
- Prices of other products
- Tastes
- Distribution of income
- Population
- Expectations about the future

    It is difficult to determine the separate influence of each of these variables if we consider what happens when everything changes at once. Instead, we consider the influence of the variables one at a time. To do this, we hold all but one of them constant. Then we let the selected variable vary and study how it affects quantity demanded. We can do the same for each of the other variables in turn, and in this way we can come to understand the importance of each. We can then combine the separate influences of the variables to discover what happens when several things change at the same time—as they often do.

    Holding all other influencing variables constant is often described by the expressions "other things being equal," "other things given," or the equivalent Latin phrase, *ceteris paribus.* When economists speak of the influence of the price of eggs on the quantity of eggs demanded, *ceteris paribus,* they refer to what a change in the price of eggs would do to the quantity of eggs demanded *if all other variables that influence the demand for eggs did not change.*

Quantity Demanded and Price

We are interested in developing a theory of how prices are determined. To do this, we need to study the relationship between the quantity demanded of each product and that product's price. This requires that we hold all other influences constant and ask, "How will the quantity demanded of a product change as its price changes?"

quantity demanded
The amount of a commodity that consumers wish to purchase in some time period.

EXTENSIONS IN THEORY 3-1

The Distinction Between Stocks and Flows

One important conceptual issue that arises frequently in economics is the distinction between stock and flow variables. Economic theories use both, and it takes a little practice to keep them straight.

As noted in the text, a flow variable has a time dimension—it is so much *per unit of time*. For example, the quantity of Grade A large eggs purchased in Edmonton is a flow variable. No useful information is conveyed if we are told that the number purchased was 2000 dozen eggs unless we are also told the period of time over which these purchases occurred. Two thousand dozen eggs per hour would indicate a much more active market in eggs than would 2000 dozen eggs per month.

In contrast, a stock variable is a variable whose value has meaning *at a point in time*. Thus the number of eggs in the egg producer's warehouse on a particular day—for example, 20 000 dozen eggs on September 3, 1999—is a stock variable. All those eggs are there at one time, and they remain there until something happens to change the stock held in the warehouse. The stock variable is just a number at a point in time, not a rate of flow of so much per unit of time.

The terminology of stocks and flows can be understood in terms of an analogy to a bathtub. At any moment, the tub holds so much water. This is the *stock*, and it can be measured in terms of the volume of water, say, 100 litres. There might also be water flowing into the tub from the tap; this *flow* is measured as so much water per unit time, say, 500 litres per hour.

The distinction between stocks and flows is important. Failure to keep them straight is a common source of confusion and even error. Note, for example, that because they have different dimensions, a stock variable and a flow variable cannot be added together without specifying some time period for which the flow persists.

We cannot add the stock of 100 litres of water in the tub to the flow of 500 litres per hour to get 600 litres. The new stock of water will depend on how long the flow persists; if it lasts for half an hour, the new stock will be 350 litres; if the flow persists for two hours, the new stock will be 1100 litres (or the tub will overflow!).

The amount of income earned is a flow; there is so much per year or per month or per hour. The amount of a consumer's expenditure is also a flow—so much spent per week or per month or per year. The amount of money in a bank account or a miser's hoard (earned, perhaps, in the past but unspent) is a stock—just so many thousands of dollars. The key test is always whether a time dimension is required to give the variable meaning. Other variables are neither stocks nor flows, but just numbers; for example, the price of one dozen eggs.

The amount of water behind the dam at any time is the stock of water; the amount moving through the gate is the flow, which is measured per unit of time.

A basic economic hypothesis is that the price of a product and the quantity demanded are related negatively, other things being equal. That is, the lower the price, the higher the quantity demanded; and the higher the price, the lower the quantity demanded.

The British economist Alfred Marshall (1842–1924) called this fundamental relation the "law of demand." In Chapter 6, we will derive the law of demand as a prediction that follows from more basic assumptions about consumer behaviour. For now, let's simply ask "why might this be so?" Products are used to satisfy desires and needs, and there is almost always more than one product that will satisfy any desire or need. Hunger may be alleviated by meat or vegetables; a desire for green vegetables can be satisfied by broccoli or spinach. The desire for a vacation may be satisfied by a trip to the ocean or to the mountains; the need to get there may be satisfied by different airlines, a bus, a car, or a train. For any general desire or need, there are many different products that will satisfy it.

Now consider what happens if income, tastes, population, and the prices of all other products remain constant and the price of only one product changes. As the price goes up, that product becomes an increasingly expensive way to satisfy a desire. Some consumers will stop buying it altogether; others will buy smaller amounts; still others may continue to buy the same quantity. Because many consumers will switch wholly or partly to other products to satisfy the same desire, less will be demanded of the product whose price has risen. As meat becomes more expensive, for example, consumers may to some extent switch to meat substitutes; they may also forgo meat at some meals and eat less meat at others.

Conversely, as the price goes down, the product becomes a cheaper method of satisfying a desire. Households will demand more of it. Consequently, they will buy less of similar products whose prices have not fallen and as a result have become expensive *relative* to the product in question. When the price of tomatoes falls, shoppers switch to tomatoes and cut their purchases of many other vegetables that now look relatively more expensive.

Demand Schedules and Demand Curves

A **demand schedule** is one way of showing the relationship between quantity demanded and the price of a product, other things being equal. It is a numerical tabulation showing the quantity that is demanded at certain prices.

The table in Figure 3-1 shows a hypothetical demand schedule for carrots. It lists the quantity of carrots that would be demanded at various prices, given the assumption that all other variables are held constant. We should note in particular that average

demand schedule
A table showing the relationship between the quantity of a commodity that buyers wish to purchase (per period of time) and the price of that commodity, other things being equal.

FIGURE 3-1   The Demand for Carrots

	Price Per Ton ($)	Quantity Demanded When Average Household Income Is $50 000 Per Year (thousands of tons per year)
U	20	110.0
V	40	90.0
W	60	77.5
X	80	67.5
Y	100	62.5
Z	120	60.0

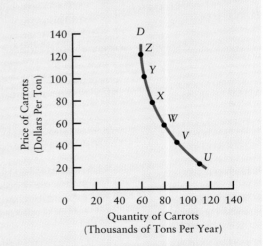

Both the table and the graph show the quantity of carrots that would be demanded at various prices, *ceteris paribus*. For example, row *W* indicates that if the price of carrots were $60 per ton, consumers would desire to purchase 77 500 tons of carrots per year, given the values of the other variables that affect quantity demanded. The demand curve, labelled *D*, relates quantity of carrots demanded to the price of carrots; its negative slope indicates that quantity demanded increases as price falls.

household income is fixed at $50 000 because later we will want to see what happens when income changes. The table gives the quantities demanded for six selected prices, but in fact a separate quantity would be demanded at each possible price from 1 cent to several hundreds of dollars.

A second method of showing the relationship between quantity demanded and price is to draw a graph. The six price-quantity combinations shown in the table are plotted in Figure 3-1. Price is plotted on the vertical axis, and quantity is plotted on the horizontal axis.

demand curve The graphical representation of the relationship between the quantity of a commodity that buyers wish to purchase (per period of time) and the price of that commodity, other things being equal.

The smooth curve drawn through these points is called a **demand curve.** It shows the quantity that purchasers would like to buy at each price. The negative slope of the curve indicates that the quantity demanded increases as the price falls. Each point on the demand curve indicates a single price-quantity combination. The demand curve as a whole shows something more.

The demand curve represents the relationship between quantity demanded and price, other things being equal.

When economists speak of demand in a particular market, they are referring not just to the particular quantity being demanded at the moment (i.e., not just to one point on the demand curve) but to the entire demand curve—to the relationship between desired purchases and all the possible prices of the product.

demand The entire relationship between the quantity of a commodity that buyers wish to purchase (per period of time) and the price of that commodity, other things being equal.

Thus, the term **demand** refers to the entire relationship between the quantity demanded of a product and the price of that product (as shown, for example, by the demand curve in Figure 3-1). In contrast, a single point on a demand schedule or curve is the quantity demanded at that point. This distinction between "demand" and "quantity demanded" is an extremely important one and we will examine it more closely later in this chapter.

Shifts in the Demand Curve

The demand schedule is drawn with the assumption that everything except the product's own price is being held constant. But what if other things change, as surely they do? For example, consider an increase in household income while price remains constant. If households increase their purchases of the product, the new quantity demanded cannot be represented by a point on the original demand curve. It must be represented on a new demand curve that is to the right of the old curve. Thus, the rise in consumer income shifts the demand curve to the right, as shown in Figure 3-2. This shift illustrates the operation of an important general rule.

A demand curve is drawn with the assumption that everything except the product's own price is held constant. A change in any of the variables previously held constant will shift the demand curve to a new position.

A demand curve can shift in two important ways. In the first case, more is bought at each price—the demand curve shifts rightward so that each price corresponds to a higher quantity than it did before. In the second case, less is bought at each price—the demand curve shifts leftward so that each price corresponds to a lower quantity than it did before.

We can assess the influence of changes in variables other than price by determining how changes in each variable shift the demand curve. Any change will shift the demand curve to the right if it increases the amount that households wish to buy, other things remaining equal. It will shift the demand curve to the left if it decreases the amount that households wish to buy, other things remaining equal.

FIGURE 3-2   An Increase in the Demand for Carrots

Price Per Ton ($) p	Quantity Demanded When Average Household Income Is $50 000 Per Year (thousands of tons per year) D_0		Quantity Demanded When Average Household Income Is $60 000 Per Year (thousands of tons per year) D_1	
20	110.0	U	140.0	U'
40	90.0	V	116.0	V'
60	77.5	W	100.8	W'
80	67.5	X	87.5	X'
100	62.5	Y	81.3	Y'
120	60.0	Z	78.0	Z'

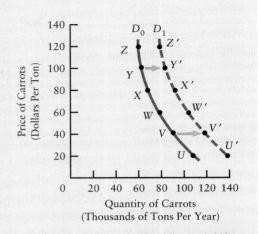

An increase in average household income increases the quantity demanded at each price. This is shown by the rightward shift in the demand curve, from D_0 to D_1. When average income rises from $50 000 to $60 000 per year, quantity demanded at a price of $60 per ton rises from 77 500 tons per year to 100 800 tons per year. A similar rise occurs at every other price.

Average Household Income.   If consumers receive more income on average, they can be expected to purchase more of most products even though product prices remain the same.[1] We therefore expect that a rise in average consumer income shifts the demand curve for most products to the right, indicating that more will be demanded at any given price. Such a shift is illustrated in Figure 3-2.

Prices of Other Goods.   We saw that the negative slope of a product's demand curve occurs because the lower its price, the cheaper the product becomes relative to other products that can satisfy the same needs or desires. These other products are called **substitutes.** Another way for the same change to come about is that the price of the substitute product rises. For example, carrots can become cheap relative to broccoli either because the price of carrots falls or because the price of broccoli rises. Either change will increase the amount of carrots that consumers wish to buy as consumers substitute away from broccoli and toward carrots. Thus a rise in the price of a substitute for a product shifts the demand curve for the product to the right. More will be demanded at each price.

substitutes Goods that can be used in place of another good to satisfy similar needs or desires.

    Complements are products that tend to be used jointly. Cars and gasoline are complements; so are CD players and speakers, golf clubs and golf balls, electric stoves and electricity, and airplane flights to Calgary and ski-lift tickets in Banff. Because complements tend to be consumed together, a fall in the price of one will increase the quantity demanded of *both* products. Thus, a fall in the price of a complement for a product will shift that product's demand curve to the right. More will be demanded at each price.

complements Goods that tend to be used jointly.

---

[1]Such products are called *normal goods*. Products for which the quantity demanded falls as income rises are called *inferior goods*. These concepts are defined and discussed in Chapter 4.

For example, a fall in the price of airplane trips to Calgary will lead to a rise in the demand for ski-lift tickets in Banff, even though the price of those lift tickets is unchanged. (So the demand curve for ski-lift tickets will shift to the right.)

Tastes.   Tastes have an effect on people's desired purchases. A change in tastes may be long-lasting, such as the shift from fountain pens to ballpoint pens or from typewriters to computers; or it may be a short-lived fad such as CB radios (a fad in the late 1970s and early 1980s) and many toys such as Pogs and Beanie Babies. In either case, a change in tastes in favour of a product shifts the demand curve to the right. More will be demanded at each price.

Distribution of Income.   If a constant total of income is distributed differently among the population, demands may change. A change in the distribution of income, therefore, will cause an increase in the demand for products bought most by households whose incomes increase and a decrease in the demand for products bought most by households whose incomes decrease. If, for example, the government increases the deductions that may be taken for children on income-tax returns and compensates by raising basic tax rates, income will be transferred from households without children to households with children. Demands for products more heavily bought by childless persons will decline, while demands for products more heavily bought by households with children will increase.

Population.   Population growth does not create new demand unless the additional people have the means to purchase goods—that is, unless they have purchasing power. If there is an increase in population with purchasing power—for example, the immigration of wealthy foreigners—the demands for all the products purchased by the new people will rise. Thus, we expect that an increase in population will shift the demand curves for most products to the right, indicating that more will be demanded at each price.

Expectations about the Future.   Our discussion has so far focused on how changes in the current value of variables may change demand. But it is also true that changes in people's *expectations about future values* of variables may change demand. For example, suppose that you are thinking about buying a house in a small town in Nova Scotia and you have learned that in the near future a large high-tech firm will be moving its head office and several hundred employees to this same small town. Since their future movement into your town will surely increase the demand for housing and thus will drive up the *future* price of houses, this expectation will lead you (and others like you) to increase your demand *today* so as to make the purchase before the price rises. Thus, the demand curve for houses will shift to the right today in anticipation of a future event.

Figure 3-3 summarizes the reasons that demand curves shift.

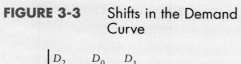

FIGURE 3-3   Shifts in the Demand Curve

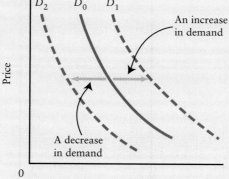

A rightward shift in the demand curve from D_0 to D_1 indicates an increase in demand; a leftward shift from D_0 to D_2 indicates a decrease in demand. An increase in demand means that more is demanded at each price. Such a rightward shift can be caused by a rise in income, a rise in the price of a substitute, a fall in the price of a complement, a change in tastes that favours that product, an increase in population, a redistribution of income toward groups that favour the product, or the anticipation of a future event that will increase the price.

A decrease in demand means that less is demanded at each price. Such a leftward shift can be caused by a fall in income, a fall in the price of a substitute, a rise in the price of a complement, a change in tastes that disfavours the product, a decrease in population, a redistribution of income away from groups that favour the product, or the anticipation of a future event that will decrease the price.

Movements Along the Curve Versus Shifts of the Whole Curve

Suppose that you read in today's newspaper that a sharp increase in the price of carrots has been caused by an increased demand for carrots. Then tomorrow you read that the rising price of carrots is reducing the typical consumer's purchases of carrots, as shoppers switch to potatoes, yams, and peas. The two stories appear to contradict each other. The first associates a rising price with rising demand; the second associates a rising price with declining demand. Can both statements be true? The answer is yes—because they refer to different things. The first describes a shift in the demand curve; the second describes a movement along a demand curve in response to a change in price.

Consider first the statement that the increase in the price of carrots has been caused by an increased demand for carrots. This statement refers to a shift in the demand curve for carrots—in this case, a shift to the right, indicating more carrots demanded at each price. This shift, as we will see later in this chapter, will increase the price of carrots.

Now consider the second statement—that fewer carrots are being bought because carrots have become more expensive. This refers to a movement along the new demand curve and reflects a change between two specific quantities demanded, one before the price increased and one afterward.

Possible explanations for the two stories are:

1. A change in tastes is shifting the demand curve for carrots to the right as more carrots are demanded at each price. This, in turn, raises the price of carrots (for reasons we will soon study in detail). This was the first newspaper story.

2. The rising price of carrots is causing each individual household to cut back on its purchase of carrots. The cutback is represented by an upward movement to the left along any particular demand curve for carrots. This was the second newspaper story.

To prevent the type of confusion caused by our two newspaper stories, economists use a specialized vocabulary to distinguish between shifts of curves and movements along curves.

We have seen that demand refers to the *entire* demand curve, whereas quantity demanded refers to the quantity that is demanded at a specific price, as indicated by a particular *point* on the demand curve. In Figure 3-1, for example, demand is given by the curve *D;* at a price of $40 per ton, the quantity demanded is 90 000 tons, as indicated by the point *V*.

Economists reserve the term **change in demand** to describe a change in the quantity demanded at *every* price. That is, a change in demand refers to a shift of the entire demand curve. The term **change in quantity demanded** refers to a movement from one point on a demand curve to another point, either on the same demand curve or on a new one.

A change in quantity demanded can result from a shift in the demand curve with the price constant; from a movement along a given demand curve due to a change in the price; or from a combination of the two. [3]

We consider these three possibilities in turn.

An increase in demand means that the whole demand curve shifts to the right; a decrease in demand means that the whole demand curve shifts to the left. At a given price, an increase in demand causes an increase in quantity demanded, whereas a decrease in demand causes a decrease in quantity demanded. For example, in Figure 3-2, the shift in the demand curve from D_0 to D_1 represents an increase in demand, and at a price of $40 per ton, quantity demanded increases from 90 000 tons to 116 000 tons, as indicated by the move from *V* to *V'*.

change in demand A change in the quantity demanded at each possible price of the commodity, represented by a shift in the whole demand curve.

change in quantity demanded A change in the specific quantity of the good demanded, represented by a change from one point on a demand curve to another point, either on the original demand curve or on a new one.

FIGURE 3-4   Shifts of and Movements Along the Demand Curve

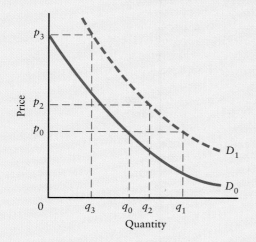

An increase in demand means that the demand curve shifts to the right, and hence quantity demanded will be higher at each price. A rise in price causes an upward movement to the left along the demand curve, and hence quantity demanded will fall. The demand curve is originally D_0 and price is p_0, which means that quantity demanded is q_0. Suppose that demand increases to D_1, which means that at any particular price, there is a larger quantity demanded; for example, at p_0, quantity demanded is now q_1. Now suppose that the price rises above p_0. This causes a movement up and to the left along D_1, and quantity demanded falls below q_1.

The net effect of these two changes can be either an increase or a decrease in the quantity demanded. In this figure, a rise in price to p_2 means that the quantity demanded q_2 is still in excess of the original quantity demanded q_0; a rise in price to p_3 means that the final quantity demanded q_3 is below the original quantity demanded q_0.

A movement down and to the right along a demand curve represents an increase in quantity demanded; a movement up and to the left along a demand curve represents a decrease in quantity demanded. For example, in Figure 3-2, with demand given by the curve D_1, an increase in price from \$40 to \$60 per ton causes a movement along D_1 from V' to W', and quantity demanded decreases from 116 000 tons to 100 800 tons.

When there is a change in demand *and* a change in the price, the overall change in quantity demanded is the net effect of the shift in the demand curve and the movement along the new demand curve. Figure 3-4 shows the combined effect of an increase in demand, shown by a rightward shift in the whole demand curve, and an upward movement to the left along the new demand curve due to an increase in price. The increase in demand causes an increase in quantity demanded at the initial price, whereas the movement along the demand curve causes a decrease in the quantity demanded. Whether quantity demanded rises or falls overall depends on the relative magnitudes of these two changes.

Supply

What determines the supply of any given product? Why do Canadian oil producers extract and market more oil when the price of oil is high? Why do Canadian cattle ranchers sell more beef when the price of cattle-feed (mostly grain) falls? We start by developing a theory designed to explain the supply of some typical product.

What Is "Quantity Supplied"?

quantity supplied
The amount of a commodity that producers wish to sell in some time period.

The amount of a product that firms wish to sell in some time period is called the **quantity supplied** of that product. Quantity supplied is a flow; it is so much per unit of time. Note also that quantity supplied is the amount that firms are willing to offer for sale; it is not necessarily the amount that they succeed in selling, which is expressed by *quantity actually sold* or *quantity exchanged*.

The quantity supplied of a product is influenced by the following variables: [4]

- Product's own price
- Prices of inputs
- Technology
- Number of suppliers

The situation with supply is the same as that with demand: There are several influencing variables, and we will not get far if we try to discover what happens when they all change at the same time. Again, we use the convenient *ceteris paribus* assumption to study the influence of the variables one at a time.

Quantity Supplied and Price

We begin by holding all other influences constant and ask, "How do we expect the quantity of a product supplied to vary with its own price?"

A basic hypothesis of economics is that the price of the product and the quantity supplied are related *positively*, other things being equal. That is, the higher the product's own price, the more its producers will supply; and the lower the price, the less its producers will supply.

In later chapters we will derive this hypothesis as a prediction from more basic assumptions about the behaviour of firms. But now we simply ask "why might this be so?" Firms will supply more because the profits that can be earned from producing a product will increase if the price of that product rises, whereas the costs of inputs used to produce it will remain unchanged. As a result, firms, which are in business to earn profits, will wish to produce more of the product whose price has risen.

Supply Schedules and Supply Curves

A rise in the price of wheat, other things being equal, will lead farmers to plant less of other crops and plant more wheat.

The general relationship just discussed can be illustrated by a **supply schedule,** which shows the relationship between quantity supplied of a product and the price of the product, other things being equal. A supply schedule is analogous to a demand schedule; the former shows what producers would be willing to sell, whereas the latter shows what households would be willing to buy, at alternative prices of the product. The table in Figure 3-5 presents a hypothetical supply schedule for carrots.

A **supply curve,** the graphical representation of the supply schedule, is illustrated in Figure 3-5. Each point on the supply curve represents a specific price-quantity combination; however, the whole curve shows something more.

The supply curve represents the relationship between quantity supplied and price, other things being equal; its positive slope indicates that quantity supplied increases when price increases.

When economists make statements about the conditions of supply, they are not referring just to the particular quantity being supplied at the moment—that is, not to just one point on the supply curve. Instead, they are referring to the entire supply curve, to the complete relationship between desired sales and all possible prices of the product.

Supply refers to the entire relationship between the quantity supplied of a product and the price of that product, other things being equal. A single point on the supply curve refers to the *quantity supplied* at that price.

supply schedule
A table showing the relationship between the quantity of some commodity that producers wish to sell (per period of time) and the price of that commodity, other things being equal.

supply curve   The graphical representation of the relationship between the quantity of some commodity that producers wish to sell (per period of time) and the price of that commodity, other things being equal.

supply   The entire relationship between the quantity of some commodity that producers wish to sell (per period of time) and the price of that commodity, other things being equal.

FIGURE 3-5   The Supply of Carrots

	Price Per Ton ($)	Quantity Supplied (thousands of tons per year)
u	20	5.0
v	40	46.0
w	60	77.5
x	80	100.0
y	100	115.0
z	120	122.5

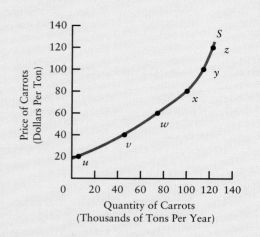

Both the table and the graph show the quantities that producers wish to sell at various prices, *ceteris paribus*. For example, row *w* indicates that if the price of carrots were $60 per ton, producers would want to sell 77 500 tons per year. The supply curve, labelled *S*, relates quantity of carrots supplied to the price of carrots; its positive slope indicates that quantity supplied increases as price increases.

Shifts in the Supply Curve

A shift in the supply curve means that at each price a quantity different from the previous one will be supplied. An increase in the quantity supplied at each price is shown in Figure 3-6. This change appears as a rightward shift in the supply curve. In contrast, a decrease in the quantity supplied at each price appears as a leftward shift. For supply, as for demand, there is an important general rule:

A change in any of the variables (other than the product's own price) that affects the quantity supplied will shift the supply curve to a new position.

Let's consider the effect of changes in several variables.

Price of Inputs.   All things that a firm uses to produce its outputs, such as materials, labour, and machines, are called the firm's *inputs*. Other things being equal, the higher the price of any input used to make a product, the less will be the profit from making that product. We expect, therefore, that the higher the price of any input used by a firm, the less the firm will produce and offer for sale at any given price of the product. A rise in the price of inputs therefore shifts the supply curve to the left, indicating that less will be supplied at any given price; a fall in the cost of inputs shifts the supply curve to the right.

Technology.   At any time, what is produced and how it is produced depend on what is known. Over time, knowledge changes; so do the quantities of individual products supplied. The enormous increase in production per worker that has been going on in industrial societies for about 200 years is due largely to improved methods of production. The Industrial Revolution is more than a historical event; it is a present reality. Discoveries in chemistry have led to lower costs of production for well-established products, such as

---

FIGURE 3-6   An Increase in the Supply of Carrots

Price Per Ton (\$) p	Quantity Supplied Before Cost-Saving Innovation (thousands of tons per year) S_0		Quantity Supplied After Innovation (thousands of tons per year) S_1	
20	5.0	u	28.0	u'
40	46.0	v	76.0	v'
60	77.5	w	102.0	w'
80	100.0	x	120.0	x'
100	115.0	y	132.0	y'
120	122.5	z	140.0	z'

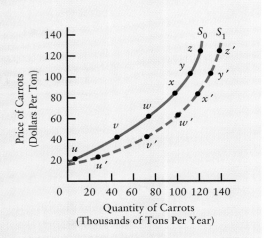

A cost-saving innovation increases the quantity supplied at each price. This is shown by the rightward shift in the supply curve, from S_0 to S_1. As a result of a cost-saving innovation, the quantity that is supplied at a price of \$100 per ton rises from 115 000 to 132 000 tons per year. A similar rise occurs at every price.

---

paints, and to a large variety of new products made of plastics and synthetic fibers. Such inventions as silicon chips have radically changed products such as computers, televisions, and telephones, and the consequent development of smaller computers has revolutionized the production of countless other nonelectronic products.

Any technological innovation that decreases production costs will increase the profits that can be earned at any given price of the product. Because increased profitability leads to increased willingness to produce, this change shifts the supply curve to the right.

Number of Suppliers.   For given prices and technology, the total amount of any product supplied depends on the number of firms producing that product and offering it for sale. For example, in Chapter 9 we will examine the situation where profits made by existing firms producing a particular good attract other firms to enter the industry in pursuit of those profits. The effect of this increase in the number of suppliers is to shift the supply curve to the right. Similarly, if the existing firms are losing money, they will eventually leave the industry; such a reduction in the number of suppliers shifts the supply curve to the left.

Movements Along the Curve Versus Shifts of the Whole Curve

As with demand, it is important to distinguish movements along supply curves from shifts of the whole curve. Economists reserve the term **change in supply** to describe a shift of the whole supply curve—that is, a change in the quantity that will be supplied at every price. The term **change in quantity supplied** refers to a movement from one point on a supply curve to another point, either on the same supply curve or a new one. In other words, an increase in supply means that the whole supply curve has shifted to the right, so that the quantity supplied at any given price has increased; a movement up and to the right along a supply curve indicates an increase in the quantity supplied in response to an increase in the price of the product.

Practise with Study Guide Chapter 3, Exercise 6.

change in supply
A change in the quantity supplied at each possible price of the commodity, represented by a shift in the whole supply curve.

change in quantity supplied   A change in the specific quantity supplied, represented by a change from one point on a supply curve to another point, either on the original supply curve or on a new one.

A change in quantity supplied can result from a change in supply, with the price constant; from a movement along a given supply curve due to a change in the price; or from a combination of the two.

The Determination of Price

So far we have considered demand and supply separately. We now come to a key question: how do the two forces of demand and supply interact to determine price?

The Concept of a Market

Originally the term "market" designated a physical place where products were bought and sold. We still use the term this way to describe places such as Granville Island Market in Vancouver, Kensington Market in Toronto, or Jean Talon Market in Montreal. Once developed, however, theories of market behaviour were easily extended to cover products such as wheat or oil, which can be purchased anywhere in the world at a price that tends to be uniform the world over. The concepts of "the wheat market" or "the oil market" extend our viewpoint well beyond the idea of a single place to which the consumer goes to buy something.

market   Any situation in which buyers and sellers can negotiate the exchange of goods or services.

For present purposes a **market** may be defined as existing in any situation (a physical place or an electronic medium) in which buyers and sellers negotiate the exchange of some product or related group of products. It must be possible, therefore, for buyers and sellers to communicate with each other and to make meaningful deals over the whole market.

Individual markets differ in the degree of *competition* among the various buyers and sellers. In the next few chapters we will confine ourselves to examining markets in which the number of buyers and sellers is sufficiently large that no one of them has any appreciable influence on the market price. This is a very rough definition of what economists call *perfectly competitive markets*. Starting in Chapter 10, we will consider the behaviour of markets in which there are small numbers of either sellers or buyers. But our initial theory of markets will actually be a very good description of the markets for such things as wheat, pork, newsprint, coffee, copper, and many other commodities.

Graphical Analysis of a Market

The table in Figure 3-7 brings together the demand and supply schedules from Figure 3-1 and 3-5. The quantities of carrots demanded and supplied at each price may now be compared.

excess demand
A situation in which, at the given price, quantity demanded exceeds quantity supplied.

excess supply
A situation in which, at the given price, quantity supplied exceeds quantity demanded.

There is only one price, $60 per ton, at which the quantity of carrots demanded equals the quantity supplied. At prices less than $60 per ton, there is a shortage of carrots because the quantity demanded exceeds the quantity supplied. This is a situation of **excess demand.** At prices greater than $60 per ton, there is a surplus of carrots because the quantity supplied exceeds the quantity demanded. This is a situation of **excess supply.** This same story can also be told in graphical terms. The quantities demanded and supplied at any price can be read off the two curves; the excess supply or excess demand is shown by the horizontal distance between the curves at each price.

FIGURE 3-7 Determination of the Equilibrium Price of Carrots

Price Per Ton ($) p	Quantity Demanded (thousands of tons per year) D	Quantity Supplied (thousands of tons per year) S	Excess Demand (+) or Excess Supply (−) (thousands of tons per year) $D - S$
20	110.0	5.0	+105.0
40	90.0	46.0	+44.0
60	77.5	77.5	0.0
80	67.5	100.0	−32.5
100	62.5	115.0	−52.5
120	60.0	122.5	−62.5

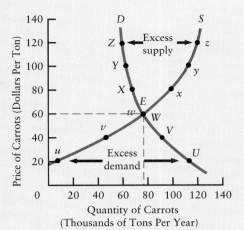

The equilibrium price corresponds to the intersection of the demand and supply curves. Equilibrium is indicated by E, which is point W on the demand curve and point w on the supply curve. At a price of $60, quantity demanded equals quantity supplied. At prices above equilibrium, there is excess supply and downward pressure on price. At prices below equilibrium, there is excess demand and upward pressure on price.

To examine the determination of market price, let's suppose first that the price is $100 per ton. At this price, 115 000 tons are offered for sale, but only 62 500 tons are demanded. There is an excess supply of 52 500 tons per year. Sellers are then likely to cut their prices to get rid of this surplus. And purchasers, observing the stock of unsold carrots, will begin to offer less money for the product. In other words, *excess supply causes downward pressure on price.*

Now consider the price of $20 per ton. At this price, there is excess demand. The 5000 tons produced each year are snapped up quickly, and 105 000 tons of desired purchases cannot be made. Rivalry between would-be purchasers may lead them to offer more than the prevailing price to outbid other purchasers. Also, sellers may begin to ask a higher price for the quantities that they do have to sell. In other words, *excess demand causes upward pressure on price.*

Finally, consider the price of $60. At this price, producers wish to sell 77 500 tons per year, and purchasers wish to buy that same quantity. There is neither a shortage nor a surplus of carrots. There are no unsatisfied buyers to bid the price up, nor are there unsatisfied sellers to force the price down. Once the price of $60 has been reached, therefore, there will be no tendency for it to change.

Equilibrium implies a state of rest, or balance, between opposing forces. The **equilibrium price** is the one toward which the actual market price will tend. It will persist, once established, unless it is disturbed by some change in market conditions which shifts the demand curve, the supply curve, or both.

The price at which the quantity demanded equals the quantity supplied is called the equilibrium price, or the market-clearing price. [5]

equilibrium price
The price at which quantity demanded equals quantity supplied. Also called the market-clearing price.

disequilibrium price
A price at which quantity demanded does not equal quantity supplied.

disequilibrium
A situation in a market in which there is excess demand or excess supply.

Any price at which the market does not "clear"—that is, quantity demanded does not equal quantity supplied—is called a **disequilibrium price.** Whenever there is either excess demand or excess supply in a market, that market is said to be in a state of **disequilibrium,** and the market price will be changing.

Figure 3-7 makes it clear that the equilibrium price occurs where the demand and supply curves intersect. Below that price, there is excess demand and hence upward pressure on the existing price. Above that price, there is excess supply and hence downward pressure on the existing price.

The Laws of Demand and Supply

Changes in any of the variables, other than price, that influence quantity demanded or supplied will cause a shift in the supply curve, the demand curve, or both. There are four possible shifts: an increase in demand (a rightward shift in the demand curve), a decrease in demand (a leftward shift in the demand curve), an increase in supply (a rightward shift in the supply curve), and a decrease in supply (a leftward shift in the supply curve).

comparative statics
The derivation of predictions by analysing the effect of a change in some exogenous variable on the equilibrium.

To discover the effects of each of the possible curve shifts, we use the method known as **comparative statics.**[2] With this method, we derive predictions by analysing the effect on the equilibrium of some change in which we are interested. We start from a position of equilibrium and then introduce the change to be studied. We then determine the new equilibrium position and compare it with the original one. The difference between the two positions of equilibrium must result from the change that was introduced because everything else has been held constant.

Each of the four possible curve shifts causes changes that are described by one of the four "laws" of demand and supply. Each of the laws summarizes what happens when an initial position of equilibrium is disturbed by a shift in either the demand curve or the supply curve. By using the term "law" to describe what happens, economists do not mean that they are absolutely certain of the outcome. The term "law" in science is used to describe a theory that has stood up to substantial testing. The laws of demand and supply are thus hypotheses that predict certain kinds of behaviour in certain situations, and the predicted behaviour occurs sufficiently often that economists continue to have confidence in the underlying theory.

The four laws of demand and supply are derived in Figure 3-8. Study the figure carefully. Previously, we had given the axes specific labels, but because it is now intended to apply to any product, the horizontal axis is simply labelled "Quantity." This means quantity per period in whatever units output is measured. "Price," the vertical axis, means the price measured as dollars per unit of quantity for the same product.

The four laws of demand and supply are as follows:

1. An increase in demand causes an increase in both the equilibrium price and the equilibrium quantity exchanged.

2. A decrease in demand causes a decrease in both the equilibrium price and the equilibrium quantity exchanged.

---

[2]The term *static* is used because we are not concerned with the actual path by which the market goes from the first equilibrium position to the second or with the time taken to reach the second equilibrium. Analysis of these movements would be described as *dynamic analysis.*

FIGURE 3-8 The Four "Laws" of Demand and Supply

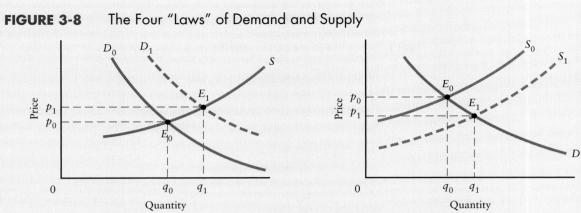

(i) The effect of shifts in the demand curve

(ii) The effect of shifts in the supply curve

The effects on equilibrium price and quantity of shifts in either demand or supply are known as the laws of demand and supply.
    A rise in demand. In part (i), suppose that the original demand and supply curves are D_0 and S, which intersect to produce equilibrium at E_0, with a price of p_0 and a quantity of q_0. An increase in demand shifts the demand curve to D_1, taking the new equilibrium to E_1. Price rises to p_1 and quantity rises to q_1.
    A fall in demand. In part (i), the original demand and supply curves are D_1 and S, which intersect to produce equilibrium at E_1, with a price of p_1 and a quantity of q_1. A decrease in demand shifts the demand curve to D_0, taking the new equilibrium to E_0. Price falls to p_0, and quantity falls to q_0.
    A rise in supply. In part (ii), the original demand and supply curves are D and S_0, which intersect to produce equilibrium at E_0, with a price of p_0 and a quantity of q_0. An increase in supply shifts the supply curve to S_1, taking the new equilibrium to E_1. Price falls to p_1, and quantity rises to q_1.
    A fall in supply. In part (ii), the original demand and supply curves are D and S_1, which intersect to produce equilibrium at E_1, with a price of p_1 and a quantity of q_1. A decrease in supply shifts the supply curve to S_0, taking the new equilibrium to E_0. Price rises to p_0, and quantity falls to q_0.

3. An increase in supply causes a decrease in the equilibrium price and an increase in the equilibrium quantity exchanged.

4. A decrease in supply causes an increase in the equilibrium price and a decrease in the equilibrium quantity exchanged.

Demonstrations of these laws are given in the caption to Figure 3-8. The intuitive reasoning behind each is as follows:

1. An increase in demand creates a shortage at the initial equilibrium price, and the unsatisfied buyers bid up the price. This rise in price causes a larger quantity to be supplied with the result that at the new equilibrium, more is exchanged at a higher price.

2. A decrease in demand creates a glut at the initial equilibrium price, and the unsuccessful sellers bid the price down. As a result, less of the product is supplied and offered for sale. At the new equilibrium, both price and quantity exchanged are lower than they were originally.

3. An increase in supply creates a glut at the initial equilibrium price, and the unsuccessful suppliers force the price down. This drop in price increases the quantity demanded, and the new equilibrium is at a lower price and a higher quantity exchanged.

4. A decrease in supply creates a shortage at the initial equilibrium price that causes the price to be bid up. This rise in price reduces the quantity demanded, and the new equilibrium is at a higher price and a lower quantity exchanged.

Practise with Study Guide Chapter 3, Exercise 3.

In this chapter, we have studied many forces that can cause demand or supply curves to shift. By combining this analysis with the four laws of demand and supply, we can link many real-world events that cause demand or supply curves to shift with changes in market prices and quantities. *Applying Economic Concepts 3-1* shows how we can use demand-and-supply analysis to examine two real-world shocks: the effects of Brazil's 1994 coffee-crop failure and the effects of the 1998 ice storm in Eastern Canada. *Applying Economic Concepts 3-2* examines the effect of ongoing technological improvement on the price of computer chips.

The theory of the determination of price by demand and supply is beautiful in its simplicity. Yet as we shall see throughout this book, it is powerful in its wide range of applications.

Prices and Inflation

The theory we have developed explains how individual prices are determined by the forces of demand and supply. To facilitate matters, we have made *ceteris paribus* assumptions. Specifically, we have assumed the constancy of all prices except the one we are studying. Does this mean that our theory is inapplicable to an inflationary world in which all prices are rising at the same time? Fortunately, the answer is no.

absolute price   The amount of money that must be spent to acquire one unit of a commodity. Also called *money price*.

The price of a product is the amount of money that must be spent to acquire one unit of that product. This is called the **absolute price** or *money price*. A **relative price** is the ratio of two absolute prices; it expresses the price of one good in terms of (relative to) another.

We have been reminded several times that what matters for demand and supply is the price of the product in question *relative to the prices of other products*; that is, what matters is the relative price.

relative price   The ratio of the money price of one commodity to the money price of another commodity; that is, a ratio of two absolute prices.

In an inflationary world, we are often interested in the price of a given product as it relates to the average price of all other products. If, during a period when all prices were increasing by an average of 10 percent, the price of oranges rose by 30 percent, then the price of oranges rose relative to the prices of other goods as a whole. Oranges became *relatively* expensive. However, if oranges had risen in price by 30 percent when other prices increased by 40 percent, then the relative price of oranges would have fallen. Although the money price of oranges rose substantially, oranges became *relatively* cheap.

It has been convenient in this chapter to analyse changes in particular prices in the context of a constant price level. We can easily extend the analysis to an inflationary period by remembering that any force that raises the price of one product when other prices remain constant will, given general inflation, raise the price of that product faster than the price level is rising. For example, a change in tastes in favour of carrots that would raise their price by 5 percent when other prices were constant would raise their price by 8 percent if, at the same time, the general price level were rising by 3 percent. In each case, the price of carrots rises 5 percent *relative to the average of all prices*.

In microeconomics, whenever we refer to a change in the price of one product, we mean a change in that product's relative price; that is, a change in the price of that product relative to the prices of all other goods.

If the price level is constant, an increase in the product's relative price requires only a rise in the money price of the product. If the price level itself is rising, an increase in the product's relative price requires that the money price of the product rise faster than the price level.

APPLYING ECONOMIC CONCEPTS 3-1

Ice Storms, Droughts, and Economics

Here are two simple examples of the demand and supply apparatus in action. Both examples show how the weather—something that changes in unpredictable and often dramatic ways—can have significant effects on either the demand or the supply of various products, with obvious implications for the observed market price.

The Weather and a Demand Shock

In January of 1998, Quebec, eastern Ontario, and parts of the northeastern United States were hit by a massive ice storm. So unprecedented was this storm in its magnitude that many electric power systems were devastated. Homes and businesses in the Montreal area went without power for as long as four weeks.

This electric power shortage had many economic effects, including lost factory production, damage to much capital stock, the death of farm livestock, and the displacement of thousands of people, especially elderly people, into shelters where they could be fed and cared for. Another effect of the power shortage, as soon as it became clear that it would last for more than just a few hours, was a sudden and substantial increase in the demand for portable gas-powered electric generators. Within just a couple of days, all stores in the greater Montreal area were sold out of such generators, and the prices for newly ordered units had increased.

Furthermore, the shortages and price increases for electric generators were not confined to the area directly hit by the ice storm. As it became clear that there was an excess demand for generators in Quebec, sellers in other parts of the country began to divert their supply toward Quebec. This reduction in supply caused shortages, and thus price increases, in other parts of the country, as far away as Edmonton.

The Weather and a Supply Shock

Brazil, which produces one-third of the world's coffee, experienced unusually severe weather in 1994. Two killing frosts in June and July and a period of drought thereafter severely damaged the next year's crop. Some experts estimated that the frosts had destroyed as much as 45 percent of Brazil's 1995 harvest.

This crop damage meant that the world's supply curve of coffee shifted in—upward and to the left. Without a change in price, there would have been excess demand for coffee, with more people wanting to buy than wanting to sell. Predictably, the market forces reacted swiftly, and coffee prices soared by nearly 100 percent on the wholesale commodity market on July 14. Consumers also felt the impact of the supply shock, with retail prices climbing by about $5 per kilogram.

This severe weather hurt coffee growers in Brazil, reducing their incomes considerably. But coffee growers elsewhere—such as Colombia, Costa Rica and Kenya—actually benefited from Brazil's misfortune. They sold their normal-size crop at the elevated world price and thus enjoyed unusually high incomes.

The Quebec ice storm in January 1998 decimated the electricity distribution system. The demand for portable electricity generators (and many other emergency products) increased sharply as a result.

APPLYING ECONOMIC CONCEPTS 3-2

Technological Progress and the Market for Computer Chips

According to a June 1996 article in the *Financial Times*,

It is only nine months since the world semiconductor industry was forging ahead. Demand for chips was so great that there was a shortage, analysts were forecasting record growth and manufacturers were unveiling plans for dozens of $1 billion chip factories....

The euphoria has been short-lived. The shortage rapidly turned into surplus, and the price of dynamic random access memory (D-RAM) chips—the basic memory chips for PCs—has dropped by about 65 percent over the past six or seven months....

Commodity chip prices normally fall by 20 percent to 30 percent each year as manufacturing costs fall. But with manufacturers scrambling to protect market share, international spot market prices have fallen below the break-even point of some Asian manufacturers.

The newspaper story points to key aspects of this market. First, the technology of producing computer chips is evolving rapidly. This causes the market supply curve to shift continually to the right. Second, the demand curve has a negative slope, and shifts in some periods.

The trend decline of "20 percent to 30 percent each year" is clearly shown in the accompanying figure. So is the abnormal period between 1992 and 1995 when chip prices actually rose slightly before falling back sharply in 1996, as discussed above. What is the explanation?

In "normal" times the primary influence is that the ongoing technological improvement causes the supply curve to shift to the right along a nearly stationary demand curve. Chip prices fall and quantity demanded increases. In the 1992–95 period, however, the demand curve shifted sharply to the right. This increase in demand was due to the increased availability (and reduced prices) of such complementary software products as multimedia games and educational programs. By 1996, the demand curve had stopped shifting to the right but the supply curve had continued to shift, since the technolog-

ical improvements continued to occur. Hence prices returned to their "usual" downward trend.

Notice that the price rises associated with the temporary boom in demand between 1992 and 1995 would have increased the quantity supplied on each rightward-shifting supply curve because the high profitability of chip production encouraged higher production at each level of capacity. The fall in price in 1996 no doubt reduced the quantity supplied along the supply curve that existed at the time. However, despite the fall in price, the supply curve continued to shift to the right in successive periods as technological progress continued to reduce the costs of production.

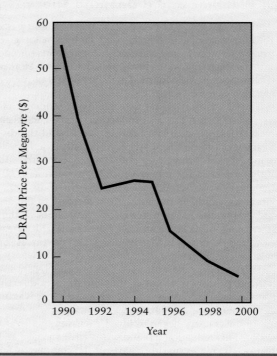

S U M M A R Y

Demand

- The amount of a product that consumers wish to purchase is called *quantity demanded*. It is a flow expressed as so much per period of time. It is determined by tastes, average household income, the product's own price, the prices of other products, the size of the population, the distribution of income among consumers, and expectations about the future.
- The relationship between quantity demanded and price is represented graphically by a demand curve that shows how much will be demanded at each market price. Quantity demanded is assumed to increase as the price of the product falls, other things held constant. Thus, demand curves are downward sloping.

- A shift in a demand curve represents a change in the quantity demanded at each price and is referred to as a *change in demand*. The demand curve shifts to the right (an increase in demand) if average income rises, if population rises, if the price of a substitute rises, if the price of a complement falls, or if there is a change in tastes in favour of the product. The opposite changes shift the demand curve to the left (a decrease in demand).
- It is important to make the distinction between a movement along a demand curve (caused by a change in the product's price) and a shift of a demand curve (caused by a change in any of the other determinants of demand).

Supply

- The amount of a product that firms wish to sell is called *quantity supplied*. It is a flow expressed as so much per period of time. It depends on the product's own price, the costs of inputs, the number of suppliers, and the state of technology.
- The relationship between quantity supplied and price is represented graphically by a supply curve that shows how much will be supplied at each market price. Quantity supplied is assumed to increase as the price of the product increases, other things held constant. Thus, supply curves are upward sloping.

- A shift in the supply curve indicates a change in the quantity supplied at each price and is referred to as a *change in supply*. The supply curve shifts to the right (an increase in supply) if the costs of producing the product fall or if, for any reason, producers become more willing to produce the product. The opposite changes shift the supply curve to the left (a decrease in supply).
- It is important to make the distinction between a movement along a supply curve (caused by a change in the product's price) and a shift of a supply curve (caused by a change in any of the other determinants of supply).

The Determination of Price

- The *equilibrium price* is the price at which the quantity demanded equals the quantity supplied. At any price below equilibrium, there will be excess demand; at any price above equilibrium, there will be excess supply. Graphically, equilibrium occurs where the demand and supply curves intersect.

- Price rises when there is excess demand and falls when there is excess supply. Thus the actual market price will be pushed toward the equilibrium price. When it is reached, there will be neither excess demand nor excess supply, and the price will not change until either the supply curve or the demand curve shifts.

• Using the method of *comparative statics,* we can determine the effects of a shift in either demand or supply. An increase in demand raises both equilibrium price and equilibrium quantity; a decrease in demand lowers both. An increase in supply raises equilibrium quantity but lowers equilibrium price; a decrease in supply lowers equilibrium quantity but raises equilibrium price. These are called the laws of demand and supply.

• The absolute price of a product is its price in terms of money; its relative price is its price in relation to other products. In an inflationary period, a rise in the *relative price* of one product means that its absolute price rises by more than the price level; a fall in its relative price means that its absolute price rises by less than the price level.

K E Y   C O N C E P T S

"Ceteris paribus" or "other things being equal"

Quantity demanded and quantity actually bought

Demand schedule and demand curve

Change in quantity demanded versus change in demand

Quantity supplied and quantity actually sold

Supply schedule and supply curve

Change in quantity supplied versus change in supply

Equilibrium, equilibrium price, and disequilibrium

Comparative statics

Laws of supply and demand

Relative price

S T U D Y   E X E R C I S E S

1. Consider households' demand for chicken meat. For each of the events listed below, state and explain the likely effect on the demand for chicken. How would each event be illustrated in a diagram?

   a. A medical study reports that eating chicken meat reduces the likelihood of suffering from particular types of heart problems.
   b. A widespread bovine disease leads to an increase in the price of beef.
   c. An increase in average household income.

2. Consider the world market for a particular quality of coffee beans. The following table shows the demand and supply schedules for this market.

Price (per kg)	Quantity Demanded	Quantity Supplied
	(millions of kg per year)	
$2.00	28	10
$2.40	26	12
$3.10	22	13.5
$3.50	19.5	19.5
$3.90	17	22
$4.30	14.5	23.5

   a. Plot the demand and supply schedules on a scale diagram.
   b. Identify the amount of excess demand or supply associated with each price.
   c. Identify the equilibrium price in this market.
   d. Suppose that government (or a collection of national governments) were somehow able to set a minimum price for coffee equal to $3.90 per kg. Explain the outcome in the world coffee market.

3. Consider the supply for grade-A beef. As the price of beef rises, ranchers will tend to sell more cattle to the slaughter houses. Yet, a central prediction from the supply-and-demand model of this chapter is that an increase in the supply of beef reduces the equilibrium price. Reconcile the apparent contradiction. Use a diagram to do so.

4. Consider the world market for wheat. Suppose there is a major failure in Russia's wheat crop due to a severe drought. Explain the likely effect on the equilibrium price and quantity in the world wheat market. Also explain why North American wheat farmers certainly benefit from Russia's drought. Draw a diagram to carefully describe and analyse the situation.

5. The *New York Times* recently stated:

   > *While the world's appetite for chocolate grows more voracious each year, cocoa farms around the globe are failing, under siege from fungal and viral diseases and insects….Researchers predict a shortfall in beans from the cacao tree, the raw material from which chocolate is made, in as little as five to ten years.*

   Describe in terms of the supply-and-demand apparatus what is described in the quote. What is the implied prediction for the equilibrium price of chocolate? What is the implied prediction for the equilibrium quantity of chocolate?

6. This is a challenging question intended for those students who like mathematics. It requires you to solve a supply-and-demand model as a system of *simultaneous equations* (meaning simply that both equations apply at the same time). Letting p be the price of the product, suppose the demand and supply functions for some product are given by

   $$Q^D = 100 - 3p$$
   $$Q^S = 10 + 2p$$

   a. Plot both the demand curve and the supply curve.
   b. What is the condition for equilibrium in this market?
   c. By imposing the condition for equilibrium, solve for the equilibrium price.
   d. Substitute the equilibrium price into either the demand or supply function to solve for the equilibrium quantity. Check to make sure you get the same answer whether you use the demand function or the supply function.
   e. Now suppose there is an increase in demand so that the new demand function is given by

   $$Q^D = 180 - 3p.$$

   Compute the new equilibrium price and quantity. Is your result consistent with the "law" of demand?
   f. Now suppose that, with the new demand curve in place, there is an increase in supply so that the new supply function is given by $Q^S = 90 + 2p$. Compute the new equilibrium price and quantity. Is your result consistent with the "law" of supply?

DISCUSSION QUESTIONS

1. Recently, a government economist predicted that this spring's excellent weather would result in larger crops of wheat and canola than farmers had expected. But the economist warned consumers not to expect prices to decrease because the cost of production was rising and foreign demand for Canadian crops was increasing. "The classic pattern of supply and demand won't work this time," the economist said. Discuss his observation.

2. What would be the effect on the equilibrium price and quantity of marijuana if its sale and consumption were legalized?

3. Classify the effect of each of the following as (i) a decrease in the demand for fish or (ii) a decrease in the quantity of fish demanded. Illustrate each diagrammatically.

   a. The government of Canada closes the Atlantic cod fishery.
   b. People buy less fish because of a rise in fish prices.
   c. The Catholic Church relaxed its ban on eating meat on Fridays.
   d. The price of beef falls and, as a result, consumers buy more beef and less fish.
   e. Fears of mercury pollution lead locals to shun fish caught in nearby lakes.
   f. It is generally alleged that eating fish is better for one's health than eating meat.

4. Predict the effect on the price of at least one product of each of the following events:

   a. Winter snowfall is at a record high in the interior of British Columbia, but drought continues in Quebec ski areas.
   b. A recession decreases employment in Oshawa automobile factories.
   c. The French grape harvest is the smallest in 20 years.
   d. The province of Ontario cancels permission for citizens to cut firewood in provincial camp grounds.

5. Are the following two observations inconsistent? (a) Rising demand for housing causes prices of new homes to soar. (b) Many families refuse to buy homes as prices become prohibitive for them.

CHAPTER 4

Elasticity

The laws of demand and supply predict the *direction* of changes in price and quantity in response to various shifts in demand and supply. However, it usually is not enough to know merely whether price and quantity simply rise or fall; it is also important to know by *how much* each changes.

In the previous chapter we discussed the coffee-crop failure in Brazil and how this drove up the world coffee price. But what did this crop failure do to the incomes of Brazilian coffee growers? If the world price increased by more (in percentage terms) than their crop shrank, their incomes would have actually *increased*; that is, the crop failure actually would have made them, as a group, better off. On the other hand, if the price increased by less than the crop shrank, their incomes would have fallen.

Measuring and describing the extent of the responsiveness of quantities to changes in prices and other variables are often essential if we are to understand the significance of these changes. Such measurement is accomplished with the concept of *elasticity*.

Price Elasticity of Demand

Suppose there is an increase in the supply of some farm crop—that is, a rightward shift in the supply curve. We saw in Figure 3-8 when we examined the laws of supply and demand that such an increase in supply will cause the equilibrium price to fall and the equilibrium quantity to rise. But by how much will each change? The answer depends on what is called the *price elasticity of demand*.

Loosely speaking, demand is said to be *elastic* when quantity demanded is quite responsive to changes in price. When quantity demanded is quite unresponsive to changes in price, demand is said to be *inelastic*.

The meaning of elasticity is illustrated in the two parts of Figure 4-1. The two parts of the figure have the same initial equilibrium, and that equilibrium is disturbed by the same leftward shift in the supply curve. But, because the demand curves are different in the two parts of the figure, the new equilibrium position is different, and hence the magnitude

FIGURE 4-1   The Effect of the Shape of the Demand Curve

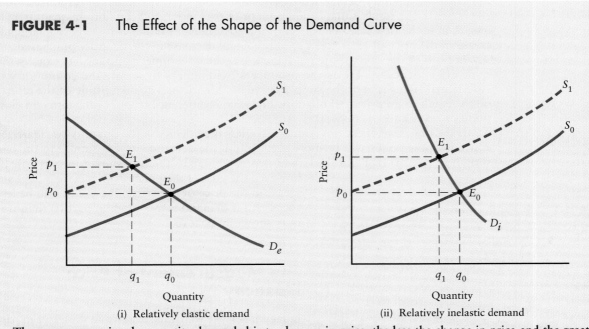

(i) Relatively elastic demand   (ii) Relatively inelastic demand

The more responsive the quantity demanded is to changes in price, the less the change in price and the greater the change in quantity resulting from any given shift in the supply curve. Both parts of the figure are drawn to the same scale. They show the same initial equilibrium and the same shift in the supply curve. In each part, initial equilibrium is at price p_0 and output q_0 and the new equilibrium is at p_1 and q_1. In part (i), the effect of the shift in supply from S_0 to S_1 is a slight rise in the price and a large decrease in quantity. In part (ii), the effect of the identical shift in the supply curve from S_0 to S_1 is a large increase in the price and a relatively small decrease in quantity.

of the effects of the increase in supply on equilibrium price and quantity are different. The demand curve in part (i) is more elastic than the demand curve in part (ii).

A shift in supply will have different quantitative effects, depending on the shape of the demand curve. The difference may be significant for government policy. Suppose the market being depicted in Figure 4-1 is the market for cigarettes, and that the government imposes a tax on each pack of cigarettes sold (as the federal government and all Canadian provincial governments do). As we will see later in this chapter, the effect of such a tax is to shift the supply curve of cigarettes upward by the amount of the tax—a reduction in supply.

Part (i) of Figure 4-1 illustrates a case in which the quantity that consumers demand is relatively responsive to price changes—that is, demand is relatively elastic. The reduction in supply pushes up the price, but, because the quantity demanded is quite responsive, only a small change in price is necessary to restore equilibrium. Thus, the effect of the government's policy is to achieve a large decrease in the production (and consumption) of cigarettes and only a small increase in price.

Part (ii) of Figure 4-1 shows a case in which the quantity demanded is relatively unresponsive to price changes—that is, demand is relatively inelastic. As before, the decrease in supply at the original price causes a shortage that increases the price. However, this time the quantity demanded by consumers does not fall much in response to the rise in price. The result is that equilibrium price rises more, and equilibrium quantity falls less, than in the first case. The effect of the government's policy is to achieve a large increase in the price of cigarettes but only a small decrease in the quantity purchased.

In both of the cases shown in Figure 4-1, the government's policy has exactly the same effectiveness as far as the producers' willingness to supply the commodity is concerned—the shifts of the supply curve are identical. The magnitude of the effects on the equilibrium price and quantity, however, is different because of the different elasticities of demand.

If the objective of the government's policy is to decrease the quantity of cigarettes consumed, the policy will be more successful if the demand curve is similar to the one shown in part (i) of Figure 4-1 than if it is similar to the one shown in part (ii). If, however, the goal of the policy is to achieve a large increase in the price of cigarettes, the policy will be less successful if demand is as shown in part (i) than if it is as shown in part (ii).

The Measurement of Price Elasticity

In Figure 4-1, we were able to say that the curve in part (i) showed a demand that was more responsive to price changes than the curve in part (ii) because two conditions were fulfilled. First, both curves were drawn on the same scale. Second, the initial equilibrium prices and quantities were the same in both parts of the figure. Let us see why these conditions matter.

First, by drawing both figures on the same scale, the curve that looked steeper actually did have the larger absolute slope. (The slope of a demand curve tells us the number of dollars by which price must change to cause a unit change in quantity demanded.)

TABLE 4-1	Price Reductions and Corresponding Increases in Quantity Demanded for Three Products

Commodity	Reduction in Price (cents)	Increase in Quantity Demanded (per month)
Cheese	40 per kilogram	7500 kilograms
T-shirts	40 per shirt	5000 shirts
CD players	40 per CD player	100 CD players

The data show, for each of the three products, the change in quantity demanded resulting from the same absolute fall in price. The data are fairly uninformative about the responsiveness of demand to price because they do not tell us either the original price or the original quantity demanded.

If we had drawn the two curves on different scales, we could have concluded nothing about the relative price changes needed to get a unit change in quantity demanded by comparing their appearances on the graph.

Second, because we started from the same price-quantity equilibrium in both parts of the figure, we did not need to distinguish between *percentage* changes and *absolute* changes. If the initial prices and quantities are the same in both cases, the larger absolute change is also the larger percentage change. However, when we wish to deal with different initial price-quantity equilibria, we need to decide whether we are interested in absolute or percentage changes. To see which is relevant, let's suppose that we have the information shown in Table 4-1. Should we conclude that the demand for portable CD players is not as responsive to price changes as the demand for cheese? After all, price cuts of 40 cents cause quite a large increase in the quantity of cheese demanded but only a small increase in the quantity demanded of CD players.

It should be obvious that a reduction in the price of 40 cents will be a large price cut for a low-priced product and an insignificant price cut for a high-priced product. All of the price reductions listed in Table 4-1 represent price reductions of 40 cents, but they are clearly different proportions of the respective prices. It is usually more revealing to know the *percentage* change in the prices of the various products. For similar reasons knowing the quantity by which demand changes is not very revealing unless the initial level of demand is also known. An increase of 7500 kilograms is quite a significant reaction to demand if the quantity formerly bought was 15 000 kilograms, but it is insignificant if the quantity formerly bought was 10 million kilograms.

Table 4-2 shows the original and new levels of price and quantity. Changes in price and quantity expressed as percentages of the *average* prices and quantities are shown in columns (1) and (2) of Table 4-3. The **price elasticity of demand,** the measure of responsiveness of quantity of a product demanded to a change in that product's price, is symbolized by the Greek letter eta, η. It is defined as follows:

price elasticity of demand (η) A measure of the responsiveness of quantity demanded to a change in the commodity's own price.

$$\eta = \frac{\text{percentage change in quantity demanded}}{\text{percentage change in price}}$$

This measure is called the price elasticity of demand, or simply *demand elasticity*. Because the variable causing the change in quantity demanded is the product's own price, the term *own-price elasticity of demand* is also used.

TABLE 4-2 Price and Quantity Information Underlying Data of Table 4-1

Product	Unit	Original Price ($)	New Price ($)	Average Price ($)	Original Quantity	New Quantity	Average Quantity
Cheese	kg	3.40	3.00	3.20	116 250	123 750	120 000
T-shirts	shirt	16.20	15.80	16.00	197 500	202 500	200 000
CD players	player	80.20	79.80	80.00	9 950	10 050	10 000

These data provide the appropriate context for the data given in Table 4-1. The table relates the 40-cent-per-unit price reduction of each product to the actual prices and quantities demanded.

TABLE 4-3	Calculation of Demand Elasticities		

Product	(1) Percentage Decrease in Price	(2) Percentage Increase in Quantity	(3) Elasticity of Demand (2) ÷ (1)
Cheese	12.5	6.25	0.5
T-shirts	2.5	2.50	1.0
CD players	0.5	1.00	2.0

Elasticity of demand is the percentage change in quantity demanded divided by the percentage change in price. The percentage changes are based on average prices and quantities shown in Table 4-2. For example, the 40-cent-per-kilogram decrease in the price of cheese is 12.5 percent of $3.20. A 40-cent change in the price of CD players is only 0.5 percent of the average price per CD player of $80.00.

The Use of Average Price and Quantity in Computing Elasticity

The caption in Table 4-3 stresses that the demand elasticities are computed using changes in price and quantity measured in terms of the *average* values of each. Averages are used to avoid the ambiguity caused by the fact that when a price or quantity changes, the change is a different percentage of the original value than it is of the new value. For example, the 40-cent change in the price of cheese shown in Table 4-2 represents an 11.8 percent change of the original price of $3.40 but a 13.3 percent change of the new price of $3.00.

Using average values for price and quantity means that the measured elasticity of demand between any two points on the demand curve, call them A and B, is independent of whether the movement is from A to B or from B to A. In the example of cheese in Tables 4-2 and 4-3, the 40-cent change in the price of cheese is unambiguously 12.5 percent of the average price of $3.20, and that percentage applies to a price increase from $3.00 to $3.40 or for a price decrease from $3.40 to $3.00.

The implications of using average values for price and quantity for calculating elasticity are as follows. Consider a change from an initial price of p_0 and quantity of q_0 to a new price of p_1 and quantity of q_1. The formula for elasticity is then

$$\eta = \frac{(q_1 - q_0)/q}{(p_1 - p_0)/p} \tag{4-1}$$

where p and q are the average price and average quantity, respectively. Thus

$$p = (p_1 + p_0)/2 \quad \text{and} \quad q = (q_1 + q_0)/2.$$

We can substitute these expressions for p and q in Equation 4-1 and, after dividing out the factors of 2, we get

$$\eta = \frac{(q_1 - q_0)/(q_1 + q_0)}{(p_1 - p_0)/(p_1 + p_0)} \tag{4-2}$$

which provides a convenient formula for calculating demand elasticity. For example, for the case of cheese in Tables 4-2 and 4-3, we have

$$\eta = \frac{7500/240\,000}{0.40/6.40} = \frac{0.03125}{0.0625} = 0.5$$

which is as in Table 4-3. There is further discussion of the use of averages to calculate elasticity and of alternative methods in the appendix to this chapter. [6]

Interpreting Numerical Elasticities

Because demand curves have negative slopes, an increase in price is associated with a decrease in quantity demanded, and vice versa. Because the percentage changes in price and quantity have opposite signs, demand elasticity is a negative number. However, we will follow the usual practice of ignoring the negative sign and speak of the measure as a positive number, as we have done in the illustrative calculations in Table 4-3. Thus the more responsive the quantity demanded (for example, CD players relative to cheese), the greater the elasticity of demand and the higher the measure (e.g., 2.0 compared with 0.5).

The numerical value of demand elasticity can vary from zero to infinity. Elasticity is zero when quantity demanded does not respond at all to a price change. As long as the percentage change in quantity demanded is less than the percentage change in price, the elasticity of demand has a value of less than one (economists sometimes say less than *unity*). When the two percentage changes are equal, elasticity is equal to one. When the percentage change in quantity demanded exceeds the percentage change in price, the elasticity of demand is greater than one.

When the percentage change in quantity demanded is less than the percentage change in price (elasticity less than 1), there is said to be **inelastic demand**. When the percentage change in quantity is greater than the percentage change in price (elasticity greater than 1), there is said to be **elastic demand**. This important terminology is summarized in part A of *Extensions in Theory 4-1*, which is found toward the end of the chapter.

A demand curve need not, and usually does not, have the same elasticity over every part of the curve. Figure 4-2 shows that a negatively sloped straight-line demand curve does not have a constant elasticity, even though it does have a constant slope. A straight-line demand curve has constant elasticity only when it is vertical or horizontal. Figure 4-3 illustrates these two cases, in addition to a third case of a particular *nonlinear* demand curve that also has a constant elasticity.

FIGURE 4-2   Elasticity Along a Straight-Line Demand Curve

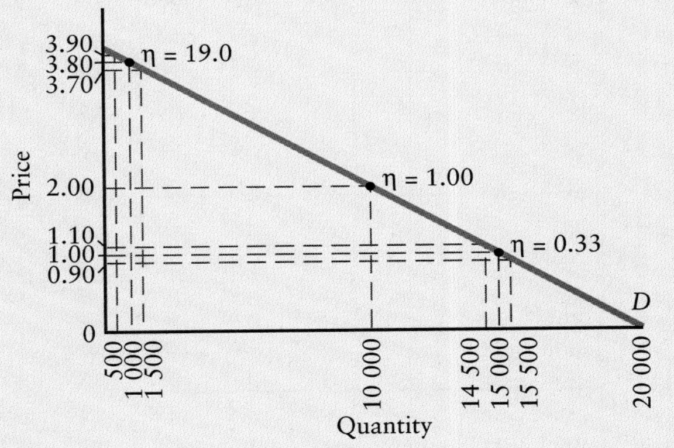

Moving down a straight-line demand curve, elasticity falls continuously. On this straight-line demand curve, a reduction in price of $0.20 always leads to the same increase (1000 units) in quantity demanded.

Near the upper end of the curve, where price is $3.80 and quantity demanded is 1000 units, a reduction in price of $0.20 (from $3.90 to $3.70) is just slightly more than a 5 percent reduction, but the 1000-unit increase in quantity demanded is a 100 percent increase. Here, elasticity is 19.

Near the lower end, at a price of $1.00 and a quantity of 15 000 units, a price reduction of $0.20 (from $1.10 to $0.90) leads to the same 1000-unit increase in quantity demanded. However, the $0.20 price reduction represents a 20 percent fall, whereas the 1000-unit increase in quantity demanded represents only a 6.67 percent increase. Here, elasticity is 0.33.

What Determines Elasticity of Demand?

The main determinant of demand elasticity is the availability of substitutes. Some products, such as margarine, broccoli, lamb, and Toyota cars, have quite close substitutes—butter, other green vegetables, beef, and Mazda cars. A change in the prices of these products, *with the prices of the substitutes remaining constant*, can be expected to cause much substitution. A fall in price leads consumers to buy more of the product and less of the substitutes, and a rise in price leads consumers to buy less of the product and more of the substitutes. Products defined more broadly, such as *all* foods or *all* clothing or *all* methods of transportation, have many fewer satisfactory substitutes. A rise in their prices can be expected to cause a smaller fall in quantities demanded than would be the case if close substitutes were available.

A product with close substitutes tends to have an elastic demand; a product with no close substitutes tends to have an inelastic demand.

inelastic demand The situation in which, for a given percentage change in price, there is a smaller percentage change in quantity demanded; elasticity less than one.

elastic demand The situation in which, for a given percentage change in price, there is a greater percentage change in quantity demanded; elasticity greater than one.

FIGURE 4-3   Three Demand Curves with Constant Elasticity

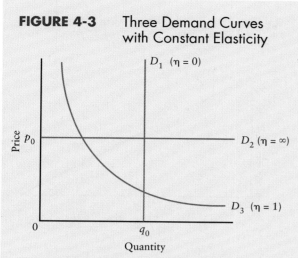

Each of these demand curves has a constant elasticity. D_1 has zero elasticity: The quantity demanded is equal to q_0, independent of the price. D_2 has infinite elasticity at the price p_0: A small price increase from p_0 decreases quantity demanded from an indefinitely large amount to zero. D_3 has unit elasticity: A given percentage increase in price brings an equal percentage decrease in quantity demanded at all points on the curve; it is a rectangular hyperbola for which price times quantity demanded is a constant.

Demand elasticity depends on the availability of substitutes. The availability of a product's substitutes, in turn, depends on how the product is defined and on the time period being considered. We explore these aspects next.

Definition of the Product

For food taken as a whole, demand is inelastic over a large price range. It does not follow, however, that any one food, such as white bread or peanut butter, is a necessity in the same sense. Individual foods can have quite elastic demands, and they frequently do.

Clothing provides a similar example. Clothing as a whole has a less elastic demand than do individual kinds of clothes. For example, when the price of wool sweaters rises, many households may buy cotton sweaters or down vests instead of buying an additional wool sweater. Thus, although purchases of wool sweaters fall, total purchases of clothing do not.

Any one of a group of related products will have a more elastic demand than the group as a whole.

Short Run and Long Run

Because it takes time to develop satisfactory substitutes, a demand that is inelastic in the short run may prove to be elastic when enough time has passed. Perhaps the most dramatic example of this principle occurred in 1973 when the Organization of Petroleum Exporting Countries (OPEC) shocked the world with its sudden and large increase in the price of oil. At that time, the short-run demand for oil proved to be highly inelastic. Large price increases were met in the short run by very small reductions in quantity demanded. In this case, the short run lasted for several years. Gradually, however, the high price of petroleum products led to such adjustments as the development of smaller, more fuel-efficient cars, economizing on heating oil by installing more efficient insulation, and replacement of fuel oil in many industrial processes with such other power sources as coal and hydroelectricity. The long-run elasticity of demand, relating the change in price to the change in quantity demanded after all adjustments were made, turned out to have an elasticity of well over unity, although the long-run adjustments took as much as a decade to work out.

The response to a price change, and thus the measured price elasticity of demand, will tend to be greater the longer the time span.

For such products as cornflakes and pillowcases, the full response to a price change occurs quickly, and there is little reason to make the distinction between short-run and long-run effects. But other products are typically used in connection with highly durable appliances or machines. A change in the price of, say, electricity and gasoline may not have its major effect until the stock of appliances and machines using these products has been adjusted. This adjustment may take several years to occur.

For products for which substitutes are developed over a period of time, it is helpful to identify two kinds of demand curves. A *short-run demand curve* shows the response of quantity demanded to a change in price for a given structure of the durable goods that use the product and for the existing sets of substitute products. A different short-run demand curve will exist for each such structure. The *long-run demand curve* shows the response of quantity demanded to a change in price after enough time has passed to ensure that all adjustments to the changed price have occurred.

The long-run demand for a product is more elastic than the short-run demand.

Figure 4-4 shows the short-run and long-run effects of an increase in supply. In the short run, the supply increase leads to a movement down the relatively inelastic short-run demand curve; it thus causes a large fall in price but only a small increase in quantity. In the long run, demand is more elastic; thus long-run equilibrium has price and quantity above those that prevailed in short-run equilibrium.

This pattern is often referred to as *overshooting* of the price. The overshooting of price that is evident in the figure is the way in which markets clear when demand is less elastic in the short run than in the long run. Note also that there is *undershooting* of quantity—that is, the equilibrium quantity rises by less in the short run than in the long run.

Elasticity and Total Expenditure

We know that quantity demanded increases as price falls, but what happens to the total expenditure on that product? It turns out that the response of total expenditure depends on the price elasticity of demand.

To see the relationship between the elasticity of demand and total expenditure, we begin by noting that total expenditure is equal to price times quantity:

$$\text{Total Expenditure} = \text{Price} \times \text{Quantity}$$

Because price and quantity move in opposite directions along a demand curve, one falling when the other rises, the change in total expenditure appears to be ambiguous. It is easily shown, however, that the direction of change in total expenditure depends on the relative percentage changes in the price and quantity. If the percentage change in price exceeds the percentage change in quantity, the price change will dominate, and total expenditure will change in the same direction as the price changes; this is the case where elasticity is less than unity. If the percentage change in the price is less than the percentage change in the quantity demanded (elasticity exceeds unity), the quantity change will dominate, and total expenditure will

Because most people cannot easily or quickly change their method of transportation, the demand for gasoline is much less elastic in the short run than in the long run.

FIGURE 4-4   Short-Run and Long-Run Equilibrium Following an Increase in Supply

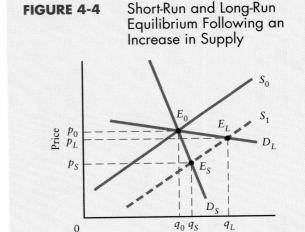

The magnitude of the changes in the equilibrium price and quantity following a shift in supply depends on the time allowed for demand to adjust. The initial equilibrium is at E_0, with price p_0 and quantity q_0. Supply then increases such that the supply curve shifts from S_0 to S_1.

On impact, the relevant demand curve is the short-run curve D_S, and the new equilibrium immediately following the supply shock is E_S. Price falls sharply to p_S, and quantity rises only to q_S. In the long run, the demand curve is the more elastic one given by D_L, and equilibrium is at E_L. The long-run equilibrium price is p_L (greater than p_S), and quantity is q_L (greater than q_S).

FIGURE 4-5   Total Expenditure and Quantity Demanded

Price ($)	Quantity Demanded	Expenditure ($)
3.80	1 000	3 800
3.00	5 000	15 000
2.50	7 500	18 750
2.00	10 000	20 000
1.50	12 500	18 750
1.00	15 000	15 000

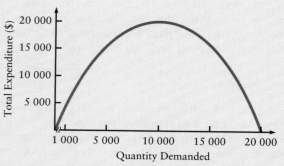

The change in total expenditure on a product in response to a change in price depends on the elasticity of demand. The table and graph are based on the demand curve shown in Figure 4-2. For quantities demanded that are less than 10 000, elasticity of demand is greater than one, and hence any increase in quantity demanded will be proportionately larger than the fall in price that caused it. In that range, total expenditure is increasing. For quantities greater than 10 000, elasticity of demand is less than one, and hence any increase in quantity demanded will be proportionately smaller than the fall in price that caused it. In that range, total expenditure is decreasing. The maximum of total expenditure occurs where the elasticity of demand equals one.

Practise with Study Guide Chapter 4, Exercises 3 and 5.

For information on OPEC and its activities, see www.opec.org.

change in the same direction as quantity changes. If the two percentage changes are equal, total expenditure is unchanged—this is the case of unit elasticity.

Figure 4-5 illustrates the relationship between elasticity of demand and total expenditure; it is based on the straight-line demand curve in Figure 4-2. Total expenditure at each of a number of points on the demand curve is calculated in the table, and the general relationship between total expenditure and quantity demanded is shown by the plotted curve. In the figure we see that expenditure reaches its maximum when elasticity is equal to 1. [7]

The following example uses this relationship between elasticity, price and total expenditure. When a bumper potato crop recently sent prices down 50 percent (a rightward shift in the supply curve), the quantity purchased increased by only 15 percent. Demand was clearly inelastic, and the result of the bumper crop was that total expenditure on potatoes *fell* sharply. Potato farmers, therefore, experienced a sharp fall in income.

A second example relates to the OPEC oil shock in the early 1970s. As the OPEC countries acted together to restrict supply and push up the world price of oil, quantity demanded fell, but only by a small percentage—much smaller than the percentage increase in price. World demand for oil (at least in the short run) was very inelastic, and the result was that total expenditure on oil *increased* dramatically. The OPEC oil producers, therefore, experienced an enormous increase in income.

Price Elasticity of Supply

price elasticity of supply (η_S)   A measure of the responsiveness of quantity supplied to a change in the commodity's own price.

The concept of elasticity can be applied to supply as well as to demand. **Price elasticity of supply** measures the responsiveness of the quantity supplied to a change in the product's price. It is denoted η_S and defined as follows:

$$\eta_s = \frac{\text{percentage change in quantity supplied}}{\text{percentage change in price}}$$

This is often called *supply elasticity*. The supply curves considered in this chapter all have positive slopes: An increase in price causes an increase in quantity supplied. Such supply curves all have positive elasticities because price and quantity change in the same direction.

There are important special cases. If the supply curve is vertical—the quantity supplied does not change as price changes—then elasticity of supply is zero. A horizontal supply curve has an infinite elasticity of supply: A small drop in price will reduce the quantity that producers are willing to supply from an indefinitely large amount to zero. Between these two extremes, elasticity of supply varies with the shape of the supply curve. Loosely speaking, steeper supply curves imply a smaller quantity response for a given change in price, and thus a lower elasticity.

Note, however, that a steeper supply curve does *not always* reflect less elastic supply. There is an important special case worth remembering. Students are quite often surprised to learn that straight-line supply curves *that pass through the origin* have a particular characteristic.

Any positively sloped straight-line supply curve through the origin has a price elasticity equal to one.

Such a supply curve is shown in Figure 4-6. To see that the price elasticity is equal to one, consider two triangles in the figure. The first has the sides p, q, and the S curve; the second has the sides Δp, Δq, and the S curve. These are similar triangles. It follows that the ratios of their sides are equal. That is,

$$p/q = \Delta p/\Delta q$$

From our earlier discussion, elasticity of supply is defined as

$$\eta_s = (\Delta q/\Delta p) \times (p/q)$$

which, by substitution, gives

$$\eta_s = (q/p) \times (p/q) = 1$$

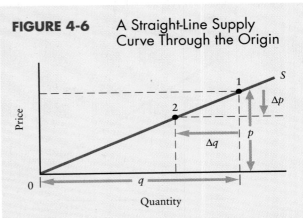

FIGURE 4-6   A Straight-Line Supply Curve Through the Origin

At every point on the supply curve, p/q equals $\Delta p/\Delta q$; hence supply elasticity equals unity at every point.

Determinants of Supply Elasticity

Because much of the treatment of demand elasticity carries over to supply elasticity, we can cover the main points quickly.

Substitution and Production Costs

The ease of substitution can vary in production as well as in consumption. If the price of a product rises, how much more can be produced profitably? This depends in part on how easy it is for producers to shift from the production of other products to the one whose price has risen. If agricultural land and labour can be readily shifted from one crop to another, the supply of any one crop will be more elastic than if they cannot. Or, if machines used to produce coats can be easily modified to produce pants (and vice versa), then the supply of both pants and coats will be more elastic than if the machines cannot be so easily modified.

Supply elasticity depends to a great extent on how costs behave as output is varied. If the costs of producing a unit of output rise rapidly as output rises, then the stimulus to expand production in response to a rise in price will quickly be choked off by increases in costs. In this case, supply will tend to be rather inelastic. If, however, the costs of producing a unit of output rise only slowly as production increases, a rise in price that raises profits will elicit a large increase in quantity supplied before the rise in costs puts a halt to the expansion in output. In this case, supply will tend to be rather elastic.

Short Run and Long Run

As with demand, length of time for response is important. It may be difficult to change quantities supplied in response to a price increase in a matter of weeks or months but easy to do so over a period of years. An obvious example is the planting cycle of crops. An increase in the price of wheat that occurs in mid-summer may lead wheat farmers to be more careful (and less wasteful) in their harvesting this fall, but it occurs too late to influence how much wheat gets planted for this years' crop. But if the high price persists, it will surely influence how much wheat gets planted next spring. Also, new oil fields can be discovered, wells drilled, and pipelines built over a period of years but not in just a few months. Thus the elasticity of oil supply is much greater over five years than over one year.

As with demand, it is useful to make the distinction between the short-run and the long-run supply curve. The *short-run supply curve* shows the response of quantity supplied to a change in price given producers' current capacity to produce the good. The *long-run supply curve* shows the response of quantity supplied to a change in price after enough time has passed to allow producers to adjust their productive capacity.

The long-run supply for a product is more elastic than the short-run supply.

Figure 4-7 illustrates the short-run and long-run effects of an increase in demand. The short-run overshooting of price and the undershooting of quantity that are evident in the figure are analogous to that shown in Figure 4-4 when we examined the short-run and long-run effects following a shift in supply. Here it arises following a shift in demand and is the market-clearing response when supply is less elastic in the short run than in the long run.

FIGURE 4-7   Short-Run and Long-Run Equilibrium Following an Increase in Demand

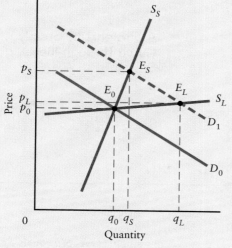

The size of the changes in the equilibrium price and quantity following a shift in demand depends on the time frame of the analysis. The initial equilibrium is at E_0, with price p_0 and quantity q_0. Demand then increases such that the demand curve shifts from D_0 to D_1.

On impact, the relevant supply curve is the short-run curve S_S, so that the new equilibrium immediately following the demand shock is at E_S. Price rises sharply to p_S, and quantity rises only to q_S. In the long run, the supply curve is the more elastic one given by S_L. The long-run equilibrium is at E_L; price is p_L (less than p_S) and quantity is q_L (greater than q_S).

An Important Example Where Elasticity Matters

So far, this chapter has been fairly tough going. We have spent much time examining price elasticity (of both demand and supply) and how to measure it. But who cares? In this section we explore the important concept of *tax incidence* and show that elasticity is crucial to determining whether consumers or producers (or both) end up being harmed by excise taxes.

The federal and provincial governments levy special sales taxes (called **excise taxes**) on many goods such as cigarettes, alcohol, and gasoline. All such taxes work in the following way. At the point of sale of the product, the sellers collect the tax on behalf of the government and then periodically remit the tax collections.

When the sellers write their cheques to the government, these firms feel—with some justification—that they are the ones paying the tax. Consumers, however, argue—again, with some justification—that *they* are the ones who are shouldering the burden of the tax because the tax causes the price of the product to rise.

The question of who *bears the burden* of a tax is called the question of **tax incidence**. A straightforward application of demand-and-supply analysis will show that tax incidence has nothing to do with whether the government collects the tax directly from consumers or from firms.

The burden of a sales (or excise) tax is distributed between consumers and sellers in a manner that depends on the relative elasticities of supply and demand.

At the beginning of this chapter we considered a government that taxed the sale of cigarettes. Let's examine that possibility again in a little more detail. We begin with Figure 4-8. To simplify the problem, we analyse the case where there is initially no tax. The equilibrium without taxes is illustrated by the solid supply and demand curves. What happens when a sales tax of t per pack of cigarettes is introduced? A sales tax means that the price paid by the consumer, called the *consumer price,* and the price received by the seller, called the *seller price,* must now differ by the amount of the tax, t.

In terms of the figure, we can analyse the effect of the tax by considering a new supply curve S' that is above the original supply curve S by the amount of the tax, t. To understand this new curve, let's consider the firm's situation at the original equilibrium quantity q_0. To supply that quantity, producers must receive p_0 per pack of cigarettes sold. However, for producers to receive p_0 when there is a tax on cigarettes, the consumer must pay a total price of $p_0 + t$—whether the consumer "pays the tax directly" by giving p_0 to the firm and t to the government or whether the consumer pays the total $p_0 + t$ to the firm and the firm then remits the tax t to

excise tax   A tax on the sale of a particular commodity.

tax incidence   The location of the burden of a tax; that is, the identity of the ultimate bearer of the tax.

FIGURE 4-8   The Effect of a Cigarette Excise Tax

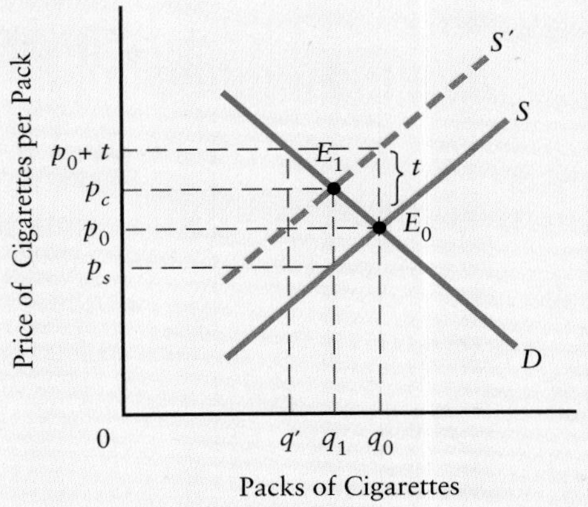

The burden of an excise tax is shared by consumers and producers. The original supply and demand curves for cigarettes are given by the solid lines S and D; equilibrium is at E_0 with price p_0 and quantity q_0. When a sales tax of t per pack is imposed, the supply curve shifts up to the dashed line S', which lies above the original supply curve by the amount of the tax t. The tax increases the consumer price and reduces the seller price. It also reduces the equilibrium quantity exchanged.

the government. Either way, the total amount that consumers must pay to obtain a given quantity from firms has increased by the amount of the tax t.

This upward shift in the supply curve for cigarettes is depicted in Figure 4-8 as the dashed curve, S'. This shift in the supply curve, caused by the tax, will generally also cause a movement *along* the demand curve, reducing the equilibrium quantity.

Consider the situation at the consumer price of $p_0 + t$. Firms will still be willing to sell the original quantity, but households will demand less because the price has risen; there is excess supply and hence pressure for the consumer price to fall.

The new equilibrium after the imposition of the sales tax occurs at the intersection of the original demand curve D with the tax-shifted supply curve S'. At this new equilibrium, E_1, the consumer price rises to p_c (greater than p_0), the seller price falls to p_s (less than p_0), and the equilibrium quantity falls to q_1.

Note that the quantity demanded *at the consumer price* is equal to the quantity supplied *at the seller price*, a condition that is required for equilibrium. As shown in the figure, compared to the original equilibrium, the consumer price is higher and the seller price is lower, although in each case the change in price is less than the full extent of the sales tax.

After the imposition of a sales tax, the difference between the consumer and seller prices is equal to the tax. In the new equilibrium, the quantity exchanged is less than that exchanged prior to the imposition of the tax.

The role of the relative elasticities of supply and demand in determining the incidence of the sales tax is illustrated in Figure 4-9. In part (i), demand is inelastic relative to

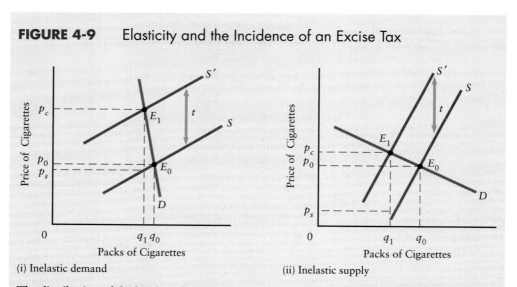

FIGURE 4-9   Elasticity and the Incidence of an Excise Tax

(i) Inelastic demand

(ii) Inelastic supply

The distribution of the burden of a sales tax between consumers and producers depends on the relative elasticities of supply and demand. In both parts of the figure, the initial supply and demand curves are given by S and D; the initial equilibrium is at E_0 with equilibrium price p_0 and quantity q_0. A tax of t per pack of cigarettes is imposed, causing the supply curve to shift up by the amount of the tax to S'. The new equilibrium is at E_1. The consumer price rises to p_c, the seller price falls to p_s, and the quantity falls to q_1. Sellers bear little of the burden of the tax in the first case (and consumers bear a lot), whereas consumers bear little of the burden in the second case (and sellers bear a lot).

supply; as a result, the fall in quantity is quite small, whereas the price paid by consumers rises by almost the full extent of the tax. Because neither the price received by sellers nor the quantity sold changes very much, sellers bear little of the burden of the tax. In part (ii), supply is inelastic relative to demand; in this case, consumers can more easily substitute away from cigarettes. There is little change in the price, and hence they bear little of the burden of the tax, which falls mostly on suppliers. Notice in Figure 4-9 that the size of the upward shift in supply is the same in the two cases, indicating the same tax increase in both cases.

When demand is inelastic relative to supply, consumers bear most of the burden of excise taxes. When supply is inelastic relative to demand, producers bear most of the burden.

Now we can examine who really pays for cigarette tax increases (or tax increases on gasoline and alcohol). The demand for cigarettes is inelastic both overall and relative to supply, suggesting that a cigarette-tax increase would be borne more by consumers than by producers. Thus, the large *reductions* in cigarette taxes which took place in the summer of 1994 in Ontario and Quebec benefited consumers more than producers. The demand for gasoline is also inelastic, but much more so in the short run than in the long run. (In the long run, drivers can change their driving routines and improve the efficiency of their vehicles, but in the short run such changes are very costly.) The supply of gasoline, given world trade in petroleum and petroleum products, is elastic relative to demand. The relatively inelastic demand and elastic supply imply that the burden of gasoline taxes falls mostly on consumers.

Applying Economic Concepts 4-1 discusses another important example of the issue of tax incidence—this time involving the burden of payroll taxes, such as the premiums that firms and workers pay for employment insurance and the Canada Pension Plan.

Practise with Study Guide Chapter 4, Exercise 9.

Other Demand Elasticities

The price of the product is not the only important variable determining demand for that product. Income and other prices also matter, and elasticity is a useful concept in measuring their effects.

Income Elasticity of Demand

One of the most important determinants of demand is the income of the customers. The responsiveness of demand to changes in income is termed the **income elasticity of demand** and is symbolized η_Y.

$$\eta_Y = \frac{\text{percentage change in quantity demanded}}{\text{percentage change in income}}$$

For most goods, increases in income lead to increases in demand—their income elasticity is positive. These are called **normal goods.** Goods for which demand decreases in response to a rise in income have negative income elasticities and are called **inferior goods.**

The income elasticity of normal goods can be greater than unity (elastic) or less than unity (inelastic), depending on whether the percentage change in the quantity

income elasticity of demand (η_Y)
A measure of the responsiveness of quantity demanded to a change in income.

normal good
A good for which quantity demanded rises as income rises—its income elasticity is positive.

inferior good
A good for which quantity demanded falls as income rises—its income elasticity is negative.

APPLYING ECONOMIC CONCEPTS 4-2

Who Really Pays for Payroll Taxes?

Some social programs in Canada are financed by **payroll taxes**—taxes collected from both firms and workers, computed as a proportion of workers' earnings. For example, the Employment Insurance program (formerly known as Unemployment Insurance) is financed by premiums paid by both firms and workers. The Canada Pension Plan is financed the same way.

When the federal government determines that such payroll taxes need to be increased (for reasons that we will discuss in Chapter 18 when we examine many aspects of Canadian social policy), an immediate question comes to the fore of the public debate: Should workers or firms be required to pay the extra taxes? There appears to be a great deal at stake in the resolution of this question. After all, neither workers nor firms want to bear the burden of extra taxes. Strikingly, however, *there is no economic difference between imposing payroll taxes on firms and imposing them on workers.* This proposition can be established by using the

same supply-and-demand analysis that we used to examine the incidence of sales taxes.

The accompanying figure illustrates a model of the labour market. The figure shows a standard demand-and-supply apparatus except that the axes have been relabelled as "Employment" and "Hourly Wage Rate."* Firms represent the demand for labour services. As the wage falls, it is profitable for firms to hire more workers (and to produce more output). Thus the demand curve for labour has a negative slope. Workers represent the supply of labour services. As the wage rises, the opportunity cost of *not working* rises, and thus workers substitute away from other activities and supply more labour services. Thus the supply curve for labour has a positive slope. The supply curve is shown to be relatively inelastic, in keeping with a considerable amount of empirical evidence showing that the quantity of labour supplied to the economy is quite unresponsive to changes in the wage rate. In the absence of any payroll taxes, the equilib-

---

payroll taxes Taxes paid by the firm and worker, computed as a percentage of the worker's total earnings.

demanded is greater or less than the percentage change in income that brought it about. It is also common to use the terms *income-elastic* and *income-inelastic* to refer to income elasticities of greater or less than unity. (See *Extensions in Theory 4-1* for a summary of the different elasticity concepts.)

The reaction of demand to changes in income is extremely important. We know that in most Western countries, economic growth caused the level of income to double every 20 to 30 years over a sustained period of at least a century. This rise in income has been shared to some extent by most citizens. As they found their incomes increasing, they increased their demands for most products, but the demands for some products, such as food and basic clothing, did not increase as much as the demands for other products. In developing countries the demand for durable goods is increasing most rapidly as household incomes rise, while in North America and Western Europe, the demand for services has risen most rapidly. The uneven impact of the growth of income on the demands for different products has important economic effects, which are studied at several points in this book.

What Determines Income Elasticity of Demand?

The variations in income elasticities shown in Table 4-4 suggest that the more basic a product, the lower its income elasticity. Food as a whole has an income elasticity of 0.2, consumer durables of 1.8. In Canada, starchy roots such as potatoes are inferior goods; their quantity demanded falls as income rises.

rium wage is w_0 and the equilibrium level of employment is E_0.

As in the analysis of excise taxes, the effect of the payroll tax is to drive a wedge between the wage paid by the firm (w_F) and the wage received by the worker (w_W). With a payroll tax of t dollars per hour, w_F rises above w_0 and w_W falls below w_0. Employment falls from E_0 to E_1. As the supply curve is drawn in the figure, however, almost all of the burden of the tax falls on workers. The lower right-hand bracket shows the amount by which the workers' take-home wage falls. The upper right-hand bracket shows the amount by which the employers' total payment per worker rises. Together, these add up to the payroll tax, shown by the left-hand bracket. Were the supply curve *perfectly* inelastic, the entire burden would fall on workers.

Quite apart from how the burden of the tax is apportioned between workers and firms, the figure also shows why many economic commentators refer to payroll taxes as "job killers"—by increasing the total cost that firms must pay for each unit of labour services, payroll taxes naturally lead firms to hire fewer workers.

The burden of payroll taxes would be shared more by firms if the supply of labour were more elastic (or if the demand were less elastic). But, as is the case with excise taxes that we discussed in the text, it is the shapes of the supply and demand curves that determine who bears the burden of payroll taxes.

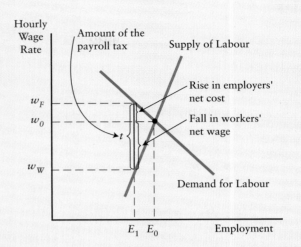

* This analysis assumes that the labour market is reasonably competitive—meaning that there are a large number of both workers and firms, none of which have the power to influence the market wage. Though this is usually a good description of the labour market, there are some situations that are not well modelled by a simple supply-and-demand apparatus. We discuss the role of labour unions, for example, in Chapter 14.

The more basic is an item in the consumption pattern of consumers, the lower is its income elasticity.

Income elasticities for any one product also vary with the level of a consumer's income. When incomes are low, consumers may eat almost no green vegetables and consume lots of starchy foods such as bread and potatoes; when incomes are higher, they may eat cheap cuts of meat and more green vegetables along with their bread and potatoes; when incomes are higher still, they are likely to eat higher quality and prepared foods of a wide variety.

The distinction between luxuries and necessities helps to explain differences in income elasticities. The case of restaurant meals is one example. Such meals are almost always more expensive, calorie for calorie, than meals prepared at home. It would thus be expected that at lower ranges of income, restaurant meals would be regarded as an expensive luxury but that the demand for them would expand substantially as consumers became richer. This is actually what happens.

What is true of individual consumers is also true of countries. Empirical studies show that for different countries at comparable stages of economic development, income elasticities are similar. However, the countries of the world are at various stages of economic development and thus have widely different income elasticities for the same products. Notice in Table 4-4 the different income elasticity of poultry in the United States, where it is a standard item of consumption, and in Sri Lanka, where it is a luxury good.

TABLE 4-4	Some Estimated Income Elasticities of Demand

Inferior goods (η_Y less than zero)	
Whole milk	−0.5
Pig products	−0.2
Starchy roots	−0.2
Inelastic normal goods (η_Y between zero and one)	
Wine (France)	0.1
All food	0.2
Poultry	0.3
Elastic normal goods (η_Y greater than one)	
Gasoline	1.1
Wine	1.4
Consumer durables	1.8
Poultry (Sri Lanka)	2.0
Restaurant meals (U.K.)	2.4

Income elasticities vary widely across commodities and sometimes across countries. The basic source of food estimates by country is the Food and Agriculture Organization of the United Nations, but many individual studies have been made. (For the United States except where noted.)

Another example of the luxury-necessity distinction is shown in Table 4-4 by the different income elasticities for wine in France and the United States. In France, wine is a much more basic part of the meal than is the case in the United States, where wine is regarded as more of a luxury. As a result, increases in income lead to much smaller increases in the demand for wine in France than in the United States.

Graphical Representation of Income Elasticity

Increases in income shift the demand curve to the right for a normal good and to the left for an inferior good. Figure 4-10 shows a different kind of graph, an *income-consumption curve*. The curve resembles an ordinary demand curve in one respect: It shows the relationship of quantity demanded to one other variable, *ceteris paribus*. The other variable is not price, however, but household income. (An increase in the price of the product, holding income constant, would shift the curves in Figure 4-10 downward.)[1]

The figure shows three different patterns of income elasticity. Goods that consumers regard as necessities will generally have income elasticities that fall as income rises. The obvious reason is that as incomes rise, it becomes possible for consumers to devote a smaller proportion of their incomes to meeting basic needs and a larger proportion to buying things that they previously could not afford. At high levels of income some of the necessities may even become inferior goods. So-called luxury goods will not tend to be purchased at low levels of income but will have high income elasticities once incomes rise enough to permit consumers to sample the better things of life now available to them.

Cross Elasticity of Demand

cross elasticity of demand (η_{XY})
A measure of the responsiveness of the quantity of one commodity demanded to changes in the price of another commodity.

The responsiveness of demand to changes in the price of *another* product is called the **cross elasticity of demand**. It is denoted η_{XY} and defined as follows:

$$\eta_{XY} = \frac{\text{percentage change in quantity demanded of good } X}{\text{percentage change in price of good } Y}$$

The change in the price of good Y causes the *demand curve* for good X to shift. If X and Y are substitutes, an increase in the price of Y leads to an increase in the demand for

---

[1]In Figure 4-10, in contrast to the ordinary demand curve, quantity demanded is on the vertical axis. This placement follows the usual practice of putting the variable to be explained (the dependent variable) on the vertical axis and the explanatory variable (the independent variable) on the horizontal axis. It is the ordinary demand curve that has the axes "backward." The explanation is buried in the history of economics and dates to Alfred Marshall's *Principles of Economics* (1890). [8] For better or worse, Marshall's scheme is now used by everybody, although mathematicians never fail to wonder at this example of the odd ways of economists.

FIGURE 4-10   Income-Consumption Curves of Different Products

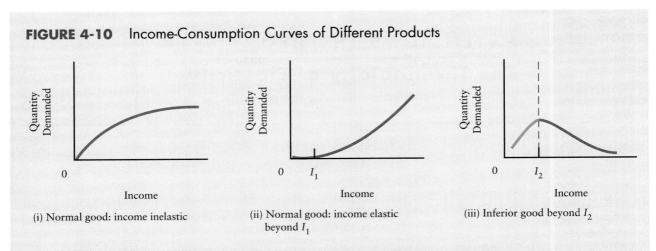

(i) Normal good: income inelastic

(ii) Normal good: income elastic beyond I_1

(iii) Inferior good beyond I_2

Different shapes of the curve relating quantity demanded to income correspond to different ranges of income elasticity. Normal goods have upward-sloping curves; inferior goods have downward-sloping curves. The good in part (i) is a typical normal good that is a necessity (the income elasticity declines as income rises). The good in part (ii) is a luxury good that is income elastic beyond income I_1. The good in part (iii) is a necessity (normal) at low incomes but becomes an inferior good at incomes beyond I_2.

X. If X and Y are complements, an increase in the price of Y leads to a reduction in demand for X. In either case, we are holding the price of X constant. We therefore measure the change in the quantity demanded of X (at its unchanged price) by measuring the shift of the demand curve for X.

Cross elasticity can vary from minus infinity to plus infinity. Complementary products, such as cars and gasoline, have negative cross elasticities. A large rise in the price of gasoline will lead to a decline in the demand for cars, as some people decide to do without a car and others decide not to buy an additional car. Substitute products, such as cars and public transport, have positive cross elasticities. A large rise in the price of cars (relative to public transport) will lead to a rise in the demand for public transport as some people shift from cars to public transport. (See *Extensions in Theory 4-1* for a summary of elasticity terminology.)

The positive or negative sign of cross elasticities tell us whether goods are substitutes or complements.

Measures of cross elasticity sometimes prove helpful in defining whether producers of similar products are in competition with each other. For example, glass bottles and tin cans have a high cross elasticity of demand. The producer of bottles is thus in competition with the producer of cans. If the bottle company raises its price, it will lose substantial sales to the can producer. In contrast, men's shoes and women's shoes have a low cross elasticity and thus a producer of men's shoes is not in close competition with a producer of women's shoes. If the former raises its price, it will not lose many sales to the latter. Knowledge of cross elasticity can be important in matters of *competition policy* in which the issue is whether a firm in one industry is or is not competing with firms in another industry. We discuss competition policy in more detail in Chapter 12.

Substitute products have a positive cross elasticity; an increase in the price of one leads to an increase in demand for the other.

EXTENSIONS IN THEORY 4-1
The Terminology of Elasticity

Term	Symbol	Numerical Measure of Elasticity	Verbal Description
A. Price elasticity of demand (supply)	η (η_S)		
Perfectly or completely inelastic		Zero	Quantity demanded (supplied) does not change as price changes.
Inelastic		Between zero and one	Quantity demanded (supplied) changes by a smaller percentage than does price.
Unit elastic		One	Quantity demanded (supplied) changes by exactly the same percentage as does price.
Elastic		Greater than one but less than infinity	Quantity demanded (supplied) changes by a larger percentage than does price
Perfectly, completely, or infinitely elastic		Infinity	Purchasers (sellers) are prepared to buy (sell) all they can at some price and none at all at a higher (lower) price.
B. Income elasticity of demand	η_Y		
Inferior good		Negative	Quantity demanded decreases as income increases.
Normal good		Positive	Quantity demanded increases as income increases:
Income-inelastic		Less than one	Less than in proportion to income increase
Income-elastic		Greater than one	More than in proportion to income increase
C. Cross elasticity of demand	η_{XY}		
Substitute		Positive	Price increase of a substitute leads to an increase in quantity demanded of this good.
Complement		Negative	Price increase of a complement leads to a decrease in quantity demanded of this good.

Practise with Study Guide Chapter 4,
Exercise 1.

S U M M A R Y

Price Elasticity of Demand   LO 1

- *Price elasticity of demand,* also called *elasticity of demand,* is a measure of the extent to which the quantity demanded of a product responds to a change in its price. Represented by the symbol η, it is defined as

$$\eta = \frac{\text{percentage change in quantity demanded}}{\text{percentage change in price}}$$

  The percentage changes are usually calculated as the change divided by the *average* value. Elasticity is defined to be a positive number, and it can vary from zero to infinity.
- When the numerical measure of elasticity is less than unity, demand is *inelastic*—the percentage change in quantity demanded is less than the percentage change in price that brought it about. When the numerical measure exceeds unity, demand is *elastic*—the percentage change in quantity demanded is greater than the percentage change in price that brought it about.

- The main determinant of the price elasticity of demand is the availability of substitutes for the product. Any one of a group of close substitutes will have a more elastic demand than will the group as a whole. Items that have few substitutes in the short run tend to develop many substitutes when consumers and producers have time to adapt.
- Since price elasticities are larger in the long run than in the short run, a shift in supply will lead to a larger change in price and a smaller change in quantity in the short run than in the long run.
- Elasticity and total expenditure are related in the following way: If elasticity is less than unity, total expenditure is positively related with price; if elasticity is greater than unity, total expenditure is negatively related with price; and if elasticity is unity, total expenditure does not change as price changes.

Price Elasticity of Supply   LO 2

- *Elasticity of supply* measures the extent to which the quantity supplied of some product changes when the price of that product changes. Represented by the symbol η_S, it is defined as

$$\eta_S = \frac{\text{percentage change in quantity supplied}}{\text{percentage change in price}}$$

- Supply tends to be more elastic in the long run than in the short run because it usually takes time for producers to alter their productive capacity in response to price changes.

An Important Example Where Elasticity Matters   LO 3 4

- The distribution of the burden of a sales tax between consumers and producers is independent of who actually remits the tax to the government. Rather, it depends on the relative elasticities of the supply and the demand for the product.

- The less elastic that demand is relative to supply, the more of the burden of an excise tax falls on the consumers.

Other Demand Elasticities

- *Income elasticity of demand* is a measure of the extent to which the quantity demanded of some product changes as income changes. Represented by the symbol η_Y, it is defined as

$$\eta_Y = \frac{\text{percentage change in quantity demanded}}{\text{percentage change in income}}$$

  The income elasticity of demand for a product will usually change as income varies. For example, a product that has a high income elasticity at a low income (because increases in income bring it within reach of the typical household) may have a low or negative income elasticity at higher incomes (because with further rises in incomes, it is gradually replaced by a superior substitute).

- *Cross elasticity of demand* is a measure of the extent to which the quantity demanded of one product changes when the price of a different product changes. Represented by the symbol η_{XY}, it is defined as

$$\eta_{XY} = \frac{\text{percentage change in quantity demanded of good } X}{\text{percentage change in price of good } Y}$$

  It is used to define products that are substitutes for one another (positive cross elasticity) and products that are complements for one another (negative cross elasticity).

KEY CONCEPTS

Price elasticity of demand
Inelastic and perfectly inelastic demand
Elastic and infinitely elastic demand
Relationship between demand elasticity and total expenditure
The burden of a sales (or excise) tax

Consumer price and seller price
Income elasticity of demand
Income-elastic and income-inelastic demands
Normal goods and inferior goods

Cross elasticity of demand
Substitutes and complements
Elasticity of supply
Short-run and long-run responses to shifts in demand and supply

STUDY EXERCISES

1. What would you predict about the *relative* price elasticity of demand for each of the following items? Explain your reasoning.

   a. food
   b. vegetables
   c. leafy vegetables (such as spinach and lettuce)
   d. leafy vegetables sold at your local supermarket
   e. leafy vegetables sold at your local supermarket on Wednesdays

2. Suppose a stamp collector buys the only two existing copies of a stamp at an auction. After the purchase, the collector goes to the front of the room and burns one of the stamps in front of the shocked audience. What must the collector believe in order for this to be a wealth-maximizing action? Explain with a demand-and-supply diagram.

3. For each of the following events, state the relevant elasticity concept. Then compute the measure of elasticity. Where appropriate, use average prices and quantities in your calculations. In all cases, assume that these are *ceteris paribus* changes.

   a. When the price of theatre tickets is reduced from $14.00 to $11.00, ticket sales increase from 1200 to 1350.
   b. As average household income in Canada increases by 10 percent, annual sales of Toyota Camrys increase from 56 000 to 67 000.
   c. After a major failure of Brazil's coffee crop sent coffee prices up from $3.00 per kg to $4.80 per kg, sales of tea in Canada increased from 7500 kg per month to 8000 kg per month.
   d. An increase in the world demand for pulp (used in producing newsprint) increases the price by 14

percent. Annual Canadian production increases from 8 million tons to 11 million tons.

4. The following table shows the demand schedule for denim jeans.

	Price (per unit)	Quantity Demanded (per year)	Total Expenditure
A	$30	400 000	
B	35	380 000	
C	40	350 000	
D	45	320 000	
E	50	300 000	
F	55	260 000	
G	60	230 000	
H	65	190 000	

a. Compute total expenditure for each row in the table.
b. Plot the demand curve and the total expenditure curve.
c. Compute the price elasticity of demand between points A and B, B and C, C and D, and so on.
d. Over what range of prices is the demand for denim jeans elastic? Explain.
e. Over what range of prices is the demand for denim jeans inelastic? Explain.

5. Consider the following straight-line supply curves. In each case, p is the price (measured in $ per unit) and Q^S is the quantity supplied of the product (measured in thousands of units per month).

i) $p = 2Q^S$
ii) $p = 4Q^S$
iii) $p = 5Q^S$
iv) $p = 10Q^S$

a. Plot each supply curve on a scale diagram. In each case, plot point A (which corresponds to price equal to $20) and point B (which corresponds to price equal to $40).
b. For each supply curve, compute the price elasticity of supply between points A and B.
c. Explain why the *slope* of a supply curve is not the same as the *elasticity* of supply.

6. This is a challenging question intended for those students who like mathematics. It will help you work through the issue of tax incidence. Consider the market for gasoline. Suppose the market demand and supply curves are as given below. In each case, quantity refers to millions of litres of gasoline per month; price is the price per litre (in cents).

$$\text{Demand: } p = 80 - 5Q^D$$
$$\text{Supply: } p = 24 + 2Q^S$$

a. Plot the demand and supply curves on a scale diagram.
b. Compute the equilibrium price and quantity.
c. Now suppose the government imposes a tax of 14 cents per litre. Show how this affects the market equilibrium. What is the new "consumer price" and what is the new "producer price"?
d. Compute the total revenue raised by the gasoline tax. What share of this tax revenue is "paid" by consumers, and what share is "paid" by producers? (Hint: if the consumer price were unchanged from the pre-tax equilibrium, we would say that consumers pay none of the tax.)

DISCUSSION QUESTIONS

1. From the following quotations, what, if anything, can you conclude about elasticity of demand?

a. "Good weather resulted in record wheat harvests and sent wheat prices tumbling. The result has been disastrous for many wheat farmers."
b. "Ridership always went up when bus fares came down, but the increased patronage never was enough to prevent a decrease in overall revenue."
c. "As the price of CD players fell, producers found their revenues soaring."

d. "Coffee to me is an essential good—I've just gotta have it no matter what the price."

e. "The soaring price of condominiums does little to

4. Interpret the following statements in terms of the relevant elasticity concept.

point, the p and q corresponding to that point are used (rather than the average p and q over an arc of the curve).

Equation 4A-1 splits elasticity into two parts. The first part, $\Delta q/\Delta p$, is related to the *slope* of the demand curve. In fact, it is the *reciprocal* of the slope. The second part, p/q, is related to the *point* on the curve at which the measurment is made.

Although point elasticity of demand refers to a price-quantity point on the demand curve, the first term in Equation 4A-1 still refers to changes over an arc of the curve. This is the part of the formula that involves approximation, and, as we shall see, it has some unsatisfactory results. Nonetheless, we can derive some interesting results by using this formula as long as we confine ourselves to straight-line demand curves.

The elasticity of a downward-sloping straight-line demand curve varies from zero at the quantity axis to infinity at the price axis.

First, notice that because a straight line has a constant slope, the ratio $\Delta p/\Delta q$ is the same everywhere on the line. Therefore, its reciprocal, $\Delta q/\Delta p$, must also be constant. The changes in η can now be inferred by inspecting the ratio p/q. Where the line cuts the quantity axis, price is zero, so the ratio p/q is zero; thus $\eta = 0$. Moving up the line, p rises and q falls, so the ratio p/q rises; thus elasticity rises. Approaching the top of

the line, q approaches zero, so the ratio becomes very large. Thus elasticity increases without limit as the price axis is approached.

Where there are two straight-line demand curves of the same slope, the one farther from the origin is less elastic at each price than the one closer to the origin.

Figure 4A-2 shows two parallel straight-line demand curves. Compare the elasticities of the two curves at any price, say, p_0. Because the curves are parallel, the ratio $\Delta q/\Delta p$ is the same on both curves. Because elasticities at the same price are being compared on both curves, p is the same, and the only factor left to vary is q. On the curve farther from the origin, quantity is larger (i.e., $q_1 > q_0$) and hence p_0/q_1 is smaller than p_0/q_0; thus η is smaller.

It follows that parallel shifts of a straight-line demand curve reduce elasticity (at each price) when the line shifts outward and increase elasticity when the line shifts inward.

For two intersecting straight-line demand curves the steeper curve is the less elastic.

In Figure 4A-3, there are two intersecting curves. At the point of intersection, p and q are common to both curves, and hence the ratio p/q is the same. Therefore, η varies only with $\Delta q/\Delta p$. On the steeper

FIGURE 4A-2 Two Parallel Straight-Line Demand Curves

For any given price, the quantities are different on these two parallel curves; thus the elasticities are different, being higher on D_0 than on D_1.

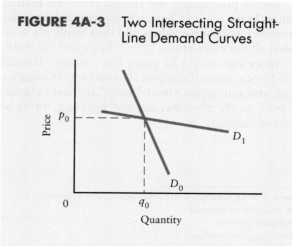

FIGURE 4A-3 Two Intersecting Straight-Line Demand Curves

Elasticities are different at the point of intersection of these demand curves because the slopes are different, being higher on D_0 than on D_1. Therefore, D_1 is more elastic than D_0 at p_0.

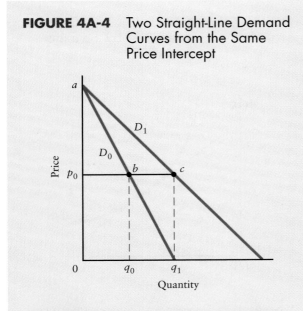

FIGURE 4A-4   Two Straight-Line Demand Curves from the Same Price Intercept

The elasticity is the same on D_0 and D_1 at any given price. This situation occurs because the steeper slope of D_0 is exactly offset by the smaller quantity demanded at any price.

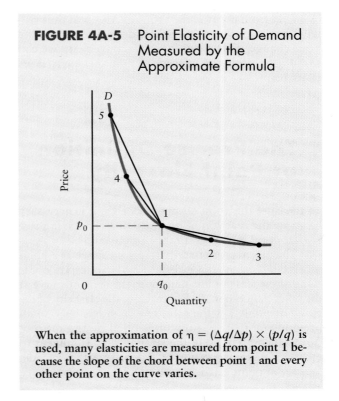

FIGURE 4A-5   Point Elasticity of Demand Measured by the Approximate Formula

When the approximation of $\eta = (\Delta q/\Delta p) \times (p/q)$ is used, many elasticities are measured from point 1 because the slope of the chord between point 1 and every other point on the curve varies.

curve, $\Delta q/\Delta p$ is smaller than on the flatter curve, so elasticity is lower.

If the slope of a straight-line demand curve changes while the price intercept remains constant, elasticity at any given price is unchanged.

This case is interesting for at least two reasons. First, when more customers having similar tastes to those already in the market enter the market, the demand curve pivots outward in this way. Second, when more firms enter a market that is shared proportionally among all firms, each firm's demand curve shifts inward in this way.

Consider in Figure 4A-4 the elasticities at point b on demand curve D_0 and at point c on demand curve D_1. We shall focus on the two triangles abp_0 on D_0 and acp_0 on D_1 formed by the two straight-line demand curves emanating from point a and by the price p_0. The price p_0 is the line segment $0p_0$. The quantities q_0 and q_1 are the line segments p_0b and p_0c, respectively. The slope of D_0 is $\Delta p/\Delta q = ap_0/p_0b$, and the slope of D_1 is $\Delta p/\Delta q = ap_0/p_0c$. From Equation 4A-1 we can

represent the elasticities of D_0 and D_1 at the points b and c, respectively, as

$$\eta \text{ at point } b = (p_0b/ap_0) \times (0p_0/p_0b) = (0p_0/ap_0)$$
$$\eta \text{ at point } c = (p_0c/ap_0) \times (0p_0/p_0c) = (0p_0/ap_0)$$

Because the distance corresponding to the quantity demanded at p_0 appears in both the numerator and the denominator and thus cancels out, the two values of the elasticity are the same. Put differently, if the straight-line demand curve D_0 is twice as steep as D_1, it has half the quantity demanded at p_0. Therefore, in Equation 4A-1 the steeper slope (a smaller Δq for the same Δp) is exactly offset by the smaller quantity demanded (a smaller q for the same p).

The demand elasticity measured from any point, according to Equation 4A-1, depends on the direction and magnitude of the change in price and quantity.

Except for a straight line (for which the slope does not change), the ratio $\Delta q/\Delta p$ will not be the same over different ranges of a curve. Figure 4A-5 shows a demand curve that is not a straight line. To measure the elasticity from point 1, the ratio $\Delta q/\Delta p$—and thus η—will vary according to the size and the direction of the price change. This result is very inconvenient; we can avoid it by using the concept of point elasticity in its exact form.

The Precise Definition of Point Elasticity

To measure the point elasticity *exactly,* it is necessary to know the reaction of quantity to a change in price *at that point,* not over a range of the curve.

The reaction of quantity to price change at a point is called dq/dp, and this is defined as the reciprocal of the slope of the straight line tangent to the demand curve at the point in question. In Figure 4A-6, the elasticity of demand at point 1 is the ratio p/q (as it has been in all previous measures), now multiplied by the ratio of $\Delta q/\Delta p$ measured along the straight line T, tangent to the curve at point 1, that is, by dq/dp. Thus the exact definition of point elasticity is

$$\eta = \frac{dq}{dp} \times \frac{p}{q} \qquad (4A\text{-}2)$$

The ratio dq/dp, as defined, is in fact the differential calculus concept of the *derivative* of quantity with respect to price.

This definition of point elasticity is the one normally used in economic theory. Equation 4A-1 is mathematically only an approximation of this expression. In Figure 4A-6, the measure of arc elasticity will come

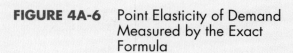

FIGURE 4A-6   Point Elasticity of Demand Measured by the Exact Formula

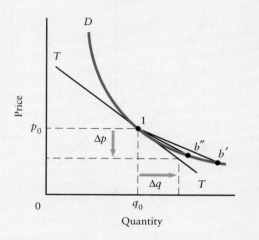

When the exact definition $\eta = (dq/dp) \times (p/q)$ is used, only one elasticity is measured from point 1 because there is only one tangent to the demand curve at that point.

closer to the measure of point elasticity as a smaller price change is used to calculate the arc elasticity. The $\Delta q/\Delta p$ in Equation 4A-1 is the reciprocal of the slope of the chord connecting the two points being compared. As the chord becomes shorter, its slope gets closer to that of the tangent T. (Compare the chords connecting point 1 to b' and b'' in Figure 4A-6.) Thus the error in using Equation 4A-1 as an approximation of Equation 4A-2 tends to diminish as the size of Δp diminishes.

An Introduction to Macroeconomics

What is macroeconomics all about? What do we mean when we talk about national income, and what is the difference (if any) between national income and national output? What is unemployment, and is it a problem? Is it possible to eliminate unemployment entirely? What do we mean by inflation, and what causes it? What are interest rates, and how are they related to inflation? Is it just a coincidence that periods of high inflation are also periods of high interest rates? What is the exchange rate, and how is this related to Canada's trade balance with the rest of the world? What determines Canada's rate of productivity growth, and how is this related to overall living standards? These are some of the questions that dominate macroeconomics and that we will examine in the next three chapters.

Chapter 19 is an overview chapter that introduces all of the major issues discussed in Chapters 22 through 36. One of the central themes of this chapter (and of macroeconomics itself) is the distinction between trends and cycles. This reflects a difference between the short run—in which our focus is on the cyclical fluctuations in macroeconomic variables—and the long run—in which our primary focus is on the trends in those same variables.

Chapter 20 explains how Gross Domestic Product (GDP) measures the value of national income, national output and national expenditure. The important distinction between real and nominal national income helps to explain why measured national income can rise even though no more goods are being produced (the answer has something to do with inflation). Finally, we examine some of the things that national income does not measure. Illegal activities, nonmarket activities, and economic "bads" (such as pollution) are just some of the omissions from measures of national income.

Chapter 21 examines the important difference between the short run and the long run in macroeconomics. A central theme of this chapter is that, in response to various shocks or policy changes, the behaviour of the macro economy over a period of just a few months is different from the behaviour over a few years. This makes the study of macroeconomics very complex, but also very interesting.

CHAPTER 19

What Macroeconomics Is All About

🔵 *LEARNING OBJECTIVES*

❶ View most macroeconomic issues as being about either long-run growth or short-run fluctuations, and see that government policy enters both categories.

❷ Understand the meaning and importance of the key macroeconomic variables, including national income, unemployment, inflation, interest rates, exchange rates, and trade flows.

Turn on the evening news or read your local newspaper, and you will likely hear talk of unemployment, inflation, recession, changes in exchange rates, and productivity growth. Almost everyone cares about economic issues. Workers are anxious to avoid the unemployment that comes with recessions and to share in the rising income that is brought about by economic growth. Firms are concerned about how interest rates, recession, and foreign competition affect their profits. Few things are more likely to bring a change of government than bad economic performance.

Macroeconomics is the study of how the economy behaves in broad outline without dwelling on much of its interesting but sometimes confusing detail. Macroeconomics is largely concerned with the behaviour of economic *aggregates*, such as total output, total investment, total exports, and the price level (the average price of all goods and services). These aggregates result from activities in many different markets and from the combined behaviour of different decision makers in households, firms, and governments.

We know perfectly well that an economy producing much wheat and few computers is different from one producing many computers but little wheat. We also know that an economy with cheap wheat and expensive computers is different from one with cheap computers and expensive wheat. Studying aggregates alone may cause us to miss these important differences, but it focuses our attention on some important issues for the economy as a whole.

In return for losing sight of some valuable detail, studying economic aggregates allows us to view the big picture. When aggregate output rises, the output of many commodities and the incomes of many people rise with it. When the price level rises, virtually everyone in the economy is forced to make adjustments. When the unemployment rate rises, many workers suffer reductions in their incomes. Such movements in economic aggregates matter for most individuals because they influence the health of the industries in which they work and the prices of the goods that they purchase. This is why macroeconomic issues get airtime on the evening news, and it is one of the important reasons why we study macroeconomics.

macroeconomics
The study of the determination of economic aggregates, such as total output, total employment, the price level, and the rate of economic growth.

Growth Versus Fluctuations

Most important macroeconomic issues can be divided into two broad categories—long-term economic growth and short-term fluctuations. Broad government policies, such as monetary policy and fiscal policy, typically make an appearance in both discussions.

Economic Growth

Both total output and output per person have risen for many decades in most industrial countries. These long-term trends have meant rising average living standards. Since the early 1970s, however, average living standards have grown less rapidly than during the preceding decades of the twentieth century. Although long-term growth gets less play on the evening news than current economic developments, it has considerably more importance for a society's prospects from decade to decade and generation to generation. For this reason, many macroeconomists devote their research time to answering this question: What caused the slowdown in worldwide growth rates that began in the 1970s?

A second set of questions regarding economic growth involves government policy. Can governments do anything to promote economic growth? Do some government policies, directed to quite different goals, have unintended consequences on the long-term rate of economic growth? What is the connection between the *monetary policy* conducted by the Bank of Canada and the rate of growth of the Canadian economy? Does the adherence to a low-inflation policy have any effects on the growth rate?

The government's *fiscal policy* also enters into the discussion of economic growth. Many economists believe that when governments spend less than they raise in tax revenue—and thus have a budget surplus—the reduced need for borrowing drives down interest rates and stimulates investment by the private sector. Such increases in investment imply a higher stock of physical capital available for future production, and thus an increase in economic growth. Do government budget surpluses increase future growth? Or do budget surpluses have no effect at all on the economy's future ability to produce?

Short-Term Fluctuations

The economy's short-term fluctuations in output and employment are often called *business cycle*s. What caused the Great Depression in the 1930s, when almost one-fifth of the Canadian labour force was out of work and massive unemployment plagued all major industrial countries? Why did the Canadian economy begin a significant recession in 1990–91, from which recovery was initially very gradual? What explains why nine years later, the Canadian unemployment rate was lower than it had been in almost thirty years?

Understanding business cycles requires an understanding of monetary policy. Most economists agree that the increase in inflation in the 1970s and early 1980s was related to monetary policy, though they also agree that other events were partly responsible. When the Bank of Canada implemented a policy in the early 1990s designed to reduce inflation, was it merely a coincidence that a significant recession followed? Most economists think not, though they also think that the slowdown in the U.S. economy was an important contributor to Canada's recession.

Government budget deficits and surpluses also enter the discussion of business cycles. Some economists think that, in recessionary years, the government ought to increase spending (and reduce taxes) in an effort to stimulate economic activity. Similarly, they believe that taxes should be raised to slow down a booming economy. Indeed, several government policies, from income taxation to unemployment insurance, are actually designed to mitigate the short-term fluctuations in national income. Other economists believe that the government cannot successfully "fine-tune" the economy by spending and taxing because our knowledge of how the economy works is imperfect and because such policies tend to be imprecise.

Key Macroeconomic Variables

In this chapter, we discuss several important macroeconomic variables, with an emphasis on why and how they matter for our well-being. Here and in Chapter 20 we also explain how the key macroeconomic variables are measured. The remainder of this book is largely about the causes and consequences of changes in each of these variables, the many ways in which they interact, and the effect they have on the well-being of Canadians.

Output and Income

The most comprehensive measure of a nation's overall level of economic activity is the value of its total production of goods and services, called *national product*.

One of the most important ideas in economics is that the production of output generates income.

For the nation as a whole, all of the value that is produced must ultimately belong to someone in the form of an income claim on that value. For example, if a firm produces $100 worth of ice cream, then that $100 must ultimately represent income for the firm's workers, the firm's suppliers of material inputs, or the firm's owners. Thus, the national product is *by definition* equal to the total income claims generated by the production of goods and services. In short, when we study national product, we are also studying national income. Figure 19-1 depicts national income and expenditure as a circular flow. You may recall first encountering the circular-flow diagram in Chapter 1. The concept is the same but now there are more flows to consider because we recognize the role of government, financial markets, and international trade.

There are several related measures of a nation's total output and total income. Their various definitions, and the relationships among them, are discussed in detail in the next chapter. In this chapter, we use the generic term *national income* to refer to both the value of total output and the value of the income claims generated by the production of that output.

Aggregating Total Output

To measure total output, quantities of many different goods are *aggregated*. To construct such totals, we add up the *values* of the different products. We cannot add tons of steel to loaves of bread, but we can add the money value of steel production to the money value of bread production. Hence by multiplying the physical output of a good by its price per unit and then summing this value for each good produced, we can calculate the quantity of total output *measured in dollars*.

This value of total output gives the money value of national output, usually called **nominal national income**. A change in this measure can be caused by a change in ei-

nominal national income   Total national income measured in current dollars. Also called current-dollar national income.

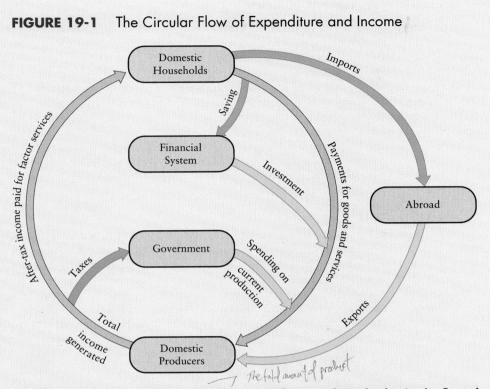

FIGURE 19-1   The Circular Flow of Expenditure and Income

National income is equal to national product. Their flows are shown by the circular flow of income and expenditure. Consider first only the red lines. In this case, the flow would be a simple circle from households to producers and back to households. Now add the blue and green lines. The blue lines represent *injections* to the circular flow (exports, investment, and government purchases) while the green lines represent *withdrawals* from the circular flow (imports, saving, and taxes). Injections and withdrawals complicate the picture but do not change the basic relationship: Domestic production creates a claim on the value of that production. When all of the claims are added up, they must be equal to the value of all of the production.

ther the physical quantities or the prices on which it is based. To determine the extent to which any change is due to quantities or to prices, economists calculate **real national income.** This measures the value of individual outputs not at current prices but at a set of prices that prevailed in some base period.

Nominal national income is often referred to as *current-dollar national income.* Real national income is often called *constant-dollar national income.* Denoted by the symbol Y, real national income tells us the value of current output measured at constant prices—the sum of the quantities valued at prices that prevailed in the base period. Since prices are held constant when computing real national income, changes in real national income reflect *only* changes in quantities. Comparing real national incomes of different years therefore provides a measure of the change in real output that has occurred during the intervening period.

Since our interest is primarily the *real* output of goods and services, we shall use the terms national income and national output to refer to *real* national income unless otherwise specified.

real national income
National income measured in constant dollars. It changes only when quantities change.

To see the most recent values for most of the macroeconomic variables discussed in this chapter, go to Statistics Canada's website: www.statcan.ca. Click on "Canadian Statistics" and then "Latest Indicators."

National Income: Recent History

One of the most commonly used measures of national income is called *gross domestic product (GDP)*. GDP can be measured in either real or nominal terms; we focus here on real GDP. The details of its calculation will be discussed in Chapter 20.

Part (i) of Figure 19-2 shows real national income produced by the Canadian economy since 1960; part (ii) shows its annual percentage change for the same period. The GDP series in part (i) shows two kinds of movement. The major movement is a positive trend that increased real output by approximately four times since 1960. This is what economists refer to as long-term economic growth.

A second feature of the real GDP series is short-term fluctuations around the trend, often described as cyclical fluctuations. Overall growth so dominates the real GDP series that the fluctuations are hardly visible in part (i) of Figure 19-2. However, as can be seen in part (ii), the growth of GDP has never been smooth. In most years, GDP increases, but in 1981 and 1991 GDP actually decreased, as shown by the negative rate of growth in the figure.

business cycle
Fluctuations of national income around its trend value that follow a wavelike pattern.

The **business cycle** refers to this continual ebb and flow of business activity that occurs around the long-term trend. We observe such cyclical fluctuations in many economic series; in particular, they are obvious from the continual oscillations in the growth rate of GDP that we see in Figure 19-2(ii).

No two business cycles are exactly the same—variations occur in duration and magnitude. Some expansions are long and drawn out, like the one that began in 1992 and was still continuing at the time this book went to press in the spring of 2000. Others come to an end before high employment and industrial capacity are reached. Nonetheless,

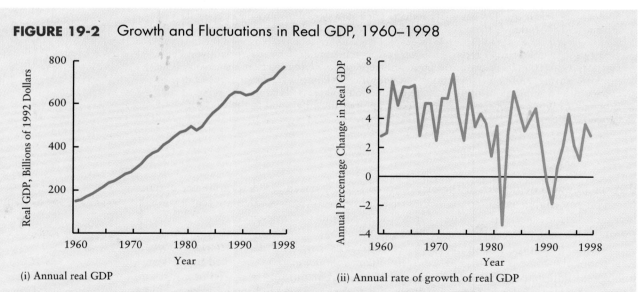

FIGURE 19-2   Growth and Fluctuations in Real GDP, 1960–1998

(i) Annual real GDP

(ii) Annual rate of growth of real GDP

Real GDP measures the quantity of total output produced by the nation's economy over the period of a year. Real GDP is plotted in part (i). It has risen steadily since 1960, with only a few interruptions. This demonstrates the long-term growth of the Canadian economy.

Short-term fluctuations are obscured by the long-term trend in part (i) but are highlighted in part (ii). The growth rate fluctuates considerably from year to year. The long-term upward trend of real GDP shows up in part (i) because most of the observations in part (ii) are positive.

(*Source:* These data are available on Statistics Canada's website: www.statcan.ca.)

fluctuations are systematic enough that it is useful to identify common factors in each of the four phases. These factors are outlined in *Applying Economic Concepts 19-1*.

Potential Output and the Output Gap

Actual national output represents what the economy *actually* produces. An important related concept is *potential* output, which measures what the economy could produce if all resources—land, labour, and productive capacity—were employed at their normal levels of utilization. This concept is usually referred to as **potential output** (but is sometimes called *full-employment output*).[1] Its symbol, Y^*, distinguishes it from actual output, indicated by Y.

The **output gap** (sometimes called the *GDP gap*) measures the difference between potential output and actual output. The gap is calculated by subtracting potential output from actual output ($Y - Y^*$). The output gap is thus positive when actual output exceeds potential output and it is negative when actual output is less than potential output.

When actual output is less than potential output, the gap measures the market value of goods and services that are not produced because the economy's resources are not fully employed. The goods and services that are not produced when the economy is operating below Y^* are permanently lost to the economy. When the economy is operating below its potential level of output—that is, when Y is less than Y^*—the output gap is called a **recessionary gap**.

In booms, actual output exceeds potential output. Actual output can exceed potential output because potential output is defined for a *normal* rate of utilization of factors of production, and there are many ways in which these normal rates can be exceeded temporarily. Labour may work longer hours than normal; factories may operate an extra shift or delay closing for routine repairs and maintenance. Although these expedients are only temporary, they are effective in the short term. When actual GDP exceeds potential GDP, there is often upward pressure on prices. Thus, when Y exceeds Y^*, we say the output gap is an **inflationary gap**.

When actual output is less than potential output, there is a recessionary gap. When actual output exceeds potential output, there is an inflationary gap.

Figure 19-3 shows potential GDP for the years since 1965. The upward trend reflects the growth in the productive capacity of the Canadian economy over this period. The figure also shows actual GDP (reproduced from Figure 19-2), which has kept approximately in step with potential GDP. The distance between the two, which is the output gap, is plotted in part (ii) of Figure 19-3. Fluctuations in economic activity are apparent from fluctuations in the size of the gap. The loss in production from unemployed resources over any time span is indicated by the overall amount of the gap over that time span. It is shown in part (ii) of the figure by the shaded area between the curve and the zero line, which represents the equality of actual output with potential output.

Why National Income Matters

National income is an important measure of economic performance in both the short run and the long run. Short-run movements in the business cycle receive the most attention in politics and in the press, but most economists agree that long-term growth—as reflected by the growth of *potential GDP*—is in many ways the more important of the two.

potential output (Y^*)
The real gross domestic product that the economy could produce if its productive resources were employed at their normal levels of utilization. Also called *potential GDP*.

Practise with Study Guide Chapter 19, Exercise 2.

output gap   Actual national income minus potential national income. Also called the *GDP gap*.

recessionary gap
A negative output gap; that is, a situation in which actual national income is less than potential income.

inflationary gap
A situation in which actual national income exceeds potential income.

---

[1]The words *real* and *actual* have similar meanings in everyday usage. When national income is measured, however, their meanings are different. *Real* national income is distinguished from *nominal* national income; and *actual* national income is distinguished from *potential* national income. The latter both refer to *real* measures of national income.

APPLYING ECONOMIC CONCEPTS 19-1

The Terminology of Business Cycles

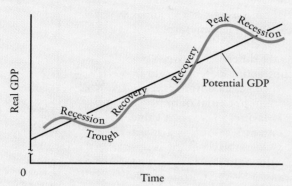

The accompanying figure shows a stylized business cycle, with real GDP fluctuating around a steadily rising level of potential GDP—the economy's normal capacity to produce output. We begin our discussion of terminology with a trough.

A *trough* is characterized by unemployed resources and a level of output that is low in relation to the economy's capacity to produce. There is thus a substantial amount of unused productive capacity. Business profits are low; for some individual companies, they are negative. Confidence about economic prospects in the immediate future is lacking, and, as a result, many firms are unwilling to risk making new investments.

The process of *recovery* moves the economy out of a trough. The characteristics of a recovery, or expansion, are many: Run-down equipment is replaced; employment, income, and consumer spending all begin to rise; and expectations become more favourable. Investments that once seemed risky may be undertaken as firms become more optimistic about future business prospects. Production can be increased with relative ease merely by reemploying the existing unused capacity and unemployed labour.

Eventually the recovery comes to a *peak* at the top of the cycle. At the peak, existing capacity is used to a high degree; labour shortages may develop, particularly in categories of key skills, and shortages of essential raw materials are likely. As shortages develop in more and more markets, a situation of general excess demand develops. Costs rise, but because prices rise also, business remains profitable.

Peaks are eventually followed by *recessions*. A **recession,** or contraction, is a downturn in economic activity. Common usage defines a recession as a fall in real GDP for two successive quarters. As output falls, so do employment and households' incomes. Profits drop, and some firms encounter financial difficulties. Investments that looked profitable with the expectation of continually rising income now appear unprofitable. It may not even be worth replacing capital goods as they wear out because unused capacity is increasing steadily. In historical discussions, a recession that is deep and long-lasting is often called a **depression.**

These terms are nontechnical but descriptive. The entire falling half of the cycle is often called a *slump,* and the entire rising half is often called a *boom.*

recession   A downturn in the level of economic activity. Often defined precisely as two consecutive quarters in which real GDP falls.

depression   A persistent period of very low economic activity with very high unemployment and high excess capacity.

Short-Term Fluctuations.   Recessions are associated with unemployment and lost output. When actual GDP is below potential GDP, economic waste and human suffering result from the failure to use the economy's resources (including its human resources) at their normal intensity of use.

Booms, although associated with high employment and high output, can bring problems of their own. When actual GDP exceeds potential GDP, inflationary pressure usually ensues, causing serious concern for any government that is committed to keeping the inflation rate low.

Long-Term Growth.   The long-run trend in real per capita national income is an important determinant of improvements in a society's overall standard of living. When income per person grows, each generation can expect, on average, to be better off than preceding ones. For example, if real per capita income grows at the relatively modest rate of 1.5

percent per year, the average person's lifetime income will be about *twice* that of his or her grandparents.[2]

In the long run, national income per person can grow for two reasons. One is growth in the amount of output produced per unit of input. It is this growth in *productivity* that has generally eliminated the low living standards that prevailed at the start of the Industrial Revolution two hundred years ago. A second source of growth in per capita income arises from changes in the amount of capital and labour supplied in the economy. If people work more hours, they will produce more output. If there are more machines and factories in operation, more output will be produced. The difference between productivity growth and the growth in the number of inputs is important. When productivity increases, more output is obtained for a given amount of effort. When total inputs increase, more output is obtained by using more resources. Income rises, but people (and other resources) are working harder.

In Canada, much of the growth in per capita income during the past three decades has been due to increases in the amounts of input of labour and capital. A relatively small part of that growth, compared to the trend of the rest of the century, is attributed to growth in productivity. This slowdown in productivity growth has created new interest in the sources of long-term growth, a subject that is one of the major themes in our discussion of macroeconomics.

Finally, it is important to remember that although economic growth makes people better off *on average,* it does not necessarily make *every* individual better off—the benefits of growth do not typically fall evenly on all members of the population. For example, if growth involves significant changes in the structure of the economy, such as a shift away from agriculture and toward manufacturing (as happened in the first part of this century), then these changes will hurt some people for extended periods of time.

Employment, Unemployment, and the Labour Force

National income and employment are closely related. If more is to be produced, either more workers must be used in production, or existing workers must produce more. The first change means a rise in employment;

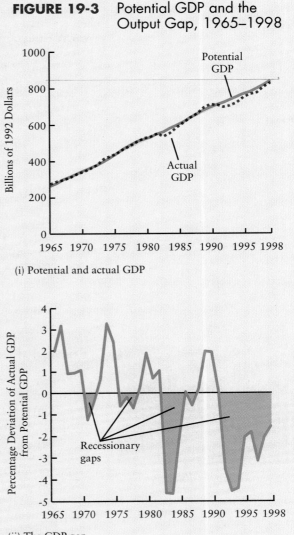

FIGURE 19-3   Potential GDP and the Output Gap, 1965–1998

(i) Potential and actual GDP

(ii) The GDP gap

Potential and actual GDP both display an upward trend. The output gap measures the difference between an economy's potential output and its actual output; the gap is expressed here as a percentage of potential output. Since 1965, potential and actual GDP have increased by more than three times. The distance between the two is the output gap, which shows clearly the cyclical behaviour. Shaded regions in part (ii) show recessionary gaps.

(*Source:* Data for potential GDP provided by the Bank of Canada.)

---

[2]We discuss several reasons in Chapter 20 why national income is not a perfect measure of well-being. The main reason is that there are many things—like leisure, non-market production, and environmental degradation—that affect our well-being but are not captured in measures of national income.

employment   The number of persons 15 years of age and older who hold jobs.

unemployment   The number of persons 15 years of age and older who are not employed and are actively searching for a job.

labour force   The total number of persons employed in both civilian and military jobs, plus the number of persons who are unemployed.

unemployment rate   Unemployment expressed as a percentage of the labour force, denoted *U*.

full employment   Employment that is sufficient to produce the economy's potential output; at full employment, all remaining unemployment is frictional and structural.

the second means a rise in output per person employed, which, as we have seen, is a rise in productivity. In the short run—a span of several months—changes in productivity tend to be very small; thus, most changes in output are accomplished by changes in employment. Over the long run, however, changes in both productivity and employment are significant.

Employment denotes the number of adult workers (defined in Canada as workers aged 15 and over) who hold jobs. **Unemployment** denotes the number of adult workers who are not employed but who are actively searching for a job. The **labour force** is the total number of people who are either employed or unemployed. The **unemployment rate** is equal to the number of unemployed people expressed as a fraction of the labour force—it represents the fraction of people wanting jobs who do not currently have one.

$$\text{Unemployment Rate} = \frac{\text{number of people unemployed}}{\text{number of people in the labour force}} \times 100 \text{ percent}$$

The level of unemployment in Canada is estimated from the Labour Force Survey conducted each month by Statistics Canada. Persons who are currently without a job but who say they have searched actively for one during the sample period are recorded as unemployed. The estimated total number of unemployed is then expressed as a percentage of the labour force to obtain the figure for the unemployment rate. *Applying Economic Concepts 19-2* discusses some difficulties in the measurement of unemployment.

Economists make the distinction between frictional, structural, and cyclical unemployment. But this distinction matters little to the individual who has difficulty finding an appropriate job.

frictional unemployment   Unemployment caused by the time that is taken for labour to move from one job to another.

structural unemployment   Unemployment due to a mismatch between characteristics required by available jobs and characteristics possessed by unemployed workers.

Frictional, Structural, and Cyclical Unemployment

When the economy is at potential GDP, economists say there is **full employment**. But it is important to understand that there will still be some unemployment even when the economy is at potential GDP. There are two main reasons why this is so.

First, there is a constant turnover of individuals in given jobs and a constant change in job opportunities. New members enter the workforce; some people quit their jobs; others are fired. It may take some time for these people to find jobs. So at any point in time, there is unemployment due to the normal turnover of labour. Such unemployment is called **frictional unemployment.**

Second, because the economy is constantly changing and adapting, at any moment there will always be some mismatch between the characteristics of the labour force and the characteristics of the available jobs. This is a mismatch between the *structure* of the supplies of labour and the *structure* of the demands for labour. Such unemployment is called **structural unemployment.** The mismatch may occur, for example, because labour does not currently have the skills that are in demand or because labour is not in the part of the country where the demand is located.

Even when the economy is said to be at full employment, some unemployment exists due to natural turnover in the labour market and to mismatch between jobs and workers.

Full employment is said to occur when the only existing unemployment is frictional and structural. At full employment, factors of production are being used at their normal intensity, and the economy is at potential GDP. At less than full employment, other types of unemployment are present as well. One major reason for lapses from full employment lies in the business cycle. During recessions, unemployment rises above its full-

APPLYING ECONOMIC CONCEPTS 19-2

Problems in Measuring Unemployment

Statistics Canada measures unemployment by its monthly Labour Force Survey. What economists want to know is how many people genuinely want a job but are unable to find one. But this is not always what the official measure of unemployment provides.

On the one hand, measured unemployment overstates the amount of "true" unemployment by including some people who are *voluntarily* out of work. For example, Canada's program of Employment Insurance provides protection against genuine hardship caused by job loss, but it also induces some people to stay out of work to collect Employment Insurance benefits for as long as the benefits last. Such people have, in fact, voluntarily withdrawn from the labour force, although to remain eligible for benefits they must make a show of looking for a job. Such people are usually included in the ranks of the unemployed because, for fear of losing their benefits, they tell the person who surveys them that they are actively looking for a job even though they are not really trying very hard to find one.

On the other hand, measured unemployment understates the amount of "true" unemployment by omitting some people who would accept a job if one were available but who did not actively look for one during the week in which the data were collected. For example,

people who have not found jobs after searching for a long time may become discouraged and stop actively looking for work. Such people have withdrawn from the labour force and are not recorded as unemployed. They are, however, unemployed in the sense that they would willingly accept a job if one were available. People in this category are referred to as *discouraged workers*. They have withdrawn from the labour market because they believe that they cannot find a job under current conditions.

In addition, there are part-time unemployed people. If some people are working six hours instead of eight hours per day because there is insufficient demand for the product that they help to make, these workers are suffering 25 percent unemployment even though none of them are reported as unemployed.

The official figures for unemployment are useful, particularly because they tell us the *direction* of changes in unemployment. It is unlikely, for example, that the official unemployment figures will be rising when "true" unemployment is actually falling. For the reasons that we have just discussed, however, they can at times give under- or over-estimates of the total number of persons who would be genuinely willing to work if they were offered a job at the going rate of pay.

---

employment level. This excess amount is called **cyclical unemployment** (or, sometimes, *deficient-demand unemployment*).

The measured unemployment rate when the economy is at full employment (that is, at potential output) is often called the *natural rate of unemployment* or the **NAIRU**, the cumbersome acronym standing for the Non-Accelerating Inflation Rate of Unemployment. Although estimates of this rate are difficult to obtain, they provide a useful benchmark against which to gauge the current performance of the economy, as measured by the actual unemployment rate. Estimates indicate that the NAIRU rose throughout the 1970s, from around 5.5 percent to a high of around 8 percent in the early 1980s, and it has now fallen to below 7 percent. (We will discuss the reasons for these changes in Chapter 30.)

Unemployment: Recent History

Figure 19-4 shows the trends in the labour force, employment, and unemployment since 1960. Despite booms and slumps, employment has grown roughly in line with the growth in the labour force (which itself grew in part because of the increasing participation of women in the labour force, especially in the 1970s and 1980s).

Although the long-term trend dominates the employment data, Figure 19-4 shows that the short-term fluctuations in the unemployment rate have been substantial. The

cyclical unemployment
Unemployment in excess of frictional and structural unemployment. Sometimes called *deficient-demand unemployment.*

NAIRU   Short for *nonaccelerating inflation rate of unemployment*. The rate of unemployment associated with potential national income. Also called the *natural rate of unemployment.*

FIGURE 19-4 Labour Force, Employment, and Unemployment, 1960–1998

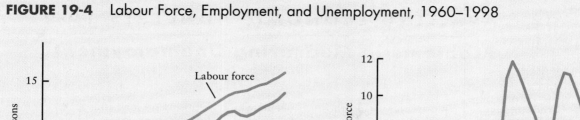

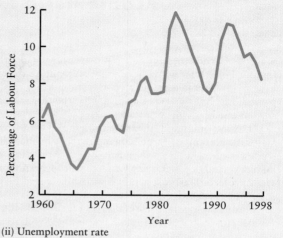

(i) Labour force and employment

(ii) Unemployment rate

The labour force and employment have grown since 1960 with only a few interruptions. The unemployment rate responds to the cyclical behaviour of the economy. The labour force and the level of employment in Canada have both almost tripled since 1960. Booms are associated with a low unemployment rate and slumps with a high unemployment rate.

(*Source:* Current labour-force statistics are available on Statistics Canada's website at www.statcan.ca.)

unemployment rate has been as low as 3.4 percent in 1966 and as high as 12.6 percent in 1982. By 1999, after the economy had been growing steadily for several years, the unemployment rate was approximately 7.5 percent, the lowest it had been in nearly 20 years.

Figure 19-4(ii) reveals an upward trend in the Canadian unemployment rate over the past few decades. For example, the cyclical low-point for unemployment in 1966 was below 4 percent, but by 1989 it was almost 8 percent. In Chapter 30 we will discuss how structural changes in the economy as well as some government labour-market policies may help to explain this upward trend.

Why Unemployment Matters

The social and political significance of the unemployment rate is enormous. The government is blamed when it is high and takes credit when it is low. Few macroeconomic policies are planned without some consideration of how they will affect unemployment. No other summary statistic carries such weight as a source of both formal and informal policy concern.

Unemployment involves economic waste and human suffering. Human effort is the least durable of economic commodities. If a fully employed economy has 16 million people who are willing to work, their services must either be used this year or wasted. When only 14.7 million people are actually employed, one year's potential output of

1.3 million workers is lost forever. In an economy in which there is not enough output to meet everyone's needs, such a waste of potential output is cause for concern.

The loss of income associated with unemployment is clearly harmful to individuals. In some cases, the loss of income pushes people into poverty. But this lost income does not capture the full cost of unemployment. A person's spirit can be broken by a long period of desiring work but being unable to find it. Research has shown that crime, mental illness, and general social unrest tend to be positively associated with long-term unemployment.

In the not-so-distant past, only personal savings, private charity, or help from friends and relatives stood between the unemployed and starvation. Today, welfare and employment insurance have created a safety net, particularly when unemployment is for short periods, as is most often the case in Canada. However, when an economic slump lasts long enough, as in the early 1980s and the early 1990s, some unfortunate people begin to exhaust their employment insurance and so part of that safety net disappears.

Inflation and the Price Level

Most people know what inflation is, even though they might not be able to define it precisely. Inflation means that prices in general are going up—not just the price of gasoline, jeans, or burritos, but the price of almost everything. If you are a typical reader of this book, inflation has not been very noticeable during your lifetime. When your parents were your age, however, high inflation was a major economic problem.

To study inflation, economists use two concepts. The first is the **price level,** which refers to the average level of all prices in the economy and is given by the symbol, P. The second is the rate of **inflation,** which is the rate at which the price level is rising.

To measure the average price level, economists construct a *price index*, which averages the prices of various commodities according to how important they are. The best-known price index in Canada is the **Consumer Price Index (CPI),** which measures the average cost of the goods and services that are bought by the typical Canadian household. *Applying Economic Concepts 19-3* shows how a price index such as the CPI is constructed.

Price indexes compare the cost of a given bundle of goods and services purchased at different times. The base period used for the CPI in 1999 was 1992, for which the average value of the index is set to 100. Thus, when we read that the CPI for January 1999 had a value of 109.2, we know that a bundle of goods and services that cost $100 in 1992 would cost $109.20 to purchase in January 1999.

The CPI is designed to measure changes in the cost of living for the average household in Canada. Because it is based on consumption for the *average* household, it does not measure accurately the change in the cost of living for *each* household. Rich, poor, young, old, single, married, urban, and rural households typically consume goods in different proportions. An increase in air fares, for example, will raise the cost of living of a frequent traveller but not affect that of a nontravelling household.

The more an individual household's consumption pattern conforms to that of the typical pattern used to create a price index, the better the index will reflect changes in that household's cost of living.

By allowing us to compare the general price level at different times, a price index such as the CPI also allows us to measure the rate of inflation. For example, the value of the CPI in January 1999 was 109.2 and in January 1998 was 108.1 The *rate of inflation* during that one-year period, expressed in percentage terms, is equal to the change in the price level divided by the initial price level, times 100:

price level   The average level of all prices in the economy, usually expressed as an index number.

inflation   A rise in the average level of all prices.

Consumer Price Index (CPI)   An index of the average prices of goods and services commonly bought by households.

To compute the rate of inflation from any point in your lifetime to today, check out the "inflation calculator" at the Bank of Canada's website: www.bank-banque-canada.ca.

APPLYING ECONOMIC CONCEPTS 19-3

How the CPI Is Constructed

Although the details are somewhat more complicated, the basic idea behind the Consumer Price Index is straight-forward, as is illustrated by the following hypothetical example.

Suppose we wish to discover what was happening to the overall cost of living for typical university students. A survey of student behaviour in 1990 shows that the average university student consumed only three goods—pizza, coffee, and photocopying—and spent a total of $200 a month on these items, as shown in Table 1.

TABLE 1   Expenditure Behaviour in 1990

Product	Price	Quantity per Month	Expenditure per Month
Photocopies	$0.10 per sheet	140 sheets	$14.00
Pizza	8.00 per pizza	15 pizzas	120.00
Coffee	0.75 per cup	88 cups	66.00
Total expenditure			$200.00

By 2000, the price of photocopying has fallen to 5 cents per copy, the price of pizza has increased to $8.50, and the price of coffee has increased to 80 cents. What has happened to the cost of living? In order to find out, we calculate the cost of purchasing the 1990 bundle of goods at the prices that prevailed in 2000, as shown in Table 2.

The total expenditure required to purchase the bundle of goods that cost $200.00 in 1990 has risen to $204.90. The increase in required expenditure is $4.90, which is a 2.45 percent increase over the original $200.00.

If we define 1990 as the *base year* for the "student price index" and assign an index value of 100 to the cost of the average student's expenditure in that year, the value of the index in 2000 is 102.45. Thus, goods and services that cost $100.00 in the base year cost $102.45 in 2000, exactly what is implied by Table 2.

The Consumer Price Index, as constructed by Statistics Canada, is built on exactly the same principles as the preceding example. In the case of the CPI, many

TABLE 2   1990 Expenditure Behaviour at 2000 Prices

Product	Price	Quantity per Month	Expenditure per Month
Photocopies	$0.05 per sheet	140 sheets	$7.00
Pizza	8.50 per pizza	15 pizzas	127.50
Coffee	0.80 per cup	88 cups	70.40
Total expenditure			$204.90

thousands of consumers are surveyed, and the prices of thousands of products are monitored, but the basic method is the same:

1. Survey the consumption behaviour of consumers.

2. Calculate the cost of the goods and services purchased by the average consumer in the year in which the original survey was done. Define this as the *base period* of the index.

3. Calculate the cost of purchasing the same bundle of goods and services in other years.

4. Divide the result of step 3 (in each year) by the result of step 2, and multiply by 100. The result is the value of the CPI for each year.

The CPI is not a perfect measure of the cost of living because it does not account for quality improvements or for changes in consumers' expenditure patterns. For example, the use of home computers is much more widespread today than it was even ten years ago, when they would have appropriately had a very small role in the CPI. Changes of this type require the underlying survey of consumer expenditure to be updated from time to time to make sure that the expenditure patterns in the survey approximately match consumers' actual expenditure patterns.

$$\text{Rate of Inflation} = \frac{109.2 - 108.1}{108.1} \times 100 \text{ percent}$$

$$= 1.02 \text{ percent}$$

Practise with Study Guide Chapter 19, Extension Exercise E1.

The inflation rate just computed is an *annual* inflation rate, often called the *year-on-year* inflation rate. When time periods are not exactly one year apart, changes in price levels are usually converted to annual rates, the average year-to-year percentage change in prices over the period measured. For example, in May 1998, the CPI was 108.4 and in February 1998 it was 108.0. During the three months separating February and May, the CPI rose by 0.37 percent. If the CPI continued to grow at 0.37 percent every three months for a whole year, the percentage increase over the year would be 1.49. Thus, we say that over the period from February 1998 to May 1998, the CPI was growing at an *annual rate* of 1.49 percent.[3]

Inflation: Recent History

If you are a typical reader of this textbook (roughly 18–22 years old), inflation has probably not been an important part of your life experience, especially if you have lived in Canada for the past decade or so. Inflation in Canada is currently around 1.5 percent per year, and has been below 2 percent since 1992. But it has not always been so. There was a time—not so long ago—when inflation in Canada was both high and unpredictable from year to year.

Figure 19-5 shows the CPI and the inflation rate (measured by the annual rate of change in the CPI) from 1960 to 1998. What can we learn from this figure? First, we learn that the price level is constantly changing. Second, we learn that the price level has not fallen at all since 1960 (in fact, the last time it fell was in 1953, and even then it fell only briefly). The cumulative effect of this sequence of repeated price increases is quite dramatic: By 1998, the price level was over seven times higher than it was in 1960. In other words, you now pay $7 for what cost $1 in 1960.

Third, we learn that although the long-term upward trend stands out when we look at the price level, the short-term fluctuations stand out when we look at the inflation rate. The sharp year-to-year swings in the inflation rate have sometimes been dramatic. The increase in the inflation rate into double-digit levels in 1974, and again in 1979, were associated with major increases in the world prices of oil and foodstuffs and with loose monetary policy. The declines in inflation that followed were delayed responses to major recessions. Note that even when the inflation rate *falls,* as it did from 1980 to 1982 and from 1990 to 1992, for example, the price level continues to rise as long as inflation remains *positive.*

Why Inflation Matters

Money is the universal yardstick in our economy. This does not mean that we care only about money—it means simply that we measure *economic values* in terms of money, and we use money to conduct our economic affairs. Things as diverse as wages, bank balances, the value of a house, and a university's endowment are all stated in terms of money. We value money, however, not for itself but for what we can purchase with it. The terms **purchasing power of money** and *real value of money* refer to the amount of goods and services that can be purchased with a given amount of money. The purchasing power of

purchasing power of money The amount of goods and services that can be purchased with a unit of money.

---

[3]Notice that 1.49 is slightly more than 0.37 × 4. The reason for this is that the growth rate of 0.37 percent per quarter is *compounded* when the annual rate is calculated. [28]

FIGURE 19-5   The Price Level and the Inflation Rate, 1960–1998

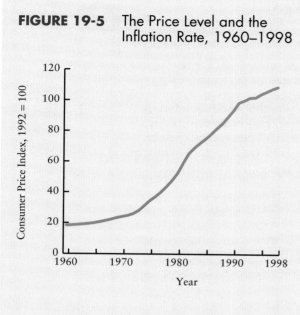

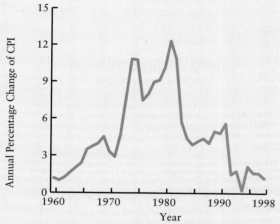

The trend in the price level has been upward over the past half century. The rate of inflation has varied from almost 0 to over 12 percent since 1960.

(*Source:* Data taken from various issues of *Bank of Canada Review* and data provided by Department of Finance.)

money is negatively related to the price level. For example, if the price level doubles, a dollar will buy only half as much, whereas if the price level halves, a dollar will buy twice as much.

Inflation also reduces the real value of anything else whose price is *fixed* in money terms. Thus, the real value of a money wage, a savings account, or the balance that is owed on a student loan is reduced by inflation.

The real effects of inflation depend to a great extent on whether the inflation is *anticipated* or *unanticipated*.

A Fully Anticipated Inflation.   We can imagine an inflation that has no real effects. There are two requirements for this to happen: first, everyone who is making any sort of financial arrangement must know what the inflation rate will be over the life of the contract and, second, *all* financial contracts must be written to incorporate the expected inflation. In this case, the real value of the financial obligations will not change when the price level changes. The real behaviour of the economy would then be exactly the same with and without inflation.

If all financial contracts are written to incorporate a fully anticipated inflation, then such an inflation will have no real effects.

For example, suppose that a firm and its workers agree that wages should go up by 3 percent in real terms. If the inflation rate is expected to be zero, they would agree to a 3 percent increase in money wages. If 5 percent inflation is expected, however, they would agree to an 8 percent increase in money wages. Five percent would be needed to maintain the purchasing power of the money wages that would be paid, and 3 percent would be needed to bring about the desired increase in purchasing power.

If all such adjustments were made, not just to labour contracts but also to life-insurance benefits, pension plans, and income-support payments, the result would be a 5 percent increase in everyone's money incomes and money assets combined with a 5 percent increase in all money prices and all money liabilities. Nothing real would have changed. People's higher money incomes would buy the same amount of goods as before, and the real value of their assets and liabilities would be unchanged.

An Unanticipated Inflation.   At the opposite extreme from a fully anticipated inflation is a completely unanticipated inflation. No one sees it coming; no one is prepared to offset its consequences. The real value of all contracts that are specified in nominal terms will change unexpectedly. Who will gain and who will lose?

An unexpected inflation benefits anyone who has an obligation to pay money and harms anyone who is entitled to receive money.

For example, consider a wage contract that specifies a wage increase of 3 percent agreed to under the assumption that the price level will remain constant. Both employers and employees expect that the purchasing power of wages paid will rise by 3 percent as a result of the contract. Now suppose, however, that the price level unexpectedly rises by 5 percent over the life of the wage contract. The combination of the 5 percent inflation and the 3 percent increase in money wages implies a reduction in the purchasing power of wages of 2 percent. Employers gain because their wage payments represent a smaller part of the value of their output than they had expected. Workers lose because their wages represent a smaller receipt of purchasing power than they had expected.

Employers and workers will be able to adjust to the new price level when they make new contracts, but some people will be locked in to their old nominal contracts for the rest of their lives. The extreme case is suffered by those who live on fixed money incomes. For example, pensions that are provided by the private sector often promise to pay a certain number of dollars per year for life. On retirement, this sum may look adequate, even generous. Twenty years later, however, inflation may have reduced its purchasing power to the poverty level. A family that retired on a fixed money income in 1980 would have found the purchasing power of that income reduced year by year until, in 1999, it would have had only 42 percent of its original value.

Intermediate Cases.   There are several reasons why virtually all real inflations fall somewhere between the two extremes that we have just discussed.

First, the inflation rate is usually variable and seldom foreseen exactly, even though its general course may be anticipated. Thus, the actual rate will sometimes be higher than expected—to the benefit of those who have contracted to pay money. At other times the inflation rate will be lower than expected—to the benefit of those who have contracted to receive money.

Second, even if the inflation rate is accurately anticipated, all adjustments to it cannot occur at the same speed. As a result, inflation redistributes income, and it does so in a haphazard way. People whose money incomes rise more slowly than prices will lose; those whose money incomes rise faster than prices will gain.

Third, even if the inflation rate is anticipated, the full set of institutions that would be needed for everyone to avoid its consequences does not exist. For example, many private pension plans are stated in money terms and employees have little choice but to take the only plan that their employers make available to them. Thus, even when inflation is predicted, some people will wind up living on fixed nominal incomes and will see their real incomes erode over time.

The Interest Rate

If a bank lends you money, it will require you to agree to a schedule for repayment. Furthermore, it will charge you **interest** for the privilege of borrowing the money. If, for example, you borrow $1000 today, repayable in one year's time, you may also be asked to pay $6.67 per month in interest. This makes $80 in interest over the year, which can be expressed as an interest rate of 8 percent per annum.

The **interest rate** is the price that is paid to borrow money for a stated period of time. It is expressed as a percentage amount per year per dollar borrowed. For example, an interest rate of 8 percent per year means that the borrower must pay 8 cents per year for every dollar that is borrowed.

There are many interest rates. A bank will lend money to an industrial customer at a lower rate than it will lend money to you—there is a lower risk of not being repaid. The

interest   The payment for the use of borrowed money.

interest rate   The price paid per dollar borrowed per period of time, expressed either as a proportion (e.g., 0.06) or as a percentage (e.g., 6 percent).

rate charged on a loan that is not to be repaid for a long time will usually differ from the rate on a loan that is to be repaid quickly.

When economists speak of "the" interest rate, they mean a rate that is typical of all the various interest rates in the economy. Dealing with only one interest rate suppresses much interesting detail. However, because interest rates commonly move together, at least for major changes, following the movement of one rate allows us to consider changes in the general level of interest rates. The *prime interest rate,* the rate that banks charge to their best business customers, is an interest rate which attracts much attention because when the prime rate changes, most other rates change in the same direction. Another high-profile interest rate is the *bank rate,* the interest rate that the Bank of Canada (Canada's central bank) charges on short-term loans to commercial banks.

Interest Rates and Inflation

nominal interest rate
The price paid per dollar borrowed per period of time.

How does inflation affect interest rates? To begin developing an answer, imagine that your friend lends you $100 and that the loan is repayable in one year. The amount that you pay her for making this loan, measured in money terms, is the **nominal interest rate.** If you pay her $108 in one year's time, $100 will be repayment of the amount of the loan (which is called the *principal*) and $8 will be payment of the interest. In this case, the nominal interest rate is 8 percent.

How much purchasing power has your friend gained or lost by making this loan? As we have already noted in our discussion of the consequences of inflation, the answer depends on what happens to the price level during the year. Intuitively, the more the price level rises, the worse off your friend will be and the better the transaction will be for you. This result occurs because the more the price level rises, the less valuable are the dollars that you use to repay the loan. The **real interest rate** measures the *real* return on a loan, in terms of purchasing power.

real interest rate
The nominal rate of interest corrected for the change in the purchasing power of money. Equal to the nominal interest rate minus the rate of inflation.

If the price level remains constant over the year, the real rate of interest that your friend earns would also be 8 percent, because she can buy 8 percent more goods and services with the $108 that you repay her than with the $100 that she lent you. However, if the price level rises by 8 percent, the real rate of interest would be zero because the $108 that you repay her buys the same quantity of goods as the $100 that she originally gave up. If she is unlucky enough to lend money at 8 percent in a year in which prices rise by 10 percent, the real rate of interest that she earns is −2 percent. The repayment of $108 will purchase 2 percent fewer goods and services than the original loan of $100.

The burden of borrowing depends on the real, not the nominal, rate of interest.

For example, a nominal interest rate of 8 percent combined with a 2 percent rate of inflation is a much greater real burden on borrowers than a nominal rate of 16 percent combined with a 14 percent rate of inflation.

Figure 19-6 shows the nominal and real interest rate paid on short-term government borrowing since 1960. Both nominal and real interest rates were high and volatile during the early part of the 1980s. During the latter part of the 1980s, nominal rates fell somewhat and became somewhat less variable, though real rates remained relatively high. In the 1990s, both real and nominal interest rates fell and stabilized.

Why Interest Rates Matter

Changes in real interest rates affect the standard of living of savers and borrowers. Many retirees, for example, rely on interest earnings from their stock of accumulated assets to provide much of their household income. In the early 1990s, as real interest rates fell to 2–3 percent (from 5–6 percent a decade earlier), many retirees experienced a significant decline in their real incomes.

In contrast, borrowers are made better off with low real interest rates. This point was dramatically illustrated during the late 1970s when homeowners who had long-term fixed-rate mortgages benefitted tremendously from several years of unanticipated inflation which resulted in negative real interest rates.

Interest rates also matter for the economy as a whole. As we shall see in Chapter 22, real interest rates help to determine the amount of investment. High real interest rates make borrowing costly, and there is less real investment than when interest rates are low. But less investment today implies less productive capacity in the future. Thus, real interest rates, through their effect on investment, affect long-term growth and *future* living standards. Changes in investment also cause swings in the business cycle. A slowdown in investment can trigger a slump; conversely, when investment increases sharply, GDP generally follows. Thus, through their effect on investment, real interest rates also affect employment and output in the short run.

The International Economy

The two important indicators of the Canadian position in the international economy are the *exchange rate,* which measures the external value of the dollar, and the *balance of payments,* which records all transactions between Canada and the rest of the world.

The Exchange Rate

If you are going on a holiday to France, you will need French francs to pay for your purchases. Many of the larger banks, as well as any foreign-exchange office, will make the necessary exchange of currencies for you; they will sell you francs in return for your Canadian dollars. If you get 4 francs for each dollar that you give up, the two currencies are trading at a rate of 1 dollar = 4 francs or, expressed another way, 1 franc = 0.25 dollars.

As our example shows, the exchange rate can be defined either as dollars per franc or francs per dollar. In this book we adopt the convention of defining the **exchange rate** between the Canadian dollar and any foreign currency as the number of Canadian dollars required to purchase one unit of foreign currency. For example, on March 10, 1999, 1 Canadian dollar was worth 3.94 French francs; expressed the other way, 1 French franc was worth 0.254 Canadian dollars. The exchange rate on that day was therefore equal to 0.254, telling us that it took just over 25 Canadian cents to purchase one French franc.

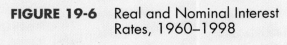

FIGURE 19-6   Real and Nominal Interest Rates, 1960–1998

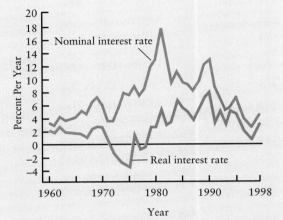

Inflation over the past four decades has meant that the real interest rate has always been less than the nominal interest rate. The data for the nominal interest rate show the average rate on three-month treasury bills in each year since 1960. The real interest rate is calculated as the nominal interest rate minus the actual rate of inflation over the same period. For the most part, the real interest rate has been below 4 percent for the past four decades. Through much of the 1970s, the real interest rate was negative, indicating that the inflation rate exceeded the nominal interest rate. The 1980s saw real interest rates rise as high as 8 percent. Since then, real rates have declined again to levels that are closer to the long-term historical average.

(*Source: Bank of Canada Review,* Spring 1999.)

exchange rate   The number of units of domestic currency required to purchase one unit of foreign currency.

---

[4]Some economists use a reverse definition of the exchange rate—the number of units of foreign currency that can be purchased by one Canadian dollar. It is up to the student, then, to examine carefully the definition that is being used by a particular writer or speaker. In this book the exchange rate is defined as the number of Canadian dollars required to purchase one unit of foreign currency because this measure emphasizes that foreign currency, like any other good or service, has a price. In this case, the price has a special name—the exchange rate.

The exchange rate is the number of Canadian dollars required to purchase one unit of foreign currency.[4]

The term **foreign exchange** refers to foreign currencies or claims on foreign currencies, such as bank deposits, cheques, and promissory notes, that are payable in foreign money. The **foreign-exchange market** is the market where foreign exchange is traded—at a price expressed by the exchange rate.

Internal Versus External Value of the Dollar

We can view the value of the Canadian dollar in two ways. The **internal value of the dollar** refers to its power to purchase goods in domestic markets. We have already seen that the internal value of the dollar is reflected by the price level—specifically, increases in the price level reduce the internal value of the dollar.

The **external value of the dollar** refers to its power to purchase foreign currencies. This is reflected by the exchange rate. A rise in the exchange rate means that it takes *more* Canadian dollars to purchase one unit of foreign currency—this is a *reduction* in the external value of the dollar and is referred to as a **depreciation** of the Canadian dollar. Conversely, a fall in the exchange rate means that it takes *fewer* Canadian dollars to purchase one unit of foreign currency—this is an *increase* in the external value of the dollar and is referred to as an **appreciation** of the dollar.

A rise in the exchange rate reflects a depreciation of the Canadian dollar; a fall in the exchange rate reflects an appreciation of the Canadian dollar.

Understanding exchange rates, appreciations, depreciations, and changes in the external value of the dollar is difficult. (Many students appear to have difficulties even after studying economics for three years!) But it is important to get these concepts straight in your mind. *Applying Economic Concepts 19-4* presents the basic definitions and interpretations one more time, and uses the more familiar example of the Canadian-U.S. exchange rate.

Figure 19-7 shows two measures of the Canadian exchange rate since 1970. The first is the Canadian-dollar price of one U.S. dollar; the second is an index of the weighted-average Canadian-dollar price of the currencies of a group of major industrial countries, called the G-10. Since the United States is Canada's largest trading partner, the U.S. dollar gets a large weight in this index, and so the two series move closely together.

For the first half of the 1970s, the external value of the Canadian dollar was relatively stable, fluctuating only modestly and showing no clear trend. From 1976 through 1986, however, the Canadian dollar depreciated sharply, by roughly 40 percent over that ten-year period. This depreciation in the Canadian dollar is reflected by a rise in the exchange rate. During this period, therefore, the external value of the Canadian dollar was *falling*. From 1986 through the early 1990s, the Canadian dollar appreciated, shown as a reduction in both measures of the exchange rate. During this period, the external value of the Canadian dollar was *rising*. By 1992, the external value of the Canadian dollar had returned approximately to where it was in 1980. In the several years following 1992, however, the Canadian dollar depreciated again significantly, by over 25 percent (its external value fell from 88 to 65 U.S. cents).

What explains the considerable volatility in Canada's exchange rate? As we will see in later chapters, both domestic policy and external events have important effects on the Canadian exchange rate. For example, most economists believe that the appreciation of the Canadian dollar between 1986 and 1992 was caused in part by the Bank of Canada's efforts to reduce the rate of inflation. The Bank's policy was

foreign exchange Actual foreign currencies or various claims on them, such as bank balances or promises to pay, that are traded on the foreign-exchange market.

foreign-exchange market The market where different national currencies, or claims to these currencies, are traded.

internal value of the dollar The purchasing power of the dollar measured in terms of domestic goods and services.

external value of the dollar The value of the dollar expressed in terms of foreign currencies. The inverse of the exchange rate.

depreciation A fall in the external value of domestic currency in terms of foreign currency; that is, a rise in the exchange rate.

appreciation A rise in the external value of the domestic currency in terms of foreign currencies; a fall in the exchange rate.

International trade is very important to the Canadian economy. Exports and imports of goods and services each represent about 40 percent of Canada's GDP.

APPLYING ECONOMIC CONCEPTS 19-4

The Exchange Rate and the External Value of the Canadian Dollar

To illustrate these important relations, we concentrate on the rates that are most familiar to all of us, those between the Canadian dollar and the U.S. dollar. Recall once again the critical definitions.

The exchange rate is the number of Canadian dollars required to buy one U.S. dollar. The external value of the Canadian dollar is its power to purchase U.S. currency. Thus, a rise in the Canada-U.S. exchange rate is a *reduction* in the external value of the Canadian dollar. A fall in the exchange rate is an *increase* in the external value of the Canadian dollar.

Consider an example. Suppose you are told that the cost of one U.S. dollar is 1.50 Canadian dollars. In this case, the exchange rate is 1.50. But what is the external value of the Canadian dollar? What we know is

$$1 \text{ U.S. dollar} = 1.50 \text{ Canadian dollars}$$

Dividing through by 1.50 tells us that

$$\frac{1 \text{ U.S. dollar}}{1.50} = 1 \text{ Canadian dollar}$$

which, doing the division, is

$$0.667 \text{ U.S. dollar} = 1 \text{ Canadian dollar, or}$$

$$66.7 \text{ U.S. cents} = 1 \text{ Canadian dollar}$$

This shows that the exchange rate and the external value of the currency are the reciprocals of each other. It follows that they move in opposite directions. Thus, when the exchange rate rises, the external value of the Canadian dollar falls—this is called a *depreciation* of the Canadian dollar. Conversely, when the exchange rate falls, the external value of the Canadian dollar rises—this is called an *appreciation* of the Canadian dollar.

It may sound confusing that a fall in the external value of the Canadian dollar is shown by a rise in the exchange rate, while a rise in the external value of the Canadian dollar is shown by a fall in the exchange rate. This, however, is no more confusing than the definition of the *internal* value of the dollar. Recall that when all Canadian prices go up, the internal value of the Canadian dollar goes down (and when all prices fall, the internal value of the Canadian dollar rises).

All you need to remember is that the exchange rate tells us how many Canadian dollars are needed to buy one U.S. dollar, and the higher that number, the less each Canadian dollar is worth.

---

controversial at the time, not least because of the effect it had on the exchange rate and the many export-oriented firms who were harmed by Canada's strong dollar. We examine the link between monetary policy and exchange rates in detail in Chapters 27 and 28.

The depreciation of the Canadian dollar from 1997 to 1999 is thought by most economists to have resulted from a nearly 30 percent decline in the world prices of commodities, many of which are important Canadian exports. The decline in commodity prices was partly caused by a significant recession that started in several Asian economies in the summer of 1997—economies that are large importers of Canadian commodities. Thus, events in faraway lands can have dramatic effects on the Canadian exchange rate. We examine the link between world commodity prices and the Canadian exchange rate in Chapter 36.

The Balance of Payments

To know what is happening to the course of international trade and international capital movements, governments keep an account of the transactions among countries. These accounts are called the **balance-of-payments accounts.** They record all international

Practise with Study Guide Chapter 19, Exercise 5.

balance-of-payments accounts A summary record of a country's transactions with the rest of the world, including the buying and selling of goods, services, and assets.

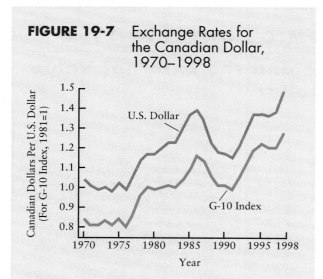

FIGURE 19-7 Exchange Rates for the Canadian Dollar, 1970–1998

The exchange rate rose—the Canadian dollar depreciated—steadily from the mid 1970s through the mid 1980s. From 1986 to 1992, the Canadian dollar appreciated; since 1992, the dollar has been depreciating. The black line shows the Canada-U.S. exchange rate, defined as the Canadian-dollar price of one U.S. dollar. The coloured line shows the Canadian dollar exchange rate in terms of ten major industrialized countries. It is expressed as an index, with the 1981 value set equal to 1. Since the United States is Canada's largest trading partner by far, the two exchange rates move closely together.

(*Source: Bank of Canada Review,* Spring 1999.)

payments that are made for the buying and selling of both goods and services, as well as financial assets such as stocks and bonds.

Figure 19-8 shows one part of the balance of payments that is most often at the centre of controversy—the balance of trade.[5] This balance, also called net exports, is the difference between the value of Canadian exports and the value of Canadian imports. As we can see from Figure 19-8, Canadian exports and imports have increased fairly closely in step with each other over the past thirty years. The trade balance has thus had mild fluctuations over the years, but has stayed at or near a roughly balanced position. Also apparent in Figure 19-8 is that Canadian trade flows (both imports and exports) began to grow more quickly after 1990. The increased importance of international trade is largely due to the Canada-U.S. Free Trade Agreement, that began in 1989, and to the North American Free Trade Agreement (which added Mexico), that began in 1993.

In Part 11 of this textbook, we explore in detail the reasons for international trade and the benefits that trade brings. At that time, we will be better able to interpret the data shown in Figure 19-8.

What Lies Ahead

This chapter has provided a quick tour of macroeconomics. The purpose of this tour has been to whet your appetite for the many complex and interesting issues that macroeconomists think about. Having read this chapter, you should have in place a basic understanding of what the central macroeconomic variables are and why they matter.

In the next chapter we discuss the measurement of GDP, and emphasize why, even though GDP is not a perfect measure of our well-being, it is viewed as the best available single measure of the country's level of economic activity. In Chapter 21 we take a brief look at the difference between the short run and the long run in macroeconomics. In particular, we see that changes in productivity and in the economy's amount of labour and capital are the main determinants of long-run changes in GDP. In contrast, short-run changes in GDP are mostly caused by changes in the economy's ability to put a given amount of labour and capital to work—the *factor utilization rate*. This difference between

---

[5]The trade balance that one reads about in the newspapers is often the *merchandise* trade balance, which counts only trade in tangible goods, but excludes trade in services such as engineering or legal services. There is no economic rationale for treating goods differently from services, and in this book unless otherwise specified, when we refer to the balance of trade we mean the balance on both goods and services.

short-run and long-run changes in GDP implies that we must think differently about the economy's short-run and long-run behaviour.

The chapters that follow lay out a short-run model of the macro economy and emphasize the determination of output, employment, and interest rates, all under the assumption that the price level is held constant. We then allow the price level to adjust to excess demand or supply and see the short-run macro model evolve into a long-run model. Once our model has been developed in this way, we will then be in a position to discuss the role of fiscal policy and monetary policy, and how the effects of such policies are generally different in the short run than in the long run.

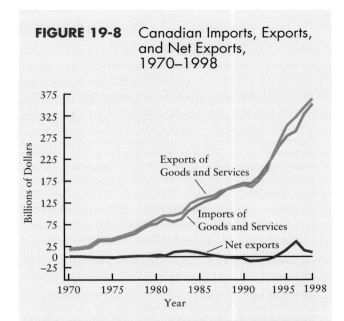

FIGURE 19-8   Canadian Imports, Exports, and Net Exports, 1970–1998

Though imports and exports have increased dramatically over the past 40 years, the trade balance has remained roughly in balance. The nominal values of imports and exports rose steadily over the past few decades, due to price increases and quantity increases. The growth of trade increased sharply after the early 1990s. The trade balance—net exports—is always close to zero.

(*Source: Bank of Canada Review,* Spring 1999; Department of Finance, Economic Reference Tables, July 1994.)

S U M M A R Y

Growth Versus Fluctuations

- Macroeconomics examines the behaviour of such broad aggregates and averages as the price level, national income, potential output, the GDP gap, employment, unemployment, the exchange rate, and the balance of payments.

- The most important macroeconomic issues can be divided into two broad categories—long-term economic growth and short-term fluctuations. Broad government policies, such as monetary policy and fiscal policy, typically make an appearance in both discussions.

Key Macroeconomic Variables

LO 2

- The value of the total production of goods and services in a nation is called its national product. Because production of output generates income in the form of claims on that output, the total is also referred to as national income. One of the most commonly used measures of national income is gross domestic product (GDP).
- Nominal national income evaluates output in current prices. Real national income evaluates output in constant base-period prices. Changes in real national income reflect changes in quantities of output produced.
- Potential output is the level of output produced when factors of production are employed at their normal intensity of use. The GDP gap is the difference between actual and potential output.
- Fluctuations of national income around its potential level are associated with the business cycle. Recoveries pass through peaks and turn into recessions that, in turn, pass through troughs to become recoveries. Although these movements are systematic rather than random, they are by no means predictably regular.
- The unemployment rate is the percentage of the labour force not employed and actively searching for a job. The labour force and employment have both grown steadily for the past half century. The unemployment rate fluctuates considerably from year to year. Unemployment imposes serious costs on the economy in the form of economic waste and human suffering.
- The average price level is measured by a price index, which measures the cost of a set of goods in one year relative to their cost in an (arbitrary) base year. The price level has displayed a continual upward trend since 1960. The inflation rate measures the rate of change of the price level. Although it fluctuates considerably, the inflation rate has been consistently positive.
- The interest rate is the price that is paid to borrow money for a stated period and is expressed as a percentage amount per dollar borrowed. The nominal interest rate is this price expressed in money terms; the real interest rate is this price expressed in terms of goods or purchasing power.
- The exchange rate is the number of Canadian dollars needed to purchase one unit of foreign currency. A rise in the exchange rate is a reduction in the external value of the Canadian dollar. The balance of payments is a record of all international transactions made by Canadian firms, households, and governments.

KEY CONCEPTS

National product and national income
Real and nominal national income
Potential and actual output
The output (or GDP) gap
Employment, unemployment, and the labour force

Full employment
Frictional, structural, and cyclical unemployment
The price level and the rate of inflation
The effects of anticipated and unanticipated inflation

Real and nominal interest rates
The exchange rate
Depreciation and appreciation of the Canadian dollar
The balance of payments

STUDY EXERCISES

1. Consider the macroeconomic data shown below for a hypothetical country's economy.

Year	Real GDP Actual (billions of $)	Real GDP Potential (billions of $)	Output Gap (% of potential)	Unemployment Rate (% of labour force)
1994	768	788	—	11.1
1995	784	796	—	10.2
1996	797	805	—	9.1
1997	811	815	—	8.3
1998	825	825	—	7.6
1999	840	836	—	7.3
2000	853	847	—	7.1
2001	862	858	—	7.3
2002	870	870	—	7.6

   a. Compute the output gap for each year.
   b. Identify the periods in which there is an inflationary output gap, and those periods in which there is a recessionary output gap.
   c. Explain how GDP can exceed potential GDP.
   d. Does real GDP ever fall in the time period shown? What is the relationship between falling GDP and a recessionary gap?
   e. What is the natural rate of unemployment in this economy? What kind of unemployment exists when unemployment is equal to the natural rate?

2. Consider the data shown below for the Canadian Consumer Price Index (CPI), drawn from the *Bank of Canada Review*.

Year	CPI (1992=100)	CPI Inflation (% change from previous year)
1987	81.5	4.35
1988	84.8	4.05
1989	89.0	——
1990	93.3	——
1991	98.5	5.57
1992	100.0	——
1993	101.8	——
1994	102.0	0.20
1995	104.2	2.16
1996	105.9	——
1997	107.6	——
1998	108.9	1.21

   a. Compute the missing data in the table.
   b. Do average prices ever fall in the time period shown? In which year do prices come closest to being stable?
   c. Across which two consecutive years is the rate of inflation closest to being stable?
   d. In a diagram with the price level on the vertical axis and time on the horizontal axis, illustrate the difference between a situation where the price level is stable and a situation where the rate of inflation is stable.

3. The data below show the nominal interest rate and the inflation rate for several developed economies (drawn from *The Economist*, March 13, 1999).

Country	Nominal Interest Rate (on 10-year government bonds)	Inflation Rate (% change in CPI from previous year)	Real Interest Rate
Australia	5.61	1.6	—
Canada	5.25	0.6	—
France	4.13	0.2	—
Germany	4.03	0.2	—
Japan	1.79	0.2	—
Switzerland	2.50	0.3	—
UK	4.71	2.4	—
USA	5.19	1.7	—

   a. Compute the real interest rate for each country, assuming that people expected the inflation rate at the time to persist.
   b. If you were a lender, in which country would you have wanted to lend in March of 1999? Explain.
   c. If you were a borrower, in which country would you have wanted to borrow in March of 1999? Explain.

4. Consider the following data drawn from *The Economist* in March 1999. Recall that the external value of the Canadian dollar is the number of units of some foreign currency needed to purchase one Canadian dollar. The Canadian exchange rate is the number of Canadian dollars needed to purchase one unit of some foreign currency.

Currency	External Value of Cdn Dollar		Cdn Dollar Exchange Rate	
	March 1999	March 1998	March 1999	March 1998
U.S. dollar	—	—	1.520	1.410
Japanese yen	0.789	0.915	—	—
British pound	—	—	2.492	2.311
Swedish krona	5.342	—	—	0.176
Brazilian real	1.441	0.801	—	—
Mexican peso	6.553	—	—	0.162

a. Provide the missing data in the table.
b. Which currencies appreciated relative to the Canadian dollar from March 1998 to March 1999?
c. Which currencies depreciated relative to the Canadian dollar from March 1998 to March 1999?
d. Using the information provided in the table, can you tell whether the Japanese yen depreciated or appreciated *against the U.S. dollar* from March 1998 to March 1999?

DISCUSSION QUESTIONS

1. Explain carefully what has happened to the CPI to justify each of the following newspaper headlines.

   a. "Prices on the rise again after a year of stability"
   b. "Inflation increases for three successive months"
   c. "Finance Minister pleased at moderation in inflation rate"
   d. "Cost-of-living increases devastating pensioners"

2. Explain why during booms it is possible for the unemployment rate to increase even while total employment is rising.

3. Evaluate the following statements about unemployment.

   a. "Unemployment is a personal tragedy and a national waste."

   b. "No one needs to be unemployed these days; just look at the Help Wanted ads in the newspapers and the signs in the stores."
   c. "Unemployment insurance is a boondoggle for the lazy and unnecessary for the industrious."

4. Consider a 10-year period over which output per worker falls, but GDP increases. How can this happen? Do you think this is likely to be good for the economy?

5. When the Canadian dollar depreciates in foreign-exchange markets, many people view this as "good" for the Canadian economy. Who is likely to be harmed by and who is likely to benefit from a depreciation of the Canadian dollar?

CHAPTER 20

The Measurement of National Income

⒧ LEARNING OBJECTIVES

❶ Recognize the problem of "double counting" and how the concept of value added solves this problem when measuring national income.

❷ Understand that the circular flow of income implies three ways of computing national income—total value added, total expenditure, and total income.

❸ Explain the basic methods of measuring national income, using either the income approach or the expenditure approach.

❹ Understand the difference between real and nominal GDP, and why GDP per worker is a better measure of living standards than just GDP itself.

❺ Recognize that many things affecting our well-being are omitted from official measures of GDP.

This chapter provides a detailed look at the measurement of national income. Once we know more precisely what is being measured and how it is measured, we will be ready to build a macroeconomic model to explain the determination of national income. Understanding how national income is measured is an important part of understanding how and why it changes. Indeed, this is a general rule of all economics and all science: Before using any data, it is essential to understand how those data are developed and what they measure.

National Output and Value Added

The central topic of macroeconomics is the overall level of economic activity—aggregate output and the income that is generated by its production. We start by asking what we mean by output.

It may seem strange to ask what we mean by output. Surely the town bakery knows what it produces, and if General Motors or Bombardier do not know their own output, what do they know? If each firm knows the value of its total output, the national income statisticians simply have to add up each separate output value to get the nation's output—or is that really all?

The reason that obtaining a total for the nation's output is not quite that simple is that one firm's output is often another firm's input. The local baker uses flour that is the output of the flour milling company, and the flour milling company, in turn, uses wheat that is the farmer's output. What is true for bread is true for most commodities.

Production occurs in stages: Some firms produce outputs that are used as inputs by other firms, and these other firms, in turn, produce outputs that are used as inputs by yet other firms.

If we merely added up the market values of all outputs of all firms, we would obtain a total greatly in excess of the value of the economy's actual output.

Consider the baker as a simple example. If we added the total value of the output of the wheat farmer, the flour mill, and the baker, we would be counting the value of the wheat three times, the value of the milled flour twice, and the value of the bread once.

The error that would arise in estimating the nation's output by adding all sales of all firms is called **double counting**. "Multiple counting" would actually be a better term because if we added up the values of all sales, the same output would be counted every time that it was sold by one firm to another.

The problem of double counting could in principle be solved by distinguishing between two types of output. **Intermediate goods** are outputs of some firms that are used as inputs by other firms. **Final goods** are products that are not used as inputs by other firms, at least not in the period of time under consideration. The term final demand refers to the purchase of final goods for consumption, for investment (including inventory accumulation), for use by governments, and for export.

If the sales of firms could be easily disaggregated into sales of final goods and sales of intermediate goods, then measuring total output would be straightforward. It would simply equal the value of all *final* goods produced by firms. However, when Stelco sells steel to the Ford Motor Company, it does not care, and usually does not know, whether the steel is for final use (say, construction of a warehouse that will not be sold by Ford) or for use as part of an automobile that will be sold again. Even in our earlier example of bread, a bakery cannot be sure that its sales are for final use, for the bread may be further "processed" by a restaurant prior to its final sale to a customer. In general, it is extremely difficult if not impossible to successfully distinguish final from intermediate goods. The problem of double counting must therefore be resolved in some other manner.

To avoid double counting, statisticians use the important concept of **value added**. Each firm's value added is the value of its output minus the cost of the intermediate goods that it purchases from other firms.

double counting   In national income accounting, adding up the total outputs of all the sectors in the economy so that the value of intermediate goods is counted in the sector that produces them as well as every time they are purchased as an input by another sector.

intermediate goods   All outputs that are used as inputs by other producers in a further stage of production.

final goods   Goods that are not used as inputs by other firms but are produced to be sold for consumption, investment, government, or exports during the period under consideration.

value added   The value of a firm's output minus the value of the inputs that it purchases from other firms.

Value Added = Revenue − Costs of Intermediate Goods

Thus a steel mill's value added is the revenue it earns from selling the steel it produces minus the value of the ore that it buys from the mining company, the value of the electricity and fuel oil that it uses, and the values of all other inputs that it buys from other firms. A bakery's value added is the revenue it earns minus the value of the flour and other inputs that it buys from other firms.

Note that a firm's value added equals the value of its output minus the value of inputs *purchased from other firms*. Earnings by factors of production, such as labour income or profits, are not purchases from other firms, and hence are not subtracted from the value of output when computing value added. Since the total value of output is simply the sum of materials inputs plus earnings by factors of production, value added is exactly equal to the sum of factor incomes.[1]

---

[1]We are ignoring here the role of indirect taxes, such as provincial sales taxes or the Goods and Services Tax (GST). Such taxes are included in the market value of a firm's output, but these taxes are remitted to the government and do not represent a payment to a factor of production.

APPLYING ECONOMIC CONCEPTS 20-1

Value Added Through Stages of Production

Because the output of one firm often becomes the input of other firms, the total value of goods sold by all firms greatly exceeds the value of the output of final products. This general principle is illustrated by a simple example in which Firm R starts from scratch and produces goods (raw materials) valued at $100; the firm's value added is $100. Firm I purchases raw materials valued at $100 and produces semi-manufactured goods that it sells for $130. Its value added is $30, because the value of the goods is increased by $30 as a result of the firm's activities. Firm F purchases the semi-manufactured (intermediate) goods for $130, works them into a finished state, and sells the final products for $180. Firm F's value added is $50. We find the value of the final goods, $180, either by counting only the sales of Firm F or by taking the sum of the values

added by each firm. This value is much smaller than the $410 that we would obtain if we merely added up the market value of the commodities sold by each firm.

For products that go through many stages of production, the product's final value is equal to the total of the values added at all stages of production.

	Transactions at Three Different Stages of Production				
	Firm R	Firm I	Firm F	All Firms	
A. Purchases from other firms	$ 0	$100	$130	$230	Total interfirm sales
B. Purchases of factors of production (wages, rent, interest, profits)	100	30	50	180	Total value added
A + B = value of product	$100	$130	$180	$410	Total value of all sales

Value Added = Income to Factors of Production

Value added is the correct measure of each firm's contribution to total output—the amount of market value that is produced by that firm.

The firm's value added is the *net value* of its output. It is this net value that is the firm's contribution to the nation's total output, representing the firm's own efforts that add to the value of what it takes in as inputs. The concept of value added is further illustrated in *Applying Economic Concepts 20-1*. In this simple example, as in all more complex cases, the value of the nation's total output is obtained by summing all the individual values added.

The sum of all values added in an economy is a measure of the economy's total output.

National Income Accounting: The Basics

The measures of national income and national product that are used in Canada derive from an accounting system called the National Income and Expenditure Accounts (NIEA). The accounts, produced by Statistics Canada, provide us with a framework for analysing the generation of national income. The National Income and Expenditure Accounts are not simply collections of economic data. They have a logical structure, based on the simple yet important idea of the circular flow of income, which you may recall from Chapter 19 (see Figure 19-1). The key point from the circular flow is:

The value of domestic output is equal to the value of the expenditure on that output, and is also equal to the total claims to income that are generated by producing that output.

The circular flow of income suggests three different ways of measuring national income. The first is simply to add up the value of all goods and services produced in the economy. This requires the concept of value added, which we discussed in the previous section. The remaining two approaches correspond to the two halves of the circular flow of income. One approach is to add up the total flow of expenditure on domestic output; the other is to add up the total flow of income claims generated by the flow of domestic production. All three measures yield the same total, which is called **gross domestic product** (GDP). When it is calculated by adding up the total value added in the economy, it is called *GDP by value added*. When it is calculated by adding up total expenditure for each of the main components of final output, the result is called *GDP on the expenditure side*. When it is calculated by adding up all the income claims generated by the act of production, it is called *GDP on the income side*.

The conventions of double-entry bookkeeping require that all value produced must be accounted for by a claim that someone has to that value. Thus the two values calculated from the income and the expenditure sides are identical conceptually and differ in practice only because of errors of measurement. Any discrepancy arising from such errors is then reconciled so that one common total is given as *the* measure of GDP. Both calculations are of interest, however, because each gives a different and useful breakdown. Also, having two independent ways of measuring the same quantity provides a useful check on statistical procedures and on unavoidable errors in measurement.

GDP from the Expenditure Side

GDP for a given year is calculated from the expenditure side by adding up the expenditures needed to purchase the final output produced in that year. Total expenditure on final output is the sum of four broad categories of expenditure: consumption, investment, government, and net exports. In the following chapters, we will discuss in considerable detail the causes and consequences of movements in each of these four expenditure categories. Here we define what they are and how they are measured. Throughout, it is important to remember that these four categories of expenditure are exhaustive—they are *defined* in such a way that all expenditure on final output falls into one of the four categories.

Consumption Expenditure

Consumption expenditure includes expenditure on all goods and services sold to their final users during the year. It includes services, such as haircuts, dental care, and legal advice; nondurable goods, such as fresh vegetables, clothing, cut flowers, and fresh meat; and durable goods, such as cars, television sets, and air conditioners. *Actual* measured consumption expenditure is denoted by the symbol C_a.

Investment Expenditure

Investment expenditure is expenditure on goods not for present consumption, including inventories, capital goods such as factories, machines and warehouses, and residential housing. Such goods are called *investment goods*.

gross domestic product (GDP)
National income as measured by the output approach; equal to the sum of all values added in the economy or, what is the same thing, the values of all final goods produced in the economy.

Practise with Study Guide Chapter 20, Exercise 3.

consumption expenditure
Household expenditure on all goods and services. Represented by the symbol C as one of the four components of aggregate expenditure.

investment expenditure
Expenditure on the production of goods not for present consumption. Represented by the symbol I.

Inventories.   Almost all firms hold stocks of their inputs and their own outputs. These stocks are called **inventories.** Inventories of inputs and unfinished materials allow firms to maintain a steady stream of production despite interruptions in the deliveries of inputs bought from other firms. Inventories of outputs allow firms to meet orders despite fluctuations in the rate of production.

The accumulation of inventories counts as current investment because it represents goods produced but not used for current consumption. These goods are included in the national income accounts at market value, which includes the wages and other costs that the firm incurred in producing them and the profit that the firm will make when they are sold. Thus, in the case of inventories of a firm's own output, the expenditure approach measures what will have to be spent to purchase the inventories when they are sold rather than what has so far been spent to produce them.

The drawing down of inventories, often called *decumulation,* counts as disinvestment because it represents a reduction in the stock of finished goods that are available to be sold.

Plant and Equipment.   All production uses capital goods, which are manufactured aids to production, such as tools, machines, and factory buildings. The economy's total quantity of capital goods is called the **capital stock.** Creating new capital goods is an act of investment and is called *business fixed investment,* often shortened to **fixed investment.**

Residential Housing.   A house or an apartment building is a durable asset that yields its utility over a long period of time. Because such an asset meets the definition of investment that we gave earlier, housing construction—the building of a *new* house—is counted as investment expenditure rather than as consumption expenditure. However, when an individual purchases a house from a builder or from another individual, an existing asset is simply transferred, and the transaction is not part of national income. Only when a new house is built does it appear as residential investment in the national accounts.

Gross and Net Investment.   The total investment that occurs in the economy is called gross investment. Gross investment is divided into two parts: replacement investment and net investment. Replacement investment is the amount of investment that just maintains the level of existing capital stock; it is called the *capital consumption allowance* or simply **depreciation.** Gross investment minus replacement investment is net investment. Positive net investment increases the economy's total stock of capital, whereas replacement investment simply keeps the existing stock intact by replacing what has been used up.

All investment goods are part of the nation's total current output, and their production creates income whether the goods produced are a part of net investment or are merely replacement investment. Thus, all of gross investment is included in the calculation of national income. *Actual* total investment expenditure is denoted by the symbol I_a.

Government Purchases

When governments provide goods and services that households want, such as highways and libraries, they are adding to the sum total of valuable output in the economy. With other government activities, the case may not seem so clear. Should expenditures by the federal government to send peacekeepers overseas, or to pay a civil servant to refile papers from a now-defunct department, be regarded as contributions to national income?

National income statisticians do not speculate about such matters. Instead they include all **government purchases** of goods and services as part of national income.

---

inventories   Stocks of raw materials, goods in process, and finished goods held by firms to mitigate the effect of short-term fluctuations in production or sales.

capital stock
The aggregate quantity of capital goods.

fixed investment
Investment in plant and equipment.

depreciation   The amount by which the capital stock is depleted through its contribution to current production. Also called *capital consumption allowance.*

government purchases   All government expenditure on currently produced goods and services, exclusive of government transfer payments. Represented by the symbol *G*.

(Government expenditure on investment goods is included as government purchases rather than investment expenditure.) *Actual* government purchases of goods and services is denoted G_a.

Cost Versus Market Value.   Government output is typically valued at cost rather than at market value. In many cases, there is really no choice. What, for example, is the market value of the law courts? No one knows. But, since we do know what it costs the government to provide these services, we value them at their cost of production.

Although valuing at cost is the only possible way to measure many government activities, it does have one curious consequence. If, because of an increase in productivity, one civil servant now does what two used to do, and the displaced worker shifts to the private sector, the government's measured contribution to national income will fall (but the private sector's contribution will rise). Conversely, if two workers now do what one worker used to do, the government's contribution will rise. Both changes could occur even though what the government actually produces has not changed. This is an inevitable but curious consequence of measuring the value of the government's output by the cost of producing it.

Government Purchases Versus Government Expenditure.   Only government *purchases* of currently produced goods and services are included as part of GDP. A great deal of government expenditure does *not* count as part of GDP. For example, when the government makes payments to a retired person through the Canada Pension Plan, it is not purchasing any currently produced goods or services from the retiree. The payment itself does not add to total output. The same is true of payments for unemployment insurance, welfare, and interest on the national debt (which transfers income from taxpayers to holders of government bonds). These are examples of **transfer payments,** which are government expenditures that are not made in return for currently produced goods and services. They are not a part of expenditure on the nation's total output and are therefore not included in GDP. (Of course, the recipients of transfer payments often choose to spend their money on consumption goods. Such expenditure then counts in the same way as any other consumption expenditure.)

Net Exports

The fourth category of aggregate expenditure arises from foreign trade. How do imports and exports influence national income? **Imports** are domestic expenditure on foreign-produced goods and services, whereas **exports** are foreign expenditure on domestically produced goods and services.

Imports.   A country's national income is the total value of final commodities produced in that country. If you buy a car that was made in Japan, only a small part of that value will represent expenditure on Canadian production. Some of it represents payment for the services of the Canadian dealers and for transportation; the rest is expenditure on Japanese products. If you take your next vacation in Italy, much of your expenditure will be on goods and services produced in Italy and thus will contribute to Italian GDP rather than to Canadian GDP.

Similarly, when a Canadian firm makes an investment expenditure on a machine that was made partly with imported raw materials, only part of the expenditure is on Canadian production; the rest is expenditure on foreign production. The same is true for government expenditure on such things as roads and dams; some of the expenditure is for imported materials, and only part of it is for domestically produced goods and services.

transfer payment
A payment to a private person or institution that does not arise out of current productive activity.

imports   The value of all goods and services purchased from firms, households, or governments in other countries.

exports
The value of all goods and services sold to firms, households, and governments in other countries.

Consumption, investment, and government expenditures all have an import content. To arrive at total expenditure *on Canadian products*, we need to subtract from total Canadian expenditure any expenditure on imports, which is given the symbol IM_a.

Exports. If Canadian firms sell goods to German households, the goods are part of German consumption expenditure but also constitute expenditure on Canadian output. Indeed, all goods and services that are produced in Canada and sold to foreigners must be counted as part of Canadian production and income; they are produced in Canada, and they create incomes for the Canadian residents who produce them. They are not purchased by Canadian residents, however, so they are not included as part of C_a, I_a, or G_a. Therefore, to arrive at the total value of expenditure on *Canadian* output, it is necessary to add in the value of Canadian exports of goods and services. Actual exports are denoted X_a.

It is customary to group actual imports and actual exports together as **net exports**. Net exports are defined as total exports minus total imports ($X_a − IM_a$), which is also denoted NX_a. When the value of Canadian exports exceeds the value of Canadian imports, net exports are positive. When the value of imports exceeds the value of exports, net exports are negative.

> **net exports** The value of total exports minus the value of total imports. Represented by the symbol *NX*.

$E > I \quad NX +$
$I > E \quad NX -$

Total Expenditures

Gross domestic product measured from the expenditure side is equal to the sum of the four expenditure categories that we have just discussed. In terms of a simple equation, we have

$$\text{GDP} = C_a + I_a + G_a + (X_a − IM_a)$$

GDP, calculated from the expenditure side, is the sum of consumption, investment, government, and net export expenditures.

These data are shown in Table 20-1 for Canada in 1998.

GDP from the Income Side

The production of a nation's output generates income equal to the value of production. Labour must be employed, land must be rented, and capital must be used. The calculation of GDP from the income side involves adding up factor incomes and other claims on the value of output until all of that value is accounted for.

TABLE 20-1 GDP from the Expenditure Side, 1998

Category	Billions of Dollars	Percent of GDP
Consumption	$536.1	59.7
Government purchases	191.8	21.4
Investment	155.8	17.4
Net exports	12.8	1.4
Statistical discrepancy	0.8	0.1
Total	$897.3	100.0

GDP measured from the expenditure side of the national accounts gives the size of the major components of aggregate expenditure. Consumption was by far the largest expenditure category, equal to 60 percent of GDP. In 1998, as in most years for Canada, net exports of goods and services were positive; thus, the other three components of aggregate expenditure added up to slightly less than total GDP.

(*Source:* These data are available at the website for Statistics Canada: www.statcan.ca)

Factor Payments

National income accountants distinguish three main components of factor incomes: wages and salaries, interest, and business profits.

Wages and Salaries. Wages and salaries are the payment for the services of labour. They include take-home pay, taxes withheld, unemployment-insurance contributions,

For the most recent data on national income, see Statistics Canada's website: www.statcan.ca.

pension fund contributions, and other fringe benefits. In total, wages and salaries represent the part of the value of production that is attributable to labour.

Interest. Interest includes interest that is earned on bank deposits, interest that is earned on loans to firms, and miscellaneous other investment income (but excludes interest income generated from loans to Canadian governments).[2]

dividends Profits paid out to shareholders of a corporation. Sometimes called *distributed profits*.

Business Profits. Some profits are paid out as **dividends** to owners of firms; the rest are retained for use by firms. The former are called *distributed profits,* and the latter are called *undistributed profits* or *retained earnings*. Both distributed and undistributed profits are included in the calculation of GDP. For accounting purposes, total profits include corporate profits, incomes of unincorporated businesses (mainly small businesses, farmers, partnerships, and professionals), and profits of government business enterprises and crown corporations (such as Canada Post).

Profits and interest together represent the payment for the use of capital—interest for borrowed capital and profits for capital contributed by the owners of firms.

The sum of wages and salaries, interest, and profits is called *net domestic income at factor cost*. It is "net" because it excludes the value of output that is used as replacement investment. It is "domestic income" because it is the income accruing to domestic factors of production. It is "at factor cost" because it represents only that part of the value of final output that accrues to factors in the form of payments due to them for their services. As we will see immediately, some part of the value of final output does not accrue to the factors at all.

Nonfactor Payments

Every time a consumer spends $10 on some item, less than $10 is generated as income for factors of production. This shortfall is due to the presence of indirect taxes and depreciation.

Indirect Taxes and Subsidies. An important claim on the market value of output arises out of indirect taxes, which are taxes on the production and sale of goods and services. In Canada, the most important indirect taxes are provincial excise and retail sales taxes which differ across provinces, and the federal Goods and Services Tax (GST), which is uniform across all provinces.

For example, if a good's market price of $10.00 includes 50 cents in sales taxes, only $9.50 is available as income to factors of production. Fifty cents worth of market value represents some government's claim on that value. Adding up income claims to determine GDP therefore necessitates including the portion of the total market value of output that is the government's claim exercised through its taxes on goods and services.

It is also necessary to subtract government subsidies on goods and services, since these payments allow factor incomes to *exceed* the market value of output. Suppose that a municipal bus company spends $150 000 producing bus rides and covers its costs by selling $140 000 in fares and obtaining a $10 000 subsidy from the local government. The total income that the company will generate from its production is $150 000, but the total market value of its output is only $140 000, with the difference made up by the subsidy. To get from total income to the market value of its total output, we must subtract the amount of the subsidy.

---

[2]The treatment of interest in the national accounts is a little odd. Interest paid by the government is considered a transfer payment whereas interest paid by private households or firms is treated as expenditure (and its receipt is counted as a factor payment). This is only one example of arbitrary decisions in national income accounting. Others are discussed in *Extensions in Theory 20-1*.

Depreciation.   Another claim on the value of final output is depreciation, or capital consumption allowance. Depreciation is the value of capital that has been used up in the process of producing final output. It is part of gross profits, but because it is needed to compensate for capital used up in the process of production, it is not part of net profits. Hence, depreciation is not income earned by any factor of production. Rather, it is value that must be reinvested just to maintain the existing stock of capital equipment.

Total Income

To measure GDP from the income side, we begin with total payments to the factors of production and add total non-factor payments. That is, GDP equals factor payment plus depreciation plus indirect taxes (net of subsidies).

From the income side, GDP is the sum of factor payments *plus* indirect taxes (net of subsidies) *plus* depreciation.

The various components of the income side of the GDP in the Canadian economy in 1998 are shown in Table 20-2. Note that one of the terms in the table is called *statistical discrepancy*. This is a "fudge factor" to make sure that the independent measures of income and expenditure come to the same total. Statistical discrepancy is a clear indication that national income accounting is not error-free. Although national income and national expenditure are conceptually identical, in practice both are measured with slight error.

Extensions in Theory 20-1 provides a discussion of the way in which arbitrary accounting decisions affect measured GDP, and whether such arbitrariness matters.

TABLE 20-2 GDP from the Income Side, 1998

Category	Billions of Dollars	Percent of GDP
Wages, salaries and supplementary income	$ 471.3	52.5
Interest and miscellaneous investment income	45.8	5.1
Business profits (including net income of farmers and unincorporated businesses)	144.6	16.1
Net Domestic Income at factor cost	661.7	73.7
Capital consumption allowance	116.2	12.9
Indirect taxes less subsidies	120.2	13.5
Statistical discrepancy	–0.8	–0.1
Total	$ 897.3	100.0

GDP measured from the income side of the national accounts gives the size of the major components of the income that is generated by producing the nation's output. The largest category, equal to about 53 percent of income, is compensation to employees, which includes wages and salaries and other benefits.

(*Source:* These data are available at the website for Statistics Canada: www.statcan.ca.)

National Income Accounting: Some Extra Issues

Now that we have examined the basics of national income accounting, we are ready to explore some more detailed issues. We discuss the distinction between GDP and the related concept of gross national product (GNP), the important difference between real and nominal GDP, and some simple measures for productivity.

GDP and GNP

A measure of national output closely related to GDP is **gross national product (GNP)**. The difference between GDP and GNP is the difference between *income produced* and *income received*. GDP measures the total output *produced in Canada* and the total income generated as a result of that production. GNP measures the total amount of income

gross national product (GNP)   The value of total incomes earned by domestically based producers and factors of production.

EXTENSIONS IN THEORY 20-1

Arbitrary Decisions in National Income Accounting

National income accounting practices contain many arbitrary decisions. For example, goods that are finished and held in inventories are valued at market value, thereby anticipating their sale, even though the actual selling price may not be known. In the case of a Ford in a dealer's showroom, this practice may be justified because the *value* of this Ford is perhaps virtually the same as that of an identical Ford that has just been sold to a customer. However, what is the correct market value of a half-finished house or an unfinished novel? Accountants arbitrarily treat goods in process at cost (rather than at market value) if the goods are being made by firms. They ignore completely the value of the unfinished novel. The arbitrary nature of these decisions is inevitable: Because people must arrive at some practical compromise between consistent definitions and measurable magnitudes, any decision will be somewhat arbitrary.

Such arbitrary decisions surely affect the size of measured GDP. But does it matter? The surprising answer,

for many purposes, is no. It is wrong to think that just because a statistical measure is imperfect (as all statistical measures are), it is useless. Simple measures often give estimates to the right order of magnitude, and substantial improvements in sophistication may make only trivial improvements in these estimates.

In 1998, for example, Canadian GDP was measured as $897.3 billion. It is certain that the market value of all production in Canada in that year was neither $100 billion nor $2000 billion, but it might well have been $800 billion or $975 billion had different measures been defined with different arbitrary decisions built in. Similarly, Canadian per capita GDP is about three times the Spanish per capita GDP and is a little less than U.S. per capita GDP. Other measures might differ, but it is unlikely that any measure would reveal the Spanish per capita GDP to be higher than Canada's, or Canada's to be significantly above that of the United States.

---

received by Canadian residents, no matter where that income was generated. How can GDP differ from GNP? GDP differs from GNP for two reasons.

First, some Canadian production creates factor income for foreigners. For example, the profit generated by the Toyota factory in Cambridge, Ontario, is income generated from production in Canada (part of GDP). But some part of this profit is sent outside of Canada to the foreign shareholders of Toyota, and this part of the profit is not part of Canadian GNP. (Note that the wages earned by the Canadian workers in the Cambridge plant count as both GDP and GNP.)

Second, many Canadian residents earn income as a result of foreign investments and factor services sold abroad. Income accruing to Canadian residents from activities undertaken abroad is part of GNP but is not part of GDP. For example, when Newbridge Networks, a high-tech communications firm based in Ottawa, earns profits from its production plant in Wales, those profits are returned to the Canadian owners of the firm. This payment represents income to Canadians (and thus is part of Canadian GNP) even though the production does not take place in Canada and so is not included in Canadian GDP.

The relative sizes of GDP and GNP depend on the balance between income from Canadian investments abroad and income from foreign investments in Canada. For most of Canada's history, Canada has been a net debtor country. Thus, the value of foreign-based assets owned by Canadian residents has been less than the value of Canadian-based assets

Toyota cars produced in Canada contribute to Canada's GDP. But the portion of profits that returns to foreign shareholders is not part of Canada's GNP.

owned by foreigners. As a result, the foreign-generated income received by Canadian residents is less than the Canadian-generated income going to foreigners. This makes Canadian GNP less than Canadian GDP. But the difference is small. In most years, GNP is only three or four percent lower than GDP.

Which Measure Is Better?

Given the difference between GDP and GNP, we are naturally led to ask if one measure is better than the other. The answer depends on what we want to measure.

GDP is superior to GNP as a measure of domestic economic activity. GNP is superior to GDP as a measure of the economic well-being of domestic residents.

If you want to know how easy it will be to find a job or whether factories are working double shifts or whether new buildings are going up right and left, look to changes in the GDP. By its definition, it is the GDP that tells us how much is being produced within a nation's borders. To know how much income is available to the residents of a country, however, one should look at the GNP, which counts income earned abroad and subtracts out income produced at home that accrues to residents of other nations. Thus, the GNP is a better measure of the economic well-being of a country's residents.

Disposable Personal Income

Both GDP and GNP are important measures of overall economic activity and of national income. Most important to consumers, however, is **disposable personal income,** the part of national income that is available to households to spend or to save. The easiest way to calculate disposable personal income is to subtract from GNP the parts of the GNP that are not available to households. Hence, we must subtract all taxes (both income and sales taxes), capital consumption allowances, retained earnings, and interest paid to institutions. However, having subtracted taxes, we need to add back in transfer payments made to households. In recent years, disposable income has represented about 65 percent of GDP.

disposable personal income   GNP minus any part of it not actually paid to households minus personal income taxes paid by households plus transfer payments to households.

Real and Nominal GDP

In Chapter 19, we distinguished between real and nominal measures of aggregate output. When we add up money values of outputs, expenditures, or incomes, we end up with what are called *nominal values*. Nominal GDP increased by 28.5 percent between 1992 and 1998. If we want to compare *real* GDP in 1998 to that in 1992, we need to determine how much of that 28.5 percent nominal increase was due to increases in prices and how much was due to increases in quantities produced. Although there are many possible ways of doing this, the underlying principle is always the same: The value of output in each period is computed by using a common set of *base-period prices*. When this is done, economists say that real output is measured in *constant dollars*.

Total GDP valued at current prices is called *nominal national income*. GDP valued at base-period prices is called *real national income*.

Any change in nominal GDP reflects the combined effects of changes in quantities and changes in prices. However, when real income is measured over different periods by using a common set of base-period prices, changes in real income reflect only changes in quantities. Table 20-3 shows real and nominal GDP for selected years in Canada since 1980.

TABLE 20-3   Nominal and Real GDP in Canada: Selected Years Since 1980 (billions of dollars)

Year	Nominal GDP (current prices)	Real GDP (1992 prices)	Implicit GDP Deflator
1980	315.2	535.0	58.9
1985	485.1	612.4	79.2
1990	678.1	705.5	96.1
1992	698.5	698.5	100.0
1995	806.8	767.9	105.1
1998	897.3	840.2	106.8

Nominal GDP tells us about the money value of output; real GDP tells us about change in physical output. Nominal GDP gives the total value of output in any year, valued at the prices of that year. Real GDP gives the total value of output in any year, *valued at prices from some base year,* in this case 1992. The comparison of real and nominal GDP implicitly defines a price index, changes in which reveal changes in the (average) prices of goods produced domestically. Note that in 1992, nominal GDP equals real GDP (measured in 1992 prices) and thus the implicit GDP deflator equals 100.

(*Source: Bank of Canada Review,* Spring 1999.)

implicit GDP deflator An index number derived by dividing GDP, measured in current dollars, by GDP, measured in constant dollars, and multiplying by 100. In effect, a price index, with current-year quantity weights, measuring the average change in price of all the items in the GDP.

The Implicit GDP Deflator

If nominal and real GDP change by different amounts over a given time period, then prices must have changed over that period. Comparing what has happened to nominal and real GDP over the same period implies the existence of a price index measuring the change in prices over that period—"implies" because no price index is used in calculating either real or nominal GDP. However, an index can be inferred by comparing these two values. Such an index is called an *implicit price index* or an *implicit deflator.* It is defined as follows:

$$\text{Implicit GDP Deflator} = \frac{\text{GDP at current prices}}{\text{GDP at base-period prices}} \times 100$$

The **implicit GDP deflator** is the most comprehensive available index of the price level because it includes all the goods and services that are produced by the entire economy. Implicit deflators use the current year's bundle of production to compare the current year's prices with those prevailing in the base period. The GDP deflator was 6.8 percent higher in 1998 than in 1992 (see Table 20-3). Thus, in 1998, it cost 6.8 percent more to produce the goods and services than it would have cost to produce the same goods and services in 1992. *Applying Economic Concepts 20-2* illustrates the calculation of real and nominal GDP and an implicit deflator for a simple hypothetical economy that produces only wheat and steel.

As we said above, a change in nominal national income can be split into a change due to prices and a change due to quantities. For example, from the data in Table 20-3 we see that in 1998, Canadian nominal GDP was 28.5 percent higher than in 1992. This increase was due to a 6.8 percent increase in prices and a 20.3 percent increase in real GDP.[3]

Output and Productivity

The rise in real GDP during this century has had two main causes:

1. an increase in the amounts of land, labour, and capital used in production; and,

2. an increase in the amount of output produced *per unit of input.*

---

[3]For large percentage changes in price and quantity, the nominal percentage change is not exactly equal to the sum of the price and the quantity changes; generally, the relationship is multiplicative. In this case, prices and quantities are respectively 1.068 and 1.203 times their original values. Thus, nominal GDP is $(1.068) \times (1.203) = 1.285$ times its original value, which is an increase of 28.5 percent. For small percentage changes, the sum is a very good approximation of the multiplicative change. If prices grow by 2 percent and quantities by 3 percent, the nominal change is $(1.02) \times (1.03) = 1.0506$, which is very close to 1.05.

APPLYING ECONOMIC CONCEPTS 20-2
Calculating Nominal and Real GDP

To see what is involved in calculating nominal GDP, real GDP, and the implicit GDP deflator, an example may be helpful. Consider a simple hypothetical economy that produces only two commodities, wheat and steel. Table 1 gives the basic data for output and prices in the economy for two years.

TABLE 1   Data for a Hypothetical Economy

| | Quantity produced | | Prices | |
	Wheat (bushels)	Steel (ton)	Wheat ($/bushel)	Steel ($/ton)
Year 1	100	20	10	50
Year 2	110	16	12	55

Table 2 shows nominal GDP, calculated by adding the money values of wheat output and of steel output for each year. In year 1, the value of both wheat and steel production was $1000, so nominal GDP was $2000. In year 2, wheat output rose to $1320, and steel output fell to $880. Since the rise in value of wheat was greater than the fall in value of steel, nominal GDP rose by $200.

TABLE 2   Calculation of Nominal GDP

Year 1: $(100 \times \$10) + (20 \times \$50) = \$2000$
Year 2: $(110 \times \$12) + (16 \times \$55) = \$2200$

Table 3 shows real GDP, calculated by valuing output in each year *at year 2 prices;* that is, year 2 is used as the base year. In year 2, wheat output rose, but steel output fell. If we use year 2 prices, the value of the fall in steel output between years 1 and 2 exceeded the value of the rise in wheat output, and so real GDP fell.

TABLE 3   Calculation of Real GDP Using Year 2 Prices

Year 1: $(100 \times \$12) + (20 \times \$55) = \$2300$
Year 2: $(110 \times \$12) + (16 \times \$55) = \$2200$

In Table 4, the ratio of nominal to real GDP is calculated for each year and multiplied by 100. This ratio implicitly measures the change in prices over the period in question and is called the *implicit GDP deflator*. The implicit deflator shows that the price level increased by 15 percent between year 1 and year 2.

TABLE 4   Calculation of the Implicit GDP Deflator

Year 1: $(2000/2300) \times 100 = 86.96$
Year 2: $(2200/2200) \times 100 = 100.00$

Throughout this box we have used year 2 as the base year. But we could just as easily have used year 1. The changes we would have computed in real GDP and the implicit deflator would have been very similar—but not identical—to the ones we did compute using year 2 as the base year. The choice of base year matters because of different *relative* prices in the different years (note that the price of steel relative to the price of wheat is lower in year 2 than in year 1). Put simply, with different relative prices in different years, the various output changes get weighted differently depending on which prices we use, and thus the *aggregate* measure of real GDP changes by different amounts. (If you want to understand this point in more detail, try doing Study Exercise #6 at the end of the chapter.)

But if it matters which year we choose as the base year, how do we choose the "right" base year? As with many other elements of national income accounting, there is some arbitrariness in the choice. There is no "right" year. The important thing is not which year to use—the important thing is to be clear about which year you are using and then, for a given set of comparisons, to be sure that you are consistent in your choice.

In other words, more inputs have been used, and each input has become more productive. Although it is useful to measure total output for some purposes, such as assessing the total size of a particular economy, for other purposes, such as studying changes in overall living standards, it is better to use output per person, which is called **per capita output.**

Per capita GDP measures the average amount of output (and income) per person.

per capita output
GDP divided by total population.

Practise with Study Guide Chapter 20,
Extension Exercise 1.

See Chapter 20 of
www.pearsoned.ca/lipsey for an
interesting discussion of why the
computer revolution has not yet
appeared in measurements of
productivity growth: Jeremy Leonard,
"Computers and Productivity in the
Information Economy," *World
Economic Affairs*.

A different way of assessing overall living standards is to consider measures of *productivity*. For example, GDP divided by the number of *employed* persons tells us the average output per employed worker. This is one measure of *labour productivity*. GDP divided by the total number of hours worked measures output per hour of labour input and provides a second measure of labour productivity.

Is the level of per capita output a better measure of average well-being than the level of productivity? The answer depends on which things determine our well-being. To the extent that the level of per capita income and consumption are the most important determinants of well-being, then per capita GDP is probably the best single measure. But if well-being also depends on the amount of leisure that we have, the level of productivity may be the better measure. Productivity improvements allow more output for an unchanged amount of input. (We can consume more without having to work harder.) In contrast, if productivity is not improving, then per capita output can increase only with an increase in inputs. (In order to consume more, we have to work harder.) In this second case, per capita income and consumption may have increased but we may be worse off overall because of the reduction in leisure.

Omissions from GDP

National income as measured in the National Income and Expenditure Accounts provides an excellent measure of the flow of economic activity in organized markets in a given year. But much economic activity takes place outside of the markets that the national income accountants survey. Although these activities are not typically included in the measure of GDP, they nevertheless use real resources and satisfy real wants and needs.

Illegal Activities

Prostitution and other illegal activities involve genuine market transactions, but they are not included in official measures of national income.

GDP does not measure illegal activities, even though many of them are ordinary business activities that produce goods and services sold in markets and that generate factor incomes. Many forms of illegal gambling, prostitution, and drug trade come into this category. To gain an accurate measure of the total demand for factors of production, of total marketable output, or of total incomes generated, we should include these activities, whether or not we as individuals approve of them. The omission of illegal activities is no trivial matter: The drug trade alone is a multibillion-dollar business.

Note that some illegal activities do get included in national income measures, although they are generally misclassified by industry. The income is included because people sometimes report their earnings from illicit activities as part of their earnings from legal activities. They do this to avoid the fate of Al Capone, the famous Chicago gangster in the 1920s and 1930s, who, having avoided conviction on many counts, was finally caught for income-tax evasion.

The Underground Economy

A significant omission from GDP is the so-called underground economy. The transactions that occur in the underground economy are perfectly legal in themselves; the only illegality involved is that such transactions are not reported for tax purposes. One example of this is the carpenter who repairs a leak in your roof and takes payment in cash or in kind to avoid taxation. Because such transactions go unreported, they are omitted from GDP.

The growth of the underground economy is facilitated by the rising importance of services in the nation's total output. It is much easier for a carpenter to pass unnoticed by government authorities than it is for a manufacturing establishment. Estimates of the value of income earned in the underground economy run from 2 percent to 15 percent of GDP. In some countries, the figures are even higher. The Italian underground economy, for example, has been estimated at close to 25 percent of that country's GDP.

Home Production

If a homeowner hires a firm to do some landscaping, the value of the landscaping enters into GDP; if the homeowner does the landscaping herself, the value of the landscaping is omitted from GDP because there is no market transaction. Such production of goods and services in the home is called *home production*. Other nonmarket activities include voluntary work such as canvassing for a political party, helping to run a volunteer day-care centre, or leading a scout troop. Both home production and volunteer activities clearly add to economic well-being, and both use economic resources. Yet neither of them is included in official measures of national income.

Compared to developing countries, the nonmarket sector in most advanced industrial economies is relatively small, although much household maintenance, education, and child care are performed at home. The omissions become very misleading when national income measures are used to compare living standards in structurally different economies. Generally, the nonmarket sector of the economy is larger in rural than in urban settings and in less developed than in more developed economies. Be cautious, then, when interpreting data from a country with a very different climate and culture. When you hear that the per capita GDP of Nigeria is about $1200 per year (compared to about $26 000 in Canada), you should not imagine that living in Nigeria is like living in Canada with only $1200.

One extremely important nonmarket activity is leisure itself. If an attorney voluntarily chooses to reduce her time at work from 2400 hours to 2200 hours per year, measured national income will fall by the attorney's wage rate times 200 hours. Yet the value to the attorney of the 200 hours of new leisure which is enjoyed outside of the marketplace must exceed the lost wages (otherwise she would choose to work the extra 200 hours), so total economic welfare must rise rather than fall. Until recently, one of the most important ways in which economic growth benefited people was by permitting increased amounts of leisure. Because the time off is not marketed, its value does not show up in measures of national income.

Economic "Bads"

When an electric power plant sends sulfur dioxide into the atmosphere, leading to acid rain and environmental damage, the value of the electricity sold is included as part of GDP, but the value of the damage done by the acid rain is not deducted. Similarly, the gasoline that we use in our cars is part of national income when it is produced, but the damage done by burning that gasoline is not deducted. To the extent that economic growth brings with it increases in pollution, congestion, and other disamenities of modern living, measurements of national income will overstate the improvement in living standards. Such measures capture the increased output of goods and services, but they fail to account for the increased output of "bads" that generally accompany economic growth.

Do the Omissions Matter?

GDP does a good job of measuring the flow of goods and services through the market sector of the economy. Usually, an increase in GDP implies greater opportunities for employment for households that sell their labour services in the market.

Unless the importance of unmeasured economic activity changes rapidly, *changes* in GDP will probably do a satisfactory job of measuring *changes* in economic opportunities.

See Chapter 20 of www.pearsoned.ca/lipsey for an excellent discussion of the role of per capita income in determining a country's overall "human development": William Watson, "If Canada Is Number One, Why Would Anyone Leave?" *World Economic Affairs*.

However, when the task at hand is measurement of the overall flow of goods and services available to satisfy people's wants, regardless of the source of the goods and services, then the omissions that we have discussed become undesirable and potentially serious. Still, in the relatively short term, changes in GDP will usually be a good measure of the direction, if not the exact magnitude, of changes in economic well-being. *Lessons from History 20-1* provides many examples from the Industrial Revolution to illustrate the point that changes in real GDP do not always capture improvements in living standards.

LESSONS FROM HISTORY 20-1
GDP and Economic Growth

GDP is not a very good indicator of the growth in well-being that accompanies long-term economic growth. The reason is that so many of the major benefits that growth provides are imperfectly measured or not measured at all by GDP. This can be dramatically illustrated by looking at some of the most important changes that accompanied the first Industrial Revolution (1784–1870).

1. In early eighteenth-century Europe, average life expectancy was around 30 years; in France, one in five children were dead by the end of the first year of life, and 50 percent of registered children were dead by age 10. Life expectancy rose dramatically during the Industrial Revolution.

2. Industrialization reduced famine and hunger. Not only did the average food intake rise, its year-to-year variation fell. It is of little consolation to a peasant that the average food consumption is above the subsistence level over the decades if fluctuations in harvests periodically drive it below the subsistence level, thus causing starvation.

3. Technological changes that accompanied the Industrial Revolution virtually eliminated many terrible diseases that had been common until that time, such as plague, tuberculosis, cholera, dysentery, smallpox, and leprosy.

4. The urbanization that accompanied industrialization increased literacy and education and broadened experience. Before then, poverty and a rural, peasant

existence, with little or no communication between the village and the outside world, tended to be associated with superstition and very narrow experience.

5. Privacy became possible when people moved from the peasant dwelling, where the entire family lived, ate, and slept in one room, to multiroom urban sites.

6. The introduction of a market economy greatly increased the mobility of persons among jobs. In the rural societies, there were few options for employment, and customary behaviour—doing what one's parents did—dominated job selection.

7. The Industrial Revolution was based on mass production of goods sold mainly to low- and middle-income people. These changed the quality of consumption. For example, instead of wooden clogs, people adopted leather shoes; instead of rough, homespun cloth, people had factory-made shirts and skirts; instead of mud floors and thatched roofs, people had wooden floors and rain-proof roofs; instead of all living in one room, parents had a room separate from their children. These things may seem trivial to us today, but they changed the way of life of ordinary people.

Throughout the late eighteenth century and all of the nineteenth century, a succession of new products continued to alter the way ordinary people lived until, by the mid-twentieth century, the ordinary working person had a structurally different way of life from his or her counterpart in the mid-eighteenth century. Statistics, however, are the same if a doubling of GDP takes the form of twice as much of the same, or of new things that enhance the quality of life. The effect on living standards is, however, much greater when new commodities replace older ones rather than just more of the same becoming available.

This box draws on material in: J. Blum, *Our Forgotten Past: Seven Centuries of Life on the Land* (London: Thames and Hudson, 1982); F. Braudel, *Structures of Everyday Life, 15th–18th Century* (New York: Harper and Row, 1981); and N. Rosenberg and L. E. Birdzell, Jr., *How the West Grew Rich* (New York: Basic Books, 1986).

SUMMARY

National Output and Value Added

LO **1** **2**

- Each firm's contribution to total output is equal to its value added, which is the value of the firm's output minus the value of all intermediate goods and services—that is, the outputs of other firms—that it uses. The sum of all the values added produced in an economy is the economy's total output, which is called gross domestic product (GDP).

National Income Accounting: The Basics

LO **3**

- From the circular flow of income, there are three ways to compute national income. One is to add up each firm's value added. The second is to add up total expenditure on domestic output. The third is to add up the total income generated by domestic residents. By standard accounting conventions, these three aggregations define the same total.
- From the expenditure side of the national accounts,

$$\text{GDP} = C_a + I_a + G_a + (X_a - IM_a)$$

C_a comprises consumption expenditures of households. I_a is investment in plant and equipment, residential construction, and inventory accumulation. G_a is government purchases of goods and services. $(X_a - IM_a)$ represents net exports of goods and services.

- GDP measured from the income side adds up all claims to the market value of production. Wages, interest, profits, depreciation (or capital consumption allowance), and indirect taxes net of subsidies are the major categories.

National Income Accounting: Some Extra Issues

LO **4** **5**

- GDP measures the value of production that is located in Canada, and gross national product (GNP) measures income accruing to Canadian residents. The difference is due to the balance between Canadian claims to incomes that are generated abroad and foreign claims to incomes that are generated in Canada. Throughout Canada's history, GNP has been slightly less than GDP.
- Real measures of national income are calculated to reflect changes in real quantities. Nominal measures of national income are calculated to reflect changes in both prices and quantities. Any change in nominal income can be split into a change in quantities and a change in prices. Appropriate comparisons of nominal and real measures yield implicit deflators.
- Economists frequently use measures of GDP, GDP per capita, and various measures of labour productivity such as GDP per employed worker or GDP per hour worked. Changes in overall living standards are better reflected by changes in productivity than by changes in GDP per capita.
- GDP and related measures of national income must be interpreted with their limitations in mind. GDP excludes production resulting from activities that are illegal, that take place in the underground economy, or that do not pass through markets. Hence GDP does not measure everything that contributes to (or detracts from) human well-being.
- Notwithstanding its limitations, GDP remains a useful measure of the total economic activity that passes through the nation's markets. Recorded *changes* in GDP will generally do an accurate job of measuring *changes* in economic activity and economic opportunities.

KEY CONCEPTS

Intermediate and final goods
Value added
GDP as the sum of all values added
GDP from the expenditure side

GDP from the income side
GNP versus GDP
Disposable personal income
Implicit GDP deflator

Per capita GDP and labour
    productivity
Omissions from GDP

STUDY EXERCISES

1. In measuring GDP from the expenditure side (GDP = $C_a + I_a + G_a + NX_a$), which of the following expenditures are included, and within which of the four categories?

   a. expenditures on automobiles by consumers C
   b. expenditures on automobiles by firms I
   c. expenditures on new machinery by Canadian-owned forest companies in Canada I
   d. expenditures on new machinery by Canadian-owned forest companies in the United States $J+$
   e. expenditures on new machinery by U.S.-owned forest companies in Canada NI
   f. reductions in business inventories I
   g. purchases of second-hand cars and trucks Γ
   h. the hiring of economic consultants by the Manitoba government G
   i. the purchase of Canadian-produced software by a firm in Japan NX

2. The list below provides some national income figures for the country of Econoland. All figures are in millions of dollars.

Wages and salaries	5000
Interest income	200
Personal consumption	3900
Personal saving	1100
Personal income taxes	200
Business profits	465
Indirect taxes	175
Subsidies	30
Government purchases	1000
Exports	350
Imports	390
Net private investment	950
Depreciation	150

   a. Using the expenditure approach, what is the value of GDP for Econoland?
   b. Using the income approach, what is the value of GDP?
   c. What is the value of net domestic income at factor cost?

3. The table below shows data for real and nominal GDP for a hypothetical economy over several years.

Year	Nominal GDP (billions of $)	Real GDP (billions of 1996 $)	Implicit GDP Deflator
1994	775.3	798.4	----
1995	814.1	838.6	----
1996	862.9	862.9	----
1997	901.5	882.5	----
1998	951.3	920.6	----
1999	998.8	950.5	----

   a. Compute the implicit GDP deflator for each year.
   b. Compute the total percentage change in nominal GDP from 1994 to 1999. How much of this change was due to increases in prices and how much was due to changes in quantities?

4. Would inflation, as measured by the rate of change in the Implicit GDP Deflator, ever be different from inflation as measured by the rate of change in the Consumer Price Index? Would it ever be the same? Explain.

5. For each of the following events, describe the likely effect on real GDP.

   a. The Quebec ice storm of 1998 increases the demand for building materials to repair damage to homes.
   b. The Quebec ice storm of 1998 damages many factories.
   c. The building of a baseball stadium in Montreal increases the demand for *Expos* tickets by Montrealers.
   d. The building of a baseball stadium in Montreal increases the demand for *Expos* tickets by residents of Vermont and New Hampshire.

6. This is a challenging question to give you practice in computing real GDP and implicit GDP deflators. Consider the following data for a hypothetical economy that produces two goods, milk and honey.

   | | Quantity Produced | | Prices | |
	Milk (litres)	Honey (kg)	Milk ($/litre)	Honey ($/kg)
Year 1	100	40	2	6
Year 2	120	25	3	6

   a. Compute nominal GDP for each year in this economy.

b. Using year 1 as the base year, compute real GDP for each year. What is the percentage change in real GDP from year 1 to year 2?

c. Using year 1 as the base year, compute the implicit price deflator for each year. What is the percentage change in real GDP from year 1 to year 2?

d. Now compute the implicit GDP deflator for each year, using year 1 as the base year.

e. Now compute the implicit GDP deflator for each year, using year 2 as the base year.

f. Explain why the measures of real GDP growth (and growth in the implicit deflator) depend on the choice of base year.

DISCUSSION QUESTIONS

1. Residents of some Canadian cities have recently become concerned about the growing proportion of their local real estate that is being bought up by foreign residents. What is the effect of this transfer of ownership on Canadian GDP and GNP?

2. What would be the effect of the following events on the measured value of Canada's real GDP? Speculate on the effects of each event on the true well-being of Canadians.

a. destruction of thousands of homes by flood water

b. destruction of hundreds of businesses by an ice storm

c. complete cessation of all imports from Europe

d. an increase in the amount of acid rain that falls

e. an increase in the amount of spending on devices that reduce pollution at a major hydroelectricity plant

f. reduction in the standard work week from 37 hours to 30 hours

g. hiring of all welfare recipients as government employees

h. outbreak of hostilities in the Middle East in which Canadian troops became involved as peacekeepers

3. A recent United Nations study concluded that Canada is the best country in which to live—that Canada has the best "quality of life." In view of the fact that Canada does not have the highest per capita real GDP in the world, explain how it can be ranked as the "best."

4. One way of estimating the size of the underground economy is to see the amount of cash Canadians are carrying relative to the total value of GDP. Why would a rapid rise in the ratio of cash held by the public to GDP indicate a rise in the underground economy? Can you offer an explanation for why this ratio has risen steadily since the introduction of the GST in 1991?

5. A company's wages and salaries are part of its value added. Suppose, however, that the cleaning and machinery maintenance that its own employees used to do are now contracted out to specialist firms who come in to do the same work more cheaply. What happens to the company's value added when a company follows this recent trend of "contracting out"? What happens to value added in the economy as a whole?

CHAPTER 21

Short-Run Versus Long-Run Macroeconomics

(LO) LEARNING OBJECTIVES

1. Recognize why economists think differently about short-run and long-run changes in macroeconomic variables.

2. Explain why any change in GDP can be decomposed into changes in: the amount of factors, the employment of factors, and the productivity of factors.

3. Realize that short-run changes in GDP are mostly caused by changes in factor utilization, whereas long-run changes in GDP are mostly caused by changes in factor supplies and productivity.

4. Recognize that fiscal and monetary policy each have different effects in the short run than in the long run.

We began our introduction to macroeconomics in Chapter 19 by emphasizing that most macroeconomic issues can be divided into two broad categories—long-run trends and short-run fluctuations. But what do we mean by the "short run" and "long run," and why is the distinction so important? These are the two questions we examine in this chapter. We will not go into a lot of theoretical or empirical detail—the necessary details will be presented in the following chapters. The purpose of this chapter is to introduce one very important idea: in response to a shock or a change in government policy, the economy behaves differently over several months than it does over several years.

This distinction between short-run and long-run behaviour makes the study of macroeconomics more challenging but it also makes it more interesting. The difference is often not fully appreciated by newspaper writers and TV news reporters. This chapter presents a brief introduction to this important distinction.

Practise with Study Guide Chapter 21, Exercise 2.

Two Examples

We begin by giving two examples of the difference between short-run and long-run behaviour.

Inflation and Interest Rates in Canada

In April of 1995, the Governor of the Bank of Canada, Gordon Thiessen, was interviewed by Peter Gzowski on CBC Radio. Thiessen was asked about the Bank's policy of reducing inflation, from about 6 percent a few years earlier, and maintaining it since then between 1 percent and 3 percent annually. Thiessen argued that the high nominal interest rates of the past were caused mostly by high inflation. The main reason for this connection between inflation and nominal interest rates is that inflation erodes the value of money. Lenders need to be compensated for the inflation-induced fall in the real value of their money between the time they lend it and the time that they are repaid. This can only be done by charging a nominal interest rate high enough to cover the reduction in value. Thus, higher inflation pushes up interest rates; lower inflation pushes them down. Thiessen also argued that in order to reduce inflation the Bank must reduce the growth rate of the money supply. This action, he admitted, tends to push up interest rates. Apparently puzzled, Peter Gzowski then asked the crucial question: how is it possible that a policy which raises interest rates can be a necessary part of reducing both inflation and interest rates?

The key to answering Gzowski's question is to understand the different short-run and long-run effects of monetary policy. In the short run, a policy by the Bank of Canada to reduce the growth rate of money will make credit more scarce (as we will see in detail in Chapter 27). This greater scarcity of credit causes both nominal and real interest rates to rise. Firms will reduce their investment in new factories, machines, and warehouses, and households will purchase fewer big-ticket items, such as cars, ski vacations, and furniture. Such reductions in expenditure will lead to a reduction in national output because firms faced with less demand for their goods have less need to produce output. But as firms scale back their production, workers get laid off and the unemployment rate increases—the economy will be in recession. Indeed, when we examine the detailed workings of monetary policy in later chapters, we will see that a monetary policy designed to reduce inflation is effective precisely because *it creates a recession.*

So much for the short-run effects of the Bank's policy. Interest rates rise and the economy slows down. But how does this reduce the inflation rate? Over a longer period of time, perhaps several years, the excess supply of labour that is a key part of the unemployment and recession puts downward pressure on wages. In other words, wages start to increase at a slower rate than before, and maybe even begin to fall. Wages, however, are one of the most important components of production costs. Thus, as wage growth declines the pressure on prices to rise also declines. That is, the rate of inflation falls. As inflation falls, and the rate of erosion of money's value falls with it, so too will nominal interest rates fall. Thus, as Gordon Thiessen said in the interview, "the best way to get low interest rates is to get low inflation."

The details of monetary policy will be discussed in Chapters 27 and 28, and this argument will be repeated in considerable detail. At that time, we will more clearly see the difference between the short-run and long-run effects of monetary policy. Economists have a special term to reflect this difference. In the long run, economists say that *money is neutral*—meaning that changes in the money supply have no long-run effect on *real* variables such as GDP, employment, and investment but do have an effect on *nominal* variables such as the price level or the rate of inflation. In the short run, however, economists say that *money is not neutral* because changes in the money supply affect real variables. Understanding this difference is crucial to understanding most debates about monetary policy.

Saving and Growth in Japan

By early in 1999, the Japanese economy had been in recession for over a year—that is, real GDP had been falling for more than a year. Moreover, Japan had experienced very low rates of employment growth and GDP growth over the previous six years. Japan's economy was stagnant. Many economists argued that the solution to Japan's economic malaise was for its firms and consumers to spend more. The problem with Japan, they argued, was simply that its firms and consumers saved "too much." On the other hand, many of these same economists acknowledged that Japan's remarkable economic success in the forty years following the Second World War—high growth rates of real GDP and low unemployment—was largely due to its high saving rate. But if "too much" saving is an important reason for Japan's economic slump during the 1990s, how can high saving be the reason for Japan's economic success over four decades? How can both these views be correct?

Once again, the key to understanding this apparent contradiction is to recognize that the short-run effect of saving is different from its long-run effect. In the short run, an increase in firms' and households' desire to save, perhaps caused by some uncertainty about future economic events, implies a reduction in expenditure. Firms spend less on investment goods; households spend less on all sorts of consumer goods. This reduction in expenditure leads to a reduction in output as firms decide to reduce their production rather than stockpile unneeded inventories. Increased saving in the short run, therefore, can be one reason why an economy such as Japan's enters an economic slump.

The high private saving rate in Japan is one reason that the Japanese economic recovery in the late 1990s was so slow.

But if an increase in firms' and households' saving can cause a recession, how can a high saving rate also explain Japan's many years of healthy economic growth? The answer is that in the long run, over periods of several years, greater saving leads to a larger pool of funds. This larger pool of available funds drives down the price of credit—the interest rate—and makes firms' investment projects more profitable. More investment in factories, machines, and warehouses leads to a higher level of potential output, and it is to this higher level of potential output that the economy converges in the long run. This long-run relationship between saving, investment, and growth explains the striking correlation that we will see in Chapter 32—countries with high long-run investment rates tend to be countries with high rates of long-run per capita GDP growth.

When we examine the short-run effects of saving in Chapter 22 and 23, and the long-run effects of saving in Chapter 32, we will note the different role that saving plays over a period of several months as compared to a period of many years. Economists have special terminology to describe this difference. Economists say that national income in the short run is *demand determined*, meaning that increases in demand will lead to increases in output. Thus, an increase in the desire to save, which is a reduction in the desire to spend, leads to less total spending and a reduction in national income. In the long run, however, economists say that national income is *supply determined*, meaning that long-run increases in output will only be possible if the supply of output increases. Such an increase in supply requires either more factors of production (like labour and capital) or greater productivity. As we will see shortly (and in detail in Chapter 32), both increases in productivity and in the amount of productive factors play an important part in explaining a country's long-run economic growth.

A Need to Think Differently

The two examples above suggest that a complete understanding of macroeconomics requires an understanding of both the short run and the long run. Such an understanding, in turn, requires us to think differently about short-run and long-run behaviour. It is one thing to say that macroeconomic variables behave differently over the short run than over the long run; it is quite another to understand *why* this is the case. A complete understanding of the various reasons will only develop gradually as you progress through the several chapters of this book. In the next section, we will introduce a simple equation to account for changes in GDP, and we will use this equation to separate the sources of short-run and long-run changes.

So far, we have been vague about the meaning of the short run and the long run. Can't we remove the mystery and say precisely what we mean by these terms? The answer is partly yes and partly no. We can be precise about *what* we mean by the short run and long run, but we can't be precise about *how much time* is involved in each. The short run is a time period over which changes in economic conditions tend to cause changes in output and employment, with relatively small changes in prices or wages. In contrast, the long run is a time period over which wage and price adjustment takes place—a process set in motion by the short-run changes in output and employment. The two "runs" are therefore not completely separate; the short run evolves into the long run with the passage of time and the adjustment of wages and prices.

Defining the precise time spans involved is much more difficult. The short run is a span of time over which wages and prices do not significantly adjust to changes in economic events. Over the long run, full wage and price adjustment takes place. But how long does the short run last? In other words, how quickly do wages and prices respond to changes in economic events? The answer depends on the context. In Chapter 25, for example, we will see that wages and prices usually fall more slowly during recessions than they increase during booms. Also, wages and prices tend to rise faster in bigger booms than in smaller ones.

For the remainder of this chapter, it is helpful to think of the short run as a span of time that lasts up to many months, maybe even three or four years. In contrast, think of the long run as anything beyond that. This is not meant to be exact—it is only a rule of thumb to help set the context for our distinction between short-run fluctuations and long-run trends.

Accounting for Changes in GDP

The simplest illustration of short-run versus long-run changes in economic activity is the behaviour of real GDP over time, as shown in Figure 21-1. The figure shows the path of Canadian real GDP and potential GDP, beginning from 1970. Actual GDP is measured by Statistics Canada. Potential GDP, as you may recall from Chapter 19, is the level of output that the economy produces when all factors of production are being utilized at their "normal" rates. But Statistics Canada can't tell us the value of potential GDP because it is not an observed variable—it must be estimated. The value of potential GDP is estimated by combining three pieces of information: the amounts of available factors of production (like the labour force and the capital stock); an estimate of these factors' "normal" rates of utilization; and an estimate of the factors' productivity.

Figure 21-1 shows two different types of changes in GDP. First, there are those changes that involve departures of actual GDP from potential GDP. For example, notice that actual GDP is equal to potential GDP at point B in 1981. As the Canadian economy entered a major recession, actual GDP then dropped below potential GDP to point C in 1982. An economic recovery then took place, taking actual GDP back to potential GDP at point D in 1986. Such changes in GDP are what economists call short-run changes in GDP—they involve primarily the opening and then closing of an output gap. In this case, the output gap between 1981 and 1986 was a recessionary output gap.

The second type of change in GDP involves changes in potential GDP, with little or no change in the output gap. For example, the change in actual GDP from point A in

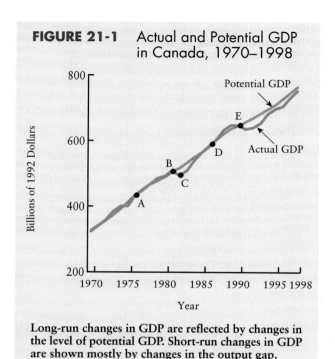

FIGURE 21-1 Actual and Potential GDP in Canada, 1970–1998

Long-run changes in GDP are reflected by changes in the level of potential GDP. Short-run changes in GDP are shown mostly by changes in the output gap.

1976 to point E in 1990 represents entirely a change in potential GDP. We know this because the output gap in both years is zero (that is, in both 1976 and 1990 GDP is equal to potential GDP). Such changes in GDP are what economists call long-run changes in GDP—they involve a change in potential GDP, with little or no change in the output gap.

When studying long-run trends in GDP, economists focus on the change in potential output. When studying short-run fluctuations, economists focus on the change in the output gap.

Figure 21-1 may make us wonder whether short-run changes in GDP have a different cause than long-run changes. After all, the discussion in the previous section suggested that output is *demand determined* in the short run but *supply determined* in the long run. Aren't the determinants of supply different from the determinants of demand? To explore this issue, we turn to a very simple accounting framework that applies to *all* changes in GDP.

GDP Accounting: The Basic Principle

Suppose we want to *account for* changes in GDP. By this we simply mean breaking down any change in GDP into its component parts. By understanding how each component changes, we may then gain some insights into how short-run changes differ from long-run changes.

To break up GDP into the parts we want to study, we do the following obvious but useful things. First, we write

$$GDP = GDP$$

This is obviously true! Next, we multiply the right-hand side of the equation by F/F, where F is the economy's total available stock of factors. This gives

$$GDP = F \times (GDP/F)$$

Next, we multiply the right-hand side by F_E/F_E, where F_E is the number of the economy's factors that are employed. This gives

$$GDP = F \times (F_E/F) \times (GDP/F_E) \qquad (21\text{-}1)$$

It may seem like we have done nothing useful since we have simply twice multiplied the right-hand side of an obviously true equation by one. But, in fact, Equation 21-1 is very useful when thinking about the different sources of change in GDP.

First, however, note that Equation 21-1 is written as if we could add together units of labour and land and capital to get a meaningful number for the economy's "available factors." But this is not actually possible since different factors are measured in different units. For example, we can't add together six workers and five machines to get a total of 11 factors. In the next section, we will focus on a single factor to avoid this problem. For now, however, our point is simplified by thinking about the economy's total available factors, F, and the number of those factors that are employed, F_E.

To make the discussion less cumbersome, let's name the three components of Equation 21-1. Instead of the term "available factors" let's call F the economy's *factor supply*. The term F_E/F is the *factor utilization rate* because it is the fraction of the total factors that are employed or utilized. Finally, the term GDP/F_E is the economy's *productivity* because it is a measure of output per unit of input employed.

Note that Equation 21-1 does nothing more than separate any change in GDP into a change in one or more of the three components, F, F_E/F, or GDP/F_E. For example, Canadian GDP increased dramatically in the fifty years between 1947 and 1997. Also, Canadian GDP increased by a few percentage points from 1997 to 1999. In both cases, the increase in GDP was only possible because one of three things, and possibly more than one, happened—either the factor supply (F) increased, the factor utilization rate (F_E/F) increased, or the level of productivity (GDP/F_E) increased.

Any change in GDP must be the result of a change in factor supply, a change in factor utilization, or a change in productivity.

The value of this accounting exercise becomes clear when we recognize that two of these components, factor supply and productivity, typically change most over long periods of time whereas the third component, factor utilization, changes mostly only over shorter periods. We discuss each component in turn.

The Long Run: Factor Supply

There are two main factors of production—labour and capital—that make up the economy's factor supply.

Labour.   The economy's supply of labour can increase for two main reasons. First, population can increase. An increase in population can be caused, in turn, either by greater immigration, an increase in birth rates, or a decrease in the mortality rate. The second way to increase the economy's supply of labour is to increase the fraction of the population that chooses to seek employment. This fraction is called the *labour-force participation rate*. In Canada, the labour-force participation rate is currently about 66 percent. It has increased steadily from the 1960s, due mostly to the increase in the participation rate of married women and the coming-of-age of the baby-boom generation.

No matter how the economy's supply of labour increases, the important point for our purposes is that such changes are mostly *long-run changes*. Population growth, through whatever means, is a very gradual process. Changes in labour-force participation also tend to be gradual. As a result, the economy's supply of labour does not usually change dramatically from year to year. Over a period of many years, however, the increase in the supply of labour can be significant.

Capital.   The economy's supply of physical capital—machines, factories, and warehouses—increases for one reason. Firms that choose to purchase or build such investment goods today are accumulating physical capital that will be used to produce output in the future. Thus, today's flow of investment expenditure adds to the economy's stock of physical capital.

As is the case for labour, the economy's stock of physical capital changes only very gradually. This is not to be confused with the very dramatic swings in investment that are often observed over the course of the business cycle. The difference is that investment is the *flow* that contributes to the *stock* of capital. But the economy's capital stock is so large compared to the annual flow of investment expenditure that even dramatic swings in the annual level of investment generate only small changes in the stock of capital.

Changes in the economy's supply of labour and capital occur only gradually. As a result, changes in factor supply are important for explaining long-run changes in output, but relatively unimportant for explaining short-run changes.

The Long Run: Productivity

The economy's level of productivity is a measure of the amount of output that is produced with a given level of input. In practice, there are several possible measures of productivity, each one measuring something slightly different. Although there is more than one measure of productivity, Equation 21-1 uses the concept of output per employed factor, GDP/F_E. An increase in productivity is called *productivity growth*. As we discussed in the previous two chapters, rising productivity—productivity growth—is an important source of rising living standards.

The economy's level of productivity changes only slowly over time. For example, a typical rate of productivity growth in Canada over the past few decades is 1 percent per year, and often less. Such low growth rates do not lead to significant changes in GDP or living standards over short periods of time, but can generate huge improvements in living conditions over many years. For example, you might not notice a two percent increase in your productivity from one year to the next, but you would surely notice the doubling that this annual growth rate would produce if it were sustained over 35 years.

The economy's level of productivity changes only gradually. As a result, productivity growth is very important for explaining long-run changes in output, but less important for explaining short-run changes.

The Short Run: Factor Utilization

The factor utilization rate is the last remaining component from our equation. Recall that it is simply the fraction of the total supply of factors that is employed. An immediate question comes to mind: Why would firms ever use fewer factors than are available to them? The answer has to do with how firms respond to changes in the demand for their product. When a firm's sales start dropping off, it must make a choice. It can continue producing at the current rate and let its inventories build up. Or it can reduce its rate of production. For a firm that is interested in maximizing profits, there is a limit to the amount of costly inventories it will be prepared to accumulate. Eventually, a reduction in demand for its product leads the firm to reduce its output and, in turn, reduce its employment of factors. Workers are laid off and equipment and other physical capital is used less intensively.

Similarly, a firm that is faced with a sudden increase in demand for its product has two alternatives. It can continue with its previous rate of production and satisfy the increased demand by letting its inventories run down. Or it can increase its rate of production by hiring more factors. Since profit-maximizing firms do not want to miss an opportunity to make a profitable sale, as would happen if the stockpile of inventories gets fully depleted, eventually the increase in demand leads them to increase production and hire more factors. Extra workers are hired, existing workers work overtime, and machines and other physical capital are used more intensively.

But these responses by firms to changes in demand are only the firms' short-run responses. A low factor utilization rate describes *excess supply* in the factor markets. Such a situation of excess supply typically causes downward pressure on factor prices. This reduction of factor prices, in turn, puts downward pressure on product prices. Similarly, in the case of the increase in demand, the situation of a high factor utilization rate describes *excess demand* in factor markets. Such excess demand causes upward pressure on factor prices. This, in turn, puts upward pressure on product prices.

The factor utilization rate fluctuates in response to changes in the demand for firms' output. Over time, however, excess supply or excess demand for factors causes an adjustment in factor prices that brings the factor utilization rate back to its "normal" level.

What do we mean by a "normal" factor utilization rate? In Chapter 19 we briefly discussed the idea of the *natural rate of unemployment*. This "natural" or "normal" rate of unemployment is the rate of unemployment against which we compare the actual unemployment rate to judge whether the labour market has excess supply or excess demand. That is, if unemployment is above the natural rate, there is an excess supply of labour; if unemployment is below the natural rate, there is an excess demand for labour. For physical capital, the utilization rate is called the *capacity utilization rate* because the amount of physical capital largely determines the productive *capacity* of a given plant or factory. As with labour, so too is there a "natural" or "normal" capacity utilization rate.

The statement that factor utilization rates eventually return to their "normal" level simply means that factor prices adjust in the long run to eliminate excess demands or excess supplies. This adjustment process will be an important topic of discussion in Chapters 24 and 25. An important implication of such long-run adjustment in factor prices is that changes in the factor utilization rate, though important for explaining short-run changes in GDP, are not an important determinant of long-run changes in GDP.

Changes in the factor utilization rate are important for explaining short-run changes in GDP. But, because factor prices adjust in the long run, the factor utilization rate returns to its "normal" level and, hence, is not important for explaining long-run changes in GDP.

GDP Accounting: An Application

We made some strong statements in the previous section regarding short-run versus long-run changes in various economic variables. Are these statements supported by the evidence? In this section, we apply the accounting concept contained in Equation 21-1 to Canadian GDP data to illustrate the basic arguments. Unfortunately, we cannot use *exactly* the same equation because, as we noted then, it is not possible to add units of labour together with units of physical capital. But, using exactly the same intuition as earlier, we can express the GDP accounting equation in terms of a single factor of production—labour. Letting L be the labour force and E be the level of employment, the new equation is:[1]

$$GDP = L \times (E/L) \times (GDP/E) \tag{21-2}$$

The basic interpretation of Equation 21-2 is the same as for Equation 21-1, except now the discussion relates only to labour. The labour force (L) is the supply of labour. The employment rate (E/L) is the fraction of the labour force actually employed (which is equal

---

[1]We get this equation by beginning with GDP = GDP. We then multiply the right-hand side by E/E and then by L/L.

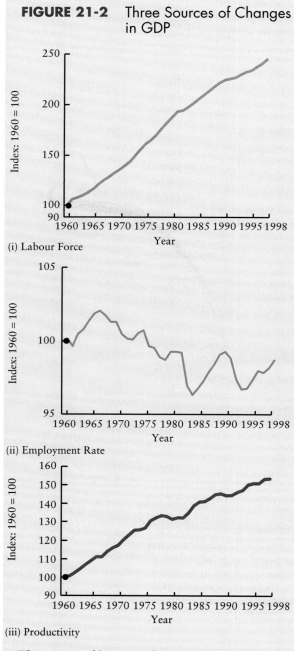

FIGURE 21-2   Three Sources of Changes in GDP

(i) Labour Force

(ii) Employment Rate

(iii) Productivity

The sources of long-run changes in GDP differ from the sources of short-run changes in GDP. Panel (i) shows the upward trend in the Canadian labour force. Panel (iii) shows the upward tend in productivity, measured as GDP per worker. Both show substantial growth over the long run, but relatively small short-run fluctuations. Panel (ii) shows the employment rate, the fraction of the labour force that is employed. It shows almost no long-run trend but considerable short-run fluctuations.

to one minus the unemployment rate). And the measure of productivity—in this case, labour productivity—is GDP/E.

Figure 21-2 shows the behaviour of these three components for Canada beginning in 1960. Each variable is expressed as an index number, with the value in 1960 set equal to 100. Expressing each variable in this way makes it easy to see each variable's percentage change over the four decades. The first panel in the figure shows the growth of the Canadian labour force. From 1960 to1998, the index number increased from 100 to 245, an increase of 145 percent. It is clear from the graph that any short-run fluctuations in the Canadian labour force are dwarfed in importance by the long-run upward trend.

Now look at the third panel, showing the growth of Canadian labour productivity. The level of GDP per person employed, expressed as an index number, increases from 100 in 1960 to 169 in 1998, an increase of 69 percent. Like the labour force, the level of labour productivity has its short-run fluctuations, but it is clear that the overriding change—the upward trend—takes place over many years.

Finally, consider the middle panel, showing the Canadian employment rate—the utilization rate of labour. Compared to the other two variables graphed in Figure 21-2, the employment rate shows much more short-run volatility and much less long-run change. The employment rate (expressed as an index number) falls slightly from 100 in 1960 to 98 in 1998, a long-run decrease of only 2 percent. There is very little change over the long run, but considerable changes are occurring over shorter periods of time.

Summing Up

To summarize, we can account for *any* change in GDP by changes in factor supply, the factor utilization rate, and productivity. But these three components typically contribute to GDP changes over different spans of time. In particular, factor supply and productivity typically change very slowly over time and hence are important for explaining long-run changes in GDP, but are not usually helpful in explaining short-run changes in GDP. In contrast, the factor utilization rate typically changes substantially over short periods of time but returns to its normal level over several years. Thus, changes in the factor utilization rate are important for explaining short-run changes in GDP but are not of central importance for explaining long-run changes.

Policy Implications

Because of this important difference between the source of short-run and long-run changes in GDP, economists think differently about short-run and long-run macroeconomic relationships. When thinking about short-run fluctuations, economists focus on understanding why actual GDP deviates from potential GDP. As we said above, such deviations are usually explained by changes in the demand for output. Thus, in understanding short-run fluctuations, economists focus on the *demand side* of the economy.

When thinking about long-run changes in GDP, however, economists focus on understanding why potential GDP changes over time. As we said above, such long-run growth has its source in the growth of factor supplies and productivity. Thus, in understanding long-run growth, economists focus on the *supply side* of the economy.

When studying short-run fluctuations, economists ignore changes in potential output and focus instead on the deviations of actual output from potential. When studying long-run changes, economists ignore such deviations and focus instead on changes in potential output.

Much of what we discuss in the chapters ahead will be explaining the details of this distinction between the short run and the long run. We will do so through the use of a formal macroeconomic model. Before we go on to build this model, however, it is useful to make one final point about what this distinction implies for the effects of macroeconomic policy. As we discussed in the examples at the beginning of this chapter, the long-run and short-run effects of policy are different.

We have discussed in this chapter how changes in demand may cause actual GDP to depart from potential GDP. For example, firms may feel optimistic about the future and increase their investment expenditure, thereby increasing the overall level of demand. Or the government may increase its purchases of goods and services, thus adding to demand. Or foreigners may decide to increase their demand for Canadian goods, thus adding to the overall demand for goods produced by Canadian firms. All of these changes would increase the overall level of demand in the economy and, in the short run, would lead actual GDP to rise above potential GDP. Conversely, any decrease in the demand for goods would, in the short run, cause actual GDP to fall below potential GDP.

We have also mentioned that the economy has an adjustment mechanism that returns the factor utilization rate to its "normal" level in the long run. In particular, when actual GDP is above potential GDP, there is an excess demand for factors. This causes factor prices to rise and thereby eliminates the excess demand, bringing actual GDP back to potential. Conversely, when actual GDP is less than potential GDP, there is an excess supply of factors. This causes factor prices to fall and eliminates the excess supply, thereby bringing actual GDP back to potential.

This adjustment process that brings the economy back to the level of potential output in the long run implies a stark result regarding the effects of macroeconomic policy:

Fiscal and monetary policies affect the short-run level of GDP because they alter the level of demand. But unless they are able to affect the level of *potential* output, they will have no long-run effect on GDP.

The consensus among economists is that monetary policy does *not* affect the level of potential output and thus does not have a long-run effect on GDP. As we will see in later chapters, monetary policy *does* affect the level of demand in the short run by changing interest rates and affecting firms' investment expenditures. But most economists believe, on the basis of both theory and considerable empirical evidence, that changes in monetary policy are *neutral* in the long run—that is, that monetary policy has long-run effects only on *nominal* variables such as nominal wages, the price level, and the rate of inflation.

There is also a broad consensus among economists that fiscal policy—in particular, a change in the level of government spending—*probably does* affect the level of potential output, but that it is *opposite* to its short-run effect on actual GDP. In the chapters ahead, we will see that when the government decides to increase its level of spending on goods and services, it will add to the overall level of demand. This stimulus to demand will, in the short run, lead to an increase in actual GDP. And in the long run, the adjustment process that we have discussed will bring the level of actual GDP back to potential GDP. In this case, however, the long-run effect of the higher level of government spending will actually be to *reduce* the level of potential GDP. The explanation is fairly involved and we will see it in detail later. But the basic story is that the higher government spending will push up interest rates and "crowd out" private spending, especially private investment. And less private investment in equipment and factories means less physical capital in the future and thus a lower level of potential output.

Looking Ahead

The discussion in this chapter has been centred around one topic—the difference between the short run and the long run in macroeconomics. We have shown that short-run movements in GDP are mostly accounted for by changes in the factor utilization rate, whereas long-run changes in GDP are mostly accounted for by changes in factor supplies and productivity. This difference forces economists to think differently about macroeconomic relationships that exist over a few months as compared to those that exist over several years.

In the next two chapters, we will explore the workings of a simple short-run model of the economy. In this model, we will see the emphasis on the demand side and understand why increases in demand usually lead to increases in actual GDP. In the following two chapters, we will discuss the adjustment process that takes the economy from the short run to the long run, so that actual GDP returns to potential GDP. With this basic macro model in place, we will then be ready to explore many interesting macroeconomic issues, such as inflation, unemployment, and government debt. A particularly important macroeconomic issue is the study of long-run economic growth, which we explore in Chapter 32.

As you learn about the formal macroeconomic model that we develop in the next few chapters, try not to lose sight of the central message in this chapter: understanding both short-run fluctuations and long-run trends is central to a complete understanding of macroeconomics and macroeconomic policy.

S U M M A R Y

Two Examples

- Macroeconomic variables behave differently over the short run than over the long run. One example: a monetary policy designed to reduce inflation and nominal interest rates in the long run requires an *increase* in interest rates in the short run. Another example: an increase in households' or firms' saving rates will reduce the level of output in the short run, but it will increase output in the long run.

- In the short run, there is some adjustment of output and employment, but little adjustment of wages and prices.

In the long run, full adjustment of wages and prices takes place.

Accounting for Changes in GDP

- All changes in GDP can be accounted for by changes in one or more of the following three variables:
  - supply of factors   LR ΔGDP
  - factor utilization rates SR ΔGDP
  - factor productivity   LR ΔGDP
- Long-run changes in GDP are caused mostly by changes in factor supplies and factor productivity; the utilization

rate of factors does not change significantly over the long run.
- Short-run changes in GDP are caused mostly by changes in the factor utilization rate; factor supplies and productivity have relatively minor short-run fluctuations.

Policy Implications

- When studying short-run fluctuations, economists focus on changes in the output gap and ignore changes in potential output. When studying long-run fluctuations, economists focus on changes in potential output and ignore changes in the output gap.

- Fiscal and monetary policies affect GDP in the short run because they affect the level of demand. Unless they are able to affect the level of *potential* output, they will have no long-run effect on GDP.

KEY CONCEPTS

Short-run fluctuations
Long-run trends

Changes in the output gap versus
  changes in potential output
Accounting for changes in GDP

Factor supplies
Factor utilization rates
Productivity

STUDY EXERCISES

1. Consider the data below for a hypothetical country.

Year	Real GDP (billions of real dollars)	Labour Force	Employment
		(millions of people)	
1950	100	1.5	1.4
1955	130	1.6	1.45
1960	175	1.75	1.55
1965	210	1.95	1.65
1970	230	2.15	1.85
1975	265	2.40	2.0
1980	300	2.70	2.2
1985	340	3.0	2.8
1990	375	3.3	3.05

a. Using the definitions in the chapter, compute the employment rate and the level of productivity (measured as GDP per worker) for each year.
b. For each 5-year period, compute the percentage change in the labour force, the employment rate, and the level of productivity. Compute the same three things over the entire 40-year period.
c. Compute the percentage change in real GDP over each 5-year period. Do it also for the entire 40-year period.
d. Based on Equation 21-1, it can be shown that the percentage change in real GDP is approximately equal to the percentage change in the labour force *plus* the percentage change in the employment rate

plus the percentage change in the level of productivity. Compare the sum of your answers from part **b.** with your answers from part **c.** Are they close?

e. For each 5-year period, what fraction of the percentage change in GDP is accounted for by the change in the employment rate?

f. Over the entire 40-year period, what fraction of the percentage change in GDP is accounted for by the change in the employment rate?

2. Go to Statistics Canada's website (*www.statcan.ca*) and look for data on capacity utilization rates in Canadian industries. The capacity utilization rate is, roughly, the fraction of the capital stock that is utilized or employed. How has this variable changed over the past several decades? Contrast the short-run versus the long-run movements.

DISCUSSION QUESTIONS

1. Figure 21-1 shows the path of actual GDP as well as the path of potential GDP. The chapter mentioned that the economy has an adjustment mechanism that brings actual GDP back to potential.

    a. Describe this adjustment process, and how it relates to the concept of market-clearing.

    b. If, following the implementation of some policy, actual GDP eventually returns to potential GDP, does this mean that policy can have no long-run effect on GDP? Constrast the long-run effects of monetary and fiscal policy.

PART EIGHT

National Income and Fiscal Policy

What determines the level of national income? Why, in the midst of a recession, does the government sometimes attempt to increase national income by spending a few billion dollars? During other recessions our elected leaders implore us to "go out and spend." Can such increased spending end a recession? At other times, when the economy has been growing quickly for several years, the government may be worried that any further spending will add to inflationary pressures. What then determines when an increase in spending leads to an increase in national income and when it leads to inflation? These are the sorts of questions you will be able to answer after reading the next four chapters.

Chapter 22 examines the determination of national income under the assumption that the price level is held constant. It introduces the simplest possible model of the macro economy to explain how equilibrium national income is determined. The key to understanding this model involves understanding the essential distinction between desired expenditure and actual expenditure. One of the key aspects of this model is the multiplier, which explains why a $1 billion increase in desired expenditure will end up increasing equilibrium national income by more than $1 billion.

Chapter 23 extends this simple model by adding a government sector and international trade. This is your introduction to fiscal policy; it is also the first time we see the relationship between the exchange rate and a country's exports and imports. Surprisingly, this more complicated model works in exactly the same way as the simple one but it allows us to consider a more realistic setting.

Chapter 24 removes the assumption of the fixed price level. We make the distinction between the demand side and the supply side of the economy and examine the important concepts of aggregate demand and aggregate supply. We then examine what is called macroeconomic equilibrium—the simultaneous determination of the equilibrium level of national income and the equilibrium price level.

Finally, Chapter 25 examines the behaviour of the economy in the long run—when the price level is free to adjust to excess demand or excess supply in the economy as a whole. We discuss the concepts of potential output, the output gap, and the Phillips Curve. The chapter ends with a detailed discussion of fiscal policy in the short run and in the long run. (Many of these issues will resurface in Chapter 31 when we examine government debt and deficits.)

CHAPTER 22

The Simplest Short-Run Macro Model

🔾 *LEARNING OBJECTIVES*

❶ Understand the difference between desired expenditure and actual expenditure.

❷ Explain the determinants of desired consumption and desired investment expenditures.

❸ Understand the meaning of equilibrium national income.

❹ Recognize the difference between movements along and shifts of the aggregate expenditure function.

❺ Explain how a change in desired expenditure affects equilibrium income, and how this change is reflected by the multiplier.

In Chapters 19 and 20, we encountered a number of important macroeconomic variables. We considered how they are measured and how they have behaved over the past several decades. We now turn to a more detailed study of what *causes* these variables to behave as they do. In particular, we study the forces that determine real national income and the price level.

Real national income and the price level are determined simultaneously. It is, however, easier to study them one at a time. So, in this chapter and the next, we simplify matters by seeing how real national income is determined *under the assumption that the price level is constant*. The simplified analysis will be an important first step toward understanding how prices and incomes are determined together, which is the subject of Chapters 24 and 25.

Our ability to explain the behaviour of real national income depends on our understanding of what determines the amount that households and firms spend. So, we begin with an examination of the expenditure decisions of households and firms.

Desired Expenditure

In Chapter 20, we discussed how national income statisticians divide *actual* GDP into its expenditure components: consumption, investment, government purchases, and net exports.

In this chapter and the next, we are concerned with a different concept. It is variously called *desired* or *planned* expenditure. Of course, all people would like to spend virtually unlimited amounts, if only they had the resources. Desired expenditure does not refer, however, to what people would like to do under imaginary circumstances; it refers to what people would like to spend out of the resources that are at their command. Recall from Chapter 20 that the *actual* values of the various categories of expenditure are indicated by C_a, I_a, G_a, and $(X_a - IM_a)$. Economists use the same letters without the subscript "a" to indicate the *desired* expenditure in the same categories: C, I, G, and $(X - IM)$.

Everyone makes expenditure decisions. Fortunately, it is unnecessary for our purposes to look at each of the millions of such individual decisions. Instead, it is sufficient to consider four main groups of decision makers: domestic households, firms, governments, and foreign purchasers of domestically produced commodities. The *actual* purchases made by these four groups account for the four main categories of expenditure that we studied in Chapter 20: consumption, investment, government purchases, and net exports. The sum of their *desired* expenditures on domestically produced output is called desired aggregate expenditure, or more simply **aggregate expenditure (*AE*)**:

$$AE = C + I + G + (X - IM)$$

Desired expenditure need not equal actual expenditure, either in total or in any individual category. For example, firms might not plan to invest in inventory accumulation this year but might do so unintentionally if sales are unexpectedly low—the unsold goods that pile up on their shelves are undesired inventory accumulation. In this case, actual investment expenditure, I_a, will exceed desired investment expenditure, I.

National income accounts measure *actual* expenditures in each of the four expenditure categories. National income theory deals with *desired* expenditures in each of these four categories.

You are probably wondering why the distinction between desired and actual expenditure is so important. The answer will become clear in the next section where we discuss the concept of *equilibrium* national income, which involves the relationship between desired and actual expenditure. For now, however, the remainder of this section examines more fully the various components of desired expenditure.

Autonomous Versus Induced Expenditure.

In what follows, it will be useful to distinguish between *autonomous* and *induced* expenditure. Components of aggregate expenditure that do *not* depend on national income are called **autonomous expenditures**. Autonomous expenditures can and do change, but such changes do not occur systematically in response to changes in national income. Components of aggregate expenditure that *do* change in response to changes in national income are called **induced expenditures**. As we will see, the induced response of desired aggregate expenditure to a change in national income plays a key role in the determination of equilibrium national income.

Important Simplifications.

Our goal in this chapter is to develop the simplest possible model of national-income determination. To do so, we focus on only two of the four components of desired aggregate expenditure—consumption and investment. Consumption is by far the largest component of aggregate expenditure; it also provides the most important link between desired aggregate expenditure and real national income. Investment is output that is used to add to the stock of physical capital rather than for current consumption purposes. It is much smaller than consumption but also

aggregate expenditure (*AE*) function   The function that relates desired aggregate expenditure to actual national income.

Because it is constant

autonomous expenditure   Elements of expenditure that do not vary systematically with national income.

induced expenditure   Any component of expenditure that is systematically related to national income.

much more volatile; understanding investment is therefore important for understanding fluctuations in real national income.

closed economy An economy that has no foreign trade.

We begin by considering a **closed economy**—that is, one that does not trade with other countries. We also suppose that there is no government and that the price level is constant. These assumptions are clearly extreme, but they serve a vital purpose. As we will see in this chapter, the presence of government and foreign trade is *not* essential to understanding the basic principles of national-income determination. By simplifying the model as much as possible, we are better able to understand the structure of this simple model.

In following chapters we will complicate our simple macro model by adding a government and international trade and then by removing the assumption of a fixed price level. The result will be a much more complete model of the macro economy. For now, however, we begin the discussion of our simplest model by considering the two crucial components of desired aggregate expenditure—consumption and investment.

Desired Consumption Expenditure

saving All disposable income that is not spent on consumption.

Households can do one of two things with their disposable income: spend it on consumption or save it. **Saving** is all disposable income that is not spent on consumption.

By definition, there are only two possible uses of disposable income—consumption and saving. When the household decides how much to put to one use, it has automatically decided how much to put to the other use.

What determines the division between the amount that households decide to consume and the amount they decide to save? The factors that influence this decision are summarized in the *consumption function* and the *saving function*.

The Consumption Function

consumption function The relationship between desired consumption expenditure and all the variables that determine it; in the simplest case, the relationship between consumption expenditure and disposable income.

The **consumption function** relates the total desired consumption expenditure of all households to the factors that determine it. It is, as we shall see, one of the central relationships in macroeconomics.

The consumption behaviour of households depends on the income that they actually have to spend, which is called their *disposable income*. Under the simplifying assumptions that we have made in this chapter, however, there are no taxes, and so all income that is generated is received by households. Therefore, disposable income, which we denote by Y_D, is equal to national income, Y.

It is not surprising that a household's expenditure is related to the amount of income that it has at its disposal. However, there is more than one way this relationship can work. To see what is involved, let's consider two quite different households.

The first household is short-sighted and spends everything it receives and puts nothing aside for a rainy day. When some overtime work results in a large paycheque, the members of the household go out and spend it. When it is hard to find work, the household's paycheque is small and its members reduce their expenditures. This household's monthly expenditure is therefore exactly equal to its current disposable income.

The second household is forward-looking. Its members think about the future as much as the present and make plans that stretch over their lifetimes. They put money aside for retirement and for the occasional rainy day when disposable income may fall temporarily. An unexpected windfall of income will be saved. An unexpected shortfall of income will be cushioned by spending some of the accumulated savings that were put aside for just such a rainy day. In short, this household's current expenditure will be closely related to its expected *lifetime income*. Fluctuations in its *current income* will have little effect on its current consumption expenditure. Economists refer to this behaviour as *consumption smoothing*.

Figure 22-1 shows the difference between our two sample households, short-sighted and forward-looking, and how their respective consumption expenditure is related to their current disposable income.

John Maynard Keynes (1883–1946), the famous English economist who developed much of the basic theory of macroeconomics—and gave his name to Keynesian economics—inhabited his theory with households whose current consumption expenditure depended mostly on their current income. But these households are not as extreme as the short-sighted households we discussed above. Keynes did not assume that households *never* saved. He simply assumed that their current level of expenditure and saving depended on their *current* level of income. To this day, a consumption function based on this assumption is called a *Keynesian consumption function*.

Practise with Study Guide Chapter 22, Exercise 1.

During the 1950s, two U.S. economists, Franco Modigliani and Milton Friedman, both of whom were subsequently awarded Nobel Prizes in economics, analysed the behaviour of forward-looking households. Their theories, which Modigliani called the *life-cycle theory* and Friedman called the *permanent-income theory*, explain some observed consumer behaviour that cannot be explained by the Keynesian consumption function.

The differences between the theories of Keynes, on the one hand, and Friedman and Modigliani, on the other, are not as great as it might seem at first sight. To see why this is so, let us return to our two imaginary households.

Even the extremely short-sighted household may be able to do some consumption smoothing in the face of income fluctuations. Most households have some money in the bank and some ability to borrow, even if it is just from friends and relatives. As a result, every change in income need not be matched by a proportional change in consumption expenditures.

In contrast, although the forward-looking household wants to smooth its pattern of consumption completely, it may not have the borrowing capacity to do so. Its bank may not be willing to lend money for consumption when the security consists of nothing more than the *expectation* that the household's income will be much higher in later years. As a result, the household's consumption expenditure might fluctuate with its current income more than it would wish.

The foregoing discussion suggests that the consumption expenditure of both types of households will fluctuate to some extent with their current disposable incomes and to some extent with their expectations of future disposable income.

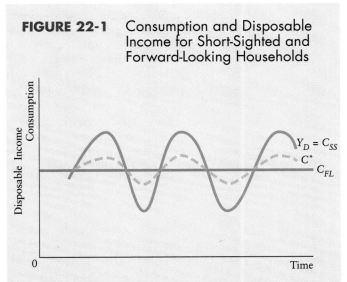

FIGURE 22-1   Consumption and Disposable Income for Short-Sighted and Forward-Looking Households

How consumption relates to current disposable income depends on whether the household is short-sighted or forward-looking. Disposable income, Y_D, is shown to fluctuate over time. If the household is short-sighted, it doesn't think about the future and thus spends all of its income each year. Its consumption rises and falls with its income, so its path of consumption, C_{SS}, is the same as the path of Y_D. A forward-looking household plans for the future and wants to smooth its consumption as much as possible. Its path of consumption is given by C_{FL}. When Y_D exceeds C_{FL}, the forward-looking household is saving; when Y_D is less than C_{FL}, the household is spending from its accumulated savings. If the economy is made up of both types of households, the *average* household will have a pattern of consumption that is smoother than C_{SS} but not as smooth as C_{FL}—a path like C^*. Aggregate consumption will rise when aggregate disposable income rises; consumption will fall when disposable income falls.

Moreover, in any economy there will be households of both types, both spendthrifts and planners, and aggregate consumption will be determined by a mix of the two types. The consumption behaviour for the *average* household in such an economy is shown in Figure 22-1 as the path C^*. Consumption fluctuates in response to changes in disposable income, rising when income rises and falling when income falls.

The consumption function describes the relationship between consumption and the variables that influence it; in the simplest theory, consumption is determined primarily by current disposable income.

When a household's income is zero, it will still consume some minimal amount (via begging, borrowing, or drawing down savings). This level of consumption expenditure is *autonomous* because it persists even when there is no income. The higher a household's income, the more it will want to consume. This part of consumption is *induced;* that is, it varies with disposable income.

Consider the schedule relating disposable income to desired consumption expenditure for a hypothetical economy that appears in the first two columns of the table in Figure 22-2. In this example, autonomous consumption expenditure is $30 billion, whereas induced consumption expenditure is 80 percent of disposable income (for every $1 increase in disposable income, there is an 80 cent increase in consumption). The equation for this simple consumption function is $C = a + b\,Y_D$ where a is equal to $30 billion and b is equal to 0.8. In what follows, we use this hypothetical example to illustrate the various properties of the consumption function.

Average and Marginal Propensities to Consume.

To discuss the consumption function concisely, economists use two technical expressions.

average propensity to consume (APC)
The level of consumption divided by the level of disposable income.

The **average propensity to consume** *(APC)* is total consumption expenditure divided by total disposable income:

$$APC = C/Y_D$$

The fourth column of the table in Figure 22-2 shows the *APC* calculated from the data in the table. Note that *APC* falls as disposable income rises.

marginal propensity to consume (MPC)
The change in consumption divided by the change in disposable income that brought it about.

The **marginal propensity to consume** *(MPC)* relates the *change* in desired consumption to the *change* in disposable income that brought it about. *MPC* is the change in desired consumption divided by the change in disposable income:

$$MPC = \Delta C/\Delta Y_D,$$

where the Greek letter Δ, delta, means "a change in." The last column of the table in Figure 22-2 shows the *MPC* that corresponds to the data in the table. Note that by construction in this example, the *MPC* is constant. [29]

The Slope of the Consumption Function.

Part (i) of Figure 22-2 shows a graph of the consumption function. The consumption function has a slope of $\Delta C/\Delta Y_D$, which is, by definition, the marginal propensity to consume. The positive slope of the consumption function shows that the *MPC* is positive; increases in income lead to increases in consumption expenditure.

The 45° Line.

Figure 22-2(i) contains a line that is constructed by connecting all points where desired consumption (measured on the vertical axis) equals disposable income (measured on the horizontal axis). Because both axes are given in the same units, this line has a positive slope equal to one; that is, it forms an angle of 45° with the axes. The line is therefore called the *45° line*.

The 45° line is a useful reference line. In part (i) of Figure 22-2, the consumption function cuts the 45° line at the break-even level of income—in this example, at $150 billion. The 45° line is also useful because its slope, which is equal to one, is greater than the slope of the consumption function, which is equal to the marginal propensity to consume. This is simply a graphic reminder that the *MPC* is less than one, and that the higher is the *MPC*, the steeper is the consumption function.

Disposable income can either be saved or spent on consumption goods. Bank deposits are one important form of saving.

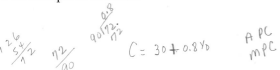

FIGURE 22-2   The Consumption and Saving Functions

Disposable Income (Y_D)	Desired Consumption (C)	Desired Saving (S)	APC = C/Y_D	ΔY_D	ΔC	MPC = $\Delta C/\Delta Y_D$
0	30	−30	—			
				30	24	0.8
30	54	−24	1.800			
				90	72	0.8
120	126	−6	1.050			
				30	24	0.8
150	150	0	1.000			
				150	120	0.8
300	270	30	0.900			
				150	120	0.8
450	390	60	0.867			
				75	60	0.8
525	450	75	0.857			
				75	60	0.8
600	510	90	0.850			

(i) Consumption function

(ii) Saving function

Both consumption and saving rise as disposable income rises. Line C in part (i) of the figure relates desired consumption expenditure to disposable income by plotting the data from the second column of the accompanying table. The consumption function cuts the 45° line at the break-even level of disposable income. Note that the level of autonomous consumption is $30 billion. The slope of the consumption function is equal to the marginal propensity to consume, which is shown in the table to be 0.8.

The relationship between desired saving and disposable income is shown in part (ii) by line S, which plots the data from the third column of the table. The vertical distance between C and the 45° line in part (i) is by definition the height of S in part (ii); that is, any given level of disposable income must be either consumed or saved. Note that the level of autonomous saving is −$30 billion.

The Saving Function

Households decide how much to consume and how much to save. As we have said, this is only a single decision—how to divide disposable income between consumption and saving. It follows that once we know the dependence of consumption on disposable income, we automatically know the dependence of saving on disposable income.

There are two saving concepts that are exactly parallel to the consumption concepts of *APC* and *MPC*. The **average propensity to save (APS)** is the proportion of disposable income that households want to save, computed by dividing total desired saving by total disposable income:

$$APS = S/Y_D$$

The **marginal propensity to save (MPS)** relates the change in desired saving to the change in disposable income that brought it about:

$$MPS = \Delta S/\Delta Y_D$$

There is a simple relationship between the saving and the consumption propensities. *APC* and *APS* must sum to one, and so must *MPC* and *MPS*. Because all disposable income is either spent or saved, it follows that the fractions of income consumed and saved must account for all income (*APC* + *APS* = 1). It also follows that the fractions of any *increment* to income consumed and saved must account for all of that increment (*MPC* + *MPS* = 1). [30]

Calculations from the table in Figure 22-2 will allow you to confirm these relationships in the case of the example given. Figure 22-2(ii) shows the saving function. Where desired consumption equals disposable income, desired saving is zero. The slope of the saving function, $\Delta S/\Delta Y_D$, is equal to the *MPS*.

Wealth and the Consumption Function

We have been analysing the Keynesian consumption function—where consumption expenditure depends only on current disposable income. But this extreme depiction of consumption behaviour can easily be combined with the more recent life-cycle and permanent-income theories of consumption. According to these theories, households save to accumulate wealth that they can use during their retirement or during periods of unexpectedly low income. Suppose that there is an unexpected rise in aggregate wealth. This could be caused by an increase in the values of the shares that households own in the stock market. The increase in wealth means that less current income needs to be saved for the future and thus households will spend a larger fraction of income on current consumption. Hence, the consumption function will be shifted upward and the saving function downward, as shown in Figure 22-3. Conversely, a fall in wealth increases the incentive to save in order to restore wealth. This change shifts the consumption function downward and the saving function upward.

Practise with Study Guide Chapter 22, Exercise 3.

Consumption and Disposable Income in Canada

We have devoted considerable time and space to discussing the consumption function, as this relationship between desired consumption and disposable income is of central importance in the determination of national income. It is worthwhile, therefore, to take a brief look at actual data to see if such a relationship exists in Canada.

Figure 22-4 plots real per capita consumption expenditure against real per capita disposable income for Canada from 1977 to 1998. The straight line drawn through the data points is the straight line that shows the single "best fit" in the relationship between consumption and disposable income. Notice also the two clusters of points above and below the line of best fit. The cluster below the line corresponds to the significant recession in the early 1990s, when households increased their saving and reduced their consumption. The cluster above the line corresponds to the boom in the late 1990s when households did the opposite.

Keep in mind that when we simply plot the data and draw the line of best fit as in Figure 22-4, we are not accounting for changes in those variables that could *shift* the consumption function. Failure to account for such changes means that the true marginal propensity to consume is not necessarily well represented by the slope of the best-fit line. A precise estimate of the marginal propensity to consume therefore requires more complicated statistical techniques. (You will learn about the appropriate estimation methods if you go on to study econometrics.) For now, however, Figure 22-4 does give us a very rough estimate of the consumption function. It suggests that the theoretical consumption function we have been discussing is indeed broadly supported by a first glance at the Canadian data.

Desired Investment Expenditure

Investment expenditure is the most volatile component of GDP, and changes in investment expenditure are strongly associated with economic fluctuations. For example, as shown by the top line in Figure 22-5, total investment in Canada fell from over 18 percent of GDP in 1989, the peak of the business cycle, to 14.5 percent of GDP in 1993, the trough of the business cycle. Then, as GDP recovered from 1993 to 1999, investment increased back up toward its previous peak.

What explains such fluctuations in investment? Here we examine three important determinants of aggregate investment expenditure—the real interest rate, changes in sales, and business confidence.

Investment and the Real Interest Rate

The real interest rate represents the real cost of borrowing money for investment purposes. A rise in the real interest rate therefore reduces the amount of desired investment expenditure. This relationship is most easily seen if we separate investment into three components: inventories, residential construction, and plant and equipment.

Inventories. Changes in inventories represent only a small percentage of private investment in a typical year. As shown by the bottom line in Figure 22-5, inventory investment has always been between –2 percent and 2 percent of GDP over the past 20 years. But the average size of such changes is not an adequate measure of their importance. Since they

FIGURE 22-3 Wealth and the Consumption Function

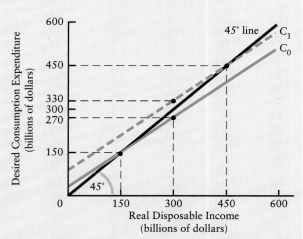

(i) The consumption function shifts upward with an increase in wealth

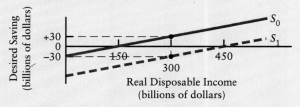

(ii) The saving function shifts downward with an increase in wealth

Changes in wealth shift the consumption function. In part (i), line C_0 reproduces the consumption function from Figure 22-2(i). An increase in wealth raises desired consumption at each level of disposable income, thus shifting the consumption function up to C_1. In the figure, the consumption function shifts up by $60 billion, so with disposable income of $300 billion, for example, desired consumption rises from $270 billion to $330 billion.

The saving function in part (ii) shifts down by $60 billion, from S_0 to S_1. Thus, for example, at a disposable income of $300 billion, desired saving falls from $30 billion to –$30 billion.

FIGURE 22-4   Consumption and Disposable Income, 1970–1998

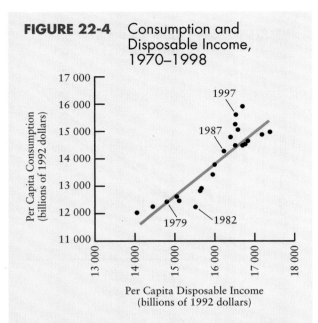

The Canadian data suggest a clear, positive relationship between consumption and income. The figure plots real per capita consumption on the vertical axis and real per capita disposable income on the horizontal axis. Each point corresponds to the data from one year. The straight line is the line which shows the single "best fit" in the relationship between consumption and income.

(*Source:* Data prior to 1992 are from Department of Finance, *Economic Reference Tables*, August 1995. Data after 1992 are from CANSIM; D28390, D28391.)

The largest part of investment by firms is the building of new plants and equipment, such as this expansion of a pulp mill in British Columbia.

are one of the more volatile elements of total investment, they have an important influence on fluctuations in investment expenditure.

When a firm ties up funds in inventories, those same funds cannot be used elsewhere to earn income. As an alternative to holding inventories, the firm could lend the money out at the going rate of interest. Hence, the higher the real rate of interest, the higher the opportunity cost of holding an inventory of a given size; the higher the opportunity cost, the smaller the inventories that will be desired.

Residential Construction.   Expenditure on residential housing is also volatile. Most houses are purchased with money that is borrowed by means of mortgages. Interest on the borrowed money typically accounts for over one-half of the purchaser's annual mortgage payments; the remainder is repayment of the original loan, called the *principal*. Because interest payments are such a large part of mortgage payments, variations in interest rates exert a substantial effect on the demand for housing.

Plant and Equipment.   Investment in plant and equipment is the largest component of domestic investment. Over one-half is financed by firms' retained earnings (profits that are not paid out to shareholders). Current profits are thus an important determinant of investment.

The rate of interest is also a major determinant of investment in plant and equipment. When interest rates are high, it is expensive for firms to borrow funds that can be used for fixed investment. At the same time, firms with cash on hand can earn high returns on interest-earning assets, again making investment in plant and equipment a less attractive alternative. Thus, high real interest rates lead to reduced investment in plant and equipment, and low real interest rates increase such investment.

The real interest rate reflects the opportunity cost associated with investment, whether it is investment in inventories, residential construction, or plant and equipment. The higher the real interest rate, the higher the opportunity cost of investment, and thus the lower the amount of desired investment.

Figure 22-5 shows these three components of investment over the past 20 years. Inventory investment is clearly the smallest of the three but in relative terms is the most volatile. Note that the three components move broadly together. They all fell in the 1981–82 recession, and again in the 1990–91 recession.

Investment and Changes in Sales

Studies show that the stock of inventories tends to rise as production and sales rise. Because the size of inventories is related to the level of sales, the *change* in inventories (which is part of current investment) is related to the *change* in the level of sales.

Suppose a firm wants to hold inventories equal to 10 percent of its sales. If sales are $100 000, it will wish to hold inventories of $10 000. If sales increase to $110 000, it will want to hold inventories of $11 000. Over the period during which its stock of inventories is being increased, there will be a total of $1000 of new inventory investment.

The higher the level of production and sales, the larger the desired stock of inventories. Changes in the rate of production and sales therefore cause temporary bouts of investment (or disinvestment) in inventories.

Changes in sales have similar effects on investment in plant and equipment. For example, if there is a general increase in consumers' demand for products that is expected to persist and that cannot be met by existing capacity, investment in new plant and equipment will be needed. Once the new plants have been built and put into operation, however, the rate of new investment will fall.

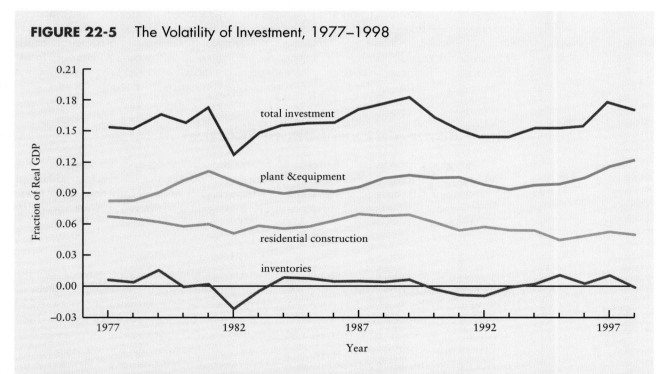

FIGURE 22-5   The Volatility of Investment, 1977–1998

Total investment as a share of GDP fluctuates considerably. In percentage terms, changes in inventories are the most volatile component of investment.

(*Source: Bank of Canada Review,* Winter 1998–99.)

Investment and Business Confidence

Investment takes time. When a firm invests, it increases its future capacity to produce output. If it can sell the new output profitably, the investment will prove to be a good one. If the new output does not generate profits, the investment will have been a bad one. When it undertakes an investment, the firm does not know if it will turn out well or badly—it is betting on a favourable future that cannot be known with certainty.

When firms expect good times ahead, they will want to invest now so that they have a larger productive capacity in the future ready to satisfy the greater demand. When they expect bad times ahead, they will not invest because they expect no payoff from doing so.

Investment depends in part on firms' forecasts of the future state of the economy.

Investment as Autonomous Expenditure

We have seen that investment is influenced by many things, and a complete discussion of the determination of national income is not possible without including all of these factors.

For the moment, however, our goal is to build the *simplest* model of the aggregate economy in which we can examine the interaction of actual national income and desired aggregate expenditure. To build this simple model, we begin by treating investment as *autonomous*—that is, it is unaffected by changes in national income.

In later chapters, we will complicate this simple model—making investment into an induced expenditure flow by linking changes in national income to changes in investment via induced changes in interest rates. For now, however, we simply assume that desired investment does not vary with changes in national income.

The Aggregate Expenditure Function

The Conference Board of Canada publishes regular surveys of business and consumer confidence. Visit their website: www.conferenceboard.ca.

aggregate expenditure (AE) function   The function that relates aggregate desired expenditure to actual national income.

The **aggregate expenditure *(AE)* function** relates the level of desired expenditure to the level of actual income. (In both cases we mean *real* as opposed to *nominal* variables.) In the simplified economy of this chapter, in which there is no government and no international trade, desired aggregate expenditure is just equal to desired consumption plus desired investment, $C + I$.

$$AE = C + I$$

The table in Figure 22-6 shows how the *AE* function can be calculated, given the consumption function from Figure 22-2 and a constant level of desired investment of $75 billion. In this specific case, all of investment expenditure is autonomous, as is the $30 billion of consumption that would be desired if national income were equal to zero. Total autonomous expenditure is therefore $105 billion—induced expenditure is just equal to induced consumption, which is equal to the *MPC* times disposable income ($0.8 \times Y_D$). Furthermore, since our simple model has no government and no taxes, disposable income, Y_D, is equal to national income, Y. Hence, desired aggregate expenditure can be written as:

$$AE = \$105 \text{ billion} + 0.8 \times Y$$

The Propensity to Spend Out of National Income

The fraction of any increment to national income that people spend on purchasing domestic output is called the economy's **marginal propensity to spend.** The marginal propensity to spend is measured by the change in desired aggregate expenditure divided by the change in national income, or $\Delta AE/\Delta Y$, the slope of the aggregate expenditure function. In this book, the marginal propensity to spend is denoted by the symbol z, which is a number greater than zero and less than one.

For the example given in Figure 22-6, the marginal propensity to spend is 0.8. If national income increases by a dollar, 80 cents will go into increased expenditure; 20 cents will go into increased saving and will not be spent.

The marginal propensity to spend should not be confused with the marginal propensity to consume.

The marginal propensity to spend is the amount of extra total expenditure induced when national income rises by $1, whereas the marginal propensity to consume is the amount of extra consumption expenditure induced when households' disposable income rises by $1.

In the simple model of this chapter, the marginal propensity to spend is equal to the marginal propensity to consume. In later chapters, however, when we add government and international trade to the model, the marginal propensity to spend differs from the marginal propensity to consume. Both here and in later chapters, it is the more general measure—the marginal propensity to spend—that is important for determining equilibrium national income.

marginal propensity to spend (MPS) The change in total desired spending on domestic output divided by the change in national income that brought it about.

FIGURE 22-6 The Aggregate Expenditure Function

National Income (Y)	Desired Consumption Expenditure (C = 30 + 0.8 × Y)	Desired Investment Expenditure (I = 75)	Desired Aggregate Expenditure (AE = C + I)
30	54	75	129
120	126	75	201
150	150	75	225
300	270	75	345
450	390	75	465
525	450	75	525
600	510	75	585
900	750	75	825

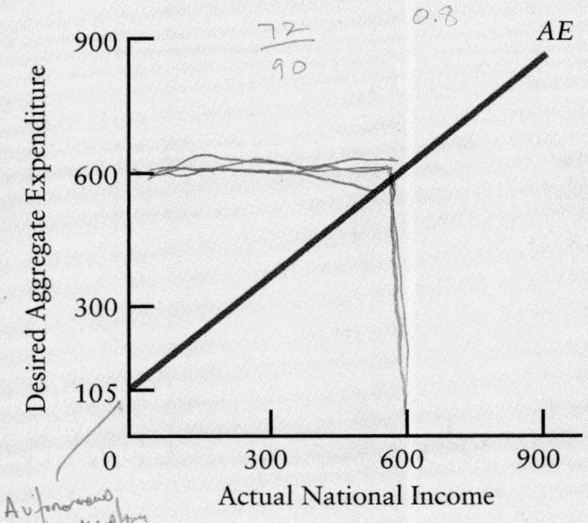

The aggregate expenditure function relates total desired expenditure to actual national income. The curve AE in the figure plots the data from the first and last columns of the accompanying table. Its intercept, which in this case is $105 billion, shows the sum of autonomous consumption and autonomous investment. Its slope is equal to the marginal propensity to spend (which in this simple economy is just the marginal propensity to consume).

Equilibrium National Income

We are now ready to see what determines the *equilibrium* level of national income. When something is in equilibrium, there is no tendency for it to change. Any conditions that are required for something to be in equilibrium are called its *equilibrium conditions*. We will see that the distinction between desired and actual expenditure is central to the equilibrium conditions for national income.

Desired Expenditure and Actual Output

Table 22-1 illustrates the determination of equilibrium national income for our simple hypothetical economy. Suppose that firms are producing a final output of $300 billion, and thus national income is $300 billion. According to the table, at this level of income, aggregate desired expenditure is $345 billion. If firms persist in producing a current output of only $300 billion in the face of an aggregate desired expenditure of $345 billion, one of two things will happen.

One possibility is that households and firms will be unable to spend the extra $45 billion that they would like to spend, so lines or waiting lists of unsatisfied customers will appear. These shortages will send a signal to firms that they can increase their sales if they increase their production. When the firms increase production, national income rises. Of course, the individual firms are interested only in their own sales and profits, but their individual actions have as their inevitable consequence an increase in GDP.

A more realistic possibility is that all spenders will spend everything that they wanted to spend. In this case, however, expenditure will exceed current output, which can happen only if some sales come from the producers' accumulated inventories. In our example, the fulfillment of plans to purchase $345 billion worth of commodities in the face of a current output of only $300 billion will reduce inventories by $45 billion. As long as inventories last, more goods can be sold than are currently being produced.

Eventually, however, inventories will run out. But before this happens, firms will increase their outputs as they see their inventories being depleted. Extra sales can then be made without a further depletion of inventories. Once again, the consequence of each individual firm's behaviour is an increase in national income. Thus, the final response to an excess of aggregate desired expenditure over actual output is a rise in national income.

For any level of national income at which aggregate desired expenditure exceeds actual income, there will be pressure for national income to rise.

TABLE 22-1 Equilibrium National Income
(billions of dollars)

National Income (Y)	Desired Aggregate Expenditure (AE = C + I)	Effect
30	129	Pressure
120	201	on income
150	225	to rise
300	345	↓
450	465	↓
525	525	Equilibrium income
600	585	↑
900	825	Pressure on income to fall

National income is in equilibrium when aggregate desired expenditure equals actual national income. The data are from Figure 22-6.

Next consider the $900 billion level of national income in Table 22-1. At this level, desired expenditure on domestically produced goods is only $825 billion. If firms persist in producing $900 billion worth of goods, $75 billion worth must remain unsold. Therefore, inventories must rise. However, firms will not allow inventories of unsold goods to rise indefinitely; sooner or later, they will reduce the level of output to the level of sales. When they do, national income will fall.

For any level of income at which aggregate desired expenditure is less than actual output, there will be pressure for national income to fall.

Finally, look at the national income level of $525 billion in Table 22-1. At this level, and only at this level, aggregate desired expenditure is equal to actual national income. Purchasers can fulfill their spending plans without causing inventories to change. There is no incentive for firms to alter output. Because everyone wishes to purchase an amount equal to what is being produced, output and income will remain steady; they are in equilibrium.

The equilibrium level of national income occurs where aggregate desired expenditure equals actual national income.

Desired Saving and Desired Investment

We have just seen that equilibrium national income occurs where desired aggregate expenditure equals actual national income. The same equilibrium can also be described as the level of national income where *desired saving equals desired investment.*

The saving-investment formulation of the model is useful because it adds perspective on how equilibrium national income is determined. Later in this book, the saving-investment formulation will illuminate a key issue in economic policy—the influence of macroeconomic policy on long-run economic growth. Since investment adds to an economy's stock of productive resources, investment is often the only way for new and better technologies to be introduced to the workplace. In the long run, the level of a country's saving, through its effect on investment, can exert an important influence on economic growth. We are not yet ready to explore this important point, but when we are, the saving-investment balance will be an important part of the story. For now, our goal is to show that the equilibrium level of national income can be examined in terms of desired saving and desired investment.

Table 22-2 repeats data from Table 22-1, with three columns added: desired consumption, desired saving (which is disposable income minus desired consumption), and investment. Careful examination of this table reveals an important point: *The difference between desired investment and desired saving is exactly equal to the difference between desired aggregate expenditure and actual national income.*

This equality is no accident, but rather comes straight from the definition of desired aggregate expenditure. To see this, suppose the difference between desired saving and desired investment is equal to some number, W. Thus,

$$S - I = W$$

Now, recall that we use Y to denote actual national income, and that desired saving is just equal to actual national income minus desired consumption, $S = Y - C$. We can therefore rewrite the equation above to get

$$Y - C - I = W$$

TABLE 22-2 The Saving-Investment Balance

National Income (Y)	Desired Aggregate Expenditure ($AE = C + I$)	Desired Consumption ($C = 30 + 0.8 \times Y$)	Desired Saving ($S = Y - C$)	Desired Investment (I)
30	129	54	−24	75
120	201	126	−6	75
300	345	270	30	75
525	525	450	75	75
600	585	510	90	75
900	825	750	150	75

National income is in equilibrium where desired saving is equal to desired investment. The data for Y, AE, and I are from Figure 22-2. At every level of national income, the difference between national income and desired aggregate expenditure is exactly equal to the difference between desired saving and desired investment.

But since desired aggregate expenditure is just the sum of desired consumption and desired investment, $AE = C + I$, we can rewrite the equation again to get

$$Y - (C + I) = W$$
$$\Rightarrow Y - AE = W$$

Thus, the difference between desired saving and desired investment is always equal to the difference between actual national income and desired aggregate expenditure.

In the simple model of this chapter, with no government and no international trade, the difference between desired saving and desired investment is exactly the same as the difference between actual national income and desired aggregate expenditure. Thus, the economy is in equilibrium when desired investment equals desired saving.

Practise with Study Guide Chapter 22, Exercise 5.

Equilibrium Illustrated

Figure 22-7 shows the determination of the equilibrium level of national income. The line labeled AE graphs the specific aggregate expenditure function that we have been working with throughout this chapter. The 45° line ($AE = Y$) graphs the equilibrium condition that aggregate desired expenditure equals actual national income. Anywhere along the 45° line, the value of desired aggregate expenditure, which is measured on the vertical axis, is equal to the value of actual national income, which is measured on the horizontal axis.[1]

Graphically, equilibrium occurs at the level of income at which the AE line intersects the 45° line. This is the level of income where desired expenditure is just equal to actual national income and hence is just sufficient to purchase total final output.

---

[1]Because it turns up in many different guises, the 45° line can cause a bit of confusion until one gets used to it. The main thing to remember is that it can be used whenever the variables plotted on the two axes are measured in the same units, such as dollars, and are plotted on the same scale. In that case, equal distances on the two axes measure the same amounts.

The equilibrium is also illustrated in part (ii) of the figure, but in terms of the saving-investment balance. The line labeled S is equal to desired saving. The line labeled I is desired investment.

Notice that the vertical distance between S and I is exactly equal to the distance between the 45° line and AE. When desired investment exceeds desired saving, desired aggregate expenditure exceeds actual national income by the same amount. When desired investment is less than desired saving, desired aggregate expenditure is less than actual national income by the same amount.

Now that we have explained the meaning of equilibrium national income, we will go on to examine the various forces that can *change* this equilibrium. We will then be well on our way to understanding some of the sources of short-run fluctuations in national income.

Changes in Equilibrium National Income

Because the AE function plays a central role in determining equilibrium national income, you should not be surprised to hear that *shifts* in the AE function are central to explaining why national income changes. To understand this influence, we must recall an important distinction we first encountered in Chapter 3—the distinction between *shifts of* a curve and *movements along* a curve.

Suppose that desired aggregate expenditure rises. This may be a response to a change in national income, or it may be the result of an increased desire to spend *at each level* of national income. A change in national income causes a *movement along* the AE function. An increased desire to spend at each level of national income causes a *shift of* the AE function. Figure 22-8 illustrates this important distinction.

Shifts of the *AE* Function

The AE function shifts when one of its components shifts—that is, when there is a shift in the consumption function or in desired investment expenditure.

Upward Shifts in the *AE* Function

What will happen if households experience an increase in wealth and thus increase their desired levels of consumption spending at each level of disposable income? What

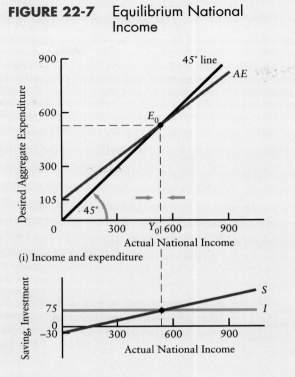

FIGURE 22-7   Equilibrium National Income

Equilibrium national income is that level of national income where desired aggregate expenditure equals actual national income. If actual national income is below Y_0 in panel (i), desired aggregate expenditure will exceed national income, and output will rise. This is shown by the arrow to the left of Y_0. If national income is above Y_0, desired aggregate expenditure will be less than national income, and production will fall. This is shown by the arrow to the right of Y_0. Only when national income is equal to Y_0 will the economy be in equilibrium.

Panel (ii) shows desired saving and desired investment on the same scale as panel (i). Equilibrium national income occurs where desired saving equals desired investment. The vertical distance between saving and investment is exactly the same as the vertical distance in part (i) between AE and the 45° line.

FIGURE 22-8   Movements Along and Shifts of the *AE* Function

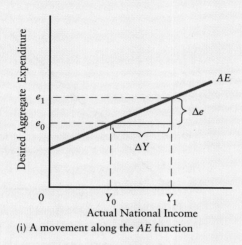

(i) A movement along the *AE* function

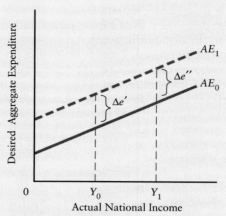

(ii) A shift of the *AE* function

A movement along the *AE* function occurs in response to a change in national income; a shift of the *AE* function indicates a different level of desired expenditure at each level of national income. In part (i), a change in income of ΔY, from Y_0 to Y_1, changes desired expenditure by Δe, from e_0 to e_1. In part (ii), a shift in the *AE* function from AE_0 to AE_1 raises the amount of desired expenditure associated with each level of national income. At Y_0, for example, desired aggregate expenditure is increased by $\Delta e'$; at Y_1, it is increased by $\Delta e''$. (If the *AE* function shifts in a parallel manner, then $\Delta e' = \Delta e''$.)

will happen if the expectation of higher future sales causes domestic auto makers to increase their planned investment?

Because any such increase in autonomous expenditure shifts the entire *AE* function upward, the same analysis applies to each of the changes mentioned. Two types of shift in *AE* can occur. First, if the same addition to expenditure occurs at all levels of income, the *AE* function shifts parallel to itself, as shown in part (i) of Figure 22-9. Second, if there is a change in the marginal propensity to spend, the slope of the *AE* function changes, as shown in part (ii) of Figure 22-9.

Figure 22-9 shows that an upward shift in the *AE* function increases equilibrium national income. After the shift in the *AE* curve, income is no longer in equilibrium at its original level because at that level desired expenditure exceeds actual national income. Given this excess demand, firms' inventories are being depleted and firms then respond by increasing production. Equilibrium national income rises to the higher level indicated by the intersection of the new *AE* curve with the 45° line.

Downward Shifts in the Saving Function.   We saw earlier that, in equilibrium, desired aggregate expenditure is equal to actual national income, and desired saving is equal to desired investment. When the *AE* function shifts and equilibrium income changes, this equality must still hold true at the new equilibrium.

Consider the case of a shift in the *AE* function that is caused by a shift in the consumption function. As we discussed earlier (see Figure 22-2), when the consumption function shifts, the saving function shifts as well, and by an equal and opposite amount. This is true because consumption and saving always adds up to disposable income.

FIGURE 22-9   Shifts in the Aggregate Expenditure Function

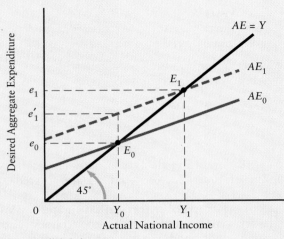

(i) A parallel shift in *AE*

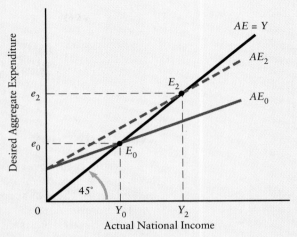

(ii) A change in the slope of *AE*

Upward shifts in the *AE* function increase equilibrium income; downward shifts decrease equilibrium income. In parts (i) and (ii), the *AE* function is initially AE_0 with equilibrium national income equal to Y_0.

In part (i), a parallel upward shift in the *AE* curve from AE_0 to AE_1 reflects an increase in desired expenditure at each level of national income. For example, at Y_0, desired expenditure rises from e_0 to e_1' and therefore exceeds national income. Equilibrium is reached at E_1, where income is Y_1. The increase in desired expenditure from e_1' to e_1, represented by a movement along AE_1, is an induced response to the increase in income from Y_0 to Y_1.

In part (ii), a nonparallel upward shift in the *AE* curve from AE_0 to AE_2 reflects an increase in the marginal propensity to spend. This leads to an increase in equilibrium national income. Equilibrium is reached at E_2, where national income is equal to Y_2.

Hence, if the consumption function shifts up by some amount at every level of income, the saving function *must* shift down by exactly the same amount.

Figure 22-10 shows a downward shift in the saving function (corresponding to an upward shift in the consumption function). Equilibrium national income occurs where desired saving equals desired investment. With desired investment fixed, a downward shift in the saving function leads to an *increase* in equilibrium national income. This is just as it should be—a downward shift in the saving function implies an upward shift in the consumption and *AE* functions.

Downward Shifts in the *AE* Function

What happens to national income if there is a decrease in the amount of consumption or investment expenditure desired at each level of income? These changes shift the *AE* function downward. A constant reduction in desired expenditure at all levels of income shifts *AE* parallel to itself. A fall in the marginal propensity to spend out of national income reduces the slope of the *AE* function. When we use the saving-investment relation, we must note that a downward shift in the consumption function implies an upward shift in the saving function, reducing the equilibrium level of income.

The Results Restated

We have derived two important general propositions from our simple model of national income determination.

1. A rise in the amount of desired aggregate expenditure associated with each level of national income will increase equilibrium national income.

2. A fall in the amount of desired aggregate expenditure associated with each level of national income will reduce equilibrium national income.

The Multiplier

We have learned how to predict the direction of the changes in national income that occur in response to various shifts in the AE function. We would like also to predict the *magnitude* of these changes.

Economists need to know the *size* of the effects of changes in expenditures. During a recession, the government sometimes takes measures to stimulate the economy. If these measures have a larger effect than estimated, demand may rise too much, and full employment may be reached while demand is still rising. As we will see in Chapters 24 and 25, this outcome will have an inflationary effect on the economy. On the other hand, if the government overestimates the impact of its measures, the recession will persist longer than necessary. In this case, there is a danger that the policy will be discredited as ineffective, even though the correct diagnosis is that too little of the right thing was done.

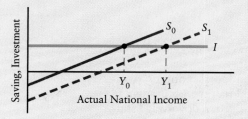

FIGURE 22-10 Shifts in Desired Saving

A downward shift in the saving function increases equilibrium national income. If the consumption function shifts up, the saving function must shift down by an equal amount, indicating a reduction in desired saving at every level of national income. Since equilibrium occurs where desired saving equals desired investment, the new equilibrium occurs at a higher national income—the economy moves from Y_0 to Y_1. The saving function has indeed shifted down, but the increase in equilibrium income has caused a movement *along* the new S_1 function and restored the level of saving to its previous level.

Defining the Multiplier

A measure of the magnitude of changes in national income is provided by the *multiplier*. We have just seen that a shift in the AE curve will cause a change in equilibrium national income. Such a shift could be caused by a change in any autonomous component of aggregate expenditure. An increase in desired aggregate expenditure increases equilibrium national income by a *multiple* of the initial increase in autonomous expenditure. That is, the increase in national income is *larger than* the initial increase in desired expenditure.

The multiplier is the change in equilibrium national income divided by the change in autonomous expenditure that brought it about. In the simple macro model, the multiplier is greater than one.

To see why the multiplier is greater than one, consider a simple example. Imagine what would happen to national income if Kimberley-Clark decided to spend $500 million per year on new paper mills. Initially, the construction of the paper mills would create $500 million worth of new national income and a corresponding amount of income for households and firms on which the initial $500 million is spent. But this is not the end of the story. The increase in national income of $500 million would cause an increase in disposable income, which would cause an induced rise in consumption expenditure.

Electricians, masons, and carpenters—who gain new income directly from the building of the paper mills—would spend some of it on food, clothing, entertainment, cars, TVs, and other commodities. When output expands to meet this demand, new incomes would be created for workers and firms in these industries. When they, in turn, spend their newly earned incomes, output would rise further. More income would be created, and more expenditure would be induced. Indeed, at this stage, we might wonder whether the increases in income would ever come to an end. To deal with this concern, we need to consider the multiplier in somewhat more precise terms.

Suppose we let autonomous expenditure be denoted by A. Now consider an increase in autonomous expenditure of ΔA, which in our example above was $500 million per year. Remember that ΔA stands for *any* increase in autonomous expenditure; this could be an increase in investment or in the autonomous component of consumption. The new autonomous expenditure shifts the AE function upward by that amount. National income is no longer in equilibrium at its original level because desired aggregate expenditure now exceeds actual income. Equilibrium is restored by a *movement along* the new AE curve.

The **simple multiplier** measures the change in equilibrium national income that occurs in response to a change in autonomous expenditure *at a constant price level*. We refer to it as "simple" because we have simplified the situation by assuming that the price level is fixed (an assumption we will remove following Chapter 23). Figure 22-11 illustrates the simple multiplier and makes clear that it is greater than one. *Applying Economic Concepts 22-1* provides a numerical example.

The Size of the Simple Multiplier

The size of the simple multiplier depends on the slope of the AE function—that is, on the marginal propensity to spend, z.

As shown in Figure 22-12, a high marginal propensity to spend means a steep AE curve. The expenditure induced by any initial increase in income is large, with the result that the final rise in income is correspondingly large. By contrast, a low marginal propensity to spend means a relatively flat AE curve. The expenditure induced by the initial increase in income is small, and the final rise in income is not much larger than the initial rise in autonomous expenditure that brought it about.

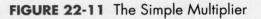

simple multiplier
The ratio of the change in equilibrium national income to the change in autonomous expenditure that brought it about, calculated for a constant price level. $\frac{\Delta Y}{\Delta AE}$

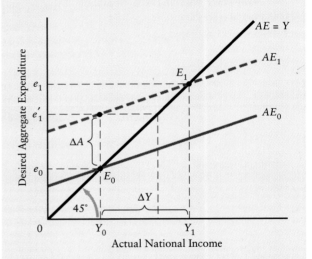

FIGURE 22-11 The Simple Multiplier

An increase in the autonomous component of desired aggregate expenditure increases equilibrium national income by a multiple of the initial increase. The initial equilibrium is at E_0, where AE_0 intersects the 45° line. At this point, desired expenditure, e_0, is equal to national income, Y_0. An increase in autonomous expenditure of ΔA then shifts the AE function upward to AE_1.

Equilibrium occurs when income rises to Y_1. Here desired expenditure, e_1, equals national income, Y_1. The increase in desired expenditure from e_1' to e_1 represents the induced increase in expenditure. It is the amount by which the overall increase in national income, ΔY, exceeds the initial increase in autonomous expenditure, ΔA. Because ΔY is greater than ΔA, the simple multiplier is greater than one ($\Delta Y/\Delta A > 1$).

APPLYING ECONOMIC CONCEPTS 22-1

The Multiplier: A Numerical Example

Consider an economy that has a marginal propensity to spend out of national income of 0.80. Suppose an increase in business confidence leads many firms to increase their spending on new buildings and factories. Specifically, suppose desired investment increases by $1 billion per year. National income initially rises by $1 billion, but that is not the end of it. The factors of production that received the first $1 billion spend $800 million. This second round of spending generates $800 million of new income. This new income, in turn, induces $640 million of third-round spending, and so it continues, with each successive round of new income generating 80 percent as much in new expenditure. Each additional round of expenditure creates new income and yet another round of expenditure.

The table carries the process through 10 rounds. Students with sufficient patience (and no faith in mathematics) may compute as many rounds in the process as they wish; they will find that the sum of the rounds of expenditures approaches a limit of $5 billion, which is five times the initial increase in expenditure. [31]

The graph of the cumulative expenditure increases shows how quickly this limit is approached. The multiplier is 5, given that the marginal propensity to spend is 0.8. Had the marginal propensity to spend been lower, say, 0.667, the process would have been similar, but it would have approached a limit of three instead of five times the initial increase in expenditure.

Round of spending	Increase in Expenditure (millions of dollars)	Cumulative Total (millions of dollars)
1 (initial increase)	1000.0	1000.0
2	800.0	1800.0
3	640.0	2440.0
4	512.0	2952.0
5	409.6	3361.6
6	327.7	3689.3
7	262.1	3951.4
8	209.7	4161.1
9	167.8	4328.9
10	134.2	4463.1
11 to 20 combined	479.3	4942.4
All others	57.6	5000.0

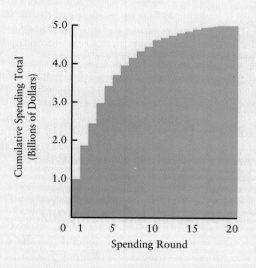

The larger the marginal propensity to spend, the steeper the *AE* function and thus the larger the simple multiplier.

We can derive the precise value of the simple multiplier by using elementary algebra. (The formal derivation is given in *Extensions in Theory 22-1*.) The result is that the simple multiplier, which is called *K*, is

$$\text{Simple Multiplier} = K = \frac{\Delta Y}{\Delta A} = \frac{1}{1-z}$$

FIGURE 22-12 The Size of the Simple Multiplier

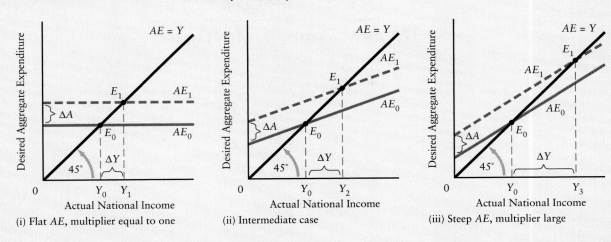

The larger the marginal propensity to spend out of national income (z), the steeper is the AE curve and the larger is the multiplier. In each part of the figure, the initial AE function is AE_0, equilibrium is at E_0, with income Y_0. The AE curve then shifts upward to AE_1 as a result of an increase in autonomous expenditure of ΔA. ΔA is the same in each part. The new equilibrium in each case is at E_1.

In part (i), the AE function is horizontal, indicating a marginal propensity to spend of zero ($z = 0$). The change in equilibrium income ΔY is only the increase in autonomous expenditure because there is no induced expenditure by the people who receive the initial increase in income. The simple multiplier is then equal to one, its minimum possible value.

In part (ii), the AE curve slopes upward but is still relatively flat (z is low). The increase in equilibrium national income to Y_2 is only slightly greater than the increase in autonomous expenditure that brought it about.

In part (iii), the AE function is quite steep (z is high). Now the increase in equilibrium income to Y_3 is much larger than the increase in autonomous expenditure that brought it about. The simple multiplier is quite large.

Recall that z is the marginal propensity to spend out of national income and is between zero and one. The *smallest* simple multiplier occurs when z equals zero. In this case, $(1 - z)$ equals one and so the multiplier equals one. On the other hand, if z is very close to one, $(1 - z)$ is close to zero and so the multiplier becomes very large. The relationship between z, the slope of the AE function, and the size of the multiplier is shown in Figure 22-12.

To estimate the size of the multiplier in an actual economy, we need to estimate the value of the marginal propensity to spend out of national income in that economy. Evidence suggests that the Canadian value is much smaller than the 0.8 that we used in our example, in large part because there are a number of withdrawals from the circular flow of income that we have not yet included in our model of the economy. In addition to saving, which we have discussed, these withdrawals include income taxes and import expenditures. For the current Canadian economy these adjustments lead to a realistic estimate of around 0.3 for z. Hence, the simple multiplier in Canada is approximately $K = 1/(1 - 0.3) = 1/0.7 = 1.43$. The simple multiplier is closer to 1.5 than to 5, as in the example.

The simple multiplier is a useful starting point for understanding the effects of changes in autonomous expenditures on equilibrium national income; however, as we shall see in subsequent chapters, many complications that make the story more complex will arise.

EXTENSIONS IN THEORY 22-1
Deriving The Simple Multiplier

Basic algebra is all that is needed to derive the exact expression for the multiplier. Readers who feel at home with algebra may want to follow this derivation. Others can skip it and rely on the graphical and numerical arguments that have been given in the text.

First, we derive the equation for the AE curve. Desired aggregate expenditure can be decomposed into autonomous expenditure and induced expenditure. In the simple model of this chapter, autonomous expenditure is just equal to investment plus autonomous consumption. Induced expenditure is just equal to induced consumption.

Hence, we can write   *induced expenditure*   *autonomous Expenditure*

$$AE = zY + A \qquad [1]$$

where A is autonomous expenditure and zY is induced expenditure, z being the marginal propensity to spend out of national income. In the simple model of this chapter, with no government and no international trade, z is equal to the marginal propensity to consume.

Now we write the equation of the 45° line,

$$AE = Y \qquad [2]$$

which states the equilibrium condition that desired aggregate expenditure equals actual national income. Equations 1 and 2 are two equations with two unknowns,

AE and Y. To solve them, we substitute Equation 1 into Equation 2 to obtain

$$Y = zY + A \qquad [3]$$

Equation 3 can be easily solved to get Y expressed in terms of A and z. The solution is

$$Y = \frac{A}{1 - z} \qquad [4]$$

Equation 4 tells us the equilibrium value of Y in terms of autonomous expenditures and the marginal propensity to spend out of national income. Now consider a \$1 increase in A. The expression $Y = A/(1 - z)$ tells us that if A changes by one dollar, the change in Y will be $1/(1 - z)$ dollars. Generally, for a change in autonomous spending of ΔA, the change in Y will be

$$\Delta Y = \frac{\Delta A}{1 - z} \qquad [5]$$

Dividing through by ΔA gives the value of the multiplier, which is designated by K:

$$K = \frac{\Delta Y}{\Delta A} = \frac{1}{1 - z} \qquad [6]$$

SUMMARY

Desired Expenditure   🔟①②

- Desired aggregate expenditure is equal to desired consumption plus desired investment plus desired government purchases plus desired net exports. It is the amount that economic agents want to spend on purchasing the national product. In this chapter, we consider only consumption and investment.

- The relationship between disposable income and consumption is called the consumption function. The constant term in the consumption function is autonomous expenditure. The part of consumption that responds to income is called induced expenditure.

- A change in disposable income leads to a change in desired consumption and desired saving. The responsiveness of these changes is measured by the marginal propensity to consume (*MPC*) and the marginal propensity to save (*MPS*), both of which are positive, and which sum to one, indicating that all disposable income is either consumed or saved.

- A change in wealth tends to cause an increase in the portion of disposable income that is consumed. The consumption function shifts up.
- Investment depends, among other things, on real interest rates, changes in sales, and business confidence. In our simplest model of the economy, investment is treated as an autonomous expenditure.

Equilibrium National Income

- Equilibrium national income is defined as that level of national income where desired aggregate expenditure equals actual national income. At incomes above equilibrium, desired expenditure falls short of national income. In this case, inventories accumulate and output will sooner or later fall. At incomes below equilibrium, desired expenditure exceeds national income. In this case, inventories are depleted and output will sooner or later rise.
- In a closed economy with no government, an alternative definition of equilibrium national income is that level of national income where desired saving equals desired investment.
- Equilibrium national income is represented graphically by the point at which the aggregate expenditure curve cuts the 45° line—that is, where desired aggregate expenditure equals national income. This is the same level of income at which the saving function intersects the investment function.

Changes in Equilibrium National Income

- Equilibrium national income is increased by a rise in either autonomous consumption or autonomous investment expenditure. Equilibrium national income is reduced by a fall in these desired expenditures.
- The magnitude of the effect on national income of shifts in autonomous expenditure is given by the multiplier. It is defined as $K = \Delta Y/\Delta A$, where ΔA is the change in autonomous expenditure.

- The simple multiplier is the multiplier when the price level is constant. It is equal to $1/(1 - z)$, where z is the marginal propensity to spend out of national income. The larger is z, the larger is the multiplier. It is a basic prediction of national income theory that the simple multiplier, relating an increase in spending on domestic output to the resulting increase in national income, is greater than one.

KEY CONCEPTS

Desired versus actual expenditure
The consumption function
Average and marginal propensities to consume
Average and marginal propensities to save

The aggregate expenditure *(AE)* function
Marginal propensity to spend
Equilibrium national income
Shifts of and movements along *AE* curves

Effect on national income of shifts in the *AE* curve
The simple multiplier
The size of the multiplier and slope of the *AE* curve

STUDY EXERCISES

1. Consider the following table for a household's consumption expenditures and disposable income. All values are expressed in real 1992 dollars.

Disposable Income (Y_D)	Desired Consumption (C)	$APC = C/Y_D$	$MPC = \Delta C/\Delta Y_D$
0	150	—	
100	225	—	—
200	300	—	—
300	375	—	—
400	450	—	—
500	525	—	—
600	600	—	—
700	675	—	—
800	750	—	—

a. Compute the average propensity to consume for each level of income and fill in the table.
b. Compute the marginal propensity to consume for each successive change in income and fill in the table.
c. Plot the consumption function on a scale diagram. What is its slope?

2. This question relates to desired saving, and is based on the table from Question 1.

a. Compute desired saving at each level of disposable income. Plot the saving function on a scale diagram. What is its slope?
b. Show that the average propensity to save plus the average propensity to consume must equal one.

3. In the chapter we explained at length the difference between *desired* expenditures and *actual* expenditures.

a. Is national income accounting based on desired or actual expenditures? Explain.
b. Suppose there were a sudden decrease in consumer expenditure. Explain why this would lead to an equally sudden increase in *actual* investment. Which type of investment would rise?
c. Illustrate the event from part **b** in a 45° line diagram. Illustrate the increase in actual investment.

4. Consider the following diagram of the *AE* function and the 45° line.

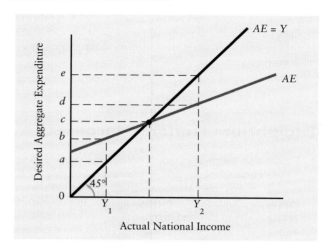

a. Suppose the level of actual national income is Y_1. What is the level of desired aggregate expenditure? Is it greater or less than actual output? Are inventories being depleted or accumulated?
b. If actual income is Y_1, explain the process by which national income changes toward equilibrium.
c. Suppose the level of actual national income is Y_2. What is the level of desired aggregate expenditure? Is it greater or less than actual output? Are inventories being depleted or accumulated?
d. If actual income is Y_2, explain the process by which national income changes toward equilibrium.

5. Suppose that you are given the following information for an economy without government spending, exports, or imports. C is desired consumption, I is desired investment, and Y is income. C and I are given by:

$$C = 1400 + 0.8Y$$
$$I = 400$$

a. What is the equation for the aggregate expenditure (*AE*) function?
b. Applying the equilibrium condition that Y = AE, determine the level of equilibrium national income.
c. Using your answer from part **b**, determine the values of consumption, saving and investment when the economy is in equilibrium.

6. Consider an economy characterized by the following equations:

$$C = 500 + 0.75Y$$
$$I = 150$$

where C is desired consumption, I is desired investment, and Y is national income.

a. Draw the aggregate expenditure function on a scale diagram along with the 45° line. What is the equilibrium level of national income?
b. The marginal propensity to spend in this economy is 0.75. What is the value of the multiplier?

c. Using your answer from part **b**, what would be the change in equilibrium national income if desired investment increased to 250? Can you show this in your diagram?

7. The "Paradox of Thrift" is a famous idea in macroeconomics—one that we will discuss in later chapters. The basic idea is that if every household in the economy tries to increase its level of desired saving, the level of national income will fall and they will end up saving no more than they were initially. Use the model and diagrams of this chapter to show how an (autonomous) increase in desired saving would reduce equilibrium income and lead to no change in aggregate saving.

DISCUSSION QUESTIONS

1. Relate the following newspaper headlines to shifts in the C, S, I, and AE functions and to changes in equilibrium national income.

a. "Revival of consumer confidence leads to increased spending."
b. "High mortgage rates discourage new house purchases."
c. "Concern over future leads to a reduction in inventories."
d. "Accelerated depreciation allowances in the new federal budget sets off boom on equipment purchases."
e. "Consumers spend as stock market soars."

2. Why might an individual's marginal propensity to consume be higher in the long run than in the short run? Why might it be lower? Is it possible for an individual's average propensity to consume to be greater than one in the short run? In the long run? Can a country's aver-

age propensity to consume be greater than one in the short run? In the long run?

3. Explain why a sudden, unexpected fall in consumer expenditure would initially cause an increase in actual investment expenditure by firms.

4. In the simple model of this chapter, aggregate investment was assumed to be autonomous. The simple multiplier was $K = 1/(1 - z)$, where z was the marginal propensity to spend. With autonomous investment, the marginal propensity to spend is simply the marginal propensity to consume. Now suppose that investment is *not* completely autonomous. That is, suppose that $I = \bar{I} + mY$, where $\bar{I}$ is autonomous investment and m is the "marginal propensity to invest" ($m > 0$). Explain how this modification to the simple model changes the simple multiplier.

CHAPTER 23

Adding Government and Trade to the Simple Macro Model

(LO) *LEARNING OBJECTIVES*

1 Understand how the government budget surplus is related to national income.

2 Understand how net exports are related to national income.

3 Recognize the difference between the marginal propensity to consume and the marginal propensity to spend.

4 Explain why net exports lead the economy to accumulate assets.

5 Understand why the presence of government and foreign trade reduces the value of the simple multiplier.

6 Explain how government can use its fiscal policy to influence the level of national income.

7 Recognize that the simple income-expenditure model of national income determination is based on the assumption of a given price level.

In Chapter 22, we developed a simplified model of national income determination in a closed economy with fixed prices. In this chapter, we add a government and a foreign sector to our simple model. In Chapters 24 and 25, we will expand the model further to explain the determination of the price level.

Adding government to the model allows us to study *fiscal policy,* the government's use of its taxing and spending powers to affect the level of national income. Adding foreign trade allows us to examine how external events—such as the 1997–98 Asian financial and economic crisis—affect the Canadian economy. Fortunately, the key elements of last chapter's theory of income determination are unchanged even after government and the foreign sector are incorporated.

Introducing Government

fiscal policy The use of the government's tax and spending policies in an effort to influence the behaviour of GDP.

A government's **fiscal policy** is defined by its plans for taxes and spending. These influence the size of national income in both the short and the long run. Our discussion of fiscal policy begins in this chapter; we go into more detail in Chapter 25 and again in Chapter 31.

Government Spending

In Chapter 20, we distinguished between government *purchases of goods and services* and government *transfer payments*. The distinction bears repeating here. Government purchases are part of GDP. When the government hires a bureaucrat, buys a paper clip, or purchases fuel for the armed forces, it is adding directly to the demands for the economy's current output of goods and services. Hence, desired government purchases, *G*, are part of aggregate desired expenditure.

The other part of government spending, transfer payments, also affects desired aggregate expenditure, but only indirectly. Consider welfare or unemployment-insurance payments, for example. These government expenditures place no demand on the nation's production of goods and services. However, when recipients spend some of these payments on consumption, their expenditure is part of aggregate expenditure. Thus, government transfer payments do affect aggregate expenditure but only through the effect that these payments have on *disposable* income. An increase in transfer payments increases disposable income, and an increase in disposable income increases households' desired consumption expenditure.

Tax Revenues

Taxes reduce households' disposable income relative to national income. In contrast, transfer payments raise disposable income relative to national income. For the purpose of calculating the effect of government policy on desired consumption expenditure, it is the net effect of the two that matters.

Net taxes are defined as total tax revenue received by the government minus total transfer payments made by the government, and it is denoted as *T*. (For convenience, the term "taxes" means "net taxes" unless explicitly stated otherwise.) Because transfer payments are smaller than total tax revenues, net tax revenues are positive. This makes disposable personal income substantially less than national income. (It was about 67 percent of GDP in 1998.)

net taxes Total tax revenue minus transfer payments, denoted *T*.

The Budget Balance

The *budget balance* is the difference between total government revenue and total government expenditure; equivalently, it equals net tax revenue minus government purchases, *T − G*. When revenues exceed expenditures, the government is said to be running a **budget surplus**. When expenditures exceed revenues, the government is said to be running a **budget deficit**.[1] When the two amounts are equal, the government has a *balanced budget*.

In the simple model of Chapter 22, all saving was private since we had no government in the model. But now we must make a distinction between *private saving* and *public saving*.

Private saving is the difference between disposable income and consumption expenditure, or the amount that households choose to save. **Public saving** is the difference between the government's tax revenues (its income) and its expenditures (its consumption). Public saving is therefore equal to the budget surplus, *T − G*.

budget surplus Any excess of current revenue over current expenditure.

budget deficit Any shortfall of current revenue below current expenditure.

private saving Saving on the part of households—the part of disposable income that is not spent on current consumption.

public saving Saving on the part of governments equal to the government budget surplus.

---

[1]When the government runs a budget deficit, it must borrow the excess of spending over revenues. It does this by issuing and selling *government bonds*. When the government runs a surplus, it uses the excess revenue to purchase outstanding government bonds. The stock of outstanding bonds is termed the *national debt*. Deficits and the national debt are the principal topics of Chapter 31.

When government runs a budget surplus, public saving is positive; when government runs a budget deficit, public saving is negative.

The Public Saving Function

In this chapter, government purchases of goods and services are treated as autonomous—that is, the level of government purchases *(G)* does not depend on the level of national income. We also treat *tax rates* as autonomous. This, however, implies that *tax revenues* are induced. As national income rises, a tax system with given tax rates will yield more revenue. For example, when income rises, people will pay more income tax in total even though the tax *rates* are unchanged.

Figure 23-1 illustrates these assumptions with a specific example using hypothetical data. It shows public saving when government purchases (*G*) are constant at $51 billion and net taxes are equal to 10 percent of national income. Notice that public saving (which is exactly equal to the government budget surplus) increases with national income. This relationship occurs because net tax revenues rise with income but, by assumption, government purchases do not. The slope of the public saving function (which can also be called the *budget surplus function*) is just equal to the income-tax rate. The position of the budget surplus function is determined by fiscal policy, as we discuss later in this chapter.

The federal Department of Finance designs and implements Canada's fiscal policy. See their website: www.fin.gc.ca.

Practise with Study Guide Chapter 23, Exercise 3.

Provincial and Municipal Governments

Most of our discussion of government spending and taxing is focused on the federal government, which generally has more discretion over its fiscal policy than do provincial and municipal governments. However, it is important to remember that the Canadian provincial and municipal governments account for *more* purchases of goods and services than does the federal government. The federal government raises about the same amount of tax revenue as do the provincial and municipal governments combined, but spends much more of its revenues on transfer payments.

FIGURE 23-1 The Public Saving (Budget Surplus) Function

National Income (Y)	Government Purchases (G)	Net Taxes ($T = 0.1 \times Y$)	Public Saving ($T - G$)
150	51	15	−36
300	51	30	−21
525	51	52.5	1.5
600	51	60	9
900	51	90	39

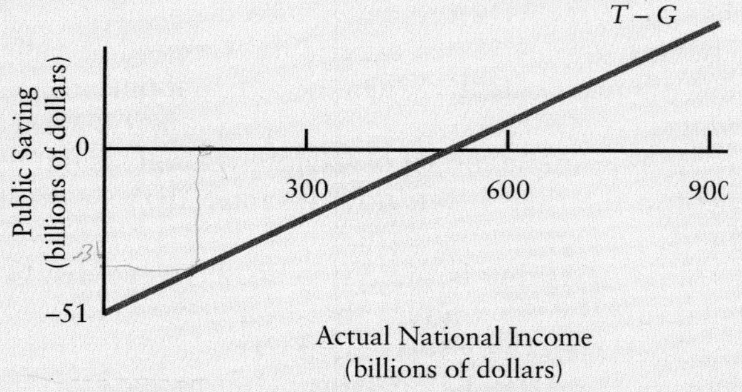

Public saving, which is just equal to the budget surplus, is negative at low levels of national income but rises with national income. The slope of the public saving function is equal to the income-tax rate, 0.1. As national income rises, public saving rises by the income-tax rate times the change in national income. Thus, when national income rises by $300 billion, public saving rises by $30 billion.

When measuring the overall contribution of government to desired aggregate expenditure and to public saving, all levels of government must be included.

As we proceed through this chapter discussing the role of government in the determination of national income, think of "the government" as the combination of all levels of government—federal, provincial, and municipal.

Introducing Foreign Trade

Of all the goods and services produced in Canada in a given year, roughly 40 percent are exported. A similar value of goods and services is imported into Canada every year. Thus, while *net* exports may not contribute much to Canada's GDP (1.4 percent in 1998), trade is tremendously important to Canada's economy.

Canada imports all kinds of goods and services, from French wine and Peruvian anchovies to Swiss financial and American architectural services. Canada also exports a variety of goods and services, including timber, nickel, automobiles, engineering services, computer software, and commuter jets. U.S.-Canadian trade is the largest two-way flow of trade between any two countries in the world today.

The Net Export Function

Exports depend on spending decisions made by foreign households and firms that purchase Canadian goods and services. Typically, exports will not change as a result of changes in Canadian national income. We therefore treat exports as autonomous expenditure.

Imports, however, depend on the spending decisions of Canadian households and firms. Almost all consumption goods have an import content. Canadian-made cars, for example, use large quantities of imported components in their manufacture. Canadian-made clothes most often use imported textiles, such as cotton or wool. And most restaurant meals contain some imported fruits, vegetables, or meats. Hence, as consumption rises, imports will also increase. Because consumption rises with national income, we also get a positive relationship between imports and national income. The **marginal propensity to import** (denoted m) is the change in imports that comes about from a $1 change in national income.

marginal propensity to import The change in import divided by the change in real GDP that brought it about. Denoted by m.

There is a positive relationship between desired imports and national income. Since exports are autonomous with respect to national income, desired net exports (exports minus imports) are negatively related to national income.

This negative relationship between net exports and national income is called the *net export function*. Data for a hypothetical economy with autonomous exports and with imports that are 10 percent of national income are illustrated in Figure 23-2. In this example, exports form the autonomous component and imports the induced component of the desired net export function.

Shifts in the Net Export Function

The net export function relates net exports $(X - IM)$, which we also denote NX, to national income. It is drawn under the assumption that everything affecting net exports, except domestic national income, remains constant. The major factors that must be held

FIGURE 23-2   The Net Export Function

National Income (Y)	Exports (X)	Imports (IM = 0.1 × Y)	Net Exports
0	72	0	72
300	72	30	42
600	72	60	12
720	72	72	0
900	72	90	−18

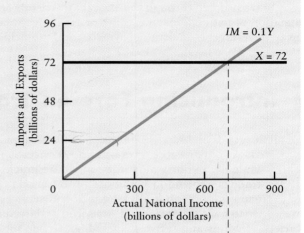

(i) Export and import functions

Net exports, defined as the difference between exports and imports, fall as income rises. The data are hypothetical. They assume that exports are constant and that imports are 10 percent of national income. In part (i), exports are constant at $72 billion while imports rise with national income. Therefore, net exports, shown in part (ii), decline with national income. The slope of the import function in part (i) is equal to the marginal propensity to import. The slope of the net export function in part (ii) is the negative of the marginal propensity to import.

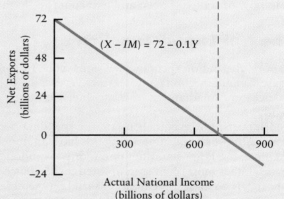

(ii) Net export function

constant are foreign national income, domestic and foreign prices, and the exchange rate. A change in any of these factors will affect the amount of net exports that will occur at each level of Canadian national income and hence will shift the net export function.

Notice that anything affecting Canadian exports will shift the net export function parallel to itself, upward if exports increase and downward if exports decrease. Also notice that anything affecting the *proportion of income* that Canadian consumers wish to spend on imports will change the *slope* of the net export function.

Foreign Income

An increase in foreign income, other things being equal, will lead to an increase in the quantity of Canadian goods demanded by foreign countries—that is, to an increase in Canadian exports. This change causes the net export function to shift upward, parallel to its original position. A fall in foreign income leads to a reduction in Canadian exports and thus to a parallel downward shift in the net export function.

Relative International Prices

Any change in the prices of Canadian goods relative to those of foreign goods will cause both imports and exports to change. These changes will shift the net export function.

Consider what happens with a rise in Canadian prices relative to those in foreign countries. The increase in Canadian prices means that foreigners now see Canadian goods as more expensive relative both to goods produced in their own country and to goods imported from countries other than Canada. As a result, the value of Canadian exports will fall.[2] The X curve shifts down in Figure 23-3. Similarly, Canadians will see imports from foreign countries become cheaper relative to the prices of Canadian-made goods. As a result, they will shift their expenditures toward foreign goods and away from Canadian goods. That is, Canadians will spend a higher fraction of national income on imports—the IM curve in Figure 23-3 will rotate up. The combination of these two effects is that the net export function shifts downward and changes its slope.

Now consider the opposite case of a fall in Canadian prices relative to prices of foreign-made goods. The decline in Canadian prices means that Canadian exports now look cheaper in foreign markets relative both to foreign goods and to goods imported from countries other than Canada. As a result, Canadian exports rise. Similarly, the same change in relative prices causes Canadian imports to fall. Thus, the net export function shifts upward and changes its slope.

A rise in Canadian prices relative to those in other countries reduces Canadian net exports at any level of national income. A fall in Canadian prices increases net exports at any level of national income.

The most important cause of a change in international relative prices is a change in the exchange rate. A fall in the external value of the Canadian dollar (a *depreciation* of the Canadian dollar) means that foreigners must pay less of their money to buy one Canadian dollar, and Canadian residents must pay more Canadian dollars to buy a unit of any foreign currency. As a result, the price of foreign goods in terms of Canadian dollars rises, and the price of Canadian goods in terms of foreign currency falls. This reduction in the relative price of Canadian goods will cause a shift in expenditure away from foreign goods and toward Canadian goods. Canadian residents will im-

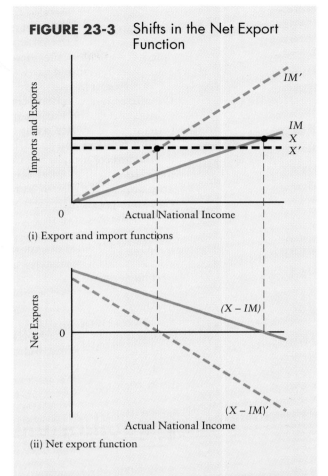

FIGURE 23-3   Shifts in the Net Export Function

(i) Export and import functions

(ii) Net export function

Changes in relative international prices shift the NX function. A rise in Canadian prices relative to foreign prices, or a rise in the external value of the Canadian dollar, lowers exports from X to X' and raises the import function from IM to IM'. This shifts the net export function downward from (X − IM) to (X − IM)'. A fall in Canadian prices has the opposite effect.

For lots of interesting information on Canada's international trade, go to the website for the Department of Foreign Affairs and International Trade: www.dfait-maeci.gc.ca.

---

[2] The rise in Canadian prices clearly leads to a reduction in the demand for Canadian goods by foreigners. But in order for the *value* of Canadian exports to fall, the price elasticity of demand for Canadian exports must exceed one (so that the quantity reduction dominates the price increase). We make this assumption, which is generally believed to be true, throughout this book.

port less at each level of Canadian national income, and foreigners will buy more Canadian exports. The net export function thus shifts upward.

A rise in the external value of the Canadian dollar (an *appreciation* of the Canadian dollar) has the opposite effect: It causes a fall in exports and a rise in imports, shifting the net export function downward.

An example may help to clarify the argument. Suppose something causes the Canadian dollar to depreciate relative to the euro (the common currency recently introduced into the European Union). The depreciation of the Canadian dollar leads Canadians to switch away from French wines and German cars, purchasing instead more B.C. wine and Ontario-made cars. This reduction in imports is reflected by the downward rotation of the *IM* curve. The depreciation of the Canadian dollar relative to the euro also stimulates Canadian exports. Quebec furniture and Maritime vacations now appear cheaper to Europeans than previously, and so their expenditure on such Canadian goods increases. This increase in Canadian exports is reflected by the upward shift in the *X* curve in Figure 23-3. The overall effect is that the net export function shifts up and becomes flatter.

One final word of caution regarding prices, exchange rates, and net exports. It is important to keep in mind that the simple model in this chapter *takes the price level and the exchange rate as given*—they are exogenous variables in this chapter. But, in the actual economy they are endogenous variables. We discuss the determination of the price level in Chapters 24 and 25 (where we still take the exchange rate as given) and the determination of the exchange rate in Chapter 36. In a more complete model of the economy, in which prices and exchange rates are determined endogenously, the relationship among prices, exchange rates, and net exports is more complicated. For now, however, we continue to take the price level and exchange rate as given, and we consider how changes in these variables affect net exports and equilibrium national income.

Equilibrium National Income

As in Chapter 22, equilibrium national income is the level of income where desired aggregate expenditure equals actual national income. The addition of government and net exports changes the calculations that we must make but does not alter the basic principles that are involved.

Desired Consumption and National Income

When there are taxes, disposal income (Y_D) is less than national income (Y). The relationship between consumption and national income involves both the relationship between consumption and disposable income and the relationship, via taxes, between disposable income and national income.

Continuing the example from Figure 23-1, suppose that disposable income is always 90 percent of national income—that is, net taxes (T) is given by the function $T = (0.1)\,Y$. Thus, whatever the relationship between C and Y_D, we can always substitute $(0.9)Y$ for Y_D. Hence, if changes in consumption were always 80 percent of changes in Y_D—that is, an *MPC* out of disposable income equal to 0.8—changes in consumption would always be 72 percent (80 percent of 90 percent) of changes in Y.

To see that this is true, let's use a little simple algebra. The consumption function is given by

$$C = 30 + (0.8)Y_D$$

and disposable income given by

$$Y_D = (0.9)Y$$

Substituting the second equation into the first gives:

$$C = 30 + (0.8)(0.9)Y$$

Therefore, $\qquad\qquad\qquad C = 30 + (0.72)Y$

Thus, we can express desired consumption as a function of Y_D or as a *different* function of Y. In this example, 0.72 is equal to the *MPC* times $(1 - t)$, where t is the income-tax rate. So, whereas 0.8 is the marginal propensity to consume out of *disposable* income, 0.72 is the marginal propensity to consume out of *national* income.

In the presence of income taxes, the marginal propensity to consume out of national income is less than the marginal propensity to consume out of disposable income.

The *AE* Function

In order to determine equilibrium national income, we must define the desired aggregate expenditure *(AE)* function. In Chapter 22, it had only consumption and investment. Now we must include government purchases and net exports to get:

$$AE = C + I + G + NX$$

Figure 23-4 illustrates the aggregate expenditure function and shows how it is constructed from its various components.

The Marginal Propensity to Spend

As in Chapter 22, the slope of the *AE* function is the *marginal propensity to spend* out of national income (z). With the addition of net taxes and net exports, however, the marginal propensity to spend is no longer simply equal to the marginal propensity to consume.

Suppose that the economy produces $1 of extra national income and that the response to this is governed by the relationships in Figure 23-4. Because 10 cents is collected by the government as net taxes, 90 cents becomes disposable income, and 80 percent of this amount (72 cents) is spent on consumption. However, 10 cents of all expenditure goes to imports, so expenditure on domestic goods, that is, aggregate expenditure, rises by only 62 cents $(72 - 10)$. Hence, z, the marginal propensity to spend, is 0.62. What is not spent on domestic output includes the 10 cents in taxes, the 18 cents of disposable income that is saved, and the 10 cents of import expenditure, for a total of 38 cents.

Equilibrium National Income

The *AE* function can be used directly to determine equilibrium national income. In Figure 23-5, the *AE* function from Figure 23-4 is drawn again, together with the 45° line. As was the case in Chapter 22, the 45° line is the *equilibrium condition* that actual national income equals desired aggregate expenditure. The equilibrium level of national income is $600 billion. When national income is equal to $600 billion, it is also equal to desired aggregate expenditure.

FIGURE 23-4 The Aggregate Expenditure Function

The aggregate expenditure function is the sum of desired consumption, investment, government purchases, and net export expenditures. The autonomous components of desired aggregate expenditure are desired investment, desired government purchases, desired export expenditures, and the constant term in desired consumption expenditure. These sum to $228 billion in the given example and this sum is the vertical intercept of the AE curve. The induced components are the second terms in desired consumption expenditure ($0.72\,Y$) and desired imports ($-0.1\,Y$).

The response of consumption to a change in national income is 0.72, calculated as the product of the marginal propensity to consume (0.8) times the fraction of national income that becomes disposable income (0.9). The response of desired aggregate expenditure to a change in national income, $\Delta AE/\Delta Y$, is 0.62. For example, as national income rises from $300 billion to $600 billion, desired aggregate expenditure increases from $414 billion to $600 billion. The slope of the AE curve, $\Delta AE/\Delta Y$, is therefore equal to $186/300 = 0.62$.

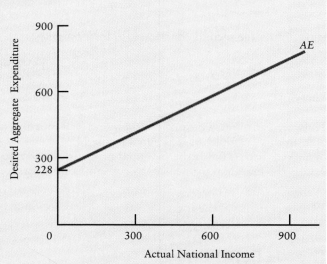

National Income (Y)	Desired Consumption Expenditure (C = 30 + 0.72 Y)	Desired Investment Expenditure (I = 75)	Desired Government Expenditure (G = 51)	Desired Net Export Expenditure (X − IM = 72 − 0.1 Y)	Desired Aggregate Expenditure (AE = C + I + G + X − IM)
0	30	75	51	72	228
150	138	75	51	57	321
300	246	75	51	42	414
600	462	75	51	12	600
900	678	75	51	−18	786

Equilibrium

Suppose that national income is less than its equilibrium amount. The forces leading back to equilibrium are exactly the same as those described in Chapter 22. When households, firms, foreign demanders, and governments try to spend at their desired amounts, they will try to purchase more goods and services than the economy is currently producing. Hence, some of the desired expenditure must either be frustrated or take the form of purchases of inventories of goods that were produced in the past. As firms see their inventories being depleted, they will increase production, thereby increasing the level of national income.

The opposite sequence of events occurs when national income is greater than the level of desired aggregate expenditure. Now the total of desired household consumption, business investment, government purchases, and net foreign demand on the economy's production is less than national output. Firms will notice that they are unable to sell all of their output. Their inventories will be rising, and sooner or later they will seek to reduce the level of output until it equals the level of sales. When they do, national income will fall.

Finally, when national income is equal to desired aggregate expenditure ($600 billion in Figure 23-5), there is no pressure for output to change. Desired consumption, investment, government purchases, and net exports just add up to national product. Firms are producing exactly the quantity of goods and services that purchasers want to use, given the level of income.

The Saving-Investment Approach

In the closed-economy model of Chapter 22, we saw an alternative way of stating the equilibrium condition for national income: At the equilibrium level of income, desired saving equals desired investment. Adding government and international trade changes the precise form that this condition takes, but not the central underlying principle. Now, instead of describing equilibrium as desired saving equals desired investment, equilibrium will be characterized by desired *national* saving equal to desired *national asset formation*. We define these new terms in turn.

Practise with Study Guide Chapter 23, Exercise 7.

National Saving

National saving is the sum of private and public saving, $S + (T - G)$. Private saving (S) is the part of disposable income that is not used for current consumption. Public saving $(T - G)$ is the part of government revenue that is not spent by governments. Between them, households and governments account for all claims to national income. Thus, the sum of what households and governments save accounts for all national saving.

   The national saving function is illustrated in Figure 23-6. The slope of this function is the sum of the slopes of its two parts, private saving and public saving. In the example that we have been using throughout this chapter, the income-tax rate, *t*, is 0.1. Thus, when national income rises by $1, public saving $(T - G)$ rises by 10 cents. (Recall that *G* is assumed to be autonomous and so does not change when national income changes.) The remaining 90 cents is added to disposable income. From this 90-cent increase in disposable income, private saving is increased by the marginal propensity to save (*MPS*), which is equal to 0.2 in our example. The total increase in saving per marginal dollar of national income is therefore $t + MPS(1 - t)$, or $0.1 + (0.2)(0.9) = 0.28$. This is the slope of the national saving function.

National Asset Formation

In Chapter 22, all of national output was either consumption or investment goods. In addition, all income that was received by households was either consumed or saved. So the saving of households was the counterpart of the economy's investment. In the closed economy of Chapter 22—and indeed in any closed economy—the only way to accumulate assets for future use is to devote some part of national product to investment, and that investment must be financed by saving. In an open economy, however, it is possible to accumulate assets in a different form—as net claims on foreigners. Net exports are central to determining the rate at which a country acquires such claims on foreigners.

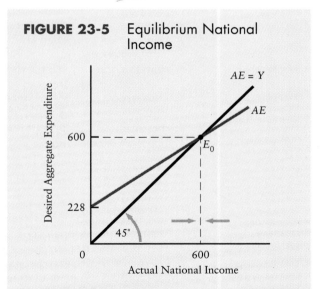

FIGURE 23-5   Equilibrium National Income

Equilibrium national income occurs at E_0, where the *AE* function intersects the 45° line. The *AE* line is taken from Figure 23-4; autonomous expenditure is $228 billion and the slope of *AE* is 0.62. If actual national income is below $600 billion, desired aggregate expenditure will exceed national income, and output will rise. If actual national income is above $600 billion, desired aggregate expenditure will be less than national income, and output will fall. Only when actual national income is $600 billion will desired aggregate expenditure equal actual national income.

Investment and net exports thus have a great deal in common: They are the two ways that current output can be used to accumulate assets. Investment, by definition, is production that will yield services in the future rather than in the present. Clearly, an economy that invests is adding to its assets.

To demonstrate that net exports also lead to asset accumulation, we must go through a number of steps. First, we note that net exports are the difference between what an economy produces and what it uses for consumption, investment, and government. An economy whose net exports are positive is producing more than it is using, with the difference sold abroad. Similarly, an economy that has negative net exports is using more than it is producing, with the difference purchased from abroad.

What happens when a country produces more or less than it uses? Here, the analogy to an individual is instructive. Suppose that you spend more than you earn and that you borrow money to cover the difference. You consequently go into debt. Now suppose that you earn more than you spend. As a result, you acquire assets (or reduce your debts). When you earn more than you spend and do nothing with the balance, you end up holding cash. If you put the money into a bank, you have a bank balance; if you buy stocks or bonds with money, you hold the stocks or bonds. Spending more than you earn reduces your net asset position, and earning more than you spend increases your net asset position.

This simple idea can be extended to the national level because a nation's balances between expenditure and income are simply the total of what individual citizens do. If a nation's firms, households, and governments sell more to other countries than they buy from them (X exceeds IM), that nation must accumulate foreign assets. These assets could be in the form of foreign currency, balances in foreign banks, foreign stocks and bonds, or even foreign lands and factories.

Conversely, if the nation's firms, households, and governments spend more abroad than they earn by selling abroad (IM exceeds X), the nation must incur foreign liabilities (or run down its foreign assets.) To finance the excess of imports over exports, funds must come from somewhere. Since they are not earned by selling current output, they must be raised by transferring assets to foreigners. As a result, a new liability is generated domestically, in the form of domestic assets held by foreigners. Again, these could be bank balances, stocks and bonds, or titles to factories and farms.

Net exports result in the accumulation of assets for the exporting country. Hence, net exports are like investment in the sense that they generate future income for the exporting country.

national asset formation   The sum of investment and net exports. The extent to which the domestic economy is accumulating assets.

To summarize, in a closed economy, **national asset formation** is just equal to investment. In an open economy, however, we must add net assets accumulated abroad (equal to positive net exports) or subtract net domestic assets accumulated by foreigners (equal to negative net exports) in order to calculate the extent to which the domestic economy is accumulating assets worldwide.

Figure 23-6 shows the national asset formation function, $I + (X - IM)$. Recall that I and X are both autonomous whereas IM rises as national income rises. The result is a negative relationship between national income and national asset formation.

Equilibrium

Figure 23-6 shows both the national saving function and the national asset formation function. With the two relationships together, we can determine the equilibrium level of national income.

When desired national saving is equal to desired national asset formation, national income is at its equilibrium level.

FIGURE 23-6   National Saving and National Asset Formation

The economy is in equilibrium when desired national saving, ($S + T − G$), equals desired national asset formation, ($I + X − IM$). The figure graphs the function from the second and third columns of the accompanying table; equilibrium national income is equal to $600 billion. When national income is less than $600 billion, desired national asset formation exceeds desired national saving and desired aggregate expenditure exceeds national income. Firms will respond to the imbalance by producing more, moving the economy toward equilibrium. When national income is above $600 billion, desired national asset formation is less than desired national saving, and desired aggregate expenditure is less than national income. Firms will reduce output to avoid accumulating excess inventories, and the economy will move toward equilibrium.

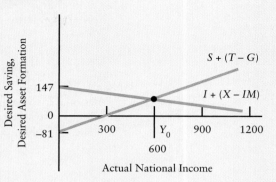

National Income (Y)	Desired National Saving ($S + T − G$)	Desired National Asset Formation ($I + X − IM$)	Saving Minus Asset Formation ($S + T − G$) − ($I + X − IM$)
0	−81	147	−228
300	3	117	−114
600	87	87	0
900	171	57	114
1200	255	27	228

To see why equilibrium occurs when desired national saving equals desired national asset formation, it is crucial to recognize that the vertical distance between the two curves in Figure 23-6 is exactly the same as the distance between the *AE* curve and the 45° line in Figure 23-4. Indeed, by picking any level of national income and comparing the tables in these two figures you will see that the difference between actual national income and desired aggregate expenditure is *always* equal to the difference between desired national saving and desired national asset formation.

Let's use a little algebra to see why this must be the case. Suppose the difference between desired national saving, $(S + T − G)$, and desired national asset formation, $(I + X − IM)$, is equal to some number which we call W. In symbols, this is

$$(S + T − G) − (I + X − IM) = W$$

Now, recall that disposable income is equal to actual income minus taxes, $Y − T$. Further, note that all of disposable income must be used up by consumption and saving. That is,

$$Y − T = C + S$$

which implies

$$S = Y − T − C$$

Now, this last equation can be substituted into our first equation above and, after a little rearranging of terms, we get

$$Y - (C + G + I + (X - IM)) = W$$

Finally, note that the expression in parentheses is simply desired aggregate expenditure, AE, and so the equation can be rewritten to be

$$Y - AE = W$$

We have just shown that the difference between desired national saving and desired national asset formation, which we called W, is exactly the same as the difference between actual national income and desired aggregate expenditure. It immediately follows that the equilibrium illustrated in Figure 23-6 is just another way of looking at the same equilibrium shown in Figure 23-5.

Changes in Equilibrium National Income

Changes in any of the components of desired aggregate expenditure will cause changes in equilibrium national income. In Chapter 22, we investigated the consequences of shifts in the consumption function and in the investment function. Here we take a first look at fiscal policy—the effects of government spending and taxes. We also consider shifts in the net export function. First, we explain why the simple multiplier is reduced by the presence of taxes and imports.

The Multiplier with Taxes and Imports

In Chapter 22, we saw that the *simple multiplier,* the amount by which equilibrium national income changes when autonomous expenditure changes by one dollar, was equal to $1/(1 - z)$, where z is the marginal propensity to spend out of national income. In the simple model of Chapter 22, with no government and no international trade, z is simply the marginal propensity to consume out of disposable income. But in the more complex model of this chapter, in which we have added government and net exports, the marginal propensity to spend out of national income is slightly more complicated. The central point here is as follows:

The presence of imports and income taxes reduces the marginal propensity to spend out of national income and thus reduces the value of the simple multiplier.

To see this, note that in Chapter 22 the marginal propensity to spend was equal to 0.8 and the multiplier was therefore equal to 5. In the example that we have developed in this chapter, with a marginal propensity to import of 0.1 and an income-tax rate of 0.1, the marginal propensity to spend is 0.62. Ten percent of a $1 increase in national income goes to taxes, leaving 90 cents of disposable income. With a marginal propensity to consume of 0.8, 72 cents is spent. Of this, 10 cents is spent on imports, leaving a total of 62 cents to be spent on domestically produced goods. Hence, the simple multiplier is $1/(1 - 0.62) = 2.63$.

Dealing with the numbers in a specific example is sometimes confusing, and it is useful to think more generally about why the presence of imports and income taxes reduces the value of the simple multiplier. With taxes and imports both increasing in response to an increase in national income, every increase in national income generates more leakages from the flow of expenditure than would be the case in the simpler world with no taxes and no imports. Thus, as national income increases, there is less induced expenditure *on domestically produced goods* and therefore the overall change in equilibrium national income is lower.

The higher is the marginal propensity to import, the lower is the simple multiplier. The higher is the income-tax rate, the lower is the simple multiplier.

We have explained why z, the marginal propensity to spend out of national income, is smaller in the presence of government and foreign trade than it is in the simple model of Chapter 22. As a result, the multiplier is also smaller. But what is z precisely equal to? In the model we have been developing in this chapter, z is given by

$$z = MPC(1-t) - m$$

where MPC is the marginal propensity to consume out of disposable income, t is the income-tax rate, and m is the marginal propensity to import. From this formula for z, it is clear that the higher is the tax rate, the lower is z (and thus the lower is the multiplier). It is also clear that the higher is the marginal propensity to import, the lower is z (and thus the lower is the multiplier).

Net Exports

Earlier in this chapter, we discussed the determinants of net exports and of shifts in the net export function. As with the other elements of desired aggregate expenditure, if the net export function shifts upward, equilibrium national income will rise; if the net export function shifts downward, equilibrium national income will fall.

Generally, exports themselves are autonomous with respect to domestic national income. Foreign demand for Canadian goods and services depends on foreign income, on foreign and Canadian prices, and on the exchange rate, but it does not depend on Canadian income. Export demand could also change because of a change in tastes. Suppose that foreign consumers develop a taste for Canadian-made furniture and desire to consume $1 billion more per year of these goods than they had in the past. The net export function (and the aggregate expenditure function) will shift up by $1 billion, and equilibrium national income will increase by $1 billion times the multiplier.

Fiscal Policy

Fiscal policy involves the use of government spending and tax policies to influence total desired expenditure so as to change the equilibrium level of national income. Because government purchases increase desired aggregate expenditure and taxation decreases it, the *directions* of the required changes in spending and taxation are generally easy to determine once we know the direction in which the government wishes to change national income. But the *timing, magnitude,* and *mixture* of the changes are more difficult issues.

Any policy that attempts to stabilize national income at or near any particular level (usually potential national income) is called **stabilization policy.** Here we introduce the idea of stabilization through fiscal policy. In Chapters 25 and 31, we return to discuss some of its complications after we have developed the required theory.

The basic idea of stabilization policy follows from what we have already learned. A reduction in tax rates or an increase in government purchases shifts the *AE* curve upward, causing an increase in equilibrium national income. An increase in tax rates or a decrease

stabilization policy
Any policy designed to reduce the economy's cyclical fluctuations and thereby to stabilize national income.

Changes in government purchases and tax rates can have significant effects on desired aggregate expenditure and thus on equilibrium national income.

in government purchases shifts the *AE* curve downward, causing a decrease in equilibrium income.

If the government has some target level of national income, it can use its taxes and expenditures in an attempt to push the economy toward that target. First, suppose that national income is well below the level of potential national income. In this case, the government would like to increase national income. The appropriate fiscal tools are to raise expenditures or to lower tax rates (or both). Second, suppose that the economy is "overheated," meaning that national income is above potential. What can the government do? The fiscal tools at its command are to reduce government expenditure and to raise tax rates, both of which have a depressing effect on national income.

Changes in Government Purchases

Suppose the government decides to reduce its purchases of all consulting services, saving $100 million per year in spending. Planned government purchases (*G*) would fall by $100 million at every level of income, shifting *AE* downward by the same amount. How much would equilibrium income change? This amount can be calculated by using the multiplier. Government purchases are part of autonomous expenditure, so a *change* in government purchases of ΔG will lead to a *change* in equilibrium national income equal to the multiplier times ΔG. In this example, equilibrium income will fall by $100 million times the multiplier.

Increases in government purchases would have the opposite effect. If the government were to spend $1 billion on new highways, equilibrium national income would rise by $1 billion times the multiplier.

Changes in Tax Rates

If tax rates change, the relationship between disposable income and national income changes. As a result, the relationship between desired consumption and national income also changes. For any given level of national income, there will be a different level of disposable income and hence a different level of consumption. Consequently, a change in tax rates will also cause a change in *z*, the marginal propensity to spend out of national income.

Consider first a decrease in tax rates. If the government decreases its rate of income tax so that it collects 5 cents less out of every dollar of national income, disposable income rises in relation to national income. Hence, consumption also rises at every level of national income. This increase in consumption results in a (nonparallel) upward shift of the *AE* curve, that is, an increase in the slope of the curve, as shown in Figure 23-7. The result of this shift will be a rise in equilibrium national income.

A rise in tax rates has the opposite effect. A rise in tax rates causes a decrease in disposable income, and hence consumption expenditure, at each level of national income. This results in a (nonparallel) downward shift of the *AE* curve and decreases the level of equilibrium national income.

Balanced Budget Changes

Another policy available to the government is to make a *balanced budget change* by altering spending and taxes equally. For example, suppose the government increases tax rates enough to raise an extra $1 billion in tax revenues that it then uses to purchase goods and services. Aggregate expenditure would remain unchanged if, and only if, the $1 billion that the government takes from the private sector in higher taxes would otherwise have been entirely spent by that sector. If so, the government's policy would reduce private expenditure by $1 billion and raise its own spending by $1 billion. Aggregate expenditure, and hence national income, would remain unchanged.

But this is not the usual case. When an extra $1 billion in taxes is taken away from households, spending on domestically produced goods falls by *less than* $1 billion. If the marginal propensity to consume out of disposable income is, say, 0.8, consumption expenditure will fall by only $800 million. If the government spends the entire $1 billion on domestically produced goods, aggregate expenditure will increase by $200 million. In this case, the balanced budget increase in government expenditure has an expansionary effect because it shifts the *AE* function upward.

In the simple model of national income determination, a balanced budget increase in government expenditure will have a mild expansionary effect on national income, and a balanced budget decrease will have a mild contractionary effect.

The **balanced budget multiplier** measures these effects. It is the change in income divided by the balanced budget change in government expenditure that brought it about. If the extra $1 billion of spending and taxes causes national income to rise by $800 million, the balanced budget multiplier is 0.8; if income rises by only $200 million, it is 0.2.

Now compare the sizes of the multipliers for a balanced budget and a deficit-financed increase in government spending. (When expenditure is increased with no corresponding increase in tax rates, we say it is deficit financed.) With a deficit-financed increase in expenditure, there is no increase in taxes and hence no resulting decrease in consumption expenditure to offset the increase in government expenditure. With a balanced budget increase in expenditure, however, the offsetting increase in tax rates and decrease in consumption do occur. Consequently, the balanced budget multiplier is smaller than the simple multiplier.

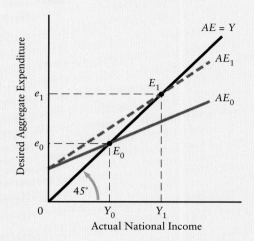

FIGURE 23-7 The Effect of Changing the Tax Rate

Changing the tax rate changes equilibrium income by shifting (and changing the slope of) the *AE* curve. A reduction in tax rates rotates the *AE* curve from AE_0 to AE_1. The new curve has a steeper slope because the lower tax rate withdraws a smaller amount of national income from the desired consumption flow. Equilibrium income rises from Y_0 to Y_1 because, at every level of national income, desired consumption, and, hence, desired aggregate expenditure is higher.

balanced budget multiplier The change in equilibrium national income divided by the tax-financed change in government expenditure that brought it about.

Limitations of the Income-Expenditure Approach

In this and the preceding chapter, we have discussed the determination of the four categories of aggregate expenditure and have seen how they simultaneously determine equilibrium national income. The basic approach is the same no matter how many categories are considered. An algebraic exposition of the model is presented in the appendix to this chapter.

The simple income-expenditure model that we have developed is based on three central concepts.

Equilibrium National Income.   The equilibrium level of national income is that level where *desired* aggregate expenditure equals *actual* national income. If actual national income exceeds desired expenditure, then the unintended accumulation of inventories eventually leads firms to reduce production—national income falls. If actual national income is less than desired expenditure, then the unintended running-down of inventories eventually leads firms to increase production—national income rises.

The Multiplier.   The multiplier measures the change in equilibrium national income that results from a change in the *autonomous* part of desired aggregate expenditure. The multiplier is equal to $1/(1 - z)$, where z is the marginal propensity to spend out of national income. In the model of Chapter 22, in which there is no government and no international trade, z is simply the marginal propensity to consume out of disposable income. The addition to the model of government and net exports reduces the value of z, and thus reduces the value of the simple multiplier.

Demand-Determined Output.   The income-expenditure model that we have examined is constructed *for a given price level*—that is, the price level is assumed to be constant. This assumption of a given price level is related to another assumption that we have been (implicitly) making. We have implicitly assumed that firms are able and willing to produce any amount that is demanded without requiring any change in prices. When this is true, national income depends only on how much is demanded—that is, national income is *demand determined*. Things get more complicated if firms are either unable or unwilling to produce enough to meet all demands without requiring a change in prices. We deal with this possibility in Chapter 24 when we consider *supply-side* influences on national income.

There are two situations in which we might expect national income to be demand determined. First, when there are unemployed resources and firms have excess capacity, firms will be prepared to provide whatever is demanded from them at unchanged prices. In contrast, if the economy's resources are fully employed and firms have no excess capacity, increases in output may only be possible with higher unit costs, and these cost increases may lead to price increases.

The second situation is where firms are *price setters*. Readers who have studied some microeconomics will recognize this term. It means that the firm has the ability to influence the price of its product, either because it is large relative to the market or, more usually, because it sells a product that is *differentiated* to some extent from the products of its competitors. Firms that are price setters often respond to changes in demand by altering their production and sales, at least initially, rather than by adjusting their prices. Only after some time has passed, and the change in demand has persisted, do such firms adjust their prices. This type of behaviour corresponds well to our short-run macro model in which changes in demand lead to changes in output (for a given price level).

The simple income-expenditure model of national income determination assumes a constant price level. In this model, national income is demand determined.

In the following chapters, we augment the income-expenditure model by making the price level endogenous to the model. We do this by considering the *supply side* of the economy—that is, those things that influence firms' abilities to produce output, such as technology and factor prices. When we consider the demand side and the supply side of the economy simultaneously, we will see that changes in desired aggregate expenditure usually cause both prices and real national income to change. This is why the simple multiplier, derived under the assumption that prices do not change, is too simple.

Nonetheless, there are three ways in which the simple income-expenditure models of Chapters 22 and 23 remain useful, even when the price level does change. First, the simple multiplier will continue to be a valuable starting place in calculating actual changes in national income in response to changes in autonomous expenditure. Second, no matter what the price level may be, the components of desired aggregate expenditure add up to actual national income *in equilibrium*. Third, no matter what the price level may be, equilibrium requires that desired national saving be equal to desired national asset formation. This last point will be especially important when we consider the determinants of national income and prices in the long run.

S U M M A R Y

Introducing Government

- Government purchases, G, is part of autonomous aggregate expenditure. Taxes minus transfer payments are called net taxes and affect aggregate expenditure indirectly. Taxes reduce disposable income, whereas transfers increase disposable income.

- The budget balance is defined as net tax revenues minus government purchases, $(T - G)$. When $(T - G)$ is positive, there is a budget surplus; when $(T - G)$ is negative, there is a budget deficit.
- When there is a budget surplus, there is positive public saving.

Introducing Foreign Trade

- Exports are foreign purchases of Canadian goods, and thus do not depend on Canadian national income. Desired imports increase as national income increases. Hence, net exports decrease as national income increases.
- Changes in international relative prices lead to shifts in the net export function. A rise in the exchange rate (a de-

preciation of the Canadian dollar) implies that Canadian goods are now cheaper relative to foreign goods. This leads to a rise in exports and a fall in imports, shifting the net export function up. A fall in the exchange rate (an appreciation of the Canadian dollar) has the opposite effect.

Equilibrium National Income

- As in Chapter 22, national income is in equilibrium when desired aggregate expenditure equals actual national income. The equilibrium condition is

  $$Y = AE, \quad \text{where } AE = C + I + G + (X - IM)$$

- The sum of investment and net exports is called *national asset formation* because investment and net exports rep-

resent the two ways in which national income that is not used in the current year can be used to generate future national income. At the equilibrium level of national income, desired national saving is equal to desired national asset formation:

  $$S + (T - G) = I + (X - IM)$$

Changes in Equilibrium National Income

- The presence of taxes and net exports reduces the value of the simple multiplier. With taxes and imports both increasing in response to an increase in national income, every increase in national income generates more leakages from the flow of expenditure.
- An increase in government purchases shifts up the *AE* function and thus increases the equilibrium level of national income. A decrease in the income-tax rate makes the *AE* function rotate upward and increases the equilibrium level of national income.
- An increase in exports can be caused by either an increase in foreign demand for Canadian goods, a fall in the Canadian price level, or a depreciation of the Canadian dollar. An increase in exports shifts the *AE* function up and increases the equilibrium level of national income.

Limitations of the Income-Expenditure Approach

- The simple income-expenditure model of national income determination is constructed for a given price level. That prices are assumed not to change in response to an increase in desired expenditure reflects a related assumption that output is demand determined. This implies that national income is demand determined.
- Output would be demand determined in two situations. One is where there are unemployed resources; the other is where firms are price setters.
- In later chapters when we consider the demand side and the supply side of the economy simultaneously, we will see that changes in desired aggregate expenditure usually cause both prices and real national income to change.

KEY CONCEPTS

Taxes, transfers, and net taxes
The budget balance
The public saving (budget surplus) function
The net export function

National saving
National asset formation
Calculation of the simple multiplier in an open economy with government

Fiscal policy and equilibrium income
The balanced budget multiplier

STUDY EXERCISES

1. Consider the following table showing national income and government tax revenues in billions of dollars. Assume that the level of government purchases is $155 billion.

National Income (Y)	Net Tax Revenues (T)	Public Saving ($T - G$)
100	45	—
200	70	—
300	95	—
400	120	—
500	145	—
600	170	—
700	195	—
800	220	—

a. Compute the level of public saving (the government budget surplus) for each level of national income and fill in the table.
b. Plot the public saving function on a scale diagram. Explain the economics of why it is upward sloping.
c. What is the tax rate? Explain.
d. Suppose the government decides to increase the level of its purchases of goods and services by $15 billion. Show in your diagram what happens to the public saving function.

2. Consider the following table showing national income and imports in billions of dollars. Assume that the level of exports is $300 billion.

National Income (Y)	Imports (IM)	Net Exports ($X - IM$)
100	85	—
200	120	—
300	155	—
400	180	—
500	215	—
600	250	—
700	285	—
800	320	—

a. Compute the level of net exports for each level of national income and fill in the table.

b. Plot the net export function on a scale diagram. Explain the economics of why it is downward sloping.

c. What is the marginal propensity to import? Explain.

d. Suppose one of Canada's major trading partners experiences a significant recession. Explain how this will affect the net export function. Show the effect in your diagram.

3. Each of the following headlines describes an event that will have an effect on desired aggregate expenditure. What will be the effect on equilibrium national income? In each case, describe how the event would be illustrated in the 45° line diagram.

a. "Minister takes an axe to the Armed Forces."

b. "Russia agrees to buy more Canadian wheat."

c. "High-tech firms to cut capital outlays."

d. "Finance Minister pledges to cut income-tax rates."

e. "U.S. imposes import restrictions on Canadian lumber."

f. "Asian slump means smaller market for B.C. lumber."

g. "Weak dollar spurs exports from Ontario manufacturers."

4. The following table shows alternative hypothetical economies and the relevant values for the marginal propensity to consume out of disposable income (MPC), the income-tax rate (t), and the marginal propensity to import, m.

Economy	MPC	t	m	z	Multiplier $K = 1/(1 - z)$
Economy A	0.75	0.2	0.15	—	—
Economy B	0.75	0.2	0.30	—	—
Economy C	0.75	0.4	0.30	—	—
Economy D	0.90	0.4	0.30	—	—

a. Recall that z, the marginal propensity to spend out of national income, is given by the simple expression

$z = MPC(1 - t) - m$. Using this expression, compute z for each of the economies and fill in the table.

b. Compare Economies A and B (they differ only by the value of m). Which one has the larger multiplier? Explain the economics of why the size of the multiplier depends on m.

c. Compare Economies B and C (they differ only by the value of t). Which one has the larger multiplier? Explain the economics of why the size of the multiplier depends on t.

d. Compare Economies C and D (they differ only by the value of MPC). Which one has the larger multiplier? Explain the economics of why the size of the multiplier depends on MPC.

5. Consider the diagram below showing the national saving function and the national asset formation function.

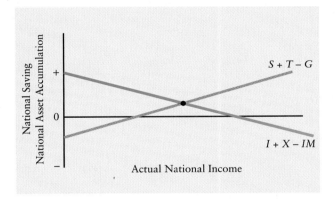

a. Explain why the national asset formation function is downward sloping. What determines its slope?

b. Explain why the national saving function is upward sloping. What determines its slope?

c. Suppose the government decided to increase its level of purchases. How would this policy change be illustrated in the diagram? What would happen to national income?

d. Suppose domestic firms decided to increase their desired investment. How would this change be illustrated in the diagram? What would happen to national income?

e. Suppose that the Canadian government reduced income-tax rates. How would this change be illustrated in the diagram? What would happen to national income?

6. This question requires you to solve a macro model algebraically. Reading the appendix to Chapter 23 will help you to answer this question. But, just in case, we lead you through it step by step. The equations for the model are as follows:

i) $C = a + bY_D$ Consumption
ii) $I = I_0$ Investment (autonomous)
iii) $G = G_0$ Government purchases (autonomous)
iv) $T = T_0 + tY$ Tax revenue
v) $X = X_0$ Exports (autonomous)
vi) $IM = mY$ Imports

a. Step 1: Substituting the tax function into the consumption function, derive the relationship between desired consumption and national income.

b. Step 2: Sum the four components of desired aggregate expenditure (C, I, G, NX). This is the aggregate expenditure (AE) function.

c. Step 3: Now recall the equilibrium condition, $Y = AE$. Form the equation $Y = AE$, where AE is your expression for the AE function from part **b**.

d. Step 4: Now collect terms and solve for Y. This is the equilibrium value of national income.

e. Step 5: Suppose the level of autonomous expenditure, which we could call A, rises by ΔA. What is the effect on the level of equilibrium national income?

DISCUSSION QUESTIONS

1. The countries of the European Union agreed in the Maastricht Treaty of 1991 to reduce their budget deficits to below 3 percent of GDP. What fiscal measures would reduce their deficits? Why might a reduction of 10 percent in government expenditure accomplish much less than a 10 percent decrease in the deficit, at least in the first instance?

2. It is typical for the federal government's forecasts of its own budget deficit to be less than the forecasts made by private-sector economists. Much of the discrepancy seems to be accounted for by assumptions about the state of the economy over the coming year. How do assumptions about the economy affect estimates of the budget deficit?

3. Classify each of the following government activities as either government purchases or transfers.

   a. Welfare payments for the poor
   b. Payments to teachers in public schools
   c. Payments to teachers at military colleges
   d. Payments on account of hospital and medical care
   e. Public Health Service vaccination programs

4. The trade deficit that the United States has with Japan has received much attention over the last 20 years. Given an economy in equilibrium, what is the relationship between saving and investment if the government budget remains balanced but there exists a trade deficit? What additional role must foreigners play in this situation? Can you explain why this situation is viewed by many Americans as troublesome? Do you agree with them?

5. In Chapter 20 we examined how national income was *measured*. Using the expenditure approach, we showed that GDP is always equal to the sum of consumption, investment, government purchases, and net exports. In Chapters 22 and 23 we examined the *determination* of national income. We showed that equilibrium national income occurs when actual national income equals the sum of desired consumption, investment, government purchases, and net exports. Does this mean that national income is always at its equilibrium level? Explain the important difference between "actual" and "desired" expenditures.

An Algebraic Exposition of the Income-Expenditure Model

We start with the definition of desired aggregate expenditure:

$$AE = C + I + G + (X - IM) \quad [1]$$

For each component of AE, we write down a behavioural function.

$$C = a + bY_D \quad \text{(consumption function)} \quad [2]$$

$$I = I_0 \quad \text{(autonomous investment)} \quad [3]$$

$$G = G_0 \quad \text{(autonomous government purchases)} \quad [4]$$

$$X = X_0 \quad \text{(autonomous exports)} \quad [5]$$

$$IM = mY \quad \text{(imports)} \quad [6]$$

where a is autonomous consumption spending, b is the marginal propensity to consume, and m is the marginal propensity to import. Obviously, the "behavioural" functions for investment, government purchases, and exports are very simple: These are all assumed to be independent of the level of national income.

Before deriving aggregate expenditure, we need to determine the relationship between national income (Y) and disposable income (Y_D), because it is Y_D that determines desired consumption expenditure. Y_D is defined as income after net taxes. In Chapter 23 we examined a very simple linear income tax of the form $T = tY$. More generally, we might imagine autonomous net taxes T_0 and induced net taxes tY, so that the tax function is given by:

$$T = T_0 + tY \quad [7]$$

Taxes must be subtracted from national income to obtain disposable income:

$$Y_D = Y - T_0 - tY = Y(1 - t) - T_0 \quad [8]$$

Substituting Equation 8 into the consumption function allows us to write consumption as a function of national income.

$$C = a - bT_0 + b(1 - t)Y \quad [9]$$

Notice that autonomous consumption now has two parts, a and $-bT_0$, where the latter term is the effect of autonomous taxes on consumption.

Now we can add up all of the components of desired aggregate expenditure, substituting Equations 3, 4, 5, 6, and 9 into Equation 1:

$$AE = a - bT_0 + b(1 - t)Y + I_0 + G_0 + X_0 - mY \quad [10]$$

Equation 10 is the AE function which shows desired aggregate expenditure as a function of actual national income.

In equilibrium, desired aggregate expenditure must equal actual national income:

$$AE = Y \quad [11]$$

Equation 11 is the equilibrium condition for the income-expenditure model. It is the equation of the 45° line in the figures in this chapter.

To solve for the equilibrium level of national income, we want to solve for the level of Y that satisfies both equations 10 and 11. That is, solve for the level of Y which is determined by the intersection of the AE curve and the 45° line. Substitute equation 11 into 10:

$$Y = a - bT_0 + b(1 - t)Y + I_0 + G_0 + X_0 - mY \quad [12]$$

Group all the terms in Y on the right-hand side, and subtract them from both sides:

$$Y = Y[b(1 - t) - m] + a - bT_0 + I_0 + G_0 + X_0 \quad [13]$$

$$Y - Y[b(1 - t) - m] = a - bT_0 + I_0 + G_0 + X_0 \quad [14]$$

Notice that $[b(1 - t) - m]$ is exactly the marginal propensity to spend out of national income, defined earlier as z. When national income goes up by one dollar, only $1 - t$ dollars go into disposable income, and only b of that gets spent on consumption. Additionally, m gets spent on imports, which are not expenditure on domestic national income. Hence $[b(1 - t) - m]$ gets spent on domestic output.

Substituting z for $[b(1 - t) - m]$ and solving Equation 14 for equilibrium Y yields

$$Y = \frac{a - bT_0 + I_0 + G_0 + X_0}{1 - z} \quad [15]$$

Notice that the numerator of Equation 15 is total autonomous expenditure, which we call A. Hence, Equation 15 can be rewritten as

$$Y = \frac{A}{1 - z} \qquad [16]$$

Notice also that if autonomous expenditure rises by some amount ΔA, Y will rise by $\Delta A/(1 - z)$. So, the simple multiplier is $1/(1 - z)$.

The Algebra Illustrated

The numerical example that was carried through Chapters 22 and 23 can be used to illustrate the preceding exposition. In that example, the behavioural equations are:

$$C = 30 + 0.8Y_D \qquad [17]$$
$$I = 75 \qquad [18]$$
$$G = 51 \qquad [19]$$
$$X - IM = 72 - 0.1Y \qquad [20]$$
$$T = 0.1Y \qquad [21]$$

T_0 is 0, so, from Equation 8, disposable income is given by $Y(1 - t) = 0.9Y$. Substituting this into

Equation 17 yields

$$C = 30 + 0.72Y$$

as in Equation 9.

Now, recalling that in equilibrium $AE = Y$, we add up all of the components of AE and set the sum equal to Y, as in Equation 12:

$$Y = 30 + 0.72Y + 75 + 51 + 72 - 0.1Y \quad [22]$$

Collecting terms yields

$$Y = 228 + 0.62Y$$

Subtracting $0.62Y$ from both sides gives

$$0.38Y = 228$$

and dividing through by 0.38, we have

$$Y = \frac{228}{0.38} = 600$$

This can also be derived by using Equation 16. Autonomous expenditure is 228, and z, the marginal propensity to spend out of national income, is 0.62. Thus, from Equation 16, equilibrium income is $228/(1 - 0.62) = 600$, which is exactly the equilibrium we obtained in Figure 23-4.

CHAPTER 24

Output and Prices in the Short Run

LO LEARNING OBJECTIVES

❶ Understand why an exogenous change in the price level shifts the *AE* curve and changes the equilibrium level of real GDP.

❷ Explain the meaning of the *AD* curve, and which factors lead it to shift.

❸ Explain the meaning of the *SRAS* curve and why changes in technology or factor prices cause it to shift.

❹ Understand the concept of macroeconomic equilibrium.

❺ Explain the effects of aggregate demand and aggregate supply shocks on real GDP and the price level.

In Chapters 22 and 23, we developed a model of national income determination in an economy with a constant price level. Of course, in any real economy, prices are changing more or less all the time. On the supply side of the economy, the prices of imported raw materials used by firms change frequently and sometimes dramatically, as when oil prices soared during 1973–1974 and 1979–1980 in response to the actions of the OPEC oil cartel. On the demand side of the economy, a major downturn in the economies of Japan and Southeast Asia, as happened in 1997 and 1998, reduced the demand for Canadian exports. This slowed a rapidly growing Canadian economy and helped to contain inflationary pressures.

Virtually all shocks to the economy affect *both* real national income and the price level. To understand why this happens, we need to drop the assumption that the price level is constant.

We make the transition to a variable price level in three steps. First, we study the consequences for national income of *exogenous* changes in the price level—changes that happen for reasons that are not explained by our model of the economy. We ask how changes in the price level affect desired aggregate expenditure. That is, we examine the *demand side* of the economy. Second, we examine the *supply side* by exploring the relationship between the price level, the prices of factor inputs, and the level of output firms would like to supply. Finally, we examine the concept of *macroeconomic equilibrium* that combines both the demand and supply sides to simultaneously determine the price level and real national income.

The Demand Side of the Economy

What happens to equilibrium GDP when the price level changes for some exogenous reason, such as a rise in the price of imported raw materials? To find out, we need to understand how the change affects desired aggregate expenditure.

Shifts in the *AE* Curve

We need to establish one key result: A change in the price level shifts the *AE* curve—downward when the price level rises and upward when the price level falls. Part of the explanation lies with how the change in the price level affects desired consumption expenditure and desired net exports.

In later chapters, we will discuss why changes in the price level also have an effect on investment, through changes in the interest rate. To fully understand why this happens, however, we need to know about the demand and supply of money. This discussion must await our treatment of money and banking in Chapters 26 and 27; for now we focus only on the effects of a change in the price level on consumption and net exports.

Changes in Consumption

One link between a change in the price level and changes in desired consumption is provided by wealth. We first consider the link between the price level and wealth, and then the link between wealth and consumption.

Much of the private sector's total wealth is held in the form of assets with a fixed nominal value. The most obvious example is money itself. We will discuss money in considerable detail in Chapters 26 and 27, but for now just note that most individuals and businesses hold money in their wallets, in their cash registers, or in their chequing accounts. What this money can buy—its real value—depends on the price level. The higher the price level, the less a given amount of money can purchase. For this reason, a rise in the domestic price level lowers the real value of money holdings. Similarly, a reduction in the price level raises the real value of money holdings.

Changes in the price level cause changes in the real value of cash held by the private sector. This leads to changes in the amount of desired consumption expenditure.

A rise in the price level lowers the real value of money held by the private sector. A fall in the price level raises the real value of money held by the private sector.

Other examples of assets that have fixed nominal values include government and corporate bonds. The bondholder has lent money to the issuer of the bond and receives a repayment from the issuer when the bond matures. What happens when there is a change in the price level in the intervening period? A rise in the price level means that the repayment to the bondholder is lower in real value. This is a decline in wealth for the bondholder. However, the issuer of the bond, having made a repayment of lower real value because of the increase in the price level, has experienced an increase in wealth. In dollar terms, the bondholder's reduction in wealth is exactly offset by the issuer's increase in wealth.

Changes in the price level change the wealth of bondholders and bond issuers, but because the changes offset each other there is no change in aggregate wealth.

What happens when the issuer of the bond is the government? It is still true that a rise in the price level leads to no change in aggregate wealth—the reduction in the bondholder's wealth being exactly offset by an increase in the government's (that is, taxpayers') wealth. But the key question here is whether the private sector *recognizes* such changes in the government's (taxpayers') wealth. This issue is hotly debated among economists. Many economists argue that when individuals hold *government* bonds, they think they are made less wealthy by an increase in the price level, even though, in principle, they have some claim—as taxpayers—on the associated increase in the government's wealth. Other economists argue that the private sector takes full account of the changes in the government's wealth when computing their own wealth because any increase in the government's wealth must ultimately accrue to the private sector in the form of lower future taxes. In this case, holders of government bonds would feel no wealthier (or less wealthy) after a change in the price level. This contentious issue of "Ricardian Equivalence" is discussed in Chapter 31 when we examine the effects of government budget deficits. For now, we simply note that a rise in the price level reduces the private sector's perception of its wealth, at least for one reason (the reduced value of money holdings) and possibly for a second reason (the reduced value of government bonds).

The second link in the chain running from changes in the price level to changes in desired consumption is provided by the relationship between wealth and consumption that we stressed in Chapter 22. In that discussion we noted that forward-looking consumers save partly to accumulate assets for future use. A change in wealth will then change households' consumption and saving behaviour. In particular, when households suffer a decrease in their wealth, they will increase their saving so as to restore their wealth to their desired level. An increase in desired saving, of course, implies a reduction in desired consumption. Conversely, when households get an increase in their wealth, they will reduce their saving and consume more, causing an upward shift in the consumption function.

A rise in the domestic price level lowers private-sector wealth; this leads to a fall in desired consumption, and thus a downward shift in the *AE* curve. A fall in the domestic price level leads to a rise in wealth and desired consumption and thus to an upward shift in the *AE* curve.

Changes in Net Exports

When the domestic price level rises, Canadian goods become more expensive relative to foreign goods. As we saw in Chapter 23, this change in relative prices causes Canadian consumers to reduce their purchases of Canadian-made goods, which have now become relatively more expensive, and to increase their purchases of foreign goods, which have now become relatively less expensive. At the same time, consumers in other countries reduce their purchases of the now relatively more expensive Canadian-made goods. We saw in Chapter 23 that these changes cause a downward shift in the net export function.

A rise in the domestic price level shifts the net export function downward, which causes a downward shift in the *AE* curve. A fall in the domestic price level shifts the net export function and hence the *AE* curve upward.

Changes in Equilibrium GDP

Because it causes downward shifts in both the net export function and the consumption function, an exogenous rise in the price level causes a downward shift in the *AE* curve, as shown in Figure 24-1. When the *AE* curve shifts downward, the equilibrium level of real GDP falls.

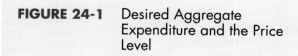

FIGURE 24-1 Desired Aggregate Expenditure and the Price Level

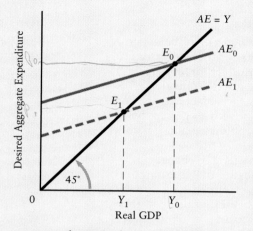

An exogenous change in the price level causes the *AE* curve to shift and thus causes equilibrium GDP to change. At the initial price level, the *AE* curve is given by the solid line AE_0, and hence equilibrium GDP is Y_0. An increase in the price level reduces desired aggregate expenditure and thus causes the *AE* curve to shift downward to the dashed line, AE_1. As a result, equilibrium GDP falls to Y_1.

Now suppose that there is a fall in the price level. Canadian goods become relatively cheaper internationally, so net exports rise. Also, the purchasing power of assets denominated in money terms is increased, so households spend more. The resulting increase in desired expenditure on Canadian goods causes the *AE* curve to shift upward. The equilibrium level of real GDP therefore rises.

In Chapters 22 and 23 the horizontal axis was labeled "Actual National Income." Notice in Figure 24-1, however, that we have labelled the horizontal axis "Real GDP." We use GDP rather than *national income* but the two are clearly the same. It is still *actual,* as opposed to *desired,* but we leave that off, also for simplicity. Finally, we add *real* because from this chapter onward the price level will be determined endogenously and thus it is necessary to distinguish changes in nominal GDP from changes in real GDP.

The Aggregate Demand Curve

We now know from the behaviour underlying the *AE* function that the price level and real equilibrium GDP are negatively related to each other. This negative relationship can be shown in an important new concept, the *aggregate demand curve.*

Recall that the *AE* curve relates real GDP to desired aggregate expenditure for a given price level, plotting real GDP on the horizontal axis. The **aggregate demand (AD) curve** relates equilibrium real GDP to the price level, again plotting GDP on the horizontal axis. Because the horizontal axes of both the *AE* and *AD* curves measure real GDP, the two curves can be placed one above the other so that the level of GDP on each can be compared directly. This is shown in Figure 24-2.

Now let us see how the *AD* curve is derived. Given a value of the price level, equilibrium GDP is determined in part (i) of Figure 24-2 at the point where the *AE* curve crosses the 45° line. In part (ii) of Figure 24-2, the combination of the equilibrium level of GDP and the corresponding value of the price level is plotted, giving one point on the *AD* curve.

As we have seen, the *AE* curve shifts when the price level changes. The new position of the *AE* curve gives rise to a new equilibrium level of GDP that is associated with the new price level. This determines a second point on the *AD* curve, as shown in part (ii) of Figure 24-2. By joining these points, we trace out the *AD* curve.

aggregate demand (AD) curve A curve showing combinations of real GDP and the price level that make desired aggregate expenditure equal to national income.

For any given price level, the *AD* curve shows the level of real GDP for which desired aggregate expenditure equals actual GDP.

Note that because the *AD* curve relates equilibrium GDP to the price level, changes in the price level that cause *shifts in* the *AE* curve cause *movements along* the *AD* curve. A movement along the *AD* curve thus traces out the response of equilibrium GDP to a change in the price level.

Practise with Study Guide Chapter 24, Exercises 1 and 2.

The Slope of the *AD* Curve

Figure 24-2 provides us with sufficient information to establish that the *AD* curve is negatively sloped.

1. A rise in the price level causes the *AE* curve to shift downward and hence leads to a movement upward and to the left along the *AD* curve, reflecting a fall in the equilibrium level of GDP.

2. A fall in the price level causes the *AE* curve to shift upward and hence leads to a movement downward and to the right along the *AD* curve, reflecting a rise in the equilibrium level of GDP.

In Chapter 3, we saw that demand curves for individual goods such as coffee, CD players, and automobiles are downward sloping. However, the reasons for the negative slope of the *AD* curve are different from the reasons for the negative slope of individual demand curves used in microeconomics. Why is this the case?

An individual demand curve describes a situation in which the price of one commodity changes *while the prices of all other commodities and consumers' money incomes are constant.* Such an individual demand curve is downward sloping for two reasons. First, as the price of the commodity rises, the purchasing power of each consumer's money income will fall, and this fall in real income will lead to fewer units of the good being purchased. Second, as the price of the commodity rises, consumers buy less of that commodity and more of the now relatively cheaper substitutes.

The first reason has no application to the *AD* curve, which relates the total demand for all output to the *price level* rather than to any particular (relative) price. All prices and total output are changing as we move along the *AD* curve. Because the value of output determines income, consumers' money incomes will also be changing along this curve.

The second reason does apply to the aggregate demand curve, but only in a limited way. A rise in the price level entails a rise in *all* domestic commodity prices. Hence, there is no incentive to substitute among domestic commodities whose prices do not change relative to each other. However, it does give rise, as we saw earlier in this chapter, to some substitution between domestic and foreign products. Domestic goods rise in price relative to imported goods, and the switch in expenditure will reduce desired aggregate expenditure on domestic output and hence will reduce equilibrium national income.

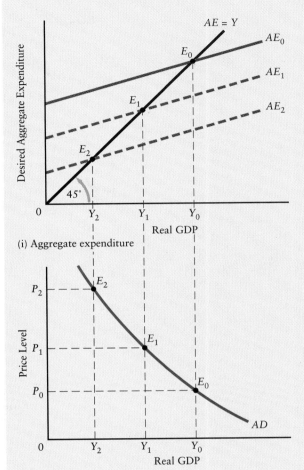

FIGURE 24-2 Derivation of the *AD* Curve

(i) Aggregate expenditure

(ii) Aggregate demand

Equilibrium GDP is determined by the *AE* curve for each given price level; the level of equilibrium GDP and its associated price level are then plotted to yield a point on the *AD* curve. When the price level is P_0, the *AE* curve is AE_0, and hence equilibrium GDP is Y_0, as shown in part (i). Plotting Y_0 against P_0 yields the point E_0 on the *AD* curve in part (ii).

An increase in the price level to P_1 causes the *AE* curve to shift downward to AE_1 and causes equilibrium GDP to fall to Y_1. Plotting this new level of GDP against the higher price level yields a second point, E_1, on the *AD* curve. A further increase in the price level to P_2 causes the *AE* curve to shift downward to AE_2, and thus causes equilibrium GDP to fall to Y_2. Plotting P_2 and Y_2 yields a third point, E_2, on the *AD* curve.

Thus, a change in the price level causes a shift in the *AE* curve but a movement along the *AD* curve.

aggregate demand shock   Any event that causes a shift in the aggregate demand curve.

Shifts in the *AD* Curve

Figure 24-3 shows a shift in the *AD* curve. Because the *AD* curve plots equilibrium GDP as a function of the price level, anything that alters equilibrium GDP *at a given price level* must shift the *AD* curve. In other words, any change—other than a change in the price level—that causes the *AE* curve to shift will also cause the *AD* curve to shift. Such a shift is called an **aggregate demand shock**.

For example, in the late 1990s, the U.S. economy was growing quickly. The U.S. economic boom led to an increase in America's demand for Canadian products, which caused an upward shift in Canada's net export function. This event, taken by itself, would shift Canada's *AE* function upward and thus would shift Canada's *AD* curve to the right. Working in the opposite direction, however, the economies of Japan and Southeast Asia experienced a significant recession in 1997 and 1998. The economic slump in these countries led to reduced demands for Canadian goods, especially raw materials. This event, taken by itself, would shift Canada's *NX* and *AE* functions down, thus shifting Canada's *AD* curve to the left.

For a given price level, a rise in the amount of desired aggregate expenditure associated with each level of national income shifts the *AE* curve upward and the *AD* curve to the right. A fall in desired aggregate expenditure shifts the *AE* curve downward and the *AD* curve to the left.

Remember the following important point. In order to shift the *AD* curve, the change in desired expenditure must be caused by something other than a change in the domestic price level. As we saw earlier in this chapter, a change in aggregate expenditure caused by a change in the domestic price level leads to a movement along (not a shift of) the *AD* curve.

FIGURE 24-3   The Simple Multiplier and Shifts in the *AD* Curve

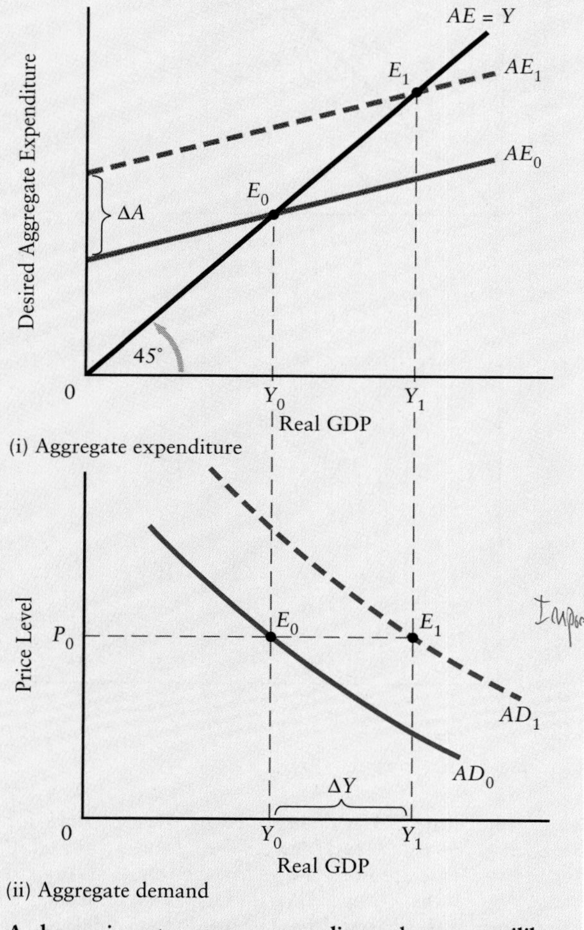

(i) Aggregate expenditure

(ii) Aggregate demand

A change in autonomous expenditure changes equilibrium GDP for any given price level. The simple multiplier measures the resulting horizontal shift in the *AD* curve. The original *AE* curve is AE_0 in part (i). Equilibrium is at E_0, with GDP of Y_0 at price level P_0. This yields point E_0 on the curve AD_0 in part (ii).

The *AE* curve in part (i) then shifts upward from AE_0 to AE_1, due to an increase in autonomous expenditure of ΔA. Equilibrium GDP now rises to Y_1, with the price level still constant at P_0. Thus, the *AD* curve in part (ii) shifts to the right to point E_1, indicating the higher equilibrium GDP of Y_1 associated with the same price level P_0. The magnitude of the shift, ΔY, is equal to the simple multiplier times ΔA.

The Simple Multiplier and the *AD* Curve

We saw in Chapters 22 and 23 that the simple multiplier measures the magnitude of the change in equilibrium national income in response to a change in autonomous expenditure *when the price level is held constant*. It follows that this multiplier gives the magnitude of the *horizontal shift* in the *AD* curve in response to a change in autonomous expenditure, as illustrated in Figure 24-3.

The simple multiplier measures the horizontal shift in the *AD* curve in response to a change in autonomous expenditure.

If the price level remains constant and firms are willing to supply everything that is demanded at that price level, the simple multiplier will also show the change in equilibrium income that will occur in response to a change in autonomous expenditure. This mention of firms' willingness to supply output brings us to a discussion of the *supply side* of the economy.

The Supply Side of the Economy

So far, we have explained how the equilibrium level of GDP is determined *when the price level is taken as given* and how that equilibrium changes as the price level is changed exogenously. We are now ready to take the important next step: adding an *explanation* for the behaviour of the price level. To do this, we need to take account of the supply decisions of firms.

The Aggregate Supply Curve

Aggregate supply refers to the total output of goods and services that firms would like to produce. An *aggregate supply curve* relates aggregate supply to the price level. It is necessary to define two types of such curves. The **short-run aggregate supply *(SRAS)* curve** relates the price level to the quantity of output that firms would like to produce and sell *on the assumption that technology and the prices of all factors of production remain constant.* The **long-run aggregate supply *(LRAS)* curve**, which we discuss in detail in the next chapter, also assumes that technology is constant. It relates the price level to the level of output firms would like to sell after factor prices have adjusted to any excess demands or supplies. For the remainder of this chapter, we confine our attention to the *SRAS* curve.

The short-run aggregate supply curve *(SRAS)* is drawn with the assumption that technology and factor prices are held constant.

The Slope of the *SRAS* Curve

To study the slope of the *SRAS* curve, we need to see how costs are related to output and then how prices are related to output.

Costs and Output.   Suppose that firms wish to increase their output above current levels. What will this do to their costs per unit of output—usually called their **unit costs?** The short-run aggregate supply curve is drawn on the assumption that technology and the prices of all factors of production remain constant. This does not, however, mean that unit costs will be constant. As output increases, less efficient standby plants may have to be used, and less efficient workers may have to be hired, while existing workers may have to be paid overtime rates for additional work. For these and other similar reasons, unit costs will tend to rise as output rises, even when technology and input prices are constant. (Readers who have studied microeconomics will recognize the *law of diminishing returns* as one reason why costs rise in the short run as firms squeeze more output out of a fixed quantity of capital equipment.)

Prices and Output.   To consider the relationship between price and output, we need to consider firms that sell in two distinct types of markets: those in which firms are *price takers* and those in which firms are *price setters*.

short-run aggregate supply *(SRAS)* curve A curve showing the relation between the price level and the quantity of aggregate output supplied on the assumption that technology and all factor prices are held constant.

long-run aggregate supply *(LRAS)* curve A curve showing the relationship between the price level and the quantity of aggregate output supplied when all markets have fully adjusted to the existing price level; a vertical line at $Y = Y^*$.

unit cost   Cost per unit of output, equal to total cost divided by total output.

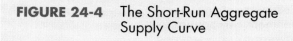

FIGURE 24-4   The Short-Run Aggregate Supply Curve

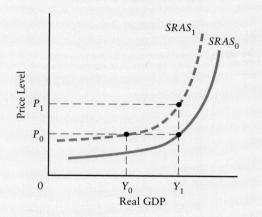

The *SRAS* curve is positively sloped, indicating that firms will provide more aggregate output only at a higher price level. The *SRAS* curve is drawn for a given level of technology and factor prices. Any change in technology or factor prices will shift the *SRAS* curve.

A shift up and to the left reflects a decrease in supply; a shift down and to the right reflects an increase in supply. Starting from (P_0, Y_1) on $SRAS_0$, suppose that there is an increase in input prices. At price level P_0, only Y_0 would be produced. Alternatively, to get output Y_1 would require a rise to price level P_1. The new supply curve is $SRAS_1$, which may be viewed as being above and to the left of $SRAS_0$. An increase in supply, caused by a decrease in input prices or an improvement in technology, would shift the *SRAS* curve downward and to the right, from $SRAS_1$ to $SRAS_0$.

Some industries, especially those that produce raw materials, contain many individual firms. In these cases, each one is too small to influence the market price, which is set by the overall forces of demand and supply. Each firm must accept whatever price is set by the market. Such firms are said to be *price takers*. When the market price changes, these firms will react by altering their level of production.

Because their unit costs rise with output, price-taking firms will produce more only if price increases and will produce less if price falls.

Many other industries, including most of those that produce manufactured products, contain few enough firms that each can influence the market price of its product. Most such firms sell products that differ from one another, although all are similar enough to be thought of as a single product produced by one industry. For example, no two kinds of automobiles are the same, but all automobiles are sufficiently alike that we have no trouble talking about the automobile industry and its product, automobiles. In such cases, each firm must quote a price at which it is prepared to sell each of its products; that is, the firm is a *price setter*. If the demand for the output of price-setting firms increases sufficiently to take their outputs into the range in which their unit costs rise, these firms will not increase their outputs unless they can pass at least some of these extra costs on through higher prices. When demand falls, they will reduce output, and competition among them will tend to cause a reduction in prices whenever their unit costs fall.

Price-setting firms will increase their prices when they expand output into the range in which unit costs are rising.

This is the basic behaviour of firms in response to the changes in demand and prices when technology and factor prices are constant, and it explains the slope of the *SRAS* curve, such as the one shown in Figure 24-4.

The actions of both price-taking and price-setting firms cause the price level and the supply of output to be positively related—the short-run aggregate supply (*SRAS*) curve is upward sloping.

The Increasing Slope of the *SRAS* Curve

In Figure 24-4 we see that the *SRAS* curve not only slopes up but also gets steeper as real GDP increases. That is, at low levels of GDP the *SRAS* curve is relatively flat, but as GDP rises the *SRAS* curve gets progressively steeper. What explains this shape?

When output is low (below potential output), firms typically have excess capacity—some plant and equipment are idle. When firms have excess capacity, only a small increase in the price of their output may be needed to induce them to expand production. Once output is pushed above normal capacity, however, unit costs tend to rise quite rapidly. Many higher-cost expedients may have to be adopted—such as standby capacity, overtime, and extra shifts. These higher-cost methods will not be used unless the selling price of the output has risen enough to cover them. The more output is expanded beyond normal capacity, the more that unit costs rise and hence the larger is the rise in price that is necessary to induce firms to increase output. This increasing slope of the *SRAS* curve is sometimes called the *first asymmetry* in the behaviour of aggregate supply. (The second, *sticky wages*, will be discussed in the next chapter.)

As we will see later in this chapter, the shape of the *SRAS* curve is crucial for determining how the effect of an aggregate demand shock is divided between a change in the price level and a change in real GDP.

Shifts in the *SRAS* Curve

Shifts in the *SRAS* curve, which are shown in Figure 24-4, are called **aggregate supply shocks**. Two sources of aggregate supply shocks are of particular importance: changes in the price of inputs and changes in productivity.

aggregate supply shock   Any event that causes a shift in the aggregate supply curve.

Changes in Input Prices.   Factor prices are held constant along the *SRAS* curve, and when they change, the curve shifts. If factor prices rise, firms will find the profitability of their current production reduced. For any given level of output to be produced, an increase in the price level will be required. If prices do not rise, firms will react by decreasing production. For the economy as a whole, there will be less output supplied at each price level than before the increase in factor prices. Or, to put it another way, there will be a higher price level for each level of output than before the increase in factor prices. Thus, if factor prices rise, the *SRAS* curve shifts upward (or to the left). This is a decrease in aggregate supply.

Changes in the prices of raw materials—such as the lumber shown here—lead to changes in firms' production costs. Such changes cause shifts in the SRAS curve.

Similarly, a fall in factor prices causes the *SRAS* curve to shift downward (or to the right). There will be more output supplied at each price level. Or, to put it differently, the same amount of output will be supplied at a lower price level. This is an increase in aggregate supply. A dramatic example of such a reduction in factor prices occurred in 1997 and 1998 when the world prices of raw materials fell by an average of 30 percent. In the many countries that use raw materials as inputs in manufacturing, the *SRAS* curve shifted to the right.

Changes in Productivity.   If labour productivity rises—that is, each worker can produce more—the unit costs of production will fall (for given wages). Lower costs typically lead to lower prices. Competing firms cut prices in attempts to raise their market shares, and the net result of such competition is that the fall in production costs is accompanied by a fall in prices. That the same output is sold at a lower price causes a shift in the *SRAS* curve downward and to the right. This shift is an increase in aggregate supply, as illustrated in Figure 24-4.

A change in either factor prices or productivity will shift the *SRAS* curve because any given output will be supplied at a different price level than previously. An increase in factor prices or a decrease in productivity shifts the *SRAS* curve to the left; an increase in productivity or a decrease in factor prices shifts it to the right.

FIGURE 24-5 Macroeconomic Equilibrium

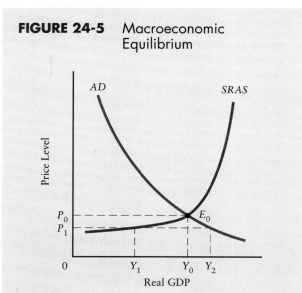

Macroeconomic equilibrium occurs at the intersection of the *AD* and *SRAS* curves and determines the equilibrium values for real GDP and the price level. Given the *AD* and *SRAS* curves in the figure, macroeconomic equilibrium occurs at E_0.

If the price level were equal to P_1, the desired output of firms would be Y_1. However, at P_1, the level of output that is consistent with expenditure decisions would be Y_2. Hence, when the price level is less than P_0, the desired output of firms will be less than the level of real GDP that is consistent with expenditure decisions. This causes upward pressure on the price level.

Similarly, for any price level above P_0, the desired output of firms exceeds the level of output that is consistent with expenditure decisions. This causes downward pressure on the price level.

The only price level where the supply decisions of firms are consistent with desired expenditure is at macroeconomic equilibrium. At P_0, firms wish to produce Y_0. When they do so, they generate a real GDP of Y_0; when real GDP is Y_0, decision makers wish to spend exactly Y_0, thereby purchasing the nation's output. Hence, all decisions are consistent with each other.

Macroeconomic Equilibrium

We have now reached our objective: We are ready to see how both real GDP and the price level are simultaneously determined by the interaction of aggregate demand and aggregate supply.

The equilibrium values of real GDP and the price level occur at the intersection of the *AD* and *SRAS* curves, as shown by the pair Y_0 and P_0 that arise at point E_0 in Figure 24-5. The combination of real GDP and price level that is on both the *AD* and *SRAS* curves is called a *macroeconomic equilibrium*.

To see why the point (Y_0, P_0) is the only macroeconomic equilibrium, first consider what Figure 24-5 shows would happen if the price level were below P_0. At this lower price level, the desired output of firms, as given by the *SRAS* curve, is less than desired aggregate expenditure. The excess desired aggregate expenditure will cause prices to be bid up. Similarly, the figure shows that when the price level is above P_0, the behaviour underlying the *SRAS* and *AD* curves is not consistent. In this case, producers will wish to supply more than the amount that is demanded at that price level. This excess of output supplied over desired aggregate expenditure will cause prices to fall.

Only at the combination of real GDP and price level given by the intersection of the *SRAS* and *AD* curves are demand behaviour and supply behaviour consistent.

Macroeconomic equilibrium thus requires that two conditions be satisfied. The first is familiar to us because it comes from Chapters 22 and 23. At the prevailing price level, desired aggregate expenditure must be equal to actual GDP—that is, households are just willing to buy all that is produced. The *AD* curve is constructed in such a way that this condition holds everywhere along it. The second requirement for equilibrium is introduced by consideration of aggregate supply. At the prevailing price level, firms must wish to produce the prevailing level of GDP, no more and no less. This condition is fulfilled everywhere along the *SRAS* curve. Only where the two curves intersect are both conditions fulfilled simultaneously.

Changes in the Macroeconomic Equilibrium

The aggregate demand and aggregate supply curves can now be used to understand how various shocks to the economy change both real GDP and the price level.

As indicated earlier, a shift in the *AD* curve is called an aggregate demand shock. A rightward shift in the *AD* curve is an increase in aggregate demand; it means that at all price levels, expenditure decisions will now be consistent with a higher level of real GDP. This is called an *expansionary shock*. Similarly, a leftward shift in the *AD* curve is a decrease in aggregate demand—that is, at all price levels, expenditure decisions will now be consistent with a lower level of real GDP. This is called a *contractionary shock*.

Also as indicated earlier, a shift in the *SRAS* curve is called an aggregate supply shock. A rightward shift in the *SRAS* curve is an increase in aggregate supply; at any given price level, more real GDP will be supplied. A leftward shift in the *SRAS* curve is a decrease in aggregate supply; at any given price level, less real GDP will be supplied.

What happens to real GDP and to the price level when either the *AD* or *SRAS* curve shifts?

A shift in either the *AD* or the *SRAS* curve leads to changes in the equilibrium values of the price level and real GDP.

Let's now examine such shocks in a little more detail.

Aggregate Demand Shocks

Figure 24-6 shows the effects of an increase in aggregate demand. This increase could have occurred because of, say, increased investment or government purchases, an increase in foreigners' demand for Canadian goods, or an increase in household consumption resulting from a reduction in personal income taxes. Whatever the cause, the increase in aggregate demand means that more domestic output is demanded at any given price level. As is shown in the figure, following an increase in aggregate demand, both the price level and real GDP rise. Conversely, a decrease in demand causes both the price level and real GDP to fall.

Aggregate demand shocks cause the price level and real GDP to change in the same direction; both rise with an increase in aggregate demand, and both fall with a decrease in aggregate demand.

The Multiplier When the Price Level Varies

We saw earlier in this chapter that the simple multiplier (which we examined in detail in Chapters 22

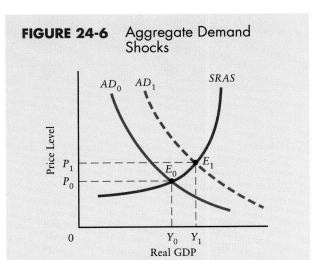

FIGURE 24-6   Aggregate Demand Shocks

Shifts in aggregate demand cause the price level and real GDP to move in the same direction. An increase in aggregate demand shifts the *AD* curve to the right, from AD_0 to AD_1. Macroeconomic equilibrium moves from E_0 to E_1. The price level rises from P_0 to P_1, and real GDP rises from Y_0 to Y_1, reflecting a movement along the *SRAS* curve.

FIGURE 24-7   The Multiplier When the Price Level Varies

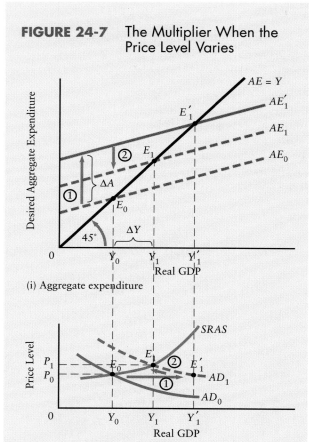

(i) Aggregate expenditure

(ii) Aggregate demand and supply

An increase in autonomous expenditure causes the AE curve to shift upward, but the rise in the price level causes it to shift part of the way down again. Hence, the multiplier is smaller than when the price level is constant. Originally, equilibrium is at point E_0 in both part (i) and part (ii). Desired aggregate expenditure then shifts by ΔA to AE_1', shifting the AD curve to AD_1. These shifts are shown by arrow 1 in both parts. But the adjustment is not yet complete.

The shift in the AD curve raises the price level to P_1 because the $SRAS$ curve is positively sloped. The rise in the price level shifts the AE curve down to AE_1, as shown by arrow 2 in part (i). This is shown as a *movement along* the new AD curve, as indicated by arrow 2 in part (ii). The new equilibrium is thus at E_1. The amount Y_0Y_1 is ΔY, the actual increase in real GDP. The multiplier, adjusted for the effect of the price increase, is the ratio $\Delta Y/\Delta A$ in part (i).

and 23) gives the extent of the horizontal shift in the AD curve in response to a change in autonomous expenditure. If the price level remains constant and firms are willing to supply all that is demanded at the existing price level (as would be the case with a horizontal $SRAS$ curve), the simple multiplier gives the increase in equilibrium national income.

But what happens in the more usual case in which the $SRAS$ curve slopes upward? As can be seen in Figure 24-6, when the $SRAS$ curve is positively sloped, the change in real GDP caused by a change in autonomous expenditure is no longer equal to the size of the horizontal shift in the AD curve. Part of the expansionary impact of an increase in demand is dissipated by a rise in the price level, and only part is transmitted to a rise in real GDP. Of course, an increase in output does occur; thus, a multiplier may still be calculated, but its value is not the same as that of the *simple* multiplier.

When the $SRAS$ curve is upward sloping, the multiplier is smaller than the simple multiplier.

Why is the multiplier smaller when the $SRAS$ curve is positively sloped? The answer lies in the behaviour that is summarized by the AE curve. To understand this, it is useful to think of the final change in real GDP as occurring in two stages, as shown in Figure 24-7.

First, with prices remaining constant, an increase in autonomous expenditure shifts the AE curve upward (from AE_0 to AE_1') and therefore shifts the AD curve to the right. This increase in autonomous expenditure is shown by a shift upward of the AE curve in part (i) of the figure and a shift to the right of the AD curve in part (ii). The horizontal shift in the AD curve is measured by the simple multiplier, but this cannot be the final equilibrium position because firms are unwilling to produce enough to satisfy the extra demand at the existing price level. The final equilibrium must be a point on the $SRAS$ curve.

Second, we take account of the rise in the price level that occurs because of the positive slope of the $SRAS$ curve. As we saw earlier in this chapter, a rise in the price level, via its effect on net exports and on wealth, leads to a downward shift in the AE curve (from AE_1' to AE_1). This second shift of the AE curve partly counteracts the initial rise in real GDP and so reduces the size of the multiplier. The second stage shows up as a downward shift of the AE curve in part (i) of Figure 24-7 and a movement upward and to the left along the new AD curve in part (ii).

The Importance of the Shape of the *SRAS* Curve

We have now seen that the shape of the *SRAS* curve has important implications for how the effects of an aggregate demand shock are divided between changes in real GDP and changes in the price level. Figure 24-8 highlights the price level and GDP effects of aggregate demand shocks by considering *AD* shocks in the presence of an *SRAS* curve that exhibits three distinct ranges.

Over the *flat* range, from 0 to Y_0, any change in aggregate demand leads to no change in prices and, as seen earlier, a response of output equal to that predicted by the simple multiplier.

Over the *intermediate* range, along which the *SRAS* curve is positively sloped, a shift in the *AD* curve gives rise to appreciable changes in both real GDP and the price level. Because of the increase in the price level, the multiplier in this case is positive, but smaller than the simple multiplier.

Over the *steep* range, very little more can be produced, however large the increase in demand. This range deals with an economy near its capacity constraints. Any change in aggregate demand leads to a sharp change in the price level and to little or no change in real GDP. The multiplier in this case is nearly zero.

The effect of any given shift in aggregate demand will be divided between a change in real output and a change in the price level, depending on the conditions of aggregate supply. The steeper the *SRAS* curve, the greater the price effect and the smaller the output effect.

Extensions in Theory 24-1 deals with the special case of a horizontal *SRAS* curve—sometimes called a *Keynesian SRAS* curve. In that case, the aggregate supply curve determines the price level by itself, and the *AD* curve then determines real GDP by itself.

Reconciliation with Previous Analysis

One of the central points of this chapter is that aggregate demand shocks typically lead to changes in *both* price level and the level of real GDP. Furthermore, with a steep enough *SRAS* curve, such aggregate demand shocks will result in no change in real GDP, but only a change in the price level. How do we reconcile this possibility with the analysis of Chapters 22 and 23, where shifts in *AE* *always* change real GDP? The answer is that each *AE* curve is drawn on the assumption that there is a constant price level. An upward shift in the *AE* curve shifts the *AD* curve to the right. However, a steep *SRAS* curve means that the price level rises significantly, and this rise shifts the *AE* curve back down, offsetting some of its initial rise.

We can see this interaction most easily if we study the extreme case, shown in Figure 24-9, in which the *SRAS* curve is vertical. An increase in autonomous expenditure shifts the *AE* curve upward, thus raising the amount demanded. However, a vertical *SRAS* curve means that

Practise with Study Guide Chapter 24, Exercise 4.

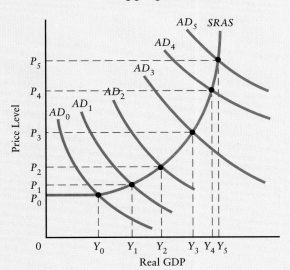

FIGURE 24-8 The Effects of Increases in Aggregate Demand

The effect of increases in aggregate demand is divided between increases in real GDP and increases in prices, depending on the slope of the *SRAS* curve. Because of the increasing slope of the *SRAS* curve, increases in aggregate demand up to AD_0 have virtually no impact on the price level. Successive further increases bring larger price increases and relatively smaller output increases. By the time aggregate demand is at AD_4 or AD_5, virtually all of the effect is on the price level.

EXTENSIONS IN THEORY 24-1

The Keynesian *SRAS* Curve

In this box, we consider an extreme version of the *SRAS* curve that is horizontal over some range of real GDP. It is called the *Keynesian short-run aggregate supply curve*, after John Maynard Keynes (1883–1946), who in his famous book *The General Theory of Employment, Interest and Money* (1936) pioneered the study of the behaviour of economies under conditions of high unemployment. Despite its name, this curve does not describe Keynes' own views on the behaviour of the price level. It is instead the version of aggregate supply used by many of Keynes' followers in their early attempts to express Keynes' work in a formal model—something Keynes himself did not do.

The behaviour that gives rise to the Keynesian *SRAS* curve can be described as follows. When real GDP is below potential GDP, individual firms are operating with excess capacity. They then respond to demand variations by altering output while keeping prices constant. In other words, they will supply whatever they can sell at their existing prices as long as they are producing below their normal capacity.*

Under these circumstances, the economy has a horizontal *SRAS* curve, indicating that any output up to potential output will be supplied at the going price level. The amount that is actually produced is then de-

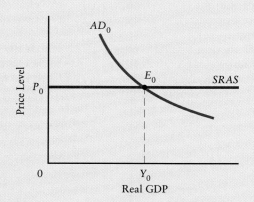

termined by the position of the *AD* curve, as shown in the figure. Thus, real GDP is said to be *demand determined*. If demand rises enough so that firms are trying to squeeze more than normal output out of their plants, their costs will rise, and so will their prices. Hence, the horizontal Keynesian *SRAS* curve applies only to levels of GDP below potential GDP.

This special case of a horizontal *SRAS* curve corresponds to the macro model that we developed in Chapters 22 and 23. Recall in that simple model that we assumed a constant price level. In other words, if the *SRAS* curve is horizontal, our macro model in this chapter is *exactly the same* as the simple version in Chapters 22 and 23. In this case, a change in autonomous expenditure, ΔA, will lead to increases in equilibrium GDP equal to ΔA times the simple multiplier. (In Figure 24-3 this is exactly the distance of the horizontal shift in the *AD* curve in response to any given ΔA.)

---

*There is considerable evidence that many firms do behave like this in the short run. One possible explanation for this is that changing prices frequently is too costly, so firms set the best possible (profit-maximizing) prices when output is at normal capacity and then do not change prices in the face of short-term fluctuations in demand.

Practise with Study Guide Chapter 24, Exercise 6.

output cannot be expanded to satisfy the increased demand. Instead, the extra demand merely forces prices up, and as prices rise, the *AE* curve shifts down again. The rise in prices continues until the *AE* curve is back to where it started. Thus, the rise in prices offsets the expansionary effect of the original shift and consequently leaves both real aggregate expenditure and equilibrium real GDP unchanged.

A vertical *SRAS* curve, however, is quite unrealistic. Most economists agree that the *SRAS* curve is shaped something like the one shown in Figure 24-8—that is, relatively flat for low levels of GDP and becoming steeper as GDP rises. This shape suggests that if GDP is below potential GDP, shifts in aggregate demand primarily affect output; whereas if GDP is above potential GDP, shifts in aggregate demand primarily affect the price level.

Of course, as we have noted already, treating technology and factor prices as constant is appropriate only when the time period under consideration is short. Hence, the *SRAS* curve is used only to analyse the economy in the short run. In the next chapter, we will see what happens in the long run when factor prices respond to changes in real GDP and the price level. First, however, our analysis of the short run needs to be rounded out with a discussion of aggregate supply shocks.

Aggregate Supply Shocks

A decrease in aggregate supply, shown by a shift to the left in the *SRAS* curve, means that less real output will be supplied at any given price level. An increase in aggregate supply, shown by a shift to the right in the *SRAS* curve, means that more real output will be supplied at any given price level.

Figure 24-10 illustrates the effects on the price level and real GDP of a decrease in aggregate supply. This decrease could have occurred because of, say, an increase in the world price of important inputs, such as oil, copper or iron ore. As can be seen from the figure, following the decrease in aggregate supply, the price level rises and real GDP falls. This combination of events is called *stagflation,* a term derived by combining *stagnation* (sometimes used to mean less than full employment) and *inflation.* Conversely, an increase in aggregate supply leads to an increase in real GDP and a decrease in the price level.

Aggregate supply shocks cause the price level and real GDP to change in opposite directions. With an increase in supply, the price level falls and GDP rises; with a decrease in supply, the price level rises and GDP falls.

Oil prices have provided two major examples of negative aggregate supply shocks in recent decades. The economy is especially responsive to changes in the price for oil because, in addition to being used to produce energy, oil is an input into plastics and many other materials that are widely used in manufacturing. Massive increases in oil prices occurred during 1973–1974 and 1979–1980, caused by the successful efforts of the OPEC countries to form a cartel and restrict the output of oil. These increases in the price of oil caused leftward shifts in the *SRAS* curve in most countries. Real GDP fell while the price level rose—stagflation. (In subsequent years the price of oil fell, shifting the *SRAS* curve back to the right, but the declines were more gradual and thus less dramatic than the initial increases.)

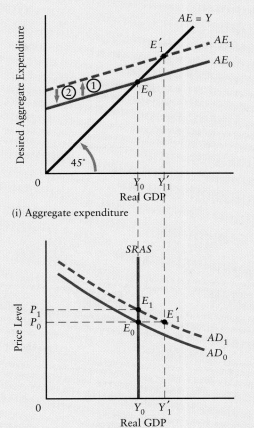

FIGURE 24-9   Demand Shocks When the *SRAS* Curve Is Vertical

(i) Aggregate expenditure

(ii) Aggregate demand and supply

In the extreme case where the *SRAS* curve is vertical, the effect of an increase in autonomous expenditure is solely to increase price level. An increase in autonomous expenditure shifts the *AE* curve upward from AE_0 to AE_1, as shown by arrow 1 in part (i). Given the initial price level P_0, equilibrium would shift from E_0 to E_1' and real GDP would rise from Y_0 to Y_1'. However, the price level does not remain constant. This is shown by the *SRAS* curve in part (ii). Instead, the price level rises to P_1. This causes the *AE* curve to shift back down all the way to AE_0, as shown by arrow 2 in part (i), and equilibrium GDP stays at Y_0. In part (ii), the new equilibrium is at E_1 with GDP at Y_0 and the price level at P_1.

For information on OPEC, see its website: www.opec.org.

FIGURE 24-10 Aggregate Supply Shocks

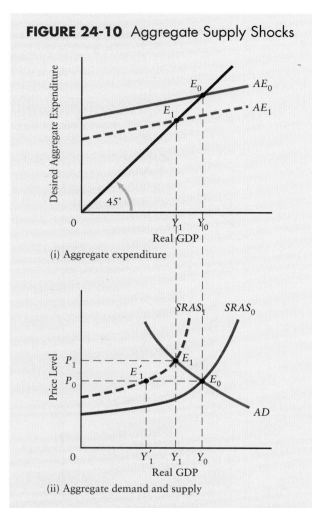

(i) Aggregate expenditure

(ii) Aggregate demand and supply

Aggregate supply shocks cause the price level and real GDP to move in opposite directions. The original equilibrium is at E_0, with GDP of Y_0 appearing in both parts of the figure. The price level is P_0 in part (ii), and at that price level, the desired aggregate expenditure curve is AE_0 in part (i).

A negative aggregate supply shock now shifts the $SRAS$ curve in part (ii) to $SRAS_1$. At the original price level of P_0, firms are now only willing to supply Y_1'. The fall in supply, with no corresponding fall in demand, causes a shortage that leads to a rise in the price level. The new equilibrium is reached at E_1, where the AD curve intersects $SRAS_1$. At the new and higher equilibrium price level of P_1, the AE curve has fallen to AE_1, as shown in part (i).

Commodity prices have provided an important recent example of a positive aggregate supply shock. The Southeast Asian countries of Indonesia, Malaysia, Thailand, and South Korea are all significant users of raw materials. When their economies plunged into a major recession in 1997 and 1998, the world demand for raw materials fell, and the prices of such goods fell as a result. From the summer of 1997 to the end of 1998, the average price of raw materials fell by approximately 30 percent.

Though this was clearly bad economic times for much of Southeast Asia, the reduction in raw materials prices was a *positive* aggregate supply shock for countries that used raw materials as inputs for production. In countries like Canada, the United States, and most of western Europe, the $SRAS$ curves shifted to the right. The effect was to increase real GDP and reduce the price level.[1]

A Word of Warning

We have discussed the effects of aggregate demand and aggregate supply shocks on the economy's price level and real GDP. Students are sometimes puzzled, however, because some events would appear to be *both* demand and supply shocks. How do we analyse such complicated shocks? For example, when OPEC restricted the supply of oil and thus drove up the world price of oil, this was clearly a negative supply shock. After all, oil is a very important input to production for so many firms and so many industries. But for Canada, which produces and exports oil, doesn't the increase in the world price of oil also imply an increase in export revenue? And doesn't this imply a *positive* aggregate demand shock?

The answer to both questions is yes. The OPEC oil shock was indeed a negative aggregate supply shock to any country that uses oil as an input (which means most countries). But for those countries that also produce and export oil—like Canada—the OPEC oil shock was also a positive aggregate demand shock. The rise in the price of oil generated an increase in income to Canadian oil producers—it is no surprise that Alberta's economy was booming throughout the 1970s.

For such countries, a complete analysis of the OPEC oil shocks involves both a leftward shift of the $SRAS$ curve and a rightward shift of the AD curve. In

---

[1]Actually, it is more correct to say that the shock reduced the price level *compared to what it otherwise would have been*. Due to ongoing inflation, the causes of which we will discuss in Chapters 28 and 29, the price level in Canada rarely falls. But we have been assuming throughout this chapter that there is no ongoing inflation, and in that setting a positive $SRAS$ shock like the one described in the text would indeed cause the price level to fall.

APPLYING ECONOMIC CONCEPTS 24-1

The Asian Crisis and the Canadian Economy

In the summer of 1997, the currencies of several countries in Southeast Asia plummeted (relative to the U.S. and Canadian dollars) as their central banks were no longer able to "peg" their exchange rates. We will discuss how such pegged exchange rates operate in Chapter 36. For now, the important point is that, for various reasons, banks, firms, and households in these countries had accumulated a large stock of debt denominated in foreign currencies, especially U.S. dollars. The sudden depreciations of their currencies—in some cases by 70 percent in just a few days—led to dramatic increases in the amount of domestic income required to pay the interest on this debt. Manufacturing firms and financial institutions went bankrupt, workers were laid off, and economic output fell sharply. By late in 1997, the economies of Malaysia, Indonesia, Thailand, South Korea, and the Philippines were suffering major recessions.

How did this Asian crisis affect Canada? It had offsetting positive and negative effects on the level of economic activity in Canada. The events in Asia generated both a *negative* aggregate demand shock and a *positive* aggregate supply shock for Canada.

To understand the demand side of the story, we must recognize that these Asian economies are important users of raw materials. When their level of economic activity declined sharply, so, too, did their demand for raw materials. Indeed, average raw materials prices fell by roughly 30 percent between the summer of 1997 and the end of 1998. But raw materials are an important export for Canada. The decline in the world's demand for raw materials implied a reduction in demand for Canadian goods. As a result, Canadian producers of copper, pork, newsprint, lumber, and iron ore suffered significantly. In terms of the simple diagram we have been using in this chapter, the demand part of the Asian crisis is represented as a leftward shift of the Canadian AD curve.

But the story does not end there. Also important to Canada is the fact that many Canadian manufacturing firms use those same raw materials as inputs for their production of car parts, pre-fabricated houses and trailers, electrical equipment, and so on. A dramatic reduction in the prices of raw materials implies a reduction in costs for manufacturing firms. This is a positive aggregate supply shock, and is illustrated by a rightward shift of the Canadian SRAS curve.

What is the overall effect on the Canadian economy? The effect of each shock taken separately is to reduce the price level—so the overall effect is unambiguously a lower price level.* In contrast, the effect on real GDP would ap-

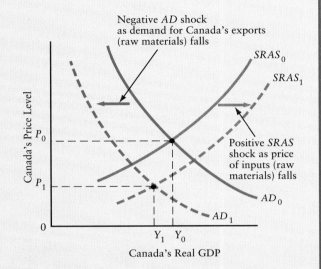

pear to be ambiguous since the AD shock reduces GDP whereas the SRAS curve increases it. But this is not quite right. Since Canada is a net exporter of raw materials (it exports more raw materials than it imports), it must experience a decrease in national income when these prices fall. In other words, the net effect of the negative demand shock and the positive supply shock is to reduce Canadian GDP. The figure is therefore drawn with the AD shock being larger than the SRAS shock and so the new equilibrium level of GDP, Y_0, is lower than in the initial equilibrium, Y_1.

In contrast, the appropriate diagram for the United States would show a similar rightward SRAS shift (because raw materials are equally important for production in the United States) but a smaller leftward AD shift (because as a share of its economy, the United States is a much smaller producer of raw materials than is Canada). Since the United States is a net importer of raw materials, its level of income must be *increased* when the prices of raw materials decline. In other words, the net effect of the negative demand shock and the positive supply shock is to increase U.S. GDP. Thus, the overall effect of the Asian crisis on the U.S. economy is different from its effect on the Canadian economy.

By the time this book went to press, in the fall of 1999, the Asian economies were on the road to economic recovery and the world prices of raw materials had begun to increase. Thus, the shifts of the AD and SRAS curves shown in the figure began to reverse themselves.

---

*Recall footnote 1 on page 572. We are assuming in this analysis that there is no ongoing inflation, so a positive SRAS shock or a negative AD shock reduces the price level. A more accurate description for the Canadian economy in 1998, with some ongoing inflation, is that the price level fell below what it otherwise would have been. This appears as a reduction in the rate of inflation.

For interesting information on the Asian crisis, see Nouriel Roubini's website: www.stern.nyu.edu/~nroubini.

this case, the equilibrium price level clearly rises. The overall effect on real GDP, however, then depends on the relative importance of the supply and demand effects. For example, the United States and Canada both use oil as an important input to production, and so the *SRAS* shifts were similar in the two countries. As a share of its economy, however, the United States produces much less oil than does Canada, and so the rightward *AD* shift in Canada was larger than in the United States. The overall effect was that the United States suffered a larger reduction in real GDP than did Canada as a result of the OPEC oil shock.

The important message here is a simple one:

Many economic events—especially changes in the world prices of raw materials—cause both aggregate demand and aggregate supply shocks. The overall effect on the economy depends on the relative importance of the two separate effects.

Applying Economic Concepts 24-1 discusses the effect of the 1997–98 Asian economic crisis on the Canadian economy. The Asian crisis represented both a negative demand shock and a positive supply shock to Canada.

SUMMARY

The Demand Side of the Economy

- The *AE* curve shows desired aggregate expenditure for each level of GDP at a particular price level. Its intersection with the 45° line determines equilibrium GDP for that price level. Equilibrium GDP thus occurs where desired aggregate expenditure equals actual GDP. A change in the price level changes household wealth and thus causes a shift in the *AE* curve: upward when the price level falls and downward when the price level rises. This leads to a new equilibrium level of real GDP.
- The *AD* curve plots the equilibrium level of GDP that corresponds to each possible price level. A change in equi-

librium GDP following a change in the price level is shown by a movement along the *AD* curve.
- A rise in the price level lowers exports and lowers consumers' spending (because it decreases consumers' wealth). Both of these changes reduce equilibrium GDP and cause the *AD* curve to have a negative slope.
- The *AD* curve shifts horizontally when any element of autonomous expenditure changes, and the simple multiplier measures the magnitude of the shift.

The Supply Side of the Economy

- The short-run aggregate supply *(SRAS)* curve, drawn for given technology and factor prices, is positively sloped because unit costs rise with increasing output and because rising product prices make it profitable to increase output.

- An increase in productivity or a decrease in factor prices shifts the *SRAS* curve to the right. This is an increase in aggregate supply. A decrease in productivity or an increase in factor prices shifts the *SRAS* curve to the left. This is a decrease in aggregate supply.

Macroeconomic Equilibrium

🔟❹❺

- Macroeconomic equilibrium refers to equilibrium values of real GDP and the price level, as determined by the intersection of the *AD* and *SRAS* curves. Shifts in the *AD* and *SRAS* curves, called aggregate demand shocks and aggregate supply shocks, change the equilibrium values of real GDP and the price level.
- When the *SRAS* curve is upward sloping, an aggregate demand shock causes the price level and real GDP to move in the same direction. The division of the effects between a change in real GDP and a change in the price level depends on the shape of the *SRAS* curve. When the *SRAS* curve is flat, shifts in the *AD* curve primarily affect real GDP. When the *SRAS* curve is steep, shifts in the *AD* curve primarily affect the price level.

- An aggregate supply shock moves equilibrium GDP along the *AD* curve, causing the price level and real GDP to move in opposite directions. A leftward shift in the *SRAS* curve causes stagflation—rising prices and falling real GDP. A rightward shift causes an increase in real GDP and a fall in the price level.
- Some events are both aggregate supply and aggregate demand shocks. Changes in the world prices of raw materials, for example, shift the *SRAS* curve. If the country (like Canada) is also a producer of such raw materials, there will also be a shift in the *AD* curve. The overall effect then depends on the relative sizes of the separate effects.

K E Y   C O N C E P T S

Effects of an exogenous change in the price level	Negative slope of the *AD* curve	The multiplier when the price level varies
Relationship between the *AE* and *AD* curves	Positive slope of the *SRAS* curve	Aggregate supply shocks
	Macroeconomic equilibrium	
	Aggregate demand shocks	

S T U D Y   E X E R C I S E S

1. Consider the effects of an exogenous increase in the domestic price level. For each of the assets listed, explain how the change in the price level would affect the wealth of the asset holder. Then explain the effect on *aggregate* (private sector) wealth.

   a. Cash holdings
   b. Deposits in a bank account
   c. A household mortgage
   d. A corporate bond that promises to pay the bondholder $10 000 on January 1, 2006
   e. A government Treasury bill that promises to pay the holder $10 000 on January 1, 2006

2. Consider the following simplified *AE* function:

   $$AE = 350 + 0.8Y + 0.1(M/P)$$

   where *AE* is desired aggregate expenditure, *Y* is real GDP, *M* is the private sector's *nominal wealth*, and *P* is the price level. Suppose that *M* is constant and equal to 6000.

   a. Explain why the expression for *AE* above makes sense. Why do *M* and *P* enter the *AE* function?
   b. Fill in the table below:

P	M/P	AE
1	—	—
2	—	—
3	—	—
4	—	—
5	—	—
6	—	—

   c. Plot each of the *AE* functions—one for each price level—on the same scale 45° line diagram.
   d. Compute the level of equilibrium national income for each of the values of *P*.
   e. Plot the pairs of price level and equilibrium national income on a scale diagram with *P* on the vertical axis and *Y* on the horizontal axis.

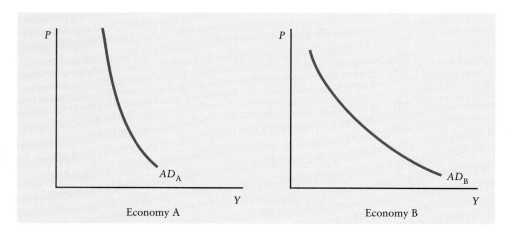

Economy A   Economy B

3. Consider the diagrams above showing the AD curves in two economies. Economy A is Autarkland—it does not trade with the rest of the world (*autarky* is a situation in which a country does not trade with other countries). Economy B is Openland—it exports to and imports from the rest of the world.

   a. Explain why an increase in the domestic price level (for a given exchange rate) reduces net exports in Openland. How would you illustrate this with the *AE* curve in the 45° line diagram?
   b. Explain why the *AD* curve is steeper in Autarkland than in Openland.
   c. If there are never any net exports in Autarkland, why isn't the *AD* curve vertical? Explain what other aspect of the economy generates a downward-sloping *AD* curve.

4. The economy of Neverland has the following *AD* and *SRAS* schedules. Denote Y_{AD} as the level of real GDP along the *AD* curve; let Y_{SRAS} be the level of real GDP along the *SRAS* curve. GDP is shown in billions of 1992 dollars.

Price Level	Y_{AD}	Y_{SRAS}
90	1100	750
100	1000	825
110	900	900
120	800	975
130	700	1050
140	600	1125

   a. Plot the *AD* and *SRAS* curves on a scale diagram.
   b. What is the price level and level of real GDP in Neverland's macroeconomic equilibrium?
   c. Suppose the level of potential output in Neverland is $950 billion. Is the current equilibrium level of real GDP greater than or less than potential?

5. Each of the following events is either a *cause* or a *consequence* of a shift in the *AD* or *SRAS* curve. Identify which it is and, if it is a cause, describe the effect on equilibrium real GDP and the price level.

   a. OPEC's actions significantly increased the world price of oil in 1979–80.
   b. During 1996–99, Canadian real GDP was growing at a healthy pace but inflation showed no signs of rising.
   c. World commodity prices declined sharply in 1997–98. Many of these commodities are both produced in Canada and are used as important inputs for Canadian firms.
   d. The end of the Cold War led to large declines in defence spending in many countries (including Canada).
   e. Canadian exports increased in response to a falling external value of the Canadian dollar in the mid 1990s.
   f. Several provinces lowered their personal income-tax rates in the late 1990s.
   g. The federal government reduced its level of government purchases (*G*) in the late 1990s.

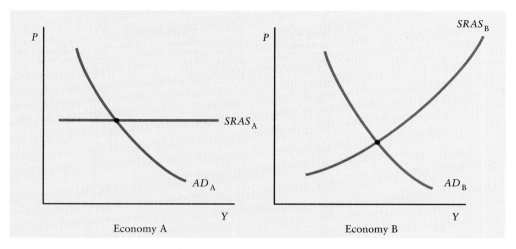

Economy A   Economy B

6. The diagrams above show the AD and SRAS curves in two different economies.

a. Explain what aspect of firms' behaviour might give rise to the horizontal SRAS curve in Economy A.

b. Explain what aspect of firms' behaviour gives rise to the upward-sloping SRAS curve in Economy B.

c. In which economy is output demand determined? Explain.

d. Consider the effects of an increase in autonomous expenditure. Which economy has the larger multiplier? Explain your reasoning.

7. This is a challenging question and involves algebraically solving the system of two equations given by the AD and SRAS curves. The equations for the curves are given by:

AD: $Y_{AD} = 710 - 30P + 5G$

SRAS: $Y_{SRAS} = 10 + 5P - 2P_{OIL}$

where Y is real GDP, P is the price level, G is the level of government purchases, and P_{OIL} is the world price of oil.

a. Explain the various terms in the AD curve. What is the value of the simple multiplier? (Hint: the simple multiplier is the change in equilibrium real GDP when some autonomous component of expenditure, like G, changes by \$1.)

b. Explain the various terms in the SRAS curve. Explain why the price of oil enters negatively.

c. Solve for the equilibrium value of real GDP and the price level.

d. Using your solution to part c, what is the effect of a change in G on equilibrium Y and P?

e. Using your solution to part c, what is the effect of a change in P_{OIL} on equilibrium Y and P?

DISCUSSION QUESTIONS

1. In 1979 and 1980, the British government greatly reduced income taxes but restored the lost government revenue by raising excise and sales taxes. These actions led to a sharp increase in the price level and a fall in output. Explain these events in terms of shifts in the aggregate demand or aggregate supply curves (or both).

2. This chapter discussed the meaning of aggregate demand and aggregate supply shocks, and several examples were given of each. But some shocks can be both demand-side shocks and supply-side shocks. Consider the prices of many commodities, such as lumber, newsprint, oil, copper, grains, and iron ore. The prices

of such commodities are determined in world markets, and are subject to significant fluctuations from year to year. For example, in 1997–98, there was a significant decline in the prices of many such commodities. Explain how such a decline in commodity prices can lead to both a decline in Canadian aggregate demand and an increase in Canadian aggregate supply. How would you determine the net effect on real GDP and the price level?

3. Show the effects on the price level and real GDP of a major union wage settlement that significantly increases wages. Is this a supply shock, a demand shock, or both?

4. Following are the combinations of output and price level given by real GDP and the CPI, respectively, for some recent years. Treat each pair as if it is the intersection of an *AD* and an *SRAS* curve. Plot these data. Then think about the possible shifts in the *AD* or *SRAS* curves that could have caused them. Is it possible to know what the underlying shifts are? Why or why not?

Year	CPI (1992 = 100)	GDP (billions of 1992 dollars)
1990	93.3	709.9
1991	98.5	697.3
1992	100.0	702.6
1993	101.8	718.2
1994	102.0	751.1
1995	104.2	767.9
1996	105.9	777.2
1997	107.6	806.7
1998	108.9	830.7

CHAPTER 25

Output and Prices in the Long Run

LO LEARNING OBJECTIVES

1 Understand how wages and other factor prices respond to recessionary and inflationary gaps, and how this shifts the *SRAS* curve.

2 Explain how the economy adjusts following an aggregate demand or aggregate supply shock.

3 Define the economy's long-run aggregate supply (*LRAS*) curve.

4 Explain the different causes of short-run and long-run changes in real GDP.

5 Explain why the paradox of thrift applies in the short run but not in the long run.

6 Recognize how lags and uncertainty place limitations on the use of fiscal policy.

This chapter examines how the economy's *long-run* values of real GDP and the price level are determined. In the previous chapter, we introduced the short-run aggregate supply (*SRAS*) curve to represent the supply side of the economy—that is, firms' willingness to supply output at various price levels. Central to our discussion of the *SRAS* curve was the assumption that all factor prices were constant. It is now time to relax the assumption of constant factor prices and examine how factor prices are influenced by the state of the economy. The flexibility of wages and other factor prices is the fundamental difference between the short run and long run in macroeconomics.

Every worker knows that the best time to ask for a raise is during a boom, and that it is difficult to get significant wage increases during a recession. Every businessperson knows that the cost of many materials tends to rise rapidly during business expansions and to fall—often dramatically—during recessions. In short, factor prices change with economic conditions, and we need to allow for these effects. To do this, we need to see what happens in a longer-term setting, when changes in real GDP induce changes in factor prices.

Before we proceed, however, there is one important point that must be made. In Chapter 24 the *SRAS* curve was drawn under the assumption of given factor prices *and* a given state of technology. In this chapter we will examine in detail how factor prices change, but throughout the chapter we will maintain the assumption that technology (and thus productivity) is constant. This allows us to focus more clearly on the process of factor-price adjustment. In Chapter 32, where we explore the details of long-run economic growth, technological change will take centre stage. But, for now, technology is held constant.

Induced Changes in Factor Prices

We must begin by reconsidering two key concepts that we first encountered in Chapter 19—potential output and the output gap.

Potential Output and the Output Gap

Recall from our discussion in Chapter 19 that *potential output* is the total output that can be produced when all productive resources—labour and capital equipment, in particular—are being used at their *normal rates of utilization*. When a nation's actual GDP diverges from its potential GDP, the difference is called the output gap (or GDP gap).

Although growth in potential output has powerful effects from one decade to the next, its change from one *year* to the next is small enough to be ignored when studying the year-to-year behaviour of real GDP and the price level. In this chapter, therefore, we view variations in the output gap as determined solely by variations in *actual* GDP around a constant level of *potential* GDP.

Figure 25-1 shows real GDP being determined by the intersection of the *AD* and *SRAS* curves. Potential output is constant, and it is shown by identical vertical lines in the two parts of the figure. In part (i), the *AD* and *SRAS* curves intersect to produce an equilibrium real GDP less than potential output. The result, as we saw in Chapter 19, is called a *recessionary output gap* because recessions are often characterized as having

FIGURE 25-1   The Output Gap

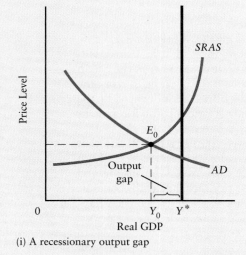
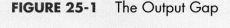

(i) A recessionary output gap

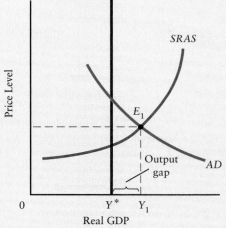

(ii) An inflationary output gap

The output gap is the difference between potential output, *Y**, and actual GDP, *Y*. Potential output is shown by the vertical line at *Y**. A recessionary gap, shown in panel (i), occurs when potential output is greater than real GDP. An inflationary gap, shown in panel (ii), occurs when real GDP is greater than potential output.

GDP below potential output. In part (ii), the *AD* and *SRAS* curves intersect to produce an equilibrium real GDP above potential output, resulting in what is called an *inflationary output gap*. The way in which an inflationary output gap puts upward pressure on prices will become clear in the ensuing discussion.

Factor Prices and the Output Gap

The output gap provides a convenient measure of the pressure on factor prices to change. When real GDP is above potential output, demand for factors will also be high. When real GDP is below potential output, demand for factors will be correspondingly low. This relationship holds for all factors of production, including labour, land, raw materials, and capital equipment. The discussion that follows is simplified, however, by focusing on one key factor, labour, and on its price, the wage rate.

When there is an inflationary gap, actual GDP exceeds potential GDP, and the demand for labour services will be relatively high. When there is a recessionary gap, actual GDP is below potential GDP, and the demand for labour services will be relatively low.

These two situations have implications for wages. In the previous chapter we referred to average costs per unit of output as *unit costs;* to focus on labour costs, we now use average wage costs per unit of output, which we refer to as *unit labour costs*.

Before we examine the effects of output gaps on wages and unit labour costs, it is worth noting that even in the absence of an output gap, the presence of ongoing inflation would influence the normal pattern of wage changes. Wage contracts often allow for changes in the price level that are expected to occur during the life of the contract. For the discussion in this chapter we make the simplifying assumption that the price level is expected to be constant; hence changes in money wages are also expected to be changes in real wages. We will discuss the distinction between changes in money wages and real wages and the important role played by expectations of price level changes in Chapter 29 when we examine the process of inflation.

Output Above Potential

Sometimes the *AD* and *SRAS* curves intersect where actual output exceeds potential, as illustrated in part (ii) of Figure 25-1. Because firms are producing beyond their normal capacity output, there is an unusually large demand for all factor inputs, including labour. Labour shortages will emerge in some industries and among many groups of workers. Firms will try to bid workers away from other firms in order to maintain the high levels of output and sales made possible by the boom conditions.

As a result of these tight labour-market conditions, workers will find that they have considerable bargaining power with their employers, and they will put upward pressure on wages. Firms, recognizing that demand for their goods is strong, will be anxious to maintain a high level of output. To prevent their workers from either striking or quitting and moving to other employers, firms will be willing to accede to some of these upward pressures.

The boom that is associated with an inflationary gap generates a set of conditions—high profits for firms and unusually large demand for labour— that causes wages and thus unit labour costs to rise.

When output is above potential, the excess demand for labour tends to push up wages.

As unit labour costs increase in response to the inflationary gap, firms reduce the quantity of output supplied for any given price level—the SRAS curve shifts up and to the left. This shift has the effect of reducing equilibrium real GDP and raising the price level. Real GDP moves back toward potential and the inflationary gap begins to close.

Output Below Potential

Sometimes the AD and SRAS curves intersect where actual output is less than potential, as illustrated in part (i) of Figure 25-1. Because firms are producing below their normal-capacity output, there is an unusually low demand for all factor inputs, including labour. There will be labour surpluses in some industries and among some groups of workers. Firms will have below-normal sales and not only will resist upward pressures on wages but will seek reductions in wages.

The slump that is associated with a recessionary gap generates a set of conditions—low profits for firms and low demand for labour—that causes wages, and thus unit labour costs, to fall.

As unit labour costs fall in response to the recessionary gap, firms increase the quantity of output supplied for any given price level—the SRAS curve shifts down and to the right. This shift has the effect of increasing equilibrium real GDP and reducing the price level. Real GDP moves back toward potential and the recessionary gap begins to close.

Adjustment Asymmetry

At this stage, we encounter an important asymmetry in the economy's aggregate supply behaviour. Boom conditions (an inflationary gap), along with labour shortages, cause wages and unit labour costs to rise. The experience of many developed economies, however, suggests that the downward pressures on wages during slumps (recessionary gaps) often do not operate as quickly as the upward pressures during booms. Even when wages fall, they tend to fall more slowly than they would rise in an equally sized inflationary gap. This *wage stickiness* implies that the rightward shift in the SRAS curve and the downward pressure on the price level are correspondingly slight.[1]

Both upward and downward adjustments to wages and unit labour costs do occur, but there are differences in the speed at which they typically operate. Booms can cause wages to rise very rapidly; recessions usually cause wages to fall only slowly.[2]

The Phillips Curve

We saw in Chapter 19 that when real GDP is equal to potential GDP, the unemployment rate is equal to the *nonaccelerating inflation rate of unemployment*, or NAIRU. This cumbersome acronym will be explained in detail in Chapter 29; economists often use the easier term, the *natural rate of unemployment*. We use U^* to designate the NAIRU (or the natural rate of unemployment).

---

[1]This is the second asymmetry in aggregate supply that we have encountered. The first involves the changing slope of the SRAS curve, discussed in Chapter 24.

[2]Though unit labour costs do tend to fall during recessionary gaps, nominal wages rarely fall. The reason is that productivity tends to increase continually, thus allowing wages to rise, even though more slowly than productivity. But such changes in productivity shift the LRAS curve to the right and complicate our analysis. In this chapter we hold productivity and thus the LRAS curve constant. We then talk of how nominal wages—and thus unit labour costs—respond to output gaps.

U^* is not zero. Instead, even when output is equal to potential, there may be significant *frictional* and *structural* unemployment. A detailed discussion of U^* and its determinants must await Chapter 30, but for now we simply note the relationship between output gaps and the gap between the unemployment rate and U^*. Our previous discussion emphasized that when real GDP exceeds potential, the excess demand for labour pushes wages up. In these situations, the unemployment rate is less than U^*. That discussion also emphasized that when real GDP is less than potential, the excess supply of labour puts downward pressure on wages. In these situations, the unemployment rate exceeds U^*.

This relationship between U^*, the actual unemployment rate, and the rate of change of wages is illustrated by one of the most famous curves in macroeconomics—the *Phillips curve*. *Extensions in Theory 25-1* discusses the Phillips curve and how it relates to the short-run aggregate supply curve. The key point is that the Phillips curve describes the adjustment process we have been discussing. A *movement along* the Phillips curve leads to a change in the rate at which the *SRAS* curve is shifting.

In Chapter 29 we will discuss the Phillips curve in more detail when we discuss the relationship between inflation and unemployment.

Inflationary and Recessionary Gaps

Now it should be clear why the output gaps are named as they are. When real GDP exceeds potential GDP, there will normally be rising unit costs, and the *SRAS* curve will be shifting upward. This will in turn push the price level up. Indeed, the most obvious event accompanying these conditions is likely to be significant inflation. The larger the excess of real GDP over potential GDP, the greater the inflationary pressure. The term *inflationary gap* emphasizes this salient feature when output exceeds potential output.

When actual output is less than potential output, as we have seen, there will be unemployment of labour and other productive resources. Unit labour costs will fall only slowly, leading to a slow downward shift in the *SRAS* curve. Hence, the price level will be falling only slowly, so that *unemployment* will be the output gap's most obvious result. The term *recessionary gap* emphasizes this salient feature that high rates of unemployment occur when actual output falls short of potential output.

The induced effects of output gaps on unit labour costs and the consequent shifts in the *SRAS* curve play an important role in our analysis of the long-run consequences of aggregate demand and aggregate supply shocks, to which we now turn.

Demand and Supply Shocks

We can now extend our study to cover the longer-run consequences of aggregate demand and aggregate supply shocks, incorporating changes in factor prices. We need to examine the effects of expansionary and contractionary shocks separately because the behaviour of unit costs is not symmetrical for the two cases. Let's begin with demand shocks.

Expansionary *AD* Shocks

Suppose the economy starts with a stable price level and that real GDP equals potential GDP as shown by the initial equilibrium in part (i) of Figure 25-2. Now suppose that this

EXTENSIONS IN THEORY 25-1

The Phillips Curve and the Shifting *SRAS* Curve

In the early 1950s, Professor A. W. Phillips of the London School of Economics was conducting pioneering research on macroeconomic policy. In his early models, he related the rate of inflation to the difference between actual and potential output. Later he investigated the empirical underpinnings of this equation by studying the relationship between the rate of increase of wages and the level of unemployment. He studied these variables because unemployment data were available as far back as the mid-nineteenth century, whereas very little data on output gaps were available when he did his empirical work. In 1958, he reported that a stable relationship had existed between these two variables for 100 years in the United Kingdom. This relationship came to be known as the Phillips curve. The **Phillips curve** provided an explanation, rooted in empirical observation, of the speed with which wage changes shifted the *SRAS* curve by changing unit labour costs.

The original Phillips curve related wage changes to the level of unemployment. But we can express the same information in a slightly different way. Note that unemployment and output gaps are negatively related—a recessionary gap is associated with high unemployment, and an inflationary gap is associated with low unemployment. We can therefore create another Phillips curve which plots wage changes against output (rather than against unemployment). Both figures show the same information.

Inflationary gaps (when $Y>Y^*$ and $U<U^*$) are associated with *increases* in wages. Recessionary gaps (when $Y<Y^*$ and $U>U^*$) are associated with *decreases* in wages.[*] Thus, a Phillips curve that plots wage changes against real GDP is upward sloping whereas a Phillips curve that plots wage changes against the unemployment rate is downward sloping. Both versions of the Phillips curve are shown in the accompanying figure.

When output is at potential, firms are at their capacity level of output and all factors are being used at their normal rates of utilization. There is neither upward nor downward pressure on wages (or other factor prices) because there is neither an excess demand nor an excess supply of labour. Hence, the Phillips curve cuts the horizontal axis at Y^* (and at U^*). This is how Phillips drew his original curve.

The Phillips curve is *not* the same as the *SRAS* curve. The *SRAS* curve has the *price level* on the vertical axis whereas the Phillip curve has the *rate of change of wages* on the vertical axis. How are the two curves related? The economy's location on the Phillips curve indicates how the *SRAS* curve is shifting as a result of the existing output gap.

For example, suppose a positive aggregate demand (or supply) shock causes real GDP to increase to Y_1 and thus

---

[*] Recall that we are assuming productivity to be constant so that changes in wages imply changes in unit labour costs. When productivity is growing, however, recessionary output gaps cause unit labour costs to fall. This only requires wages to be growing more slowly than productivity, not to be actually falling.

Phillips curve
Originally, a relationship between the unemployment rate and the rate of change of money wages. Now often drawn as a relationship between actual GDP and the rate of price inflation.

situation is disturbed by an increase in autonomous expenditure, perhaps caused by an upturn in business confidence and a resulting boom in investment spending. Figure 25-2(i) shows the effects of this aggregate demand shock in raising both the price level and real GDP. The AD curve shifts from AD_0 to AD_1, and real GDP rises above potential GDP. An inflationary gap opens up.

We have seen that an inflationary gap leads to increases in wages, which cause unit costs to rise. The *SRAS* curve shifts to the left as firms respond to the higher input costs by increasing their output prices. As seen in part (ii) of the figure, the upward shift of the *SRAS* curve causes a further rise in the price level, but this time the price rise is associated with a *fall* in output.

The cost increases (and the consequent upward shifts of the *SRAS* curve) continue until the inflationary gap has been removed—that is, until in part (ii) real GDP returns to Y^*. Only then is there no excess demand for labour, and only then do wages and unit costs, and hence the *SRAS* curve, stabilize.

produces an inflationary gap. The excess demand for labour puts upward pressure on wages and the economy moves along the Phillips curve to point A, where wages begin rising. The increase in wages, as we have seen both in this chapter and the previous one, increases unit costs and causes the $SRAS$ curve to shift up and to the left. Thus, each point on the Phillips curve determines the rate at which the $SRAS$ curve is shifting. To complete the example, note that as the $SRAS$ curve shifts to the left, the level of GDP will fall and the inflationary gap will begin to close. The economy thus moves back along the Phillips curve to where it started.

Note that the convex shape of the Phillips curve is not accidental—it reflects the adjustment asymmetry we mentioned in the text. The convexity of the Phillips curve im-plies that an inflationary gap of a given amount will lead to faster wage increases than an equally sized recessionary gap will lead to wage reductions. In other words, an inflationary gap will cause the $SRAS$ curve to shift up more quickly than a recessionary gap will cause the $SRAS$ curve to shift down.

Finally, you might be wondering what would happen if the Phillips curve were to shift. And what would cause such a shift? As we will see in Chapter 29 when we discuss the phenomenon of sustained inflation, an important cause of shifts of the Phillips curve is changes in firms' and households' *expectations* of future inflation. For now, the best way to think of the Phillips curve is as an easy graphical way of describing the process of wage adjustment in response to output gaps.

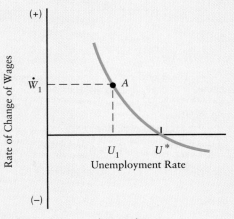

(i) Wage changes and unemployment

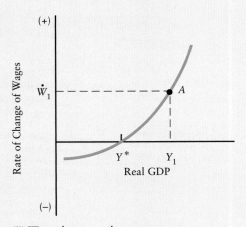

(ii) Wage changes and output

The ability to get more output from the economy than its underlying potential output is only a short-term possibility. When real GDP is greater than Y^*, inflationary forces are set in motion that bring GDP back to Y^*.

An adjustment mechanism eventually eliminates any boom caused by a demand shock by returning real GDP to its potential level.

Practise with Study Guide Chapter 25, Exercise 2.

Contractionary AD Shocks

Suppose again that the economy starts with stable prices and real GDP equal to potential, as shown in part (i) of Figure 25-3. Now assume that there is a *decline* in aggregate demand. This negative aggregate demand shock might be a reduction in investment expenditure, or perhaps a decline in the world demand for Canadian lumber or computer software.

FIGURE 25-2   The Long-Run Effect of a Positive Aggregate Demand Shock

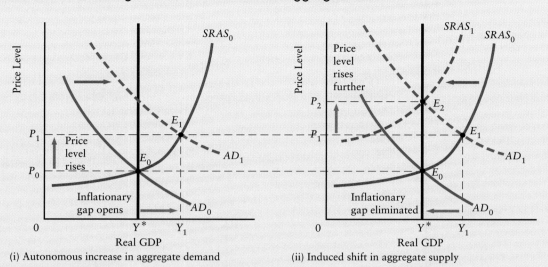

(i) Autonomous increase in aggregate demand   (ii) Induced shift in aggregate supply

A rightward shift of the *AD* curve first raises prices and output along the *SRAS* curve. It then induces a shift of the *SRAS* curve that further raises prices but lowers output along the new *AD* curve. In part (i), the economy is in equilibrium at E_0, at its level of potential output, Y^*, and price level P_0. The *AD* curve then shifts from AD_0 to AD_1. This moves equilibrium to E_1, with income Y_1 and price level P_1, and opens up an inflationary gap.

In part (ii), the inflationary gap results in an increase in wages and other input costs, shifting the *SRAS* curve leftward. As this happens, output falls and the price level rises along AD_1. Eventually, when the *SRAS* curve has shifted to $SRAS_1$, output is back to Y^* and the inflationary gap has been eliminated. However, the price level has risen to P_2. The long-run result of the aggregate demand shock is therefore a higher price level with no change in real GDP.

The first effects of the decline are a fall in output and some downward adjustment of prices, as shown in part (i) of the figure. As real GDP falls below potential, a recessionary gap is created, and unemployment rises. At this point we must analyse two separate cases. The first is where wages fall quickly in response to the excess supply of labour. The second is where wages fall only slowly.

Flexible Wages

Suppose wages (and other factor prices) fall quickly in response to the recessionary gap. The *SRAS* curve would therefore shift quickly to the right as the lower wages lead to reduced unit costs.

As shown in part (ii) of Figure 25-3, the economy would move along the new *AD* curve, with falling prices and rising output, until real GDP was quickly restored to potential, Y^*. We conclude that if wages were to fall rapidly whenever there was unemployment, the resulting shift in the *SRAS* curve would quickly restore full employment.

Flexible wages that fall rapidly during periods of unemployment provide an automatic adjustment mechanism that pushes the economy back toward potential output.

Sticky Wages

Boom conditions, along with labour shortages, do cause wages to rise, shifting the *SRAS* curve upward. In general, the bigger the inflationary gap, the faster wages will rise and

FIGURE 25-3   The Long-Run Effect of a Negative Aggregate Demand Shock

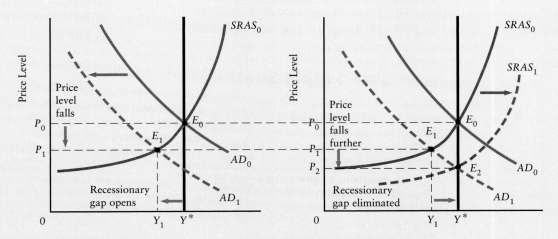

A leftward shift of the *AD* curve first lowers the price level and GDP along the *SRAS* curve and then induces a (slow) shift of the *SRAS* curve that further lowers prices but raises output along the new *AD* curve. In part (i), the economy is in equilibrium at E_0, at its level of potential output, Y^*, and price level P_0. The *AD* curve then shifts to AD_1, moving equilibrium to E_1, with income Y_1 and price level P_1, and opens up a recessionary gap.

Part (ii) shows the adjustment back to potential output that occurs from the supply side of the economy. The fall in wages shifts the *SRAS* curve to the right. Real GDP rises, and the price level falls further along the new *AD* curve. Eventually, the *SRAS* curve reaches $SRAS_1$, with equilibrium at E_2. The price level stabilizes at P_2 when real GDP returns to Y^*, closing the recessionary gap.

the more quickly the *SRAS* curve will shift upward. However, as we noted earlier when we encountered the second asymmetry of aggregate supply, the experience of many economies suggests that wages typically do not fall rapidly in response to even large recessionary gaps. It is sometimes said that wages are "sticky" in the downward direction. This does not mean that wages never fall, only that they tend to fall more slowly in a recessionary gap than they rise in an equally sized inflationary gap. When wages are sticky, the analysis is the same as when wages are flexible, and thus Figure 25-3 tells the right story. The only difference is that the *SRAS* curve shifts more slowly when wages are sticky and thus the recessionary gap remains open for longer. An important implication of sticky wages is that high unemployment may not be quickly eliminated.

If wages are downwardly sticky, the economy's adjustment mechanism is sluggish and thus recessionary gaps tend to persist.

The weakness of the adjustment mechanism does not mean that slumps must always be prolonged. Rather, this weakness means that speedy recovery back to potential output must be generated mainly from the demand side. If wages are downwardly sticky and the economy is to avoid a persistent recessionary gap, a quick recovery requires a rightward shift of the *AD* curve. The possibility that government *stabilization policy* might accomplish such a rightward shift in the *AD* curve is an important and contentious issue in macroeconomics, one that we will return to often throughout the remainder of this book.

The slow adjustment of wages and prices when output is below potential means that the recessionary effects of negative shocks sometimes persist for long periods.

The difference in the speed of adjustment of wages (and other factor prices) is the important asymmetry in the behaviour of aggregate supply that we noted earlier in this chapter. This asymmetry helps to explain two key facts about the Canadian economy. First, unemployment can persist for quite long periods without causing decreases in wages and prices of sufficient magnitude to remove the unemployment. Second, booms, along with labour shortages and production beyond normal capacity, do not persist for long periods without causing increases in wages and the price level.

Aggregate Supply Shocks

We have discussed the long-run effects of aggregate demand shocks, and the economy's automatic adjustment mechanism that returns real GDP to its potential level, Y^*. The same adjustment process operates following an aggregate supply shock.

Consider an economy that has a stable price level and real GDP at its potential level, as illustrated by point E_0 in part (i) of Figure 25-4. Suppose there is an increase in the world price of an important input, such as oil. As we have mentioned several times in this book, the OPEC oil shocks of 1973–74 and 1979–80 involved enormous increases in the price of oil and, to date, are surely the best examples that economists have of large negative aggregate supply shocks.

An increase in the price of oil increases unit costs for firms and causes the $SRAS$ curve to shift to the left. Real GDP falls and the price level increases—this is *stagflation*.

FIGURE 25-4   The Long-Run Effect of a Negative Aggregate Supply Shock

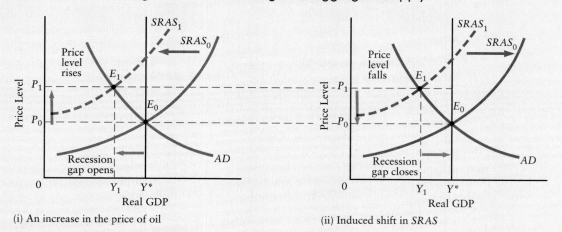

(i) An increase in the price of oil   (ii) Induced shift in $SRAS$

A leftward shift of the $SRAS$ curve caused by an increase in input prices causes real GDP to fall and the price level to rise. The economy's adjustment mechanism then reverses the $SRAS$ shift and returns the economy to its starting point.

The economy begins at point E_0 in part (i). The increase in the price of oil increases unit costs and causes the $SRAS$ curve to shift up to $SRAS_1$. Real GDP falls to Y_1 and the price level rises to P_1. A recessionary gap is created.

In part (ii), the excess supply of labour associated with the recessionary gap causes wages to fall, possibly slowly. As wages fall, unit costs fall and so the $SRAS$ curve shifts back down to $SRAS_0$. The economy is finally in long-run equilibrium at Y^* and P_0, its starting point.

The short-run equilibrium is at point E_1 in Figure 25-4. With the opening of a recessionary gap, the economy's adjustment mechanism comes into play, though sticky wages reduce the speed of this adjustment.

The recessionary gap caused by the negative supply shock causes firms to shut down and workers to be laid off. The excess supply of labour (and other factors) eventually pushes wages down and begins to reverse the initial increase in unit costs caused by the increase in the price of oil. This adjustment is shown in part (ii) of the figure. As wages fall, the *SRAS* curve shifts back toward its starting point, and real GDP rises back toward its potential level, Y^*. Eventually, the economy returns to its initial point, E_0.

We leave it to the reader to analyse the long-run effects of a positive aggregate supply shock, such as the dramatic reduction in the world price of raw materials that occurred in 1997 and 1998. The logic of the analysis is exactly the same as illustrated in Figure 25-4, except that the initial shift in the *SRAS* curve is to the right, creating an inflationary gap.

Exogenous changes in input prices cause the *SRAS* curve to shift, creating an output gap. The adjustment mechanism then reverses the initial *SRAS* shift and brings the economy back to potential output and the initial price level.

Economic Shocks and Business Cycles

Aggregate demand and aggregate supply shocks are a major source of fluctuations in real GDP around potential. As we have seen, a positive demand shock, such as increase in desired investment, will lead to an increase in output and prices. This will be followed by a fall in output and a further increase in prices as the adjustment mechanism restores the economy to long-run equilibrium. Depending on the nature and magnitude of the shock, the adjustment will take many months, maybe even a year or two.

Similarly, a positive supply shock, such as a reduction in the world price of an important input, will cause real GDP to rise and the price level to fall. As the adjustment mechanism comes into play, real GDP will fall back to potential and the price level will rise back to its initial level. As with a demand shock, the full adjustment may take many months.

No matter what the cause of the expansionary shock, the economy will not respond instantaneously. In many industries, it takes weeks or months or even longer to bring new or mothballed capacity into production and to hire and train new workers. Because of these lags in the economy's response, changes in output are spread out over a substantial period of time. An increase in demand or supply may lead to a gradual increase in output that lasts several months. Then, as output does change, the adjustment mechanism comes into play, eventually returning real GDP to its potential level.

Thus, a positive shock—demand or supply—initially leads to an increase in output and then, as the adjustment mechanism begins to operate, is followed by a reduction in output back to potential. Conversely, a negative demand or supply shock initially leads to a reduction in output and then, as the (slower) adjustment mechanism comes into play, is eventually followed by an increase in output back to potential. In both cases, the impact effect of the shock is reversed by the economy's adjustment mechanism. Shocks, therefore, generate *cyclical* movements in real GDP. Such shocks are the fundamental cause of *business cycles*.

Both aggregate demand and aggregate supply are subject to continual random shocks. The economy's adjustment mechanism can convert these shocks into cyclical fluctuations in real GDP.

The Long-Run Aggregate Supply Curve

long-run aggregate supply (LRAS) curve
A curve showing the relationship between the price level and the quantity of aggregate output supplied when all markets have fully adjusted to the existing price level; a vertical line at $Y = Y^*$.

The economy's adjustment mechanism leads us to an important concept: the **long-run aggregate supply (LRAS) curve.** This curve relates the price level to real GDP after wage rates and all other input costs have been fully adjusted to eliminate any unemployment or overall labour shortages. (Recall that we are holding technology, and thus productivity, constant.)

Once all the adjustments have occurred, any excess demand or excess supply of labour will have been eliminated. In other words, full employment will prevail, and output will be at its potential level, Y^*. The value of Y^* depends on real variables such as factor supplies and technology, but is independent of nominal variables like the price level. It follows that the LRAS curve is vertical at Y^*, as shown in Figure 25-5. The LRAS curve is sometimes called the *Classical aggregate supply curve* because the Classical economists were mainly concerned with the behaviour of the economy in long-run equilibrium.[3]

The economy's long-run aggregate supply (LRAS) curve is vertical at the level of potential output, Y^*.

Notice that the vertical LRAS curve does not represent the same thing as the vertical portion of the SRAS curve (see Figure 24-8). Over the vertical range of the SRAS curve, the economy is at its utmost limit of productive capacity, when no more output can be squeezed out under any circumstances. In contrast, the vertical shape of the LRAS curve is due to the workings of an adjustment mechanism that brings the economy back to its potential output, even though output may differ from potential for considerable periods of time. It is called the long-run aggregate supply curve because it describes what happens as a result of adjustments that occur over an extended period of time.

Long-Run Equilibrium

Figure 25-5 shows the equilibrium output and the price level as they are determined by the intersection of the AD curve and the vertical LRAS curve. Because the LRAS curve is vertical, shifts in the AD curve change the price level but not the level of equilibrium output, as shown in part (i). By contrast, a shift in the LRAS curve changes both output and the price level, as shown in part (ii). For example, a rightward shift of the LRAS curve increases real GDP and leads to a fall in the price level.

In the long run, total output is determined solely by conditions of aggregate supply, and the role of aggregate demand is only to determine the price level.

Consider the effect of an increase in government purchases in a situation where the economy begins in long-run equilibrium. In part (i) of Figure 25-5 it is clear that the long-run effect of an increase in government purchases is to increase the price level but to leave the level of real GDP unchanged at Y_0^*. What the figure does not show, how-

---

[3]The Classical school of economic thought began with Adam Smith (1723–1790) and was developed through the work of David Ricardo (1772–1823), Thomas Malthus (1766–1834) and John Stuart Mill (1806–1873). These economists emphasized the long-run behaviour of the economy. Beginning in the middle of the nineteenth century, Neoclassical economists devoted much time and effort to studying short-term fluctuations. *The General Theory of Employment, Interest and Money* (1936), written by John Maynard Keynes (1883–1946), was in a long tradition of the study of short-term fluctuations. Where Keynes differed from the Neoclassical economists was in approaching the issues from a macroeconomic perspective that emphasized fluctuations in real expenditure flows. Each of the economists mentioned in this footnote, along with several others, are discussed in more detail in the timeline at the back of the book.

ever, is that while the *level* of GDP may be unchanged, the *composition* of GDP has changed.

To see how the composition of GDP is affected by the increase in G, consider what happens as the price level rises from P_0 to P_1 in part (i) of the figure. For a given stock of nominal assets (money and bonds), the rise in the price level reduces the wealth of the private sector and thus reduces household consumption. In addition, for a given exchange rate, the rise in the domestic price level makes Canadian goods more expensive relative to foreign goods, and thus reduces Canada's net exports. (You will recall that these are the two reasons why the AD curve is downward sloping, as we discussed at the beginning of Chapter 24.) Thus, the increase in government purchases, by creating an inflationary gap and forcing up the price level, has "crowded out" some elements of private expenditure—in this case, consumption and net exports.

So, while real GDP is the same at points E_0 and E_1 in part (i) of Figure 25-5, the composition of the GDP is different. Specifically, G is higher at E_1 than it is at E_0; C and NX are lower at E_1 than at E_0.

Why do we care about the composition of GDP? Recall from Chapter 23 that net exports and investment are similar in the sense that they both imply *asset accumulation* for the domestic economy. Thus, other things equal, the more of GDP that is used for asset accumulation, the higher national income will be in the future. Thus, "crowding out" is potentially important if it hinders the economy's prospects for long-run growth. In later chapters we will examine a type of crowding out (of investment) that reduces the economy's long-run growth. In order to do that, however, we must learn some details about money and interest rates, which we examine in Chapters 26 and 27. Until then, our discussion about the composition of GDP is summarized as follows:

The vertical *LRAS* curve shows that given full adjustment of input prices, potential output is compatible with any price level, although its composition among consumption, investment, government, and net exports may vary at different price levels.

FIGURE 25-5   Long-Run Equilibrium and Aggregate Supply

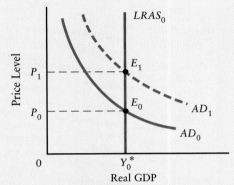

(i) A rise in aggregate demand

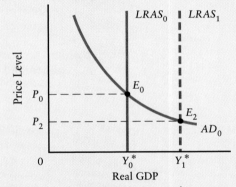

(ii) A rise in long-run aggregate supply

Because the *LRAS* curve is vertical, aggregate supply determines the long-run equilibrium value of real GDP at Y^*. Given Y^*, aggregate demand determines the long-run equilibrium value of the price level. In both parts of the figure, the initial long-run equilibrium is at E_0, so the price level is P_0 and real GDP is Y_0^*.

In part (i), a shift in the AD curve from AD_0 to AD_1 moves the long-run equilibrium from E_0 to E_1. This raises the price level from P_0 to P_1 but leaves real GDP unchanged at Y_0^* in the long run.

In part (ii), a shift in the *LRAS* curve from $LRAS_0$ to $LRAS_1$ moves the long-run equilibrium from E_0 to E_2. This raises real GDP income from Y_0^* to Y_1^* and lowers the price level from P_0 to P_2.

National Income in the Short and Long Run

In Chapter 21 we discussed the difference between short-run and long-run macroeconomics. Without developing any formal theory at that time, we described how output is affected by changes in demand in the short run, whereas changes in supply are the crucial factor determining output in the long run. Now, after developing some formal macroeconomic theory, we have come full circle. We now have the theoretical tools to *understand* this important distinction between the short run and the long run.

1. In the short run, the economy is in equilibrium at the level of real GDP and prices where the *SRAS* curve intersects the *AD* curve.

2. In the long run, the economy is in equilibrium at potential output, the position of the vertical *LRAS* curve. The price level is determined where the *AD* curve intersects the *LRAS* curve.

The position of the *LRAS* curve is at Y^*, which is determined by past economic growth. Since in the long run output equals Y^*, it follows that economic growth explains long-run movements in output. In contrast, deviations of actual output from potential output—output gaps—are short-run phenomena and are generally associated with *business cycles*. Changes in total real output may therefore take place either because of long-term growth or because of business cycles.

This suggests a need to distinguish three ways in which Y can increase. The first two relate to short-run changes in Y; the third is a long-run change in Y. These are illustrated in Figure 25-6. In each case, the economy begins with real GDP equal to Y^*.

Aggregate Demand Shocks.   As shown in part (i) of Figure 25-6, an increase in aggregate demand will yield a one-time increase in real GDP. The demand shock

FIGURE 25-6   Three Ways that Real GDP Can Increase

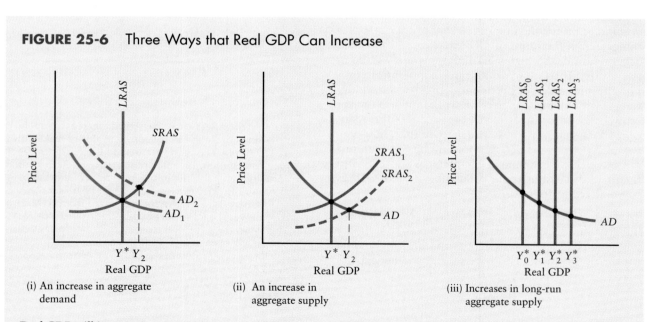

(i) An increase in aggregate demand

(ii) An increase in aggregate supply

(iii) Increases in long-run aggregate supply

Real GDP will increase in response to an increase in aggregate demand or an increase in aggregate supply. The increase will be permanent only if the *LRAS* curve shifts. In the cases shown in parts (i) and (ii), any increase in GDP beyond potential is temporary because the inflationary gap will cause wages and other factor prices to rise; this will cause the *SRAS* curve to shift upward and hence cause real GDP to converge to Y^*.

In part (iii), the *LRAS* curve shifts to the right, causing potential output to increase. Whether or not actual GDP increases immediately depends on what happens to the *AD* and *SRAS* curves. Because, in the absence of other shocks, actual output eventually converges to potential output, a rightward shift in the *LRAS* curve eventually leads to an increase in actual output. If the shift in the *LRAS* curve is recurring, real GDP will grow continually.

pushes Y beyond Y^* (a shift from AD_1 to AD_2). The inflationary gap will cause wages and other costs to rise, shifting the *SRAS* curve to the left. This drives Y back toward potential so that the only lasting effect is on the price level.

Aggregate Supply Shocks.   Increases in aggregate supply will also lead to a temporary increase in real GDP. Part (ii) of Figure 25-6 shows the effects of an increase in aggregate supply caused, for example, by the reduction of input prices. This will shift the *SRAS* curve to the right but will have no effect on the *LRAS* curve and hence on potential output. The shock will thus cause Y to rise above Y^*, but the increase will eventually be reversed by the economy's adjustment mechanism.

Increases in Long-Run Aggregate Supply.   Part (iii) of Figure 25-6 shows the effects of shocks that shift the *LRAS* curve. There are several possible explanations for such a shift. For example, a once-and-for-all change in a labour-market policy that reduces the level of structural unemployment will lead to a one-time rightward shift in the *LRAS* curve. Another example might be a one-time improvement in the education system that makes workers more productive, shifting the *LRAS* curve to the right. More important, however, are the ongoing changes such as population growth, capital accumulation, or improvements in productivity—these all cause a continual rightward shift in the *LRAS* curve, giving rise to a continual increase in the level of potential output.

Unlike the case of *AD* or *SRAS* shocks, the changes in real GDP in part (iii) of Figure 25-6 are permanent effects—no natural adjustment mechanism will bring real GDP back to its previous level of potential. Indeed, GDP is equal to potential GDP, but potential GDP has increased.

In the long run, only changes to the level of Y^* can change the level of real GDP.

In Chapter 32 we will study changes in potential output over long periods of time. To complete this chapter, however, we return briefly to a topic that we first discussed in Chapter 23—fiscal policy. Now that we understand the distinction between the short run and the long run, we are ready to discuss some details about the effects of government spending and taxation.

Fiscal Policy and the Business Cycle

In Chapter 23, we briefly considered the basic concepts of fiscal stabilization policy. In principle, this policy can be used in attempts to stabilize real GDP at or near some desired level (usually potential output). In the remainder of this chapter, we look into taxing and spending as tools of fiscal stabilization policy. We will return to the subject in more detail in Chapter 31, after we have discussed money and the banking system.

So far in this chapter we have discussed shocks and economic fluctuations but have not looked at any actual data. If significant fluctuations don't really exist, there is not much point in thinking about fiscal stabilization policy, for there would be no fluctuations to stabilize. A quick look at Figure 25-7, however, should assure you that economic fluctuations are the rule rather than the exception. There is no single "correct" way to measure fluctuations in the level of economic activity because different macroeconomic variables fluctuate in different degrees. But many of them travel broadly together. Figure 25-7 shows that the changes in three key variables—real GDP, the number of housing starts, and firms' capacity utilization rate—are considerable on a year-to-year basis. The government could use its fiscal policy tools—expenditure and taxation—to try to smooth these fluctuations.

FIGURE 25-7   Fluctuations in Economic Activity, 1970–1998

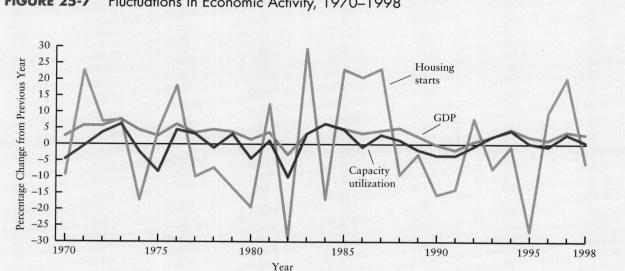

Fluctuations follow similar, but not identical, paths for various measures of economic activity. Fluctuations are easily seen in these three series—the annual percentage changes in real GDP, annual housing starts, and the capacity utilization rate.

(*Source:* Department of Finance, *Economic Reference Tables*, August 1995, and *Bank of Canada Review*, Winter 1998–99.)

Because government expenditure increases aggregate demand and taxation decreases it, the *direction* of the required changes in spending and taxation is generally easy to determine once we know the direction of the desired change in real GDP. However, the *timing, magnitude,* and *mixture* of the changes are more difficult issues.

There is no doubt that the government can exert a major influence on real GDP. Prime examples are the massive increases in military spending during major wars. Canadian federal expenditure during World War II rose from 12.2 percent of GDP in 1939 to 41.8 percent in 1944. At the same time, the unemployment rate fell from 11.4 percent to 1.4 percent. Economists agree that the increase in government spending helped to bring about the rise in output and the associated fall in unemployment.

In the heyday of fiscal policy, from about 1945 to about 1970, many economists were convinced that the economy could be stabilized adequately just by varying the size of the government's taxes and expenditures. That day is past. Today, most economists are aware of the many limitations of fiscal policy.

The Basic Theory of Fiscal Stabilization

A reduction in tax rates or an increase in government purchases will shift the *AD* curve to the right, causing an increase in real GDP. An increase in tax rates or a cut in government expenditure will shift the *AD* curve to the left, causing a decrease in real GDP.

FIGURE 25-8   The Closing of a Recessionary Gap

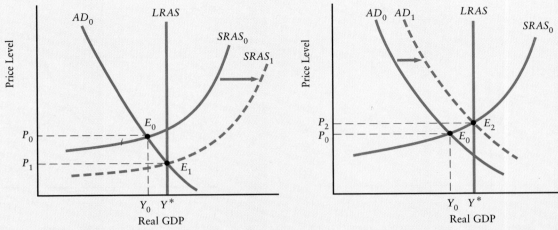

(i) A recessionary gap closed by the induced change in factor prices

(ii) A recessionary gap closed by a rightward shift in *AD*

A recessionary gap may be closed by a (slow) rightward shift of the *SRAS* curve or an increase in aggregate demand.
Initially, equilibrium is at E_0, with real GDP at Y_0 and the price level at P_0. There is a recessionary gap.

As shown in part (i), the gap might be removed by a shift in the *SRAS* curve to $SRAS_1$, as will eventually happen when wages and other factor prices fall in response to excess supply. The shift in the *SRAS* curve causes a movement down and to the right along AD_0 to a new equilibrium at E_1, achieving potential output Y^* and lowering the price level to P_1.

As shown in part (ii), the gap might also be removed by a shift of the *AD* curve to AD_1, caused by an expansionary fiscal policy or a recovery of private-sector spending. The shift in the *AD* curve causes a movement up and to the right along $SRAS_0$. This movement shifts the equilibrium to E_2, raising output to Y^* and the price level to P_2.

How Fiscal Stabilization Works

A more detailed look at how fiscal stabilization works will help to show some of the complications that arise when implementing fiscal policy.

A Recessionary Gap.   The closing of a recessionary gap is illustrated in Figure 25-8. There are two ways the gap can be closed. First, the recessionary gap may eventually drive wages and other factor prices down enough to shift the *SRAS* curve to the right and thereby reinstate potential output. The evidence, however, is that this process takes a substantial period of time.

Second, the *AD* curve could shift to the right, restoring the economy to potential output. The government can cause such a shift by using expansionary fiscal policy (or, as we shall see in Chapter 27, expansionary monetary policy). The advantage of using fiscal policy rather than allowing the economy's natural adjustment mechanism to operate is that it may substantially shorten what would otherwise be a long recession. One disadvantage is that the use of fiscal policy may stimulate the economy just before private-sector spending recovers on its own. As a result, the economy may overshoot its potential output, and an inflationary gap may open up. In this case, fiscal policy that is intended to promote economic stability can actually cause instability.

FIGURE 25-9   The Closing of an Inflationary Gap

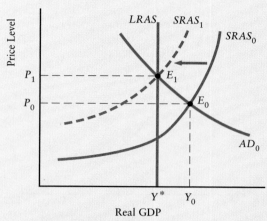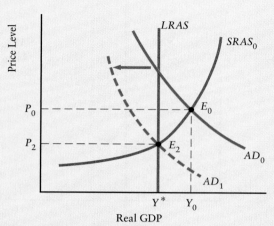

(i) An inflationary gap closed by the induced change in factor prices   (ii) An inflationary gap closed by a leftward shift in AD

An inflationary gap may be removed by a leftward shift of the *SRAS* curve, a reduction in private-sector demand, or a policy-induced reduction in aggregate demand. Initially, equilibrium is at E_0, with real GDP at Y_0 and the price level at P_0. There is an inflationary gap.

As shown in part (i), the gap might be removed by a shift in the *SRAS* curve to $SRAS_1$, as will eventually happen when wages and other factor prices rise in response to the excess demand. The shift in the *SRAS* curve causes a movement up and to the left along AD_0. This movement establishes a new equilibrium at E_1, reducing output to its potential level Y^* and raising the price level to P_1.

As shown in part (ii), the gap might also be removed by a shift in the *AD* curve to AD_1 caused by, for example, a contractionary fiscal policy. The shift in the *AD* curve causes a movement down and to the left along $SRAS_0$. This movement shifts the equilibrium to E_2, lowering income to Y^* and the price level to P_2.

An Inflationary Gap.   Figure 25-9 shows how an inflationary gap can be closed. First, wages and other factor prices may be pushed upward by the excess demand. The *SRAS* curve will therefore shift to the left, eventually closing the gap, reducing output back to Y^*. Second, the *AD* curve can shift to the left, restoring equilibrium output at Y^*. The government, by raising taxes or cutting spending, can induce such a shift, reducing aggregate demand sufficiently to close the inflationary gap. The advantage of this approach is that it avoids the inflationary increase in prices that accompanies the first method. One disadvantage is that if private-sector expenditures fall because of natural causes, real GDP may be pushed below potential, thus opening up a recessionary gap.

This discussion leads to a key proposition:

When the economy's adjustment mechanism is slow to operate, or produces undesirable side effects such as rising prices, there is a potential stabilization role for fiscal policy.

The Paradox of Thrift

The theory of national income determination predicts that an increase in national saving (either an increase in private-sector saving or an increase in the government's budget surplus) will shift the *AD* curve to the left and hence *reduce* the equilibrium level of real GDP in the short run. The contrary case, a decrease in saving and increase in expenditure, shifts the *AD* curve to the right and hence increases real GDP in the short run. Thus, frugality on the part of individuals, which may seem to be prudent behaviour for each individual taken separately, ends up reducing short-run real GDP. This prediction is known as the *paradox of thrift*—the paradox being that what may be good for any individual when viewed in isolation ends up being undesirable for the economy as a whole.

The policy implication of this prediction is that a major and persistent recession can be battled by encouraging governments, firms, and households to spend more, *not* to save more. In times of unemployment and recession, frugality will only make things worse. This prediction goes directly against the idea that we should tighten our belts when times are tough. The notion that it is not only possible but even *desirable* to spend one's way out of a recession touches a sensitive point with people raised on the belief that success is based on hard work and frugality, not on prodigality; as a result, the idea often arouses great hostility.

As is discussed in *Lessons from History 25-1*, the implications of the paradox of thrift were not generally understood during the Great Depression of the 1930s. Most governments, faced with depression-induced reductions in tax revenues, reduced their expenditures to balance their budgets. As a result, many economists argue that the fiscal policies at the time actually made things worse. When Milton Friedman (many years later) said, "We are all Keynesians now," he was referring to the general acceptance of the view that the government's budget is much more than just the revenue and expenditure statement of a very large organization. Whether we like it or not, the sheer size of the government's budget inevitably makes it a powerful tool for influencing the economy.

The paradox of thrift concentrates on shifts in aggregate demand that have been caused by changes in saving (and hence spending) behaviour. That is why it applies only in the short run, when the *AD* curve plays an important role in the determination of real GDP.

In the long run, however, the paradox of thrift does not apply. Remember that in the long run, aggregate demand is *not* the determinant of real GDP—only the position of the *LRAS* curve determines long-run real GDP. In the long run, the more people and governments save, the larger is the supply of funds available for investment. And the more that people invest, the greater is the growth of potential output, shifting the *LRAS* curve to the right.

The paradox of thrift—the idea that an increase in saving reduces the level of real GDP—is only true in the short run when the level of aggregate demand is relevant for determining real GDP. In the long run, a larger amount of saving increases investment and thus increases the level of potential output.

At this point it would be useful to re-read the brief discussion at the beginning of Chapter 21 regarding Japan's economic malaise during the late 1990s. There we posed a puzzling question: If Japan's high saving rate is partly responsible for its economic stagnation during the 1990s, how can its high saving rate also be responsible for its remarkable growth from the 1950s to the 1990s? As we said in Chapter 21, many economists believe that both statements are true. The solution to this apparent contradiction is to recognize that the paradox of thrift is an important short-run phenomenon but does not apply in the long run. In other words, a high rate of saving may well reduce real GDP in the short run, but after the economy's adjustment mechanism operates (which may take some time), the higher saving will eventually increase investment and long-run growth.

Automatic Stabilizers

In Chapter 23, we considered the *budget surplus function* (the function showing how the government's budget surplus changes as national income changes). The *discretionary* fiscal policy that we have been discussing in this chapter involves *shifts* in the budget surplus function. Expansionary policies, whether they involve increases in government purchases

LESSONS FROM HISTORY 25-1

Fiscal Policy in the Great Depression

The Great Depression, which is usually dated as beginning with the massive stock-market crash on October 29, 1929, was by far the most dramatic economic event this century. As the accompanying figure shows, Canadian real GDP plummeted by almost 30 percent from its peak in 1929 to its low point in 1933. The price level actually *fell* beginning in 1930 and declined by about 20 percent over the next five years. The unemployment rate increased from 3 percent in 1929 to an unparalleled 19.3 percent four years later. To put these numbers in perspective, by today's standards a very serious recession (like the most recent one in 1991–92) sees real GDP fall by 2 percent, the unemployment rate rise to 11 percent, and prices continue rising but perhaps at a slower rate. The economic events of the 1930s certainly deserve to be called the Great Depression!

As we will see in this box, however, the Great Depression was not just a catastrophic event that happened exogenously—its depth and duration were made worse by some fundamental mistakes in policy.

Failure to understand the implication of the paradox of thrift led many countries to adopt disastrous policies during the Great Depression. In addition, failure to understand the role of built-in stabilizers has led many observers to conclude, erroneously, that fiscal expansion was tried in the Great

Depression but failed. Let us see how these two misperceptions are related.

The Paradox of Thrift in Action

In 1932, Canadian Prime Minister R. B. Bennett said, "We are now faced with the real crisis in the history of Canada. To maintain our credit we must practice the most rigid economy and not spend a single cent." His government that year brought down a budget based on the principle of trying to balance revenues and expenditures, and it included *increases* in tax rates.

In the same year, Franklin Roosevelt was elected U.S. president on a platform of fighting the Great Depression with government policies. In his inaugural address he urged, "Our great primary task is to put people to work. . . . [This task] can be helped by insistence that the federal, state, and local governments act forthwith on the demand that their costs be drastically reduced. . . . "

Across the Atlantic, King George V told the British House of Commons in 1931, "The present condition of the national finances, in the opinion of His Majesty's ministers, calls for the imposition of additional taxation and for the effecting of economies in public expenditure."

For information on the Federal Department of Finance, the ministry in charge of fiscal policy, see: www.fin.gc.ca.

or decreases in net taxes, reduce the budget surplus (increase the deficit) at every level of real GDP, shifting the *AD* curve to the right. Contractionary policies increase the surplus (reduce the deficit) at every level of real GDP, shifting the *AD* curve to the left.

Even when the government does not attempt to stabilize the economy via discretionary fiscal policy, the upward slope of the budget surplus function means that there are fiscal effects that cause the budget to act as an "automatic stabilizer" for the economy.

procyclical Moving in the same direction as the business cycle—up in booms and down in slumps.

The budget surplus increases as real GDP increases because tax revenues rise and some transfer payments, especially unemployment insurance, fall. Thus, net taxes move in the same direction as real GDP. (Unless there are changes in policy, government purchases are generally unaffected by cyclical movements in the economy.) With **procyclical** net tax revenues, disposable income moves in the same direction as real GDP but does not move by as much. The government keeps a share of the increased real GDP when it rises. When real GDP falls, the fall in taxes and the rise in transfers make disposable income fall by less.

In Chapter 23, for example, we assumed that the net income tax rate was 10 percent of national income. This assumption implies that a 1 dollar rise in national income would increase disposable income by only 90 cents, dampening the multiplier effect of

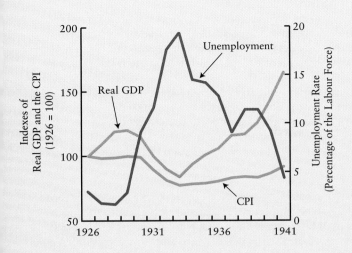

into depression. The various governments did not advocate programs of massive deficit-financed spending to shift the *AD* curve to the right. Instead, they hoped that a small amount of government spending in addition to numerous policies designed to stabilize prices and to restore confidence would lead to a recovery of private investment expenditure that would substantially shift the *AD* curve. To have expected a massive revival of private investment expenditure as a result of the puny increase in aggregate demand that was instituted by the federal government now seems hopelessly naive.

When we judge these policies from the viewpoint of modern theory, their failure is no mystery. Indeed, Professor E. Cary Brown of MIT, after a careful study, concluded, "Fiscal policy seems to have been an unsuccessful recovery device in the thirties—not because it did not work, but because it was not tried." Once the massive, war-geared expenditure of the 1940s began, output responded sharply and unemployment all but evaporated, as seen clearly in the figure.

The performance of the Canadian and U.S. economies from 1930 to 1945 is well explained by the theory of national income determination that we have developed in the last few chapters. It is clear that the governments did not effectively use fiscal policy to stabilize their economies. War brought the Depression to an end because war demands made acceptable a level of government expenditure sufficient to remove the recessionary gap. Had the Canadian and American administrations been able to do the same, it might have ended the waste of the Great Depression many years sooner.

As the paradox of thrift predicts, these policies tended to worsen, rather than cure, the Depression.

Interpreting the Deficit in the 1930s

Government deficits did increase in the 1930s, but they were not the result of a program of deficit-financed public expenditure. Rather, they were the result of the fall in tax revenues, brought about by the fall in real GDP as the economy sank

---

any change in autonomous expenditure. Generally, the wedge that income taxes place between national income and disposable income reduces the marginal propensity to spend out of national income, thereby reducing the size of the multiplier. The effect is to stabilize the economy, reducing the fluctuations in national income that are caused by changes in autonomous expenditure. Because no policies need to be changed to achieve this result, these properties of the government budget that cause the multiplier to be reduced are called **automatic fiscal stabilizers.**

Limitations of Discretionary Fiscal Policy

According to the foregoing discussion, returning the economy to potential output would simply be a matter of cutting taxes and raising government spending, in some combination. Why do so many economists believe that such policies would be "as likely to harm as help"? Part of the answer is that the execution of discretionary fiscal policy is anything but simple.

Lags. To change fiscal policy requires making changes in taxes and government expenditures. The changes must be agreed on by the cabinet and passed by parliament.

automatic fiscal stabilizers Elements of the tax and transfer systems that automatically lessen the magnitude of the fluctuations in national income caused by changes in autonomous expenditures.

The political stakes in such changes are generally very large; taxes and spending are called "bread-and-butter issues" precisely because they affect the economic well-being of almost everyone. Thus, even if economists agreed that the economy would be helped by, say, a tax cut, politicians would likely spend a good deal of time debating *whose* taxes should be cut and by *how much*. The delay between the initial recognition of a recessionary or inflationary gap and the enactment of legislation to change fiscal policy is called a **decision lag.**

decision lag   The period of time between perceiving some problem and reaching a decision on what to do about it.

Once policy changes are agreed on, there is still an **execution lag,** adding time between the enactment and the implementation of the change. Furthermore, once policies are in place, it will usually take still more time for their economic consequences to be felt. Because of these lags, it is quite possible that by the time a given policy decision has any impact on the economy, circumstances will have changed such that the policy is no longer appropriate.

execution lag   The time that it takes to put policies in place after a decision has been made.

Temporary Versus Permanent Policy Changes.   To make matters even more frustrating, tax measures that are known to be temporary are generally less effective than measures that are expected to be permanent. If households know that a given tax cut will last only a year, they may recognize that the effect on their long-run consumption possibilities is small and may adjust their short-run consumption relatively little. Thus, the more closely household consumption expenditure is related to lifetime income rather than to current income, the smaller will be the effects on current consumption of tax changes that are known to be of short duration. Or, to use the language that we used when introducing the consumption function in Chapter 22, the more forward-looking are households, the smaller will be the effects of temporary changes in taxes.

The Role of Discretionary Fiscal Policy.   All of these difficulties suggest that attempts to use discretionary fiscal policy to "fine tune" the economy are fraught with difficulties. **Fine tuning** refers to the use of fiscal (and monetary) policy to offset virtually all fluctuations in private-sector spending so as to hold real GDP at or near its potential level at all times. However, neither economic nor political science has yet advanced far enough to allow policymakers to undo the consequences of every aggregate demand or supply shock. Nevertheless, many economists still argue that when a recessionary gap is large enough and persists for long enough, *gross tuning* may be appropriate. **Gross tuning** refers to the occasional use of fiscal and monetary policy to remove large and persistent output gaps. Other economists believe that fiscal policy should not be used for economic stabilization under any circumstances. Rather, they would argue, tax and spending behaviour should be the outcome of public choices regarding the long-term size and financing of the public sector and should not be altered for short-term considerations. We return to these debates in Chapter 31.

fine tuning   The attempt to maintain national income at its full-employment level by means of frequent changes in fiscal or monetary policy.

gross tuning   The use of macroeconomic policy to stabilize the economy such that large deviations from full employment do not persist for extended periods of time.

Fiscal Policy and Growth

The desirability of using fiscal policy to stabilize the economy depends a great deal on the speed with which the economy's own adjustment mechanism returns the economy to potential output. If the adjustment mechanism works very quickly, there is little value to discretionary fiscal policy. If the adjustment mechanism works slowly, however, there may well be a role for fiscal policies that can be used to shift aggregate demand.

Fiscal stabilization policy will generally have consequences for economic growth—for the rightward shifting of the *LRAS* curve over time. In an economy at or near potential output, the more expansive is its fiscal policy, the lower will be national saving and national asset formation and, consequently, the lower will be future economic growth. Of course, if the economy would otherwise stay in recession for a period of years, the gain in output in the near term may outweigh the longer-term consequences of a smaller stock of productive assets. After all—and this was part of Keynes' message—the state of the world at potential output is not very interesting to members of a society who are a long way from it.

Stability, growth, and the effect of economic policy on both are among the key subjects of this book. With the tools that we have developed so far, we can begin to see how they fit together. Once we add a better understanding of money and monetary policy, presented in the next three chapters, we will be able to complete the story.

S U M M A R Y

Induced Changes in Factor Prices

LO 1

- Potential output is treated as given and is represented by a vertical line at Y^*. The output gap is equal to the horizontal distance between Y^* and the actual level of real GDP, Y, as determined by the intersection of the AD and $SRAS$ curves.
- An inflationary gap means that Y is greater than Y^*, and hence there is excess demand in the labour market. As a

result, wages rise causing unit costs to rise. The $SRAS$ curve shifts leftward, and the price level rises.
- A recessionary gap means that Y is less than Y^*, and hence there is excess supply in the labour market. Although there is some resulting tendency for wages to fall, the strength of this force is typically weaker than is the case with an inflationary gap. Because unit costs will fall only slowly, the output gap will persist for some time.

Demand and Supply Shocks

LO 2 3

- Beginning from a position of potential output, an expansionary demand shock creates an inflationary gap, causing wages to rise. Unit costs rise, shifting the $SRAS$ curve to the left and bringing output back to its potential level.
- Beginning from a position of potential output, a contractionary demand shock creates a recessionary gap. Because factor prices tend to be sticky downwards, the automatic adjustment process tends to be slow, and a recessionary gap tends to persist for some time.
- Aggregate supply shocks, such as those caused by changes in the price of inputs, lead the $SRAS$ curve to shift, changing real GDP and the price level. But the economy's ad-

justment mechanism reverses the shift in $SRAS$, bringing the economy back to its initial level of output and prices.
- Demand and supply shocks are important sources of business cycles. As a shock works its way through the economy and the adjustment mechanism comes into play, real GDP will often exhibit a cyclical pattern.
- The long-run aggregate supply ($LRAS$) curve relates the price level and real GDP after all wages and other input prices have been adjusted fully to long-run equilibrium. The $LRAS$ curve is vertical at the level of potential output, Y^*.

National Income in the Short and Long Run

LO 4

- In the short run, macroeconomic equilibrium is determined by the intersection of the AD and $SRAS$ curves. In the long run, the economy is in equilibrium when real GDP is equal to potential output—the economy is therefore on the $LRAS$ curve. In the long run, the price level is

determined by the intersection of the AD and $LRAS$ curves.
- Shocks to the AD or $SRAS$ curves can change real GDP in the short run. Only shifts in the $LRAS$ curve can change output in the long run.

Fiscal Policy and the Business Cycle

- In principle, fiscal policy can be used to stabilize output at or near potential output. To remove a recessionary gap, governments can shift *AD* to the right by cutting taxes and increasing spending. To remove an inflationary gap, governments can pursue the opposite policies.
- In the short run, increases in desired saving on the part of firms, households, and governments leads to further reductions in real GDP. This phenomenon is often called the paradox of thrift. In the long run, the paradox of thrift does not apply, and increased saving will lead to increased asset accumulation and economic growth.
- Because government tax and transfer programs tend to reduce the size of the multiplier, they act as automatic stabilizers. When real GDP changes, disposable income changes by less because of taxes and transfers.

- Discretionary fiscal policy is subject to decision lags and execution lags that limit its ability to take effect quickly. Some economists argue that these limitations are so severe that discretionary fiscal policy should never be used for stabilization because it will end up increasing instability. Others argue that the automatic adjustment mechanism works so slowly that discretionary fiscal policy can play a useful role in stabilizing the economy.
- Fiscal policy has very different effects in the short and long run. The same fiscal policies (reduced taxes and increased spending) that stimulate the economy in the short run will, if pursued when the economy is at potential output, reduce national saving, asset formation, and economic growth in the long run.

K E Y   C O N C E P T S

The output gap and factor prices
Wages and unit labour costs
Inflationary and recessionary gaps
Asymmetry of wage adjustment: flexible and sticky wages

Long-run effects of *AD* and *SRAS* shocks
The long-run aggregate supply (*LRAS*) curve
Fiscal stabilization policy

Decision lags and execution lags
Automatic stabilizers
Fine tuning and gross tuning

S T U D Y   E X E R C I S E S

1. The following diagram shows two economies, A and B. Both are in short-run equilibrium at point *E*, where the *AD* and *SRAS* curves intersect.

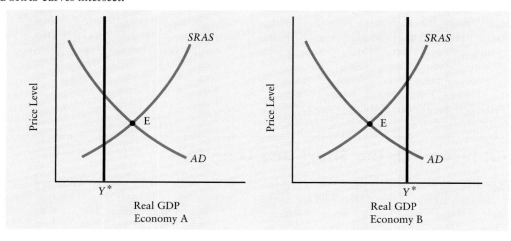

a. Explain why in Economy A wages and other factor prices will begin to rise, and why this will increase unit costs.

b. Following your answer in part **a**, show the effect on the *SRAS* curve. Explain what happens to real GDP and the price level.

c. Explain why in Economy B wages and other factor prices will begin to fall, and why this will decrease unit costs.

d. Following your answer in part **c**, show the effect on the *SRAS* curve. Explain what happens to real GDP and the price level.

2. The table shows several possible situations for the economy in terms of output gaps and the rate of change of wages. Real GDP is measured in billions of dollars. Assume that potential output is $800 billion.

Situation	Real GDP	Output Gap	Rate of Wage Change	Shift of SRAS Curve (+/0/−)
A	775	—	−2.0 %	—
B	785	—	−1.2 %	—
C	795	—	−0.2 %	—
D	800	—	0.0 %	—
E	805	—	1.0 %	—
F	815	—	2.4 %	—
G	825	—	4.0 %	—
H	835	—	5.8 %	—

a. Compute the output gap $(Y-Y^*)$ for each situation and fill in the table.

b. Explain why wages rise when output is greater than potential but fall when output is less than potential.

c. For each situation, explain whether the economy's *SRAS* curve is shifting up, shifting down, or is stationary. Fill in the table.

d. Plot the Phillips curve on a scale diagram for this economy. (See *Extensions in Theory 25-1* for a review of the Phillips curve.)

3. Consider an economy that is in equilibrium with output equal to Y^*. There is then a sudden and significant reduction in the world's demand for this country's goods.

a. Illustrate the initial equilibrium in a diagram.

b. What kind of shock occurred—aggregate demand or aggregate supply? Show the effects of the shock in your diagram.

c. Explain the process by which the economy will adjust back toward Y^* in the long run. Show this in your diagram.

d. Explain why policymakers may want to use a fiscal expansion to restore output back to Y^* rather than wait for the process you described in part **c**. What

role does downward wage stickiness play in the policymakers' thinking?

4. Consider an economy that is in equilibrium with output equal to Y^*. There is then a sudden and significant reduction in the world price of an important raw material, such as iron ore.

a. Illustrate the initial equilibrium in a diagram.

b. What kind of shock occurred—aggregate demand or aggregate supply? Show the effects of the shock in your diagram.

c. Explain the process by which the economy will adjust back toward Y^* in the long run. Show this in your diagram.

5. We explained in the chapter how shocks—demand or supply—tend to lead to cyclical fluctuations in real GDP and the price level. The following diagram shows the time paths of real GDP and the price level for an economy that begins at $Y=Y^*$ and is then subjected to a shock that shifts the *AD* curve to the right. We define t^* as the time the shock hits the economy; we define t^{**} to be the time when the economy has adjusted fully and is back in long-run equilibrium.

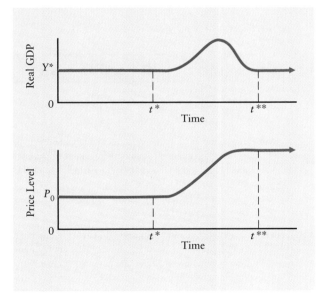

a. Draw the same types of diagrams for a negative *AD* shock. How does t^{**} for this shock compare to t^{**} for the positive *AD* shock?

b. Draw the same types of diagrams for a positive *SRAS* shock. How does t^{**} for this shock compare to t^{**} for the positive *AD* shock?

c. Draw the same types of diagrams for a negative *SRAS* shock. How does t^{**} for this shock compare to t^{**} for the positive *SRAS* and *AD* shock?

6. In our discussion of fiscal stabilization policy, we explained how income taxes and transfers affected the size of the multiplier. The accompanying diagrams show the initial equilibrium of two hypothetical economies that are each about to experience a $10 billion increase in autonomous net exports. Economy A has high (net) tax rates whereas Economy B has low (net) tax rates. Both economies have the same *SRAS* curve.

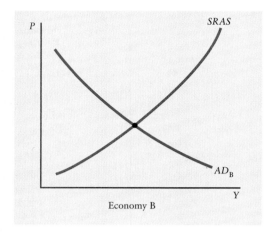

Economy B

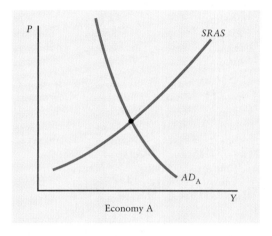

Economy A

a. Explain why Economy A is shown to have a steeper *AD* curve than Economy B.
b. Explain which economy has the larger multiplier, and why.
c. Illustrate the shifts in the *AD* curves that result from the increases in net exports. (Hint: you may want to review at this point the relationship between the *AD* curve and the *AE* curve, which we discussed in Chapter 24.)

DISCUSSION QUESTIONS

1. Discuss the following two statements in terms of short- and long-run aggregate supply curves.

   a. "Starting from potential output, an increase in government spending can produce more output and employment at the cost of a once-and-for-all rise in the price level."
   b. "Increased government spending can never lead to a permanent increase in output."

2. Politicians are sometimes accused of adopting policies that bring "short-term gain at the cost of long-term pain," whereas statesmen offer "short-term pain to buy long-term gain." What policies that shift aggregate demand or aggregate supply curves might come under one or the other of these descriptions?

3. If downward flexibility of money wages would allow the automatic adjustment mechanism to eliminate recessionary gaps quickly, why do workers usually resist wage cuts during times of economic slump?

4. Which of the following would be built-in stabilizers?

   a. Employment insurance payments
   b. Cost-of-living escalators in government contracts and pensions
   c. Income taxes
   d. Free university tuition for unemployed workers after six months of unemployment, provided that they are under 30 years old and have had five or more years of full-time work experience since high school

5. During 1998 and 1999, the Canadian economy was experiencing a sufficiently high rate of growth of real GDP that many economists predicted an increase in inflation. Yet inflation, if anything, declined slightly. At the same time, world commodity prices continued their decline that began in mid 1997. Explain the behaviour of the Canadian economy—high growth and falling inflation—in terms of aggregate demand and aggregate supply curves. What role, if any, is played by the falling commodity prices? What role is played by the U.S. economy, which at this point was experiencing very strong growth?

PART NINE

Money, Banking, and Monetary Policy

What is money, and where does it come from? Is the amount of money in the Canadian economy equal only to the actual value of bills and coins in circulation, or do accounts at commercial banks matter? If bank accounts matter, does this mean commercial banks can create money? Does the Bank of Canada control interest rates or are these rates determined by market forces? How does the Bank's monetary policy affect real GDP and employment? These are the sorts of questions you will be able to answer after reading the next three chapters.

Chapter 26 traces the development of money, from the use of barter in ancient economies to deposit money that is so important today. We will examine the Canadian banking system, from the commercial banks to the Bank of Canada, Canada's central bank. The idea of money creation will then be examined, and we will see that commercial banks do indeed create money. Finally, we will discuss several formal measures of the Canadian money supply.

Chapter 27 begins with a discussion of the demand for money. Here we see the various reasons why households and firms hold money, and why the level of interest rates is so important in these decisions. We then examine the concept of monetary equilibrium, and it is here that we consider the Bank of Canada's role in determining interest rates. We also see how changes in the Bank of Canada's policy can affect interest rates, aggregate expenditure, and eventually real GDP and the price level.

In Chapter 28 we focus on monetary policy. We will explore some of the details of how the Bank of Canada's actions influence the commercial banking system. The Bank's policy variables, policy instruments, and policy targets will all be discussed, and it is here that we discuss the lags and uncertainty that make the conduct of monetary policy so difficult. We then give a brief review of the past three decades of monetary policy in Canada. This discussion will help to put together the lessons learned throughout this part of the book.

CHAPTER 26

The Nature of Money

LEARNING OBJECTIVES

1 Understand the Classical dichotomy and how this relates to the neutrality of money.

2 Explain the various functions of money.

3 Understand the historical origins of money.

4 Recognize that modern banking systems comprise both privately owned commercial banks and government-owned central banks.

5 Explain how commercial banks create money through the process of taking deposits and making loans.

6 Know what is included in various measures of the money supply.

In the next three chapters, we examine the significance of money in market economies. The role of money may seem obvious—money is what people use to buy things. Yet as we shall see, increasing the amount of money circulating in Canada would not make the average Canadian better off in the long run. Although money allows those who have it to buy someone else's output, the total amount of goods and services available for everyone to buy depends on the total output produced, not on the total amount of money that people possess. In short, an increase in the quantity of money will not increase the level of potential real GDP, Y^*. Still, without money, modern economies could not function, and most economists would agree that the quantity of money, although it cannot affect Y^*, can and does affect short-run movements in national income.

Two Perspectives on Money

Theories on the role of money in a market economy have been evolving for several centuries.

The Classical View

In the eighteenth and nineteenth centuries, economists articulated the independence of Y^* from monetary factors in terms of an economic theory that distinguished sharply between the "real sector" of the economy and the "monetary sector" of the economy. This approach led to a view that is now referred to as the *Classical dichotomy.*

According to the **Classical dichotomy**, the allocation of resources, and hence the determination of real GDP, is determined only by the real sector of the economy. It is *relative prices* that matter for this process. Early economists argued that the price level is determined in the monetary sector of the economy. If the quantity of money were doubled, other things being equal, the prices of all commodities and money income would also double. Relative prices would remain unchanged, and the real sector of the economy would be unaffected.

According to the Classical economists, the allocation of resources—and the determination of real GDP—depends only on relative prices. An increase in the money supply leads to a proportionate increase in all money prices, with no change in the allocation of resources or the level of real GDP.

The doctrine that the quantity of money influences the level of money prices but has no effect on the real part of the economy is called the **neutrality of money**. Because early economists believed that the most important questions—How much does the economy produce? What share of it does each group in society get?—were answered in the real sector, they spoke of money as a "veil" behind which occurred the real events that affected material well-being.

Classical dichotomy
The view that national income is determined only by the real sector of the economy and that changes in the money supply lead only to changes in the price level.

neutrality of money
The doctrine that the money supply affects only the absolute level of prices and has no effect on relative prices, the allocation of resources, or the distribution of income.

The Modern View

Most modern economists still accept the neutrality of money in the long run when all the forces causing change have fully worked themselves out. However, they do not accept the neutrality of money when the economy is adjusting to the various forces that cause it to change—that is, when the economy is not in a state of long-run equilibrium. Consequently, they reject the Classical dichotomy as a description of the economy in the short run.

The view that the neutrality of money holds in the long run leads modern economists to stress the strong link between changes in the money supply and changes in the price level, at least over long periods of time. Figure 26-1 shows a scatter-plot of inflation and money growth for 82 countries over the four decades following the Second World War. Each point in the figure represents the rates of inflation and money supply growth for one country averaged over the forty-year period. The vertical axis measures each country's average annual inflation rate—that is, the average annual rate of increase of the price level. The horizontal axis measures each country's average annual rate of growth of the money supply (which we will define precisely later in the chapter). As is clear in the figure, there is a positive relationship between money supply growth and inflation, as reflected by the tight bunching of points around the upward-sloping line, the "line of best fit" between money supply growth and inflation. The slope of the line of best fit is 0.97, indicating that two countries that differ in their money growth rates by 10 percent will, on average, differ in their inflation rates by 9.7 percent.

To see how much Canada's price level has increased from anytime in the past fifty years to today, see the Bank of Canada's "inflation calculator" at: www.bank-banque-canada.ca.

FIGURE 26-1 Inflation and Money Growth Across Many Countries

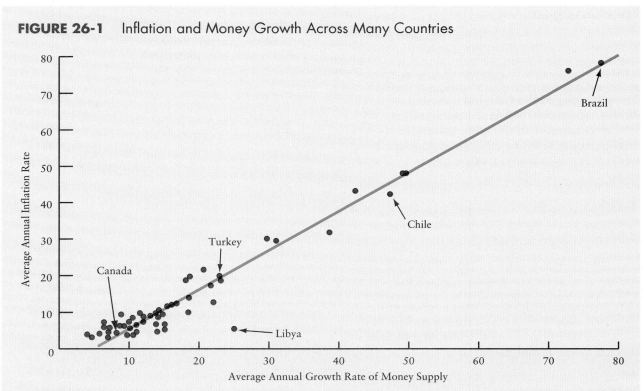

Countries with higher inflation rates tend also to be countries with higher rates of growth of the money supply. This figure plots long-run data for many countries. Each point shows the average annual inflation rate and the average annual growth rate of the money supply for a specific country over the post World War II period (the precise years vary slightly across countries). For all countries, the inflation data refer to the rate of change of the consumer price index; the money supply data refer to the growth rate of currency. The positive relationship between inflation and money supply growth (with a slope of the best-fit line very close to one) is consistent with the proposition of long-run money neutrality.

(*Source:* The data are from the International Monetary Fund's *International Financial Statistics,* as compiled by R.J. Barro and R.F. Lucas.)

Most modern economists believe that money is neutral in the long run. Long-run neutrality implies that, in the absence of other shocks to the economy, changes in money and changes in the price level are closely linked over long periods of time.

The Nature of Money

What exactly is money? In this section, we describe the functions of money and briefly outline its history.

What Is Money?

money A medium of exchange that can also serve as a store of value and a unit of account.

medium of exchange Anything that is generally acceptable in return for goods and services sold.

In economics, **money** has usually been defined as any generally accepted medium of exchange. A **medium of exchange** is anything that will be widely accepted in a society in exchange for goods and services. Although its medium-of-exchange role is perhaps its most important one, money also acts as a *store of value* and as a *unit of account*. Different kinds of money vary in the degree of efficiency with which they fulfill these functions. As we shall see, the *money supply* is measured by using different definitions for different purposes.

Money as a Medium of Exchange

If there were no money, goods would have to be exchanged by barter. **Barter** is the system whereby goods and services are exchanged directly with each other. The major difficulty with barter is that each transaction requires a *double coincidence of wants:* anyone who specialized in producing one commodity would have to spend a great deal of time searching for satisfactory transactions. For example, the barber who needs his sink repaired would have to find a plumber who wants a haircut. In a world of many different goods and many different people, the effort required to make transactions would be extreme.

> **barter** A system in which goods and services are traded directly for other goods and services.

The use of money as a medium of exchange solves this problem. People can sell their output for money and then use the money to buy what they wish from others.

The double coincidence of wants is unnecessary when a medium of exchange is used.

By facilitating transactions, money makes possible the benefits of specialization and the division of labour, which in turn contribute to the efficiency of the economic system. It is not without justification that money has been called one of the great inventions contributing to human freedom and well-being.

To serve as an efficient medium of exchange, money must have a number of characteristics. It must be readily acceptable. It must have a high value relative to its weight (otherwise it would be a nuisance to carry around). It must be divisible, because money that comes only in large denominations is useless for transactions having only a small value. Finally, it must be difficult, if not impossible, to counterfeit.

Money as a Store of Value

Money is a convenient way to store purchasing power; goods may be sold today for money and the money may then be stored until it is needed for some future purchase. To be a satisfactory store of value, however, money must have a relatively stable value. A rise in the price level is also a decrease in the purchasing power of money. When the price level is stable, the purchasing power of a given sum of money is also stable; when the price level is highly variable, so is the purchasing power of money, and the usefulness of money as a store of value is undermined.

Between the early 1970s and the early 1990s, inflation in Canada was high enough and sufficiently variable to diminish money's usefulness as a store of value. Since 1992, inflation has been both low and relatively stable, thus increasing money's role as a store of value. Even Canada's high-inflation experience, however, is very modest compared to that in some other countries, such as Chile in the mid 1970s, Bolivia in the mid 1980s, and Romania and Brazil in the early 1990s. Perhaps the most infamous experience of *hyperinflation* comes from Germany in the early 1920s. This case is discussed in *Lessons from History 26-1*.

Money as a Unit of Account

Money may also be used purely for accounting purposes without having a physical existence of its own. For instance, a government store in a truly communist society might say that everyone had so many "dollars" to use each month. Goods could then be assigned prices and each consumer's purchases recorded, the consumer being allowed to buy until the allocated supply of dollars was exhausted. These dollars need have no existence other

LESSONS FROM HISTORY 26-1

Hyperinflation

Hyperinflation is generally defined as inflation that exceeds 50 percent per month. At this rate of inflation a chocolate bar that costs $1 on January 1 would cost $129.74 by December 31 of the same year. When prices are rising at such rapid rates, is it possible for money to maintain its usefulness as a medium of exchange or as a store of value? There are several examples from history that have allowed economists to study the role of money during hyperinflation. This historical record is not entirely reassuring. In a number of instances, prices rose at an ever-accelerating rate until a nation's money ceased to be a satisfactory store of value, even for the short period between receipt and expenditure, and hence ceased also to be useful as a medium of exchange.

The most spectacular example of hyperinflation is the experience of Germany in the period after World War I. The index shows that a good purchased for one 100-mark note in July 1923 would cost *10 million* 100-mark notes only four months later! Although Germany had experienced substantial inflation during World War I, averaging more than 30 percent per year, the immediate postwar years of 1920 and 1921 gave no sign of explosive inflation. Indeed, prices were relatively stable until 1922 and 1923 when they exploded. On November 15, 1923, the German mark was officially repudiated, its value wholly destroyed. How could such a dramatic increase in prices happen?

When inflation becomes so rapid that people lose confidence in the purchasing power of their currency, they rush to spend it. People who have goods become increasingly reluctant to accept the rapidly depreciating money in exchange. The rush to spend money accelerates the increase in prices until people finally become unwilling to accept money on any terms. What was once money ceases to be money. The price system can then be restored only by repudiation of the old monetary unit and its replacement by a new unit.

About a dozen hyperinflations in world history have been documented, among them the collapse of the continental during the American Revolution in 1776, the ruble during the Russian Revolution in 1917, the drachma during and after the German occupation of Greece in World War II, the pengö in Hungary in 1945 and 1946, the Chinese national currency from 1946 to 1948, and the Bolivian peso in 1984 and 1985. Every one of these hyperinflations was accompanied by great increases in the money supply; new money was printed to give governments purchasing power that they could not or would not obtain by taxation. Further, every one occurred in the midst of a major

political upheaval in which grave doubts existed about the stability and the future of the government itself.

Is hyperinflation likely in the absence of civil war, revolution, or collapse of the government? Most economists think not. Further, it is clear that high inflation rates over a period of time do not mean the inevitable or even likely onset of hyperinflation, however serious the distributive and social effects of such rates may be.

During hyperinflation money loses its value so quickly that people cease to accept it as a means of payment. At that point, money may as well be used for wallpaper.

Date	German Wholesale Price Index (1913 = 1)
January 1913	1
January 1920	13
January 1921	14
January 1922	37
July 1922	101
January 1923	2 785
July 1923	74 800
August 1923	944 000
September 1923	23 900 000
October 1923	7 096 000 000
November 1923	750 000 000 000

than as entries in the store's books, yet they would serve as a perfectly satisfactory unit of account.

Whether they could also serve as a medium of exchange between individuals depends on whether the store would agree to transfer dollar credits from one customer to another at the customer's request. Canadian banks transfer dollars credited to deposits in this way each time you make a purchase with your ATM card. Thus, a bank deposit can serve as both a unit of account and a medium of exchange. Notice that the use of *dollars* in this context suggests a further sense in which money is a unit of account. People think about values in terms of the monetary unit with which they are familiar.

The Origins of Money

The origins of money go far back in antiquity. Most primitive tribes are known to have made some use of it.

Metallic Money

All sorts of commodities have been used as money at one time or another, but gold and silver proved to have great advantages. They were precious because their supplies were relatively limited, and they were in constant demand by the wealthy for ornament and decoration. Hence, these metals tended to have high and stable prices. Further, they were easily recognized, they were divisible into extremely small units, and they did not easily wear out. Thus, precious metals came to circulate as money and to be used in many transactions.

Before the invention of coins, it was necessary to carry the metals in bulk. When a purchase was made, the requisite quantity of the metal was carefully weighed on a scale. The invention of coinage eliminated the need to weigh the metal at each transaction, but it created an important role for an authority, usually a monarch, who made the coins and affixed his or her seal, guaranteeing the amount of precious metal that the coin contained. This was clearly a great convenience, as long as traders knew that they could accept the coin at its "face value." The face value was nothing more than a statement that a certain weight of metal was contained therein.

However, coins often could not be taken at their face value. The practice of clipping a thin slice off the edge of the coin and keeping the valuable metal became common. This, of course, served to undermine the acceptability of coins, even if they were stamped. To get around this problem, the idea arose of minting the coins with a rough edge. The absence of the rough edge would immediately indicate that the coin had been clipped. This practice, called *milling,* survives on Canadian dimes, quarters, and "twoonies" as an interesting anachronism to remind us that there were days when the market value of the metal in the coin was equal to the face value of the coin.

Not to be outdone by the cunning of their subjects, some rulers were quick to seize the chance of getting something for nothing. The power to mint placed rulers in a position to work a very profitable fraud. They often used some suitable occasion— a marriage, an anniversary, an alliance—to remint the coinage. Subjects would be ordered to bring their coins in to the mint to be melted down and coined afresh with a new stamp. Between the melting down and the recoining, however, the rulers had only to toss some further inexpensive base metal in with the molten gold. This *debasing* of the coinage allowed the ruler to earn a handsome profit by minting more new coins than the number of old ones collected, and putting the extras in the royal vault.

The result of debasement was inflation. The subjects had the same number of coins as before and hence could demand the same quantity of goods. When rulers paid their bills, however, the recipients of the extra coins could be expected to spend them. This caused a net increase in demand, which in turn bid up prices. Thus, debasing of the coinage was a common cause of increases in prices.

Gresham's Law.   The early experience of currency debasement led to the observation known as **Gresham's law,** after Sir Thomas Gresham (1519–1579), an adviser to the Elizabethan court, who coined the phrase "bad money drives out good."

Gresham's law   The theory that "bad," or debased, money drives "good," or undebased, money out of circulation.

When Queen Elizabeth I came to the throne of England in the middle of the sixteenth century, the coinage had been severely debased. Seeking to help trade, Elizabeth minted new coins that contained their full face value in gold. However, as fast as she fed these new coins into circulation, they disappeared. Why?

Suppose that you possessed one of these new coins and one of the old ones, each with the same face value, and had to make a purchase. What would you do? You would use the debased coin to make the purchase and keep the undebased one; you part with less gold that way. Suppose that you wanted to obtain a certain amount of gold bullion by melting down the gold coins (as was frequently done). Which coins would you use? You would use new, undebased coins because you would part with less face value that way (it would take more of the debased coins than the new coins to get a given amount of gold bullion). The debased coins (bad money) would thus remain in circulation, and the undebased coins (good money) would disappear—the "bad" money would drive out the "good" money.

Gresham's law predicts that when two types of money are used side by side, the one with the greater intrinsic value will be driven out of circulation.

Gresham's insights have proved helpful in explaining the experience of a number of modern high-inflation economies. For example, in the 1970s, inflation in Chile raised the value of the metallic content in coins above their face value. Coins quickly disappeared from circulation as private citizens sold them to entrepreneurs who melted them down for their metal. Only paper currency remained in circulation and was used even for tiny transactions such as purchasing a pack of matches. Gresham's law is one reason why modern coins, unlike their historical counterparts, are merely tokens that contain a metallic value that is only a small fraction of their face value.

Paper Money

The next important step in the history of money was the evolution of paper currency. Artisans who worked with gold required secure safes, and the public began to deposit gold with such goldsmiths for safekeeping. Goldsmiths would give their depositors receipts promising to hand over the gold on demand. When a depositor wished to make a large purchase, he could go to his goldsmith, reclaim some of his gold, and hand it over to the seller of the goods. If the seller had no immediate need for the gold, he would carry it back to the goldsmith for safekeeping.

If people knew the goldsmith to be reliable, there was no need to go through the cumbersome and risky business of physically transferring the gold. The buyer needed only to transfer the goldsmith's receipt to the seller, who would accept it as long as he was confident that the goldsmith would pay over the gold whenever it was needed. If the seller wished to buy a good from a third party, who also knew the goldsmith to be reliable, this transaction could also be effected by passing the goldsmith's receipt from the buyer to the seller. This transferring of paper receipts rather than gold was essentially the invention of paper money.

When it first came into being, paper money represented a promise to pay so much gold on demand. In this case, the promise was made first by goldsmiths and later by banks. Such paper money was *backed* by precious metal and was *convertible on demand* into this metal. In the nineteenth century, private banks commonly issued paper money, called **bank notes,** nominally convertible into gold. As with the goldsmiths, each bank issued its own notes, and these notes were convertible into gold at the issuing

bank notes   Paper money issued by commercial banks.

bank. Thus, in the nineteenth century, bank notes from many different banks circulated side by side, each of them being backed by gold at the bank that issued them.

Fractionally Backed Paper Money.   Early on, many goldsmiths and banks discovered that it was not necessary to keep one ounce of gold in the vaults for every claim to one ounce circulating as paper money. This is because at any one time, some of the bank's customers would be withdrawing gold, others would be depositing it, and most would be trading in the bank's paper notes without any need or desire to convert them into gold. As a result, the bank was able to issue more money redeemable in gold than the amount of gold that it held in its vaults. This was good business because the money could be invested profitably in interest-earning loans to households and firms. To this day, banks have many more claims outstanding against them than they actually have in reserves available to pay those claims. We say that the currency issued in such a situation is *fractionally backed* by the reserves.

The major problem with a fractionally backed convertible currency was maintaining its convertibility into the precious metal behind it. The imprudent bank that issued too much paper money would find itself unable to redeem its currency in gold when the demand for gold was even slightly higher than usual. It would then have to suspend payments, and all holders of its notes would suddenly find that the notes were worthless. The prudent bank that kept a reasonable relationship between its note issues and its gold reserves would find that it could meet a normal range of demand for gold without any trouble.

If, for whatever reason, the public lost confidence in the banks and demanded redemption of its currency *en masse,* the banks would be unable to honour their pledges. The history of nineteenth- and early-twentieth-century banking on both sides of the Atlantic is full of examples of banks that were ruined by "panics," or sudden runs on their gold reserves. When these happened, the banks' depositors and the holders of their notes would find themselves with worthless pieces of paper.

Fiat Money

As time went on, currency (notes and coins) issued by private banks became less common, and central banks took control of the currency. In time, *only* central banks were permitted to issue currency. Originally, the central banks issued currency that was fully convertible into gold. In those days, gold would be brought to the central bank, which would issue currency in the form of "gold certificates" that asserted that the gold was available on demand. The gold supply thus set some upper limit on the amount of currency. This practice of backing the currency with gold is known as a **gold standard.**

However, central banks, like private banks before them, could issue more currency than they had in gold because in normal times only a small fraction of the outstanding currency was presented for payment at any one time. Thus, even though the need to maintain convertibility into gold put an upper limit on note issuance, central banks had substantial discretionary control over the quantity of currency outstanding.

During the period between the World Wars (1919–1939), almost all of the countries of the world abandoned the gold standard; their currencies were thus no longer convertible into gold. Money that is not convertible by law into anything valuable derives its value from its acceptability in exchange. Such **fiat money** is widely acceptable because it is declared by government order, or *fiat,* to be legal tender. **Legal tender** is anything that by law must be accepted when offered either for the purchase of goods or services or to discharge a debt.

Today, a few countries preserve the fiction that their currency is backed by gold, but no country allows its currency to be converted into gold on demand. Gold backing for Canadian currency was eliminated in 1940, although note issues continued to carry

gold standard
A currency standard whereby a country's currency is convertible into gold at a fixed rate of exchange.

fiat money   Paper money or coinage that is neither backed by nor convertible into anything else but is decreed by the government to be accepted as legal tender.

legal tender
Anything that by law must be accepted for the purchase of goods and services or in discharge of a debt.

the traditional statement "will pay to the bearer on demand" until 1954. Today's Bank of Canada notes simply say, "This note is legal tender." It is, in other words, fiat money pure and simple.

If fiat money is acceptable, it is a medium of exchange. If its purchasing power remains stable, it is a satisfactory store of value. If both of these things are true, it serves as a satisfactory unit of account. Today, almost all currency is fiat money.

Many people are disturbed to learn that present-day paper money is neither backed by nor convertible into anything more valuable—that it consists of nothing but pieces of paper whose value derives from common acceptance and from confidence that it will continue to be accepted in the future. Many people believe that their money should be more "substantial" than this. Yet money is, in fact, nothing more than pieces of paper.

Modern Money: Deposit Money

Early in the twentieth century, private banks lost the authority to issue bank notes, and this authority was reserved for central banks (which we discuss shortly). Yet, as we shall see, they did not lose the power to create *deposit money*. (A number of terms that will be encountered as we discuss modern money and the institutions related to it are discussed in *Applying Economic Concepts 26-1*.)

Today's bank customers frequently deposit coins and paper money with the banks for safekeeping, just as in former times they deposited gold. Such a deposit is recorded as a credit to the customer's account. A customer who wishes to pay a debt may come to the bank and claim the money in dollars and then pay the money to other persons who may themselves redeposit the money in a bank.

As with gold transfers, this is a tedious procedure. It is more convenient to have the bank transfer claims to money on deposit. As soon as cheques, which are written instructions to the bank to make a transfer, became widely accepted in payment for commodities and debts, bank deposits became a form of money called *deposit money*. **Deposit money** is defined as money held by the public in the form of deposits in commercial banks that can be withdrawn on demand. Such deposits are called *demand deposits;* the most important of which are chequing accounts. Cheques, unlike bank notes, do not circulate freely from hand to hand; hence cheques themselves are not currency. However, a balance in a demand deposit *is* money; the cheque transfers money from one person to another. Because cheques are easily drawn and deposited and are relatively safe from theft, they are widely used. In recent years, the development of debit cards has taken the place of cheques for many transactions. The use of a debit card instantly (electronically) transfers funds from the bank account of the purchaser to the bank account of the seller—it thus has the same effect as a cheque, only faster.

Thus, when commercial banks lost the right to issue notes of their own, the form of bank money changed, but the substance did not. Today, banks have money in their vaults (or on deposit with the central banks), just as they always did. Once it was gold; today it is the legal tender of the times—fiat money. It is true today, just as in the past, that most of the bank's customers are content to pay their bills by passing among themselves the bank's promises to pay money on demand. Only a small proportion of the transactions made by the bank's customers are made in cash.

Bank deposits are money. Today, just as in the past, banks create money by issuing more promises to pay (deposits) than they have cash reserves available to pay out.

deposit money
Money held by the public in the form of demand deposits with commercial banks.

APPLYING ECONOMIC CONCEPTS 26-1

A Guide to Financial Assets

Throughout this and subsequent chapters, we will encounter many different types of financial assets, or *securities*. It is important to understand the meaning of some of the more commonly used terms.

Equity refers to assets such as stocks or shares that represent evidence of partial ownership of a firm and hence provide a claim on the earnings of that firm; the return on equity depends on the performance of the firm. Equity is also often called *capital*; unless the context makes it clear, care must be taken to distinguish between use of the term capital to refer to the actual plant, equipment, and machinery that constitute a firm's physical assets and use of the term to refer to the financial assets that represent a claim on the firm's earnings.

Debt refers to assets issued by firms and governments that promise to pay a specified rate of interest over a specified period of time. Unless the firm in question goes bankrupt and cannot meet its obligations, the return on debt does not depend on the earnings of the firm—the interest must be paid whether the firm is profitable or not and thus represents a prior claim on the firm's earnings before any payment to equity holders is made.

Most debt instruments, often called *bonds*, promise to pay a stated sum of money as interest each year and to repay the principal (often called the *face value* or the *redemption value*) of the bond at some future maturity date, often many years distant. The time until the maturity date is called the *term to maturity*, or simply the *term*, of the bond. Some bonds, called *perpetuities*, pay interest forever and never repay the principal.

Very-short-term bonds that promise a single payment (combining interest and principal) are called *money-market instruments* and include *treasury bills* (short-term government bonds), certificates of deposit (CDs), banker's acceptances, and commercial paper. The price paid for one of these instruments is less than the amount that the instrument pays on maturity, and the difference is called the *discount*. For example, the government issues three- and six-month treasury bills each week that are priced on a discount basis. The difference between the purchase price and the payment on maturity represents the interest on the bill.

The ownership of most financial assets is transferable, and hence they can be bought and sold in financial markets. As with anything else that is bought and sold, the price of financial assets fluctuates in response to shifts in supply and demand. In the next chapter we will look more carefully at the determination of the price of financial assets.

One important characteristic of financial assets is their *riskiness*, which refers to the possibility that the future payments will not be made in full or at all. Typically, investors are thought to be risk-averse—that is, the riskier an asset is, the higher is the yield it will have to offer to induce investors to buy it.

Another important characteristic of financial assets is their *liquidity*, which refers to their usefulness as a ready means of payment. Money can always be used as a means of payment and hence is a perfectly liquid asset. Since other financial assets can be sold in the market and hence are convertible into cash, they appear to be just as liquid as money. However, the markets for some assets are such that they cannot always be instantly sold, or at least not at anything other than a "bargain-basement" price; to receive the price that is justified by the asset's risk and return, some time and expense must be incurred.

The Canadian Banking System

Many types of institutions make up a modern banking system such as exists in Canada today. The **central bank** is the government-owned and government-operated institution that serves to control the banking system. Through it, the government's monetary policy is conducted. In Canada, the central bank is the Bank of Canada, often called just the Bank.

central bank   A bank that acts as banker to the commercial banking system and often to the government as well. Usually a government-owned institution that controls the banking system and is the sole money-issuing authority.

Financial intermediaries are privately owned institutions that serve the general public. They are called *intermediaries* because they stand between savers, from whom they accept deposits, and investors, to whom they make loans. For many years, government regulations created a sharp distinction among the various types of financial intermediaries by limiting the types of transactions that each could engage in. The past two decades have seen a sweeping deregulation of the financial system so that many of these traditional distinctions no longer apply. In this book, we use the term *commercial banks* to extend to all financial intermediaries that create deposit money, including chartered banks, trust companies and credit unions.

The Bank of Canada

All advanced free-market economies have, in addition to commercial banks, a central bank. Many of the world's early central banks were private, profit-making institutions that provided services to ordinary banks. Their importance, however, caused them to develop close ties with government. Central banks soon became instruments of the government, though not all of them were publicly owned. The Bank of England (the "Old Lady of Threadneedle Street"), one of the world's oldest and most famous central banks, began to operate as the central bank of England in the seventeenth century, but it was not formally taken over by the government until 1947.

The similarities in the functions performed and the tools used by the world's central banks are much more important than the differences in their organization. Although our attention is given to the operations of the Bank of Canada, its basic functions are similar to those of the Bank of England, the Federal Reserve System in the United States, or the new European Central Bank.

Organization of the Bank of Canada

The Bank of Canada commenced operations on March 11, 1935. It is a publicly owned corporation; all profits accruing from its operations are remitted to the Government of Canada. The responsibility for the Bank's affairs rests with a board of directors composed of the governor, the senior deputy governor, the deputy minister of finance, and 12 directors. The governor is appointed by the directors, with the approval of the federal cabinet, for a seven-year term. Since the Bank's inception, there have been six governors:

- Graham Towers (1935–54)
- James Coyne (1955–61)
- Louis Rasminsky (1961–73)
- Gerald Bouey (1973–87)
- John Crow (1987–94)
- Gordon Thiessen (1994–)

The organization of the Bank of Canada is designed to keep the operation of monetary policy free from day-to-day political influence. The Bank is not responsible to Parliament for its day-to-day behaviour in the way that the Department of Finance is for the operation of fiscal policy. In this sense, the Bank of Canada has considerable autonomy in the way it carries out monetary policy. Despite this considerable autonomy, however, the Bank of Canada is not completely independent. The *ultimate* responsibility for the Bank's actions rest with the government, since it is the government which must answer to Parliament. This system is known as "joint responsibility," and it dates back to 1967.

Under the system of joint responsibility, the governor of the Bank and the minister of finance consult regularly. In the case of fundamental disagreement over policy, the minister of finance has the option of issuing an explicit *directive* to the governor. In such a case (which has not happened since the inception of joint responsibility), the governor would simply carry out the minister's directive (or resign), and the responsibility for monetary policy would rest with the government. In the absence of such a directive, however, responsibility for monetary policy rests with the governor of the Bank.

The system of joint responsibility keeps the conduct of monetary policy free from day-to-day political influence while ensuring that the government retains ultimate responsibility for monetary policy.[1]

For information on the Bank of Canada, see its website: www.bank-banque-canada.ca.

Basic Functions of the Bank

A central bank serves four main functions: as a banker for private banks, as a bank for the government, as the regulator of the nation's money supply, and as a supporter of financial markets. The first three functions are reflected in Table 26-1, which shows the balance sheet of the Bank of Canada.

Banker to the Chartered Banks.   The central bank accepts deposits from the chartered banks and will, on order, transfer them to the account of another bank. In this way, the central bank provides the chartered banks with the equivalent of a chequing account and with a means of settling debts to other banks. The deposits of the chartered banks with the Bank of Canada—also called *reserves*—appear in Table 26-1. In

TABLE 26-1   Assets and Liabilities of the Bank of Canada, March 1999 (millions of dollars)

Assets		Liabilities	
Government of Canada securities	30 042	Notes in circulation	30 882
Advances to banks	737	Government of Canada deposits	12
Foreign-currency assets	323	Deposits of banks (reserves)	1 115
Other assets	1 696	Foreign-currency liabilities	159
		Other liabilities and capital	630
Total	32 798	Total	32 798

The balance sheet of the Bank of Canada shows that it serves as banker to the commercial banks and to the Government of Canada and as issuer of our currency; it also suggests the Bank's role as regulator of money markets and the money supply. The principal liabilities of the Bank are the basis of the money supply. Bank of Canada notes are currency, and the deposits of the commercial banks give them the reserves they need to create deposit money. The Bank's holdings of Government of Canada securities arise from its operations designed to regulate the money supply and financial markets.

(*Source: Bank of Canada Review,* Spring 1999)

---

[1] This system was motivated by the "Coyne Affair" in 1961. James Coyne, then governor of the Bank of Canada, disagreed with the minister of finance over the conduct of monetary policy and was eventually forced to resign. Louis Rasminsky then accepted the position as governor of the Bank on the condition that the Bank of Canada Act be modified to incorporate the idea of joint responsibility. The Bank of Canada Act was so amended in 1967. For a discussion of the early history of the Bank of Canada, see George Watts, *The Bank of Canada: Origins and Early History* (Carleton University Press, 1993).

March 1999 the banks had $1.11 billion on reserve at the Bank of Canada. Notice that the cash reserves of the chartered banks deposited with the central bank are liabilities of the central bank, because it promises to pay them on demand.

Historically, one of the earliest services provided by central banks was that of "lender of last resort" to the banking system. Central banks would lend money to private banks that had sound investments (such as government securities) but were in urgent need of cash. If such banks could not obtain ready cash, they might be forced into insolvency, because they could not meet the demands of their depositors, in spite of their being basically sound. Today's central banks continue to be lenders of last resort.

Banker to the Federal Government.   Governments, too, need to hold their funds in an account into which they can make deposits and on which they can write cheques. The government of Canada keeps some of its chequing deposits at the Bank of Canada, replenishing them from much larger accounts kept at the chartered banks. In March 1999 the federal government had only $12 million in deposits at the Bank of Canada.

When the government requires more money than it collects in taxes, it needs to borrow, and it does so by issuing government securities (short-term treasury bills or longer-term bonds). Most are sold directly to the public, but occasionally the government raises funds by selling securities to the central bank which "buys" them by crediting the government's account with a deposit for the amount of the purchase. In March 1999, the Bank of Canada held $30 billion in government of Canada securities. These securities are an asset for the Bank of Canada but a liability for the government. (It is largely by earning interest on these securities that the Bank of Canada earns a profit every year—a profit that is eventually remitted to the government.)

We will see in Chapter 28 that the Bank's holdings of government securities and its control over the location of government deposits (switching them between the central bank and the commercial banks) are the primary tools for the conduct of monetary policy.

Regulator of the Money Supply.   One of the most important functions of a central bank is to regulate the *money supply*. Though we have not yet defined the money supply precisely—and there are several different definitions of the money supply that we will encounter—we will see that most measures of the money supply include currency plus deposits held at commercial banks. From Table 26-1, it is clear that the overwhelming proportion of a central bank's liabilities (its promises to pay) are either currency (notes and coins) or the reserves of the chartered banks. These reserves, in turn, underlie the deposits of households and firms—in exactly the same way that the nineteenth century goldsmith's holdings of gold underlay its issue of notes.

Thus, by changing its liabilities (currency plus reserves), the Bank of Canada can change the money supply. The Bank of Canada can change the levels of its assets and liabilities in many ways and, as its liabilities rise and fall, so does the money supply. In Chapter 28, we will explore in detail how this happens and how the Bank uses this ability to conduct monetary policy.

Regulator and Supporter of Money Markets.   Central banks usually assume a major responsibility to support the country's financial system and to prevent serious disruption by wide-scale panic and resulting bank failures.

Various institutions—including chartered banks, credit unions, and trust companies—are in the business of borrowing on a short-term basis and lending on a long-term basis. Large, unanticipated increases in interest rates tend to squeeze these institutions. The average rate they earn on their investments rises only slowly as old contracts mature and new ones are made, but they must either pay higher rates to hold on to their deposits or accept wide-scale withdrawals that could easily bring about insolvency. To prevent such financial disasters, central banks often buy and sell government bonds either to slow the rate of change in interest rates or to narrow the range over which the rates are allowed to fluctuate.

Conflicts Among Functions.   The several functions of the Bank of Canada are not always compatible. For example, we will see in Chapter 27 that a policy designed to reduce the rate of inflation requires the Bank to raise short-term interest rates. The resulting squeeze makes life uncomfortable for banks and other financial institutions and makes borrowing expensive for the government. If the Bank of Canada acts to ease those problems, say, by lending money to chartered banks, it is relaxing its anti-inflationary policy. The Bank must strive to balance conflicting objectives. We discuss a number of aspects of this conflict in Chapter 28.

Commercial Banks in Canada

All Canadian banks owned in the private sector are referred to as **commercial banks.** The Canadian banking system is controlled by the provisions of the Bank Act, first passed in 1935 and revised several times since. Under the Bank Act, charters can be granted to financial institutions to operate as banks and, until 1980, there were only a few chartered banks, most of which were very large and each of which operated under identical regulatory provisions.

> **commercial bank**
> A privately owned, profit-seeking institution that provides a variety of financial services, such as accepting deposits from customers and making loans and other investments.

The 1980 revisions to the Bank Act allowed foreign banks to commence operations in Canada, although it severely limited the scale and scope of their activity. Subsequent revisions have removed some of these restrictions and made it easier to obtain new banking charters, but the revisions have maintained the distinction between these newer institutions and banks operating under what are essentially the pre-1980 provisions of the Bank Act. The original provisions, in slightly modified form, are now known as Schedule A of the Bank Act; the foreign banks and the new, smaller domestic banks operate under Schedules B and C. The term *chartered banks* is usually reserved for the Schedule A banks.

The chartered banks have common attributes: they hold deposits for their customers; they permit certain deposits to be transferred by cheque from an individual account to other accounts held in any bank branch in the country; they make loans to households and firms; they invest in government securities.

Banks are not the only financial institutions in the country. Many other privately owned, profit-seeking institutions, such as trust companies and credit unions, accept savings deposits and grant loans for specific purposes. Finance companies make loans to households for practically any purpose—sometimes at very high interest rates. Department stores and credit-card companies will extend credit so that purchases can be made on a buy-now, pay-later basis.

For information and history of Canada's largest chartered bank, see the Royal Bank's website: www.royalbank.com. Go to "corporate information" and then "history."

The chartered banks are subject to federal regulations and until recently were required to hold reserves with the Bank of Canada against their deposit liabilities. Other institutions do not face reserve requirements, but most are subject to various federal and provincial regulations concerning ownership and control and the types of financial activities they are allowed to engage in. Thus, there are differences among all types of financial institutions, not just between banks and others.

The Canadian chartered banks have historically been such a stable and dominant group that the terms *chartered banks* and *banking system* have been considered virtually synonymous. However, events over the past 15 years have broken this identification. Especially important have been sweeping changes in the structure and functioning of international financial markets; some of these developments are discussed further in *Applying Economic Concepts 26-2.*

APPLYING ECONOMIC CONCEPTS 26-2

The Globalization of Financial Markets

Technological innovations in communication over the past two decades have led to a globalization of the financial service industry. Computers, satellite communication systems, reliable telephones with direct worldwide dialing, fax machines, and the widespread use of the Internet have put people in instantaneous contact anywhere in the world.

As a result of these new technologies, borrowers and lenders can learn about market conditions and then move their funds instantly in search of the best loan rates. Large firms need transaction balances only while banks in their area are open. Once banks close for the day in each centre, the firms will not need these balances until tomorrow's reopening; hence the funds can be moved to another market, where they are used until it closes. They are then moved to yet another market. Funds are thus free to move from London to New York to Tokyo and back to London on a daily rotation. This is a degree of global sophistication that was inconceivable before the advent of the computer, when international communication was much slower and costlier than it now is. To facilitate the movement in and out of various national currencies, increasing amounts of bank deposits are denominated in foreign rather than domestic currencies.

One of the first developments in this movement toward globalization was the growth of the foreign-currency markets in Europe in the 1960s. Initially, the main currency involved was the U.S. dollar, which is why *Eurodollar* markets were the first to develop. Today, the *Eurobond* market is an international market where bonds of various types, denominated in various national currencies, are issued and sold to customers located throughout the world. The customers are mainly public corporations, international organizations, and multinational enterprises. The *Eurocurrency* market is a market for short-term bank deposits and bank loans denominated in various currencies.

The increasing sophistication of information transfer has led to a breakdown of the high degree of specialization that characterized financial markets in earlier decades. When information was difficult to obtain and analyse, an efficient division of labour called for a host of specialist institutions, each with expertise in a narrow range of transactions. As a result of the new developments in communication technology, economies of large scale led to the integration of various financial operations within one firm. For example, in Canada and many other countries, banks will sell you securities (in mutual funds) and, similarly, the mutual-fund companies will now sell you banking services. As the scale of such integrated firms increases, these firms find it easier to extend their operations geographically as well as functionally.

The forces of globalization and Canadian banks' perceived need to achieve larger scale in order to compete successfully against larger foreign-based banks led the four largest Canadian chartered banks to attempt to merge in 1998 (Royal Bank with Bank of Montreal, and CIBC with Toronto Dominion). The proposed mergers, however, were prevented by the Canadian government on the grounds that they would unduly lessen competition in the Canadian banking industry. Many critics argue that globalization has made the eventual consolidation of Canadian banks all but inevitable. Globalization, they argue, means that governments that are slow to relax their regulations will see their country's financial firms lose ground to fierce international competitors.

Whether Canadian banks will merge, and to what extent the Canadian financial-services industry will be opened-up to further international competition, is yet to be determined. But it is clear that the globalization of financial markets is real and is showing no signs of slowing down.

Dramatic reductions in communications costs over the past few decades have meant that financial markets in one country are closely linked to those in the rest of the world.

Interbank Activities

Commercial banks have a number of interbank cooperative relationships. For example, banks often share loans. Even the biggest bank cannot meet all the credit needs of a giant corporation, and often a group of banks will offer a "pool loan," agreeing on common terms and dividing the loan up into manageable segments.

Another form of interbank cooperation is the bank credit card. Visa and MasterCard are the two most widely used credit cards, and each is operated by a group of banks.

Probably the most important form of interbank cooperation is cheque clearing and collection. Bank deposits are an effective medium of exchange only because banks accept each other's cheques. If a depositor in the Bank of Montreal writes a cheque to someone who deposits it in the Toronto Dominion Bank, the Bank of Montreal now owes money to the Toronto Dominion Bank. This creates a need for the banks to present cheques to each other for payment. The same is true for transactions made with bank ATM cards.

Millions of such transactions take place in the course of a day, and they result in an enormous sorting and bookkeeping job. Multibank systems make use of a **clearing house** where interbank debts are settled. At the end of the day, all the cheques drawn by the Bank of Montreal's customers and deposited in the Toronto Dominion Bank are totalled and set against the total of all the cheques drawn by the Toronto Dominion's customers and deposited in the Bank of Montreal. It is necessary only to settle the difference between the two sums. The actual cheques are passed through the clearing house back to the bank on which they were drawn. Both banks are then able to adjust the individual accounts by a set of book entries. A flow of cash between banks is necessary only when there is a net transfer of cash from the customers of one bank to those of another. This flow of cash is accompanied by a daily transfer of deposits held by the chartered banks with the Bank of Canada.

See Chapter 26 of www.pearsoned.ca/lipsey for an interview with the Royal Bank's Chairman on the need for bank mergers: "A Case for Bank Mergers," *World Economic Affairs.*

clearing house An institution where interbank indebtedness, arising from the transfer of cheques between banks, is computed and offset and net amounts owing are calculated.

Banks as Profit Seekers

Banks are private firms that seek to make profits in the same sense as firms making neckties or bicycles. A chartered bank provides a variety of services to its customers: a safe place to store money, the convenience of demand deposits that can be transferred by personal cheque or a debit card, a safe and convenient place to earn a modest but guaranteed return on savings, and often financial advice and estate-management services.

Table 26-2 is the combined balance sheet of the chartered banks in Canada. The bulk of a bank's liabilities are deposits owed to its depositors. The principal assets of a bank are

TABLE 26-2 Consolidated Balance Sheet of the Canadian Chartered Banks, February 1999 (millions of dollars)

Assets		Liabilities	
Reserves (including deposits with Bank of Canada)	3 865	Demand deposits	56 310
Government of Canada securities	74 673	Savings deposits	292 499
Mortgage and nonmortgage loans	536 439	Time deposits	131 165
Canadian securities (corporate and provincial		Government of Canada deposits	5 976
and municipal governments)	66 462	Foreign-currency liabilities	636 120
Foreign-currency assets	612 931	Shareholders' equity	61 238
Other assets	95 141	Other liabilities	206 203
Total	1 389 511	Total	1 389 511

Reserves are only a tiny fraction of deposit liabilities. If all the commercial banks' customers who held demand deposits tried to withdraw them in cash, the banks could not meet this demand without liquidating about $52 billion of other assets. This would be impossible without assistance from the Bank of Canada.

(*Source: Bank of Canada Review,* Spring 1999.)

the *securities* it owns (including government bonds), which pay interest or dividends, and the interest-earning *loans* it makes to individuals and to businesses. A bank loan is a liability to the borrower (who must pay it back) but an asset to the bank.

Banks attract deposits by paying interest to depositors and by providing them with services such as clearing cheques, automatic-teller machines, debit cards, and the provision of regular monthly statements. Banks earn profits by lending and investing money deposited with them for more than they pay their depositors in terms of interest and other services provided.

Competition for Deposits

Competition for deposits is active among banks and between banks and other financial institutions. Financial deregulation, which removed restrictions on the activities of various financial institutions, has contributed to this competition. Interest paid on deposits, special high-interest certificates of deposit (CDs), advertising, personal solicitation of accounts, giveaway programs for new deposits to existing accounts, and improved services are all forms of competition for funds. Among the special services are payroll-accounting and pension-accounting schemes for corporate customers. Banks also establish locked deposit-boxes in which retail customers of large companies send their payments, with the bank then crediting them to the company's account. All of these services are costly to the bank, but they serve as inducements for customers to make deposits.

Reserves

All bankers would as a matter of convenience and prudence keep sufficient cash on hand to be able to meet depositors' day-to-day requirements for cash. However, just as the goldsmiths of long ago discovered that only a fraction of the gold they held was ever withdrawn at any given time and, just as banks of long ago discovered that only a small fraction of convertible bank notes was actually converted, so too do modern bankers know that only a small fraction of their deposits will be withdrawn in cash at any one time.

The reserves needed to assure that depositors can withdraw their deposits on demand will be quite small in normal times.

In abnormal times, however, nothing short of 100 percent would do the job if the commercial banking system had to stand alone. When a few bank failures cause a general loss of confidence in banks' ability to redeem their deposits, the results can be devastating. Until relatively recently, such an event—or even the rumour of it—could lead to a "run" on banks as depositors rushed to withdraw their money. Faced with such a panic, banks would have to close until they had borrowed enough funds or sold enough assets to meet the demand or until the demand subsided. However, banks could not instantly turn their loans into cash because the borrowers would have the money tied up in such things as real estate or business enterprises. Neither could the banks obtain cash by selling their securities to the public because payments would be made by cheques, which would not provide cash to pay off depositors.

The difficulty of providing sufficient reserves to meet abnormal situations is alleviated by the central bank. Because it controls the supply of bank reserves, the central bank can provide all the reserves that are needed to meet any abnormal situation. It can do this in two ways. First, it can lend reserves directly to commercial banks on the security of assets that are sound but not easy to liquidate quickly, such as interest-earning residential or commercial mortgages. Second, it can enter the open market and buy all the securities that commercial banks need to sell. Once the public finds that deposits can be turned into cash, any panic will usually subside and any further drain of cash out of banks will cease.

The possibility of panic withdrawals is also greatly diminished by the provision of deposit insurance, provided in Canada by the Canada Deposit Insurance Corporation (CDIC), a crown corporation. The CDIC guarantees that depositors will get their money back even if a bank fails completely. Most depositors will not withdraw their money as long as they are certain they can get it when they need it. Although deposit insurance confers a number of benefits on the operation of the financial system, it has also been subject to considerable criticism in recent years. This is explored in more detail in *Applying Economic Concepts 26-3*.

Target Reserves

We have seen that commercial banks hold reserves in order to meet temporary cash drains that arise when a bank's payments exceed its receipts. Receipts occur when the bank's customers deposit either cash or cheques drawn on other banks; payments are required either when cheques drawn by the bank's customers are deposited in other banks or when customers make cash withdrawals. A bank with no access to reserves will be unable to meet even a temporary cash drain and will be forced to suspend payments. This is something that banks must avoid at almost any cost, so that banking panics can be avoided.

A bank's **reserve ratio** is the fraction of its deposit liabilities that it *actually* holds as reserves, either as cash or as deposits with the central bank. A bank's **target reserve ratio** is the fraction of its deposits it *wishes* to hold as reserves.

In the past, legislation contained in the Bank Act required the chartered banks to hold reserves. These requirements were thought necessary to ensure the stability of the banking system. The reserves that the Bank Act required the banks to hold were called *required reserves*. Starting in the early 1980s, however, Canadian banks argued that the legal requirement to hold some of their assets as non-interest-bearing reserves placed them at a disadvantage relative to their competitors that were not subject to such requirements. The competitors included both foreign commercial banks and Canadian nonbank financial institutions, such as trust companies and credit unions. Globalization of financial markets had brought domestic financial institutions into direct competition with foreign ones, and continuing deregulation of financial markets had enhanced the competition between banks and nonbank financial institutions. After much deliberation, the government responded to these complaints by phasing out all legal reserve requirements early in the 1990s.

Despite the fact that Canadian banks are no longer legally required to hold reserves against their deposits, the banks' actual reserve ratio is greater than zero. Commercial banks hold some reserves for the simple reason that it is quite costly for them to borrow funds from the Bank of Canada to make up for any shortfall they may have. (Commercial banks pay the bank rate on any overdrafts from the Bank of Canada.)

Look again at Table 26-2. Notice that the banking system's cash reserves of just under $4 billion are less than one-half of 1 percent of its total liabilities of almost $1.4 trillion. If the holders of even 5 percent of its deposits demanded cash, the banks would be unable to meet the demand without outside help. Reserves can be as low as they are because the banks know that the Bank of Canada will help them out in time of temporary need. The Canadian banking system is thus a **fractional-reserve system,** with commercial banks holding reserves—either as cash or as deposits at the Bank of Canada—of much less than 100 percent of their deposits.

reserve ratio   The fraction of its deposits that a commercial bank holds as reserves in the form of cash or deposits with a central bank.

target reserve ratio   The fraction of its deposits that a commercial bank wants to hold as reserves.

fractional-reserve system   A banking system in which commercial banks keep only a fraction of their deposits in cash or on deposit with the central bank.

APPLYING ECONOMIC CONCEPTS 26-3

Deposit Insurance and the Financial System

Deposit insurance, provided in Canada by the government-owned Canada Deposit Insurance Corporation (CDIC), assures depositors that their funds are secure whatever the fate of their deposit institution. This is a great boon for depositors, but experience has shown that it is a double-edged sword.

The obvious benefit of deposit insurance is that it provides security to depositors. This greater security makes it less likely that a bank panic will start, thereby increasing the stability of the financial system.

On the other hand, deposit insurance creates an incentive for banks to pursue riskier investments than they would if depositors had to worry about losing their deposits should the institution fail. Because of deposit insurance, depositors have no reason to select banks according to the riskiness of their investments. They are free instead to select the bank that pays the highest interest without worrying about the associated risk.

Deposit insurance is thus an example of an important class of government institutions that create situations whereby "heads the private investor wins, tails the taxpayer loses." Financial institutions take in depositors' insured funds; if the owners place them in risky ventures that pay off, the owners get the profits; if the owners place the funds in ventures that fail often enough to bring down the whole institution, the taxpayers must meet the bill by repaying those who provided the capital (the depositors). Canadian financial institutions have occasionally failed, including two western banks in the mid 1980s. When those institutions went under, depositors were repaid by the CDIC. Although the legal ceiling on deposit insurance was $60 000, deposits in excess of that amount were also repaid, using taxpayer money. This created the precedent that ceilings on deposit insurance were not to

be taken seriously. Any amount would be likely to be repaid. Hence, no investor need worry about the financial probity of the investments made by the institutions in which his or her money was deposited.

Two types of reforms are possible. One type would keep deposit insurance and provide the necessary accompanying regulations. The implications of deposit insurance for the investment behaviour of financial intermediaries suggest that if deposit insurance is to be maintained, other regulations concerning capital requirements and investment standards need to be applied. In addition, the deposit insurance system might be reformed in order to relate the cost of insurance for a particular institution to the risks implied by that institution's asset position.

The other type of reform would take deregulation to its logical conclusion of ending deposit insurance. Many economists believe that if deregulation of financial institutions is regarded as desirable, it should be accompanied by a removal of deposit insurance, so that the people who use the funds will be accountable to those who provide them.

The Canada Deposit Insurance Corporation guarantees depositors that their deposits (up to a limit) are secure no matter what happens to the financial institution accepting their deposit.

In Chapter 28 we will study how the Bank of Canada can influence the money supply under a zero required reserve system after we have examined how the money supply is itself determined. Our analysis of the money supply process is based on the following behaviour of the commercial banks:

Commercial banks strive to maintain some target ratio of reserves to deposits. In the past, this target ratio was legally imposed; today, it is determined by the banks themselves.

excess reserves
Reserves held by a commercial bank in excess of its target reserves.

Any reserves in excess of target reserves are called **excess reserves.** All that matters for what follows is that there is some target reserve ratio, no matter how small.

Money Creation by the Banking System

We noted before that the *money supply* refers to both currency and deposits at commercial banks. The fractional-reserve system provides the leverage that permits commercial banks to create new deposits, and thus to create new money. The process is important, so it is worth examining in some detail.

Some Simplifying Assumptions

To focus on the essential aspects of how banks create money, suppose that banks can invest in only one kind of asset—loans—and that there is only one kind of deposit—a demand deposit.

Two other assumptions are provisional. When we have developed the basic ideas concerning the banks' creation of money, these assumptions will be relaxed.

1. *Fixed reserve ratio.* We assume that all banks have the same target reserve ratio which does not change. In our numerical illustration, we will assume that the target reserve ratio is 20 percent (0.20); that is, for every $5 of deposits the banks wish to hold $1 in cash reserves, investing the rest in new loans.

2. *No cash drain from the banking system.* We also assume that the public holds a fixed amount of currency in circulation. Thus any transfers of funds between individuals will not cause changes in the total amount of currency available for the banks to hold as reserves.

The Creation of Deposit Money

A hypothetical balance sheet, showing assets and liabilities, is shown for the Toronto Dominion (TD) Bank in Table 26-3. TD has assets of $200 of reserves, held partly as cash on hand and partly as deposits with the central bank, and $900 of loans outstanding to its customers. Its liabilities are $100 to investors who contributed capital to start the bank and $1000 to current depositors. The bank's ratio of reserves to deposits is 0.20 (200/1000), exactly equal to its target reserve ratio.

New Deposits

In what follows, we are interested in knowing how the commercial banking system can "create money" when confronted with a new deposit. But what do we mean by a new deposit? By "new," we mean a deposit of

TABLE 26-3 The Initial Balance Sheet of the Toronto Dominion (TD) Bank

Assets ($)		Liabilities ($)	
Cash and other reserves	200	Deposits	1000
Loans	900	Capital	100
	1100		1100

The TD Bank has a reserve of 20 percent of its deposit liabilities. The commercial bank earns money by finding profitable investments for much of the money deposited with it. In this balance sheet, loans are its earning assets.

cash that is new to the *commercial banking system*. There are three examples. First, an individual might immigrate to Canada and bring cash with them. When that cash is deposited into a commercial bank, it constitutes a new deposit to the (Canadian) banking system. A second example is an individual that had some cash stashed under his bed (or in a safe-deposit box) and who has now decided to deposit it into an account at a commercial bank. The final example is the most interesting, but is also the most complicated. If the Bank of Canada were to purchase a government security from an individual or from a firm, it would purchase that asset with a cheque drawn on the Bank of Canada. When the individual or firm deposits the cheque with their commercial bank, it would be a new deposit to the commercial banking system.

The important point to keep in mind here is that the *source* of the new deposit is irrelevant to the process of money creation by the commercial banks. In the discussion that follows, we use the example of the Bank of Canada buying government securities from firms or households as a way of generating a new deposit. But this is not central. We use this example because, as we shall see in Chapter 28, this is one way that the Bank of Canada conducts its monetary policy. But the general process of money creation that we are about to describe applies to *any* new deposit.

TABLE 26-4   TD's Balance Sheet Immediately After a New Deposit of $100

Assets ($)		Liabilities ($)	
Cash and other reserves	300	Deposits	1100
Loans	900	Capital	100
	1200		1200

The deposit raises liabilities and assets by the same amount. Because both cash and deposits rise by $100, the bank's actual reserve ratio, formerly 0.20, increases to 0.27. The bank has excess reserves.

TABLE 26-5   TD's Balance Sheet After Making a New Loan of $80

Assets ($)		Liabilities ($)	
Cash and other reserves	220	Deposits	1100
Loans	980	Capital	100
	1200		1200

TD lends its surplus cash and suffers a cash drain. The bank keeps $20 as a reserve against the initial new deposit of $100. It lends $80 to a customer, who writes a cheque to someone who deals with another bank. When the cheque is cleared, TD suffers an $80 cash drain. Comparing Tables 26-3 and 26-5 shows that the bank has increased its deposit liabilities by the $100 initially deposited and has increased its assets by $20 of cash reserves and $80 of new loans. It has also restored its target reserve ratio of 0.20.

A Single New Deposit

Suppose that the Bank of Canada buys $100 worth of securities on the open market. It issues a cheque to the seller, and that individual or firm opens an account with TD and deposits the $100 cheque. This is a wholly new deposit for the commercial bank, and it results in a revised balance sheet (Table 26-4). As a result of the new deposit, TD's cash assets and deposit liabilities have both increased by $100. More important, TD's ratio of reserves to deposits has increased from 0.20 to 0.27 (300/1100). The bank now has $80 in excess reserves; with $1100 in deposits, its target reserves are only $220.

TD can now lend the $80 in excess reserves that it is holding. Table 26-5 shows the position after this has been done and after the proceeds of the loan have been withdrawn to be deposited to the account of a customer of another bank. TD once again has a 20 percent reserve ratio.

So far, of the $100 initial deposit at TD, $20 is held by TD as reserves against the deposit and $80 has been lent out in the system. As a result, other banks have received new deposits of $80 stemming from the loans made by TD; persons receiving payment from those who borrowed the $80 from TD will have deposited those payments in their own banks. Note that even though the *banking system* suffers no cash drain, TD does suffer a cash drain because most of the $80 goes to other banks and is not redeposited at TD.

The banks that receive deposits from the proceeds of TD's loan are called second-round banks, third-round banks, and so on. In this case, the second-round banks receive new deposits of $80, and when the cheques clear, they have new reserves of $80. Because they desire to hold only $16 in additional reserves to support the new deposits, they have $64 of excess reserves. They now increase their loans by $64. After this money has been spent by the borrowers and has been deposited in other, third-round banks, the balance sheets of the second-round banks will have changed, as in Table 26-6.

The third-round banks now find themselves with $64 of new deposits. Against these they want to hold only $12.80 as reserves, so they have excess reserves of $51.20 that they can immediately lend out. Thus, there begins a long sequence of new deposits, new loans, new deposits, and new loans. These stages are shown in Table 26-7.

The banking system has created new deposits and thus new money, although each banker can honestly say, "All I did was invest my excess reserves. I can do no more than manage wisely the money that I receive." At the end of the process depicted in Table 26-7, the change in the combined balance sheets of the entire banking system is shown in Table 26-8.

If v is the target reserve ratio, the ultimate effect on the deposits of the banking system of a new deposit will be $1/v$ times the new deposit. [32]

In our example in which there was an initial new deposit of $100, this $100 was also the amount by which reserves increased in the banking system as a whole. This is because the entire amount of new cash eventually ends up in reserves held against a much larger volume of new deposits. Identifying a new deposit as the change in reserves in the banking system permits us to state our central result slightly differently.

With no cash drain from the banking system, a banking system with a target reserve ratio of v can change its deposits by $1/v$ times any change in reserves.

Recalling that the Greek letter delta, Δ, means "the change in," we can express this result in a simple equation. We have

$$\Delta \text{Deposits} = \frac{\Delta \text{Reserves}}{v}$$

The "multiple expansion of deposits" that we have just described applies in reverse to a withdrawal of funds. Deposits of the banking system will fall by $1/v$ times the amount withdrawn from the banking system.

Excess Reserves and Cash Drains

The two simplifying assumptions that were made earlier can now be relaxed.

TABLE 26-6 Changes in the Balance Sheets of Second-Round Banks

Assets ($)		Liabilities ($)	
Cash and other reserves	+16	Deposits	+80
Loans	+64		
	+80		+80

Second-round banks receive cash deposits and expand loans. The second-round banks gain new deposits of $80 as a result of the loan granted by TD. These banks keep 20 percent of the cash that they acquire as their reserve against the new deposit, and they can make new loans using the other 80 percent.

TABLE 26-7 The Sequence of Loans and Deposits After a Single New Deposit of $100

Bank	New Deposits	New Loans	Addition to Reserves
TD	100.00	80.00	20.00
2nd-round bank	80.00	64.00	16.00
3rd-round bank	64.00	51.20	12.80
4th-round bank	51.20	40.96	10.24
5th-round bank	40.96	32.77	8.19
6th-round bank	32.77	26.22	6.55
7th-round bank	26.22	20.98	5.24
8th-round bank	20.98	16.78	4.20
9th-round bank	16.78	13.42	3.36
10th-round bank	13.42	10.74	2.68
Total for first 10 rounds	446.33	357.07	89.26
All remaining rounds	53.67	42.93	10.74
Total for banking system	500.00	400.00	100.00

The banking system as a whole can create deposit money whenever it receives new deposits. The table shows the process of the creation of deposit money on the assumptions that all the loans made by one set of banks end up as deposits in another set of banks (the next-round banks), that the target reserve ratio (v) is 0.20, and that banks always lend out any excess reserves. Although each bank suffers a cash drain whenever it grants a new loan, the system as a whole does not, and in a series of steps it increases deposit money by $1/v$, which, in this example, is five times the amount of any increase in reserves that it obtains.

Practise with Study Guide Chapter 26, Exercise 4.

Excess Reserves

If banks do not choose to invest their excess reserves, the multiple expansion that we discussed will not occur. Go back to Table 26-4. If TD had been content to hold 27 percent in reserves, it might well have done nothing more. Other things being equal, banks will choose to invest their excess reserves because of the profit motive, but there may be times when they believe that the risk is too great. It is one thing to be offered a good rate of interest on a loan, but if the borrower defaults on the payment of interest and principal, the bank will be the loser. Similarly, if the bank expects interest rates to rise in the future, it may hold off making loans now so that it will have reserves available to make more profitable loans after the interest rate has risen.

Deposit creation does not happen automatically; it depends on the decisions of bankers. If banks do not choose to use their excess reserves to expand their investments, there will not be an expansion of deposits.

Recall that we have said that the money supply includes both currency and bank deposits. What we have just seen is that the behaviour of commercial banks is central to the process of deposit creation. It follows that the money supply is thus at least partly determined by the commercial banks—in response, for example, to changes in national income, interest rates, and expectations of future business conditions.

Cash Drain

Suppose that firms and households find it convenient to keep a fixed *fraction* of their money holdings in cash (say, 5 percent) instead of a fixed *number* of dollars. In that case, an extra $100 that gets injected into the banking system will not all stay in the banking system—only $95 will remain on deposit, and the rest will be added to currency in circulation. In such a situation, any multiple expansion of bank deposits will be accompanied by a cash drain to the public. This cash drain will reduce the maximum expansion below what it was when the public was content to hold all its new money as bank deposits.

Practise with Study Guide Chapter 26, Exercise 6.

In the case of a cash drain, the relationship between the eventual change in deposits and an injection of cash into the banking system is slightly more complicated. If $X is injected into the system then ultimately reserves will increase by $X. But if c is the ratio of cash to deposits that people want to maintain, the final change in deposits will be given by: [33]

$$\Delta \text{Deposits} = \frac{\Delta \text{Reserves}}{c + v}$$

For example, suppose the Bank of Canada were to enter the open market and purchase $1000 of government securities. As the previous bondholders deposit their $1000 into their bank accounts, there is an injection of $1000 into the banking system. If commercial banks' target reserve ratio was 10 percent and there was *no* cash drain, the eventual expansion of deposits would be $10 000 ($\Delta$Deposits = $1000/0.10). But if there were also a cash drain of 10 percent, the eventual expansion of deposits would only be $5000 ($\Delta$Deposits = $1000/(0.10 + 0.10)).

TABLE 26-8   Change in the Combined Balance Sheets of All the Banks in the System Following the Multiple Expansion of Deposits

Assets ($)		Liabilities ($)	
Cash and other reserves	+100	Deposits	+500
Loans	+400		
	+500		+500

The reserve ratio is returned to 0.20. The entire initial deposit of $100 ends up as reserves of the banking system. Therefore, deposits rise by (1/0.2) times the initial deposit—that is, by $500.

The Money Supply

Several times in this chapter we have mentioned the *money supply* without ever defining it precisely. But now that you are familiar with the balance sheets of the Bank of Canada and the commercial banking system, and are comfortable with the idea of deposit creation by the commercial banks, we are ready to be more precise about what we mean by the money supply.

The total stock of money in the economy at any moment is called the **money supply** or the *supply of money*. Economists use several alternative definitions for the money supply, most of which are regularly reported in the *Bank of Canada Review*—a quarterly publication of the Bank of Canada. Each definition of the money supply includes the amount of currency in circulation *plus* some types of deposit liabilities of the financial institutions. The different definitions vary only by which deposit liabilities are included. We begin by looking at the different kinds of deposits.

money supply   The total quantity of money in an economy at a point in time. Also called the *supply of money.*

Kinds of Deposits

Over the past 20 years or so, banks have evolved a bewildering array of different types of deposits. From our point of view, the most important distinction is between deposits that can be transferred by cheque, called "chequable," and those that cannot, called "nonchequable." Chequable deposits are media of exchange; nonchequable ones are not.

Until recently, the distinction lay between *demand deposits,* which earned little or no interest but were chequable, and *savings deposits,* which earned a higher interest return but were nonchequable.

Today, however, it is so easy to transfer funds from accounts that are technically nonchequable to other accounts that are chequable that the distinction becomes quite blurred. The deposit that is genuinely tied up for a period of time now takes the form of a **term deposit,** which has a specified withdrawal date, a minimum of 30 days into the future, and which pays a much reduced interest rate in the event of early withdrawal. Term and other nonchequable deposits pay significantly higher interest rates than do chequable deposits.

term deposit   An interest-earning bank deposit, legally subject to notice before withdrawal (in practice, the notice requirement is not normally enforced).

Nonbank financial institutions such as brokerage firms now offer *money market mutual funds* and *money market deposit accounts.* These accounts earn high interest and are chequable, although some are subject to minimum withdrawal restrictions and others to prior notice of withdrawal.

The long-standing distinction between money and other highly liquid assets used to be that, narrowly defined, money was a medium of exchange that did not earn interest, whereas other liquid assets earned interest but were not media of exchange. Today, this distinction has almost completely broken down.

Definitions of the Money Supply

M1   Currency plus demand deposits plus other chequable deposits.

M2   M1 plus saving deposits at the chartered banks.

Different definitions of the money supply include different types of deposits. The narrowly defined money supply, called **M1,** includes currency and deposits that are themselves usable as media of exchange (such as chequable deposits). A broader definition, **M2,** includes M1 plus savings accounts at the chartered banks. A still broader measure, **M2+**, includes M2 plus the deposits held at the financial institutions that are *not* chartered banks, such as trust companies and credit unions.

M1 concentrates on the medium-of-exchange function of money. M2 and M2+ contain assets that serve the temporary store-of-value function and are in practice quickly convertible into a medium of exchange. Table 26-9 shows the principal elements in these definitions of the money supply. The details of the differences are not important at this stage; what matters is that, broadly defined, money comprises a spectrum of closely related financial assets that their holders regard as highly substitutable for each other.

TABLE 26-9 Three Measures of the Money Supply in Canada, January 1999 (millions of dollars)

Currency	30 016
+ Demand deposits	52 490
= M1	82 506
+ Personal saving deposits and nonpersonal notice deposits	325 791
= M2	408 297
+ Deposits at trust and mortgage loan companies, credit unions, and caisses populaires	144 702
+ Money market mutual funds and deposits at other institutions	85 694
= M2+	638 693

The three widely used measures of the money supply are M1, M2, and M2+. The narrowest definition, M1, concentrates on what can be used directly as media of exchange, and thus includes only currency and demand deposits. The broader definitions then add in deposits that serve the store-of-value function but can be readily converted to a medium of exchange. M2 is thus M1 plus saving deposits. M2+ is M2 plus deposits at the nonbank financial institutions.

(*Source: Bank of Canada Review,* Spring 1999.)

Near Money and Money Substitutes

Over the past two centuries, what has been accepted by the public as money has expanded from gold and silver coins to include bank notes and bank deposits subject to transfer by cheque. Until recently, most economists would have agreed that money stopped at that point. No such agreement exists today.

The problem of deciding what constitutes money arises because some assets may provide relatively poor ways to meet the store-of-value function whereas others may perform poorly as media of exchange. For example, during times of high inflation, currency may serve well as a medium of exchange but poorly as a store of value (because the rising price level erodes the purchasing power of cash). In contrast, heavy gold bars may serve well as a store of value but poorly as a medium of exchange (because they are both heavy and difficult to divide into small units).

If we concentrate only on the medium-of-exchange function of money, money certainly consists of the assets included in M1, and most economists would argue that it extends to those included in M2 and M2+. Some of these assets that are effective media of exchange, however, are poor stores of value because they earn little or no interest. Assets that earn higher interest—like term deposits—will do a better job of meeting the store-of-value function than will currency or demand deposits. At the same time, however, these other assets are less capable of fulfilling the medium-of-exchange function.

Assets that fulfill adequately the store-of-value function and are readily converted into a medium of exchange but are not themselves a medium of exchange are sometimes called **near money**. Term deposits are a characteristic form of near money. When you have such a term deposit, you know exactly how much purchasing power you hold (at current prices), and, given modern banking practices, you can turn your deposit into a medium of exchange—cash or a chequing deposit—at a moment's notice (though you may pay a penalty in the form of reduced interest if you withdraw the funds before the end of the specified term).

Why then does everybody not keep his or her money in such deposits instead of in demand deposits or currency? The answer is that the inconvenience of continually shifting money back and forth may outweigh the interest that can be earned. One week's interest on $100 (at 10 percent per year) is only about 20 cents, not enough to cover bus fare to the trust company, the cost of mailing a letter, or the time lining up at an automatic teller machine. For money that will be needed soon, it would hardly pay to shift it to a term deposit.

In general, whether it pays to convert cash or chequable deposits into higher interest-earning term deposits for a given period will depend on the inconvenience and other transactions costs of shifting funds and on the amount of interest that can be earned.

Things that serve as temporary media of exchange but are not a store of value are sometimes called **money substitutes.** Credit cards are a prime example. With a credit card, many transactions can be made without either cash or a cheque. The evidence of credit, the credit slip you sign and hand over to the store, is not money, because it cannot be used to make other transactions. The credit card serves the short-run function of a medium of exchange by allowing you to make purchases, even though you have no cash or bank deposit currently in your possession. But this is only temporary; money remains the final medium of exchange for these transactions when the credit account is settled.

money substitute
Something that serves as a temporary medium of exchange but is not a store of value.

Choosing a Measure

Since the eighteenth century, economists have known that the amount of money in circulation is an important economic variable. As theories became more carefully specified in the nineteenth and early twentieth centuries, they included a variable called the "money supply." But for theories to be useful (and especially for the predictions to be testable), we must be able to identify real-world counterparts of these theoretical variables.

The specifics of the definition of money have changed and will continue to change over time. New monetary assets are continually being developed to serve some, if not all, of the functions of money, and they are more or less readily convertible into money. There is no single, timeless definition of money and what is only near money or a money substitute. Indeed, as we have seen, the Bank of Canada uses several definitions of money, and these definitions change from year to year.

The Role of the Bank of Canada

In this chapter, we have seen that the commercial banking system, when confronted with a new deposit, can create a multiple expansion of bank deposits. This shows how the reserves of the banking system are systematically related to the money supply. We have also seen a glimpse of how the Bank of Canada can affect the reserves of the banking system—we will see in Chapter 28 that the Bank of Canada has almost complete control over these reserves. Thus, the Bank of Canada controls reserves, and the commercial banking system turns those reserves into bank deposits.

This is the basis for the view taken throughout the remainder of this book that the Bank of Canada controls the money supply. In the next two chapters, we examine how the Bank uses this power to conduct monetary policy, and how monetary policy affects interest rates, real GDP, and the price level.

S U M M A R Y

Two Perspectives on Money

LO 1

- Early economists regarded the economy as being divided into a real sector and a monetary sector. The real sector is concerned with production, allocation of resources, and distribution of income, determined by relative prices. The level of prices at which all transactions take place is determined by the monetary sector—that is, by the demand for and supply of money. With the demand for money being constant, an increase in the money supply would cause all equilibrium money prices to increase, but relative prices, and hence everything in the real sector, would be left unaffected.
- Today, most economists do not hold the view that changes in the money supply will only affect the price level, except as a description of the economy in long-run equilibrium. Most economists believe that changes in the supply of money have important short-run effects on real GDP, employment, and unemployment.

The Nature of Money

LO 2 3

- A number of functions of money may be distinguished. Generally, money acts as a medium of exchange, a store of value, and a unit of account.
- Money arose because of the inconvenience of barter, and it developed in stages: from precious metal to metal coinage, to paper money convertible to precious metals, to token coinage and paper money fractionally backed by precious metals, to fiat money, and to deposit money. Societies have shown great sophistication in developing monetary instruments to meet their needs.

The Canadian Banking System

LO 4

- The banking system in Canada consists of two main elements: the Bank of Canada (which is the central bank) and the commercial banks. The Bank of Canada is a publicly owned corporation that is responsible for the day-to-day conduct of monetary policy. Though the Bank has considerable autonomy in its policy decisions, ultimate responsibility for monetary policy resides with the government.
- Commercial banks are profit-seeking institutions that allow their customers to transfer demand deposits from one bank to another by means of cheques or debit cards. They create money as a by-product of their commercial operations by making or liquidating loans and various other investments.

Money Creation by the Banking System

LO 5

- Because most customers are content to pay by cheque or debit card rather than with cash, banks need only small reserves to back their deposit liabilities. It is this *fractional-reserve* aspect of the banking system that enables commercial banks to create deposit money.
- When the banking system receives a new cash deposit, it can create new deposits to some multiple of this amount. The amount of new deposits created depends on the banks' target reserve ratio, the amount of cash drain to the public, and whether the banks choose to hold excess reserves.

The Money Supply 🔟 6

- The money supply—the stock of money in an economy at a specific moment—can be defined in various ways. M1, the narrowest definition, includes currency and chequable deposits. M2 includes M1 plus savings deposits and smaller term deposits. M2+ includes M2 plus deposits at non-bank financial institutions and money-market mutual funds.

- Near money includes interest-earning assets that are convertible into money on a dollar-for-dollar basis but that are not currently included in the definition of money. Money substitutes are things such as credit cards that temporarily serve as a medium of exchange but are not money.

K E Y   C O N C E P T S

The real and monetary sectors of the economy

Medium of exchange, store of value, and unit of account

Fully backed, fractionally backed, and fiat money

The banking system and the Bank of Canada

Target reserve ratio and excess reserves

The creation of deposit money

Demand and term deposits

The money supply

Near money and money substitutes

S T U D Y   E X E R C I S E S

1. Which of the following items can be considered money in the Canadian economy? Explain your answers by discussing the three functions of money—medium of exchange, store of value, and unit of account.

   a. A $100 Bank of Canada note
   b. A Visa credit card
   c. A well-known painting by Robert Bateman
   d. An interest-earning savings account
   e. A U.S. Treasury bill payable in three months
   f. A share of Nortel stock

2. The table below shows the balance sheet for the Regal Bank, a hypothetical commercial bank. Assume that the Regal Bank has achieved its target reserve ratio.

   Balance Sheet: Regal Bank

Assets		Liabilities	
Reserves	$ 200	Deposits	$4000
Loans	$4200	Capital	$ 400

   a. What is the Regal Bank's target reserve ratio?
   b. What is the value of the owners' investment in the bank?
   c. Suppose that someone makes a new deposit to the Regal Bank of $100. Draw a new balance sheet showing the *immediate* effect of the new deposit. What is the Regal Bank's new reserve ratio?

3. Consider a new deposit to the Canadian banking system of $1000. Suppose that all commercial banks have a target reserve ratio of 10 percent and there is no cash drain. The following table shows how deposits, reserves, and loans change as the new deposit permits the banks to "create" money.

Round	ΔDeposits	ΔReserves	ΔLoans
First	$1000	$100	$900
Second	—	—	—
Third	—	—	—
Fourth	—	—	—
Fifth	—	—	—

a. The first round has been completed in the table. Now, recalling that the new loans in the first round become the new deposits in the second round, complete the second round in the table.

b. Using the same approach, complete the entire table.

c. You have now completed the first five rounds of the deposit-creation process. What is the total change in deposits *so far* as a result of the single new deposit of $1000?

d. This deposit-creation process will go on forever, but it will have a *finite* sum. In the text, we showed that the eventual total change in deposits is equal to $1/v$ times the new deposit, where v is the target reserve ratio. What is the eventual total change in deposits in this case?

e. What is the eventual total change in reserves? What is the eventual change in loans?

4. Consider a new deposit of $5000 to the Canadian banking system. Suppose that all commercial banks have a target reserve ratio of 8 percent and that there is no cash drain.

a. Using a table like that shown in the previous question, show the change in deposits, reserves, and loans for the first three "rounds" of activity.

b. Compute the eventual total change in deposits, reserves, and loans.

5. Consider an individual who immigrates to Canada and deposits $3000 into the Canadian banking system. Suppose that all commercial banks have a target reserve ratio of 10 percent and that individuals choose to hold cash equal to 10 percent of their bank deposits.

a. In the text, we showed that the eventual total change in deposits is equal to $1/(v+c)$ times the new deposit, where v is the target reserve ratio and c is the ratio of cash to deposits. What is the eventual total change in deposits in this case?

b. What is the eventual total change in reserves?

c. What is the eventual total change in loans?

6. Consider an individual who moves from Europe to Canada and brings with him his life savings of $40 000, which he deposits in a Canadian bank. For each of the cases below, compute the overall change in deposits and reserves in the Canadian banking system as a result of this new deposit.

a. 10 percent target reserve ratio; no cash drain; no excess reserves

b. 10 percent target reserve ratio; 5 percent cash drain; no excess reserves

c. 10 percent target reserve ratio; 5 percent cash drain; 5 percent excess reserves

DISCUSSION QUESTIONS

1. A Canadian who receives a U.S. coin has the option of spending it at face value or taking it to the bank and converting it to Canadian money at the going rate of exchange. When the rate of exchange was near par (in the early 1970s), so that $1 Canadian was within 3 cents of $1 U.S., U.S. and Canadian coins circulated side by side, exchanged at face value. Use Gresham's law to predict which coinage disappeared from circulation in Canada when the Canadian dollar fell to 67 cents U.S. Why did a 3-cent differential not produce this result?

2. During hyperinflations in several foreign countries after World War II, American cigarettes were sometimes used in place of money. What made them suitable?

3. Suppose that on January 1, 1999, a household had $100 000, which it wished to hold for use one year later. Calculate, using resources available, which of the following would have been the best store of value over that period. Will the best store of value over that period necessarily be the best over the next 24 months?

a. The (Canadian) dollar

b. Stocks whose prices moved with the Toronto Stock Exchange (TSE) 300

c. An Ontario Hydro 9.0 percent bond coming due in June 2002

d. Gold

4. If all depositors tried to turn their deposits into cash at once, they would find that there are not sufficient reserves in the system to allow all of them to do this at the same time. Why then do we not still have panicky runs on the banks? Would it be better for the Bank of Canada to impose a 100 percent reserve requirement? What effect would such a reserve requirement have on the banking system's ability to create money? Would it preclude any possibility of a panic?

5. Compared to a few years ago, credit and bank cards are used extensively today to facilitate purchase of goods and services all over the world. Does this distort the true measure of money in the economy? Should credit and bank cards be incorporated in the definitions of M1 or M2?

CHAPTER 27

Money, Output, and Prices

 LEARNING OBJECTIVES

1. Explain how the present value of an asset is related to the market interest rate.

2. Know the three motives for holding money.

3. Understand how changes in the demand for money or the supply of money influence the interest rate.

4. Explain the transmission mechanism of monetary policy.

5. Distinguish between the short-run and long-run effects of changes in the money supply.

In Chapter 26, we saw how commercial banks lend their excess reserves to create bank deposits. The banking system transforms a given amount of reserves into the nation's money supply. We then concluded that chapter by saying that because the Bank of Canada can control the reserves in the banking system, the Bank of Canada effectively controls Canada's money supply. What we have not yet discussed, however, is how the Bank of Canada controls the reserves of the banking system. We leave that discussion until the next chapter when we discuss the details of monetary policy. For now, just think of the supply of money as being determined by the Bank of Canada.

In this chapter, we focus on how money affects the economy. Understanding the role of money, however, requires an understanding of the interaction of money supply and money demand. To examine the nature of money demand, we begin by examining how households decide to divide their total holdings of assets between money and interest-earning assets (which here are called "bonds"). Once that is done, we put money supply and money demand together to examine *monetary equilibrium*. Only then can we ask how changes in the supply of money or in the demand for money affect the economy—interest rates, real GDP, and the price level. We begin with a discussion of financial assets and interest rates.

Understanding Financial Assets

At any moment, households have a stock of wealth that they hold in many forms. Some of it is money in the bank or in the wallet, some may be in treasury bills and bonds, and some may be in stocks and shares.

Economists often simplify the analysis of financial assets by considering only two types of assets—money and bonds.

To simplify our discussion, we will group wealth into just two categories, which we call "money" and "bonds." By money we mean all assets that serve as a medium of exchange—that is, paper money, coins, and deposits on which cheques can be drawn. By bonds we mean all other forms of wealth; this includes interest-earning financial assets and claims on real capital (equity). This simplification can take us quite a long way because it serves to emphasize the important distinction between interest-earning and non-interest-earning assets. For some issues, however, it is necessary to treat debt and equity as distinct assets, in which case at least three categories—money, bonds, and stocks—are used. For our purposes, however, we continue with the simple division of wealth into either "money" or "bonds."

Present Value and the Interest Rate

present value (PV)
The value now of one or more payments or receipts made in the future; often referred to as *discounted present value.*

Recall from Chapter 26 that a bond is a financial asset that promises to make one or more specified payments at specified dates in the future. The **present value** *(PV)* of any asset refers to the value now of the future payments that the asset offers. Present value depends on the interest rate because when we calculate present value, the interest rate is used to *discount* the future payments. We can see this relationship between the interest rate and present value by considering two extreme examples.

A Single Payment One Year Hence

We start with the simplest case. How much would you be prepared to pay *now* to purchase a bond that will return a single payment of $100 in one year's time?

Suppose that the interest rate is 5 percent. Now ask how much you would have to lend out at that interest rate today in order to have $100 a year from now. If we use *PV* to stand for this unknown amount, we can write $PV \times (1.05) = \$100$. Thus, $PV = \$100/1.05 = \$95.24$.[1] This tells us that the present value of a $100 receivable in one year's time is $95.24; if you lend out $95.24 for one year at 5 percent interest you will get back the $95.24 plus $4.76 in interest, which makes $100.

What if the interest rate had been 7 percent? At that interest rate, the present value of the $100 receivable in one year's time would be $100/1.07 = $93.46, which is less than the present value when the interest rate was 5 percent.

A Perpetuity

Now consider another extreme case—a *perpetuity* that promises to pay $100 per year to its holder *forever*. The present value of the perpetuity depends on how much $100 per year is worth, and this again depends on the interest rate.

A bond that will produce a stream of income of $100 per year forever is worth $1000 at 10 percent interest because if you invest $1000 at 10 percent per year that investment will yield $100 interest per year forever. However, the same bond is worth

---

[1]Notice that in this type of formula, the interest rate is expressed as a decimal fraction where, for example, 5 percent is expressed as 0.05, so $1 + i$ equals 1.05.

$2000 when the interest rate is 5 percent per year because you must invest $2000 at 5 percent per year to get $100 interest per year.

A General Statement

Most bonds are not as simple as in these two extreme examples because they have several payments over many years and are then redeemable for cash. But the same basic relationship between interest rates and the present value of the asset applies.

The present value of any asset that yields a given stream of payments over time is negatively related to the interest rate.

Further details on the calculation of present value are given in *Extensions in Theory 27-1*.

Practise with Study Guide Chapter 27, Exercise 1.

Present Value and Market Price

Present value is important because it establishes the market price for an asset.

The present value of an asset is also the amount that someone would be willing to pay now to own the future stream of payments delivered by the asset.

To understand this concept, let us return to our example of a bond that promises to pay $100 one year from now. When the interest rate is 5 percent, the present value is $95.24. To see why this is the maximum that anyone would pay for this bond, suppose that some sellers offer to sell the bond at some other price, say, $98. If, instead of paying this amount for the bond, a potential buyer lends its $98 out at 5 percent interest, it would have at the end of one year more than the $100 that the bond will produce. (At 5 percent interest, $98 yields $4.90 in interest, which when added to the principal makes $102.90.) Clearly, no well-informed individual would pay $98—or, by the same reasoning, any sum in excess of $95.24—for the bond.

Now suppose that the bond is offered for sale at a price less than $95.24, say, $90. A potential buyer could borrow $90 to buy the bond and would pay $4.50 in interest on the loan. At the end of the year, the bond yields $100. When this is used to repay the $90 loan and the $4.50 in interest, $5.50 is left as profit. Clearly, it would be worthwhile for someone to buy the bond at the price of $90 or, by the same argument, at any price less than $95.24.

This discussion should make clear that the present value of an asset determines its market price. If the market price of any asset is greater than the present value of its income stream, no one will want to buy it, and this excess supply will push down the market price. If the market value is below its present value, there will be a rush to buy it, and this excess demand will push up the market price.

The equilibrium market price of any asset will be the present value of the income stream that it produces.

The Interest Rate and Market Price

The foregoing discussion leads us to two important propositions, both of which stress the negative relationship between interest rates and asset prices:

1. If the interest rate falls, the present value of an asset with a given income stream will rise.

EXTENSIONS IN THEORY 27-1

Calculating Present Value

An asset held now will generate a stream of returns in the future. What that stream of future income is worth now is called the asset's *present value (PV)*. This box provides some details concerning the calculation of present value that will prove helpful for understanding the material in the text.

The Present Value of a Single Future Payment

The numerical examples given in the text are easy to generalize. In calculating the present value of a payment one year hence, we divided the sum that is receivable in the future by 1 plus the rate of interest. In general, the present value of R dollars one year hence at an interest rate of i per year is

$$PV = \frac{R}{(1 + i)}$$

What happens to our calculation if the bond still offers a single future payment but the payment is receivable at a date later than one year from now? For example, what is the present value of $100 to be received *two* years hence if the interest rate is 5 percent? This is $100/(1.05 × 1.05) = $90.70. We can check this answer by seeing what would happen if $90.70 were lent out for two years. In the first year the loan would earn interest of 0.05 × $90.70 = $4.54, and hence after one year, the lender would receive $95.24. In the second year the interest would be earned on this entire amount; interest earned in the second year would thus equal 0.05 × $95.24 = $4.76. Therefore, in two years the lender would have $100. (Payment of interest in the second year on the interest income earned in the first year is called *compound interest*.)

In general, the present value of R dollars received t years in the future at an interest rate of i percent is

$$PV = \frac{R}{(1 + i)^t}$$

This formula simply discounts the sum R by the interest rate i repeatedly—once for each of the t periods that pass until the sum becomes available. If we look at the for-mula, we see that the higher is i or t, the higher is the whole term $(1 + i)^t$. This term, however, appears in the denominator, indicating that PV is *negatively* related to both i and t. (Try manipulating the formula yourself with different numbers to see that this is the case.)

The Present Value of a Sequence of Payments

Suppose now that we wish to calculate the present value of a bond that promises a sequence of payments for a given number of periods. Let R_1, R_2, R_3, and so on represent the payment promised after period 1, period 2, period 3, and so on, and let the last period for which a payment is promised be period T.

If we also suppose that the interest rate remains constant at i percent, the present value of this bond can be written as follows:

$$PV = \frac{R_1}{1 + i} + \frac{R_2}{(1 + i)^2} + \frac{R_3}{(1 + i)^3} + \ldots + \frac{R_T}{(1 + i)^T}$$

The Present Value of a Perpetual Stream of Payments

Now consider the value that a buyer would place on a perpetuity for R dollars—that is, on a bond that produces a stream of payments of R per year *forever*. To find the present value of R payable every year in the future, we ask how much money would have to be invested now at an interest rate of i per year to obtain R every year in the future. This present value is simply $i \times PV = R$, where PV is the sum required. In other words,

$$PV = \frac{R}{i}$$

Here, as before, PV is related to the rate of interest: The higher the interest rate, the less the present value of any particular stream of future receipts, and hence the lower the price that anyone would be prepared to pay to purchase the bond.

2. A rise in the market price of an asset with a given income stream is equivalent to a decrease in the rate of return earned by the asset.

The first proposition is illustrated by the following example. When the interest rate is 8 percent, you would have to pay $92.59 now for a bond promising to pay you $100 one year from now ($92.59 × 1.08 = $100). When the interest rate is 12 percent, you would have to pay $89.29 for the same bond ($89.29 × 1.12 = $100). Thus, the higher the interest rate, the lower the present value of the asset.

The second proposition is illustrated as follows. If you buy for $89.29 a bond that promises to pay $100 one year from now, then your asset will earn a 12 percent rate of return. But if you must pay $92.59 for the same bond, the rate of return will be only 8 percent. Thus, the higher asset price implies a lower rate of return.

Stocks and Bonds

We have been discussing the relationship between interest rates and the present value of an asset that generates a stream of returns in the future. Bonds generate a stream of interest payments whereas stocks generate a stream of dividend payments. As we said at the beginning of this section, however, for understanding the demand for money it is helpful to lump together all such assets and call them "bonds." This does not imply that stocks and the stock market are not important, however.

For the remainder of this chapter we focus on the distinction between bonds and money. In the next chapter, where we discuss the details of monetary policy, we discuss the stock market more completely.

The Demand for Money

The amount of money balances that everyone in the economy wishes to hold is called the **demand for money.** Because households are choosing how to divide their given stock of wealth between money and bonds, it follows that if we know the demand for money, we also know the demand for bonds. For a given amount of wealth, if people wish to hold $1 billion more money, they must also wish to hold $1 billion less of bonds.

When economists say that in February 1999 the quantity of money demanded was $410 billion, they mean that on that date the public wished to hold money balances that totaled $410 billion. But why do firms and households wish to hold money balances at all? There is a cost to holding any money balance because the money could have been used to purchase bonds, which earn higher interest than money.

The opportunity cost of holding any money balance is the interest that could have been earned if the money had been used instead to purchase bonds.

The opportunity cost of holding money is equal to the *nominal* rate of interest. Recall from Chapter 19 the distinction between real and nominal interest rates caused by the presence of inflation. However, because in this chapter we make the simplifying assumption that there is no ongoing inflation, the nominal and real rates of interest are the same.

demand for money
The total amount of money balances that the public wishes to hold for all purposes.

Households and firms will only choose to hold money if it provides services that are valued at least as highly as the opportunity cost of holding it. Three important services that are provided by money balances give rise to three motives for holding money: the *transactions, precautionary,* and *speculative* motives.

The Transactions Motive

Most transactions require money. Money passes from households to firms to pay for the goods and services produced by firms; money passes from firms to households to pay for the factor services supplied by households to firms. Money balances that are held to finance such flows are called **transactions balances.**

In an imaginary world in which the receipts and disbursements of households and firms were perfectly synchronized, it would be unnecessary to hold transactions balances. If every time a household spent $10 it received $10 as partial payment of its income, no transactions balances would be needed. In the real world, however, receipts and disbursements are not perfectly synchronized.

Consider the balances that are held by firms because of wage payments. Suppose, for purposes of illustration, that firms pay wages every Friday and that households spend all their wages on the purchase of goods and services, with the expenditure spread out evenly over the week. On Friday morning, firms must therefore hold balances equal to the weekly wage bill; on Friday afternoon, households will hold these balances.

Over the week, households' balances will be drawn down as a result of purchasing goods and services. Over the same period, the balances held by firms will build up as a result of selling goods and services until, on the following Friday morning, firms will again have amassed balances equal to the wage bill that must be met that day.

What determines the size of the transactions balances to be held? It is clear that in our example total transactions balances vary with the value of the wage bill. If the wage bill increases for any reason, the transactions balances held by firms and households for this purpose will also increase. As it is with wages, so it is with all other transactions: The size of the balances held is positively related to the value of the transactions.

It is not surprising then that the value of transactions is, in turn, positively related to national income. A greater value of output and income, after all, leads to greater spending by households and firms in the economy. Thus, a rise in national income leads to a rise in the total value of transactions and hence to an associated rise in the demand for transactions balances.

The larger the value of national income, the more transactions are made and thus the larger will be the value of transactions balances.

transactions balances Money balances held to finance payments because payments and receipts are not perfectly synchronized.

People hold money in order to make transactions. As income rises, the volume of transactions also rises, and so people typically decide to hold more money.

The Precautionary Motive

precautionary balances Money balances held for protection against the uncertainty of the timing of cash flows.

Many goods and services are sold on credit. The seller can never be certain when payment will be made, and the buyer can never be certain of the day of delivery and hence when payment will fall due. As a precaution against cash crises, when receipts are abnormally low or disbursements are abnormally high, firms and households carry money balances. **Precautionary balances** provide a cushion against uncertainty about the timing of cash flows. The larger are such balances, the greater is the protection against running out of money because of temporary fluctuations in cash flows.

The seriousness of the risk of a cash crisis depends on the costs of being caught without sufficient money balances. A firm is unlikely to be pushed into insolvency, but it may incur considerable costs if it is forced to borrow money at high interest rates to meet a temporary cash crisis. (As we saw in Chapter 26, this is the same reason why commercial banks hold reserves even though they are not required by law to do so.)

The protection provided by a given quantity of precautionary balances depends on the volume of payments and receipts. A \$100 precautionary balance provides a large cushion for a household whose volume of payments per month is \$800 and a small cushion for a firm whose monthly volume is \$25 000. For firms, fluctuations of the sort that create the need for precautionary balances tend to vary directly with the size of the firm's cash flow. To provide the same degree of protection as the value of transactions rises, more money is necessary. Since the value of transactions rises with national income, precautionary balances need to be higher when national income is higher.

The precautionary motive arises because households and firms are uncertain about the timing of payments and receipts. Precautionary balances rise when national income rises.

The Speculative Motive

Money can also be held to provide a hedge against the uncertainty inherent in fluctuating prices of other financial assets. For the typical household this motive is probably irrelevant. But for the manager of a mutual fund or a wealthy individual managing her portfolio, such **speculative balances** are important.

When a household or firm holds bonds, they earn interest that they would not earn if they were instead holding money. But because the market prices of bonds fluctuate in response to changes in market interest rates, the rate of return earned by the bondholder is uncertain. In other words, bonds are a risky asset.

In choosing between holding money or holding bonds, wealth holders must balance the extra interest income that they could earn by holding bonds against the risk that bonds carry. At one extreme, if a household or a firm holds all its wealth in the form of bonds, it earns extra interest on its entire wealth, but it also exposes its entire wealth to risk. At the other extreme, if the household or firm holds all its wealth in the form of money, it earns less interest income, but it faces no risk. Wealth holders usually do not take either extreme position. They hold part of their wealth as money and part of it as bonds—that is, they *diversify* their holdings.

Bonds are a risky asset. Risk-averse households and firms choose to hold money to diversify their portfolio.

How do individuals decide how much of their total wealth to hold in the form of money and how much to hold as bonds? The speculative motive leads households and firms to add to their money holdings until the reduction in risk obtained by the last dollar added is just balanced (in each wealth holder's view) by the cost in terms of the interest forgone on that dollar.

When the interest rate falls, the opportunity cost of holding money falls. This decrease leads to the holding of more money as wealth holders modify their portfolios by substituting away from bonds and toward money. When the interest rate rises, the opportunity cost of holding money increases. This rise leads to the holding of less money.

The speculative motive implies that the demand for money varies negatively with the interest rate.

speculative balances
Money balances held as a hedge against the uncertainty of the prices of other financial assets.

Real and Nominal Money Balances

In referring to the demand for money, it is important to distinguish real from nominal values. Real values are measured in purchasing power units; nominal values are measured in money units.

First, consider the demand for money in real terms. This demand is the number of units of purchasing power that the public wishes to hold in the form of money balances. For example, in an imaginary one-product wheat economy, this demand would be measured by the number of bushels of wheat that could be purchased with the money balances held. In a more complex economy, it could be measured in terms of the number of "baskets of goods" represented by a price index, such as the Consumer Price Index, that could be purchased with the money balances held. When economists speak of the demand for money in real terms, they speak of the amount demanded in constant dollars:

The real demand for money is the nominal quantity demanded divided by the price level.

For example, in the decade from 1989 to 1999, the *nominal* quantity of M2 balances held in Canada increased from $295.7 billion to $410.1 billion, an increase of 38.7 percent. Over the same period, however, the price level, as measured by the CPI, rose from 89.0 to 110.0—an increase of 23.4 percent. Such increases in the price level imply that the increase in *real* money balances was much less than the increase in nominal money balances. The *real* value of M2 increased by only 12.2 percent over that 10-year period.

Our discussion has identified two fundamental determinants of the demand for real money balances—real GDP and the interest rate. But what is the role of the price level?

A change in the price level does not affect the demand for real money balances, but it does affect the demand for nominal money balances.

To see why this is the case, consider the following example. Suppose real GDP and the interest rate were held constant but the price level doubled. Since real GDP is constant, the *real* value of transactions will also be unchanged. The constant interest rate implies that the opportunity cost of holding money is unchanged. Thus, the demand for *real* money balances will be unaffected by the doubling of the price level. However, since all goods and services now cost twice as much as before in dollar terms, households and firms will need to hold twice as many *nominal* dollars. That is, the doubling of the price level will lead to a doubling of the *nominal* demand for money.

Other things being equal, the nominal demand for money balances varies in direct proportion to the price level.

Total Demand for Money

In the preceding few pages we have discussed the three motives for households and firms to hold money—the transactions motive, the precautionary motive, and the speculative motive. Together, these make up the total demand for money. But it is important to keep in mind that these three motives are not "visible" in any way—it is not possible to say that an individual, for example, is holding this amount of money for transactions purposes and that amount for precautionary purposes. All we can observe is that an individual is holding a given amount of money, and we view each of the three motives as being partially responsible for that individual's behaviour.

Figure 27-1 summarizes the influences of real GDP, the nominal interest rate, and the price level—the three variables that account for most of the short-term variations in the nominal quantity of money demanded. The function relating money demanded to the rate of interest is often called the **liquidity preference *(LP)* function.** This name reflects the idea that as the interest rate falls, individual wealth holders choose to hold a larger share of their wealth in the most liquid asset—money. That is, they express their preference for liquidity.

liquidity preference (*LP*) function   The function that relates the demand for money to the nominal rate of interest.

Monetary Forces and National Income

We are now in a position to examine the relationship between money, on the one hand, and the equilibrium values of real GDP and the price level, on the other. The first step in explaining this relationship is a new one: the link between *monetary equilibrium* and aggregate demand. The second is familiar from earlier chapters: the effects of shifts in aggregate demand on equilibrium values of real GDP and the price level.

Monetary Equilibrium and Aggregate Demand

As we have just seen, the demand for money is determined by the behaviour of households and firms as they decide how much of their wealth to hold in the form of money. In the last chapter we saw that the money supply is determined by the Bank of Canada and the commercial banking system.

FIGURE 27-1   The Demand for Money as a Function of Interest Rates, Income, and the Price Level

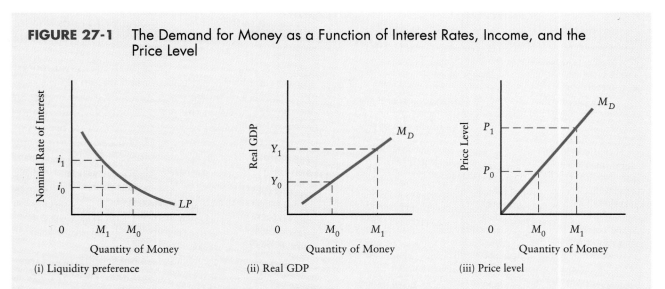

(i) Liquidity preference   (ii) Real GDP   (iii) Price level

The quantity of money demanded varies negatively with the nominal rate of interest and positively with both real GDP and the price level. In part (i), the quantity of money demanded is shown varying negatively with the nominal interest rate along the liquidity preference function. When the interest rate rises from i_0 to i_1, households and firms reduce the quantity of money demanded from M_0 to M_1. In part (ii), money demand varies positively with real GDP. When GDP rises from Y_0 to Y_1, households and firms increase the quantity of money demanded from M_0 to M_1. In part (iii), money demand varies in direct proportion to the price level (hence the line is a ray from the origin). When the price level doubles from P_0 to P_1, households and firms double the quantity of money demanded from M_0 to M_1.

**monetary
equilibrium**
A situation in which the
demand for money equals
the supply of money.

Monetary equilibrium occurs when the quantity of money demanded equals the quantity of money supplied. In Chapter 4, we saw that in a competitive market for some commodity the price will adjust to establish equilibrium. In the market for money, the interest rate is that "price" that adjusts to bring about equilibrium.

In this section we first examine how the demand for money and the supply of money interact to determine the interest rate. We then examine how changes in either the demand for or the supply of money affect aggregate demand. This is the *transmission mechanism*.

Interest Rate Determination

When a single household or firm finds that it is holding a smaller fraction of its wealth in money than it wishes, it can sell some bonds and add the proceeds to its money holdings. Such behaviour by an individual firm or household will have a negligible effect on the economy.

But what happens when *all* of the firms and households in the economy try to add to their money balances? They all try to sell bonds to add to their money balances, but what one person can do, all persons cannot do simultaneously. At any moment, the economy's total supply of money and bonds is fixed; there is just so much money, and there are just so many bonds in existence. Thus, as everyone tries to sell bonds, an excess supply of bonds develops. But since people are simply trying to switch between a given amount of bonds and money, the excess supply of bonds implies an excess demand for money, as shown at interest rate i_1 in Figure 27-2.

What happens when there is an excess supply of bonds? Like any other good or service, an excess supply causes a fall in the price. But as we saw earlier in the chapter, a fall in the price of bonds implies an increase in the interest rate. As the interest rate rises, people economize on money balances because the opportunity cost of holding such balances is rising. Eventually, the interest rate will rise enough that people will no longer be trying to add to their money balances by selling bonds. At that point, there is no longer an excess supply of bonds, and the interest rate will stop rising. The demand for money again equals the supply, as at point E in Figure 27-2.

Suppose now that firms and households hold larger money balances than they would like. That is, there is an excess supply of money, as at interest rate i_2 in Figure 27-2. The excess supply of money implies an excess demand for bonds—people are trying to "get rid of" their excess money balances by acquiring bonds. But when all households try to buy bonds, they bid up the price of bonds, and the interest rate falls. As the interest rate falls, households and firms become willing to hold larger quantities of money. The interest rate falls until firms and households stop trying to convert bonds into money. In other

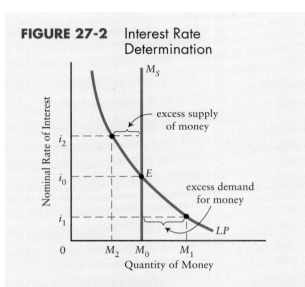

FIGURE 27-2   Interest Rate Determination

The interest rate rises when there is an excess demand for money and falls when there is an excess supply of money. The fixed quantity of money M_0 is shown by the completely inelastic supply curve M_S. The demand for money is given by LP; its negative slope indicates that a fall in the rate of interest causes the quantity of money demanded to increase. Monetary equilibrium is at E, with a rate of interest of i_0.

If the interest rate is i_1, there will be an excess demand for money of $M_0 M_1$. Bonds will be offered for sale in an attempt to increase money holdings. This will force the rate of interest up to i_0 (the price of bonds falls), at which point the quantity of money demanded is equal to the fixed available quantity of M_0. If the interest rate is i_2, there will be an excess supply of money $M_2 M_0$. Bonds will be demanded in return for excess money balances. This will force the rate of interest down to i_0 (the price of bonds rises), at which point the quantity of money demanded is equal to the fixed supply of M_0.

words, it continues until everyone is content to hold the existing supply of money and bonds, as at point *E* in Figure 27-2.

Monetary equilibrium occurs when the rate of interest is such that the quantity of money demanded equals the quantity of money supplied.

The determination of the interest rate depicted in Figure 27-2 is often called the *liquidity preference theory of interest*. This name reflects the fact that a demand to hold money (rather than bonds) is a demand for the more liquid of the two assets—a preference for liquidity.

The Transmission Mechanism

The mechanism by which changes in the demand for and supply of money affect aggregate demand is called the **transmission mechanism.** It operates in three stages: The first is the link between monetary equilibrium and the interest rate, the second is the link between the interest rate and investment expenditure, and the third is the link between investment expenditure and aggregate demand.

transmission mechanism   The channels by which a change in the demand or supply of money leads to a shift of the aggregate demand curve.

Changes in the Interest Rate.   The interest rate will change if the equilibrium depicted in Figure 27-2 is disturbed by a change in either the supply of money or the demand for money. For example, as shown in Figure 27-3(i), an increase in the supply of money, with an unchanged liquidity preference function, creates an excess supply of

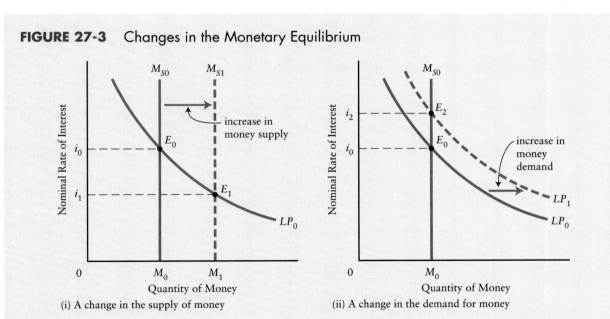

FIGURE 27-3   Changes in the Monetary Equilibrium

(i) A change in the supply of money

(ii) A change in the demand for money

Shifts in the supply of money or in the demand for money cause the equilibrium interest rate to change. In both parts of the figure, the money supply is shown by the vertical curve M_{S0}, and the demand for money is shown by the negatively sloped curve LP_0. The initial monetary equilibrium is at E_0, with corresponding interest rate i_0. In part (i), an increase in the money supply causes the money supply curve to shift to the right, from M_{S0} to M_{S1}. The new equilibrium is at E_1, where the interest rate is i_1. In part (ii), an increase in the demand for money causes the LP curve to shift to the right from LP_0 to LP_1. The new monetary equilibrium occurs at E_2, and the new equilibrium interest rate is i_2.

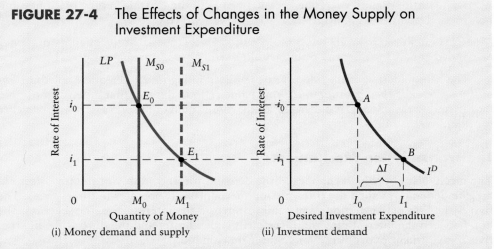

FIGURE 27-4   The Effects of Changes in the Money Supply on Investment Expenditure

Increases in the money supply reduce the interest rate and increase desired investment expenditure. Equilibrium in the money market, in panel (i), is at E_0, with a quantity of money of M_0 and an interest rate of i_0. The corresponding level of investment expenditure is I_0 (point A) in panel (ii). The Bank of Canada then increases the money supply to M_1. This reduces the interest rate to i_1 and increases investment expenditure by ΔI to I_1 (point B).

money at the original interest rate. As we have seen, an excess supply of money leads firms and households to attempt to buy bonds, thus driving up the price of bonds and pushing down the interest rate.

As shown in Figure 27-3(ii), an increase in the demand for money, with an unchanged supply of money, creates an excess demand for money at the original interest rate. Firms and households try to acquire more money by selling their holdings of bonds. This drives down the price of bonds and pushes up the interest rate.

Changes in either the demand for or the supply of money cause changes in the interest rate.

Changes in Desired Investment.   The second link in the transmission mechanism relates interest rates to desired investment expenditure. We saw in Chapter 22 that investment, which includes expenditure on inventory accumulation, residential construction, and business fixed investment, responds to changes in the real rate of interest. Other things being equal, a decrease in the real rate of interest makes borrowing cheaper and generates new investment expenditure. This negative relationship between desired investment and the interest rate is labelled I^D in Figure 27-4.

The first two links in the transmission mechanism are shown in Figure 27-4.[2] We concentrate for the moment on changes in the money supply, although, as we have seen already, the process can also be set in motion by changes in the demand for money. In part (i), we see that a change in the money supply causes the rate of interest to change in the

---

[2] In part (i) of Figure 27-4, it is the nominal interest rate that affects money demand. In part (ii), however, it is the real interest rate that influences desired investment expenditure. It is therefore worth emphasizing that we are continuing with the assumption that there is no inflation and so the nominal and real interest rates are the same. This allows us to use the same vertical axis in the two parts of the figure.

opposite direction. In part (ii), we see that a change in the interest rate causes the level of desired investment expenditure to change in the opposite direction.

An increase in the money supply leads to a fall in the interest rate and an increase in investment expenditure. A decrease in the money supply leads to a rise in the interest rate and a decrease in investment expenditure.

Changes in Aggregate Demand.   Now that we see how monetary disturbances lead to changes in desired aggregate expenditure, we are back on familiar ground. In Chapter 24, we saw that a shift in the aggregate expenditure curve (caused by something *other than* a change in the price level) leads to a shift in the *AD* curve. This situation is shown again in Figure 27-5.

A change in the money supply, by causing a change in desired investment expenditure and hence a shift in the *AE* curve, causes the *AD* curve to shift. An increase in the money supply causes an increase in desired investment expenditure and therefore a rightward shift of the *AD* curve. A decrease in the money supply causes a decrease in desired investment expenditure and therefore a leftward shift of the *AD* curve.

The entire transmission mechanism is illustrated in Figure 27-6 for the case of an expansionary monetary shock. An increase in money supply or a decrease in money demand tends to reduce interest rates and increase aggregate demand.

An Open-Economy Modification

So far, the emphasis in our discussion of the transmission mechanism has been on the effect that a change in the interest rate has on desired investment. In an open economy, however, where financial capital flows easily across borders, the transmission mechanism is a little more complex.

Financial capital is very mobile across international boundaries. Bondholders, either in Canada or abroad, are able to substitute between Canadian bonds, U.S. bonds, German bonds or bonds from almost any country you can think of. Bonds from different countries are generally not *perfect* substitutes for each other because of varying amounts of political and economic instability. But bonds from similar countries—Canada and the United States, for example—are often viewed as very close substitutes.

The ability of bondholders to easily substitute between bonds from different countries implies that monetary disturbances will generally lead to capital flows, which in turn will cause changes in exchange rates and changes in exports and imports.

FIGURE 27-5   The Effects of Changes in the Money Supply on Aggregate Demand

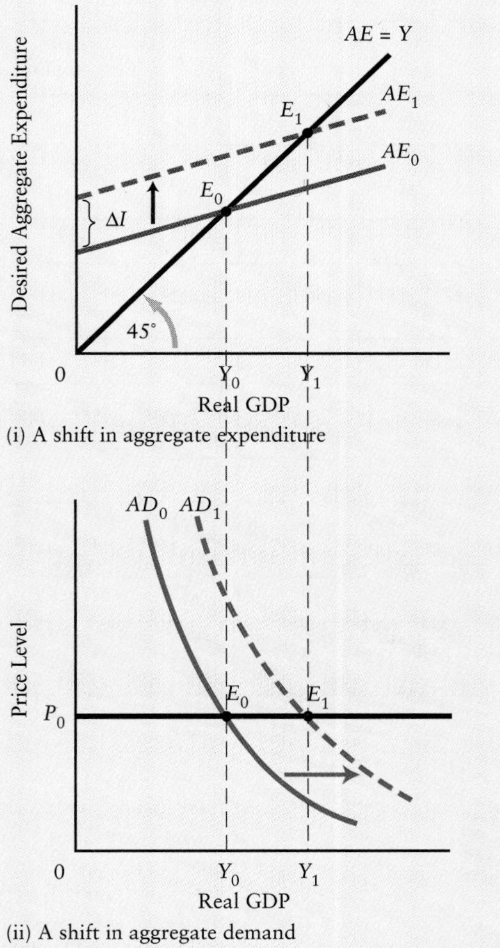

(i) A shift in aggregate expenditure

(ii) A shift in aggregate demand

Changes in the money supply cause shifts in the aggregate expenditure and aggregate demand functions. In Figure 27-4, an increase in the money supply increased desired investment expenditure by ΔI. In part (i) of this figure, the aggregate expenditure function shifts up by ΔI (which is the same as ΔI in Figure 27-4), from AE_0 to AE_1. At the fixed price level P_0, equilibrium GDP rises from Y_0 to Y_1, as shown by the horizontal shift in the aggregate demand curve from AD_0 to AD_1 in part (ii).

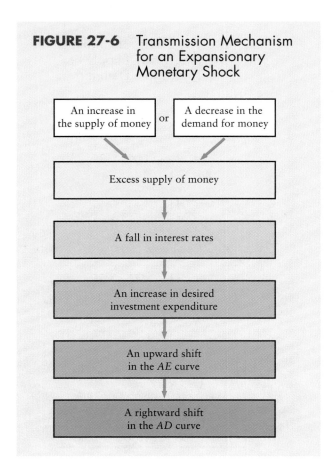

FIGURE 27-6   Transmission Mechanism for an Expansionary Monetary Shock

An increase in the supply of money	or	A decrease in the demand for money

Excess supply of money

A fall in interest rates

An increase in desired investment expenditure

An upward shift in the *AE* curve

A rightward shift in the *AD* curve

Practise with Study Guide Chapter 27, Exercise 5.

In an open-economy with capital mobility, monetary disturbances lead to capital flows, exchange rate changes and changes in net exports.

The Open-Economy Transmission Mechanism

To understand how capital mobility adds this second channel to the transmission mechanism, consider an example. Suppose the Bank of Canada decides to increase the money supply. As shown in Figure 27-4, the increase in money supply reduces the interest rate and increases desired investment expenditure. This is the first channel of the transmission mechanism. But the story does not end there.

The reduction in Canadian interest rates also makes Canadian bonds less attractive relative to foreign bonds. Canadian and foreign investors alike will sell some of their Canadian bonds and buy more of the high-return foreign bonds. But in order to buy foreign bonds, it is necessary first to exchange Canadian dollars for foreign currency. The increase in the demand for foreign currency causes the Canadian dollar to depreciate relative to other currencies.

An increase in the Canadian money supply reduces Canadian interest rates and leads to a capital outflow. This causes the Canadian dollar to depreciate.

As the Canadian dollar depreciates, however, Canadian goods and services become less expensive relative to those from other countries. This change in international relative prices causes households and firms—both in Canada and abroad—to substitute away from foreign goods and toward Canadian goods. Imports fall and exports rise.

So the overall effect of the increase in the Canadian money supply is not just a fall in interest rates and an increase in investment. Because of the international mobility of financial capital, the low Canadian interest rates also lead to a capital outflow, a depreciation of the Canadian dollar, and an increase in Canadian net exports. This increase in net exports, of course, *strengthens* the positive effect on aggregate demand already coming from the increase in desired investment.

This complete open-economy transmission mechanism is shown in Figure 27-7. This figure is based on Figure 27-6, but simply adds the second channel of the transmission mechanism that works through capital mobility, exchange rates and net exports.

In an open economy with capital mobility, an increase in the money supply results in an increase in aggregate demand for two reasons. First, there is a reduction in interest rates that causes an increase in investment. Second, the lower interest rate causes a capital outflow, a currency depreciation, and a rise in net exports.

Our example has been that of a monetary expansion. A monetary contraction would have the opposite effect, but the logic of the mechanism is the same. A reduction in the

Canadian money supply would raise Canadian interest rates and reduce desired investment expenditure. The higher Canadian interest rates would attract foreign financial capital as bondholders sell low-return foreign bonds and purchase high-return Canadian bonds. This action would increase the demand for Canadian dollars in the foreign-exchange market and thus appreciate the Canadian dollar. Finally, the appreciation of the Canadian dollar would increase Canadians' imports of foreign goods and reduce Canadian exports to other countries. Canadian net exports would fall.

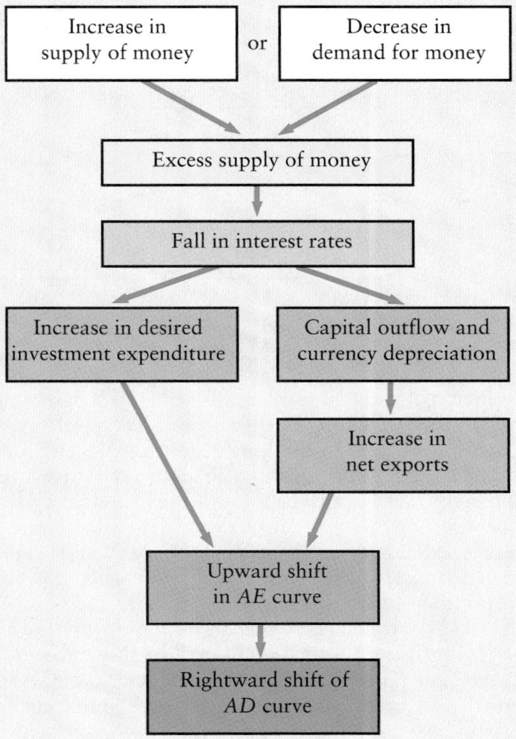

The Slope of the *AD* Curve

We can now use the transmission mechanism to add to the explanation (given in Chapter 24) of the negative slope of the *AD* curve. In Chapter 24, we mentioned two reasons for the negative slope of the *AD* curve: the change in wealth, and the substitution between domestic for foreign goods, both of which occur when the price levels changes. A third effect operates through interest rates. And we are now in a position to understand this third effect.

The essential feature of this third effect is that a rise in the price level raises the money value of transactions. This leads to an increased demand for money, which brings the transmission mechanism into play. People try to sell bonds to add to their money balances; but, collectively, all they succeed in doing is forcing up the interest rate. The rise in the interest rate then reduces desired investment expenditure and so reduces equilibrium national income.

This effect is important because, empirically, the interest rate is the most important link between monetary factors and real expenditure flows. This reason for the negative slope of the *AD* curve is discussed in more detail in the appendix to this chapter.

FIGURE 27-7 The Open-Economy Transmission Mechanism for an Expansionary Monetary Shock

The Strength of Monetary Forces

In the previous section we saw that a change in the money supply leads to a change in interest rates. The change in interest rates, in turn, leads to changes in investment and (through capital flows and changes in the exchange rate) net exports. Thus, a change in the money supply leads to a change in desired aggregate expenditure and therefore to a shift in the *AD* curve.

What will be the effect on real GDP and the price level of the change in the money supply? Because a change in the money supply leads to a shift in the *AD* curve, we know from our analysis in Chapter 25 that the short-run effects will differ from the long-run effects.

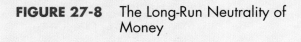

FIGURE 27-8   The Long-Run Neutrality of Money

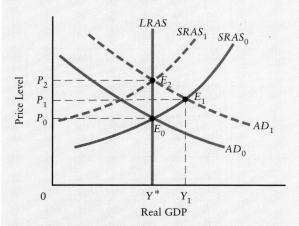

An increase in the money supply leads to a rightward shift in the *AD* curve, but because it has no effect on potential income, in the long run it has no effect on real GDP and results only in a change in the price level. The economy is initially in equilibrium at E_0, with price level of P_0 and real GDP of Y^*. An increase in the money supply causes the *AD* curve to shift rightward from AD_0 to AD_1. Real GDP rises to Y_1, and the price level rises to P_1. The inflationary gap of Y^*Y_1 sets the adjustment mechanism in action, driving up wages and causing the *SRAS* curve to shift up and to the left. The process comes to a halt when real GDP has returned to its potential level, Y^*, thus eliminating the inflationary gap, and the price level has increased to P_2. In the long run, the monetary expansion has no effect on any real variables—money is *neutral*.

Long-Run Effects on Real GDP

We saw in Chapter 25 that any shock—either to aggregate demand or aggregate supply—that creates an output gap sets in place an adjustment mechanism that will eventually close that gap and return real GDP to its potential level, Y^*. The operation of this adjustment mechanism following an increase in the money supply is illustrated in Figure 27-8.

Although a change in the money supply causes the *AD* curve to shift, it has no effect on the level of real GDP in the long run.

Figure 27-8 shows that the only long-run effect of a shift in the *AD* curve following a change in the money supply is a change in the price level. This result is often referred to as the *neutrality of money*, as discussed at the beginning of Chapter 26.

Short-Run Effects on Real GDP

We now focus on the effects of a change in the money supply on the short-run equilibrium level of real GDP. As we will see, there are several factors that determine the short-run strength of monetary changes.

The Role of Aggregate Demand

The size of the shift in the *AD* curve in response to an increase in the money supply depends on the amount of investment expenditure that is stimulated. This in turn depends on the strength of the two key linkages that make up the transmission mechanism.

The first consideration is how much interest rates fall in response to an increase in the money supply. Interest rates must fall to induce households and firms to hold the increased amount of money. The more interest sensitive the demand for money is (the flatter is the *LP* curve), the less interest rates must fall.

The second consideration is how much investment expenditure increases in response to the fall in interest rates. Desired investment expenditure increases in response to a fall in the interest rate. The more interest sensitive desired investment expenditure is (the flatter is the I^D curve), the greater the response will be.

It follows that the size of the shift of the *AD* curve in response to a change in the money supply depends on the shapes of the *LP* and I^D curves. The influence of the shapes of the two curves is shown in Figure 27-9 and can be summarized as follows:

1. The steeper (less interest-sensitive) the *LP* curve, the greater the effect on interest rates of a given change in the money supply.

2. The flatter (more interest-sensitive) the I^D curve, the greater the effect on investment expenditure a change in the interest rate will have and hence the larger will be the shift in the *AD* curve.

The combination that produces the largest shift in the *AD* curve for a given change in the money supply is a steep *LP* curve and a flat *I^D* curve. This combination is illustrated in Figure 27-9(i). It accords with the view that monetary policy is relatively effective as a means of influencing real GDP in the short run. The combination that produces the smallest shift in the *AD* curve is a flat *LP* curve and a steep *I^D* curve. This combination is illustrated in Figure 27-9(ii). It accords with the view that monetary policy is relatively ineffective in the short run.

FIGURE 27-9   Two Views on the Strength of Monetary Changes

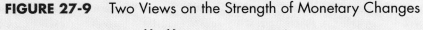

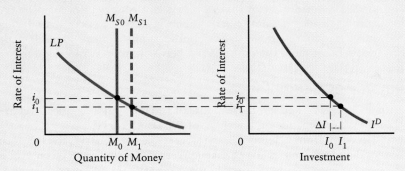

(i) Changes in the money supply effective

(ii) Changes in the money supply ineffective

The strength of the effect of a change in the money supply on investment and hence on aggregate demand depends on the interest elasticity of both the demand for money and desired investment expenditure. Initially, in parts (i) and (ii), the money supply is M_{S0}, and the economy has an interest rate of i_0 and investment expenditure of I_0. The central bank then expands the money supply from M_{S0} to M_{S1}. The rate of interest thus falls from i_0 to i_1, as shown in each of the left panels. This causes an increase in investment expenditure of ΔI, from I_0 to I_1, as shown in each of the right panels.

In part (i), the demand for money is highly interest-inelastic, so the increase in the money supply leads to a large fall in the interest rate. Further, desired investment expenditure is highly interest-elastic, so the large fall in interest rates also leads to a large increase in investment expenditure. Hence, in this case, the change in the money supply will be very effective in stimulating aggregate demand.

In part (ii), the demand for money is more interest-elastic, so the increase in the money supply leads to only a small fall in the interest rate. Further, desired investment expenditure is interest-inelastic, so the small fall in interest rates leads to only a small increase in investment expenditure. Hence, in this case, the change in the money supply will be less effective in stimulating aggregate demand.

The effectiveness of monetary policy in inducing short-run changes in real GDP depends on the slopes of the LP and I^D curves. The steeper is the LP curve, and the flatter is the I^D curve, the more effective is monetary policy.

Figure 27-9 characterizes a famous debate among economists during the 1950s and early 1960s. Some economists, following the ideas of John Maynard Keynes, argued that changes in the money supply led to relatively small changes in interest rates and that investment was relatively insensitive to changes in the interest rate. These economists, who called themselves *Keynesians*, concluded that monetary policy was not a very effective method of stimulating aggregate demand—they therefore emphasized the value of using fiscal policy (as Keynes himself had argued during the Great Depression). Another group of economists, led by Milton Friedman, who then was at the University of Chicago, argued that changes in the money supply caused sharp changes in interest rates which, in turn, led to significant changes in investment expenditure. These economists called themselves *Monetarists* and concluded that monetary policy was a very effective tool for stimulating aggregate demand.[3]

Several decades later, however, this debate between Keynesians and Monetarists is all but over. A great deal of empirical research devoted to uncovering the relationship between interest rates and money demand suggests that money demand is relatively insensitive to changes in the interest rate. That is, the LP curve is quite steep and, as a result, changes in the money supply cause relatively large changes in interest rates (as argued by the Monetarists). The evidence is much less clear, however, on the slope of the I^D curve. Though the evidence confirms that I^D is clearly downward sloping, there is no consensus on whether the curve is steep or flat. Part of the problem facing researchers is that an important determinant of investment is not observable. Firms' expectations about the future have a significant effect on their investment decisions but this variable is not easily measured by researchers. The unobservability of this variable makes it very difficult to precisely estimate the relationship between interest rates and investment.

The Role of Aggregate Supply

As we saw in Chapters 24 and 25, the response of real GDP and the price level to any given shift in the AD curve depends on the slope of the $SRAS$ curve.

As you will recall from Chapter 24, the steeper the $SRAS$ curve, the larger the change in the price level and the smaller the change in real GDP following a given shift in the AD curve. Many economists think that when the level of real GDP is near or above its potential level, the $SRAS$ curve is very steep.

When the economy is operating near or above its potential level of output, increases in aggregate demand (including those caused by increases in the money supply) will lead to small increases in real GDP but will have a substantial effect on the price level.

What Lies Ahead

In this and the previous chapter we incorporated money into our macro model. You now know what money is and how it is created by the banking system. You also know how the money market determines the interest rate. Finally, you have seen in general

---

[3]Monetarists argued that monetary policy was very effective for stimulating aggregate demand but they *did not* advocate an "activist" monetary policy. One of their concerns was that an activist monetary policy would destabilize the economy. We address these issues in Chapter 28.

terms how monetary disturbances—changes in the demand or supply for money—affect real GDP and the price level.

What we have not yet discussed is how the Bank of Canada influences the money supply and what factors it must consider when doing so. What are the Bank's objectives? How does it achieve these objectives? With the basics of money now in place, we are ready to discuss the details of monetary policy. We do so in the next chapter.

SUMMARY

Understanding Financial Assets

- For simplicity, we divide all forms of wealth into "money," which is a medium of exchange, and "bonds," which earn a higher interest return than money and can be turned into money by being sold at a price that is determined on the open market.

- The price of bonds varies negatively with the rate of interest—a rise in the interest rate lowers the prices of all bonds.

The Demand for Money

- The opportunity cost of holding money (rather than bonds) is the interest earnings that are forgone—the interest that would have been earned had bonds been held instead of money.
- Despite the opportunity cost of holding money, households and firms hold money for three reasons—the transactions, precautionary, and speculative motives. Taken together, they have the effect of making the real demand for money vary positively with real GDP, and negatively with the nominal interest rate.
- The real demand for money is independent of the price level. The nominal demand for money varies in direct proportion with the price level.
- The liquidity preference *(LP)* function is the relationship between money demand and the nominal interest rate (holding real income and the price level constant).

Monetary Forces and National Income

- The interest rate is determined by the interaction of the demand for money and the supply of money. An excess demand for money balances leads people to sell bonds. This pushes the price of bonds down and the interest rate up. An excess supply of money balances leads people to buy bonds. This pushes the price of bonds up and the rate of interest down. Monetary equilibrium is established when people are willing to hold the fixed stock of money (and therefore bonds) at the current rate of interest.

- A change in the (real) interest rate causes desired investment to change along the investment demand *(I^D)* curve. This shifts the AE function and causes equilibrium GDP to change. The AD curve also shifts.
- The link between money and aggregate demand is known as the transmission mechanism. A decrease in the supply of money raises interest rates, reduces desired investment expenditure, and thus reduces aggregate demand. An increase in the supply of money reduces interest rates, in-

creases desired investment expenditure, and thus increases aggregate demand.

- In an open economy with capital mobility there is a second part to the transmission mechanism. An increase in the money supply reduces interest rates and makes domestic bonds less attractive than foreign bonds. The capital outflow causes a depreciation of the Canadian dollar that stimulates net exports, and thus increases aggregate demand. A decrease in the money supply raises interest rates, causes a capital inflow, appreciates the currency and reduces net exports.

- The negatively sloped AD curve indicates that the higher the price level, the lower the equilibrium national income. The explanation lies in part with the effect of money on the adjustment mechanism: Other things being equal, the higher the price level, the higher the demand for money and the rate of interest; the lower the aggregate expenditure function, the lower the equilibrium income.

The Strength of Monetary Forces

- Changes in the money supply affect real GDP via shifts in the AD curve. But such changes do not affect potential output. Hence, changes in the money supply can affect output in the short run but not in the long run.

- The steeper the LP curve and the flatter the I^D curve, the greater the effect on aggregate demand of a given change in the money supply. The steeper the $SRAS$ curve, the smaller the transitory effect on real GDP of a given shift in the AD curve.

KEY CONCEPTS

Interest rates and bond prices
The transactions, precautionary, and speculative motives for holding money
The liquidity preference *(LP)* function

Monetary equilibrium
The transmission mechanism
The investment demand (I^D) curve

Money and the adjustment mechanism
The strength of monetary forces

STUDY EXERCISES

1. The following table shows the stream of income produced by several different assets. In each case, P_1, P_2, and P_3 are the payments made by the asset in years 1, 2 and 3.

Asset	(i)	P_1	P_2	P_3	Present Value
Treasury Bill	8%	$1000	$0	$0	—
Bond	7%	$0	$0	$5000	—
Bond	9%	$200	$200	$200	—
Stock	10%	$50	$40	$60	—

a. For each asset, compute the asset's present value. (Note that the market interest rate, i, is not the same in each situation.)
b. Explain why the market price for each asset is likely to be the asset's present value.

2. What motives for holding money—transactions, precautionary, or speculative—do you think explain the following holdings? Explain.

a. Currency in the cash register of the local grocery store at the start of each working day.
b. Money to meet Stelco's bi-weekly payroll deposited in the local bank.
c. A household tries to keep a "buffer" of $1000 in their saving account.
d. An investor sells bonds for cash, which he then deposits in a low-return bank account.
e. You carry $20 in your pocket even though you have no planned expenditures.

3. The diagram opposite shows the demand for money and the supply of money.

   a. Explain why the *LP* function is downward sloping.
   b. Suppose the interest rate is at i_A. Explain how firms and households attempt to satisfy their excess demand for money. What is the effect of their actions?
   c. Suppose the interest rate is at i_B. Explain how firms and households attempt to dispose of their excess supply of money. What is the effect of their actions?
   d. Now suppose there is an increase in the transactions demand for money (perhaps because of growth in real GDP). Beginning at i^*, explain what happens in the money market. How is this shown in the diagram?

4. The following diagrams show the determination of monetary equilibrium and the demand for investment. The economy begins with money supply M_{S0}, liquidity preference curve *LP*, and investment demand I^D. The interest rate is i_0 and investment is I_0.

   a. Beginning at the initial equilibrium, suppose the Bank of Canada increases the money supply. What happens in the money market and what happens to desired investment expenditure?

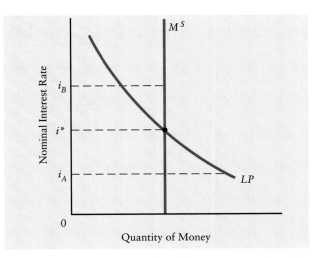

   b. Beginning in the initial equilibrium, suppose there is a reduction in the demand for money (caused, perhaps, by bonds becoming more attractive to firms and households). What happens in the money market and what happens to desired investment expenditure?
   c. Explain why an increase in money supply can have the same effects as a reduction in money demand.

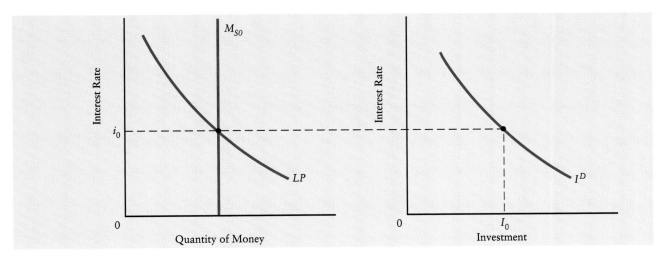

5. In the text we discussed why, in an open economy with international capital mobility, there is a second part to the monetary transmission mechanism. (It may be useful to review Figure 27-7 when answering this question.)

   a. Explain why an increase in Canada's money supply makes Canadian bonds less attractive relative to foreign bonds.
   b. Explain why Canada's bonds being less attractive leads to a depreciation of the Canadian dollar.
   c. Why would such a depreciation of the Canadian dollar lead to an increase in Canada's net exports?

   d. Now suppose that the Bank of Canada does not change its policy at all, but the Federal Reserve (the U.S. central bank) increases the U.S. money supply. What is the likely effect on Canada? Explain.

6. In the text we discussed the debate between Keynesians and Monetarists regarding the effectiveness of monetary policy in changing real GDP (see Figure 27-9 to review). Using the same sort of diagram, discuss two conditions in which a change in the money supply would have *no* effect on real GDP.

DISCUSSION QUESTIONS

1. Historically, construction of new houses has been one of the most interest-sensitive categories of aggregate expenditure. Recently, the financial press have carried a number of stories suggesting that because of financial deregulation and innovations in housing finance, this interest sensitivity has apparently decreased. If this is true, what are the implications for monetary policy?

2. Suppose that you alone know that the Bank of Canada is going to engage in policies that will decrease the money supply sharply, starting next month. How might you make speculative profits by purchases or sales of bonds now?

3. In recent years, central bankers in Canada and elsewhere (especially the United States) have expressed concern about the dramatic increases in stock-market values. In December 1996, U.S. Federal Reserve Chairman, Alan Greenspan, alarmed the markets by referring to investors' "irrational exuberance."

   a. Explain why central bankers might be concerned about "excessive" increases in stock-market values.
   b. Explain how a policy-induced increase in interest rates would affect the stock market.

   c. Suppose prices in the stock market fell sharply for reasons unrelated to domestic interest rates. What would be the likely effect on aggregate demand?

4. In 1997–98, there was a significant recession in the Southeast Asian economies of Malaysia, Indonesia, Thailand, and South Korea.

   a. Explain the likely effects of these events on the demand for Canadian exports. What would be the effect on Canadian aggregate demand?
   b. Suppose the Bank of Canada viewed its monetary policy as being appropriate (for keeping output close to potential) before this "Asian Crisis" occurred. What would you then predict to be the bank's response to the crisis?

5. In the text we discussed how capital mobility in an open economy added a second part to the transmission mechanism. In this setting, discuss why changes in the Federal Reserve's policy in the United States are carefully watched—and often matched—by the Bank of Canada.

Interest Rates and the Slope of the *AD* Curve

The *AD* curve relates the price level to the equilibrium level of real GDP. Its negative slope means that the higher the price level, the lower the equilibrium GDP. In Chapter 24 we explained the slope of the aggregate demand curve by arguing that a change in the price level changed the wealth of firms and households (by changing the real value of money and bond holdings). We also argued that a change in the price level changed the prices of Canadian goods relative to foreign goods, and so affected net exports. What we *did not say* in Chapter 24, however, is that a third reason for a negatively sloped *AD* curve is due to the changes in the interest rate that are caused by the change in the price level. We omitted this argument then for the simple reason that we had not yet introduced the concepts of money demand, money supply, and the determination of interest rates. But we now have the tools in hand to do this.

Let us look at the monetary transmission mechanism in detail. Although the argument contains nothing new, it does require that you follow carefully through several steps.

We start with an initial equilibrium position, corresponding to a given price level P_0, shown by the 0 subscripts in the two figures. Figure 27A-1 shows the determination of the interest rate by the conditions of monetary equilibrium in part (i); that in turn determines the level of desired investment spending by the investment demand curve in part (ii). Figure 27A-2 shows the *AE* curve, drawn for that level of investment spending, and the determination of equilibrium real GDP in part (i); that level of real GDP is then plotted against the price level to give point A on the *AD* curve in part (ii).

A rise in the price level raises the money value of transactions and increases the quantity of nominal money demanded at each possible value of the interest rate. As a result, the *LP* function shifts upward, raising the equilibrium interest rate and reducing the level of desired investment expenditure. The reduction in investment spending in turn causes the *AE* curve to shift downward, leading to a reduction in the equilibrium level of national income.

The negative relationship between the price level and equilibrium real GDP shown by the *AD* curve

FIGURE 27A-1 Changes in the Price Level: Interest Rates and Investment

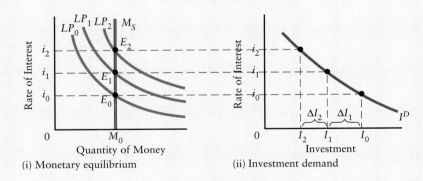

(i) Monetary equilibrium

(ii) Investment demand

Changes in the price level influence the demand for money and hence cause the level of interest rates and desired investment spending to change. In part (i), the money supply is fixed at M_0. Initially, money demand is given by LP_0, equilibrium is at E_0, and the interest rate is i_0. Given that interest rate, desired investment spending is I_0, as shown in part (ii) by the I^D curve.

An increase in the price level causes an increase in the demand for money, and hence the *LP* curve shifts upward to LP_1. Monetary equilibrium is at E_1, the interest rate rises to i_1, and desired investment spending falls by ΔI_1 to I_1. A further increase in the price level causes a further increase in the demand for money, to LP_2. Monetary equilibrium is at E_2, the interest rate rises to i_2, and desired investment spending falls by ΔI_2 to I_2.

occurs because, other things being equal, a rise in the price level raises the quantity of money demanded. This increase in money demand pushes up the interest rate, which then reduces investment and equilibrium GDP. Note the qualification "other things being equal." It is important for this process that the nominal money *supply* remain constant. The adjustment mechanism operates because the demand for money increases when the price level rises whereas the money supply remains constant. The attempt to add to money balances by selling bonds is what drives the interest rate up and reduces desired expenditure, thereby reducing equilibrium GDP. (This argument is conducted in terms of the nominal supply of and demand for money. Arguing in terms of the real demand and supply of money leads to identical results. [34])

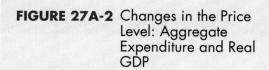

FIGURE 27A-2 Changes in the Price Level: Aggregate Expenditure and Real GDP

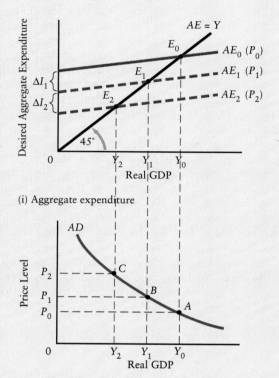

(i) Aggregate expenditure

(ii) Aggregate demand

Changes in the price level lead to changes in desired aggregate expenditure and hence in the equilibrium level of real GDP. Equilibrium GDP is determined in part (i). At a given initial price level—hence with an initial level of desired investment spending of I_0 from Figure 27A-1—desired aggregate expenditure is shown by AE_0. Equilibrium is at E_0, and equilibrium real GDP is Y_0. In part (ii), Y_0 is plotted against P_0 to give point A on the AD curve.

An increase in the price level causes a decrease of ΔI_1 in the level of desired investment spending, as determined in Figure 27A-1 and shown in part (i) here. Thus, the AE curve shifts down to AE_1. Equilibrium is at E_1, and equilibrium real GDP falls to Y_1. In part (ii), the higher price level P_1 is plotted against the lower equilibrium level of income Y_1 as point B on the AD curve.

CHAPTER 28

Monetary Policy in Canada

LEARNING OBJECTIVES

① Explain the two methods by which the Bank of Canada changes the money supply.

② Understand the difference between the Bank's policy variables and its policy instruments.

③ Recognize why the Bank of Canada cannot target the money supply and the interest rate independently.

④ Explain why monetary policy affects real GDP and the price level only after long lags.

⑤ Have a basic understanding of the main challenges that the Bank of Canada has faced over the past two decades.

In the previous two chapters, we saw how money supply and money demand interact to determine interest rates. Further, we saw how monetary disturbances—changes in either the demand for money or the supply of money—affect interest rates, desired aggregate expenditure and, thus, the level of real GDP.

We also saw how commercial banks, through the process of making loans and new deposits, are able to affect the money supply. But there is still one important piece missing from our analysis. Though we discussed some of the functions of the Bank of Canada in Chapter 26, we have not yet examined how the Bank of Canada influences the level of reserves in the commercial banking system. And it is these reserves that form the basis of commercial-bank lending. Until we have examined the operations of the Bank of Canada in more detail, we do not have a full picture of the determinants of the money supply.

In this chapter, we examine the Bank of Canada's monetary policy—how it sets the level of reserves in the banking system to affect interest rates, the exchange rate, real GDP and, eventually, the price level.

The Bank of Canada and the Money Supply

Deposit money is by far the most important part of the money supply. It accounts for about 65 percent of M1, the narrowest definition of money, and for about 90 percent of

M2, the broader measure. As we have seen, the ability of banks to create such deposit money depends on their target level of reserves. These reserves, in turn, are determined by the Bank of Canada. Thus, the ability of the central bank to affect the money supply is critically related to its ability to determine the reserves of the commercial banking system.

In the following sections, we discuss two ways in which the Bank of Canada alters the reserves of the banking system and hence influences the money supply. In Chapter 26, we identified the *target reserve ratio* of the commercial banks as the ratio of reserves they wished to hold relative to their deposit liabilities. At this stage of our discussion of the money supply, we suppose that the target reserve ratio is constant.

Open-Market Operations

open-market operations   The purchase and sale of government securities on the open market by the central bank.

One tool that the Bank of Canada can use for influencing the supply of money is the purchase or sale of government securities on the open market. These actions are known as **open-market operations.** Just as there are stock markets, there are active and well-organized markets for government securities. Anyone, including you, the Toronto Dominion Bank, Ford Motor Company, or the Bank of Canada can enter this market to buy or sell negotiable government securities at whatever price the market establishes. But there is an important difference between the purchase and sale of government securities *among members of the private sector* and *between the central bank and the private sector.* As we shall see, whenever the Bank of Canada is involved in either the purchase or the sale of government securities, the reserves of the entire banking system are altered, and this change affects the money supply.

At the start of 1999, the Bank of Canada held about $30 billion in government securities. In a typical year, the Bank of Canada may make a *net* addition of $1–2 billion to these holdings. During the year, however, its *gross* purchases and sales of government securities on the open market amount to many times this amount. What is the effect of these open-market purchases and sales?

TABLE 28-1   Initial Balance Sheet Changes Caused by an Open-Market Purchase from a Household

Private households	
Assets	Liabilities
Bonds −100 000	No change
Deposits +100 000	

Commercial banks	
Assets	Liabilities
Reserves +100,000	Demand deposits+100 000

Bank of Canada	
Assets	Liabilities
Bonds +100 000	Commercial bank deposits +100 000

An open-market purchase by the Bank of Canada from the private sector increases commercial bank reserves and thus, through an expansion of bank lending, increases the money supply. When the Bank of Canada buys a $100 000 bond from a household, the household gains money and gives up a bond. The commercial banks gain a new deposit of $100 000 and thus new reserves of $100 000. Commercial banks can now engage in a multiple expansion of deposit money, as analysed in Chapter 26.

Open-Market Purchases

When the Bank of Canada buys a treasury bill or a bond from a household or a firm, it pays for the bond with a cheque drawn on itself and payable to the seller. The seller deposits this cheque in a commercial bank, which then presents the cheque to the Bank of Canada for payment. The Bank of Canada then makes a book entry, increasing the deposit of the commercial bank at the central bank, and thus adds to the commercial bank's reserves.

Table 28-1 shows the changes in the balance sheets of the several parties involved in a Bank of Canada purchase of $100 000 in government securities from a household. At the end of these transactions, the central bank has acquired a new asset in the form of a security and a new liability in the form of a deposit by the commercial bank. The seller has reduced its security holdings and increased its deposits. The commercial bank has increased its deposit liabilities and its reserves by the amount of the transaction. When the Bank of Canada buys securities on the open market, the entire banking system gains new reserves.

Given a constant target reserve ratio, after the transactions shown in Table 28-1 are completed, the commercial banks have excess reserves—that is, reserves over and above those needed to maintain their target reserve ratio. To see this, simply note that deposits and reserves have increased by the same amount ($100 000 in this case). As long as the target reserve ratio is less than 100 percent (and it would typically be only a tiny fraction of that), there are now excess reserves. Thus, the commercial banks are in a position to expand their loans and deposits.

When the central bank buys securities on the open market, the reserves of the commercial banks are increased. These banks can then expand deposits, thereby increasing the money supply.

Open-Market Sales

When the Bank of Canada sells a security to a household or firm, it receives in return the buyer's cheque drawn against a deposit in a commercial bank. The Bank of Canada presents the cheque to the commercial bank for payment. Payment is made by a book entry that reduces the commercial bank's deposit at the central bank, and hence reduces its reserves.

The changes in this case are the opposite of those shown in Table 28-1. The central bank has reduced its assets by the value of the security it sold and reduced its deposit liabilities to the banks. The household or firm has increased its holdings of securities and reduced its deposit with a commercial bank. The commercial bank has reduced its deposit liability to the household or firm and reduced its reserves (on deposit with the central bank) by the same amount. In each case, the asset change is balanced by a liability change.

Given a constant target reserve ratio, the commercial bank finds that by suffering an equal reduction in its reserves and its deposit liabilities, its actual ratio of reserves to deposits falls below its target ratio. Banks will then take steps to restore their reserve ratios. The necessary reduction in deposits can be accomplished by not granting new loans when old ones are repaid or by selling (liquidating) existing investments.

When the central bank sells securities on the open market, the reserves of the commercial banks are decreased. These banks must in turn contract deposits, thereby decreasing the money supply.

Although the process just described reflects the mechanics of an open-market sale by the Bank of Canada, it does not fully capture some of the subtleties involved in the Bank's selling of securities. For example, how is the Bank sure that it can always find a willing buyer? Or every time the Bank successfully sells government securities and thus decreases the reserves of the banking system, is this necessarily a "contractionary" monetary policy? These issues are examined in *Extensions in Theory 28-1*.

Shifting Government Deposits

In addition to open-market operations, the Bank of Canada has a second general method for changing the level of reserves in the banking system. As the government's *fiscal agent,* the Bank of Canada manages a large amount of government funds. It maintains

EXTENSIONS IN THEORY 28-1

Open-Market Sales and "Contractionary" Monetary Policy

This box looks at two additional issues that arise whenever the Bank of Canada conducts an open-market sale of government securities (which reduces the reserves of the banking system and is thus called a *contractionary monetary policy*).

Can the Bank of Canada Always Find a Buyer?

One way in which the Bank pursues a contractionary monetary policy is to sell government securities, thus reducing the reserves available to the banking system. What if the public does not wish to buy the securities that the Bank wants to sell? Can the Bank force them to do so?

The answer is that there is always a price at which the public will buy. The Bank must be prepared in its open-market operations to lower the price of securities as far as necessary in order to sell them. This fall in price is, as we have seen, the same thing as an increase in the interest rate. If the Bank wishes to pursue a contractionary policy by selling government securities, it will have to accept that interest rates must rise.

Do Reserves Actually Fall?

In every year since 1950, real GDP growth and inflation have ensured that nominal national income has risen. As a result, the demand for money has grown. In every year in the period, the nominal money supply has grown, reflecting the Bank's decision to supply additional reserves to the banking system to meet the growing demand for money. Does this mean that the Bank has never followed a contractionary monetary policy?

The answer is no. When real income growth and inflation result in a continually growing nominal national income, the stance of monetary policy depends upon the rate at which the money supply is allowed to grow *relative to the rate of growth of the demand for money*. A contractionary monetary policy occurs when the growth in the money supply is held below the rate of growth in the demand for money; it does not require a fall in the absolute size of the money supply.

For example, if the nominal demand for money is growing at 4 percent per year, the Bank of Canada can follow a contractionary policy if it limits the rate of growth of the money supply to 2 percent. This would create an excess demand for money, causing interest rates to rise. The higher interest rates, in turn, would feed through the transmission mechanism to slow the growth in spending and, hence, slow the growth in real GDP.

government accounts on its own books, into which funds are deposited and from which funds are withdrawn. In addition, it manages some government accounts with the chartered banks. Alterations in the amount held in these accounts will affect the reserves of the chartered banks. The process of shifting government accounts from the Bank of Canada to the chartered banks (or in the other direction) is referred to as *cash management*.

Cash management—the shifting of government deposits between the Bank of Canada and the chartered banks—is a major tool used by the Bank of Canada in its day-to-day operations.

Suppose, for example, that the Bank of Canada transfers $100 000 from the government's account at the Bank to the government's account with a chartered bank. The transactions involved are illustrated in Table 28-2. From the government's view, nothing substantial has changed, since its deposits with one financial institution will have fallen, but its deposits with another have risen by the same amount. However, the chartered bank in question will find that its deposit liabilities and reserves will each have increased by $100 000, and hence its ratio of reserves to deposits will have risen. With an unchanged target reserve ratio, the bank will have excess reserves. As with the situation following a Bank of Canada purchase of government securities on the open market, the chartered bank will wish to loan out some of its excess reserves, thus setting in motion an expansion of deposits.

A transfer of government deposits from the chartered banks to the Bank of Canada has the opposite effect. The reserves and deposit liabilities of the banking system fall by the same amount, thus driving the actual reserve ratio below the target reserve ratio. Banks will now have insufficient reserves and will begin to call in existing loans and stop making new ones, setting in motion a process of deposit contraction.

When government deposits are transferred between the Bank of Canada and the chartered banks, the reserves of the chartered banks are changed. Such changes in reserves, through the expansion or contraction of lending, lead to changes in the money supply.

Effects on the Money Supply

Recall from Table 26-2 that the Bank of Canada holds government securities among its assets and government deposits among its liabilities. Either through open-market operations or switching these government deposits, the Bank can significantly change the reserves of the commercial banks.

Open-market operations and control of government deposits give the Bank of Canada potent tools for affecting the size of commercial-bank reserves and thus for affecting the money supply.

TABLE 28-2 Initial Balance Sheet Changes Caused by a Transfer of Government Deposits from the Bank of Canada to a Commercial Bank

Commercial bank		
Assets	Liabilities	
Reserves +100 000	Government deposits	+100 000

Bank of Canada		
Assets	Liabilities	
No change	Government deposits	−100 000
	Commercial bank deposits	+100 000

A transfer of government deposits from the Bank of Canada to a commercial bank increases bank reserves and, thus, through an expansion of bank lending, increases the money supply. When the Bank of Canada transfers $100 000 of government deposits to a commercial bank, the commercial bank's account with the Bank of Canada is credited with a deposit of $100 000. The commercial bank's increase in its deposit liabilities to the government is balanced by the increase in its reserves on deposit with the Bank of Canada. Since its deposits and its reserves have increased by the same amount, it has excess reserves and the potential is created for multiple expansion of deposit money as analysed in Chapter 26.

Though the details of an open-market operation differ from the details of switching government deposits, both actions have the same basic result: They change the reserves of the banking system, and this change in reserves then gets transformed, through commercial-bank lending, into changes in the money supply. In the remainder of this chapter, we focus on the Bank's control of reserves, ignoring the precise way in which these reserves are altered.

Practise with Study Guide Chapter 28, Exercise 1.

Monetary Policy with Zero Required Reserves

In many countries, commercial banks are *required* to hold some fraction of their deposit liabilities in reserves, either in their own vaults or as deposits at the central bank. In the past, Canadian banks faced such requirements as well, but these were eliminated in the early 1990s.

As we observed in Chapter 26, even without legal requirements to hold reserves, banks would still choose to hold quite large reserves if they did not have a central bank to fall back on, for the simple reason that there is considerable uncertainty over how many customers will enter the bank on any given day wanting the value of their deposits in cash. Today, however, in the absence of reserve requirements, the commercial banks know that as long as their balance sheets show them to be solvent, the Bank of Canada will provide them, on a temporary basis, with whatever liquidity they require.

Borrowing from the central bank is not free, however. When commercial banks borrow from the Bank of Canada, they are charged interest on their loan—the interest rate they are charged is called the **bank rate**. The bank rate changes quite frequently and draws considerable public attention when it does. See *Applying Economic Concepts 28-1* for some detailed information about how the bank rate is determined.

bank rate   The rate of interest at which the Bank of Canada makes loans to commerical banks.

The current Canadian policy of "zero required reserves" is really a policy that requires the banks to have zero (or positive) reserves on *average* over a four-week averaging period. Thus, if a commercial bank has a negative balance of $10 million for one day they are required to balance that shortfall with positive reserves of $10 million on some other day during the four-week averaging period. The $10 million negative balance is financed by a loan from the Bank of Canada, which charges an interest rate equal to the bank rate. The $10 million positive balance is effectively a loan from the commercial bank to the Bank of Canada on which the Bank pays half a percentage point below the bank rate.

Since commercial banks pay a higher interest rate on negative balances than they earn on positive balances, they have an incentive to avoid negative balances. In addition, since the rate they earn on positive balances is typically less than what they could earn in the market, they also have an incentive to avoid positive balances.

Commercial banks have an incentive to maintain zero balances at the Bank of Canada.

Monetary policy now works in the same way as described in the earlier sections. When the Bank of Canada buys government securities in the open market, the commercial banks find themselves with excess reserves. They will expand their loans until the excess reserves drain away. When the Bank sells government securities, the commercial banks find themselves short of reserves and hence suffer increased risk of being forced to borrow reserves from the Bank. They will cut down on their loans in an attempt to restore their reserves.

A Review of the Transmission Mechanism

We have now seen how the Bank of Canada can alter the money supply: The Bank of Canada, through its open-market operations or the switching of government deposits, changes the reserves of the banking system. The commercial banks, facing a different level of reserves, then alter their loans and deposits to change the money supply. Before turning to a more detailed discussion of the policy choices faced by the Bank, we briefly review the analysis in Chapter 27 of the effects of changes in the money supply on the economy—this is a review of the *transmission mechanism*.

Suppose the Bank of Canada increases the reserves of the banking system (either through an open-market purchase or by switching government deposits toward the chartered banks). This action leads to an increase in the money supply and thus a fall in interest rates. This reduction in interest rates has two effects. First, lower interest rates lead to an increase in desired investment. Second, lower interest rates lead to a capital outflow as Canadian bonds become less attractive relative to foreign ones, and this capital

APPLYING ECONOMIC CONCEPTS 28-1
Monetary Policy and the Bank Rate

When commercial banks find it necessary to borrow funds temporarily from the Bank of Canada—such as when their reserves at the Bank are negative (overdrawn)—they are charged an interest rate on their loan. The bank rate is the interest rate at which the Bank of Canada makes loans to the commercial banks.

Commercial banks in need of temporary financing are not forced to borrow from the Bank of Canada, however. They can also borrow from each other or from investment dealers. The interest rate for these loans, which are often overnight (or just a few days), is called the **overnight rate.**

A higher bank rate (or a higher overnight rate) induces the commercial banks to hold more reserves in view of the higher cost of borrowing they would have to incur if they should suffer a loss of cash and are forced to seek a loan either from the Bank or from the overnight market. Thus, other things equal, an increase in the bank rate increases the target reserve ratio of the commercial banks and thus reduces the amount by which a given level of reserves in the banking system can be expanded into bank deposits.

The bank rate is set at the upper end of a range that the Bank of Canada announces as its *desired* range for the overnight rate. By moving this range (which is one-half of a percentage point wide) up or down, the Bank signals to the financial markets where it thinks the overnight rate needs to be in order to accomplish its policy goals. Since commercial banks can borrow from the Bank of Canada at the bank rate (the upper end of the range), they won't be prepared to pay a higher rate to other lenders in the overnight market. Conversely, since commercial banks can lend money to the Bank of Canada (by keeping positive balances there) and earn an interest rate given by the lower end of the desired range, they won't be prepared to lend money for a lower rate to other borrowers in the overnight market. Thus, by announcing this desired range, the Bank of Canada is able to control the range of the overnight rate.

If the overnight rate does not move quickly into the Bank's desired range, the Bank takes action to change the overnight rate. It does this by changing the reserves in the banking system. An increase in reserves (through either an open-market purchase or a switch of government deposits toward the commercial banks) puts commercial banks in the position of having excess reserves. As they try to lend these funds on the overnight market, the overnight rate falls. A decrease in reserves (through either an open-market sale or a switch of government deposits away from the commercial banks) puts commercial banks in the position of having deficient reserves. As they try to borrow funds in the overnight market, the overnight rate rises.

---

outflow depreciates the Canadian dollar and stimulates net exports. As a result of both the higher investment and the higher net exports, there is an increase in aggregate demand. The *AD* curve shifts to the right, and the equilibrium level of real GDP rises.

The opposite occurs when the Bank of Canada reduces the reserves of the banking system (through an open-market sale or switching government deposits away from the chartered banks). As reserves fall, the commercial banks reduce their loans and the money supply falls, thus raising interest rates. The higher interest rates have two effects. First, desired investment falls. Second, capital flows into Canada in pursuit of high-return Canadian bonds, causing an appreciation of the Canadian dollar and thus reducing net exports. The lower investment and lower net exports implies a reduction in aggregate demand. The *AD* curve shifts to the left, and the equilibrium level of real GDP falls.

Thus, monetary policy works through the transmission mechanism to shift the *AD* curve and thus to change equilibrium GDP. An *expansionary* monetary policy is one that

overnight rate   The interest rate that commercial banks charge each other for very-short-term loans.

See the Bank of Canada's website for information about Canada's monetary policy: www.bank-banque-canada.ca.

shifts the *AD* curve to the right and increases real GDP; a *contractionary* monetary policy is one that shifts the *AD* curve to the left and reduces real GDP.

Policy Variables and Policy Instruments

policy variables   The variables that the government seeks to influence, such as real GDP and the price level.

The Bank conducts monetary policy to influence real GDP and the price level. These ultimate objectives of the Bank's policy are called **policy variables.** The variables that it *directly* controls to achieve these objectives are called its **policy instruments.** The Bank also has **intermediate targets,** which are neither the ultimate objective of policy nor variables under the direct control of the Bank. Intermediate targets nevertheless play a key role in the execution of monetary policy; their importance lies in their close relationship to policy variables.

policy instruments
The variables that the government can control directly to achieve its policy objectives.

intermediate targets
Variables that the government cannot control directly and does not seek to control ultimately, yet that have an important influence on policy variables.

Policy Variables

The Bank of Canada's twin policy variables are real GDP and the price level. Recall from Chapter 27 that monetary policy operates by influencing aggregate demand; the resulting link between the Bank's monetary actions and the determination of the price level and real GDP is summarized in Figure 28-1.

Short Run: Nominal GDP

We also saw in Chapter 27 that the short-run effects of a shift in the *AD* curve are divided between the price level and real output in a manner determined by the slope of the *SRAS*

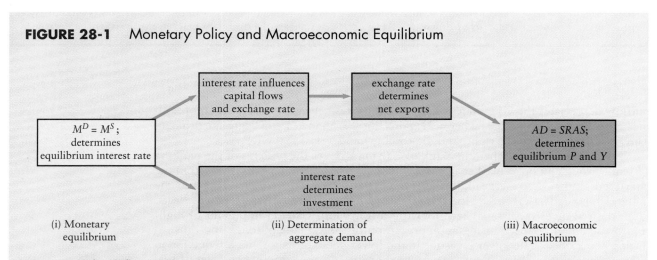

FIGURE 28-1   Monetary Policy and Macroeconomic Equilibrium

interest rate influences capital flows and exchange rate → exchange rate determines net exports

$M^D = M^S$; determines equilibrium interest rate

$AD = SRAS$; determines equilibrium P and Y

interest rate determines investment

(i) Monetary equilibrium

(ii) Determination of aggregate demand

(iii) Macroeconomic equilibrium

Monetary policy influences aggregate demand through the transmission mechanism; macroeconomic equilibrium then determines the price level and the level of real output. Monetary equilibrium requires that the interest rate be such that money supply equal the quantity of money demanded. Changes in the money market give rise to changes in the interest rate and hence, via the transmission mechanism, to changes in desired aggregate expenditure (net exports and investment). Aggregate demand and short-run aggregate supply then determine the price level and the level of real GDP.

curve. However, the Bank has no control over this slope. Thus, although the Bank cares about the separate reactions of the price level and of real output, there is little that it can do in the short run to control them independently.

Monetary policy is therefore not capable of pushing the price level (P) and real GDP (Y) toward independently determined targets simultaneously. For this reason, central banks often focus on nominal GDP (PY) as the target for monetary policy in the short run.

Long Run: The Price Level

We have seen that in the long run, when the level of wages is fully adjusted to the price level, the *LRAS* curve is vertical. The vertical *LRAS* curve implies that the only long-run impact of monetary policy will be on the price level. The absence of any long-run impact of monetary policy on real output, as we discussed in Chapter 26, is referred to as the *neutrality* of money. The long-run neutrality of money has led many central banks to focus on the price level (or its rate of change, the rate of inflation) as the long-run target for monetary policy. For example, the central banks in Sweden, Canada, and New Zealand have all adopted formal inflation targets in recent years.

Policy Instruments

Having selected its policy variables and formulated targets for their behaviour, the Bank of Canada must decide how to achieve these targets. Because the Bank can control neither real output nor the price level directly, it must employ its *policy instruments,* which it does control directly, to influence aggregate demand in the desired manner.

The Bank of Canada's policy instrument is the level of reserves in the banking system. It can adjust reserves either through open-market operations or by the switching of government deposits.

The reserves of the banking system, together with the currency in circulation, make up the Bank of Canada's liabilities (see Tables 26-1 and 26-2). Commercial bank reserves are held on deposit with the Bank of Canada and are the Bank's liability because they can be redeemed on demand. The Bank's monetary liabilities, as we saw in Chapter 26, form the *base* on which commercial banks can expand and create deposits. For this reason, the Bank's liabilities are often referred to as the *monetary base*. Therefore, economists say that the Bank's policy instrument is the monetary base. It is this monetary base that the Bank is changing when it conducts open-market operations or when it switches government deposits.

Intermediate Targets

Major changes in the direction of monetary policy are made only infrequently. Decisions regarding the implementation of policy must, however, be made almost daily. Given the values that the Bank of Canada wishes its policy variables to take on, and given the current state of the economy, are increases or decreases in the monetary base called for? How big an increase, or how big a decrease? Such questions must be answered continually in the Bank's day-to-day operations.

Daily information about the policy variables, however, is rarely available. Inflation and unemployment rates are available only on a monthly basis and with a considerable lag. National income figures are available even less frequently; they appear on a quarterly basis. Thus, the policy makers do not know exactly what is happening to the policy variables when they make their daily decisions regarding the Bank's policy instruments.

How, then, does the Bank of Canada make decisions? Central banks have typically used *intermediate targets* to guide them when implementing monetary policy in the very short run. To serve as an intermediate target, a variable must satisfy two criteria. First, information about it must be available on a frequent basis, daily if possible. Second, its movements must be closely correlated with those of the policy variable, so that changes in it can reasonably be expected to indicate that the policy variable is also changing (or will do so in the near future).

Consistency of Intermediate Targets

The two most commonly used intermediate targets have been the money supply and the interest rate. However, these two variables are not independent of each other; recall that the liquidity preference function relates the quantity of money demanded to the rate of interest. This relationship and its implications for the Bank's choice of intermediate targets are reviewed in Figure 28-2.

The Bank of Canada cannot use its control of the monetary base to influence both the interest rate and the money supply independently.

Because the money supply and interest rates are closely related (along the *LP* function), it might appear not to matter whether the Bank chooses to target the interest rate or instead chooses to target the money supply. For example, if the Bank wishes to remove an inflationary gap by reducing aggregate demand, it will sell government securities and thus drive their prices down and interest rates up. These open-market sales will also reduce the monetary base and thus contract the money supply. It is largely immaterial whether the Bank seeks to force interest rates up or to contract the money supply; doing one accomplishes the other. Similarly, driving interest rates down by means of open-market purchases of government securities will tend to expand the money supply as the public gains money in return for the securities that it sells to the Bank.

But the world is not quite as simple as we have just described. Whether the Bank uses interest rates or the money supply as an intermediate target can actually matter in some situations. Let's see why this is the case.

Choice of Intermediate Targets

Prior to the early 1970s, the Bank of Canada primarily used the interest rate as its intermediate target. Many economists, especially Monetarists, criticized this choice. They pointed out that since interest rates tended to vary directly with the business cycle, rising on the upswing and falling on the downswing, it was difficult for the central bank to determine the impact of its monetary policy by observing the interest rate alone. They cited historical examples in which central banks wished to restrain a boom and were convinced that they were doing so because interest rates were rising

FIGURE 28-2   Alternative Intermediate Targets

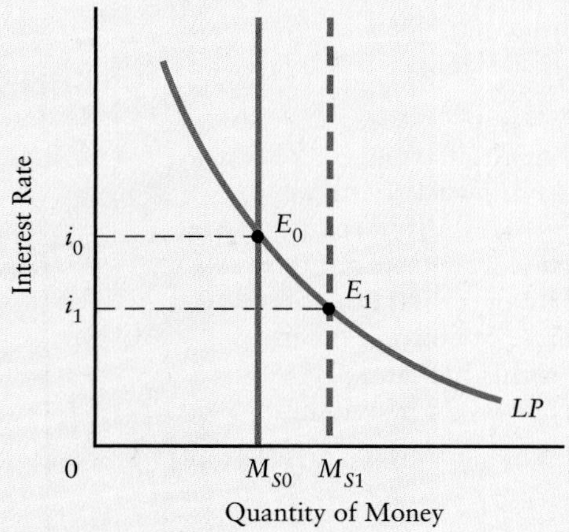

For a given liquidity preference function, the Bank of Canada cannot choose independent targets for the money supply and the interest rate. If the Bank chooses a target of M_{S0} for the money supply, it must accept the interest rate of i_0. If it then decides to increase the money supply to M_{S1}, it must accept the lower interest rate of i_1.

If the Bank chooses a target of i_0 for the interest rate, it must accept the money supply of M_{S0}. If it then decides to reduce the interest rate to i_1, it must accept the higher money supply of M_{S1}.

sharply, only to later determine that it was the boom itself that was driving up the demand for money and thus driving up interest rates.

This experience with focusing on interest rates led to changes in intermediate targets.

In the 1970s, the Bank of Canada began to focus on the money supply as its intermediate target.

At the outset, the measure that was used for this purpose was the narrowly defined money supply, M1. However, it soon became clear that problems also arose when the Bank focused exclusively on M1 as its intermediate target.

To understand the problems associated with focusing on a single measure of the money supply, note that changes in the money supply are reliable indicators of the direction of monetary policy *only if the demand for money is stable.* However, the demand for money can be unstable for two reasons. First, we have just seen that money demand tends to rise in booms and fall in slumps, as fluctuations in real GDP lead to similar changes in the transactions demand for money. Second, the demand for *any particular monetary aggregate* can change quite substantially as firms and households *substitute* one type of financial asset for another. For example, households might reduce their deposits in chequing accounts and increase their deposits in saving accounts. This would be a reduction in M1 but, because M2 includes both chequing and saving deposits, there would be no change in M2. But if the Bank is only monitoring M1, then this reduction in the money supply (as defined by M1) suggests that monetary policy is becoming tighter. In fact, however, all that is happening is a substitution of one type of asset for another. The Bank's response to the problems caused by the instability of money demand was again to change its intermediate targets.

In the early 1980s, dissatisfaction with M1 as an intermediate target led the Bank of Canada to monitor several monetary aggregates rather than just one.

Even the monitoring of several different monetary aggregates, however, does not solve the problem of the instability of money demand. There are times when the current state of monetary policy needs to be gauged by measures other than money supply magnitudes, and interest rates can provide valuable additional information.

For example, during the last half of the 1970s, slow growth in all measures of the money supply suggested (to those who were monitoring only the money supply) that monetary policy was fairly tight. However, decreases in the demand for money that were not fully recognized at the time meant that the money supply was growing quite rapidly *relative to demand,* and hence monetary policy was much more expansionary than was thought at the time. More attention to interest rates would have given an important signal of this, because throughout this period interest rates were quite low. Figure 28-3 illustrates the general lesson.

Practise with Study Guide Chapter 28, Exercise 3.

Changes in the demand for money imply that the stance of monetary policy cannot be judged only by looking at measures of the money supply. In such cases, interest rates provide additional information about monetary policy.

The Role of the Exchange Rate

As we have seen, the transmission mechanism of monetary policy in an open economy involves changes in both the interest rate and the exchange rate. So you should not be surprised to learn that the Bank of Canada pays close attention to movements in the exchange rate.

As with interest rates, however, care must be taken in drawing inferences about monetary policy from changes in the exchange rate. Care must be taken because the exchange rate can change for different reasons, which have different implications for

FIGURE 28-3 Intermediate Targets When the Demand for Money Shifts

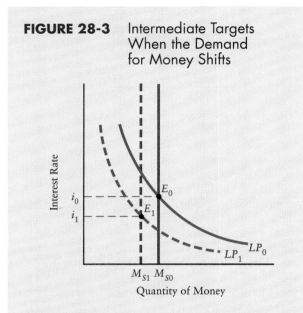

Shifts in the liquidity preference function change the relationship between the money supply and the interest rate. The demand for money is initially given by the LP function, LP_0. It then shifts to the left to the dashed LP function, LP_1—this is a reduction in the demand for money.

Suppose that, following the shift in the LP function, the money supply falls from M_{S0} to M_{S1} and so the interest rate falls from i_0 to i_1. If the Bank were to focus on the fall in the money supply (and did not recognize the reduction in money demand), it would conclude that monetary policy had tightened. But if it focused on the fall in the interest rate (and did not recognize the reduction in money demand), it would conclude that monetary policy had loosened.

Since the combination of demand and supply shifts led to a reduction in the interest rate, the truth is that money supply fell by less than money demand. From the discussion in *Extensions in Theory 28-1*, this reduction in money supply would *not* be viewed as a contractionary monetary policy. Indeed, given the reduction in money demand, the *smaller* reduction in money supply would be viewed as an *expansionary* monetary policy.

the desired direction of monetary policy. Here are two examples to illustrate this point. In both cases, suppose that we begin in a situation where real GDP is equal to its potential level.

First, suppose that Canada's trading partners are booming and thus demanding more Canadian exports. Foreigners' heightened demand for Canadian goods creates an increase in demand for the Canadian dollar in foreign-exchange markets. The Canadian dollar therefore appreciates. But the increase in demand for Canadian goods also adds directly to Canadian aggregate demand. If this shock persists, it will therefore add to domestic inflationary pressures. In this case, if the Bank notes the appreciation of the dollar (and correctly determines its cause), it can take early action to offset the positive demand shock by tightening monetary policy.

A second example involves an increase in demand for Canadian *assets* rather than Canadian goods, and has quite different implications from the first example. Suppose that investors, because of events happening elsewhere in the world, decide to liquidate some of their foreign assets and purchase more Canadian assets instead. In this case, the increase in demand for Canadian assets leads to an increase in demand for the Canadian dollar in foreign-exchange markets. This causes an appreciation of the Canadian dollar. As the dollar appreciates, however, Canadian exports become more expensive to foreigners. There will be a reduction in Canadian net exports and thus a reduction in Canadian aggregate demand. If this shock persists, it will reduce inflationary pressure in Canada. In this case, if the Bank notes the appreciation of the dollar (and correctly determines its cause), it can take early action to offset the negative demand shock by loosening monetary policy.

Notice in both examples that the Canadian dollar appreciated as a result of the external shock, but the causes of the appreciation were different. In the first case, there was a positive demand shock to net exports, which then caused the appreciation, which in turn dampened the initial increase in net exports. But the overall effect on the demand for Canadian goods was positive. In the second case, there was a positive shock to the asset market, which then caused the appreciation, which in turn reduced the demand for net exports. The overall effect on the demand for Canadian goods was negative. Thus, in the first case, the appropriate monetary policy was contractionary, whereas in the second case the appropriate monetary policy was expansionary.

Changes in the exchange rate can signal the need for changes in the stance of monetary policy. But care must be taken to identify the cause of the exchange-rate change.

Since the early 1990s, the Bank of Canada has formalized the role of the exchange rate by constructing what it calls the Monetary Conditions Index (MCI). The MCI is a weighted average of the interest rate and the exchange rate. *Applying Economic Concepts 28-2* discusses how the Bank uses the MCI as an intermediate target.

APPLYING ECONOMIC CONCEPTS 28-2

The Monetary Conditions Index as an Intermediate Target

Because monetary policy in an open economy works through changes in both the interest rate and the exchange rate, the Bank of Canada closely monitors what it calls the *Monetary Conditions Index (MCI)*. The MCI is an index that reflects changes in short-term interest rates (typically the 90-day rate on corporate bonds) and the exchange rate. The Bank uses its policy instrument—changes in bank reserves—to alter the MCI so that it is consistent with the Bank's longer-term inflation goals. In this box, we explain the MCI and how the Bank uses it to conduct its monetary policy.

The Monetary Conditions Index

Suppose we let i be the current interest rate and e be the current exchange rate. Recall from Chapter 19 that e is defined as the number of Canadian dollars required to purchase one unit of foreign currency, so an increase in e is a depreciation of the Canadian dollar. Further, let i_B and e_B be the values taken by i and e in some base year (the Bank currently uses 1987 as the base year). The MCI is then defined to be

$$MCI = (i - i_B) - \theta (e - e_B)$$

where θ is a positive parameter estimated by the Bank's economists to be about 1/3. (We discuss θ in a moment.)

To see how the MCI is influenced by monetary policy, consider what would happen if the Bank engineered a monetary contraction. The Bank reduces reserves to the banking system and this reduces the money supply. For given money demand, the reduction in money supply pushes up interest rates. But that is not the end of the story in an open economy. The high interest rates on Canadian bonds then attract foreign purchasers, who must buy Canadian dollars in order to purchase these high-yield bonds. The increase in demand for the Canadian dollar leads to an appreciation of the Canadian dollar, which is a fall in e. Thus, as a result of the reduction in the money supply, i has increased and e has fallen. On both counts, the MCI increases. By similar reasoning, a monetary expansion reduces i, raises e, and thus lowers the MCI.

Following this logic, the Bank refers to an increase in the MCI as a tightening of *monetary conditions*; a reduction in the MCI is referred to as a loosening of monetary conditions.

How the Bank Uses the MCI

As we will see later in this chapter, the Bank of Canada in 1991 announced formal *inflation-control targets*. Suppose that the Bank's target is to keep inflation between 1 and 3 percent (this is indeed the Bank's current goal). Given this long-term inflation target, how is the MCI used as an intermediate target?

The economists at the Bank use complex statistical methods to estimate the relationship between their policy instrument—changes in reserves—and real GDP and inflation. Since monetary policy works by changing i and e, and thus the MCI, they need to know the relationship between the MCI and real GDP. This is where θ comes in. The estimate of θ of 1/3 reflects the empirical finding by the Bank's economists that a 3 percent change in e has roughly the same impact on real GDP as a 1 percentage point change in i. The Bank must also make predictions of what events are likely to occur in the world economy that will affect the level of economic activity in Canada.

Given all this information, the Bank must arrive at an estimate of the level of the *current* MCI that is consistent with its inflation target *6–8 quarters in the future*. Given this desired level of the MCI, the Bank then uses its policy instrument (changes in reserves) to alter the MCI so that it is consistent with the desired level.

After the Bank has adjusted its policy instruments to get the MCI to its desired level, it must continue to monitor the economy, both within Canada and in the rest of the world. As new information becomes available, and as unforeseen events occur, the Bank revises its estimate of where the current MCI ought to be in order to reach the inflation target 6 to 8 quarters in the future.

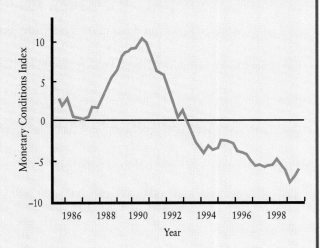

This box draws on the discussion in Charles Freedman, "The Role of Monetary Conditions and the Monetary Conditions Index in the Conduct of Policy," *Bank of Canada Review*, Autumn 1995.

Lags in the Conduct of Monetary Policy

In Chapter 27 we encountered one difference between two groups of macroeconomists involved in a debate that was prominent in the 1950s and 1960s. *Monetarists* argued that monetary policy was potentially very powerful in the sense that a given change in the money supply would lead to a substantial change in aggregate demand, whereas *Keynesians* were associated with the view that monetary policy was much less powerful.

This debate had some of its roots in differing interpretations of the causes of the Great Depression, especially as it occurred in the United States amid a large number of commercial-bank failures. Now that you better understand the role of central banks and commercial banks in the determination of the money supply, you can better understand this debate. One interesting part of the debate is why Canada and the United Kingdom had collapses in economic activity similar in magnitude to that in the United States even though they did not suffer the same banking crisis. *Lessons from History 28-1* provides a brief summary of this interesting debate.

The debate between the Monetarists and the Keynesians, however, involved more than just the *size* of the effect of a change in the money supply on national income; it also focused on the question of whether active use of monetary policy in an attempt to stabilize output and the price level was likely to be successful, or whether it would instead lead to an increase in fluctuations in those variables. This debate is as important today as it was then, and at its centre is the role of *lags*.

Execution Lags

Experience has shown that lags in the operation of policy can actually cause stabilization policy to be destabilizing. In Chapter 25, we discussed how decision and implementation lags might limit the extent to which active use of fiscal policy can be relied upon to stabilize the economy. Although both of these sources of lags are much less relevant for monetary policy, the full effects of monetary policy nevertheless occur only after quite long time lags. *Execution lags,* lags that occur after the decision has been made to implement the policy, can have important implications for the conduct of monetary policy.

There are three reasons why a change in monetary policy does not affect the economy instantly.

Deposit Creation Takes Time

Open-market operations or the switching of government deposits affect the reserves of the banks. This process takes place more or less instantly. But the full increase in the money supply occurs only when the commercial banks have granted enough new loans and made enough investments to expand the money supply by the full amount that is possible by existing reserve ratios. This process can take quite a long time.

Changes in Expenditure Take Time

A change in the money supply leads to a change in the interest rate. This, in turn, affects interest-sensitive expenditures. But it takes time for new investment plans to be drawn up, approved, and put into effect. It may take a year or more before the full increase in investment expenditure occurs in response to a fall in interest rates. In an open economy like Canada's, the change in the interest rate also leads to capital flows and a change in the exchange rate. These changes occur very quickly. But the effect on net exports takes more time while purchasers of internationally traded goods and services switch to lower-cost suppliers.

The Multiplier Process Takes Time

Changes in investment and net export expenditures brought about by a change in monetary policy set off the multiplier process that increases national income. This process, too, takes some time to work out.

Furthermore, although the end result is fairly predictable, the speed with which the entire expansionary or contractionary process works itself out can vary in ways that are hard to predict. Thus, though the effects of monetary policy might be reasonably straightforward to predict, the timing of those effects is difficult to predict.

Monetary policy is capable of exerting expansionary and contractionary forces on the economy, but it operates with a time lag that is long and variable.

Economists at the Bank of Canada estimate that it takes between 9 and 12 months for a change in monetary policy to have an effect on real GDP, and a further 9 to 12 months for the policy to have an effect on the price level.

Destabilizing Policy?

To see the significance of execution lags for the conduct of monetary policy, consider a simple example. To begin, suppose that the lag is known to be exactly 18 months. If on January 1, the Bank of Canada determines that the economy needs a stimulus, it can increase the reserves of the banking system within the day and the money supply can then begin to increase. By the end of that month a significant increase may be registered.

However, because the full effects of this policy take time to work out, the policy may prove to be destabilizing. By October, a substantial inflationary gap may have developed because of cyclical forces unrelated to the Bank's monetary policy. However, since the effects of the monetary expansion that was initiated nine months earlier are just beginning to be felt, an expansionary monetary stimulus is adding to the existing inflationary gap.

If the Bank now applies the monetary brakes by contracting the money supply, the full effects of this move will not be felt for another 18 months. By that time, a contraction may have already set in because of the natural cyclical forces of the economy. Thus, the delayed effects of the monetary policy may turn a minor downturn into a major recession.

The long execution lag of monetary policy makes monetary fine-tuning difficult; the policy may have a destabilizing effect.

We supposed in this example that the execution lag was known with certainty to be 18 months. In this case, it could be built into the Bank's calculations. But the fact that the lag is actually highly variable makes this nearly impossible. Of course, when a persistent gap has existed and is predicted to continue for a long time, monetary policy may be stabilizing even when its effects occur after a long time lag.

Political Difficulties

Long execution lags in the workings of monetary policy also imply political difficulties for the central bank.

LESSONS FROM HISTORY 28-1

Two Views on the Role of Money in the Great Depression

In most peoples' minds, the Great Depression began with the stock market crash of October 1929. In the United States, Canada, and Europe, the decline in economic activity over the next four years was massive. From 1929 to 1933, real output fell by roughly 25 percent, one quarter of the labour force was unemployed by 1933, the price level fell by over 25 percent, and businesses failed on a massive scale. In the six decades that have followed, no recession has come close to the Great Depression in terms of reduced economic activity, business failures, or unemployment.

The Great Depression has naturally attracted the attention of economists and, especially in the United States, these few years of experience have served as a kind of "retrospective laboratory" in which they have tried to test their theories.

For a discussion of these two views, and some attempts to discriminate between them, see Peter Temin, *Did Monetary Forces Cause the Great Depression?* (New York: Norton, 1976). For the classic statement of the Monetarist view, see Milton Friedman and Anna Schwartz, *A Monetary History of the United States 1867–1960* (Princeton: Princeton University Press, 1963).

The Basic Facts

The stock market crash of 1929, and other factors associated with a moderate downswing in business activity during the late 1920s, caused the U.S. public (firms and households) to wish to hold more cash and fewer demand deposits. The banking system, however, could not meet this increased demand for liquidity without help from the Federal Reserve System (the U.S. central bank). As we saw in Chapter 26, because of the fractional-reserve banking system, commercial banks are never able to satisfy from their own reserves a large and sudden demand for cash—their reserves are always only a small fraction of total deposits.

The Federal Reserve had been set up to provide just such emergency assistance to commercial banks that were basically sound but were unable to meet sudden demands by depositors to withdraw cash. However, the Fed refused to extend the necessary help, and successive waves of bank failures followed as a direct result. During each wave, hundreds of banks failed, ruining many depositors and thereby worsening an already severe depression. In the second half of 1931, almost 2000 U.S. banks were forced to suspend operations. One consequence of these failures was a sharp drop in the money supply; by 1933, M2 was 33 percent lower than it had been in 1929.

Figure 28-4 shows a situation in which the current inflation rate is at the bottom of the Bank's 1–3 percent target band, but the expectation of future events suggests that inflation will be rising sharply. This situation was faced by the Bank of Canada in the spring of 1997. At that time, the Canadian economy was experiencing healthy growth. But a fast-growing U.S. economy, through its growing demand for Canadian exports, was expected to increase Canadian growth sharply, which would then increase inflationary pressures.

What is the political problem? Remember that because of the time lags involved, any policy change that occurs today has no effect on real GDP for roughly 9 months and the full effect on the price level does not occur for 18–24 months. If the economy is at point *A* in Figure 28-4, and inflation is expected to rise in the near future, then monetary policy must be changed *now* in order to counteract this future inflation. But this is politically difficult because the *current* inflation rate is low. The Bank finds itself in the awkward position of advocating a tightening of monetary policy, in order to fight the expectation of future inflation, at a time when the *current* inflation rate suggests no need for tightening. But if the goal is to keep inflation within the target range, such *preemptive* monetary policy is necessary because of the unavoidable time lags.

Competing Explanations

To Monetarists, these facts seem decisive: To them, the fall in the money supply was clearly the major cause of the fall in output and employment that occurred during the Great Depression. Monetarists see the Great Depression as perhaps the single best piece of evidence of the strength of monetary forces, and the single best lesson of the importance of monetary policy. In their view, the increased cash drain that led to the massive monetary contraction could have been prevented had the Federal Reserve quickly increased the level of reserves in the commercial banking system. In this case, the rise in the monetary base would have offset the increase in the cash drain, so that the money supply (currency plus bank deposits) could be maintained.

Keynesians argue that the fundamental cause of the Great Depression was a reduction in autonomous expenditure. They cite a large decline in housing construction (in response to a glut of housing) and a reduction in consumption driven largely by pessimism caused by the stock market crash. Although Keynesians accept the argument that the Fed's behaviour was perverse, and exacerbated an already bad situation, they do not attribute a pivotal role to the Fed or to the money supply. Indeed, they see the fall in the money supply as a *result* of the decline in economic activity (through a reduced demand for loans and thus reduced bank lending) rather than as its cause.

Lessons from Canada's Experience

Canada has been used as a "control" in this retrospective laboratory, for the simple reason that Canada had broadly the same magnitude of economic collapse as did the United States, but *did not* have the same magnitude of bank failures. Unfortunately, Canada's experience is not able to resolve the disagreement—both sides of the debate offer explanations of the Canadian experience consistent with their central arguments.

Keynesians look to Canada's experience to support their view that money was not central to the cause of the economic collapse in the United States. They point out that in Canada, where the central bank came to the aid of the banking system, bank failures were much less common during the Great Depression, and as a consequence, the money supply did not shrink drastically as it did in the United States. Thus, their argument is that since Canada did not escape the Great Depression, but it *did* escape the collapse in the money supply, then money must not have been the central cause of the U.S. economic collapse.

Monetarists accept the point that Canada did not have a massive reduction in the money supply, but they argue that the economic contraction in the United States (which *was* caused by the collapse in the money supply) spilled over into Canada, largely through a dramatic reduction in demand for Canadian goods. This spillover implies a large decline in autonomous export expenditure for Canada, and thus a decline in Canadian national income. Thus, Monetarists essentially argue that money in the United States was an important contributor to the economic decline in Canada.

Time lags in monetary policy require that decisions regarding a loosening or tightening of monetary conditions be forward-looking. This often creates political difficulties for the central bank.

A Monetary Rule?

Monetarists have criticized the Bank for fine-tuning, and the poor record of monetary policy as a short-run stabilizer, especially in the late 1970s and early 1980s, has lent force to their criticisms. Monetarists in Canada have argued that:

- monetary policy is a potent force of expansionary and contractionary pressures;
- monetary policy works with long and variable lags;
- the Bank has been prone to sharp reversals of its policy stance.

Given these three premises, Monetarists have concluded that monetary policy has sometimes had a destabilizing effect on the economy, the policy itself accentuating rather than dampening the economy's natural cyclical swings.

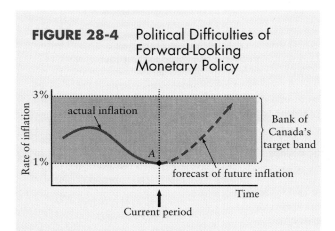

FIGURE 28-4   Political Difficulties of Forward-Looking Monetary Policy

Since monetary policy works only with a considerable time lag, central-bank actions to keep inflation within its target range must be taken in advance of expected future events. Suppose the economy is currently at point *A* with inflation at the lower bound of the target range. If events in the near future are expected to cause inflation to rise sharply, then monetary policy must be tightened immediately to keep inflation within the desired range. The central bank then faces the politically awkward situation of tightening policy at a time when *current* inflation is low.

Monetarists argue from this position that the stability of the economy would be much improved if the Bank *stopped trying to stabilize it.* What then should the Bank do? Because growth of population and of productivity leads to a rising level of real output, Monetarists think the Bank ought to expand the money supply year in and year out at a constant rate that is equal to the long-run rate of growth of real GDP. When the growth rate shows signs of long-term change, the Bank can adjust its rate of monetary expansion. It should not, however, alter this rate with a view to stabilizing the economy against short-term fluctuations.

Many other economists disagree with the Monetarists' position against fine tuning. They argue that an appropriate monetary policy of fine tuning can, *in principle,* reduce cyclical fluctuations below what they would be under a constant-rate rule. Monetarists respond, however, by arguing that whatever may be true of the *best conceivable* monetary policy, the Bank's *actual* policy over the past many years has made cyclical fluctuations larger than they would have been under a constant-rate rule. They argue that attempts to use monetary policy to fine-tune the economy inevitably are fraught with dangers.

There is another argument against a constant-rate rule, however. Experience has shown that the demand for money sometimes can shift quite substantially. A stable money supply rule in the face of demand instability guarantees monetary shocks, rather than monetary stability (recall Figure 28-3). Such demand instability undermines confidence in the appropriateness of a monetary rule. The daunting challenge that faces central banks in this situation is to offset such shifts in the demand for money while not overreacting and thereby destabilizing the economy.

20 Years of Canadian Monetary Policy

This section describes a few key episodes in recent Canadian monetary history. This is not done to teach history for its own sake, but because the lessons of past experience and past policy mistakes, interpreted through the filter of economic theory, provide our best hope for improving our policy performance in the future.

By 1980, partly as a result of the two OPEC oil shocks, in 1974 and 1979–80, inflation in Canada was over 12 percent. The Bank of Canada (and also the U.S Federal Reserve) embarked on a strict policy of monetary restraint aimed at fighting inflation. Interest rates rose sharply, as shown in Figure 28-5. The result of this aggressive disinflation policy was, in both countries, the most serious recession since the 1930s.

These high interest rates, and the recession they wrought, were more severe than might have been expected from the relatively moderate slowdown in the rate of growth of the money supply induced by the central banks.

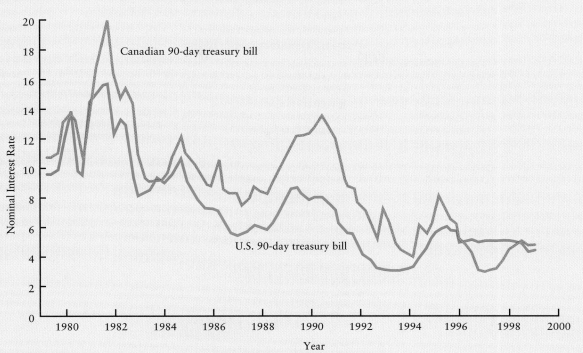

FIGURE 28-5   Short-Term Interest Rates, Canada and the United States, 1979–1999

Canadian nominal interest rates have been highly variable over the period shown. They increased with the rising inflation from 1980 to mid 1981. They then fell as inflation fell through most of the 1980s. Starting in 1988, the rates rose steadily under the impact of the Bank of Canada's anti-inflation policy, eventually reaching a level five percentage points above U.S. rates by the end of 1990. As the inflation rate tumbled in mid 1992, interest rates, which began to decline in 1990, by 1993 reached levels lower than they had been seen since the 1960s. These low interest rates continued (with some ups and downs) through to the middle of 1996 when Canadian rates fell below U.S. rates. Throughout 1996 and 1997, Canadian rates remained below U.S. rates. By mid 1998, however, Canadian interest rates rose slightly above those in the United States.

(*Source: Bank of Canada Review,* various issues; and *Economic Report of the President,* various issues.)

An unanticipated surge in the demand for money led to a much tighter monetary policy than the Bank had intended.

In other words, this unplanned tight monetary policy did not occur because money supply fell more than intended, but because money demand increased sharply. With the dramatic fall in inflation and the serious recession, the Bank eased monetary policy in the second half of 1982.

Economic Recovery: 1983–1987

In early 1983, a sustained recovery began, and by mid 1987, real GDP had moved back toward potential. Much of the growth was centred in the export-oriented manufacturing industries in Ontario and Quebec. The first four years of the recovery saw cumulative output growth of 15.7 percent.

The main challenge for monetary policy in this period was to create sufficient liquidity to accommodate the recovery without triggering a return to the high inflation rates that prevailed at the start of the decade.

In other words, the Bank of Canada had to increase the money supply to *accommodate* the recovery-induced increase in money demand *without* increasing the money supply so much that it refueled inflationary pressures.

In spite of much debate and uncertainty, the Bank handled this "reentry" problem quite well. The Bank allowed a short but rapid burst of growth in the nominal money supply, thus generating the desired increase in real money balances. Once the new level of real balances was achieved, money growth was cut back to a rate consistent with low inflation, allowing for the underlying rate of growth in real income. The trick with this policy was that to avoid triggering expectations of renewed inflation, the Bank had to generate a one-shot increase in the *level* of the money supply without creating the impression that it was raising the long-term *rate of growth* of the money supply.

In late 1983 and early 1984, when growth in monetary aggregates first started to surge, many voiced the fear that the Bank was being overly expansionary and was risking a return to higher inflation. As the reentry problem came to be more widely understood and as inflationary pressures failed to reemerge, these criticisms subsided, and the consensus appeared to be that the Bank had done a commendable job of handling the reentry problem.

Rising Inflation: 1987-1990

By mid 1987, many observers began to worry that Canadian policy makers were too complacent in accepting the 4 percent range that Canadian inflation had settled into. Further, there was concern that inflationary pressures were starting to build—monetary aggregates were growing quickly, real output growth was strong, unemployment was falling, and an inflationary gap was opening.

In 1987, many economists argued that if monetary policy was not tightened, Canada would experience gradually increasing inflation until once again a severe monetary restriction would be necessary.

Inflation slowly crept upward. A monetary restriction designed to reduce inflation would obviously impose costs in the form of lower output and higher unemployment. Was the Bank prepared to inflict such costs, especially given that Canada had emerged from a deep recession only five years earlier?

Disinflation: 1990-92

In January 1988, Bank of Canada Governor John Crow announced that monetary policy would henceforth be guided less by short-term stabilization issues and more by the goal of long-term "price stability." Specifically, he said that "monetary policy should be conducted so as to achieve a pace of monetary expansion that promotes stability in the value of money. This means pursuing a policy aimed at achieving and maintaining stable prices."[1]

---

[1]John W. Crow, "The Work of Canadian Monetary Policy," speech given at the University of Alberta, January 18, 1988; reprinted in *Bank of Canada Review,* February 1988.

This explicit adoption of price stability as the Bank's only target set off a heated debate about the appropriate stance for monetary policy. The debate was fueled by Crow's decision to give a high profile to his policy by repeatedly articulating and defending it in speeches and public appearances. Some critics said that price stability was unobtainable. Others said the costs of reaching it would be too large in terms of several years of recessionary gaps. Supporters said that the long-term gains from having a stable price level would exceed the costs of getting there.

Despite the Bank's explicit policy of "price stability," the actual inflation rate increased slightly in the years immediately following John Crow's policy announcement, from about 4 percent in 1987 to just over 5 percent in 1990.

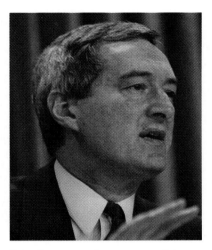

John Crow was the governor of the Bank of Canada from 1987 to 1994. In 1988 he announced that "price stability" would thenceforth be the Bank of Canada's objective.

The controversy reached new heights when in 1990 the country (and much of the world) entered a sustained recession. Maintaining the policy of tight money with high interest rates seemed perverse to many when the economy was already suffering from too little aggregate demand to sustain potential output.

Furthermore, the high Canadian interest rates attracted foreign funds. Foreigners who wished to buy Canadian bonds needed Canadian dollars, and their demands led to an appreciation of the Canadian dollar. This increased the price of Canadian exports while reducing the price of Canadian imports, putting Canadian export and import-competing industries at a competitive disadvantage, and further increasing the unemployment that had been generated by the worldwide recession.

In spite of heavy political pressure to lower interest rates, and of criticism from many economists who might have supported a move toward price stability in less depressed times, the Bank stood by its tight monetary policy. Indeed, in 1991, it formally announced *inflation-control targets* for the next several years. Beginning in 1992, inflation was to lie within the 3–5 percent range, with the range falling to 2–4 percent by 1993 and to 1–3 percent by the end of 1995.

The result of this commitment to tight money was an unprecedented differential between Canadian and U.S. interest rates (see Figure 28-5), and a high value of the Canadian dollar, which temporarily hurt the international competitiveness of Canadian goods.

As a result of the tight monetary policy of the Bank, the inflation rate fell sharply, from about 5 percent in 1990 to less than 2 percent in 1992. For 1993 and 1994, inflation hovered around 2 percent. Furthermore, short-term nominal interest rates fell from a high of 12 percent in 1990 to about 6 percent by the end of 1993. Recall that the nominal interest rate is equal to the real interest rate plus the rate of inflation. So this decline in nominal interest rates was the eventual result of the tight money policy that reduced inflation. The differential between Canadian and U.S. rates also fell and the Canadian dollar depreciated. Figure 28-5 tells the story in detail.

Price-Stability: 1992–?

Clearly, the Bank had succeeded in coming close to its target of price stability. Controversy continued, however, on two issues. First, was the result worth the price of a deeper, possibly more prolonged recession than might have occurred if the Bank had been willing to accept 3–4 percent inflation? Second, would the low inflation rate be sustainable once the recovery took the economy back toward potential income? If the inflation rate were to rise to 4 percent during the post-1993 recovery, then the verdict might well be that the cost of temporarily reducing the rate to below 2 percent was not worth the transitory gains.

The debate over the Bank's disinflation policy became centred on Governor John Crow, especially during the federal election campaign of 1993. Some called for the non-renewal of Crow's term as Governor (which would end in 1994), and his replacement with someone more concerned with the costs of disinflation. Others argued that the Bank's policy of "price stability" under Crow's stewardship was the right policy for the times, and that the long-run benefits of low inflation would be worth the costs required to achieve it.[2]

In 1994, the minister of finance appointed Gordon Thiessen, the former deputy governor of the Bank, to be the new governor. With some irony, the minister of finance, whose party had been severe critics of Crow's policy while they were in opposition, affirmed the previous monetary policy of the Bank and urged the new governor to maintain the hard-won low inflation rate. The new governor also affirmed the policy of price stability, and extended the formal inflation target of 1 to 3 percent.

For the next five years, the rate of inflation continued to hover between 1 and 2 percent. The main challenge for the Bank in the next few years was to keep inflation low while at the same time encouraging the economy to progress through what was viewed as a fragile economic recovery. Excessive stimulation of the economy would lead to the rise of inflation which would sacrifice the hard-won gains achieved only a few years earlier. On the other hand, insufficient stimulation would itself be an obstacle to economic recovery. By 2000, real GDP in Canada was close to its potential level and inflation was just below 2 percent.

Gordon Thiessen became the governor of the Bank of Canada in 1994 after inflation had hovered around 2 percent for about two years.

Concerns in the Late 1990s

During the late 1990s, three issues complicated the conduct of Canadian monetary policy. One was the "Asian Crisis" of 1997–98. The second was the remarkable growth in the Canadian and U.S. stock markets. The third was the possibility that inflation had become *too low*.

The Asian Crisis

Beginning in the summer of 1997, the economies of Thailand, Malaysia, Indonesia, and South Korea fell into serious recessions.[3] Since these countries are major importers of raw materials, their recessions led to a large decline in the world's demand for raw materials. As a result, the world price of raw materials fell by an average of about 30 percent in the subsequent year. Since Canada is a major producer and exporter of raw materials, this decline in the demand for raw materials was a negative aggregate demand shock for Canada. The decline in Canada's net exports led to a leftward shift in Canada's *AD* curve.

Working in the opposite direction, however, was the expansionary supply-side effect of lower raw materials prices for the many Canadian manufacturing firms that use raw

---

[2]For a very readable account of Canadian monetary policy from 1988 to 1993, see William Robson and David Laidler, *The Great Canadian Disinflation* (Toronto: C. D. Howe Institute, 1993).

[3]An important part of the cause of these recessions was the sudden collapse of their currencies, which were previously pegged in value to the U.S. dollar. We examine fixed and flexible exchange rates in detail in Chapter 36.

materials as inputs. Remember from Chapter 24 that reductions in input prices shift the *SRAS* curve to the right and increase real GDP—a positive supply shock.

This positive supply shock was especially important for the United States, a major importer and user of raw materials. The impact of the Asian Crisis on the U.S. economy produced a third effect on Canada as the quickly growing U.S. economy increased its demand for Canadian goods and services.

The Asian Crisis therefore produced a complicated combination of forces on the Canadian economy, including

- a negative *AD* effect from the reduction in demand (and thus the prices) for Canadian exports
- a positive *SRAS* effect from the lower-price inputs for Canadian manufacturing firms
- a positive *AD* effect from the increase in U.S. demand for Canadian goods (caused, in turn, by the positive *SRAS* effect in the United States)

In the spring of 1997, before the Asian Crisis had begun, the Canadian economy was growing and steadily closing a recessionary gap. The combination of forces created by the Asian Crisis presented problems for the Bank of Canada and for the appropriate direction for monetary policy. Especially difficult was judging the relative strengths of the three separate effects. As it turned out, Canada's recessionary gap continued to shrink as the economy grew steadily. By 1999, the Asian economies were on their way to a healthy recovery.

The Stock Market

A rising stock market can cause problems for the conduct of monetary policy. From 1994 through 1999, U.S. and Canadian stocks enjoyed unprecedented bull markets. The Dow Jones Industrial Average (an index of U.S. stock prices) increased from about 3500 in mid 1994 to about 11 000 in late 1999, an average annual increase of 26 percent. The Toronto Stock Exchange (TSE) 300 Index increased from roughly 4000 to 8000 over the same period, an average annual increase of 14 percent.

The concern for the Bank of Canada during this time was that the increase in wealth generated by these stock-market gains would stimulate consumption expenditures in what was already a steadily growing economy, thus increasing inflationary pressures. A second concern by 1998–99 was that the stock market had reached such heights that, in the views of many commentators, a "crash" (or a "correction" when it is less dramatic) was imminent. The concern was that a large stock market crash would reduce household wealth significantly and thus cause a major and sudden reduction in aggregate demand.

The appendix to this chapter contains a brief discussion of the stock market and how it is related to macroeconomic developments.

Is Inflation Too Low?

The third problem faced by the Bank during the late 1990s was, ironically, caused by its success in reducing inflation and maintaining it at a low level. Some economists argued that Canadian inflation had reached *too low* a level, and that the cost of having such low inflation was that Canadian unemployment was higher than would otherwise be the case. Indeed, these economists used the comparison between Canada and the United States as evidence. They noted that Canada's significantly higher unemployment rate and slightly lower inflation rate suggested that there may indeed be costs associated with pushing inflation too low.

Central to their argument is the importance of *downward nominal wage rigidity*— the inability of wages to fall, in dollar terms, in response to a reduction in demand. In

See Chapter 28 of www.pearsoned.ca/lipsey for an interesting discussion of how monetary policy responded to the Asian crisis: Stephen Poloz, "How Will Central Banks Cope with a Non-Inflationary World?" *World Economic Affairs*.

Chapter 24 we discussed this idea but referred to it as *sticky wages*—the idea that wages rise faster in response to excess demand than they fall in response to excess supply. These economists argued that when nominal wages are sticky downward, and inflation is very low, the invariable result is higher *permanent* unemployment. This argument was first put forward by James Tobin, the 1981 Nobel Laureate from Yale University. The argument was made recently in Canada by Pierre Fortin from the Université du Québec à Montréal.

Other economists, including many at the Bank of Canada, agreed that nominal wages may be temporarily sticky downward as the economy adjusts to an environment of very low inflation. But as firms and workers get used to a low-inflation environment, wages will become as flexible downward as they are upward. These economists do not believe, therefore, that there will be a long-run effect from low inflation on Canada's unemployment rate.

This is a contentious issue, both on theoretical and empirical grounds, and the debate is not yet settled. We address it in more detail in the next chapter when we examine inflation—its causes, costs, and cures.

SUMMARY

The Bank of Canada and the Money Supply   **LO ❶**

- The major tool the Bank of Canada uses to control the supply of money is control of reserves of the commercial banking system through open-market operations and by switching government deposits between itself and the chartered banks. Purchases of bonds on the open market or switching government deposits toward the chartered banks increases the reserves of the banking system.

Sales on the open market or withdrawing government deposits away from the chartered banks reduces bank reserves.

- The Bank of Canada now operates a system of zero required reserves, which means that each commercial bank's reserves must average to zero (or a positive amount) over a four-week averaging period.

Policy Variables and Policy Instruments   **LO ❷❸**

- The Bank's policy variables are real GDP and the rate of inflation. To influence these, the Bank works through policy instruments that it can control and that will in turn influence its policy variables. Intermediate targets are used to guide decisions about policy instruments.

- Because changes in reserves have an effect on both the interest rate and the exchange rate, the Bank uses a combination of the two—the Monetary Conditions Index—as an intermediate target.

- To reduce real GDP, the Bank reduces bank reserves. This drives up the interest rate and causes an appreciation of the Canadian dollar, reducing investment and net exports and shifting the *AD* curve to the left. To increase real GDP, the Bank increases reserves, driving down the interest rate and causing a depreciation of the Canadian dollar, shifting the *AD* curve to the right.

Lags in the Conduct of Monetary Policy

- Though the Bank can change the reserves of the banking system more or less instantly, it takes time for this change in reserves to be transformed into a change in bank deposits and thus a change in the money supply.
- Once interest rates change in response to a change in the money supply, it takes time for firms and households to change their expenditure. Even once those new plans are carried out, it takes time for the multiplier process to work its way through the economy, eventually increasing equilibrium national income.
- Not only is there a significant lag from when bank reserves are changed to when national income changes, but this time lag is itself uncertain. Monetary policy is thus said to work with "long and variable lags."

- The existence of such long and variable lags have led some economists to argue that the Bank of Canada should not use monetary policy in an attempt to stabilize national income. They argue that attempts to stabilize will in fact be destabilizing, and advocate the use of a monetary rule whereby bank reserves are increased at a constant rate.
- Others argue that such a monetary rule would be undesirable, especially since experience shows that the demand for money is unstable. They argue that the Bank of Canada could *in principle* reduce fluctuations in national income by responding to sudden changes in money demand.

20 Years of Canadian Monetary Policy

- In the early 1980s, the Bank of Canada embarked on a policy of tight money to reduce inflation. This policy contributed to the severity of the recession.
- A sustained economic recovery occurred from 1983 to 1987. The main challenge for monetary policy during this time was to create sufficient liquidity to accommodate the recovery without triggering a return to the high inflation rates that prevailed at the start of the decade.
- In 1988, when inflation was between 4 and 5 percent, the Bank of Canada announced that monetary policy would no longer be guided by short-term stabilization and instead would be guided by the long-term goal of "price stability." By 1992, the Bank's tight money policy had reduced inflation to below 2 percent.
- Controversy concerned two issues. First, was the cost in terms of lost output, heavy unemployment and a temporary reduction in international competitiveness worth the benefit in terms of long-term stable currency? Second, could the low inflation rate be sustained?
- This controversy was partly responsible for the 1994 change in the Bank of Canada's Governor, from John Crow to Gordon Thiessen. Despite this administrative change, the stated policy of price stability continued. By 1999, the rate of inflation had been hovering between 1 and 2 percent for about seven years.
- In the late 1990s, the central challenges faced by the Bank included (1) how to respond to the Asian Crisis, (2) how to respond to the rising stock market, and (3) whether very low inflation might involve permanent costs in the form of higher unemployment.

K E Y   C O N C E P T S

Open-market operations
Shifting government deposits
The bank rate

Policy variables
Policy instruments
Intermediate targets
The Monetary Conditions Index
    (MCI)

Variability of monetary policy
Monetary rules
Lags in the effect of monetary policy
Shifts in the demand for money

STUDY EXERCISES

1. Suppose the Bank of Canada enters the open market and sells $100 000 of government securities to a wealthy Canadian household. The three balance sheets below are for the *changes* in assets and liabilities for the household, commercial banks, and the Bank of Canada.

Household		Commercial Banks		Bank of Canada	
Assets	Liabilities	Assets	Liabilities	Assets	Liabilities
Bonds ——		Reserves ——	Deposits ——	Bonds ——	Commercial bank deposits —
Deposits —					

   a. How do the household's assets and liabilities change as a result of the open-market sale? Fill in the left-hand table.
   b. If the household pays for the government securities with a cheque drawn on its account at a commercial bank, what are the immediate effects on assets and liabilities for the commercial banks? Fill in the middle table.
   c. What are the changes for the Bank of Canada? Fill in the right-hand table.
   d. Explain how this open-market sale will affect the total money supply.

2. Suppose the Bank of Canada transfers $100 000 of government deposits from the government's account at the Bank of Canada to the government's account in a commercial bank. The two balance sheets below are for the *changes* in assets and liabilities for commercial banks and the Bank of Canada.

Commercial Banks		Bank of Canada	
Assets	Liabilities	Assets	Liabilities
Reserves —	Deposits —	Bonds —	Commercial bank deposits —
			Government deposits —

   a. What are the immediate effects on assets and liabilities for the commercial banks? Fill in the left-hand table.
   b. What are the changes for the Bank of Canada? Fill in the right-hand table.

   c. Explain how this transfer of government deposits will affect the total money supply.

3. In the text we stated that the Bank of Canada's long-run policy variable is the price level (or its growth rate, the rate of inflation).

   a. How is this choice of a long-run policy variable related to the idea of long-run money neutrality?
   b. If money were not neutral in the long run, do you think the Bank might choose a different long-run policy variable? Explain.

4. The diagram below shows the demand for money (the *LP* function) and the supply of money.

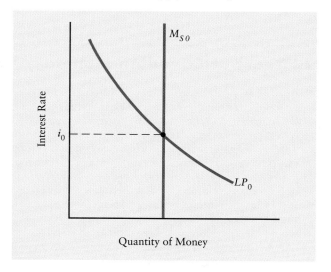

   a. Explain (and show in the diagram) why the Bank of Canada cannot have independent targets for the money supply and the interest rate.
   b. Suppose the Bank leaves the money supply unchanged but that the demand for money increases. Show this in the diagram. What happens to interest rates? What happens to investment?
   c. In the situation of part **b**, explain why monetary policy has been contractionary even though the Bank did not change the money supply.

5. Milton Friedman for many years was a professor of economics at the University of Chicago, and was the most influential Monetarist of his generation. He is known for accusing the Federal Reserve (the U.S. central bank) of following "an unstable monetary policy," arguing that although the Fed "has given lip service to controlling the quantity of money... it has given its heart to controlling interest rates."

a. Explain why, if the *LP* function were approximately stable, targeting the quantity of money would produce a "stable" monetary policy. Show this in a diagram.

b. Explain why, if the *LP* function moves suddenly and in unpredictable ways, targeting the quantity of money produces an "unstable" monetary policy. Show this in a diagram.

c. What has the Canadian experience suggested about the relative likelihood of the conditions in part **a** as opposed to those in part **b**?

6. Suppose it is mid 1999 and the stock market has been growing rapidly for the past four years. Some economists argue that the stock market has become "overvalued" and thus a "crash" is imminent.

a. How does a rising stock market affect aggregate demand? Show this in an *AD/SRAS* diagram.

b. For a central bank that is trying to keep real GDP close to potential, explain what challenges are posed by a rapidly rising stock market.

c. Suppose the stock market "crashes," falling suddenly by 30 percent. How does this affect aggregate demand? Show this in an *AD/SRAS* diagram.

d. Consider the policy dilemma faced by the central bank when prices in the stock market are very high and are continuing to rising rapidly. What are the implications of tightening monetary policy in such a situation? What are the implications of leaving monetary policy unchanged?

DISCUSSION QUESTIONS

1. Describe the chief tools of monetary policy available to the Bank of Canada, and indicate whether—and if so, how—they might be used for the following purposes:

   a. To create a mild tightening of bank credit
   b. To signal that the Bank of Canada favours a sharp curtailment of bank lending
   c. To permit an expansion of bank credit with existing reserves
   d. To supply banks and the public with a temporary increase of currency for Christmas shopping

2. It is often said that an expansionary monetary policy is like "pushing on a string." What is meant by this statement? How does this contrast with a contractionary monetary policy?

3. In 1988, the Bank of Canada announced that it was committed to achieving "price stability," but it did not commit itself to a particular target growth rate for any monetary aggregate that would be consistent with achieving its price stability target. Why do you think it failed to make such a commitment?

4. In 1993, with 11 percent unemployment, a slow recovery just underway and inflation in the 1 to 2 percent range, the Bank permitted a rapid expansion of M1. Was this inflationary? Why might the Bank have adopted this policy? What is meant by the "reentry" problem?

5. The term "moral suasion" is generally used to describe attempts by central banks to enlist the cooperation of private financial institutions in the pursuit of some objective of monetary policy. In a country such as Canada, where there are only a few banks, the central bank can easily communicate its view to the chartered banks. Using the balance sheets of the Bank of Canada and the commercial banking system, explain how an attempt by the Bank of Canada to persuade commercial banks to increase their lending would affect bank reserves and total bank deposits. How is this question related to Question 2?

6. Suppose the Canadian economy has real GDP equal to potential and that nothing significant is expected to change in the near future. Then the Canadian dollar suddenly depreciates—apparently permanently—by 5 percent against the U.S. dollar. Explain why the appropriate response of monetary policy depends on the *cause* of the depreciation. In particular, make a distinction between:

   a. a depreciation caused by a reduction in demand for Canadian exports of raw materials; and
   b. a depreciation caused by a reduction in demand for Canadian bonds that are now perceived as less attractive than U.S. bonds.

The Stock Market

An organized market in which stocks or bonds are bought and sold is called a *securities market*. Securities markets that deal in shares, or equities, are known as *stock markets*. Two of the best known stock markets are the Toronto Stock Exchange and New York Stock Exchange. The trading of *existing* shares on the stock market indicates that ownership is being transferred; it does not indicate that companies are raising new money from the public, although firms also do raise funds by issuing new shares.

The Function of Stock Markets

When a household buys shares—either existing or newly issued—it becomes one of the firm's owners. If, at some future date, the household wishes to cease being a shareholder in the firm, the household can simply sell the shares. It can do so only by persuading someone else to buy its shares in the company.

Stock markets are important because they allow people to put their savings into assets that may earn a good rate of return and are, in general, very liquid.

For example, if I want to invest in a particular stock that I think will earn a high return, I may do so, even though I know that I will want my money back after only a year. And I can be confident that I will be able to sell the stock a year from now. Nevertheless, although stock markets provide for the quick sale of stocks, they do not guarantee the price at which stocks can be sold. The price at any time is the one that equates the demand and supply for the particular stock, and rapid fluctuations in stock prices are common.

Prices on the Stock Market

Stock market values sometimes display cumulative upward movements, or *bull markets*. They also sometimes display cumulative downward movements, or *bear markets*. The Great Depression of the 1930s was preceded by the stock market crash of 1929, which caused what is still the largest percentage loss of stock values ever to be suffered by investors worldwide.

Figure 28A-1 shows the path of the Toronto Stock Exchange 300 Index since 1980. Notice the signifi-

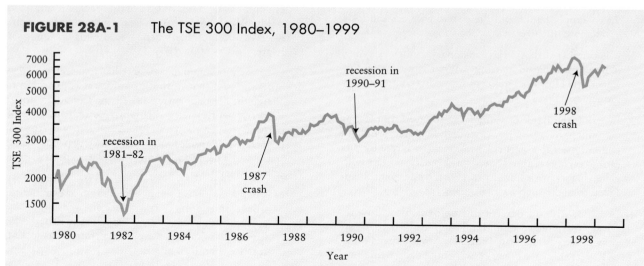

FIGURE 28A-1   The TSE 300 Index, 1980–1999

The Toronto Stock Exchange 300 Index has increased at an annual average rate of 6.5 percent over the past 20 years. There is clearly an upward long-run trend to the price of shares in the TSE 300 Index. But the sharp reduction during the 1981–82 recession is clear, as are the sudden "crashes" of October 1987 and July 1998. Note that the vertical scale is logarithmic. This means that equal distances on the scale represent *proportional* changes.
(*Source: The International Bank Credit Analyst,* June 1999)

cant decline from 1981 to 1982 during a recession, and also the sharp "crashes" in October 1987 and July 1998. The long-term trend, however, is clearly positive. Over the past twenty years, prices on the TSE 300 have increased at an average annual rate of roughly 6.5 percent.

There is clearly some association between fluctuations in the stock market and those in the economy, but is there a causal connection? Do stock market fluctuations cause business cycle fluctuations, or is it the other way around?

Causes of Stock Market Swings

Before we can answer these questions, we need to know a little about how stock markets function. In particular, what causes stock market prices to fluctuate?

When investors buy a company's stocks, they are buying rights to share in the stream of dividends to be paid out by that company. They are also buying an asset that they can sell in the future for a gain or a loss.

The value of a stock thus depends on two factors: first, what people expect the stream of future dividend payments to be, and, second, what price people expect to receive when the stock is sold. (If the price rises, the owner earns a *capital gain*: if the price falls, the owner suffers a *capital loss*.) Both influences make dealing in stocks an inherently risky operation. Will the company be profitable in future years, and thus be more likely to pay high dividends? Will the price of the stock rise so that current shareholders will earn a capital gain if they sell their shares?

The Influence of Present and Future Business Conditions

Many influences affect stock market prices, including the state of the business cycle and the stance of government policies.

Cyclical Forces.   If investors expect a firm's earnings to increase, the firm will become more valuable and the price of its stock will rise. Such influences cause stock prices to move with the business cycle, being high when current profits are high and low when current profits are low. These influences also cause stock prices to vary with a host of factors that influence expectations of future profits. A poor crop, destruc-

tion of trees by acid rain, an announcement of new defence spending, a change in the exchange rate, and a change in the governing political party can all affect profit expectations and hence stock prices.

Policy Factors.   Changes in monetary policy affect the economy by first changing interest rates. Such changes, or just the expectation of them, will have effects on stock prices. For example, suppose that the threat of future inflation leads the Bank of Canada to tighten monetary policy sharply, thus raising interest rates. Shareholders will now want to sell their shares for two reasons. First, higher interest rates imply that any given stream of future dividends now has a lower present value (see Chapter 27). Second, higher interest rates will reduce the flow of profits (and dividends) from firms as the economy slows down (which is exactly the intention of the monetary tightening). For both reasons, stocks will be a less attractive investment relative to the alternatives (mainly bonds), and so holders of stocks will decide to sell. Everyone cannot do this, however, because only so many stocks are available to be held at any given time. As all investors try to sell their stocks, prices fall. The fall will stop only when the expected rate of return to investment in stocks, based on their lower purchase price, makes stocks as attractive as alternative investments. Then investors will no longer try to shift out of stocks *en masse*.

Speculative Booms

In addition to responding to a host of factors that reasonably can be expected to influence the earnings of companies, stock prices often develop an upward or downward movement of their own, propelled by little more than speculation that feeds on itself.

In major stock market booms, people begin to expect rising stock prices and hurry to buy while stocks are cheap. This action bids up the prices of shares and creates the capital gains that justify the original expectations. Such a situation is an example of *self-realizing expectations*. Investors get rich on paper, in the sense that the market value of their holdings rises. Money making now looks easy to others, who also rush in to buy stocks, and new purchases push prices up still further. At this stage attention to the firm's actual profits all but ceases. If a stock can yield, say, a 50 percent capital gain in one year, it does not matter much if dividends rise or fall slightly. Everyone is "making money," so more people become attracted to the get-rich-quick opportunities. Their attempts to buy push prices up even further.

Eventually, something breaks the period of unrestrained optimism. Some investors may begin to worry about the very high prices of stocks in relation not only to current dividends but also to possible future dividends, even when generous allowances for growth are made. Or it may be that the prices of stocks become depressed slightly when a sufficiently large number of persons try to sell out in order to realize their capital gains. As they offer their stocks on the market, they cannot find purchasers without some fall in prices. Even a modest price fall may be sufficient to persuade others that it is time to sell. However, every share that is sold must be bought by someone. A wave of sellers may not find new buyers at existing prices, causing prices to fall. Panic selling may now occur.

This is a very simple and stylized description of a speculative cycle, yet it describes the basic elements of market booms and busts that many believe have recurred throughout stock market history. In the United States, it happened in the Jay Cooke panic of 1873 and in the Grover Cleveland panic of 1893.[1] The biggest boom of all began in the mid 1920s and ended on Black Tuesday, October 29, 1929. The collapse was dramatic, with U.S. stocks losing about 50 percent of their value in about two months. Nor did it stop there. For four years stock prices continued to decline, until the average value of stock on the New York Stock Exchange had fallen from its 1929 high of $89.10 per share to $17.35 per share by late 1933.

Speculative behaviour means that stock market prices do not always just reflect the fundamentals that underlie the expected profitability of companies; in this sense, the stock market is sometimes said to be overvalued or undervalued. However, the extent of the over- or undervaluation is difficult to determine, and hence it is hard to predict when, and by how much, prices will "correct." For example, consider the long upswing that increased prices on the TSE by 75 percent between January 1995 and the summer of 1999 (the bull market in the United States was even more dramatic). During this period, the Canadian economy was experiencing a healthy recovery, and the rising stock prices no doubt reflected the resulting favourable profit outlook of companies. However, many doubted that the full increase was justified by underlying business opportunities and hence felt that there may have been a speculative component to the rise in stock values. These people argued (and were

still arguing when this book went to press in the fall of 1999) that a "correction" was long overdue.

Stock Market Swings: Cause or Effect of Business Cycles?

Stock markets tend often to lead, and sometimes to follow, booms and slumps in business activity. In both cases the causes usually run from real business conditions, whether actual or anticipated, to stock market prices. This is the dominant theme: the stock market as a reflector.

Stock market fluctuations are usually a consequence, rather than a cause, of the business cycle.

For example, an economy that is growing steadily over a number of years will generally have rising profits. The increase in profits will cause stock market prices to rise. Conversely, an economy that enters a recession with high unemployment and bankruptcies will naturally have low profits. These low profits will cause stock market prices to fall.

Though we have said that stock market movements are *usually* the consequence of the business cycle, it is *sometimes* true that the stock market is the cause of the business cycle. The value of the stock market influences the wealth of households, which ultimately own the market, either directly or through their pension funds. (The direct holding of stocks by households has become much more common in the past decade with the widespread availability of mutual funds.) And, as we saw in Chapter 22, changes in household wealth lead to changes in desired consumption spending. Thus, as prices rise in the stock market, the increase in household wealth will generally lead to increases in aggregate demand. This will naturally have an effect on real GDP and the price level. In addition, firms use the stock market to issue new shares in order to finance investment spending. When stock market prices are high, they find this a very attractive way to raise new money and thus may choose to undertake new investments, thereby adding to aggregate demand.

For these reasons, many people believed that the dramatic fall in stock value in the October 1987 crash would cause households to curtail their consumption spending in response to their perceived fall in wealth. On this basis many forecasters predicted that the stock market crash would lead to a serious downturn in economy. After the event, such gloom-and-doom forecasts turned out to be inaccurate; apparently, people

[1]For a wonderful discussion of the history of speculative booms (and their aftermath), see John Kenneth Galbraith, *A Short History of Financial Euphoria*, 1990, Viking Press.

did not perceive the fall in the stock market as an indication that their *permanent* incomes or wealth had fallen dramatically, and hence they did not reduce their consumption spending.

Investment Marketplaces or Gambling Casinos?

Stock markets fulfill many important functions. It is doubtful that the great aggregations of capital that are needed to finance modern firms could be raised under a private-ownership system without them. There is no doubt, however, that they also provide an unfortunate attraction for many naive investors, whose get-rich-quick dreams are more often than not destroyed by the fall in prices that follows the occasional speculative booms that they help to create.

To some extent public policy has sought to curb the excesses of stock market speculation through supervision of security issues. Public policy seeks, among other things, to prevent both fraudulent or misleading information and trading by "insiders" (those in a company who have confidential information).

All in all, the stock market is both a real marketplace and a place to gamble. As in all gambling situations, players who are less well informed and less clever than the average player tend to be losers in the long term.

For information on the Toronto Stock Exchange, see its website: www.tse.com.

PART TEN

Macroeconomic Problems and Policies

What causes sustained inflation and how can it be reduced? What is the "natural" rate of unemployment, and how is it affected by labour-market policies such as unemployment insurance? Do government budget deficits raise interest rates, or do they have little or no effect on key macroeconomic variables? Can the market be left to its own to provide long-run economic growth, or are government policies to encourage growth necessary? What explains the different rates of economic growth in developed versus developing countries? These are the sorts of questions you will be able to answer after reading the next five chapters.

This part of the book contains five chapters on key macroeconomic issues. The chapters may be read in any order and each one may be read independently of the others. Chapter 29 discusses the causes of inflation. We will see the important distinction between cyclical inflation and sustained inflation. We examine the Bank of Canada's role in maintaining a sustained inflation, as well as its role in ending one.

In Chapter 30 we discuss unemployment. Two different theories of cyclical unemployment are considered—New Classical and New Keynesian. We then discuss the natural rate of unemployment—often called the Nonaccelerating Inflation Rate of Unemployment (NAIRU). We examine what determines the NAIRU and why several labour-market policies have the unintended consequence of increasing the NAIRU.

Chapter 31 returns us to the issues of fiscal policy, examining in detail government deficits, surpluses, and government debt. We will see how to judge the stance of fiscal policy, as well as the important connection between government deficits and national saving. We will consider under which conditions government deficits raise interest rates, and what happens as a result.

Chapters 32 and 33 examine economic growth. Chapter 32 emphasizes the theory of economic growth, discussing some established theories based on capital accumulation as well as some more recent theories based on endogenous technical change. Chapter 33 then examines the issue of economic growth in the developing economies and examines why some countries have had such slow rates of growth. We then discuss some of the recent views about which policies these countries might implement to improve their growth rates.

CHAPTER 29

Inflation

(LO) LEARNING OBJECTIVES

1 Explain how wage changes are driven by both excess demand and inflationary expectations.

2 Show how constant inflation can be incorporated into the basic macroeconomic model.

3 Understand the effects of aggregate demand and supply shocks on inflation and real GDP.

4 Explain how the Bank of Canada may validate demand and supply shocks.

5 Explain the three phases of a disinflation.

6 Understand how the cost of disinflation can be measured by the sacrifice ratio.

7 Have a general understanding of Canadian inflation policy over the past two decades.

---

inflation A rise in the average level of all prices. Often expressed as the annual percentage change in the Consumer Price Index.

If you are a typical reader of this book, you were born in the late 1970s or early 1980s. By the time you were old enough to notice some economic developments going on around you, it was the early 1990s. By that time, the rate of inflation in Canada was less than 5 percent per year. Thus, unless you are older than the typical student taking a course in introductory economics, or you have come to Canada recently from a high-inflation country, inflation has not been a significant phenomenon in your life. But it is not so long ago that inflation was considered to be a serious problem in Canada (and many other countries as well).

Recall from Chapter 19 that **inflation** is a rise in the average level of prices—that is, a rise in the price level. If you look again at Figure 19-5 in Chapter 19, you will see that inflation was relatively low throughout the 1960s. Starting in the late 1960s, the inflation rate slowly rose, reaching the double-digit range by the mid 1970s. It fell only slightly during the late 1970s, despite a concerted anti-inflationary policy, and rose again to the double-digit level in 1980. It remained quite high during the recession of 1981–1982, fell dramatically to 4 percent in 1983, and remained near that figure through 1987. Although this was an improvement over the double-digit inflation rates experienced earlier, 4 percent was, historically, a high inflation rate to be experienced at the end of a serious recession.

During the latter half of 1988, after several years of a vigorous economic recovery, the inflation rate crept up to over 5 percent, where it stayed through 1989 and the early part of 1990. The Bank of Canada's attempt to reduce inflation—first back to the 4 percent level and then down to below 2 percent—caused renewed controversy about the methods, the costs, and the benefits of fighting inflation. By mid 1999, inflation was between 1 and 2 percent and had been there for about 7 years. In recent years some economists have begun questioning whether inflation at such low levels is actually *bad* for the economy.

We now turn to the subject of inflation in detail. What causes inflation? What are the costs of reducing it? Can inflation be prevented from rising into the double-digit range again? Can inflation ever be too low?

To compute the total inflation from the day of your birth to today, check out the "inflation calculator" at the Bank of Canada's website: www.bank-banque-canada.ca.

Adding Inflation to the Model

In the previous several chapters we examined the effects of shocks to aggregate demand and aggregate supply. Such shocks influenced the values of both real GDP and the price level. Following these shocks, the economy's adjustment mechanism always brought the economy back to the potential level of real GDP with a stable price level. In other words, any inflation that we have so far seen in our macroeconomic model was temporary—it only existed while the economy was adjusting to its long-run equilibrium.

In this chapter we want to understand how a *sustained* inflation can exist, and how we modify our model to account for its presence. After all, even though inflation in Canada is very low, it still appears to be sustained at a rate of between 1 and 2 percent per year.

As we will soon see, the key to understanding sustained inflation is to understand the role of *inflation expectations*. When combined with excess demand or excess supply, as reflected by the economy's output gap, such expectations give us a more complete understanding of why wages (and therefore prices) change. Let's begin our analysis by examining in more detail why wages change.

Why Wages Change

In Chapter 25, increases in wages led to increases in unit costs because we maintained the assumption that technology (and thus productivity) was held constant. We continue with that assumption in this chapter. Thus, as wages and other factor prices rise, unit costs increase and the *SRAS* curve shifts up. Conversely, when wages and other factor prices fall, unit costs fall and the *SRAS* curve shifts down.

But what are the forces that cause wages (and, similarly, other factor prices) to change? Two of the main forces are the demand for labour and expectations of future inflation.[1] Much of what we discuss in the case of labour demand was first seen in Chapter 25, but the points are important enough to bear repeating.

Labour Demand and the NAIRU

In Chapter 25, we encountered three propositions about how changes in money wages were influenced by the relationship between aggregate demand and aggregate supply:

---

[1]Wages may be affected by other forces that are associated with neither excess demand nor expectations of inflation, such as government guidelines, union power, and employers' optimism. Because there are many such forces that tend to act independently of one another, they may be regarded as random shocks and must be analysed as separate causes for shifts in the *SRAS* curve.

The ways, Changes in wages are related to AD, AS

1. The excess demand for labour that is associated with an inflationary gap puts upward pressure on money wages.

2. The excess supply of labour associated with a recessionary gap puts downward pressure on money wages.

3. The absence of either an inflationary or a recessionary gap means that demand forces do not exert any pressure on money wages.[2]

When real GDP is equal to its potential level (Y^*), the unemployment rate is said to be equal to the NAIRU, which stands for the *nonaccelerating inflation rate of unemployment*. The use of this particular name will be explained later in this chapter. Another name sometimes used in place of NAIRU is the *natural rate of unemployment*, but NAIRU is now the more common usage. It is designated here by the symbol U^*.

The NAIRU is not zero. Instead, even when output equals potential output, there may be a substantial amount of *frictional* and *structural* unemployment caused, for example, by the movement of people between jobs or between regions. When real output exceeds potential output ($Y > Y^*$), the unemployment rate will be less than the NAIRU ($U < U^*$). When real output is less than potential output ($Y < Y^*$), the unemployment rate will exceed the NAIRU ($U > U^*$).

We have seen that wages and unit costs react to various pressures of demand. These demand pressures can be stated either in terms of the relationship between actual and potential output or in terms of the relationship between the actual unemployment rate and the NAIRU. When $Y > Y^*$ (or $U < U^*$), there is an inflationary gap characterized by excess demand for labour. Wages and unit costs tend to rise. Conversely, when $Y < Y^*$ (or $U > U^*$), there is a recessionary gap characterized by excess supply of labour. Wages and unit costs tend to fall.

This relationship between the excess demand or supply of labour and the rate of change of money wages is represented by the Phillips Curve, which we first discussed in Chapter 25.

Expected Inflation

A second force that can influence wages is *expectations* of future inflation. Suppose that both employers and employees expect 4 percent inflation next year. Workers will start negotiations from a base of a 4 percent increase in money wages, which would hold their *real wages* constant. Firms will also be inclined to begin bargaining by conceding at least a 4 percent increase in money wages because they expect that the prices at which they sell their products will rise by 4 percent. Starting from that base, workers may attempt to obtain some desired increase in their real wages. At this point, such factors as profits and bargaining power become important.

The expectation of some specific inflation rate creates pressure for wages to rise by that rate and hence for unit costs to rise at that rate.

The key point is that money wages can be rising even if no inflationary gap is present. As long as people *expect* prices to rise, their behaviour will put upward pressure on money wages, causing unit costs to rise, thus shifting the *SRAS* curve upward.

---

[2]As in Chapter 25, we are holding productivity constant in our analysis in this chapter. Otherwise, output gaps would cause changes in wages *relative to productivity*.

The Formation of Expectations

The way people form their expectations about future inflation may have an important effect on that inflation. Generally, we can distinguish two main patterns: One is to look backward at past experience; the other is to look at current circumstances for a clue as to what may happen in the near future.

The first type of expectations are called *backward-looking*. People look at the past in order to predict what will happen in the future. The simplest possible form of such expectations is to expect the past to be repeated in the future. According to this view, if inflation has been 5 percent over the past year, people will expect it to be 5 percent next year. This expectation, however, is quite naive. Everyone knows that the inflation rate does change, and therefore the past cannot be a perfectly accurate guide to the future.

A less naive version has people revise their expectations in light of the mistakes that they made in estimating inflation in the past. For example, if you thought that this year's inflation rate was going to be 5 percent but it turned out to be only 3 percent, you might revise your estimate of next year's rate down somewhat from 5 percent.

Backward-looking expectations tend to change slowly because some time must pass before a change in the actual rate of inflation provides enough past experience to cause expectations to adjust.

The second main type of expectations are those that look to current conditions to estimate what is likely to happen in the future. One version of this type assumes that people look to the government's current macroeconomic policy to form their expectations of future inflation. They are assumed to understand how the economy works, and they form their expectations by predicting the outcome of the policies now being followed. In an obvious sense, such expectations are *forward-looking*.

A strong version of forward-looking expectations is called **rational expectations.** Rational expectations are not necessarily always correct; rather, the *rational expectations hypothesis* assumes that people make the best possible use of all the available information. One implication is that they will not continue to make persistent, systematic errors when forming their expectations. Thus, if the economic system about which they are forming expectations remains stable, their expectations will be correct *on average*. Sometimes next year's inflation rate will turn out to be above what people expected it to be; at other times, it will turn out to be below what people expected it to be. On average over many years, however, the actual rate will not, according to the rational expectations theory, be consistently under- or overestimated.

Forward-looking expectations can adjust quickly to changes in events. Instead of being based on past inflation rates, expected inflation is based on expected economic conditions and government policies.

The importance of rational expectations in the study of macroeconomics is reflected by the fact that the economist most closely associated with the development of the idea, Robert E. Lucas Jr. of the University of Chicago, was awarded the Nobel Prize in 1995 for his work in this area.

Assuming that expectations are solely backward-looking seems overly naive. People do look ahead and assess future possibilities rather than just blindly reacting to what has gone before. Yet the assumption of "fully rational" forward-looking expectations requires workers and firms to have a degree of understanding of the economy that few economists would claim to have.

Of course, people will not make the same error of consistently underpredicting (or overpredicting) the inflation rate for decades, but evidence suggests that they can do so

Practise with Study Guide Chapter 29, Exercise 2.

rational expectations
The theory that people understand how the economy works and learn quickly from their mistakes so that even though random errors may be made, systematic and persistent errors are not.

for substantial periods, especially when they do not fully understand the causes of current inflation. Every past period of inflation has led to intense debate among economists about its causes, cures, and probable future course. If professional economists are uncertain, it would be surprising if wage and price setters made correct predictions on average over any short period of time.

The actual process of wage setting probably combines forward-looking behaviour with expectations based on the experience of the recent past. Depending on the circumstances, expectations will sometimes tend to rely more on past experience and at other times more on present events whose effects are expected to influence the future.

Overall Effect

We can now think of changes in money wages as resulting from two different forces:

$$\begin{array}{c} \text{Change in} \\ \text{Money Wages} \end{array} = \begin{array}{c} \text{Excess-} \\ \text{Demand} \\ \text{Effect} \end{array} + \begin{array}{c} \text{Expectational} \\ \text{Effect} \end{array}$$

It is important to realize that what happens to wages is the *net* effect of the two forces. Consider two examples.

First, suppose that both labour and management expect 3 percent inflation next year and are therefore willing to allow money wages to increase by 3 percent. Doing so would leave *real* wages unchanged. Suppose as well that there is a significant inflationary gap with an associated labour shortage. The demand pressure causes wages to rise by an additional 2 percentage points. The final outcome is that wages rise by 5 percent, the net effect of a 3 percent increase due to expected inflation and a 2 percent increase due to demand forces.

For the second example, assume again that expected inflation is 3 percent, but that this time there is a recessionary gap. The associated heavy unemployment exerts downward pressure on wage bargains. Hence, the demand effect now works to dampen wage increases, say, to the extent of 2 percentage points. Wages therefore rise by 1 percent, the net effect of a 3 percent increase due to expected inflation and a 2 percent decrease due to demand forces.

From Wages to Prices

We saw in Chapter 24 and 25 that shifts in the SRAS curve depend on what happens to factor prices. We have just seen that inflationary gaps and expectations of future inflation put pressure on wages to rise and hence cause the SRAS curve to shift upward. Recessionary gaps and expectations of future deflation put pressure on wages to fall and hence cause the SRAS curve to shift downward.

The net effect of the two forces acting on wages—excess demand and inflation expectations—determines what happens to the SRAS curve.

If the net effect of the demand and expectational forces is to raise wages, then the SRAS curve will shift up. This shift will cause the price level to rise—that is, the forces pushing up wages will be *inflationary*. On the other hand, if the net effect of the demand and expectational forces is to reduce wages, then the SRAS curve will shift down—the forces reducing wages will be *deflationary*.

This link between wages and prices implies that our previous decomposition of wage changes into separate forces also holds for inflation. But because the SRAS curve can also shift for reasons unrelated to changes in wages, we must complicate the story slightly. Specifically, we must consider the effect of non-wage supply shocks on the *SRAS* curve and thus on the price level. The best example of a non-wage supply shock is a change in the prices of raw materials. We can then decompose actual inflation into its three component parts:

$$\text{Actual Inflation} = \text{Excess-Demand Inflation} + \text{Expected Inflation} + \text{Supply-Shock Inflation}$$

For example, consider an economy that begins with real GDP equal to potential GDP and expectations of inflation are zero. In this case, the first two terms on the right-hand side are zero. But if an adverse supply shock occurs, such as a significant increase in the price of imported raw materials, then the *SRAS* curve shifts up and the price level rises. Actual inflation will be positive. As we will see later in the chapter, such supply shocks are not uncommon, and they generate problems for the conduct of monetary policy.

Having discussed the component parts of the inflation process, we are now in a position to see how sustained inflation can be included in our macroeconomic model.

Constant Inflation

We now know what forces cause wages to change, and how the change in wages leads to changes in the price level. So what would a constant inflation of, say, 5 percent per year look like in our macroeconomic model? To answer this question we need to consider two things. First, we must distinguish between the excess demand and expectational components of inflation. Second, we must consider the way people form their expectations of inflation. In what follows, we simplify the setting by assuming that no supply shocks occur (we address them later in the chapter).

Actual and Expected Inflation

Suppose the inflation rate is 5 percent per year and has been 5 percent for several years. This is what we mean by a *constant* inflation. In such a setting, people with backward-looking expectations about inflation will expect the actual level to continue into the future. Furthermore, in the absence of any announcements that the central bank will be attempting to alter the rate of inflation, people with forward-looking expectations will expect the actual inflation rate to continue. Thus, for the economy as a whole, the expected rate of inflation will equal the actual rate of inflation.

The Conference Board of Canada conducts a regular survey about people's expectations about inflation. See their website at: www.conferenceboard.ca.

If inflation and monetary policy have been constant for several years, the expected rate of inflation will equal the actual rate of inflation.

In the absence of temporary supply shocks, the equality of actual and expected inflation implies something about the amount of demand inflation. Since actual inflation equals excess-demand inflation plus expected inflation, it immediately follows that actual and expected inflation can only be equal if there is *no* excess-demand inflation. This, in turn, implies that there is no inflationary (or recessionary) gap—real GDP must equal its potential level, Y^*.

If expected inflation equals actual inflation, real GDP must be equal to potential GDP.

Expectational Inflation

But if there is no excess demand, what is causing the inflation? The answer is that peoples' *expectations* are causing inflation. Figure 29-1 shows a constant inflation that is purely

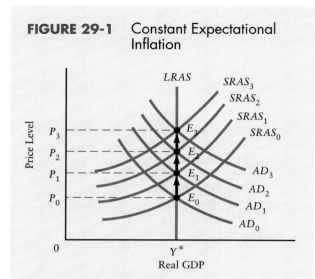

FIGURE 29-1   Constant Expectational Inflation

A constant expectational inflation is only possible when $Y=Y^*$. Expectations of a constant rate of inflation cause wages and thus the *SRAS* curve to shift upward at a uniform rate from $SRAS_0$ to $SRAS_1$ to $SRAS_2$. Monetary validation is causing the *AD* curve to shift upward at the same time from AD_0 to AD_1 to AD_2. As a result, real GDP remains at Y^*. The constant inflation rate takes the price level from P_0 to P_1 to P_2. Wage costs are rising due to expectations of inflation, and these expectations are being fulfilled.

expectational. But as we will now see, in order for a purely expectational inflation to continue, the central bank must be *validating* the expectations by constantly increasing the money supply. Let's see how this works.

Suppose that both workers and employers expect 4 percent inflation over the coming years and that employers are therefore prepared to increase wages by 4 percent per year. As wages rise by 4 percent, the *SRAS* curve shifts up by that amount. But, in order for 4 percent to be the *actual* rate of inflation, the intersection of the *SRAS* and *AD* curves must be shifting up at the rate of 4 percent. This requires the *AD* curve to be shifting up at the same 4 percent rate—this *AD* shift is caused by the growth of the money supply. So in this case there is no excess-demand inflation ($Y=Y^*$), and actual and expected inflation are equal. When the central bank increases the money supply at such a rate that the expectations of inflation end up being correct, it is said to be *validating* the expectations.

Constant inflation with $Y=Y^*$ occurs when the rate of monetary growth, the rate of wage increase, and the expected rate of inflation are all consistent with the actual inflation rate.

The key point about constant, purely expectational inflation is that there is no excess-demand effect operating on wages. Wages rise at the expected rate of inflation. The labour shortages that accompany an inflationary gap are absent, as are the labour surpluses that accompany a recessionary gap.

Shocks and Policy Responses

We have now seen how our macroeconomic model can incorporate a constant rate of inflation. Analysing constant inflation is very useful because it helps us understand some details about our macroeconomic model. But it is a special case because, as we saw above, there was no inflationary (or recessionary) gap putting pressure on inflation. We now want to go on and understand some more complicated situations where an aggregate demand or supply shock creates an output gap, and this gap, in turn, creates inflationary pressures. In this case, we will see how inflationary gaps and expectations both are important for understanding inflation.

Demand Shocks

demand inflation
Inflation arising from excess aggregate demand, that is, when actual GDP exceeds potential GDP.

Inflation that is caused by a rightward shift in the *AD* curve is called **demand inflation**. The shift in the *AD* curve could have been caused by a reduction in taxes, by an increase in such autonomous expenditure items as investment, government, and net exports, or by an increase in the money supply.

Major demand-shock inflations occurred in Canada during and after World Wars I and II. In these cases, large increases in government expenditure without fully offsetting increases in taxes led to general excess demand. More generally, demand inflation sometimes occurs at the end of a strong upswing, as rising output causes excess demand to develop simultaneously in the markets for labour, intermediate goods, and final output.

To begin our study of demand inflation, suppose that an initial long-run equilibrium is disturbed by a rightward shift in the AD curve. This shift causes the price level and output to rise. It is important next to distinguish between the case in which the Bank of Canada validates the demand shock and the case in which it does not.

No Monetary Validation

Because the initial rise in AD takes output above potential, an inflationary gap opens up. The pressure of excess demand soon causes wages to rise, shifting the SRAS curve upward and to the left. As long as the Bank of Canada holds the money supply constant, the rise in the price level moves the economy upward and to the left along the new AD curve, reducing the inflationary gap. Eventually, the gap is eliminated, and equilibrium is established at a higher but stable price level, with output at its potential level. In this case, the initial period of inflation is followed by further inflation that lasts only until the new equilibrium is reached.

The case of a non-validated demand shock was examined in detail in Chapter 25. It is shown again in Figure 29-2.

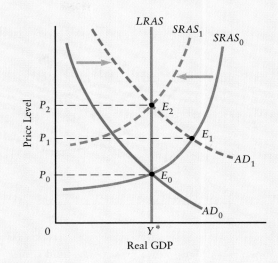

FIGURE 29-2 A Demand Shock with No Validation

A demand shock that is not validated produces temporary inflation, but the economy's adjustment process eventually restores potential GDP and stable prices. The initial long-run equilibrium is at P_0 and Y^*. A positive demand shock shifts AD_0 to AD_1, generating an inflationary gap. The excess demand puts upward pressure on wages, thus shifting $SRAS_0$ to $SRAS_1$. There is inflation as the economy moves from E_0 to E_1 to E_2, but at E_2 the price level is stable.

Monetary Validation

Suppose that after the demand shock has created an inflationary gap, the Bank of Canada increases the money supply whenever output starts to fall. This case takes us beyond our discussions in earlier chapters. It is analysed in Figure 29-3.

Two forces are now brought into play. Spurred by the inflationary gap, the increase in wages causes the SRAS curve to shift upward and to the left. Fueled by the expansionary monetary policy, however, the AD curve shifts to the right. As a result of both of these shifts, the price level rises, but real GDP need not fall. Indeed, if the shift in the AD curve *exactly* offsets the shift in the SRAS curve, real GDP and the inflationary gap will remain constant.

Continued validation of a demand shock turns what would have been transitory inflation into sustained inflation fueled by monetary expansion.

Supply Shocks

Any rise in the price level originating from increases in costs that are *not caused by excess demand* in the markets for factors of production is called **supply inflation**.

supply inflation
A rise in the price level originating from increases in costs that are not caused by excess demand in the domestic markets for factors of production.

FIGURE 29-3   A Demand Shock with Validation

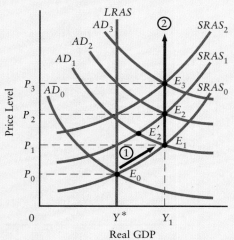

Monetary validation of a positive demand shock causes the *AD* curve to shift further to the right, offsetting the leftward shift in the *SRAS* curve and thereby leaving an inflationary gap despite the ever-rising price level. An initial demand shock shifts equilibrium from E_0 to E_1, taking output to Y_1 and the price level to P_1. The resulting inflationary gap then causes the *SRAS* curve to shift to the left. This time, however, the Bank of Canada validates the demand shock by increasing the money supply. As the money supply is increased, the *AD* curve shifts to the right. By the time the aggregate supply curve has reached $SRAS_1$, the aggregate demand curve has reached AD_2. Now instead of being at E_2', equilibrium is at E_2. Output remains constant at Y_1 leaving the inflationary gap constant while the price level rises to P_2.

The persistent inflationary gap continues to push the *SRAS* curve to the left, while the continued monetary validation continues to push the *AD* curve to the right. As long as this monetary validation continues, the economy moves along the vertical path of arrow 2.

An example of a supply shock is a rise in the costs of imported raw materials. Another is a rise in domestic wage costs per unit of output. The rise in wage costs may occur, as we saw earlier, because of generally held expectations of future inflation. If both employers and employees expect inflation, money wages are likely to rise in anticipation of that inflation. These shocks cause the *SRAS* curve to shift upward.[3] Though negative supply shocks are quite common (occurring, for example, every time the prices of raw materials increase), the most significant examples occurred in 1974 and 1979–80 when OPEC restricted the supply of oil and sharply increased world oil prices. We discuss the 1974 OPEC oil shock shortly.

The initial effects of any negative supply shock are that the equilibrium price level rises while equilibrium output falls. The rise in the price level shows up as a temporary burst of inflation. These effects were first discussed in Chapter 24. Although we now wish to go beyond that earlier discussion, we will begin by repeating it in Figure 29-4, which compares the original equilibrium with the equilibrium after the supply shock.

As with the case of a demand shock, what happens next depends on how the Bank of Canada reacts. If the Bank responds by increasing the money supply, it validates the supply shock; if it holds the money supply constant, the shock is not validated.

No Monetary Validation

The leftward shift in the *SRAS* curve in Figure 29-4 causes the price level to rise and pushes output below its potential level, opening up a recessionary gap. Pressure mounts for money wages and other factor prices to fall. As wages and other factor prices fall, unit costs will fall. Consequently, the *SRAS* curve shifts rightward, increasing equilibrium output while reducing the price level. The *SRAS* curve will continue to shift, stopping only when real GDP is returned to its potential level and the price level is returned to its initial value of P_0. Thus, the period of inflation accompanying the original supply shock is eventually followed by a period of *deflation* (negative inflation) that continues until the initial long-run equilibrium is reestablished.

A major concern in this case is the speed of the adjustment, which in earlier chapters was referred to as the second asymmetry of aggregate supply. If wages do not fall rapidly in the face of excess supply in the labour market, the adjustment back to potential output can take a very long time. For example, suppose that the original shock raised costs

---

[3]Such changes in factor prices shift the *SRAS* curve but do not affect the *LRAS* curve. We discuss changes in the *LRAS* curve in Chapter 32 when we examine the process of technological change and long-term economic growth.

by 6 percent. To reverse this shock, unit costs must fall by 6 percent. If money wages fell by only 2 percent per year it would take three years to complete the adjustment.[4]

Whenever factor prices fall only slowly in the face of excess supply, the recovery to potential output after a nonvalidated negative supply shock will take a long time.

Concern that such a lengthy adjustment will occur is the motive that often lies behind the strong pressure on the Bank of Canada to validate negative supply shocks.

Monetary Validation

Now let us see what happens if the money supply is changed in response to a negative supply shock. Suppose that the central bank decides to validate the supply shock because it believes that factor prices fall only slowly. The monetary validation shifts the AD curve to the right and causes both the price level and output to *rise*. As the recessionary gap is eliminated, the price level rises further, rather than falling back to its original value as it did when the supply shock was not validated. These effects are also illustrated in Figure 29-4.

Monetary validation of a negative supply shock causes the initial rise in the price level to be followed by a further rise, resulting in a higher price level than would occur if the recessionary gap were relied on to reduce factor prices.

The most dramatic example of a supply-shock inflation came in the wake of the first OPEC oil-price shock. In 1974, the countries who were members of the Organization of Petroleum Exporting Countries (OPEC) agreed to restrict output. Their action caused a dramatic increase in the prices of petroleum and many petroleum-related products such as fertilizer and chemicals. The resulting increase in industrial costs shifted $SRAS$ curves upward in all industrial countries. At this time, the Bank of Canada validated the supply shock with large increases in the money supply, whereas the Fed (the U.S. central bank) did not. As the theory predicts, Canada experienced a large increase in its price level but almost no recession, and the United States experienced a much smaller increase in its price level but a severe recession.

[4]Nominal wages rarely fall because there is ongoing productivity growth that offsets the effect on wages of excess supply. But in this chapter we are holding productivity constant so that we can focus on the causes and consequences of inflation. Productivity growth is addressed in Chapter 32.

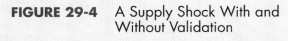

FIGURE 29-4   A Supply Shock With and Without Validation

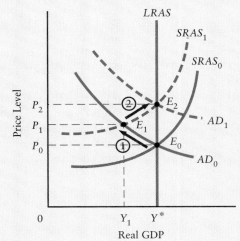

Adverse supply shocks initially raise prices while lowering output. An adverse supply shock causes the $SRAS$ curve to shift leftward from $SRAS_0$ to $SRAS_1$, as shown by arrow 1. Equilibrium is established at E_1. If there is no monetary validation, the reduction in factor prices makes the $SRAS$ curve shift slowly back to the right, to $SRAS_0$. If there is monetary validation, the AD curve shifts from AD_0 to AD_1, as shown by arrow 2. This reestablishes equilibrium at E_2 with output equal to potential output but with a higher price level, P_2.

A contract settlement that raises wages for a large number of workers will increase firms' costs and shift the SRAS curve upward and to the left.

For information on OPEC, see their website: www.opec.org.

Is Monetary Validation of Supply Shocks Desirable?

Suppose the central bank validates a negative supply shock and thus prevents what could otherwise be a protracted recession. Expressed in this way, monetary validation sounds like a good policy. Unfortunately, however, there is also a possible cost associated with this policy. The effect of the monetary validation is to extend the period of inflation. If this inflation leads firms and workers to expect *further* inflation, then point E_2 in Figure 29-4 will not be the end of the story. As expectations for further inflation develop, the *SRAS* curve will continue to shift upward. But if the central bank continues its policy of validation, then the *AD* curve will also continue to shift upward. It may not take long before the economy is in a *wage-price spiral*.

Once started, a wage-price spiral can be halted only if the Bank of Canada stops validating the supply shocks that are causing the inflation. But the longer it waits to do so, the more firmly held will be the *expectations* that it will continue its policy of validating the shocks. These entrenched expectations may cause wages to continue rising even after validation has ceased. Because employers expect prices to rise, they go on granting wage increases. If expectations are entrenched firmly enough, the wage push can continue for quite some time, in spite of the downward pressure caused by the rising unemployment associated with the growing recessionary gap.

Because of this possibility, many economists argue that the wage-price spiral should not be allowed to begin. One way to ensure that it does not begin is to refuse to validate any supply shock whatsoever.

To some economists, caution dictates that no supply shock should ever be validated, lest a wage-price spiral be created. Other economists are willing to risk validation in order to avoid the significant, though transitory, recessions that otherwise accompany them.

Accelerating Inflation

Consider a situation where a demand or supply shock increases real GDP above Y^*. Furthermore, suppose the central bank tries to maintain real GDP at this higher level. Can the central bank achieve this objective? If so, what is the effect on inflation?

acceleration hypothesis   The hypothesis that when real GDP is held above potential, the persistent inflationary gap will cause inflation to accelerate.

What happens to the rate of inflation is predicted by the **acceleration hypothesis,** which holds that when the central bank engages in whatever rate of monetary expansion is needed to hold the inflationary gap constant, the actual inflation rate will *accelerate.* The Bank of Canada may start by validating 3 percent inflation, but soon 3 percent will become 4 percent and, if the Bank insists on validating 4 percent, the rate will become 5 percent, and so on without limit, until the Bank finally stops its validation.

There are several steps in the reasoning behind this hypothesis. The first concerns the development of inflationary expectations.

Expectational Effects

Recall our earlier discussion in this chapter about how actual inflation can be decomposed into its component parts of excess demand, expectations, and non-wage supply shocks. It is worth restating:

$$\text{Actual Inflation} = \text{Excess-Demand Inflation} + \text{Expected Inflation} + \text{Supply-Shock Inflation}$$

To illustrate the importance of expectations in accelerating inflation, suppose that the inflationary gap creates sufficient excess demand to push up wages by 2 percent per year. As a result, the *SRAS* curve will also tend to be rising at 2 percent per year.

When inflation has persisted for some time, however, people may come to expect that the inflation will continue. The expectation of 2 percent inflation will tend to push up wages by that amount *in addition to* the demand pressure. As the demand effect on wages is augmented by the expectational effect, the *SRAS* curve will begin to shift upward more rapidly. When expectations are for a 2 percent inflation and demand pressure is also pushing wages up by 2 percent, the overall effect will be a 4 percent increase in wages. Sooner or later, however, 4 percent inflation will come to be expected, and the expectational effect will rise to 4 percent. This new expectational component of 4 percent, when added to the demand component, will create an inflation rate of 6 percent. And so this cycle will go on. As long as there is a demand effect arising from an inflationary gap and as long as actual inflation is equal to the demand effect plus the expectational effect, the inflation rate cannot stay constant because expectations will always be revised upward toward the actual inflation rate.

More Rapid Monetary Validation Required

The second step in the argument is that if the Bank of Canada still wishes to hold the level of output constant, it must increase the rate at which the money supply is growing. This action is necessary because to hold real GDP constant, the *AD* curve must be shifted at an increasingly rapid pace to offset the increasingly rapid shifts in the *SRAS* curve, which are driven by the continually rising rate of expected inflation.

An Increasing Rate of Inflation

The third step in the argument is that the rate of inflation must now be increasing because of the increasingly rapid upward shifts in both the *AD* and *SRAS* curves. The rise in the actual inflation rate will in turn cause an increase in the expected inflation rate. This will then cause the actual inflation rate to increase, which will in turn increase the expected inflation rate, and so on. The net result is a *continually increasing rate of inflation*. Now we see the reason for the name NAIRU. At any level of unemployment less than the NAIRU, real GDP is above Y^*, and the inflation rate tends to accelerate. Thus, the NAIRU is the lowest level of unemployment consistent with a *nonaccelerating* rate of inflation.

According to the acceleration hypothesis, as long as an inflationary gap persists, expectations of inflation will be rising, which will lead to increases in the actual rate of inflation.

The tendency for inflation to accelerate is discussed further in *Extensions in Theory 29-1*, which examines how expected inflation affects the position of the Phillips curve.

Inflation as a Monetary Phenomenon

A long-standing debate among economists concerns the extent to which inflation is a monetary phenomenon. Does it have purely monetary causes—changes in the demand or the supply of money? Does it have purely monetary consequences—only the price level is affected? One slogan that states an extreme position on this issue was popularized

EXTENSIONS IN THEORY 29-1
The Phillips Curve and Accelerating Inflation

As we first saw in Chapter 25, the Phillips curve describes the relationship between unemployment (or output) and the rate of change of wages. The Phillips curve was born in 1958 when Professor A.W. Phillips from the London School of Economics noted a relationship between unemployment and the rate of change of wages over a period of 100 years in the United Kingdom. Phillips was interested in studying the short-run behaviour of an economy subjected to cyclical fluctuations. In the years following Phillips's study, however, some economists treated the Phillips curve as estab-

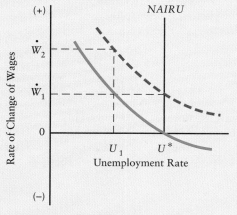

(i) Wage changes and unemployment

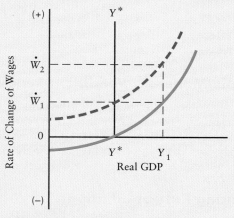

(ii) Wage changes and output

many years ago by Milton Friedman: "Inflation is *everywhere* and *always* a monetary phenomenon." To consider these issues, let us summarize what we have learned already. First, look at the *causes* of inflation:

- *Cause 1:* On the demand side, anything that shifts the AD curve to the right will cause the price level to rise.
- *Cause 2:* On the supply side, anything that increases factor prices will shift the SRAS curve to the left and cause the price level to rise.
- *Cause 3:* Unless continual monetary expansion occurs, the increases in the price level must eventually come to a halt.

The first two points provide the sense in which, in regard to causes, a temporary burst of inflation need not be a monetary phenomenon. It need not have monetary causes, and it need not be accompanied by monetary expansion. The third point provides the sense in which *sustained* inflation *must* be a monetary phenomenon. If a rise in prices is to continue indefinitely, it *must* be accompanied by continuing increases in the money supply. This is true regardless of the cause that set the inflation in motion.

Now, let us summarize the *consequences* of inflation, assuming that real GDP was initially at its potential level.

lishing a long-term tradeoff between inflation and unemployment.

Suppose the government stabilizes output at Y_1 (and hence the unemployment rate at U_1), as shown in the accompanying figures. To do this, it must validate the ensuing wage inflation, which is indicated by $\dot{W}_1$ in the figure. The government thus seems to be able to choose among particular combinations of inflation and unemployment, in which lower levels of unemployment are attained at the cost of higher rates of inflation.

In the 1960s, Phillips curves were fitted to the data for many countries, and governments made decisions about where they wished to be on the tradeoff between inflation and unemployment. Then, in the late 1960s, in country after country, the rate of wage and price inflation associated with any given level of unemployment began to rise. Instead of being stable, the Phillips curves began to shift upward. The explanation lay primarily in a shifting relationship between the pressure of demand and wage increases due to inflationary expectations, as we discussed in the text.

It was gradually understood that the original Phillips curve concerned only the influence of demand and left out inflationary expectations. This omission proved important and unfortunate. An increase in expected inflation shows up as an upward shift in the original Phillips curve that was drawn in Chapter 25. The importance of expectations can be shown by drawing what is called an **expectations-augmented Phillips curve**, as seen here. The heights of the Phillips curves above the axis at Y^* and at U^* show the expected inflation rate. These distances represent the amount that wages will rise when neither excess demand nor excess supply pressures are being felt in labour markets. The actual wage increase is shown by the augmented (dashed) curve, with the increase in wages exceeding expected inflation whenever $Y > Y^*$ ($U < U^*$) and falling short of expected inflation whenever $Y < Y^*$ ($U > U^*$).

Now we can see what was wrong with the idea of a stable inflation-unemployment tradeoff. Targeting a particular output Y_1 or unemployment U_1 in the figures is fine only if no inflation is expected. But getting to Y_1 or U_1 itself requires some inflation ($\dot{W}_1$). And once this rate of inflation comes to be expected, people will demand that much just to hold their own. The Phillips curve will shift upward to the position shown in the figures. Now there is inflation $\dot{W}_2$ because of the combined effects of expectations and excess demand. However, this higher rate is above the expected rate ($\dot{W}_1$). Once this higher rate comes to be expected, the Phillips curve will shift upward once again.

As a result of the combination of excess-demand inflation and expectational inflation, the inflation rate associated with any given positive output gap ($Y > Y^*$ or $U < U^*$) rises over time. This is the phenomenon of accelerating inflation that we discussed in the text.

The shifts in the Phillips curve are such that most economists agree that in the long run, when inflationary expectations have fully adjusted to actual inflation, there is no tradeoff between inflation and unemployment. That is, they believe that the long-run Phillips curve is a vertical line at the NAIRU.

---

expectations-augmented Phillips curve The relationship between unemployment and the rate of increase of money wages that arises when the demand and expectations components of inflation are combined.

- *Consequence 1:* In the short run, demand-shock inflation tends to be accompanied by an *increase* in real GDP above its potential level.
- *Consequence 2:* In the short run, supply-shock inflation tends to be accompanied by a *decrease* in real GDP below its potential level.
- *Consequence 3:* When all costs and prices are adjusted *fully* (so that the relevant aggregate supply curve is the *LRAS* curve), shifts in either the *AD* or *SRAS* curve leave real GDP unchanged and affect only the price level.

The first two points provide a sense in which, in terms of consequences, inflation is not, in the short run, a purely monetary phenomenon. The third point provides the sense in which inflation is a purely monetary phenomenon from the point of view of long-run equilibrium.

There is still plenty of room for debate, however, on how long the short run will last. Most economists believe that the short run can be long enough for inflation to have major real effects.

We have now reached three important conclusions:

- *Conclusion 1:* Without monetary validation, demand shocks cause temporary bursts of inflation that are accompanied by inflationary gaps. The gaps are removed as rising

Not Responsible for anything in this Chapter.

factor prices push the *SRAS* curve to the left, returning real GDP to its potential level, but at a higher price level.

- *Conclusion 2:* Without monetary validation, negative supply shocks cause temporary bursts of inflation that are accompanied by recessionary gaps. The gaps are removed as factor prices fall, restoring real GDP to its potential and the price level to its initial level.
- *Conclusion 3:* Only with continuing monetary validation can inflation initiated by either supply or demand shocks continue indefinitely.

Reducing Inflation

Suppose an economy has had a sustained rate of inflation for several years. What must the central bank do to reduce the rate of inflation? What are the costs involved in doing so?

The Process of Disinflation

disinflation The process of reducing the rate of inflation.

Disinflation means a reduction in the rate of inflation. In recent years, Canada has had two notable periods of disinflation—in 1981–82 when inflation fell from 12 percent to 4 percent, and in 1990–92 when inflation fell from 5 percent to just over 1 percent.

Reducing the rate of inflation takes time and involves major costs. The process begins when the Bank of Canada stops validating the ongoing inflation. It does this by lowering the rate of growth of the money supply below the rate of growth of money demand, thus creating an excess demand for money. This action forces up interest rates and lowers real aggregate demand, reducing any existing inflationary gap. We will soon see that it is usually necessary for the Bank to go further, creating a substantial recessionary gap that persists until the inflation is eliminated.

The process involves many costs. The recessionary gap hurts all who suffer in recessions, including the unemployed workers and the owners of firms who lose profits and risk bankruptcy. Unemployed resources mean lower output than would otherwise be produced. The temporary rise in interest rates hurts borrowers, including people with mortgages and firms with large loans. Among these groups who are most exposed and may lose their wealth are young households with large mortgages and small firms that have taken on large debts to finance expansions.

Disinflation is thus a classic case of a policy that brings short-term pain for long-term gain. Inevitably, the question arises: Are the future benefits worth the immediate costs?

Reducing sustained inflation quickly incurs high costs for a short period of time; reducing it slowly incurs lower costs but for a longer period of time.

The process of reducing sustained inflation can be divided into three phases. In the first phase, the monetary validation is stopped and the inflationary gap is eliminated. In the second phase, the economy still suffers from declining output and rising prices—stagflation. In the final phase, the economy experiences both increasing output and increasing prices, but the inflation then comes to an end. We now examine these three phases in detail.

The starting point for our analysis is an economy with an inflationary gap $(Y > Y^*)$ and rising inflation.[5]

Practise with Study Guide Chapter 29, Exercise 3.

---

[5]In the simpler case where the economy begins with $Y = Y^*$ and constant inflation, only the second and third phases are relevant.

Phase 1: Removing Monetary Validation

The first phase consists of slowing the rate of monetary expansion, thereby slowing the rate at which the *AD* curve is shifting upward. The simplest case is when the Bank of Canada adopts a "cold-turkey approach" in which the rate of monetary expansion is cut to zero so that the upward shift in the *AD* curve is halted abruptly. This halt implies a large and rapid increase in both nominal and real interest rates.

At this point, a controversy often breaks out—as it did in the early 1980s and early 1990s—over the effects that the increase in interest rates has on inflation. One group will point out that the rise in the interest rate increases business costs and that passing on the extra costs through higher prices adds to inflation. They will condemn the Bank's tight monetary policy as inflationary. A second group will argue that the rising interest rate signifies a slowdown in the rate of monetary expansion, without which inflation cannot be curbed.

The first group is correct in pointing out that the rise in interest rates may cause a one-time increase in the price level. The rise in interest costs may shift the *SRAS* curve upward, just as a rise in wage costs does. This rise in interest costs, however, has only a *one-time effect* on the price level. The first group is wrong, therefore, in asserting that the Bank's policy of driving up interest rates is contributing to a long-term increase in the rate of inflation.

The second group is correct in saying that the rise in the interest rate is a necessary part of an anti-inflationary policy. As long as the price level continues to rise, the rise in the interest rate reduces desired aggregate expenditure, thus reducing equilibrium real GDP by moving leftward along a fixed *AD* curve.

Now suppose that the Bank resists the pleas to hold down interest rates. It continues with its no-validation policy. The *AD* curve stops shifting, but under the combined influence of the present inflationary gap and expectations of continued inflation, wages continue to rise. Hence, the *SRAS* curve continues to shift upward. Eventually, the inflationary gap will be removed, as shown in part (i) of Figure 29-5.

If demand were the only influence on wages, the story would be ended. At $Y = Y^*$, there would be no upward demand pressure on wages and other factor prices. The *SRAS* curve would be stabilized, and the economy would remain at full employment with a stable price level.

Phase 2: Stagflation

Governments around the world have often wished that things were really so simple. However, wages depend not only on current excess demand but also on inflation expectations. Once inflation expectations have been established, it is not always easy to get people to revise them downward, even in the face of announced changes in monetary policies. Hence, the *SRAS* curve continues to shift upward, causing the price level to continue to rise and output to fall. This is phase 2, shown in part (ii) of Figure 29-5.

Expectations can cause inflation to persist even after its original causes have been removed. What was initially a demand and expectational inflation due to an inflationary gap becomes a pure expectational inflation.

The ease with which the Bank of Canada can end such an inflation depends on how easy it is to change these expectations of continued inflation. This change is more difficult to the extent that expectations are backward-looking and easier to the extent that expectations are forward-looking.

To the extent that people look mainly to past inflation rates to determine their expectations of the future, they will be slow to change their expectations. As the actual inflation rate falls below the expected rate, a long time will be required for the downward

FIGURE 29-5   Eliminating a Sustained Inflation

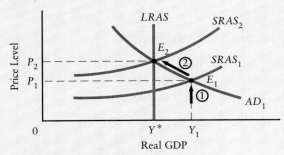

(i) Phase 1: Removing the inflationary gap

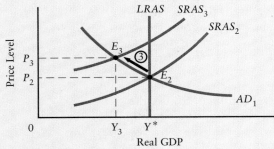

(ii) Phase 2: Stagflation

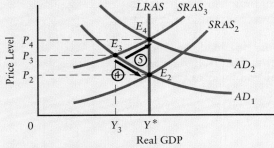

(iii) Phase 3: Recovery

(i) Phase 1: The elimination of a sustained inflation begins with a demand contraction to remove the inflationary gap. The initial position is one where fully validated inflation is taking the economy along the path shown by arrow 1. When the curves reach $SRAS_1$ and AD_1, the Bank stops expanding the money supply, thus stabilizing aggregate demand at AD_1. Wages continue to rise, taking the $SRAS$ curve leftward. The economy moves along arrow 2, with output falling and the price level rising. When aggregate supply reaches $SRAS_2$, the inflationary gap is removed, income is Y^*, and the price level is P_2.

(ii) Phase 2: Expectations and wage momentum lead to stagflation, with falling output and continuing inflation. The economy moves along the path shown by arrow 3. The driving force is now the $SRAS$ curve, which continues to shift because inflation expectations cause wages to continue rising. The recessionary gap grows as output falls. Inflation continues, but at a diminishing rate. If wages stop rising when output has reached Y_3 and the price level has reached P_3, the stagflation phase is over, with equilibrium at E_3.

(iii) Phase 3: After expectations are reversed, recovery takes output to Y^*, and the price level is stabilized. There are two possible scenarios for recovery. In the first, the recessionary gap causes wages to fall (slowly), taking the $SRAS$ curve back to $SRAS_2$ (slowly), as shown by arrow 4. The economy retraces the path originally followed in part (ii) back to E_2. In the second scenario, the Bank increases the money supply sufficiently to shift the AD curve to AD_2. The economy then moves along the path shown by arrow 5. This restores output to potential at the cost of further temporary inflation that takes the price level to P_4. Potential output and a stable price level are now achieved.

adjustment to take place. The longer a given rate has persisted, the more firmly will people expect that rate to persist.

To the extent that expectations are forward-looking, people will take notice of the Bank's changed behaviour and revise their expectations of future inflation downward in the light of the new monetary policy. If people fully understand the Bank's policies as soon as they are implemented, if they have full confidence that the Bank will stick to its policies, if they know exactly how much time will be required for the Bank's policies to have effect, and if they adjust their expectations exactly in line with this knowledge, there is little need for any recessionary gap to develop. Once the inflationary gap has been removed, expectations will immediately be revised downward, so there will then be no pressure on wages to rise because of either demand or expectational forces. In Figure 29-5, Y would not fall below Y^* because the $SRAS$ curve would stop shifting upward at $SRAS_2$. The inflation would be eliminated at almost no cost.

How long inflation persists after the inflationary gap has been removed depends on how quickly expectations of continued inflation are revised downward.

When the $SRAS$ curve does continue to shift upward, causing Y to fall below Y^*, the emerging recessionary gap has two effects. First, unemployment is rising; hence the demand influence on wages becomes negative. Second, as the recession deepens and monetary restraint continues, people revise their expectations of inflation downward. When they have no further expectations of inflation, there are no further increases in wages, and the $SRAS$ curve stops shifting. The stagflation phase is over. Inflation has come to a halt, but a large recessionary gap now exists.

Phase 3: Recovery

The final phase is the return to potential output. When the economy comes to rest at the end of the stagflation, the situation is exactly the same as when the economy is hit by a negative supply shock. The move back to potential output can be accomplished in either of two ways. First, the recessionary gap can be relied on to reduce factor prices, thereby shifting the $SRAS$ curve downward, reducing prices but increasing real GDP. Second, the money supply can be increased to shift the AD curve upward, increasing both prices and real GDP. These two possibilities are illustrated in part (iii) of Figure 29-5.

Some economists worry about relying on the $SRAS$ curve to shift downward to return the economy to potential output. Their concern is primarily that it will take too long for prices and wages to fall sufficiently to shift the $SRAS$ curve—though output will eventually return to potential, the long adjustment period will be characterized by high unemployment. These economists have a preference for a monetary expansion to get output back to potential.

Other economists worry about a temporary burst of monetary expansion because they fear that expectations of inflation may be rekindled when the Bank increases the money supply. And, if inflationary expectations *are* revived, the Bank will then be faced with a tough decision—either it must let another recession develop to break these new inflation expectations, or it must validate the inflation to reduce unemployment. In the latter case, the Bank is back where it started, with validated inflation on its hands—and diminished credibility.

The Cost of Disinflation

The foregoing discussion of the process of disinflation makes the cost of disinflation pretty clear:

The cost of disinflation is the cost of the recession that is generated in the process.

As we said earlier, the size and duration of the recession depends to a large extent on how quickly inflation expectations are revised downward. If expectations are backward looking and thus slow to adjust to the changes in policy, the recession will be deep and protracted. Conversely, if expectations are forward looking and quick to adjust to changes in policy, the recession may be mild and of short duration.

The main cost of disinflation is the reduction in economic activity that is a necessary part of the process. Increases in unemployment and plant closures are typical.

sacrifice ratio   The cumulative loss in real GDP, expressed as a percentage of potential output, divided by the percentage-point reduction in the rate of inflation.

But *how costly* is the process of disinflation? Economists have derived a simple measure of the costs of disinflation based on the depth and length of the recession and on the amount of disinflation. This measure is called the **sacrifice ratio**, and is defined to be the cumulative loss of real GDP due to a given disinflation (expressed as a percentage of potential GDP) divided by the number of percentage points by which inflation has fallen. For example, the 1990–92 disinflation in Canada reduced inflation by roughly four percentage points. Suppose that the cumulative loss of real GDP due to that disinflation was equal to $80 billion and that potential GDP at the time was equal to $800 billion. The cumulative loss of output would then be 10 percent of potential output. The sacrifice ratio would therefore have been 10/4 = 2.5. The interpretation of this number is that it "costs" 2.5 percent of real GDP for each percentage point of inflation that is reduced.

The numbers in the above example are hypothetical, but typical estimates of the sacrifice ratio for many developed countries range between 2 and 4. Figure 29-6 illustrates the time paths of real GDP and inflation following a disinflation and shows how to compute the sacrifice ratio. Note an important assumption that is implicit whenever measuring the sacrifice ratio in this way. The assumption is that all changes in the path of real GDP are *caused by* the disinflation.

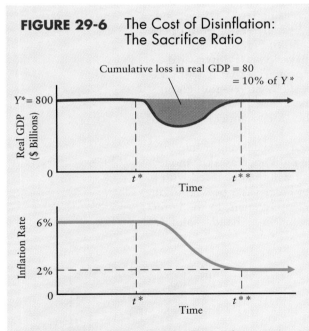

FIGURE 29-6   The Cost of Disinflation: The Sacrifice Ratio

The sacrifice ratio is larger the deeper the recession and the longer it takes real GDP to return to potential. In this example, the economy begins with Y = Y* and inflation of 6 percent. At *t**, the disinflation begins. A recessionary gap opens up and inflation falls only slowly. By *t***, real GDP has returned to Y* and inflation has been reduced by 4 percentage points. In this figure, the cumulative loss of real GDP is 10 percent of Y* and inflation has fallen by 4 percentage points. The sacrifice ratio is therefore 10/4 = 2.5.

Inflation in Canada

In this chapter's final section, we continue the discussion of Canadian inflation policy that we began in Chapter 28. We begin our study with the inflation of the 1970s. See Figure 29-7 for the time path of the annual inflation rate in Canada over the past three decades. In the discussion that follows, it will be useful to refer back to this figure frequently.

The early 1970s witnessed quite expansionary fiscal and monetary policies. The money supply was expanded rapidly, and an inflationary gap opened up as real GDP exceeded its potential level. As a result, inflation began to rise. Expansion continued until early 1974, and inflation rose throughout that period. Then a worldwide recession began, and Canada did not escape its effects. As a recessionary gap began to open up, the normal expectation was that inflation would diminish. Just then, however, the first OPEC shock hit. The prices of oil and other petroleum products soared. This negative supply shock reduced the growth of real GDP and sent inflation into the double-digit range. The result was stagflation.

The Rise of Inflation: 1975–1980

Rather than viewing the stagflation as the result of rising oil prices, Canadian policy makers interpreted the stagflation as accelerating wage-push inflation in a

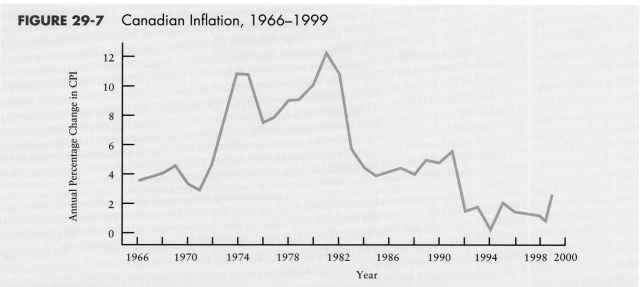

FIGURE 29-7 Canadian Inflation, 1966–1999

Canada's recent experience with inflation is varied. From about 4 percent in the late 1960s, inflation rose dramatically to a high of over 12 percent in 1980–1981. It then fell to about 4 percent by 1984. It hovered between 4 and 5 percent for the next few years, eventually creeping up to 6 percent in 1990. It then fell to about 2 percent by 1992 and then hovered between 1 and 2 percent for the next seven years. By the end of 1999, with a fast-growing economy, the inflation rate had risen above 2 percent. Inflation in this figure is measured as the annual percentage change in the Consumer Price Index (all items).

(*Source: Bank of Canada Review*, various issues.)

time of world recession. Having failed in an attempt to secure the agreement of organized labour in a voluntary policy of reducing wage demands, the government decided to impose **wage and price controls.** An Anti-Inflation Board was set up and given power to control wages and prices for 3 years. At roughly the same time, the Bank of Canada adopted the policy of "monetary gradualism" by announcing its intention to gradually reduce the rate of growth of the money supply.

wage and price controls Direct government intervention into wage and price formation with legal power to enforce the government's decisions on wages and prices.

Whether by accident or by design, the two policies made a coherent package. The monetary policy was meant to reduce the speed with which the *AD* curve was shifting upward. Wage-and-price controls were meant to reduce the speed with which the *SRAS* curve was shifting upward. If the upward rush of the two curves could be slowed at the same rate, the inflation rate could be reduced without having to endure the stagflation phase (phase 2 in Figure 29-5), which occurs when the *AD* curve rises more slowly than the *SRAS* curve.

At first, all seemed to go well. The inflation rate fell in successive years starting in 1975. Then in 1979 and in 1980, a new setback appeared in the form of a substantial supply shock. The cause was another large increase in the world price of oil, due to a second round of OPEC output restrictions. As a result, the 1980 inflation rate became once again as high as it had been just before wage and price controls were introduced.

The Fall of Inflation: 1981–1984

By the beginning of the 1980s, rapid inflation seemed firmly entrenched, and a major controversy arose over how to reduce it. Most people agreed on the goal of returning to a much lower inflation rate, but there was disagreement as to the means of achieving that goal.

Some economist—especially those that believed peoples' expectations of inflation adjust quickly—advocated breaking the entrenched inflation with monetary restraint in the manner analysed earlier in this chapter. Since they felt that there would be a short Phase 2, they were willing to rely exclusively on monetary policy to bring about the transition from a high- to a low-inflation environment.

Other economists agreed that a low rate of monetary growth was a necessary condition for returning to a low rate of inflation. However, because they felt that Phase 2 would be long—some talked in terms of 5 to 10 years—they were reluctant to use monetary policy *alone* during the transition. As a result, these economists advocated using wage and price controls once again in conjunction with a restrictive monetary policy.

In 1981, with inflation above 12 percent, the Bank of Canada chose to follow the United States in adopting a highly restrictive monetary policy. A serious recession eventually moderated wage and price increases. When it came, the fall in inflation was dramatic: from a peak of 12 percent in mid 1981 to around 4 percent by early 1984. By 1984, the restrictive monetary policy had thus succeeded in reducing inflation to a level not seen since the early 1960s. But the sharp reduction in inflation had also contributed to a major recession with all its attendant costs, including unemployment, lost output, business bankruptcies, and foreclosed mortgages.

The results came out somewhere between the extremes that had been predicted. Thus, as so often happens with great debates, neither the extreme pessimists nor the extreme optimists were right—the truth lay somewhere in between. Whatever the reasons, during the early 1980s, inflation fell faster than many economists had expected, but the slump was deeper and more prolonged than many others had expected.

Recovery: 1985–1990

For several years following 1984, the Canadian inflation rate stabilized at around 4 percent, and it was a time of low inflation in the world as a whole. There was no reason for the inflation rate to rise, since there was no inflationary gap in the Canadian economy. Indeed, since there was actually a *recessionary gap* during this period, the actual inflation seemed to be purely expectational: People expected a 4 percent inflation rate, and the Bank validated that inflation rate through a continued monetary expansion. Thus, inflation persisted at a rate of about 4 percent.

Since there was a recessionary gap during this period, why did inflation not fall further? The answer here seems to be that the weak demand forces that work toward deceleration when there is excess supply were swamped by the forces of expectational inflation and random shocks.

By 1988, a long period of expansion was bringing Canadian real GDP close to its potential level. The inflation rate began to creep upward, exceeding 5 percent in 1989 and reaching 6 percent for a few months in 1990.

As we discussed in Chapter 28, the Bank of Canada in 1988, under the leadership of Governor John Crow, announced that monetary policy would no longer be guided by short-term stabilization issues and instead would be guided by the long-term goal of price stability. This important shift in policy indicated that henceforth the Bank of Canada would be prepared to fight inflation while more-or-less ignoring the short-term pain that such battles would produce.

Disinflation: 1991–1992

In 1989 the Bank of Canada reacted by adopting a restrictive monetary policy. Interest rates were driven up and, as discussed in Chapter 28, the Canadian dollar appreciated, putting tradable-goods producers under heavy competitive pressure. The country's economic expansion proved remarkably resilient. The inflationary gap and the high inflation rate persisted for over a year, in spite of very high interest rates and a strong Canadian dollar. Finally, by the middle of 1990, the inflation rate began to fall. By autumn, it had returned to the 4 percent plateau from which it had accelerated two years earlier. The Bank, however, persisted in its tight policy.

By late 1990, the economy was clearly into a recession and many who supported the Bank's long-term policy of price stability nonetheless called for a little fine tuning to offset some of the short-term pain associated with monetary restraint. They felt that the Bank could mitigate the recession by easing up on its tight monetary policy, returning to it once the next recovery had begun. The Bank responded by reiterating the importance of driving the inflation rate close to zero over a period of a few years.

As a way of formalizing the Bank's shift in policy away from short-term stabilization and toward long-term price stability, the Bank of Canada and the federal Department of Finance announced in 1991 a series of *inflation-control targets*. Beginning in 1992, the Bank would aim at having the rate of inflation in the 3–5 percent range. The target range declined gradually so that by the end of 1995 it was 1 to 3 percent.

This policy sparked enormous controversy. Some critics felt that the costs of reducing the inflation rate below 4 percent, as reflected by the sacrifice ratio, would be excessive. They preferred to have the economy adjust to that rate rather than undergo the costs of reducing the rate to 2 percent, let alone to zero. Other critics, while accepting price stability as the ultimate goal, argued that the policy should not be pursued when the economy was already in the midst of a serious recession.

Supporters pointed out that 4 percent inflation was a high inflation rate by historical standards. They argued that price stability was the best long-run goal. To the critics who said, "yes, but not now," the supporters replied that reducing a sustained inflation is always costly, and there will always be strong arguments for not incurring these costs at present. They felt that the commitment to price stability must be honoured and the costs accepted, since the longer that attempt was postponed, the more entrenched would inflation expectations become and, thus, the greater would be the costs of finally reducing inflation.

In the event, the Bank stuck to its policy. The recession was indeed severe. Canadian interest rates stayed well above U.S. rates, and the Canadian dollar remained high on foreign-exchange markets. However, the inflation rate responded as theory predicts and, by the end of 1992, the Bank was able to declare victory against inflation. Inflation was well below 2 percent.

Recovery and Low Inflation: 1993–?

The subsequent economic recovery was considered to be a fragile one, at least for 1991 and 1992. Many people blamed the Bank for the deep recession that Canada suffered, and much of the disagreement over the Bank's policy became focused on the Governor, John Crow. In 1994, the minister of finance in the newly elected Liberal government appointed Gordon Thiessen as the new governor of the Bank of Canada. At the same time, both the finance minister and Mr. Thiessen affirmed the recent monetary policy of the Bank and announced that the formal inflation targets of 1 to 3 percent would continue. So, political considerations dictated a change in the governor while economic considerations dictated no change in monetary policy.

By 1995, economic growth had picked up considerably, even though the unemployment rate seemed to decline only slowly. The Bank's main challenge during this period of recovery was to provide enough growth in the money supply to allow a healthy recovery while at the same time not expanding so much that inflationary pressures would build. From 1995 to 1999, the rate of inflation was mostly within the established 1 to 3 percent target range, though in 1998 it temporarily dropped below the bottom of the range. By early 2000, real GDP was very close to potential GDP, the economy was growing quickly, and inflationary pressures began to build. The bank began to tighten monetary policy in an effort to keep inflation from rising.

Two Current Debates

The Bank of Canada's success in achieving and maintaining low inflation has led to two interesting debates regarding low inflation. You may recognize both debates from the business pages of Canada's newspapers. Both can be posed as questions. Is inflation dead? Is inflation too low?

The Death of Inflation?

With inflation falling rapidly in many countries in the last few years, and with the apparent success in maintaining inflation at very low levels, some economists and policy makers have started asking an inevitable question: Is inflation dead?

Many arguments have been made in defence of the view that inflation is no longer a threat, and they all involve the greater competition that comes from globalization. As we have noted earlier in this book, globalization—the sharp reductions in the cost of transportation and communication in the past two decades—presents domestic firms and workers with greater competition than they would otherwise have. If firms can easily ship their products to various countries quickly and efficiently, then domestic firms face greater competition from abroad. Similarly, if firms can easily relocate their factories to produce in lower-cost countries, then domestic workers face greater competition from abroad. As a result, domestic firms are less likely to raise prices and domestic workers are less likely to push for wage increases. In short, globalization increases the competitive pressures in the economy, thus reducing the economy's inflationary forces.

Most economists, however, reject this view that the ongoing process of globalization spells an end to inflation. While recognizing that competitive forces may well be enhanced by globalization, most economists argue that such increases in competition will have one-time effects on wages and prices, but will not influence the long-run rate of inflation. (In their view, the increase in competition is best thought of as a one-time shift in the *LRAS* curve to the right.) Central to this argument, as we have seen in this chapter, is the view that *sustained* inflation is indeed a monetary phenomenon—that is, sustained inflation is only possible when there is continual growth in the money supply. Thus, though individual demand and supply shocks may affect inflation temporarily, the long-run rate of inflation is ultimately determined by monetary policy.

In this view, inflation is dead only if central banks maintain their current commitment to keeping inflation at very low levels. Any future negative supply shock, followed by monetary validation, could easily tip any individual country—or group of countries—back into an inflationary wage-price spiral.

See Chapter 29 of www.pearsoned.ca/lipsey for an excellent debate on the death of inflation: John Crow, "The Death of Inflation and Other Metaphors," and Roger Bootle, "The Death of Inflation," *World Economic Affairs.*

Since sustained inflation is ultimately determined by monetary policy, inflation will only remain low if central banks maintain their commitment to low inflation.

Costs of Very Low Inflation?

Canada's inflation rate fell very quickly from 5 percent in 1991 to below 2 percent in 1992. It then remained between 1 and 2 percent for the next seven years. The U.S. Federal Reserve was not as aggressive in their drive to reduce inflation; inflation in the United States did not decline as much or as sharply as in Canada. Interestingly, the Canadian and U.S. economies appeared to perform differently throughout the 1990s. Especially apparent was the difference in unemployment rates between the two countries. From 1985 to 1990, when both economies were growing steadily, the Canadian unemployment rate was just over 2 percentage points higher than the U.S. rate. Beginning in 1991, however, as Canada's sharp disinflation began, the gap increased to 4 percentage points.

Some economists point to the widening gap in unemployment rates as evidence that there are costs associated with very low inflation.[6] These economists argue not only that the process of disinflation involves *temporary* costs in terms of reduced output and higher unemployment, but more controversially that there are *permanent* costs associated with maintaining inflation at very low levels.

That very low inflation may permanently raise unemployment is an argument originally put forward in 1972 by James Tobin, an economist from Yale University who was awarded the Nobel Prize in economics in 1981. In Canada, the argument was made recently by Pierre Fortin of the Université du Québec à Montréal. Central to Tobin's and Fortin's arguments is the importance of downward rigidity in nominal wages—a more extreme version of what we called *wage stickiness* in Chapter 25. Specifically, these economists believe that nominal wages will rise in the presence of excess demand but they will not fall in the presence of excess supply. Why does this wage rigidity lead to higher unemployment when inflation is very low but not when inflation is higher?

Their argument is rather involved, and to understand it we need to proceed carefully. The argument is summarized by the following four points:

- First, the various sectors within the economy are continually being subjected to demand shocks. At any given time, some sectors are expanding while others are contracting. These demand shocks lead to changes in the demand for labour in the various sectors and thus necessitate changes in real wages, rising in expanding sectors and falling in contracting sectors.
- Second, if nominal wages cannot fall because of wage rigidity, then the only way *real* wages can fall is if the price level rises.
- Third, inflation at moderate levels (3–5 percent) is high enough to bring about the necessary drop in real wages in most of the contracting sectors. This is because the pattern of demand shocks across sectors is such that even the sectors with the sharpest contractions require real-wage declines of only 5 percent.
- Finally (and this is the key point), if inflation is very low (1–2 percent), the contracting sectors *cannot* achieve the necessary reduction in real wages through inflation. Firms will instead choose to lay off their workers. Thus, when inflation is very low, the layoffs in the contracting sectors will outnumber the newly hired workers in the expanding sectors. The result is *permanently* higher unemployment.

---

[6]In Chapter 30 we discuss some other explanations for why Canada's unemployment rate is higher than the U.S. rate.

This view is not shared by all economists. The main point of contention is the cause and extent of the downward rigidity in nominal wages. Many economists believe that while nominal wages may be very slow to fall in response to excess supply, this wage stickiness is largely a result of workers' having lived in an inflationary environment for many years. In such an environment, if prices have been rising at 5, 8, or 10 percent annually, it is easy to understand why workers are reluctant to accept an actual decline in their nominal wages. But as low inflation becomes a more permanent part of the economic environment, workers will naturally come to view occasional reductions in nominal wages as one of the unpleasant but inevitable aspects of economic life. If this is true, then the downward rigidity of nominal wages will eventually disappear as Canada's experience with low inflation continues. In this case, real GDP will eventually return to Y^*, unemployment will eventually return to U^*, and low inflation will not involve permanent costs.

This debate is currently unsettled. Much theoretical and empirical research is directed at determining the extent of nominal wage rigidity and how it is related to the overall inflation rate, but it will probably take several years before a consensus emerges on just how important this potential cost of low inflation really is.[7]

Conclusion

Throughout the history of economics, inflation has been recognized as a harmful phenomenon. This view was given renewed strength as a result of the worldwide experiences of high inflation rates since the early 1970s. The resolve is there, at least in advanced industrial countries, to prevent another outbreak of rapid inflation and, should one occur for reasons of unavoidable supply-side shocks, to prevent it from continuing long enough to become firmly entrenched in people's expectations.

It is clear from experience that reducing the inflation rate by any significant amount usually has costs in terms of reduced output and increased unemployment. It is also clear from past policy debates that every time the Bank undertakes to do this, controversy will break out, whatever the current inflation rate. One side will argue that any reduction in the inflation rate is too costly and the other side will argue that these consequences must be accepted as the price of keeping some control over the inflation rate. Otherwise, the rate would slowly ratchet up under the impacts of supply- and demand-side shocks that the Bank was never allowed to counter because of fear of the short-run costs of doing so.

---

[7]The resurrection of Tobin's ideas is found in G. Akerlof, W. Dickens, and G. Perry, "The Macroeconomics of Low Inflation", *Brookings Papers on Economic Activity*, 1996. The argument for Canada was made by Pierre Fortin in "The Great Canadian Slump," *Canadian Journal of Economics*, 1997. For an assessment of the general argument, see Seamus Hogan, "What Does Downward Nominal-Wage Rigidity Imply for Monetary Policy?" *Canadian Public Policy*, 1998.

S U M M A R Y

Adding Inflation to the Model

- Sustained price inflation will be accompanied by closely related growth in wages and other factor prices such that the *SRAS* curve is shifting upward. Factors that influence shifts in the *SRAS* curve can be divided into two main components: demand and expectations. Random supply-side shocks will also exert an influence.
- The influence of demand can be expressed in terms of inflationary and recessionary gaps, which relate real output to potential output, or in terms of the difference between the actual rate of unemployment and the NAIRU.
- Expectations of inflation tend to cause wage increases equal to the expected price-level increases. Expectations

can be backward-looking, forward-looking, or some combination of the two.
- With a constant rate of inflation, expected inflation will eventually come to equal actual inflation. This implies that there is no demand pressure on inflation—that is, real GDP equals its potential level.
- Constant inflation of X percent per year is shown graphically in the macroeconomic model by the AD and $SRAS$ curves shifting up by X percent per year, keeping real GDP equal to Y^*.

Shocks and Policy Responses

- The initial effects of positive demand shocks are a rise in the price level and a rise in real GDP. If the inflation is unvalidated, output returns to its potential level while the price level rises further (as the *SRAS* curve shifts upward). Monetary validation allows demand inflation to proceed without reducing the inflationary gap (*AD* curve continues to shift upward).
- The initial effects of negative supply shocks are a rise in the price level and a fall in real GDP. If inflation is unvalidated, output will slowly return to its potential level as the price level slowly falls to its preshock level (*SRAS* curve

slowly shifts down). Monetary validation allows supply inflation to continue in spite of a persistent recessionary gap (*AD* curve shifts up with monetary validation).
- If the Bank of Canada tries to keep real GDP constant at some level above Y^*, the actual inflation rate will accelerate. Constant inflation is only possible when there are no demand pressures on inflation—that is, when $Y = Y^*$.
- Aggregate demand and supply shocks have temporary effects on inflation. But *sustained* inflation is a monetary phenomenon.

Reducing Inflation

- The process of ending a sustained inflation can be divided into three phases. Phase 1 consists of ending monetary validation and allowing the upward shift in the *SRAS* curve to remove any inflationary gap that does exist. In Phase 2, a recessionary gap develops as expectations of further inflation cause the *SRAS* curve to continue to shift upward even after the inflationary gap is removed. In Phase 3, the economy returns to poten-

tial output, sometimes aided by a one-time monetary expansion that raises the *AD* curve to the level consistent with potential output at the present price level.
- The cost of disinflation is the recession that is created in the process. The sacrifice ratio is a measure of this cost and is calculated as the cumulative loss in real GDP (expressed as a percentage of Y^*) divided by the reduction in inflation.

Inflation in Canada

LO 7

- In the early 1980s, inflation peaked at around 13 percent. The Bank of Canada followed the United States in pursuing a tight-money policy. In Canada, inflation fell to around 4 percent by 1984, but the recession Canada experienced in the early 1980s was severe. During the next four years amidst a healthy economic recovery, inflation hovered between 4 and 5 percent, then toward the end of the recovery it crept up until reaching over 5 percent in 1989.
- In 1988, the Bank of Canada announced an important shift in policy. Henceforth, monetary policy would no longer be guided by short-term stabilization issues and instead would be guided by the long-term goal of price stability. As a means of formalizing this shift in policy,

the Bank and the federal department of finance announced a series of inflation-control targets, beginning in the 3–5 percent range for 1992 and falling to the 1–3 percent range by the end of 1995. The 1–3 percent range has been extended beyond 2002.
- Despite controversy, the Bank stuck to its policy and lowered inflation to below 2 percent by 1992. For the next seven years, inflation hovered between 1 and 2 percent.
- The persistence of low inflation has led to two current debates. First, is inflation no longer a threat? Second, are there costs associated with maintaining inflation at very low levels?

KEY CONCEPTS

Temporary and sustained inflation
The NAIRU
Rational expectations
Expectational, demand, and supply
  pressures on inflation

Monetary validation of demand and
  supply shocks
Expectations-augmented Phillips curve
Accelerating inflation
Ending sustained inflation

Sacrifice ratio
Inflation in the 1980s and 1990s
Inflation-control targets

STUDY EXERCISES

1. The table below shows several macroeconomic situations, each with a given amount of excess demand (or supply) for labour and a level of inflation expectations. Both are expressed in percent per year. For example, in Case A excess demand for labour is pushing wages up by 4 percent per year, and expected inflation is pushing wages up by 3 percent per year.

Case	Demand	Inflation Expectations	Total Wage Change	SRAS Shift
A	+4	+3	—-	—-
B	+4	0	—-	—-
C	0	+3	—-	—-
D	−3	0	—-	—-
E	−3	+4	—-	—-

a. For each case, identify whether there is an inflationary or a recessionary output gap.
b. For each case, what is the total effect on nominal wages? Fill in the third column.
c. For each case, in which direction is the SRAS curve shifting (up or down)? Fill in the last column.

2. This exercise requires you to compute inflationary expectations based on a simple formula, and it will help you to understand why backward-looking expectations adjust slowly to changes in economic events. Suppose that the *actual* inflation rate in year t is denoted Π_t. *Expected* inflation for year $t+1$ is denoted Π^e_{t+1}. Now, suppose that workers and firms form their expectations according to:

$$\Pi^e_{t+1} = \theta \Pi^T + (1-\theta)\Pi_t$$

where Π^T is the central bank's announced *inflation target*. This simple equation says that people's expectations for inflation at $t+1$ are a weighted average of last year's inflation rate and the central bank's currently announced target. We will use this equation to see how the size of θ determines the extent to which expectations are backward looking. Consider the table below, which shows the data for a reduction in inflation from 10 percent to 2 percent.

Year (t)	Π_t	Π^T	Π^e_{t+1}
1	10	2	—
2	9	2	—
3	6	2	—
4	3	2	—
5	2	2	—
6	2	2	—
7	2	2	—
8	2	2	—

a. Assume that θ is equal to 0.1. Compute expected inflation for each year and fill in the table.
b. On a scale diagram, plot the time path of actual inflation, expected inflation, and the inflation target.
c. Now assume that θ equals 0.9. Repeat parts **a** and **b**.
d. Which value of θ corresponds to more backward-looking expectations? Explain.
e. Given the different speed of adjustment of inflationary expectations, predict which disinflation is more costly in terms of lost output—the one with $\theta=0.1$ or with $\theta=0.9$. Explain.

3. The diagram below shows an *AD/SRAS* diagram. The economy is in long-run equilibrium with real GDP equal to Y* and the price level is stable at P_0.

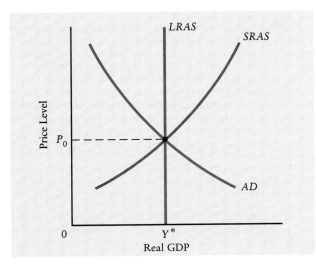

a. Suppose the central bank announces that it will make a one-time increase in the money supply and this will shift the *AD* curve up by 5 percent. Show the likely effect of this announcement on the *SRAS* curve.
b. Why does the shift of the *SRAS* curve in part **a** depend on whether workers and firms believe the central bank's announcement?
c. In a new *AD/SRAS* diagram, show how a sustained and constant inflation of 5 percent is represented.
d. Explain why a constant inflation is only possible when real GDP is equal to Y*.

4. The diagram below shows an *AD/SRAS* diagram. Suppose the economy is hit by some positive aggregate demand shock—say an increase in the demand for Canada's exports. This increases real GDP to Y_1.

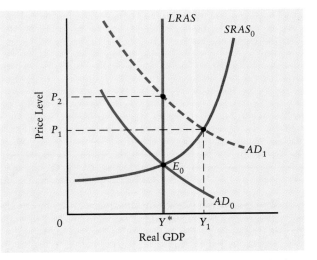

a. Explain what happens if the Bank of Canada does not react to the shock. Show this in the diagram.
b. Now suppose that the Bank decides to maintain real GDP at Y_1—that is, it decides to validate the shock. Explain how this is possible, and show it in a diagram
c. What is the effect on inflation from the policy in part **b**? Is inflation constant or is it rising? Explain.

5. The diagram on the next page shows an *AD/SRAS* diagram. Suppose the economy is hit by some negative aggregate supply shock—say an increase in wages driven by a major union settlement. This reduces real GDP to Y_1.

a. Explain what happens if the Bank of Canada does not react to the shock. Show this in the diagram.
b. Now suppose that the Bank decides to offset the shock's effect on real GDP—that is, it validates the shock. Explain how this is possible, and show it in a diagram.

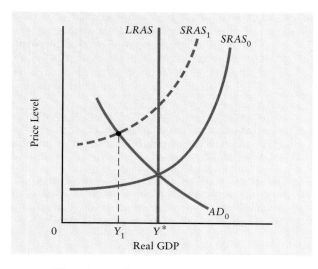

c. What danger do many economists see in validating such supply shocks? What is the alternative?

6. The table below shows some data on various disinflations. In each case, assume that potential GDP is equal to $900 billion.

Case	Inflation Reduction	Cumulative GDP Loss	Sacrifice Ratio
A	5 percentage points	$100 billion	—
B	2	30	—
C	6	60	—
D	8	80	—

a. In each case, compute the sacrifice ratio.
b. Explain why the sacrifice ratio can be expected to be smaller when expectations are more forward looking.
c. Explain why the sacrifice ratio can be expected to be smaller when central-bank announcements are more credible.

DISCUSSION QUESTIONS

1. Why might the cost of disinflation vary from one inflationary period to another? Are there reasons to think that the cost might be higher the longer inflation has persisted? What might the Bank of Canada do to reduce the cost?

2. What sources of inflation are suggested by each of the following quotations?

   a. A newspaper editorial in Manchester, England: "If American unions were as strong as those in Britain, America's inflationary experience would have been as disastrous as Britain's."
   b. An article in *The Economist:* "Oil price collapse will reduce inflation."
   c. A Canadian newspaper article in October 1990: "The combination of the Kuwaiti crisis and an emerging recession is a sure recipe for worldwide stagflation."
   d. A newspaper headline in May 1999: "Bank's fast growth of M1 will spur inflation."

3. Discuss the apparent conflict between the following views. Can you suggest how they might be reconciled using aggregate demand and aggregate supply analysis?

   a. "A rise in interest rates is deflationary, because ending entrenched inflation with a tight monetary policy usually requires that interest rates rise steeply."
   b. "A rise in interest rates is inflationary, because interest is a major business cost and, as with other costs, a rise in interest will be passed on by firms in the form of higher prices."

4. What is the relationship between the sacrifice ratio and the central bank's credibility?

   a. Explain why a more credible policy of disinflation reduces the costs of disinflation.
   b. Explain how you think the Bank of Canada might be able to make its disinflation policy more credible.
   c. Can the Bank's policy responses to negative supply shocks influence the credibility it is likely to have when trying to end a sustained inflation? Explain.

5. In Chapter 21, we discussed the costs of inflation. In this chapter, we examined the costs of *reducing* inflation. Suppose that you are the Governor of the Bank of Canada and that inflation has been high and roughly constant for a number of years. You have two policy

choices: you can continue to validate the ongoing inflation; or you can attempt to eliminate the sustained inflation. Outline the issues involved when making this choice. List and explain the costs of ongoing inflation, and also the costs of a potential disinflation. Explain how you make your policy decision.

6. In January 1991, the federal government introduced the Goods and Services Tax (GST). If you were to suppose that the GST was a *new* tax (in fact, it replaced an existing tax), what would be the effect on the *SRAS* curve? Is the introduction of the GST (or an increase in its rate) inflationary? Does it increase inflation permanently?

7. In the summer of 1999 at a time when U.S. GDP was slightly above potential, a story in *The Globe and Mail* reported that the release of strong employment-growth data for the United States led to a plunge in prices on the U.S. stock market.

   a. Explain why high employment growth would lead people to expect the U.S. central bank to tighten its monetary policy.
   b. Explain why higher U.S. interest rates would lead to lower prices of U.S. stocks.
   c. How would you expect this announcement to affect Canada? (At the time, there was still a small recessionary gap in Canada.)

CHAPTER 30

Unemployment

LEARNING OBJECTIVES

1. Understand how employment and unemployment change over the short and long runs.

2. Explain the difference between the New Classical and New Keynesian views of cyclical unemployment.

3. Understand the causes of frictional and structural unemployment.

4. Explain the various forces that cause the NAIRU to change.

5. Understand how various policies might be used to reduce unemployment.

When the level of economic activity changes, so do the levels of employment and unemployment. Figure 19-5 in Chapter 19 shows the course of unemployment in Canada over the past few decades. It is clear from that figure that the unemployment rate follows a cyclical path, rising during recessions and falling during expansions. In addition, the unemployment rate appears to have experienced a long-term increase. What are the sources of these cyclical fluctuations? What are the sources of this long-term increase?

In macroeconomics, economists distinguish between the NAIRU, which you will recall is the unemployment that occurs when real GDP is equal to its potential (Y^*), and *cyclical* unemployment, which is the unemployment associated with fluctuations of real GDP around its potential. We will see in this chapter that short-run fluctuations in unemployment are mainly changes in cyclical unemployment. In contrast, the long-term upward trend in unemployment is due to gradual increases in the NAIRU. Before examining these types of unemployment in detail, we briefly review the Canadian experience with employment and unemployment.

Employment and Unemployment

Considered over the long term, the most striking features revealed by Figure 19-5(i) are trend increases in both total employment and the total labour force. Over the decades, the pace of creation of new jobs has been roughly equal to the growth in the number of potential workers. Less obvious in Figure 19-5(i), but more clear in Figure 19-5(ii), are the substantial year-to-year fluctuations in the unemployment rate.

Over the span of many years, increases in the labour force are more-or-less matched by increases in employment. But from year to year the unemployment rate fluctuates because changes in the labour force are not exactly matched by changes in employment.

Changes in Employment

The level of employment in Canada has increased dramatically over the past few decades. In 1959, there were approximately 5 million Canadians employed. By 1999, total employment was just under 15 million. The actual level of employment, of course, is determined both by the demand for labour and by the supply of labour. How have the two "sides" of the Canadian labour market been changing?

On the supply side, the labour force has expanded virtually every year since the end of World War II. The causes have included a rising population, which boosts entry into the labour force of people born 15 to 25 years previously; increased labour force participation by various groups, especially women; and net immigration of working-age persons.

On the demand side, many existing jobs are eliminated every year, and many new jobs are created. Economic growth causes some sectors of the economy to decline and others to expand. Jobs are lost in the sectors that are contracting and created in sectors that are expanding. Furthermore, even in stable industries, many firms disappear and many new ones are set up. The net increase in employment is the difference between all the jobs that are lost and all those that are created.

In most years, enough new jobs have been created both to replace old jobs that have been eliminated and to provide jobs for the increased numbers of people in the labour force. The result has been a net increase in employment in almost all years.

Changes in Unemployment

In the early 1980s, worldwide unemployment rose to high levels. The unemployment rate remained high in many advanced industrial countries and only began to come down, and even then very slowly, during the latter half of the decade. Canadian experience reflected these international developments rather closely. From a high of 11.9 percent in 1983, the Canadian unemployment rate fell to 7.5 percent in 1989, a point that many economists at the time thought was close to the Canadian NAIRU.

With the onset of another recession in the early 1990s, the unemployment rate then rose through 1990 and 1991, reaching 11.3 percent by 1992. During the next few years, the unemployment rate fell only slowly as the Canadian recovery was weak; by early 1994 the unemployment rate was still above 10 percent. But the speed of the Canadian recovery quickened and unemployment began to drop. By early 2000, after five years of healthy economic recovery, the unemployment rate was 6.8 percent, the lowest it had been in more than twenty years.

During periods of rapid economic growth, the unemployment rate usually falls. During recessions or periods of slow growth, the unemployment rate usually rises.

Flows in the Labour Market

We know that many existing jobs are eliminated every year, as industries contract and firms either shrink or close down altogether. Similarly, new jobs are continually being created, as other industries expand and new firms are born. The focus on the labour market, however, tends to be on the overall level of employment and unemployment rather than on the amount of *job creation* and *job destruction*. This focus can often lead us to the conclusion that few changes are occurring in the labour market when in fact the truth is exactly the opposite.

For example, the Canadian unemployment rate was roughly constant at 9.5 percent from 1995 to 1996. Does this mean that no jobs were created during the year? Or that the Canadian labour market was stagnant during this period? No. In fact, workers were finding jobs at the rate of roughly 400 000 *per month*. At the same time, however, other workers were leaving jobs or entering the labour force at roughly the same rate. This tremendous number of flows *out of unemployment* was being approximately matched by the number of flows *into unemployment*. The net result was that total unemployment changed only slightly.

The level of activity in the labour market is better reflected by the flows into and out of unemployment than by the overall unemployment rate.

By looking at the *gross flows* in the labour market, we are able to see economic activity that is hidden when we just look at the overall level of employment and unemployment (which is determined by *net* flows). Indeed, these gross flows are typically so large that they dwarf the net flows. See *Applying Economic Concepts 30-1* for more discussion of the gross flows in the Canadian labour market, and how these gross-flows data can be used to compute the average length of unemployment spells.

Consequences of Unemployment

Economists view unemployment as a social "bad" just as they view output as a social "good." But this does not mean that *all* unemployment is bad, just as we know that all output—such as noise or air pollution—is not good. Indeed, we will see later in this chapter that some unemployment is socially desirable as it reflects the necessary time spent searching to make appropriate matches between firms and workers.

We examine two costs of unemployment. The first is reflected by the loss in output. The second is the harm done to the individuals who are unemployed.

Lost Output

Every person counted as unemployed is willing and able to work but unable to find a job. Hence, the unemployed are valuable resources whose contribution to producing output is wasted. The output counterpart of unemployment is the recessionary gap—output that is not produced. In a world of scarcity with many unsatisfied wants, this loss represents a serious waste of resources.

Personal Costs

For the typical worker in Canada, being unemployed is no longer the disaster that it once was. Most spells of unemployment are short (see *Applying Economic Concepts 30-1* for a simple estimate of the average duration of unemployment spells) and many workers experiencing temporary unemployment have access to the unemployment insurance program. But this does not mean there are no problems associated with unemployment. The effects of long-term unemployment, in terms of the disillusioned who have given up trying to make it within the system and who contribute to social unrest,

For data on current employment and unemployment in Canada, see Statistics Canada's website: www.statcan.ca. Click on "Canadian Statistics" and then on "Labour."

Practise with Study Guide Chapter 30, Multiple-Choice Questions 1–7.

should be a matter of serious concern to the "haves" as well as the "have-nots." The loss of self-esteem and the dislocation of families that often result from situations of prolonged unemployment are genuine tragedies.

The general case for concern about high unemployment has been eloquently put by Princeton economist Alan Blinder:

> A *high-pressure economy provides opportunities, facilitates structural change, encourages inventiveness and innovation, and opens doors for society's underdogs. . . . All these promote the social cohesion and economic progress that make democratic mixed capitalism such a wonderful system when it works well. A low-pressure economy slams the doors shut, breeds a bunker mentality that resists change, stifles productivity growth, and fosters both inequality and mean-spirited public policy. All this makes reducing high unemployment a political, economic, and moral challenge of the highest order.*[1]

Cyclical Unemployment

As we saw in Chapter 19, economists classify unemployment into three types—cyclical, frictional and structural. The last two together make up the NAIRU, which is the level of unemployment that exists when real GDP equals potential GDP. Thus we can really divide unemployment into two broad groups. We examine frictional and structural unemployment in the next section when we study the NAIRU. **Cyclical unemployment** is the difference between the actual level of unemployment and the amount that exists when real GDP is at its potential level.

When real GDP is at its potential level, there is no cyclical unemployment—all unemployment then is either frictional or structural.

People who are cyclically unemployed are normally presumed to be suffering **involuntary unemployment** in that they are willing to work at the going wage rate but are unable to find appropriate jobs. The persistence of cyclical unemployment poses a challenge to economic theory.

cyclical unemployment
Unemployment in excess of frictional and structural unemployment; it is due to a shortfall of real GDP below potential GDP.

involuntary unemployment
Unemployment due to the inability of qualified persons who are seeking work to find jobs at the going wage rate.

Why Does Cyclical Unemployment Exist?

To see what is involved in this challenge, suppose that the fluctuations in aggregate demand cause real output to fluctuate around its potential level. This fluctuation will cause the demand for labour in each of the economy's labour markets to fluctuate as well, rising in booms and falling in slumps. If all of the labour markets had fully flexible wage rates, wages would fluctuate to keep quantity demanded in each individual market equal to quantity supplied in that market. We would observe cyclical fluctuations in employment and in the wage rate but no changes in unemployment. This behaviour is illustrated in Figure 30-1.

With perfectly flexible wages, employment and real wages would be procyclical (rising in booms and falling in slumps) but there would be no involuntary unemployment.

---

[1]A. S. Blinder, "The Challenge of High Unemployment," *American Economic Review* 78 (1988), 2:1.

APPLYING ECONOMIC CONCEPTS 30-1

Stocks and Flows in the Canadian Labour Market

In most reports about changes in unemployment, both in Canada and abroad, emphasis is typically on the changes in the *stock* of unemployment—that is, on the number of people who are unemployed at a particular point in time. But as we said in the text, the focus on the stock of unemployment can often hide much activity in the labour market—activity that is revealed by looking at *gross flows* in the labour market.

What Are Labour-Market Flows?

In the accompanying figure, three series of data are shown for Canada from 1976 to 1992—a period that includes the major recessions of 1981 and 1991. The top line is the stock of unemployment—the actual *number* of people unemployed at a specific point in time (it is not the unemployment *rate*). During the severe recession of the early 1980s, unemployment peaked at approximately 1.6 million people, and then fell during the recovery until 1989. With the onset of the next recession in 1990–1991, unemployment rose again, exceeding 1.5 million in early 1992.

The two lower lines in the figure show *gross flows* in the labour market. The orange line shows the *monthly* flow into unemployment. This flow into unemployment represents either:

- workers losing their jobs through layoffs or plant closure; or
- workers quitting their jobs to search for a different job; or
- new entrants to the labour force searching for a job.

Note that the monthly flow into unemployment varies between 300 000 and 500 000 *per month* and also tends to rise and fall together with the overall stock of unemployment.

The green line shows the monthly flow out of unemployment. This outflow represents either:

- unemployed individuals finding new jobs; or
- unemployed individuals becoming discouraged and leaving the labour force.

Note that the monthly flow out of unemployment is roughly the same size as the monthly inflow (300 000–500 000 per month).

What is the connection between the flows and the stocks in the labour market? Whenever the flows into unemployment exceed the flows out of unemployment, the stock of unemployment rises. Conversely, whenever the flows out of unemployment exceed the flows into unemployment, the stock of unemployment falls.

Using Flows Data

There are two reasons why looking at flows can be very useful when we think about the labour market. First, they show the tremendous amount of activity in the labour market even though the stock of unemployment may not be changing. For example, throughout the year 1983 the stock of unemployment in Canada was roughly constant at 1.4 million persons. But during those 12 months, roughly 500 000 persons *per month* either became

---

New Classical economics An approach to explaining macroeconomic fluctuations in which fluctuations in economic activity are explained by shocks to technology and tastes rather than to markets that fail to clear.

The hypothetical situation that we have just described is not what we actually observe. Instead, we see cyclical fluctuations not only in employment but also in unemployment. Furthermore, the changes in wage rates that do occur are insufficient to equate demand and supply, as is shown in Figure 30-2. Unemployment exceeds the NAIRU in slumps and is below it in booms. Although wages do tend to vary over the cycle, the fluctuations are not sufficient to remove all cyclical variations in unemployment. Why is this so?

Two types of explanation have been advanced in recent years. The line of explanation that we consider first is associated with what is called **New Classical economics.** The explanation assumes that labour markets are always in equilibrium in the sense that quantity demanded is continually equated with quantity supplied.

unemployed or ceased being unemployed. This number reflects the massive amount of regular turnover that exists in the Canadian labour market—turnover that is the essence of what economists call *frictional unemployment*.

The second reason why looking at flows is useful is that the relationship between the flows and the stock can tell us something about the amount of time the average unemployed person spends unemployed. If U_s is the stock of unemployment, and U_o is the monthly outflow from unemployment, then one simple estimate of the average duration of an unemployment spell is

To see this, consider the situation in 1989, at the peak of the business cycle. At that time, the stock of unemployment was approximately 1 million people and the outflow from unemployment was at a rate of approximately 400 000 persons per month. Thus, the average unemployed person in 1989 could expect to leave unemployment in about 2½ months (1 000 000 people/400 000 people per month = 2.5 months). In contrast, by early 1992, at the depth of the subsequent recession, the expected duration of an unemployment spell was over 3½ months (1 600 000/450 000 = 3.6).

$$\frac{\text{Average duration of}}{\text{unemployment spell}} = \frac{U_s}{U_o}$$

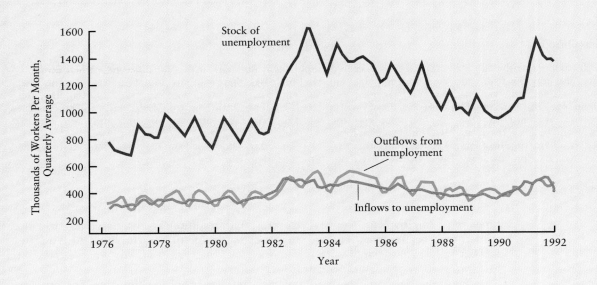

New Classical Theories[2]

Two major characteristics of New Classical theories are that agents continuously optimize and markets continuously clear; hence there can be no involuntary unemployment. These theories then seek to explain employment as the outcome of voluntary decisions made by individuals who are choosing to do what they do, including spending some

[2]The source of the label "New Classical" is that many of the arguments put forward by this group of economists are essentially more detailed and precise versions of arguments that would have been very familiar to the Classical economists, from Adam Smith and David Ricardo to Alfred Marshall.

FIGURE 30-1   Employment and Wages in a Competitive Labour Market

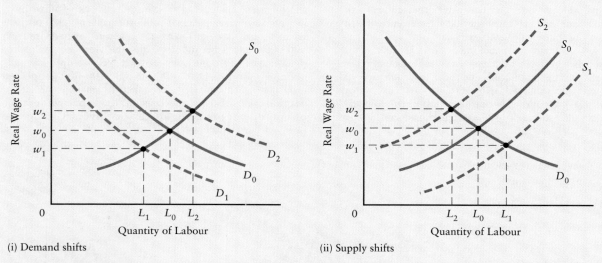

(i) Demand shifts   (ii) Supply shifts

In a perfectly competitive labour market, real wages and employment fluctuate in the same direction when demand fluctuates and in opposite directions when supply fluctuates; in both cases, there is no involuntary unemployment. The figure shows a perfectly competitive market for one type of labour. In part (i), the demand curves D_1, D_2, and D_0 are the demands for this market when there is a slump, when there is a boom, and when real GDP is at its potential level. As demand rises from D_1 to D_0 to D_2, real wages rise from w_1 to w_0 to w_2, and employment rises from L_1 to L_0 to L_2. At no time, however, is there any involuntary unemployment.

In part (ii), the supply of labour fluctuates from S_1 to S_0 to S_2, and wages fluctuate from w_1 to w_0 to w_2. In this case, wages fall when employment rises, and vice versa, but again there is no involuntary unemployment.

time out of employment. Notice the contrast with traditional Keynesian (and early monetarist) macroeconomics. Theories in this class assume that unemployment is a sign of market failure, associated with non-market-clearing prices and/or wages, and that a high proportion of unemployment is involuntary.

One New Classical explanation of cyclical fluctuations in employment assumes that they are caused by fluctuations in the willingness of people to supply their labour, as shown in part (ii) of Figure 30-1. If the supply curves of labour fluctuate cyclically (supply increases during booms and falls during slumps) there will be cyclical variations in employment. This explanation of cyclical behaviour in the labour market has two problems. First, the wage will tend to rise in slumps and fall in booms, which is not what we observe. Second, there will still be no systematic cyclical *unemployment* because labour markets always clear, leaving everyone who wishes to work actually working. Supply-induced fluctuations in employment form part of the basis of what is called real business cycle (RBC) theory, which is discussed in *Extensions in Theory 30-1*.

A second line of explanation lies in errors on the part of workers and employers in predicting the course of the price level over the business cycle. To see the argument, start by supposing that all of the economy's markets are in equilibrium, that there is full employment, that prices are stable, and that the actual and expected rates of inflation are zero. Now suppose the government increases the money supply by 5 percent. Through the transmission mechanism that we studied in Chapter 27, the increase in the money supply leads to an increase in desired aggregate expenditure. For simplicity, suppose there is an increase

EXTENSIONS IN THEORY 30-1

Real Business Cycle Theory

Real business cycle (RBC) theory attempts to explain cyclical fluctuations in the context of models in which wages and prices adjust very quickly to shocks. These models contrast sharply with the models we have discussed in this book in which fluctuations in output arise largely because wages and prices adjust gradually to shocks. In such models, if wages and prices were able to adjust instantly to all shocks, then output would always be equal to potential output—there would never be inflationary or recessionary gaps. The extreme flexibility of wages and prices is therefore a distinguishing feature of RBC models.

Key Propositions and Criticisms

The view of the business cycle found in RBC models is that short-run fluctuations in real GDP are caused by fluctuations in the vertical *LRAS* curve. In this view, unemployment is always equal to the NAIRU, and it is the NAIRU itself that fluctuates. Thus, the explanation of cyclical fluctuations that arises in RBC models is based on the role of supply shocks originating from sources such as oil price changes, technical progress, and changes in tastes.

The RBC approach is controversial. The major claims in its favour include:

1. It has been able to explain the recent behaviour of the economy quite well statistically, while downplaying the role for aggregate demand fluctuations in the business cycle.

2. It suggests that an integrated approach to understanding cycles and growth may be appropriate, as both reflect forces that affect the *LRAS* curve. The distinction it makes is that some shocks are temporary (and hence have cyclical effects) whereas others are permanent (and therefore affect the economy's long-term growth).

3. It provides valuable insights into how shocks, regardless of their origin, spread over time to the different sectors of the economy. By abstracting from monetary issues, it is possible to address more details concerning technology and household choice involving intertemporal tradeoffs between consumption, labour supply, and leisure.

Critics of the RBC approach focus on some implausible results and express concern about its assumptions of individuals' behaviour. More important, they are sceptical about a model in which monetary issues are completely ignored. For example, they point out that RBC models are unable to provide insights into the short-term correlation between money and output that is at the heart of the traditional macro model and for which a considerable amount of empirical evidence exists, in Canada as well as many other countries. Furthermore, RBC models are unable to provide insights into empirical regularities involving nominal variables, such as prices that apparently vary less than quantities and nominal prices that vary procyclically.

Policy Implications

Because the RBC approach gives no role to aggregate demand in influencing business cycles, it provides no role for stabilization operating through monetary and fiscal policies. Indeed, the models predict that the use of such demand-management policies can be *harmful*.

The basis for this prediction is the proposition in RBC models that cycles represent *efficient* responses to the shocks that are hitting the economy. Policymakers may mistakenly interpret cyclical fluctuations as deviations from potential output caused by shifts in either the *AD* or *SRAS* curves. The policymakers may try to stabilize output and thereby distort the maximizing decisions made by households and firms. This distortion will in turn cause the responses to the real shocks (as opposed to nominal, monetary shocks) to be inefficient.

Although a small minority of economists espouse RBC models as complete or even reasonable descriptions of the business cycle, and hence only a minority take seriously the strict implications for policy, many accept the view that real supply-side disturbances can play an important role in business cycles. Moreover, since the RBC approach emphasizes the importance of markets always clearing in response to changes in technology or other shocks, many economists that view RBC models as a poor description of the economy in the short run believe that many of the insights from the RBC approach are invaluable when thinking about the behaviour of the economy in the long run.

in desired expenditure on *all* goods; the demand for each good shifts to the right, and all prices, being competitively determined, rise. Individual decision makers see their selling prices go up and mistakenly interpret the increase as a rise in their own relative price. The reason is that they expect the overall inflation rate to be zero. Firms will produce more, and workers will work more since both groups think they are getting an increased *relative* price for what they sell. Thus, total output and employment rise.

When both groups eventually realize that their own relative prices are in fact unchanged, output and employment fall back to their initial levels. The extra output and employment occur only while people are being fooled. When they realize that *all* prices have increased by 5 percent, they revert to their initial behaviour. The only difference is that now the price level is 5 percent higher, leaving relative prices unchanged.

In both variants of the New Classical approach to explaining employment fluctuations, the labour markets are clearing. In the case of a reduction in the supply of workers (see part (ii) of Figure 30-1), employment falls because workers decide that they no longer want to work. In the case of workers' mistakenly viewing a change in the price level as a change in relative prices, employment falls because workers decide not to work when they think their real wage is low. In both cases, there is no involuntary unemployment.

New Classical explanations assume that labour markets clear, and then they look for reasons why employment fluctuates. They imply, therefore, that people who are not working have voluntarily withdrawn from the labour market for one reason or another; there is no involuntary unemployment.

New Keynesian Theories[3]

Many economists find the New Classical explanations implausible. They believe that people correctly read market signals but react in ways that do not cause markets to clear at all times. These economists—who refer to themselves as New Keynesians—believe that many people who are recorded as unemployed are involuntarily unemployed in the sense that *they would accept an offer of work in jobs for which they are trained, at the going wage rate, if such an offer were made.* These economists concentrate their efforts on explaining why wages do not quickly adjust to eliminate involuntary unemployment. If wages do not respond quickly to shifts in supply and demand in the labour market, quantity supplied and quantity demanded may *not* be equated for extended periods of time. Labour markets will then display unemployment during recessions and excess demand during booms, as shown for a typical labour market in Figure 30-2.

New Keynesian theories start with the everyday observation that wages do not change every time demand or supply shifts. When unemployed workers are looking for jobs, they do not knock on employers' doors and offer to work at lower wages than are being paid to current workers; instead, they answer want ads and hope to get the jobs offered but are often disappointed. Nor do employers, seeing an excess of applicants for the few jobs that are available, go to the current workers and reduce their wages until there is no one who is looking for a job; instead, they pick and choose until they fill their needs and then hang a sign saying "No Help Wanted."

---

[3]The source of the label "New Keynesian" is that many of the arguments put forward by these economists are closely related to the ideas put forward by John Maynard Keynes in *The General Theory of Employment, Interest and Money* (1936).

Long-Term Employment Relationships

One set of theories explains the familiar observations made in the preceding paragraph as results of the advantages to both workers and employers of relatively long-term and stable employment relationships. Workers want job security in the face of fluctuating demand. Employers want workers who understand the firm's organization, production, and marketing plans. Under these circumstances, both parties care about things in addition to the wage rate, and wages become somewhat insensitive to fluctuations in current economic conditions. Wages are, in effect, regular payments to workers over an extended employment relationship rather than a device for fine-tuning the current supplies and demands for labour. Given this situation, the tendency is for employers to "smooth" the income of employees by paying a steady money wage and letting profits and employment fluctuate to absorb the effects of temporary increases and decreases in demand for the firm's product.

A number of labour-market institutions work to achieve these results. For example, many long-term contracts provide for a schedule of money wages over a period of several years. Similarly, fringe benefits, such as pensions and health care, tend to bind workers to particular employers. Another example is pay that rises with years of service. This helps to bind the employee to the company, whereas seniority rules for layoffs bind the employer to the long-term worker.

In labour markets in which long-term relationships are important (as is the case in many labour markets), the wage rate does not fluctuate to continuously clear the market.

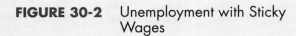

FIGURE 30-2   Unemployment with Sticky Wages

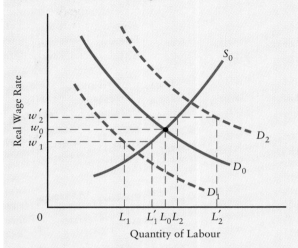

When the wage rate does not change enough to equate quantity demanded with quantity supplied, there will be unemployment in slumps and labour shortages in booms. When demand is at its normal level D_0, the market is cleared with wage rate w_0, employment is L_0, and there is no unemployment. In a recession, demand falls to D_1, but the wage only falls to w_1'. As a result, L_1 of labour is demanded and L_1' is supplied. Employment is determined by the quantity demanded at L_1. The remainder of the supply for which there is no demand, L_1L_1', is unemployed. In a boom, demand rises to D_2, but the wage rate rises only to w_2'. As a result, the quantity demanded is L_2', whereas only L_2 is supplied. Employment rises to L_2, which is the amount supplied. The rest of the demand cannot be satisfied, making excess demand for labour of L_2L_2'.

Because wages are thus insulated from short-term fluctuations in demand, any market clearing that occurs does so through fluctuations in the volume of employment rather than in wages. Of course, wages must respond to permanent shifts in market conditions—for example, the permanent and unexpected decline in the demand for the output of a particular industry.

Long-term employment relationships are important in the Canadian economy. According to a recent Statistics Canada survey of full-time workers, the average time spent with the same employer—what is referred to as *job tenure*—is just under nine years. Further, over half of them have been with their employer for six years or longer.

Menu Costs and Wage Contracts

A typical large manufacturing firm sells hundreds of differentiated products and employs hundreds of different types of labour. Changing prices and wages in response to every minor fluctuation in demand is a costly and time-consuming activity. Many firms therefore find it optimal to keep their price lists (*menus*) constant for significant periods of time. Since manufacturing firms are often operating in imperfectly competitive markets, they have some discretion over price. Hence, firms often react to small changes in demand by holding prices constant and responding with changes in output and employment. If many firms behave this way, output and employment will respond to changes in aggregate demand.

The Canadian evidence is consistent with the existence of sluggish price adjustment by firms, especially those in manufacturing industries. This, of course, is where Keynesian economics came in with an assumption of price stickiness. The New Keynesian literature attempts to model such sticky prices as resulting from firms' optimal response to adjustment costs.

Money wages tend to be inflexible in the short term because wage rates are generally set only occasionally. Wages are often set on an annual basis; in some unionized contracts wages are set for up to three years. Such inflexibility of wages implies that changes in aggregate demand and supply will tend to cause changes in unemployment.

Efficiency Wages

The idea of *efficiency wages* forms the core of another strand of New Keynesian thinking about why wages do not readily fall in response to excess supply in labour markets. For any of a number of reasons, employers may find that they get more output per dollar of wages paid—that is, a more *efficient* workforce—when they pay labour somewhat more than the minimum amount that would induce workers to work for them.

Suppose it is costly for employers to monitor workers' performance on the job, so that some workers will be able to shirk duties with a low probability of being caught. Given prevailing labour-market institutions, it is generally impossible for employers to levy fines on employees for shirking on the job since the employees could just leave their jobs rather than pay the fines. So firms may instead choose to pay a wage premium—an efficiency wage—to the workers, in excess of the wage that the workers will get elsewhere in the labour market. With such a wage premium, workers will be reluctant to shirk because, if they get caught and laid off, they will then lose this wage premium.

Efficiency-wage theory predicts that firms may find it profitable to pay high enough wages so that working is a clearly superior alternative to being laid off.

Several economists have observed that workers who believe that they are well treated work harder than those who believe that they are treated badly. This gives a reason for paying an efficiency wage—provided that the increased output from treating workers well covers the increased cost of doing so.

Union Bargaining

The final New Keynesian theory to be considered assumes that those already employed ("insiders") have more say in wage bargaining than those currently not employed ("outsiders"). Employed workers are often represented by a union which negotiates the wage rate with firms. The union will generally represent the interests of the insiders but will not necessarily reflect the interests of the outsiders. Insiders will naturally wish to bid up wages even though to do so will harm the employment prospects of the outsiders. Hence this theory generates an outcome to the bargaining process between firms and unions in which the wage is set higher than the market-clearing level, just as with efficiency wages. The consequence is involuntary unemployment.

In addition to explaining the existence of involuntary unemployment, this theory adds one important insight regarding international differences in unemployment. In some countries unions bargain at the level of the firm; in others they bargain at the level of the whole industry or the whole economy. Where bargaining is decentralized, as in Canada and the United States, the union can push for higher wages for the insiders without worrying about the effects on outsiders or on the rest of the economy. However, where bargaining is centralized, as in much of western Europe, the effects on the rest of the economy become internalized into the bargaining process, because union negotiators are bargaining on behalf of all workers (and all potential workers), rather than just the current group of insiders.

This theory leads to the following predictions. Decentralized bargaining with strong unions will lead to higher than market-clearing wages, and higher unemployment as the outsiders are excluded from jobs. In contrast, centralized bargaining will produce an outcome closer to the market-clearing outcome (because outsider concerns are voiced), so unemployment will be low. In situations where unionization is low or unions are weak, the outcome will be close to the market-clearing outcome. This analysis may explain why unemployment is relatively high in EU countries (where unions are strong and bargaining is decentralized), lower in Scandinavia (where unions are also strong but bargaining is centralized), and even lower in Canada and the United States (where unions are relatively weak and the extent of unionization is much lower).

The basic message of New Keynesian theories of unemployment is that labour markets cannot be relied upon to eliminate involuntary unemployment by equating labour demand and labour supply.

New Keynesian theories have concentrated on explaining why wages do not fluctuate to quickly clear labour markets. They therefore help to explain the existence of involuntary unemployment in the face of fluctuations in aggregate demand. These demand fluctuations are, however, still a necessary part of the explanation of cyclical fluctuations. They leave the emphasis on counter-cyclical monetary or fiscal policies whenever the automatic adjustment mechanism does not work fast enough.

Convergence of Theories?

We have examined two classes of theories of cyclical unemployment. In the New Classical theories, wages and prices adjust instantly to clear markets and so real GDP is always equal to potential GDP. Unemployment fluctuates, but it is always equal to the NAIRU, U^*. Using the terminology we introduced earlier, there is no *cyclical* unemployment in New Classical models because there is never a difference between U^* and the actual unemployment rate, U.

In contrast, New Keynesian models emphasize the gradual adjustment of wages and prices and thus the existence of periods in which real GDP is either above or below potential GDP. In these models, unemployment fluctuates around the value of U^*—that is, there is a clear distinction between the actual unemployment rate, U, and the NAIRU, U^*.

Note, however, that the sharp contrast between New Classical and New Keynesian models applies only to the short-run behaviour of the economy. It is in the short run that the extent of wage and price flexibility distinguishes these two classes of models. In the long run, however, even the staunchest New Keynesians accept the proposition that wages and prices adjust to eliminate output gaps and thus return real GDP to its potential level and the unemployment rate to the NAIRU.

Both New Classical and New Keynesians agree that in the long run wage and price flexibility brings the unemployment rate back to U^*.

Let's restate the difference between New Keynesian and New Classical models another way. In New Keynesian models there is a meaningful difference between the short

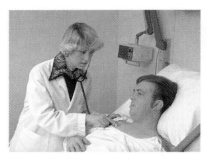

The quick adjustment of wages to excess demands and supplies is not a characteristic of labour markets in which employees and firms have long-term relationships, such as in the health-care sector.

run and the long run that is determined by the degree of wage and price flexibility. In New Classical models, however, wages and prices adjust instantly, so there is no similar distinction between the short run and the long run. But, since *both* classes of models agree that wages and prices are flexible in the long run, they have the same predictions regarding the long-run effects of policy.

For example, New Keynesians argue that a monetary expansion will raise real GDP above Y^* and reduce U below the NAIRU. In the long run, however, output will return to Y^*, U will return to U^* and the only long-run effect of the monetary expansion will be a higher price level. New Classical economists agree on this predicted long-run effect, but they argue that the short-run real effects on output and unemployment will either be absent or of much shorter duration since wages and prices adjust very quickly.

New Keynesians and New Classical economists agree that the actual unemployment rate is equal to the NAIRU in the long run. Our next job is to understand why the NAIRU changes. We turn to this topic now.

The NAIRU

The NAIRU is composed of frictional and structural unemployment. Our interest is in why the NAIRU changes over time and in the extent that economic policy can affect the NAIRU.

Frictional Unemployment

frictional unemployment
Unemployment caused by the time that is taken for labour to move from one job to another.

search unemployment
Unemployment caused by people continuing to search for a good job rather than accepting the first job they are offered after they become unemployed.

As we saw in Chapter 19, **frictional unemployment** results from the normal turnover of labour. An important source of frictional unemployment is young people who enter the labour force and look for jobs. Another source is people who leave their jobs. Some may quit because they are dissatisfied with the type of work or their working conditions; others may be fired. Whatever the reason, they must search for new jobs, which takes time. Persons who are unemployed while searching for jobs are said to be frictionally unemployed or in **search unemployment.**

The normal turnover of labour causes frictional unemployment to persist, even if the economy is at potential output.

How "voluntary" is frictional unemployment? Some of it is clearly voluntary. For example, a worker may know of an available job but may not accept it so she can search for a better one. An extreme New Classical view regards *all* frictional unemployment as voluntary. Critics of that view argue that many frictionally unemployed workers are involuntarily unemployed because they lost their jobs through no fault of their own (e.g., their factories may have closed down) and have not yet located specific jobs that they know to be available *somewhere* for which they believe they are qualified.

Extensions in Theory 30-2, which discusses search unemployment in more detail, shows that the distinction between voluntary and involuntary unemployment is not always as clear as it might at first seem.

EXTENSIONS IN THEORY 30-2

Voluntary Versus Involuntary Unemployment

Frictional unemployment is *involuntary* if the job seeker has not yet found a job for which his or her training and experience are suitable. Frictional unemployment is *voluntary* if the unemployed person is aware of available jobs for which he or she is suited but is searching for better options. But how should we classify an unemployed person who refuses to accept a job at a lower skill level than the one for which she is qualified? What if she turns down a job for which she is trained because she hopes to get a higher wage offer for a similar job from another employer?

In one sense, people in search unemployment are voluntarily unemployed because they could almost always find some job; in another sense, they are involuntarily unemployed because they have not yet succeeded in finding the job for which they feel they are suited at a rate of pay that they believe is attainable.

Workers do not have perfect knowledge of all available jobs and rates of pay, and they may be able to gain information only by searching the market. Facing this uncertainty, they may find it sensible to refuse a first job offer, for the offer may prove to be a poor one in light of further market information. But too much search—for example, holding off while being supported by others in the hope of finding a job better than a job for which one is really suited—is an economic waste. Thus, search unemployment is a gray area: Some of it is useful, and some of it is wasteful.

It is socially desirable for there to be sufficient search unemployment to give unemployed people time to find an available job that makes the best use of their skills. How long it pays for people to remain in search unemployment depends on the economic costs of being unemployed. By lowering the costs of being unemployed, unemployment insurance tends to increase the amount of search unemployment. This may or may not increase economic efficiency, depending on whether or not it induces people to search beyond the point at which they acquire new and valuable information about the labour market.

Structural Unemployment

Structural adjustments in the economy can cause unemployment. When the pattern of demand for goods changes, the pattern of the demand for labour changes. Until labour adjusts fully, structural unemployment develops. **Structural unemployment** is caused by a mismatch between the structure of the labour force—in terms of skills, occupations, industries, or geographical locations—and the structure of the demand for labour.

structural unemployment Unemployment due to a mismatch between characteristics required by available jobs and characteristics possessed by the unemployed labour.

Natural Causes

Changes that accompany economic growth shift the structure of the demand for labour. Demand rises in such expanding areas as British Columbia's lower mainland or Ontario's Ottawa valley and falls in declining areas such as Newfoundland and parts of Quebec. Demand rises for workers with certain skills, such as computer programming and electronics engineering, and falls for workers with other skills, such as stenography, assembly line work, and middle management. To meet changing demands, the structure of the labour force must change. Some existing workers can retrain and some new entrants can acquire fresh skills, but the transition is often difficult, especially for already experienced workers whose skills become economically obsolete.

Increases in international competition can also cause structural unemployment. As the geographical distribution of world production changes, so does the composition of production and of labour demand in any one country. Labour adapts to such shifts by changing jobs, skills, and locations, but until the transition is complete, structural unemployment exists.

Structural unemployment will increase if there is either an increase in the pace at which the structure of the demand for labour is changing or a decrease in the pace at which labour is adapting to these changes.

Policy Causes

Government policies can influence the speed with which labour markets adapt to changes. Some countries, including Canada, have adopted policies that *discourage* movement among regions, industries, and occupations. These policies (which may be desirable for other reasons) tend to *raise* structural unemployment rather than lower it.

Policies that discourage firms from replacing labour with machines may protect employment over the short term. However, if such policies lead to the decline of an industry because it cannot compete effectively with innovative foreign competitors, more serious structural unemployment can result in the long run.

Minimum-wage laws can cause structural unemployment by pricing low-skilled labour out of the market. As was explained in Chapter 14, minimum-wage laws have two effects when they are imposed on competitive markets: They reduce employment of the unskilled, and they raise the wages of the unskilled who retain their jobs.

Unemployment insurance also contributes to structural unemployment, for at least two reasons.[4] First, the Canadian UI system ties workers' benefits to the regional unemployment rate in such a way that unemployed workers can collect UI benefits for more weeks in regions where unemployment is high than where it is low. The UI system therefore encourages unemployed workers to remain in high-unemployment regions rather than encouraging them to move to regions where employment prospects are more favourable.

Second, workers are only eligible for unemployment insurance if they have worked for a given number of weeks in the previous year—this is known as the *entrance requirement*. In some cases, however, these entrance requirements are very low and thus seasonal workers are encouraged to work for a few months and then collect unemployment insurance and wait for the next season, rather than finding other jobs during the off season.

The Frictional-Structural Distinction

For information on Canada's Employment Insurance program, see the website for Human Resources Development Canada: www.hrdc-drhc.gc.ca.

As with many distinctions, the one between frictional and structural unemployment is not precise. In a sense, structural unemployment is really long-term frictional unemployment. Consider, for example, what would happen if there was an increase in world demand for Canadian-made car parts but at the same time a decline in world demand for Canadian-assembled cars. This change would require labour to move from one sector (the car-assembly sector) to another (the car-parts manufacturing sector). If the reallocation were to occur quickly, we call the unemployment *frictional;* if the reallocation were to occur slowly, we call the unemployment *structural.*

---

[4]Canada's unemployment-insurance program was renamed Employment Insurance (EI) in 1996. Unemployment insurance is a more general term, however, and so we continue to use it here.

The major characteristic of both frictional and structural unemployment is that there are as many unfilled vacancies as there are unemployed persons.

In the case of pure frictional unemployment, the job vacancy and the searcher are matched—the only problem is that the searcher has not yet located the vacancy. In the case of structural unemployment, the job vacancy and the searcher are mismatched in one or more relevant characteristics, such as occupation, industry, location, or skill requirements.

In practice, structural and frictional unemployment cannot be separated. But the two of them, taken together, *can* be separated from cyclical unemployment. Specifically, when real GDP is at its potential level, the *only* unemployment (by definition) is the NAIRU, which comprises frictional and structural unemployment. For example, most economists agree that real GDP in Canada was approximately equal to potential GDP in late 1999. At that time, the unemployment rate was about 7 percent, and thus the NAIRU was approximately 7 percent. In contrast, seven years earlier in 1992, the unemployment rate was 11.5 percent. To the extent that the underlying frictions and structural change in the economy were unchanged between 1992 and 1999, we can conclude that in 1992, 4.5 percentage points of the actual unemployment rate were due to cyclical factors and the rest was due to frictional and structural factors.

Why Does the NAIRU Change?

We know that structural unemployment can increase because the pace of change accelerates or the pace of adjustment to change slows down. An increase in the rate of growth, for example, usually speeds up the rate at which the structure of the demand for labour is changing. The adaptation of labour to the changing structure of demand may be slowed by such diverse factors as a decline in education and new regulations that make it harder for workers in a given occupation to take new jobs in other areas or occupations. Any of these changes will cause the NAIRU to rise. Changes in the opposite direction will cause the NAIRU to fall.

Demographic Shifts

Because people usually try several jobs before settling into one for a longer period of time, young or inexperienced workers have higher unemployment rates than experienced workers. The proportion of inexperienced workers in the labour force rose significantly as the baby boom generation of the 1950s entered the labour force in the 1970s and 1980s. Because birthrates were low in the 1960s, some demographically induced fall in this type of unemployment has been occurring over the past decade.

During the 1960s and 1970s women tended to have higher unemployment rates than men. Since this was true at all points of the business cycle, the higher unemployment was higher frictional and structural unemployment. Thus, when female labour-force participation rates increased dramatically in the 1960s and 1970s, the NAIRU naturally increased. In recent years, however, female unemployment rates have dropped below the rates for men, and so continued increases in female participation will, if anything, tend to decrease the NAIRU.

Young workers have higher unemployment rates than do older workers. As the share of younger workers in the labour force increases, so will the economy's NAIRU.

Greater labour-force participation by groups with high unemployment rates increases the level of NAIRU.

See Figure 30-3 for Canadian unemployment rates for various demographic groups in 1999. Notice especially the significantly higher

FIGURE 30-3   Unemployment Rates by Demographic Groups, 1999

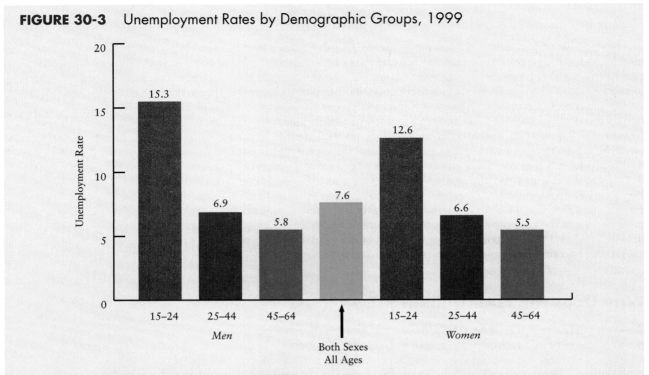

Unemployment is unevenly spread among different groups in the labour force. In 1999, when the overall unemployment rate was 7.6 percent, the unemployment rates for youths (of both sexes) was considerably higher.

(*Source:* These data are available on Statistics Canada's website: www.statcan.ca)

unemployment rates for youth of both sexes. These data form the basis for the often-heard view that while overall unemployment may be at acceptable levels, youth unemployment may be a serious problem.

Hysteresis

Some models of unemployment show that the size of the NAIRU can be influenced by the size of the actual current rate of unemployment. Such models get their name from the Greek word *hysteresis,* meaning "lagged effect."

One mechanism that can lead to hysteresis arises from the importance of experience and on-the-job training. Suppose that a recession causes a significant group of new entrants to the labour force to encounter unusual difficulty obtaining their first jobs. As a result, this unlucky group will be slow to acquire the important skills that workers generally learn in their first jobs. When demand increases again, this group of workers will be at a disadvantage relative to workers with normal histories of experience, and the unlucky group may have unemployment rates that will be higher than average. Hence, the NAIRU will be higher than it would have been had there been no recession.

Another force that can cause such effects is emphasized by commentators in western Europe, which has a more heavily unionized labour force than does either Canada or the United States. In times of high unemployment, people who are currently employed ("insiders") may use their bargaining power to ensure that their own status is maintained and prevent new entrants to the labour force ("outsiders") from competing effectively. In an *insider-outsider* model of this type, a period of prolonged, high unemployment—whatever its initial cause—will tend to become "locked in." If outsiders are denied access to the labour market, their unemployment will fail to exert downward pressure on wages, and the NAIRU will tend to rise.

Increasing Structural Change

The amount of resources being moved between industries and regions increased in the mid 1970s and appears to be carrying on through the 1980s and 1990s. In part, this is the result of the increasing integration of the Canadian economy with the rest of the world and the globalization of world markets. Most economists would argue that this integration has been beneficial overall, for reasons we discuss in Chapters 34 and 35. One less fortunate consequence, however, is that Canadian labour markets are increasingly affected by changes in demand and supply conditions anywhere in the world—changes that require adjustments throughout the world's trading nations. Although evidence is difficult to obtain, some observers argue that the increasing pace and the changing nature of technological change since the mid 1970s has contributed to an increase in the level of structural unemployment.

Policy and Labour-Market Flexibility

We mentioned briefly above how policies can affect structural unemployment and thus affect the NAIRU. It is worthwhile emphasizing again the important role that government policy can have on the NAIRU.

Our discussion in the previous several pages suggests that one important cause of unemployment is *inflexibility* in the labour market. If wages are inflexible, then shocks to labour demand or supply can cause unemployment. If workers are unable or unwilling to move between regions or between industries, then changes in the structure of the economy can cause unemployment. If it is costly for firms to hire workers, then firms will find other ways of increasing output (such as switching to more capital-intensive methods of production). In general, since the economy is always being buffeted by shocks of one sort or another, the more inflexibility there is in the labour market, the higher unemployment will be.

This relationship suggests a general point about the effect of government policy on the NAIRU:

Any government policy that reduces labour-market flexibility is likely to increase the NAIRU.

Consider two examples.

The first example is unemployment insurance (UI). UI provides income support to eligible unemployed workers and thus reduces the costs to the worker of being unemployed. This income support will typically lead the worker to search longer for a new job and thus increase the unemployment rate. This longer search may be desirable since by reducing the cost of unemployment the worker is able to conduct a thorough search for a job that is an appropriate match for his or her specific skills. On the other hand, if the UI system is so generous that workers have little incentive to accept reasonable jobs—instead holding out for the "perfect" job—then the increase in unemployment generated by the UI system will be undesirable.

In general, however, the basic message should be clear. The more generous is the unemployment insurance system, the less motivated unemployed workers will be to quickly accept a new job. This reduction in labour-market flexibility will increase the NAIRU.

The second example concerns policies designed to increase job security for workers. In most western European countries, firms that lay off workers are required either to give

See Chapter 30 of www.pearsoned.ca/lipsey for a debate on the effects of mandated job security: Seamus Hogan, "Should Governments Mandate Job Security?" and Marc Van Audenrode, "A Partial Defence of Job Security Provisions," *World Economic Affairs.*

See Chapter 30 of www.pearsoned.ca/lipsey for a discussion of the likely effects of France's recent policy of shortening the length of the work week: Jan Olters, "Some Doubts About France's 35-Hour Week," *World Economic Affairs.*

several months notice before doing so or, in lieu of such notice, are required to make severance payments equal to several months worth of pay. In Italy, for example, a worker who has been with the firm for ten years is guaranteed either 20 months notice before termination or a severance payment equal to 20 months worth of pay.

Such job-security provisions reduce the flexibility of firms. But this inflexibility on the part of the firms is passed on to workers. Any policy that forces the firm to incur large costs for laying off workers is likely to lead the same firm to be very hesitant about hiring workers in the first place. Given this reduction in labour-market flexibility, such policies are likely to increase the NAIRU.

Such mandated job security is relatively rare in Canada and the United States. Its rarity contributes to the general belief among economists that North American labour markets are much more flexible than those in Europe. Many economists see this as the most important explanation for why unemployment rates in Canada and the United States are significantly below the unemployment rates in Europe, and have been for the past two decades.

Reducing Unemployment

As the Canadian economy grew steadily from 1993 to 1999, the unemployment rate dropped from 11.3 percent to 7 percent. Unemployment in the United States declined by a similar amount, as the U.S. economy was also experiencing steady economic growth. In both cases, most economists viewed the decline in unemployment as a desirable reduction in *cyclical* unemployment.

Despite the reduction in Canada's unemployment rate in the late 1990s, however, many economists have been puzzled at the growing unemployment *gap* between Canada and the United States. Beginning in the early 1980s, the Canadian unemployment rate has increased relative to the U.S. rate. By the late 1990s, the gap was approximately four percentage points. What is the cause of the gap? *Applying Economic Concepts 30-2* examines this issue and concludes that an important part of the answer lies in how the unemployed are counted in the two countries.

In the remainder of this chapter we briefly examine what can be done to reduce unemployment. Other things being equal, all governments would like to reduce unemployment. The questions are "Can it be done?" and "If so, at what cost?"

Practise with Study Guide Chapter 30, Exercise 2.

Cyclical Unemployment

We do not need to say much more about cyclical unemployment because its control is the subject of stabilization policy, which we have studied in several earlier chapters. A major recession that occurs because of natural causes can be countered by monetary and fiscal policies to reduce cyclical unemployment.

There is room for debate, however, about *how much* the government can and should do in this respect. Advocates of stabilization policy call for expansionary fiscal and monetary policies to reduce such gaps, at least when they last for sustained periods of time. Advocates of a hands-off approach say that normal market adjustments can be relied on to remove such gaps and that government policy, no matter how well intentioned, will only make things worse. They call for setting simple rules for monetary and fiscal policy that would make discretionary stabilization policy impossible. This matter was discussed in detail at the end of Chapter 25.

Whatever may be argued in principle, however, policymakers have not yet agreed to abandon such stabilization measures in practice.

Frictional Unemployment

The turnover that causes frictional unemployment is an inevitable part of the functioning of the economy. Some frictional unemployment is a natural part of the learning process for young workers. New entrants to the labour force (many of whom are young) have to try several jobs to see which is most suitable, and this leads to a high turnover rate among the young and hence high frictional unemployment.

To the extent that frictional unemployment is caused by ignorance regarding where the appropriate jobs are, increasing the knowledge of workers about market opportunities may help. But such measures have a cost, and that cost has to be balanced against the benefits.

Unemployment insurance is one method of helping people cope with unemployment. It has reduced significantly the human costs of the bouts with unemployment that are inevitable in a changing society. Nothing, however, is without cost. Although unemployment insurance alleviates the suffering caused by some kinds of unemployment, it also contributes to search unemployment, as we have already observed.

Supporters of unemployment insurance emphasize its benefits. Critics emphasize its costs. As with any policy, a rational assessment of the value of unemployment insurance requires a balancing of its undoubted benefits against its undoubted costs. Many Canadians believe that when this calculation is made, the benefits greatly exceed the costs, although many also recognize the scope for reform of certain aspects of the program.

Many provisions have been added over the years to the unemployment insurance scheme to focus it more on people in general need and to reduce its effect of raising the unemployment rate. For example, workers must be actively seeking employment in order to be eligible for UI. Also, workers who voluntarily quit their jobs (without cause) are not eligible to collect UI. Finally, a system of *experience rating* has recently been proposed to distribute the costs more in proportion to the benefits. In the absence of experience rating all firms pay the same UI tax; this implicitly subsidizes those firms who create the most unemployment and taxes most heavily those firms who create the least unemployment. Under experience rating, firms with histories of sizable layoffs pay more than those with better layoff records.

Structural Unemployment

The reallocation of labour among occupations, industries, skill categories, and regions that gives rise to structural unemployment is an inevitable part of a market economy. There are two basic approaches to reducing structural unemployment: Try to arrest the changes that the economy experiences or accept the changes and try to speed up the adjustments. Throughout history, labour and management have advocated both approaches and governments have tried them both.

Ever since the beginning of the Industrial Revolution, workers have resisted the introduction of new techniques that replace the older techniques at which they were skilled. Such resistance is understandable. New techniques often destroy the value of the knowledge and experience of workers skilled in the displaced techniques. Older workers may not even get a chance to start over with the new technique. Employers may prefer to hire younger persons who will learn the new skills faster than older workers who are set in their ways of thinking. But, from society's point of view, new techniques are beneficial because they are a major source of economic growth. From the point of view of the workers they displace, new techniques can be an unmitigated disaster.

Over the long term, policies that subsidize employment in declining industries run into increasing difficulties. Agreements to hire unneeded workers raise costs and can hasten the decline of an industry threatened by competitive products. An industry that

APPLYING ECONOMIC CONCEPTS 30-2

The Canada–U.S. Unemployment Gap

In recent years economists have been examining why the gap between the Canadian and U.S. unemployment rates has been growing. As the accompanying figure shows, the last year in which the two countries had the same unemployment rate was 1981. Since then the Canadian unemployment rate has exceeded the U.S. rate by an average of two percentage points in the 1980s and by four percentage points in the 1990s. What is the cause of this gap? Does the gap reflect a more poorly functioning Canadian economy?

Craig Riddell from the University of British Columbia and David Card from the University of California at Berkeley have shown that an important part of the explanation lies in the difference between *unemployment* and *non-participation* in the labour force. In short, a randomly selected individual in each country who is not working is more likely to be considered unemployed in Canada but out of the labour force in the United States. This difference naturally increases the Canadian unemployment rate relative to that in the United States. Let's look at this in more detail.

Decomposing the Unemployment Rate

It is helpful to first define some terms. We will use the following symbols to represent the important labour-market variables:

U = number of persons who are unemployed
LF = number of persons in the labour force
POP = number of persons in the working-age population
N = number of persons in the working-age population who are *not* working

Recall that the unemployment rate is simply the fraction of the labour force that is unemployed, U/LF. We can write this differently as

$$U/LF = (U/N) \times (N/POP) \times (POP/LF)$$

It should be clear that this equation always holds since we could cancel the Ns and the POPs to simply get U/LF = U/LF. But this longer equation allows us to see that any change in the unemployment rate *must be* due to a change in one (or more) of these three separate variables. What are these three variables?

An individual can be non-employed either by being out of the labour force or by being in the labour force but unemployed. The ratio U/N is simply the fraction of the total non-working persons who are classified as unemployed. Clearly, a rise in U/N, other things equal, raises the unemployment rate. The second variable, N/POP, is the fraction of the working-age population that is *not* working. This is one minus the country's *employment rate*. A reduction in the employment rate, other things equal, means a rise in N/POP and thus an increase in the unemployment rate. The third variable, POP/LF, is simply the inverse of the labour-force participation rate. A fall in the participation rate, other things equal, means a rise in POP/LF and thus an increase in the unemployment rate.

Growing Labour-Force Attachment in Canada

Card and Riddell argue that the U/N ratio is the key variable for explaining the Canada-U.S. unemployment gap. They refer to U/N as a measure of *labour-force attachment*—since the non-working individuals who are classified as unemployed are "attached" to the labour force.

Card and Riddell find that between 1981 and 1998, fully two-thirds of the Canada-U.S. unemployment gap is explained by an increase in the Canadian U/N ratio relative to that in the United States. One quarter of the gap is accounted for by a lower employment rate (higher N/POP) and less than

is declining because of economic change becomes an increasingly large burden on the public purse as economic forces become less and less favourable to its success. Sooner or later, public support is withdrawn, followed by a precipitous decline.

As we assess these remedies for structural unemployment, it is important to realize that although they are not viable in the long run for the entire economy, they may be the best alternatives for the affected workers during their lifetimes.

There is often a genuine conflict between the private interest of workers threatened by structural unemployment, whose interests lie in preserving existing jobs, and the social interest served by reallocating resources to where they are most valuable.

10 percent of the gap is explained by lower labour-force participation (higher POP/LF).

To put it differently, the principal cause of the rising Canada-U.S. unemployment gap appears to be a change in the way that non-employed Canadians spend their time relative to their U.S. counterparts. When not working, Canadians in the past two decades have become more likely to continue searching for jobs, and thus to be officially counted among the unemployed. In contrast, non-working Americans have become relatively more likely to be counted among the non-participants.

Causes of the Greater Attachment

Two main reasons are offered for why Canadians appear to have a greater attachment to the labour force. First, there are slight but significant differences in how the unemployed are classified in the two countries. In order to be considered unemployed in the United States, individuals must be "actively" searching for work. In contrast, Canadians must only be "passively" looking for work. So, for example, an individual who *only* reads the help-

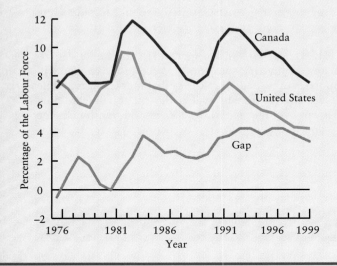

wanted ads in the newspaper would be classified as unemployed in Canada but as out of the labour force in the United States. This difference alone, although it sounds like a minor point, appears to explain one quarter of the unemployment gap.

Card and Riddell suggest that the greater generosity and availability of the Canadian unemployment-insurance system is also very important for explaining why Canadians have a greater attachment to the labour force. The greater generosity obviously improves the insurance value of the program for those workers who may lose their jobs. But by reducing the costs associated with being unemployed, it also results in longer job search and higher measured unemployment (for a given level of employment).

Is It a Problem?

In order to know whether a rise in unemployment is undesirable, we must know why the increase occurred. To the extent that the higher Canadian unemployment rate is due to poorer employment growth in Canada, this may represent a problem. Some economists argue that tight fiscal and monetary policies, especially in the 1990s, are largely responsible for the rise in the N/POP ratio in Canada relative to that in the United States.

But the findings by Card and Riddell are that the clear majority of the unemployment gap is due to a rise in labour-force attachment (U/N) in Canada. Is this a problem? As Riddell says, "The implications for individuals' welfare of a rise in unemployment that is not associated with a decline in employment are much less obvious." The greater labour-force attachment arising from the different classification of similar workers is obviously not a problem for individual well-being. However, the greater labour-force attachment arising from a more generous UI system may be a problem. As we said earlier in this chapter, an overly generous UI system may encourage unemployed workers to search *too much*, holding out for the "perfect" job match rather than accepting a merely "good" job offer.

This box is based on Craig Riddell, "Canadian Labour-Market Performance in International Perspective," *Canadian Journal of Economics*, November 1999.

A second general approach to dealing with structural change is to accept the decline of specific industries and the loss of specific jobs that go with them and to try to reduce the cost of adjustment for the workers affected. A number of policies have been introduced in Canada to ease the adjustment to changing economic conditions.

One such policy is publicly subsidized education and retraining schemes. The public involvement is motivated largely by imperfections in capital markets that make it difficult for workers to borrow funds for education, training or retraining. A major component of labour-market policies is a system of loans and subsidies for higher education.

Another policy is motivated by the difficulty in obtaining good information about current and future job prospects. In recent years, the development of the Internet has

To learn more about the National Job Bank or the Electronic Labour Exchange, see HRDC's website: www.hrdc-drhc-gc.ca.

greatly improved the flow of this type of information. Human Resources Development Canada (HRDC), for example, operates two Internet-based services to speed up and improve the quality of matches between firms and workers. The HRDC National Job Bank allows workers to search various regions of the country for jobs of specific types. The Electronic Labour Exchange allows firms (or workers) to specify certain characteristics and skills and then match these characteristics with workers (or firms) on the "other side" of the labour market.

Policies to increase retraining and to improve the flow of labour-market information will tend to reduce the amount of structural unemployment.

Conclusion

Over the years, unemployment has been regarded in many different ways. Harsh critics see it as proof that the market system is badly flawed. Reformers regard it as a necessary evil of the market system and a suitable object for government policy to reduce its incidence and its harmful effects. Others see it as overblown in importance and believe that it does not reflect any real inability of workers to obtain jobs if they really want to work.

Most government policy has followed a middle route. Fiscal and monetary policies have sought to reduce at least the most persistent of recessionary gaps, and a host of labour-market policies have sought to reduce the incidence of frictional and structural unemployment. Such social policies as unemployment insurance have sought to reduce the sting of unemployment for the many who were thought to suffer from it for reasons beyond their control.

As global economic competition becomes more and more severe and as new knowledge-driven methods of production spread, the ability to adjust to economic change will become increasingly important. Countries that succeed in the global marketplace, while also managing to maintain humane social welfare systems, will be those that best learn how to cooperate with change. This will mean avoiding economic policies that inhibit change while adopting social policies that reduce the human cost of adjusting to change. This is an enormous challenge for future Canadian economic and social policies.

S U M M A R Y

Employment and Unemployment   10 1

- Canadian employment and the Canadian labour force have increased along a strong upward trend throughout all of this century. The unemployment rate has fluctuated significantly; over the past forty years it has also shown an upward trend.
- Looking only at the level of employment or unemployment misses a tremendous amount of activity in the labour market as individuals flow from unemployment to employment or from employment to unemployment. In

recent years in Canada, approximately 400 000 people *per month* flow between employment and unemployment. This level of gross flows reflects the turnover which is a normal part of any labour market.
- It is useful to distinguish among several types of unemployment: cyclical unemployment, which is associated with output gaps; frictional unemployment, which is caused by the length of time it takes to find a first job and to move from job to job as a result of normal labour

turnover; and structural unemployment, which is caused by the need to reallocate resources among occupations, regions, and industries as the structure of demand and supply changes.

- Together, frictional unemployment and structural unemployment make up the NAIRU, which is then expressed as a percentage of the total labour force. The actual unemployment rate is equal to the NAIRU when real output is equal to potential output.

Cyclical Unemployment   LO 2

- There is a long-standing debate among economists regarding the causes of cyclical unemployment.
- New Classical theories look to explanations that allow the labour market to be cleared continuously by perfectly flexible wages and prices. Such theories can explain cyclical variations in employment but do not predict the existence of involuntary unemployment.
- New Keynesian theories have focused on the long-term nature of employer-worker relationships in which wages tend to respond only a little, and employment tends to

respond a lot, to changes in the demand and supply of labour. More recent New Keynesian theories have examined the possibility that it may be efficient for employers to pay wages that are above the level that would clear the labour market (efficiency wages).

- This debate only applies to the short-run behaviour of the economy. Both classes of models, for example, predict that in the long run, monetary expansions or contractions affect only the price level, and do not affect output, employment, or unemployment.

The NAIRU   LO 3 4

- The NAIRU will always be positive because it takes time for labour to move between jobs both in normal turnover (frictional unemployment) and in response to changes in the structure of the demand for labour (structural unemployment).
- Because different workers have different sets of skills and because different firms require workers with different sets of skills, some unemployment—resulting from workers searching for appropriate job matches with employers—is socially desirable.

- Anything that increases the rate of turnover in the labour market, or the pace of structural change in the economy, will likely increase the NAIRU.
- Unemployment insurance also increases the NAIRU by encouraging workers to continue searching for an appropriate job. Policies that mandate job security increase the costs to firms of laying off workers. This makes them reluctant to hire workers in the first place and thus increases the NAIRU.

Reducing Unemployment   LO 5

- Cyclical unemployment can be reduced by using monetary or fiscal policies to close recessionary gaps. Frictional and structural unemployment can be reduced by making it easier to move between jobs and by raising the cost of

staying unemployed (e.g., by reducing unemployment insurance benefits).

- In a growing, changing economy populated by people who wish to change jobs for many reasons, it is neither possible nor desirable to reduce unemployment to zero.

KEY CONCEPTS

Gross flows in the labour market
Cyclical, frictional, and structural unemployment
New Classical and New Keynesian theories of unemployment
Long-term employment relationships
Efficiency wages
Hysteresis
The components of the NAIRU
Determinants of the size of the NAIRU
Policies to reduce the NAIRU
Labour-market flexibility

STUDY EXERCISES

1. The following table shows the pattern of real GDP, potential GDP, and the unemployment rate for several years in Cycleland.

Year	Real GDP (billions of dollars)	Potential GDP (billions of dollars)	Unemployment Rate (%)
1991	790	740	6.3
1992	800	760	6.5
1993	780	780	6.8
1994	750	800	8.2
1995	765	810	8.4
1996	790	830	8.4
1997	815	850	8.0
1998	845	870	7.5
1999	875	890	7.2
2000	900	900	7.0
2001	930	920	6.8

a. On a scale diagram, draw the path of real GDP and potential GDP (with time on the horizontal axis).
b. On a separate diagram (below the first one) show the path of the unemployment rate.
c. For which years is it possible to determine the value of NAIRU?
d. Does the NAIRU change over the ten-year period? Provide one reason (based on the text) that NAIRU could increase.

2. The diagram below shows a simple $AD/SRAS$ diagram. The economy begins at E_0 with real GDP equal to potential GDP.

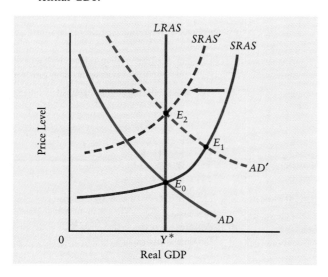

a. At E_0, the unemployment rate is 8%. What type of unemployment is this?
b. A positive aggregate demand shock now shifts the AD curve to AD'. At E_1 the unemployment rate is only 6.5% Is there cyclical unemployment at E_1?
c. Describe the economy's adjustment process to E_2.
d. What is the unemployment rate at E_2?

3. The diagram below shows a simple $AD/SRAS$ diagram. The economy begins at E_0 with real GDP equal to potential GDP.

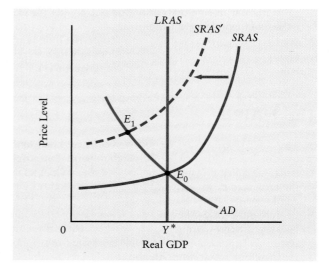

a. At E_0, the unemployment rate is 6%. What type of unemployment is this?
b. A negative aggregate supply shock now shifts the $SRAS$ curve to $SRAS'$. At E_1 the unemployment rate is 7.5% Is there cyclical unemployment at E_1? How much?
c. If monetary and fiscal policy do not react to the shock, describe the economy's adjustment process to its long-run equilibrium.
d. What is the unemployment rate at the economy's long-run equilibrium? Explain.

4. The diagram on the next page shows a perfectly competitive labour market. The initial equilibrium is with wage w^* and employment L^*.

a. Suppose the demand for labour decreases to D'_L. If wages are perfectly flexible, what is the effect on wages and employment? Show this in the diagram.
b. Is there any involuntary unemployment in part a?
c. Now suppose that wages can only adjust half as much as in part a—that is, wages are sticky. What is

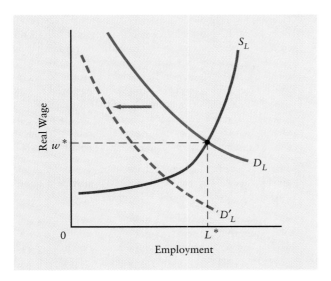

the effect on wages and employment in this case? Show this in the diagram.

d. Is there any involuntary unemployment in part **c**? How much?

5. Consider an economy that begins with real GDP equal to potential. There is then a sudden increase in the prices of raw materials, which shifts the *SRAS* curve up and to the left.

   a. Draw the initial long-run equilibrium in an *AD/SRAS* diagram.

   b. Now show the immediate effect of the supply shock in your diagram.

   c. Suppose that wages and prices in this economy adjust instantly to shocks. Describe what happens to unemployment in this economy. Explain.

d. If wages and prices adjust only slowly to shocks, what happens to unemployment? Explain.

e. Explain why the key difference between New Keynesian and New Classical theories of unemployment involves the degree of wage and price flexibility.

6. The table below shows the percentage of the labour force accounted for by youths (15–24 years old) and older workers (25 years and older) over several years. Suppose that, due to their lower skills and greater turnover, youths have a higher unemployment rate than older workers (see Figure 30-3).

| | Percentage of Labour Force | |
Year	Youths	Older Workers
1.	20	80
2.	21	79
3.	22	78
4.	23	77
5.	25	75
6.	27	73
7.	29	71
8.	31	69

a. Suppose that in year 1 real GDP is equal to potential GDP, and the unemployment rate among older workers is 6% but is 14% among youths. What is the economy's NAIRU?

b. Now suppose that for the next eight years real GDP remains equal to potential. Compute the value of NAIRU for each year.

c. Explain why NAIRU rises even though output is always equal to potential.

DISCUSSION QUESTIONS

1. Interpret the following statements from newspapers in terms of types of unemployment.

   a. "Recession hits local factory; 2000 laid off."

   b. "Of course, I could take a job as a dishwasher, but I'm trying to find something that makes use of my high school training," says a local teenager in our survey of the unemployed.

   c. "Retraining is the best reaction to the increased use of robots."

   d. "Uneven upturn: Signs of recovery in Alberta, but Ontario is still in recession."

2. Discuss the following views. Is it possible that both views are right? Explain.

   a. "Canadian workers should resist automation, which is destroying their jobs," says a labour leader.

   b. "Given the fierce foreign competition faced by Canadian firms, it's a case of automate or die," says an industrialist.

3. "No one needs to be out of work if he or she really wants a job; just look at the Help Wanted signs in many fast-food businesses and retail shops." Does the existence of the unfilled vacancies suggested in the quotation

imply that there need be no cyclical unemployment as long as workers are not excessively fussy about the kinds of jobs they will take?

4. What differences in approach toward the problem of unemployment are suggested by the following facts?

   a. In the 1960s and 1970s, Britain spent billions of dollars on subsidizing firms that would otherwise have gone out of business in order to protect the jobs of the employees.
   b. Sweden has been a pioneer in spending large sums to retrain and to relocate displaced workers.

5. Advocates of discretionary fiscal policy often argue that the government can reduce unemployment by increasing spending on such things as highways, bridges, sewer systems, and so on. What do you think of such a policy to "create jobs"? Is such a policy equally likely to create jobs during a recession as when the economy is operating at potential output? Explain.

6. Consider two hypothetical countries. In Country A, 20 percent of the labour force is unemployed for half the time and employed for the other half; the remaining 80 percent of the labour force is never unemployed. In Country B, 100 percent of the labour force is unemployed for 10 percent of the time and employed for the other 90 percent of the time. Note that both countries have an overall unemployment rate of 10 percent. Discuss which of these countries seems to have the more serious unemployment problem, and explain why.

7. There is a great deal of debate over the appropriate level of generosity for Canada's unemployment insurance program (Employment Insurance).

   a. Explain what problem can be caused by having a UI system that is too generous.
   b. Explain what problem can be caused by having a UI system that is not generous enough.
   c. If UI generosity were reduced and the NAIRU declined as a result, is this necessarily a desirable outcome?

CHAPTER   31

Budget Deficits and Surpluses

 LEARNING OBJECTIVES

❶ Understand how the government's annual budget deficit (or surplus) is related to its stock of debt.

❷ Explain the difference between the overall budget deficit and the primary budget deficit.

❸ Explain the meaning of the cyclically adjusted budget deficit, and how it can be used to measure the stance of fiscal policy.

❹ Understand Ricardian equivalence.

❺ Explain how deficits crowd out investment and net exports.

❻ Explain why a high stock of debt may hamper monetary and fiscal policy.

❼ Discuss several different proposals for balancing the budget.

Until the late 1990s, no single measure associated with the government was the focus of more attention and controversy than the size of the government budget deficit. Some people argued that the deficit was an economic time bomb, waiting to explode and cause serious harm to our living standards. Others argued that the only real danger posed by deficits was from the dramatic policy changes proposed to eliminate them. By 1999, however, after nearly two decades of debate about the budget deficit, the focus had shifted abruptly to what the governments—federal and provincial—should do with their budget surpluses. Just as debates once raged over the harmful effects of high government budget deficits, debates currently rage about whether governments that are facing budget surpluses should increase spending, reduce taxes, or use the surpluses to reduce the outstanding stock of government debt.

In this chapter, we examine various issues surrounding the government budget. We begin by considering the simple arithmetic of government budgets. This tells us how the deficit or surplus in any given year is related to the outstanding stock of debt. We then explore why deficits and debt matter for the performance of the economy—as well as what changes we can expect over the near future if Canadian governments are successful in maintaining either balanced budgets or budget surpluses.

Facts and Definitions

There is a simple relationship between the government's expenditures, its tax revenues, and its borrowing.

The Government's Budget Constraint

Just like any individual, government expenditures must be financed either by income or by borrowing. The difference between individuals and governments, however, is that governments typically do not earn income by selling products or labour services; instead, they earn income by levying taxes. Thus, all government expenditure must be financed either by tax revenues or by borrowing. This point is illustrated by the following simple equation, which is called the government's *budget constraint*:

$$\text{Government Expenditure} = \text{Tax Revenue} + \text{Borrowing}$$

debt-service payments Payments which represent the interest owed on a current stock of debt.

There are three broad components to government expenditures. The first is the government's purchases of goods and services, G. The second is transfers to individuals or firms, such as unemployment insurance or industrial subsidies, denoted TR. The third component is interest payments on the outstanding stock of debt. This is referred to as **debt-service payments**, denoted $i \times D$, where i is the interest rate and D is the stock of government debt. If we let T represent the government's tax revenues, we can rewrite the government's budget constraint as

$$G + TR + i \times D = T + \text{Borrowing}$$

or, subtracting T from both sides,

$$(G + TR + i \times D) - T = \text{Borrowing}$$

This equation simply says that any excess of total government spending over tax revenues must be financed by government borrowing.

budget deficit Any shortfall of current revenue below current expenditure.

The government's annual **budget deficit** is the excess of total government expenditure over total revenues in a given year. From the budget constraint above, this annual deficit is exactly the same as the amount borrowed by the government during the year. Since the government borrows by issuing bonds and selling them to lenders, borrowing by the government increases the government's outstanding stock of debt. Since D is the outstanding stock of government debt, ΔD is the *change* in the stock of debt during the course of the year. The budget deficit can therefore be written as

$$\text{Budget Deficit} = \Delta D = (G + TR + i \times D) - T$$

The government's annual budget deficit is the excess of total expenditure over total tax revenues in a given year. It is also equal to the change in the stock of government debt during the year.

Notice two points about budget deficits. First, a change in the size of the deficit requires a change in the level of expenditures *relative* to the level of tax revenues.

For a given level of tax revenues, a smaller deficit can come about only through a reduction in government expenditures; conversely, for a given level of expenditures, a smaller deficit requires an increase in tax revenues. Second, since the deficit is equal to the amount of new government borrowing, the stock of government debt will rise whenever the budget deficit is positive. Even a drastic reduction in the size of the annual budget deficit is therefore not sufficient to reduce the outstanding stock of government debt; the stock of debt will fall only if the budget deficit becomes *negative*. In this case, there is said to be a **budget surplus.**

A deficit increases the stock of debt; a surplus reduces it.

budget surplus   Any excess of current revenue over current expenditure.

The Primary Budget Deficit

The total level of government expenditure comprises purchases of goods and services (G), transfer payments (TR), and debt-service payments ($i \times D$). Since at any point in time the outstanding stock of government debt—determined by *past* government borrowing—cannot be influenced by current government policy, the debt-service component of total expenditures is beyond the control of the government. In contrast, the other components of the government's budget are said to be *discretionary* because the government can choose to change the levels of G, TR or T. To capture the part of the total deficit that is attributable to discretionary expenditures and revenues, the government's **primary budget deficit** is defined as the difference between the total budget deficit and the debt-service payments:

primary budget deficit   The difference between the government's overall budget deficit and its debt-service payments.

$$\begin{aligned} \text{Primary} \atop \text{Budget Deficit} &= {\text{Total} \atop \text{Budget Deficit}} - {\text{Debt-Service} \atop \text{Payments}} \\ &= (G + TR + i \times D - T) - i \times D \\ &= (G + TR) - T \end{aligned}$$

The government's primary budget deficit shows the extent to which tax revenues are able to finance the *discretionary* part of total expenditure. Another name for discretionary expenditure is the government's *program spending*.

It is possible that the government has an overall budget deficit but a *primary* budget surplus, indicating that tax revenues more than cover program spending but are insufficient to fully cover debt-service payments as well. For example, in the 1996–1997 fiscal year, the federal government had an overall budget deficit of $13.7 billion while debt-service payments were $45.2 billion. There was thus a primary budget *surplus* in that year of $31.5 billion—that is, total tax revenues exceeded program expenditures by $31.5 billion. By the next fiscal year, the federal government had eliminated the deficit and actually had an overall budget surplus of $3.2 billion. Debt-service payments were $44 billion, so the primary budget surplus was $47.2 billion.

The primary budget deficit is the difference between the overall budget deficit and the level of debt-service payments. In recent years, the federal government has had a primary budget surplus, indicating that tax revenues were more than sufficient to cover program expenditures.

For an illustration of the government's budget constraint, and of the distinction between overall budget deficits and primary budget deficits, see Figure 31-1. This distinction becomes very important when we examine changes in the debt-to-GDP ratio later in the chapter.

FIGURE 31-1   An Illustration of the Government's Budget Constraint

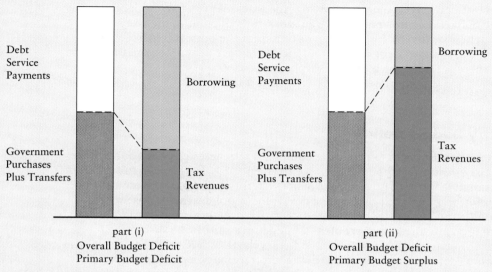

The sum of all expenditures by government must be financed either by tax collection or by borrowing. The deficit is the difference between total expenditures and total tax collection; it is also equal to the total level of borrowing. In both parts of the figure, the government's budget constraint is illustrated by the fact that the two bars are the same height, showing that total expenditures must be equal to tax revenues plus borrowing. In both parts there is an overall budget deficit because tax revenues are not sufficient to finance total expenditures (and so there is positive borrowing). In part (i), taxes are not even enough to cover government purchases and transfers, and so there is a primary budget deficit. In part (ii), taxes are more than enough to cover government purchases and transfers, and so there is a primary budget surplus (even though there is an overall budget deficit).

Deficits and Debt in Canada

Federal Government

For the most recent federal budget forecasts, see the website for the Department of Finance: www.fin.gc.ca.

In a growing economy, many macroeconomic variables such as the levels of government expenditure and tax revenue tend also to grow. As a result, rather than looking at the absolute size of the government deficit or debt, economists focus on government debt and deficits in relation to the overall size of the economy. Some budget deficits that would be unmanageable in a small country like New Zealand might be quite acceptable for a larger country like Canada, and trivial for a huge economy like the United States. Similarly, a government budget deficit that seemed crushing in Canada in 1899 might appear trivial in 1999 because the size of the Canadian economy is many times larger now than it was then.

The path of federal budget deficits since 1970 is shown in Figure 31-2. The top panel shows total federal spending and total federal tax revenues as percentages of GDP. The bottom panel shows the total federal deficit as a percentage of GDP. Persistent deficits began in the mid 1970s and lasted until the mid 1990s.

The substantial increase in the budget deficit in the early 1980s reflects the combined effects of the severe recession in 1982, some mild discretionary fiscal expansion, and increased interest payments on the government's debt. This last element was due in part to the higher real interest rates in the early 1980s and the accumulation of the deficits in the late 1970s which added to the stock of government debt. The effects of a strong economic recovery in the late 1980s, combined with active measures on the part of the federal government, then resulted in a reduction in the deficit. By 1989, at the beginning of a significant economic downturn, the deficit was just over 3 percent of GDP. The recession of 1991 again pushed up the deficit, but by then the large stock of federal government debt made the federal government reluctant to let the deficit rise considerably. As a result, by 1993, two years into a slow economic recovery, the federal budget deficit had increased only to about 5 percent of GDP. As the recovery progressed further, and the federal government continued its policy of reducing the deficit, the deficit fell rapidly until finally being eliminated in the 1997–98 fiscal year.

As we saw in the previous section, a deficit implies that the stock of government debt is rising. Thus, the persistent deficits that began in the 1970s have their counterpart in a steadily rising stock of government debt. Figure 31-3 shows the path of Canadian federal government debt since 1940. At the beginning of the Second World War, the stock of federal debt was equal to about 45 percent of GDP. The enormous increase in the debt-to-GDP ratio over the next five years reflects wartime borrowing used to finance military expenditures. From 1946 to 1974, however, there was a continual decline in the debt-to-GDP ratio. The economy was growing quickly during this period. But equally important was that the federal government in the post-war years typically ran significant budget surpluses. These two factors explain the dramatic decline in the debt-to-GDP ratio between 1946 and 1974.

By 1975 the federal debt was only 14 percent of GDP. The large and persistent budget deficits beginning in the mid 1970s, however, along with a general slowdown in the rate of economic growth, led to a significant upward trend in the debt-to-GDP ratio. The ratio climbed steadily from 1979 to 1996 and then, with the significant reductions in the deficit beginning in 1996, the debt-to-GDP ratio began to fall.

Provincial Governments

Canada is relatively special among developed countries in the sense that its provincial governments are responsible for a significant fraction of total government revenues and expenditures. In many countries, sizable regional governments either do not exist, as in New Zealand, or are often required to run balanced budgets, as is the case for about two

FIGURE 31-2   Federal Government Expenditures, Revenues, and Deficit, 1970–1998

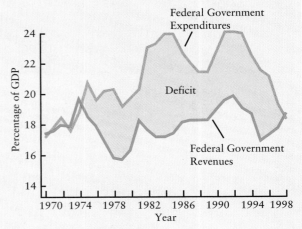

(i) Revenues and expenditures

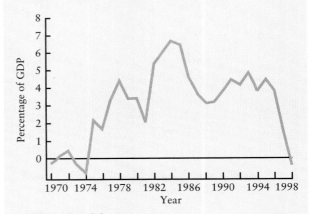

(ii) The budget deficit

The federal budget was in deficit every year between 1975 and 1997. In 1998, the federal government had a budget surplus of 0.4 percent of GDP. The graphs in part (i) show expenditures and revenues of the federal government, both as a percentage of GDP. The difference is the federal deficit, shown in part (ii).

(*Source: Economic Reference Tables*, Department of Finance. Recent data are available on the Department of Finance website: www.fin.gc.ca.)

The Canadian government ran very large budget deficits to finance Canada's participation in the Second World War. As a result, Canada's debt increased to 110 percent of GDP by 1946.

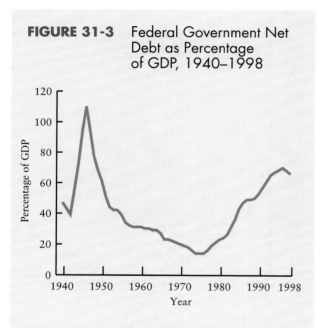

FIGURE 31-3   Federal Government Net Debt as Percentage of GDP, 1940–1998

The federal government's debt-to-GDP ratio fell dramatically after the Second World War and continued falling until 1975. It then increased markedly for the next two decades. In the late 1990s when government deficits were reduced and the economy was in a healthy recovery, the debt-to-GDP ratio began to fall.

(*Source:* Statistics Canada, CANSIM database.)

thirds of the fifty states in the United States. In contrast, the size of Canadian provincial governments—measured by their spending and taxing powers relative to that of the federal government—means that an examination of government debt and deficits in Canada would not be complete without paying attention to the provincial governments' fiscal positions.

For example, in the 1997–98 fiscal year, the federal government had $166 billion of tax revenues, representing 17 percent of GDP. In the same year, the combined provincial and territorial governments had only slightly less tax revenues—a total of $150 billion, or 16.9 percent of GDP.

When examining the size and effects of budget deficits or surpluses, it is important to consider all levels of government—federal, provincial, and municipal.

During the 1970s, the provincial governments were running budget deficits and so the stock of provincial government debt was increasing. But the deficits were small enough that this debt was not growing relative to GDP. During the 1980s and early 1990s, however, provincial deficits grew dramatically. The provincial debt grew from roughly 4 percent of GDP in 1980 to 20 percent in 1993. Since then, most provincial governments have reduced or eliminated their deficits, and some are operating small surpluses.

An International Perspective

Figure 31-4 shows how the size of government debt in Canada compares with those in the other major developed economies.[1] Canada's debt (combining all levels of government) is slightly above average among the G7 countries. The two high-debt countries are Japan and Italy. Italy, with a debt-to-GDP ratio of almost 120 percent, has been a high-debt country for many years. Japan, in contrast, has only recently become a high-debt country. In the late 1990s, in an attempt to stimulate its stagnant economy, Japan increased its government spending considerably. As a result of the fiscal expansion and a significant recession, Japan's debt-to-GDP ratio increased by 40 percentage points between 1995 and 2000.

---

[1]These data are not directly comparable with those in Figure 31-3 for two reasons. First, Figure 31-4 shows the debt of all levels of government combined, whereas Figure 31-3 shows just federal government debt. Second, Figure 31-4 shows *gross* debt whereas Figure 31-3 shows *net* debt. Gross debt is higher than net debt in Canada because some federal debt is held as an asset by provincial governments.

Some Analytical Issues

In the next section we discuss some potential effects of budget deficits and surpluses on the aggregate economy. Before doing this, however, we must examine some basic analytical issues: deficits and the stance of fiscal policy; changes in the debt-to-GDP ratio; and the relationship between government deficits and national saving.

The Stance of Fiscal Policy

In Chapters 23 and 25 we examined some basic issues surrounding **fiscal policy,** which is the use of government spending and tax polices to alter real GDP. We noted there that changes in expenditure and taxation normally lead to changes in the government's budget deficit or surplus. Thus, it is tempting to view changes in the government's budget deficit as the result of changes in fiscal policy. For example, we could interpret a decrease in the deficit as indicating a contractionary fiscal policy, since the fall in the deficit is associated with either a reduction in government expenditures or an increase in tax revenue (or both). Was the dramatic fall in the Canadian federal budget deficit between 1995 and 1999 *purely* the result of fiscal policy?

No. In general, only some changes in the deficit are due to discretionary changes in the government's expenditure or taxation policies. Other changes have nothing to do with explicit changes in policy, but instead are the result of changes in the level of economic activity that are outside the influence of government policy. If our goal is to judge the stance of fiscal policy, however, it is only the changes in the deficit *caused by changes in policy* that are relevant.

The Budget Deficit Function

To see why the budget deficit can rise or fall even when there is no change in fiscal policy, recall the equation defining the government's budget deficit. Since government transfers are payments by the government to the private sector, and taxes are payments made by the private sector to the government, it is convenient to rewrite the government's budget deficit by combining taxes and transfers to get

$$\text{Budget Deficit} = (G + i \times D) - (T - TR)$$

The key point now is that the level of taxes and transfers typically depends on the level of national income, even with unchanged policy. For example, as income rises the level of revenue raised through income taxation also rises. Furthermore, as national income (real GDP) rises there are typically fewer transfers (such as welfare or unemployment insurance) made to the private sector. Thus, $(T - TR)$ increases when national income increases. In contrast, the level of government purchases and debt-service payments can

FIGURE 31-4   Consolidated Government Gross Debt, G7 Countries, 2000

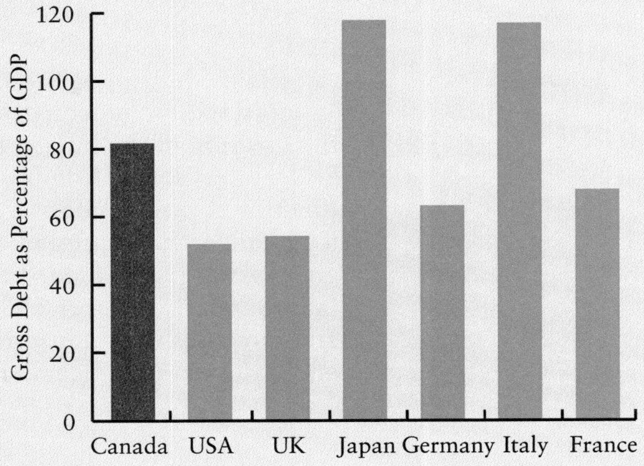

(bar chart: Gross Debt as Percentage of GDP, y-axis from 0 to 120)

Canada	~82
USA	~52
UK	~54
Japan	~118
Germany	~63
Italy	~117
France	~68

Canada's government debt is slightly above average by the standards of the richest developed countries. The debt-to-GDP ratios shown here are forecasts for the year 2000 made in 1999. The data are for all levels of government combined.

(Source: These data are available on the website for the Organization for Economic Cooperation and Development (OECD): www.oecd.org.)

fiscal policy   The use of the government's tax and spending policies in an effort to influence the level of GDP.

For macroeconomic data that are comparable across countries, see the OECD's website: www.oecd.org.

be viewed as more-or-less independent of the level of national income, at least over short periods of time. Thus, with no changes in expenditure or taxation policies, the budget deficit will tend to increase in recessions and fall in booms. That is, as national income rises, the government's budget deficit falls.

For a given spending and taxing policy, the budget deficit rises as real GDP falls, and falls as real GDP rises.

budget deficit function A relationship which plots the government's budget deficit as a function of the level of real GDP.

Figure 31-5 plots this basic relationship, which is called the **budget deficit function.** When the government determines its expenditure and taxation polices, it determines the *position* of the budget deficit function. A more expansionary fiscal policy shifts the budget deficit function up. A more contractionary fiscal policy shifts the budget deficit function down. In contrast, a change in the level of real GDP in the absence of any policy change will represent a *movement along* the budget deficit function. Thus, for a given set of policies, the budget deficit will decrease when Y rises and increase when Y falls. Similarly, for a given level of Y, an expansionary fiscal policy shifts the function up and increases the budget deficit; a contractionary fiscal policy shifts the function down and reduces the budget deficit.

Fiscal policy determines the position of the budget deficit function. Changes in real GDP lead to movements along a given budget deficit function.

FIGURE 31-5   The Budget Deficit Function and Cyclical Adjustment

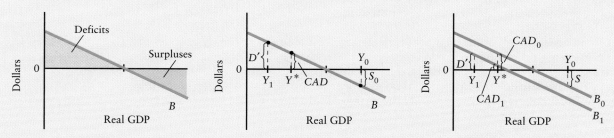

(i) The budget deficit function   (ii) Change in the measured deficit   (iii) Change in the cyclically adjusted deficit

The budget deficit can change either because of a change in fiscal policy or because of a change in real GDP. Parts (i) and (ii) illustrate the same budget deficit function, showing that the budget deficit declines (budget surplus rises) as real GDP rises. The budget deficit function is labelled *B*.

Part (ii) defines the cyclically adjusted deficit (CAD) as the budget deficit that would exist if real GDP were equal to *Y**. In the example, the CAD is a deficit. At a sufficiently high income Y_0, the actual budget would be in surplus by an amount S_0. At output lower than *Y**, such as Y_1, the actual budget would be in deficit by *D′*, more than the amount of the CAD. Along the curve in part (ii), fiscal policy is unchanged. The deficit (and surplus) changes only because real GDP changes.

Part (iii) shows how the actual deficit (or surplus) might move in a different direction from the CAD. Suppose that the economy starts at Y_0, with fiscal policy given by B_0. If fiscal policy is made more restrictive, through some combination of higher taxes and lower government purchases, the budget deficit function shifts to B_1. At the same time, if output should fall to Y_1, the budget surplus of *S* will turn into a deficit of *D′*. By looking at the actual budget balance, one would see the budget move from surplus to deficit, suggesting, incorrectly, that fiscal policy had become more stimulative. Focusing on the CAD, however, the level of budget balance at *Y** makes it clear that B_1 is more restrictive than B_0; that is, the CAD is smaller with the fiscal policy given by B_1 than that given by B_0.

The Cyclically Adjusted Deficit

Given the problem of using the budget deficit to gauge the stance of fiscal policy, economists define the **cyclically adjusted deficit (CAD)** as the budget deficit that would exist with the current set of policies if real GDP were equal to potential GDP, Y^*. This is also called the *structural budget deficit* or the *full-employment budget deficit*. This is shown in parts (ii) and (iii) of Figure 31-5. All changes in the cyclically adjusted deficit reflect changes in the stance of fiscal policy, because they come only from shifts in the budget deficit function.

Figure 31-6 shows the cyclically adjusted deficit in Canada, and plots it together with the actual budget deficit. Both are expressed as percentages of GDP and represent the combined budget deficits of all levels of government. Unlike the actual budget deficit, which can be precisely measured, the cyclically adjusted deficit can only be estimated. The

reason is that its value depends on the value of potential GDP, Y^*, which itself is not directly observable and hence must be estimated. Note from Figure 31-6 that the actual deficit is larger than the cyclically adjusted deficit during times of recessionary gaps such as 1981–1985 and 1990–1997. This relationship reflects the fact that during these periods actual GDP is less than potential GDP and thus actual tax revenues are *less than they would be if output were equal to potential.* Conversely, the actual budget deficit is less than the cyclically adjusted deficit during periods of inflationary gaps, such as 1986–1990, reflecting the fact that during these periods actual GDP is greater than potential and thus tax revenues are *greater than they would be if output were equal to potential.* In those years where the actual deficit is approximately equal to the cyclically adjusted deficit, such as 1985, 1990, and 1999, real GDP is approximately equal to potential.

The stance of fiscal policy is shown by the *changes* in the cyclically adjusted deficit. For example, the dramatic rise in the cyclically adjusted deficit from 1981 to 1985 reveals a considerable fiscal expansion; the decline from 1985 through 1988 reveals a fiscal contraction. From 1989 to 1995, the path of the cyclically adjusted deficit suggests that the stance of fiscal policy was roughly constant. Since 1995, the decline in the cyclically adjusted deficit reflects a very considerable fiscal contraction.

The stance of fiscal policy—that is, whether fiscal policy is expansionary or contractionary—is determined by changes in the cyclically adjusted deficit.

cyclically adjusted deficit (CAD) An estimate of what the government budget deficit would be if real GDP were at its potential level.

FIGURE 31-6 The Actual and Cyclically Adjusted Deficit, Combined Government, 1982–2000

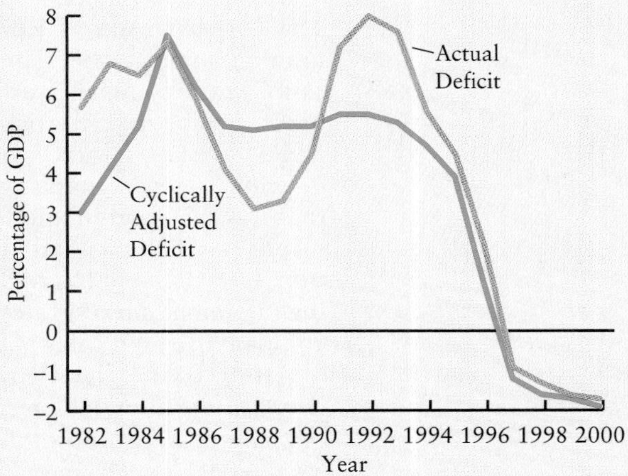

The difference between the actual budget deficit and the cyclically adjusted budget deficit reveals the level of output compared to potential. The changes in the cyclically adjusted deficit show changes in the stance of fiscal policy. The actual budget deficit is above the cyclically adjusted budget deficit when output is below potential; the actual deficit is less than the cyclically adjusted deficit when output is above potential. An increase in the cyclically adjusted deficit reveals a fiscal expansion; a decrease reveals a fiscal contraction. The values for 1999 and 2000 are forecasts.

(*Source: OECD Economic Outlook,* June 1999)

The Debt-to-GDP Ratio

We discussed above that in order to gauge the importance of government deficits and debt they should be considered relative to the size of the economy. Public debate, however, is often couched in terms of the absolute size of the budget deficit. Here we examine the link between the overall budget deficit, the primary budget deficit, and changes in the debt-to-GDP ratio.

Changes in the Debt-to-GDP Ratio

With a little work, it is possible to write a simple expression that relates the government's primary budget deficit to the change in the debt-to-GDP ratio. (To see the complete derivation of this equation, see *Extensions in Theory 31-1.*) The equation is:

$$\Delta d = x + (r - g) \times d$$

where d is the debt-to-GDP ratio, x is the government's *primary* budget deficit as a percentage of GDP, r is the real interest rate, g is the growth rate of real GDP, and Δd is the *change* in the debt-to-GDP ratio.

This simple equation shows that there are two separate forces which tend to increase the debt-to-GDP ratio. First, if the real interest rate exceeds the growth rate of real GDP (if r exceeds g), then the debt-to-GDP ratio will rise, and Δd will be positive. Second, if the government has a *primary* budget deficit (if x is positive) then the debt-to-GDP ratio will rise.

The Importance of Real Interest Rates.   It is the *real* interest rate, and not the nominal interest rate, that is important for determining the change in the debt-to-GDP ratio. Many commentators argue that high nominal interest rates are largely responsible for increasing the government's debt-service requirements and thus pushing up the deficit and debt. But this view is only partly correct. Although it is the nominal interest rate that determines how a given stock of debt will accumulate over time, this view misses the point that it is the accumulation of the *real* stock of debt that matters in terms of the government's *real* financial liabilities. And as we saw in Chapter 29 when we discussed inflation, high nominal interest rates are often associated with high inflation. Thus, although high nominal interest rates increase the government's debt-service requirements, the accompanying high inflation reduces the real value of the government's debt. The accumulation of the government's stock of *real* debt therefore depends on the difference between the nominal interest rate and the rate of inflation. This difference is simply the real interest rate, r. It follows, therefore, that changes in the debt-to-GDP ratio (which is a *real* variable) depend on the difference between the growth rate of the real stock of debt, r, and the growth rate of real GDP, g.

The Role of the Primary Deficit.   If our focus is to be on the debt-to-GDP ratio, rather than on the absolute size of the debt, then tracking the behaviour of the overall budget deficit may be misleading. Suppose that $r = g$ and thus the second term in the equation above is zero. Further, suppose that the government is running a small primary surplus, so that total tax revenues more than cover program spending. In this case, the primary surplus (x is negative) implies that the debt-to-GDP ratio is *falling;* but it is entirely possible that the overall budget deficit is positive, revealing simply that the debt-service payments exceed the primary surplus.

Stabilizing the Debt-to-GDP Ratio

Suppose the government's goal is to prevent further increases in the debt-to-GDP ratio. If the real interest rate exceeds the growth rate of real GDP—a reasonable description of the Canadian economy over the past two decades—then a government with a positive stock of outstanding debt *must* run a primary surplus in order to stabilize the debt-to-

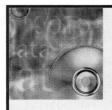

EXTENSIONS IN THEORY 31-1

Changes in the Debt-to-GDP Ratio

This box derives the simple equation in the text describing the change in the debt-to-GDP ratio. Let d be the debt-to-GDP ratio and let Δd be the amount by which d changes annually. Since d is a ratio, its change over time depends on the change in the numerator relative to the change in the denominator. That is, the debt-to-GDP ratio will increase if the stock of debt grows more quickly than GDP; it will decrease if the stock of debt grows less quickly than GDP. Representing the *percentage change* in d as $\Delta d/d$, we have*

$$\frac{\Delta d}{d} = \frac{\Delta D}{D} - \frac{\Delta \text{GDP}}{\text{GDP}}$$

Now think about each of these terms separately. As you will recall from the first section of this chapter, the change in the stock of debt, ΔD, is equal to the amount of new government borrowing—that is, it is equal to the budget deficit. From the government's budget constraint, this is equal to $(G + TR + i \times D - T)$. The second term in the equation above is the growth rate of GDP. Note that the growth rate of GDP depends on both the rate of growth of real output and the rate of inflation. If we let g be the rate of growth of *real* GDP and π be the rate of inflation, then $g + \pi$ is the growth rate of (nominal) GDP. We therefore rewrite the expression above to get

---

*For any variable X that is equal to the ratio of two other variables, Y/Z, the percentage change in X is closely approximated by the percentage change in Y minus the percentage change in Z. The lower are the rates of change of Y and Z, the better is this approximation.

$$\frac{\Delta d}{d} = \frac{G + TR - T + i \times D}{D} - (g + \pi)$$

Now we multiply both sides by d to get an expression for the absolute change in the debt-to-GDP ratio:

$$\Delta d = \frac{G + TR - T + i \times D}{D} \times d - (g + \pi) \times d$$

Since d is equal to D/GDP, it follows that d/D is equal to $1/\text{GDP}$. Our equation can thus be simplified:

$$\Delta d = \frac{G + TR - T + i \times D}{\text{GDP}} - (g + \pi) \times d$$

Now recall that $(G + TR - T)$ is the primary budget deficit. Let x be this primary budget deficit *as a percentage of GDP* and express the debt-service payments also as a percentage of GDP. This gives

$$\Delta d = x + i \times d - (g + \pi) \times d$$

Finally, recall that the real interest rate is equal to the nominal interest rate minus the rate of inflation,

$$r = i - \pi$$

We now combine terms to get

$$\Delta d = x + (r - g) \times d$$

which is the equation shown in the text.

GDP ratio. Furthermore, the larger is the real interest rate relative to the growth rate of GDP, the larger is the primary surplus required to stabilize the debt-to-GDP ratio.

To see this, let x^* be the value of the primary budget deficit that is consistent with a stable debt-to-GDP ratio—that is, x^* is the value of x such that Δd equals zero. From our equation above, setting Δd equal to zero results in

$$x^* = -(r - g) \times d$$

This equation shows the basic point that if the debt-to-GDP ratio is being pushed up by a real interest rate which exceeds the real growth rate of GDP, then a stable debt-to-GDP ratio is only possible with a value of x which is negative—that is, a primary budget surplus.

If the real interest rate exceeds the growth rate of real GDP, then stabilizing the debt-to-GDP ratio requires a primary budget surplus.

For an illustration of this central point, consider some of the numbers facing the federal minister of finance at the time of the March 1999 budget. The real interest rate on government debt was about 4 percent while the real growth rate of the economy was about 2.8 percent. Given the existing debt-to-GDP ratio of about 0.65, these data implied a value of x^* equal to $-(0.040 - 0.028) \times (0.65) = -0.0078$. Thus, the federal government would have had to run a primary surplus of about 0.8 percent of GDP in order to keep the debt-to-GDP ratio constant. As it turned out, the actual primary surplus in 1999 was much bigger than necessary to stabilize the debt-to-GDP ratio. The primary surplus was about 5 percent of GDP (an overall surplus of 0.4 percent and debt-service payments of about 4.6 percent), so the debt-to-GDP ratio declined.

Government Deficits and National Saving

As we will see in the next section, the effects of government deficits on real GDP and interest rates depend in large part on the relationship between government deficits and national saving. We therefore examine this important issue now.

Defining Terms

As we saw in Chapter 22, private saving is the difference between disposable income and consumption. And as we saw in Chapter 23, government saving is the difference between government tax revenues and government purchases. That is, government saving is equal to the budget surplus. National saving is the sum of government saving and private saving:

$$\text{National Saving} = \text{Private Saving} + \text{Government Saving}$$

Since government saving is equal to the budget surplus, an increase in the budget deficit is a reduction in government saving.

$$\text{National Saving} = \text{Private Saving} - \text{Government Budget Deficit}$$

The effect of budget deficits on the level of national saving thus depends on the link between budget deficits and private saving. For example, suppose that the government budget deficit increases by $1 billion. If this *reduction* in government saving leads to an *increase* in private saving by exactly $1 billion, there will be no change in national saving. On the other hand, if private saving rises by less than $1 billion, national saving will fall as a result of the increase in the budget deficit.

What is the link between the government deficit and the level of private saving? The answer lies in recognizing that—eventually—all government expenditures must be paid for out of taxes. Earlier in the chapter we said that expenditures during any given year could be financed either by tax revenues or by borrowing. But money borrowed in one year must *eventually* be repaid. Thus, borrowing today means higher taxes in the future to repay that debt.

Government debt is a postponed tax liability. An increase in the deficit today must be matched by an increase in taxes at some point in the future.

The link between government deficits and private saving then rests on the extent to which the current population of taxpayers recognizes the requirement for higher future taxes when the government increases its current borrowing. For example, if the government decides to reduce taxes this year by $5 billion and issue $5 billion in new bonds, do the taxpayers recognize that those bonds will need to be repaid with higher taxes ($5 billion plus interest) in the future?

Ricardian Equivalence

The link between government deficits and private saving is associated with the idea of **Ricardian Equivalence,** named after the Classical economist David Ricardo (1772–1823), and brought back to prominence among modern-day economists through the work of Robert Barro, currently at Harvard University. The central proposition of Ricardian Equivalence is that consumers recognize government borrowing as a future tax liability and thus they view taxes as *equivalent* to government borrowing in terms of the effect on their own wealth. Therefore, a reduction in taxes and an increase in borrowing (or the reverse case) do not affect the wealth of the private sector and thus does not affect their consumption behaviour.

An example to help you understand the basic idea of Ricardian Equivalence is illustrated in Figure 31-7. Suppose that the government decides to reduce current taxes by $5 billion *with unchanged government expenditures,* and thus decides to increase its current borrowing by $5 billion. If current taxpayers recognize that an increase in government borrowing of $5 billion today represents an increase in their future taxes of

Ricardian Equivalence The proposition that the method of financing government spending (taxes or borrowing) has no effect on national saving because private saving will just offset any government dissaving.

FIGURE 31-7 A Tax Reduction and Ricardian Equivalence

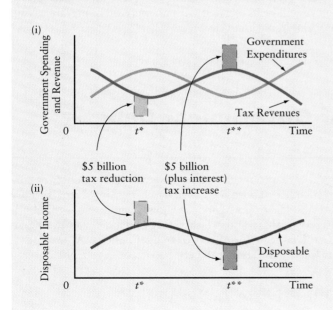

For an unchanged path of government expenditures, a reduction in taxes today must be matched with an increase in future taxes. Ricardian consumers will not feel wealthier as a result. Part (i) shows the initial path of government taxes and expenditures, with the associated deficits and surpluses. Part (ii) shows the initial path of disposable income for the private sector.

If the government reduces taxes by $5 billion in year t^*, the deficit will be increased by that amount. Disposable income at t^* will also increase by $5 billion. But in some future year, say t^{**}, the government will need to raise taxes by $5 billion (plus interest) to repay that debt. When this happens, the deficit will fall but so will disposable income. Ricardian consumers recognize that there is no change in their lifetime wealth and hence they do not spend more at t^* when their disposable income rises. Non-Ricardian consumers do not foresee the tax increase at t^{**} and thus *do* feel wealthier at t^*—they will increase their consumption at t^*.

$5 billion (plus interest), then the current generation of taxpayers will not feel any more or less wealthy as a result of the reduction in current taxes, and consequently will not change their level of current expenditure on goods and services. But, if their consumption is unchanged and their disposable income is higher by $5 billion, then their current saving must increase by the full amount of the reduction in government saving. Thus, "Ricardian" consumers faced with a change in the government deficit will adjust their private saving so as to keep national saving constant.

Now suppose that current taxpayers do perceive an increase in their wealth when their current taxes are reduced. There are several reasons why this might be so. One possibility is that individuals might be short-sighted and thus tend to place more emphasis on current tax reductions than on tax increases in the distant future. This would certainly be true if today's generation of taxpayers knew that the future tax increases would have to be paid by other people. Another possibility is that there may be a great deal of uncertainty about the government's future spending plans so that it is unclear whether the current tax reduction will be offset by future tax increases or matched by future expenditure reductions. Whatever the reason, suppose that the current generation *feels* wealthier as a result of the reduction in current taxes. We then expect them to increase their current expenditures on goods and services. As a result of the higher expenditures, private saving of such "non-Ricardian" individuals will therefore increase by less than the reduction in government saving, leading to an overall reduction in national saving.

"Ricardian" consumers will not feel wealthier as a result of the government borrowing because they recognize the increase in their future tax liabilities. "Non-Ricardian" consumers do not recognize this future liability and thus feel wealthier when the government borrows.

Whether taxpayers recognize the future tax liabilities associated with government deficits is ultimately an empirical question. Most evidence suggests that Ricardian Equivalence does not hold completely. That is, the evidence suggests that an increase in the government deficit by $5 billion will be associated with an increase in private saving by less than $5 billion and thus a fall in national saving.

Most evidence suggests that an increase in the government deficit leads to a decrease in the level of national saving.

The Effects of Government Debt and Deficits

Let's now examine why we should care about the size of the government deficit or surplus. We begin with the important idea that deficits *crowd out* private-sector activity and thereby harm future generations. The opposite idea is equally important—that budget surpluses *crowd in* private-sector activity and are therefore beneficial to future generations. In this section, we pose the issue as the effects of budget deficits. At the end of the section we review the arguments by discussing the effects of budget surpluses.

Do Deficits Crowd Out Private Activity?

crowding out   The offsetting reduction in private expenditure caused by the rise in interest rates that follows an expansionary fiscal policy.

It is useful to make the distinction between closed and open economies. We consider the two cases separately.

Investment in Closed Economies

In a closed economy, the amount of national saving is exactly equal to the amount of domestic investment; after all, the only way that a closed economy can save is to accumulate physical capital. Suppose in a closed economy there is an increase in the budget deficit brought about by a reduction in taxes. What is the effect on domestic investment? As we saw in the previous section, the answer to this question depends on the degree to which taxpayers are Ricardian—that is, on the degree to which current taxpayers recognize that today's deficit must be financed by higher future taxes. If taxpayers are not purely Ricardian, then private saving will rise by less than the fall in government saving. This response implies a decrease in the supply of national saving. The resulting excess demand for funds will put upward pressure on the domestic real interest rate. But as the real interest rate increases, those components of aggregate demand that are sensitive to the interest rate—investment in particular—will fall. The result is what is called the **crowding out** of domestic investment; it is shown in Figure 31-8.

If government borrowing to finance the deficit drives up the interest rate, some private investment will be crowded out.

Net Exports in Open Economies

The effect of budget deficits in an open economy is a little different. Consider once again the possibility that the Canadian government reduces taxes and thus increases its budget deficit. Furthermore, suppose that taxpayers are not purely Ricardian so that private saving rises by less than the fall in government saving. What is the effect of such a fall in national saving in an open economy like Canada's? As real interest rates rise in Canada, foreigners are attracted to the higher-yield Canadian assets and thus foreign financial capital flows into Canada. But since Canadian dollars are required in order to buy Canadian interest-earning assets, this capital inflow increases the demand for Canadian dollars and thus increases the external value of the Canadian dollar (the Canadian dollar appreciates).

This appreciation makes Canadian goods more expensive relative to foreign goods, inducing an increase in imports and a reduction in exports, thereby reducing Canada's net exports. In an open economy like Canada, therefore, a rise in the government deficit leads to an appreciation of the currency and to a crowding out of net exports.

FIGURE 31-8 The Crowding Out of Investment

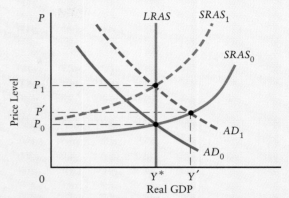

(i) Aggregate demand and supply

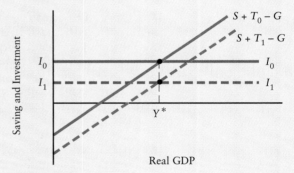

(ii) Saving and investment

For a closed economy whose real GDP equals potential, an increase in the budget deficit will cause a reduction in national saving and investment. Consider a closed economy that is in long-run equilibrium at Y^* and P_0 in part (i). The same position is shown in part (ii) as saving equal to investment at Y^* and I_0. Suppose that the government reduces its taxes from T_0 to T_1, thus increasing the budget deficit. This raises desired aggregate expenditure (and lowers desired national saving) at all levels of income. In part (i), the new short-run equilibrium is at Y' and P'. The adjustment mechanism will then cause factor prices to rise, shifting the SRAS curve from $SRAS_0$ to $SRAS_1$. The new long-run equilibrium will be at Y^* and P_1.

The effect of this change on saving and investment can be seen in part (ii). At the new long-run equilibrium, real income is unchanged at Y^*, but the price level is higher. This implies that the demand for money will have increased, causing a rise in interest rates. These higher interest rates will reduce desired investment expenditure, shown in the figure as a reduction from I_0 to I_1.

In an open economy, instead of driving up interest rates sufficiently to crowd out private investment, the government budget deficit tends to attract foreign financial capital, appreciate the domestic currency, and crowd out net exports.

The Long-Term Burden of the Debt

In a closed economy, a rise in the government deficit pushes up interest rates and crowds out domestic investment. In an open economy a rise in the government deficit appreciates the currency and crowds out net exports. Despite the apparent differences in these two effects, they both imply a *long-term burden of government debt*.

A Closed Economy.   The overall effect of the increase in the government deficit in a closed economy is a rise in the real interest rate and a fall in the level of domestic investment. But less current investment means that there will be a smaller stock of physical capital in the future, and thus a reduced ability to produce goods and services in the future. This reduction in future production possibilities, which implies lower consumption levels for future generations, is the long-term burden of the debt.

An Open Economy.   The overall effect of the increase in the government deficit in an open economy is an appreciation of the currency and a reduction in net exports. Recall from Chapter 23, however, that such a reduction in net exports implies a reduction in the country's *national asset formation*. This in turn increases the need for the domestic economy to make interest or dividend payments to foreigners in the future. Instead of having a smaller future capital stock as a result of the government's budget deficit, the country has an unchanged capital stock but *less of it is owned by domestic residents*. This reduced ownership lowers the domestic residents' future stream of income because payments must be paid to the foreign owners of the domestic capital stock. This reduction in the future stream of income for domestic residents is the long-term burden of the public debt in an open economy.

In both open and closed economies, the long-term burden of public debt takes the form of reduced consumption for future generations.

Does Government Debt Harm Future Generations?

The previous discussion reveals an important aspect of the costs of government debt and deficits:

Government deficits generate a redistribution of resources away from future generations toward the current generation.

After all, the government deficits are being used to finance goods and services that are provided to the current generation, but that will be financed by taxes levied on future generations.

This last sentence suggests that current government deficits are always financing goods and services that are provided to the current generation. Is this really true? Some government spending is on goods and services that will continue to be used well into the future. For example, if the government increases its current borrowing to finance the building of bridges or the expansion of highways, future generations will receive some of the benefits of this government spending. And, given that future generations will reap the benefits of some of these projects, it may be appropriate that future generations pay some of the taxes required to finance such projects.

Whether current government deficits impose a burden on future generations depends on the nature of the government goods and services being financed by the deficit. At one extreme, the government borrowing may finance a project that generates a return only to future generations, and thus the future generations may not be made worse off by today's budget deficit. An example might be the government's financing of long-term medical research projects that generate a return only in the distant future. At the other extreme, the government deficit may finance some government program that benefits only the current generation, and thus the future generations are inappropriately saddled with the future tax bill. An example might be the government's financing of a world's fair such as Expo '86 in Vancouver or a major sporting event, like the 1999 Pan Am Games in Winnipeg.

Budget deficits used to finance investment projects may not harm future generations because the future generations will benefit from the investment.

The concern that deficits may be inappropriately placing a financial burden on future generations has led some economists to advocate the idea of *capital budgeting* by the government. Under this scheme, the government would essentially classify all of its expenditures as either consumption or investment; the former would be spending that mostly benefits the current generation while the latter would be spending that mostly benefits future generations.

With capital budgeting, government deficits could be used to minimize the undesirable redistributions of income between generations. For example, the government might be committed to borrowing no more in any given year than the expenditures classified as investments. In this way, future generations would receive benefits from current government spending that are approximately equivalent to the future taxes they will pay.

Does Government Debt Hamper Economic Policy?

The costs imposed on future generations by government debt are very real. Unfortunately, the fact that these costs sometimes occur in the very distant future often leads us to ignore their importance. But other costs associated with the presence of government debt are more immediately apparent. In particular, government debt may make the conduct of monetary and fiscal policy more difficult.

Monetary Policy

To see how a large stock of government debt can hamper the conduct of monetary policy, consider a country that has a high debt-to-GDP ratio and that has a real interest rate above the growth rate of GDP. As we saw previously, the debt-to-GDP ratio will continue to grow in this situation unless the government starts running significant primary budget *surpluses*. But such primary surpluses require either increases in taxation or reductions in program spending, both of which are politically unpopular. If such primary surpluses look unlikely to be achieved in the near future, both foreign and domestic creditors may come to expect that the government will put pressure on the central bank to purchase—or *monetize*—an increasing portion of its deficit. Such monetization means that the money supply is increasing and will eventually be reflected in higher inflation. Any ensuing inflation would thus erode the real value of the bonds held by creditors. Such fears of future debt monetization will lead to expectations of future inflation and thus will put upward pressure on nominal interest rates and on some prices and wages. Thus, even in the absence of any actions by the central bank to increase the rate of growth of the money supply, a large government debt may lead to the *expectation* of future inflation, thus hampering the task of the central bank in keeping inflation and inflationary expectations low.

In December 1995, before the federal government had been successful in reducing its large annual budget deficits and thus slowing the rise of the debt-to-GDP ratio, the Governor of the Bank of Canada, Gordon Thiessen, appeared before the House of Commons Standing Committee on Public Accounts. His comments to that committee expressed this view that high levels of government debt generate concerns on the part of creditors.

> *. . . We would probably all agree . . . that our society needs to sort out its views about acceptable levels of taxation and the size of government, and those views can influence the amount of debt our society can afford to carry. However, when you reach a high debt-to-GDP ratio, what is sustainable is also very much influenced by the willingness of investors in financial markets to hold your debt.*
>
> *I do not mean to imply that financial markets might suddenly decide to stop lending to Canadian governments. What happens, as recent experience has shown, is that at very high levels of debt, there may be an increasing nervousness among lenders so that they would only continue to hold Canadian government debt at much higher interest rates.*[2]

Fiscal Policy

In Chapter 23 we saw that fiscal policy could potentially be used to stabilize aggregate demand and thereby stabilize real output. For example, in a recession the government might reduce tax rates or increase spending to stimulate aggregate demand; in a booming economy, the government might reduce spending or increase tax rates to prevent the economy from overheating. Having cyclically-adjusted budget deficits in recessions and cyclically-adjusted budget surpluses in booms is one obvious way of implementing *counter-cyclical fiscal policy.*

How does the presence of government debt affect the government's ability to conduct such counter-cyclical fiscal policy? Perhaps the easiest way to answer this question is to recall the equation that describes the change in the debt-to-GDP ratio:

$$\Delta d = x + (r - g) \times d$$

This equation shows that the size of the *change* in the debt-to-GDP ratio depends on the *level* of the debt-to-GDP ratio. For example, if the real interest rate exceeds the growth rate of real GDP, so that $r - g$ is positive, then the increase in the debt-to-GDP ratio (Δd) will be higher if d is already high than if it is low (for any given value of x).

With this relationship in mind, consider the dilemma faced during a recession by a government that is considering an expansionary fiscal policy. On the one hand, the short-run benefits in terms of raising the level of real GDP seem clear; on the other hand, the same government may be wary of taking actions that lead to large increases in the debt-to-GDP ratio.

If the stock of outstanding government debt is small relative to the size of the economy, then the government has a great deal of flexibility in conducting counter-cyclical fiscal policy. The small value of d implies that d will be rising only slowly in the absence of a primary deficit. Thus, there may well be room for the government to increase the primary deficit—either by increasing program spending or by reducing tax rates—without generating a large increase in the debt-to-GDP ratio. But the government has significantly less flexibility if the stock of outstanding government debt is already very large. In this case, the high value of d means that even in the absence of a primary budget deficit, d will be increasing quickly. Thus, any increase in the primary deficit brought

---

[2]Comments by Gordon Thiessen in the *Bank of Canada Review,* Winter 1995–1996.

about by the counter-cyclical fiscal policy runs the danger of generating increases in the debt-to-GDP ratio that may be viewed by creditors as unsustainable.

The idea that a large and rising stock of government debt could "tie the hands" of the government in times when it would otherwise want to conduct counter-cyclical fiscal policy was brought to the fore of Canadian economic policy by the late Douglas Purvis of Queen's University (and a coauthor on this textbook for many years). Purvis argued in the mid 1980s that Canadian government deficits must be brought under control quickly so that the debt would not accumulate to the point where the government would have no room left for fiscal stabilization policy. These warnings were not heeded. By the onset of the next recession in 1990, the federal government had added roughly $200 billion to the stock of debt and, predictably, the government felt unable to use discretionary fiscal policy to reduce some of the effects of the recession.

The Current "Fiscal Dividend"

We have been discussing the effects of government debt and deficits on the economy. As we saw earlier, government deficits were an important part of the Canadian economic environment for over twenty years from the early 1970s to the mid 1990s. But by 1998, after several years of devoted deficit fighting, the federal government had its first surplus in over twenty years, and most of the provinces had also eliminated their budget deficits.

By late 1999, it appeared that the federal government would be running significant budget surpluses for the next several years. According to forecasts made by the Department of Finance in November 1999, the projected surplus for the 1999–2000 fiscal year was $9.5 billion. Furthermore, *if the government maintained its 1999 fiscal stance*, the growth of the economy was expected to lead to an annual surplus of roughly $30 billion by the 2004–05 fiscal year. The *cumulative* surplus between 1999 and 2005 was projected to be roughly $100 billion. Such forecasts naturally sparked a considerable debate about how best to spend this "fiscal dividend"—a term used to describe the budget "return" from several years' "investment" in fiscal cutbacks.

Some people argued the need to restore spending in health care, education, and other social programs to the levels that existed in 1995, before the federal government reduced their transfer payments to the provinces. Others argued the need to reduce income-tax rates, in part to stem an alleged "brain drain"—the exodus of highly trained workers—from Canada to the United States. A third group advocated delaying any spending increases or tax reductions until after a few years' of budget surpluses could make a noticeable reduction in the stock of government debt. The Liberal government of Jean Chrétien advocated a so-called 50-50 rule whereby half of any projected surpluses would be used to boost spending and half would be used to finance some combination of tax reductions and debt repayment. For example, a projected surplus of $20 billion might be used to finance higher spending of $10 billion, lower taxes of $5 billion, and debt repayment of $5 billion. Note, however, that these actions would largely eliminate the projected surplus. In our example, the projected surplus of $20 billion becomes—after the 50-50 rule is imposed—an actual surplus of only $5 billion.

If this 50-50 rule is followed into the near future, with some part of each projected surplus being used to repay the debt, then the federal government will record a stream of budget surpluses, at least for the next few years. What will be the effect on the Canadian economy of such surpluses? To analyse the economic effects of budget surpluses, we need only to reverse the arguments that we have developed in this chapter. After all, an increase in the budget surplus is just the same as a reduction in the budget deficit. But it will be useful to review and summarize these arguments. If the Canadian federal and provincial governments succeed in running budget surpluses over the next few years, our economic theory tells us we should start to see the following things:

- Assuming that consumers are *not* fully Ricardian, the rise in the government budget surplus will raise the level of national saving.
- The rise in national saving will put downward pressure on interest rates and "crowd in" investment.
- The lower interest rates will lead to less capital inflow and thus the Canadian dollar will depreciate, leading to a rise in Canada's net exports.
- As the surpluses continue, the stock of government debt will actually be falling. Combined with a growing economy, this will make the debt-to-GDP ratio fall relatively sharply.
- The lower debt-to-GDP ratio will reduce bondholders' fears of future monetization and thus reduce inflation expectations.
- The lower debt-to-GDP ratio will restore the government's flexibility to use countercyclical fiscal policy if the economy enters another recession.

Balanced Budgets

As we have seen in this chapter, government budget deficits contribute to aggregate demand and thus have the potential to be used as an integral part of a fiscal policy designed to stabilize real GDP. However, we have also seen that government budget deficits crowd out private economic activity and impose a long-term burden, either through a reduced stock of physical capital or through greater foreign indebtedness. A tradeoff therefore appears to exist between the desirable short-run stabilizing role of deficits and the undesirable long-run costs of government debt. This tradeoff has been the source of constant debate. Here we examine some possible solutions involving different concepts of a balanced budget.

Before going on, however, note that not everyone agrees that the accumulation of government debt represents a problem. One argument often seen in the popular press is that debt itself is not a problem—the problem is that the debt is held by foreigners rather than by domestic residents. Foreign ownership of the debt is alleged to be undesirable because interest payments are made to foreigners, reducing the income available for Canadians. Such claims have even led to the proposal that the Canadian government issue new "Canada-only" bonds to Canadians and then use the newly raised funds to redeem foreign-held government debt. *Applying Economic Concepts 31-1* explains why such a policy would be unlikely to change Canadian national income.

We now go on to examine different concepts of balanced budgets.

See Chapter 31 of www.pearsoned.ca/lipsey for an interview with Paul Martin in which he discusses some of the political difficulties of reducing the budget deficit: "Regaining Canada's Fiscal Levers," *World Economic Affairs.*

Annually Balanced Budgets

Much current rhetoric of fiscal restraint calls for the government budget to be balanced every year. Though there has clearly been a significant move toward deficit reduction in Canada over the past few years, both federally and among the provinces, there has been little emphasis placed on the idea that governments should be constrained to balance their budgets *every year.*

Balancing the budget on an annual basis would be extremely difficult to achieve. The reason is that a significant portion of the government budget is beyond the short-term control of the government, and a further large amount is hard to change quickly. For example, the entire debt-service component of government expenditures is determined by past borrowing and thus cannot be altered by the current government. In addition, as we saw in our discussion of the cyclically adjusted deficit, changes in real GDP that are beyond the control of the government lead to significant changes in tax revenues (and transfer payments) and thus generate significant changes in the budget deficit.

APPLYING ECONOMIC CONCEPTS 31-1

A Common Myth About Government Debt

In 1999 about one-quarter of the federal government's debt was held outside of Canada. Thus, of the $44 billion in interest payments made on the government debt in 1999, roughly $11 billion was paid to foreigners. This fact has led many commentators in the popular press to suggest that Canada "reclaim" its national debt and keep these "lost" interest payments. These observers seem to believe that if more of the Canadian government debt were held within Canada, then Canada would be a richer country.

How do we "reclaim" the debt? The federal government simply has to issue new debt to Canadians and use the proceeds of this borrowing to redeem existing debt held by foreigners. By so doing, the fraction of government debt held by Canadians would be increased and the fraction held by foreigners decreased. Advocates of this proposal argue that the result would be higher Canadian income in the long run as fewer interest payments are sent to foreign creditors.

Proponents of this view fail to recognize the importance of an *integrated* world capital market and the fact that government bonds are only one type of asset held by creditors. Suppose that the federal government issued $1 billion of new "Canadians-only" bonds to Canadians and used the proceeds to redeem an equal amount of existing foreign-held federal government debt. Two questions must be addressed: (1) What would make Canadians buy such bonds?; and (2) What would happen to Canada's net foreign indebtedness as a result? We deal with these two issues in turn.

In order to convince Canadians to buy $1 billion worth of these new bonds, these same Canadians must somehow be convinced to divert $1 billion from some other use. For example, they could give up $1 billion worth of consumption to buy these bonds or they could sell $1 billion worth of their holdings of private corporate bonds to buy these new government bonds. In the first case, the reduction in consumption implies an increase in private saving. But it is difficult to see why Canadians would be prepared to increase their private saving simply in response to a change in the ownership of the federal government debt. One thing that might convince them to increase their saving is if these new bonds offered a rate of return greater than that of other assets available on

the market. But, in this case, it is hard to see how the federal government can improve its fiscal position by issuing new high-interest-rate bonds to raise funds used to redeem existing lower-interest-rate bonds.

Suppose, then, that these new "Canadians-only" bonds are *not* successful in increasing the amount of total private saving. Instead, the issuance of these bonds simply leads some Canadians to sell $1 billion of their holdings of private corporate debt so that they can hold the new bonds. The government then takes the $1 billion raised by the selling of the new bonds and redeems $1 billion worth of foreign-held debt. The total amount of government debt is unchanged, but less of the total debt is held by foreigners. The story does not end there, however. Recall that Canadians were able to buy these new bonds only by selling off some of their current holdings of private corporate debt. But with an unchanged pool of Canadian savings, these corporate bonds *must* be bought by foreigners. Thus, total private corporate debt is unchanged, but *more* of it is held by foreigners. Now, while it is true that the federal government has $1 billion less foreign-held debt, the private sector has $1 billion *more* foreign-held debt. And, as the government will now be making fewer interest payments to foreign creditors, the Canadian economy as a whole—the private plus public sectors—will be making the same interest payments to foreigners as before. Thus, the issuing of "Canadians-only" bonds, and the reduction in foreign-held government debt, has no effect on the stream of income available to domestic residents.

Is there some way that the Canadian economy can reduce its foreign indebtedness? Yes, but with a highly integrated global capital market like the one that exists today, schemes like Canadians-only bonds will not work. The only way that the Canadian economy can reduce its indebtedness to foreign creditors is to increase its national saving rate. This requires either an increase in private saving or an increase in public saving (that is, a reduction in the deficit), or both. Thus, if the Canadian budget surpluses continue over the next few years, we should observe a gradual decline in Canadian foreign indebtedness.

Even if it were possible for the government to perfectly control its path of spending and revenues on a year-to-year basis, it would probably be *undesirable* to balance the budget every year. We saw above that government tax revenues (net of transfers) tend to fall in recessions and rise in booms. In contrast, the level of government purchases is more-or-less independent of the level of real GDP. As a result, fiscal policy contains a

FIGURE 31-9   Balanced and Unbalanced Budgets

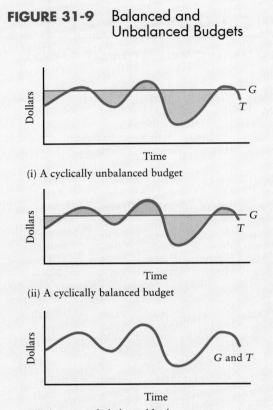

(i) A cyclically unbalanced budget

(ii) A cyclically balanced budget

(iii) A constantly balanced budget

An annually balanced budget is a destabilizer; a cyclically balanced budget is a stabilizer. The flow of tax receipts (net of transfers) T is shown varying over the business cycle; in parts (i) and (ii), government purchases G is shown at a constant rate.

In part (i), deficits (red areas) are common and surpluses (green areas) are rare because the average level of expenditure exceeds the average level of taxes. Such a policy will tend to stabilize the economy against cyclical fluctuations, but public saving is negative, on average.

In part (ii), the level of government purchases have been reduced until it is approximately equal to the average level of tax receipts. The budget is now balanced cyclically. The policy still tends to stabilize the economy against cyclical fluctuations because of deficits in slumps and surpluses in booms. However, public saving is higher than in part (i).

In part (iii), a constantly balanced budget has been imposed. Deficits have been prevented, but the level of government purchases now varies over the business cycle, which tends to destabilize the economy by accentuating the cyclical swings in real GDP.

built-in stabilizer; in recessions, the increase in the budget deficit stimulates aggregate demand whereas in booms the budget surplus reduces aggregate demand.

But things would be very different with an annually balanced budget. With a balanced budget, government expenditures would be *forced* to adjust to the changing level of tax revenues. In a recession, when tax revenues naturally decline, a balanced budget would require either a *reduction* in government expenditures or an *increase* in tax rates, thus generating a major *destabilizing* force on real GDP. Similarly, as tax revenues naturally rise in an economic boom, the balanced budget would require either an increase in government expenditures or a reduction in taxes, thus risking an overheating of the economy.

An annually balanced budget would accentuate the swings in real GDP.

Cyclically Balanced Budgets

One alternative to the extreme policy of requiring an annually balanced budget is to require that the government budget be balanced over the course of a full economic cycle, as shown in Figure 31-9. Budget deficits would be permitted in recessions as long as they were matched by surpluses in booms. In this way, the built-in stabilizers could still perform their important role, but there would be no persistent build-up of government debt. In principle, this is a desirable treatment of the tradeoff between the short-run benefits of deficits and the long-run costs of debt.

Despite its appeal, the idea of cyclically balanced budgets has its problems as well. Perhaps the most important problem with a cyclically balanced budget is an operational one. In order to have a law that requires the budget to be balanced over the cycle, it is necessary to be able to *define* the cycle unambiguously. But there will always be disagreement about what stage of the cycle the economy is currently in, and thus there will be disagreement as to whether the current government should be increasing or reducing its deficit. Compounding this problem is the fact that politicians will have a stake in the identification of the cycle. Those who favour increased deficits will argue that this year is an unusually bad year and thus an increase in the deficit is justified; deficit "hawks," in contrast, will always tend to find this year to be unusually good, and thus a time to run budget surpluses.

Though a budget balanced over the course of the business cycle is in principle a desirable way of reconciling short-term stabilization with long-term prudence, the business cycle may not be well enough defined to make this policy operational.

A second problem is largely political. Suppose that one government runs large deficits for a few years and then gets replaced in an election. Would the succeeding government then be bound to run budget surpluses? What one government commits itself to in one year does not necessarily restrict what it (or its successor) does in the next year. It is this problem which leads many in the U.S. to suggest a Constitutional Amendment to deal with deficits; once the Constitution is altered, any government is bound by it until, through a very lengthy process, it is changed again.

Allowing for Growth

A further problem with any policy that requires a balanced budget—whether over one year or over the business cycle—is that the emphasis is naturally on the overall budget deficit. But, as we saw earlier in this chapter, what determines the change in the debt-to-GDP ratio is the growth of the debt *relative* to the growth of the economy. With a growing economy, it is possible to have positive overall budget deficits—and thus a growing debt—and still have a falling debt-to-GDP ratio. Thus, to the extent that the debt-to-GDP ratio is the relevant gauge of a country's debt problem, focus should be placed on the debt-to-GDP ratio rather than on the budget deficit itself.

Some economists view a stable (or falling) debt-to-GDP ratio as the appropriate indicator of fiscal prudence. Their view permits a deficit such that the stock of debt grows no faster than GDP.

By this standard, the deficits of the late 1990s have been "prudent" because they have led to a growth rate in the stock of debt smaller than the growth rate of real GDP, and thus a reduction in the debt-to-GDP ratio. For example, in 1996, the debt-to-GDP ratio reached its recent maximum of 70 percent. The combined effects of a rapidly growing economy and some planned expenditure reductions then led to a decline in the annual budget deficit from $32 billion in 1996 to $13.6 billion in 1997 and to a surplus of $3.2 billion in 1998. With the 1999 forecast of budget surpluses for the next 4 years, the debt-to-GDP ratio was estimated to reach 55 percent by the year 2004.

For some forecasts and analysis of the government's fiscal options, see the Royal Bank's website: www.royalbank.ca. Go to "corporate information" and then "economics".

S U M M A R Y

Facts and Definitions   🔟❶❷

- The government's budget deficit is equal to total government expenditure minus total government revenue. Since the government must borrow to finance any shortfall in its revenues, the annual deficit is equal to the increase in the stock of government debt during the course of a year. Whenever the deficit is positive, the stock of government debt is growing.
- The primary budget deficit is equal to the excess of the government's program spending over total tax revenues.

The difference between the total budget deficit and the primary deficit is the debt-service payments.
- In 1975, the Canadian federal government net debt was 14 percent of GDP. Large and persistent budget deficits beginning in the 1970s increased the stock of debt so that by 1996 the federal government net debt was equal to about 70 percent of GDP. By 2000, after several years of fiscal contraction, the budget was balanced and the debt was about 60 percent of GDP.

Some Analytical Issues

LO 3 4

- Since taxes (net of transfers) tend to rise when real GDP rises, the overall budget deficit tends to rise during recessions and fall during booms. This tendency makes the budget deficit a poor measure of the stance of fiscal policy.
- The cyclically adjusted deficit is the budget deficit that would exist with the current set of fiscal policies if real GDP were equal to potential GDP. Changes in the cyclically adjusted deficit reflect changes in the stance of fiscal policy.
- The change in the debt-to-GDP ratio from one year to the next is given by

$$\Delta d = x + (r - g) \times d$$

where d is the debt-to-GDP ratio, x is the primary deficit as a percentage of GDP, r is the real interest rate, and g is the growth rate of real GDP. If r exceeds g, then a primary surplus is required to stabilize the debt-to-GDP ratio.

- National saving equals government saving plus private saving. An increase in the government budget deficit represents a fall in government saving. The link between budget deficits and private saving depends on the extent to which taxpayers recognize the future tax liabilities associated with current government deficits. When taxpayers are purely Ricardian, any change in government saving is exactly offset by an equal and opposite change in private saving, leaving national saving unchanged. Available evidence suggests that an increase in the government's budget deficit will not be fully offset by an increase in private saving and thus will decrease national saving.

The Effects of Government Debt and Deficits

LO 5 6

- In a closed economy, an increase in the budget deficit leads to a reduction in national saving and a rise in real interest rates. This increase in interest rates reduces the amount of investment and leads to a long-term decline in the domestic capital stock.
- In an open economy, an increase in the budget deficit initially pushes up real interest rates. But this attracts foreign financial capital, which drives up the external value of the currency. As the currency appreciates, there is a reduction in net exports. The capital inflow implies an increase in the country's net foreign indebtedness.
- In either open or closed economies, the long-term burden of government debt is a redistribution of resources away from future generations and toward current generations.

- A large debt-to-GDP ratio may lead creditors to expect increases in inflation, as the government attempts to finance deficits through the creation of money. Such increases in inflationary expectations hamper the conduct of monetary policy.
- A large debt-to-GDP ratio also limits the extent to which the government can conduct counter-cyclical fiscal policy without risking large increases in the debt-to-GDP ratio which may be viewed by creditors as unsustainable.

Balanced Budgets

LO 7

- Since tax revenues (net of transfers) naturally rise as real GDP increases, a policy to balance the budget on an annual basis forces either expenditures to rise or tax rates to fall during booms. This produces destabilizing fiscal policy.
- Cyclically balanced budgets, in principle, permit the short-run benefits of deficits to be realized without incurring the long-run costs of debt accumulation. Implementation of this policy is difficult, however, since the identification of the business cycle is very controversial.
- In a growing economy, it is more sensible to focus on changes in the debt-to-GDP ratio than on balancing the budget over some horizon.

K E Y   C O N C E P T S

Government's budget constraint
Primary budget deficit
The relationship between deficits and
 the national debt
Debt-service payments

Debt-to-GDP ratio
National, government, and private
 saving
Ricardian Equivalence
Crowding out of investment

Crowding out of net exports
Long-term burden of the debt
Annually balanced budget
Cyclically balanced budget

S T U D Y   E X E R C I S E S

1. The table below shows government spending data over eight years in Debtland. All figures are in billions of dollars. The symbols used are as defined in the text.

	(1)	(2)	(3)	(4)	(5)	(6)	(7)
Year	G	T	TR	iD	Total Deficit	Primary Deficit	Stock of Debt
1995	150	175	25	25	—	—	—
1996	155	180	25	26	—	—	—
1997	160	185	25	27	—	—	—
1998	165	190	23	26	—	—	—
1999	165	195	20	25	—	—	—
2000	165	200	20	24	—	—	—
2001	160	205	20	23	—	—	—
2002	155	210	20	22	—	—	—

a. Compute debtland's overall budget deficit in each year and complete column 5 in the table. (Since we are computing the deficit, a negative number indicates a surplus.)

b. Compute Debtland's primary budget deficit in each year and complete column 6 in the table.

c. Suppose the initial stock of debt (in 1994) was $400 billion. Noting that the deficit in 1995 adds to the stock of debt, what is the stock of debt by the end of 1995?

d. Compute the stock of debt for each year and complete column (7) in the table.

e. Suppose you know that Debtland's debt-to-GDP ratio was the same in 2002 as in 1994. How much did GDP grow between 1994 and 2002?

2. The figure below shows the budget deficit function for a country.

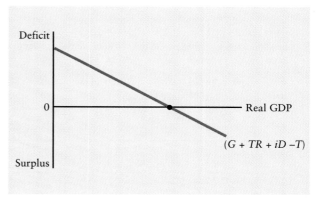

a. Explain why the budget deficit function is downward sloping.

b. If the government increases its level of purchases (G), what happens to the deficit at any level of real GDP? Show this in the diagram.

c. If the government increases its level of tax revenues (T), what happens to the deficit at any level of real GDP? Show this in the diagram.

d. Explain why a rise in the actual budget deficit does not necessarily reflect an expansionary fiscal policy. How would a fiscal expansion appear in the diagram? A fiscal contraction?

3. The U.S. government was slightly ahead of the Canadian government in reducing its budget deficit. The following table shows the actual budget deficit and the cyclically adjusted deficit (both as a percentage of GDP) for the United States from 1989 to 1997.

Year	Actual deficit	CAD
1989	2.8	2.9
1990	3.9	3.2
1991	4.6	3.4
1992	4.7	3.7
1993	3.9	3.7
1994	3.0	2.8
1995	2.3	2.6
1996	1.4	1.6
1997	0.3	1.0

a. On a scale diagram (with the year on the horizontal axis) graph the actual deficit and the cyclically adjusted deficit.
b. Identify the periods when U.S. fiscal policy was expansionary.
c. Identify the periods when U.S. fiscal policy was contractionary.
d. Look back at Figure 31-6. How does the stance of U.S. fiscal policy compare with Canada's?

4. The following table shows hypothetical data from 1995 to 2001 that can be used to compute the change in the debt-to-GDP ratio. The symbols used are as defined in the text.

	(1)	(2)	(3)	(4)	(5)
Year	x	r	g	d	Δd
1995	0.03	0.045	0.025	0.70	—
1996	0.02	0.04	0.025	—	—
1997	0.01	0.035	0.025	—	—
1998	0.00	0.035	0.025	—	—
1999	−0.01	0.03	0.025	—	—
2000	−0.02	0.03	0.025	—	—
2001	−0.03	0.025	0.025	—	—

a. Remember from the text that the change in the debt-to-GDP ratio (Δd) during a year is given by $\Delta d = x + (r-g)d$. Compute Δd for 1995.
b. Column 4 is the debt-to-GDP ratio. Note that d in 1996 is equal to d from 1995 plus Δd in 1995. Compute d in 1996.
c. Using the same method, compute d and Δd for each year, and complete columns 5 and 6.
d. Plot d in a scale diagram with the year on the horizontal axis. What discretionary variable was most responsible for the observed decline in d?
e. Note that as the primary deficit x falls between 1995 and 2001, there is also a downward trend in the real interest rate. Can you offer an explanation for this?

5. The diagram below shows an *AD/SRAS* diagram. The economy begins at E_0 with output equal to Y^*. Suppose the government in this closed economy increases its budget deficit by borrowing to increase the level of G, thus causing the *AD* curve to shift to the right.

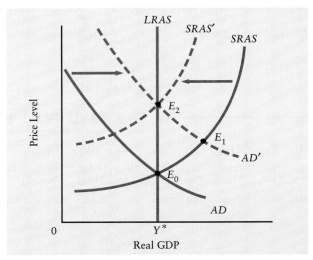

a. How does the interest rate at E_1 compare with that at E_0? Explain.
b. Given your answer to part **a**, how does investment at E_1 compare to investment at E_0?
c. Explain the economy's adjustment toward E_2. What happens to the interest rate and investment?
d. What is the long-run effect of the government deficit? How would this be reflected in the diagram?

6. The diagram below shows an *AD/SRAS* diagram. The economy begins at E_0 with output equal to Y^*. Suppose

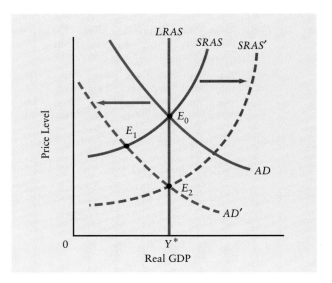

the government in this closed economy decreases its budget deficit by increasing T (and keeping G unchanged), thus causing the AD curve to shift to the left.

a. How does the interest rate at E_1 compare with that at E_0? Explain.

b. Given your answer to part **a**, how does investment at E_1 compare to investment at E_0?

c. Explain the economy's adjustment toward E_2. What happens to the interest rate and investment?

d. What is the long-run effect of the government deficit? How would this be reflected in the diagram?

e. Comparing the short-run and the long-run effects of this policy, what dilemma does the government face in reducing its deficit?

DISCUSSION QUESTIONS

1. Evaluate each of the following proposals to "control the deficit" in order to avoid the long-run burden of the debt.

   a. Maintain a zero cyclically adjusted deficit.
   b. Keep the debt-to-GDP ratio constant.
   c. Limit government borrowing in each year to some fixed percentage of national income in that year.

2. Judith Maxwell, former chairperson of the now disbanded Economic Council of Canada, warned in 1991 that "when interest rates are higher than the economic growth rate, the ratio of debt to GDP acquires dangerous upward momentum." Discuss why this is so. How does the primary deficit enter the analysis?

3. In the federal budget of 1995, the minister of finance announced some significant expenditure reductions which would reduce the deficit. In the budget of 1996, he announced no new expenditure cuts yet still predicted the deficit to fall. Explain how these statements by the minister of finance should be interpreted.

4. Paul Martin, the federal minister of finance who is credited with reducing Canada's budget deficit in the late 1990s, stressed the importance of using very conservative forecasts for economic growth. Explain the role of forecasts, and why Martin chose to use conservative ones.

5. In the text we discussed the effects of government budget deficits. In the past few years, however, the Canadian federal deficit has fallen markedly, from 3 percent of GDP in 1989 (the peak of the business cycle) to a *surplus* of 0.5 percent of GDP in 1999 (close to a peak in the business cycle). Discuss the likely short-term and long-term effects that you would expect to follow such a sustained *reduction* in the deficit.

6. A government official recently exclaimed, "The Prime Minister's policies are working! Lower interest rates combined with staunch fiscal policy have reduced the deficit significantly." What do interest rates have to do with government spending and taxes when it comes to deficit management?

CHAPTER 32

Economic Growth

LEARNING OBJECTIVES

❶ Understand how small differences in growth rates can generate large differences in income over many years.

❷ Explain the costs and benefits of economic growth.

❸ List the four fundamental determinants of growth in real GDP.

❹ Understand the main elements of Neoclassical growth theory.

❺ Have a general knowledge of the new growth theories based on endogenous technical change and increasing returns.

❻ Explain why resource exhaustion provides society with incentives for technological improvements.

The Centre for the Study of Living Standards is an Ottawa-based research institute that studies the determinants of economic growth. Visit their website at www.csls.ca.

Economic growth is the single most powerful engine for generating long-term increases in living standards. What happens to our material living standards over time depends largely on the growth in real GDP in relation to the growth in population—that is, it depends on the growth of real per capita GDP. Growth in real per capita GDP does not necessarily make *everybody* in Canada better off. But it does mean that the *average* standard of living is higher.

What determines the growth rate of per capita GDP in Canada? Is this something that is beyond our control, or are there some government policies that can stimulate economic growth? If there are, what are the costs of such policies, and are the benefits worth the costs?

In this chapter we examine this important issue of economic growth, beginning with some basic concepts and then moving on to explore the costs and benefits of growth. In the remainder of the chapter we consider various theories of economic growth, an area in which much new research is being done. Finally, we examine the idea that there may be *limits to growth*.

The Nature of Economic Growth

Over the past century, most residents of most countries in the industrialized world have become materially better off decade by decade. Children have typically been substantially better off than their parents were at the same age. Beginning in the mid 1970s, however, the engine of growth faltered. Growth rates fell, though they remained positive. Although we still live in a very wealthy society, many observers speak of the end of the dream that each generation can expect to be much better off than its predecessors.

Over the long run, the main cause of rising real GDP is **economic growth**—the increase in potential output due to changes in factor supplies (labour and capital) and in the productivity of factors (output per unit of factor input). The removal of a serious recessionary gap might cause a once-and-for-all increase in real GDP by, at the very most, 5 percent. However, a growth rate of 3 percent per year raises potential GDP by 10 percent in three years, doubles it in about 24 years, and quadruples it in 47 years. Even a 1 percent growth rate doubles potential GDP over one normal lifetime of about 70 years.

economic growth
Increases in real potential GDP.

Because growth can go on over very long periods, it is a much more powerful method of raising living standards than the removal of recessionary gaps.

Table 32-1 illustrates the cumulative effect of what you might think are very small differences in growth rates. Notice that if one country grows faster than another, the gap in their respective living standards will widen progressively. If, for example, Canada and France start from the same level of income but Canada grows at 3 percent per year while France grows at 2 percent per year, Canada's income will be twice France's in 72 years. [35] You may not think that it matters much whether the economy grows at 2 percent or 3 percent per year, but your children and grandchildren certainly will.

TABLE 32-1 The Cumulative Effect of Economic Growth

Year	\multicolumn{5}{c}{Annual Growth Rate}
	1%	2%	3%	5%	7%
0	100	100	100	100	100
10	111	122	135	165	201
30	135	182	246	448	817
50	165	272	448	1 218	3 312
70	201	406	817	3 312	13 429
100	272	739	2 009	14 841	109 660

Small differences in growth rates make enormous differences in levels of potential GDP over a few decades. Let potential GDP be 100 in year 0. At a growth rate of 3 percent per year, it will be 135 in 10 years, 448 after 50 years, and over 2000 in a century. Notice the difference between 2 percent and 3 percent growth—even small differences in growth rates make big differences in future income levels.

Efficiency and Equity

Observing that sustained economic growth is the most important force for raising living standards over the long term in no way implies the unimportance of policies designed to increase economic efficiency or to redistribute income in the pursuit of greater equity.

Improving Efficiency

If, at any moment in time, real GDP could be increased by removing certain inefficiencies in the economy, such gains would be valuable. After all, as long as scarcity exists (and it always does), any increase in real GDP is welcome. Furthermore, inefficiencies may themselves act to reduce the growth rate. For example, government subsidies to failing firms that may be criticized on grounds of productive and allocative efficiency may also reduce growth rates by reducing the incentive to innovate.

Improving Equity

Economic growth has made the poor vastly better off than they would have been if they had lived 100 years ago. Yet that is little consolation when they see that they cannot afford many things that are currently available to citizens with higher incomes. After all, people compare themselves with others in their own society, not with their counterparts at other times or in other places. Because people care about relative differences among individuals, governments in most countries continue to have policies to redistribute income and to make such basic services as education and health care available to all people, regardless of their ability to pay for them.

Interrelationships Among the Goals

Economists once assumed that the goals of improving equity, increasing economic efficiency, and ensuring growth could each be treated independently. But it is now understood that equity, efficiency, and economic growth are interrelated. For example, policies that redistribute income to the poor in ways that provide large disincentives to work may adversely affect economic growth. It follows that policies designed to reduce inefficiencies or improve equity should be examined carefully for any effects that they may have on economic growth, and policies designed to influence growth need to be examined for their effects on economic efficiency and income distribution. A policy that reduces growth may be a bad bargain, even if it increases the immediate efficiency of the economy or creates a more equitable distribution of income. Similarly, a policy that increases growth may be a bad bargain if it achieves that higher growth only by misallocating resources or by redistributing income in ways that are deemed to be undesirable.

Benefits of Growth

Let's look in more detail, first, at the benefits of growth and then at its costs. *Applying Economic Concepts 32-1* and *32-2* outline some of the commonly heard arguments on both sides of the growth debate.

Average Living Standards

For all who share in it, economic growth is a powerful means of improving living standards. A family that is earning $35 000 today can expect an income of about $42 600 within 10 years (in constant dollars) if it shares in a 2 percent growth rate, $51 800 if the rate is 4 percent.

A family often finds that an increase in its income can lead to changes in the pattern of its consumption—extra money buys important amenities of life and also allows them to save more for the future. Similarly, economic growth that raises average income may change the whole society's consumption patterns. Not only do expanding markets in a rapidly growing country make it profitable to produce more cars, but the government is led to construct more highways and to provide more recreational areas for its affluent and mobile population.

One illustration of the basic point that patterns of demand change as a country becomes wealthier is to note the different attitudes toward environmental protection in rich and poor countries. In developing countries, most of the resources of the country are devoted to providing basic requirements of life such as food, shelter, and clothing. These countries typically do not have the "luxury" of being concerned about environmental degradation. Some may consider this a short-sighted view, but the fact is that the concerns associated with hunger *today* are much more urgent than the concerns associated with *future* environmental problems. In contrast, richer countries are wealthy enough that they can easily provide the basic requirements of life and devote significant resources to environmental protection.

Alleviation of Poverty

Not everyone benefits equally from growth. Many of the poorest are not even in the labour force and hence are unlikely to share in the higher wages that, along with profits,

APPLYING ECONOMIC CONCEPTS 32-1

An Open Letter from a Supporter of the "Growth Is Good" School

Dear Ordinary Citizen:

You live in the world's first civilization that is devoted principally to satisfying *your* needs rather than those of a privileged minority. Past civilizations have always been based on leisure and high consumption for a tiny upper class, a reasonable living standard for a small middle class, and hard work with little more than subsistence consumption for the great mass of people.

The continuing Industrial Revolution is based on mass-produced goods for you, the ordinary citizen. It ushered in a period of sustained economic growth that has dramatically raised consumption standards of ordinary citizens. Consider a few examples: travel, live and recorded music, art, good food, universal literacy, inexpensive books, and a genuine chance to be educated. Most important, there is leisure to provide time and energy to enjoy these and thousands of other products of the modern developed economy.

Would any ordinary family seriously prefer to go back to the world of 150 or 500 years ago in its same *relative* social and economic position? Surely the answer is no. However, for those with incomes in the top 1 or 2 percent of the income distribution, economic growth has destroyed much of their privileged consumption position. They must now vie with the masses when they visit the world's beauty spots and be annoyed, while lounging on the terrace of a palatial mansion, by the sound of charter flights carrying ordinary people to inexpensive holidays in faraway places. Many of the rich complain bitterly

about the loss of exclusive rights to luxury consumption, and it is not surprising that they find their intellectual apologists.

Whether they know it or not, the antigrowth economists are not the social revolutionaries they think they are. They say that growth has produced pollution and wasteful consumption of all kinds of frivolous products that add nothing to human happiness. However, the democratic solution to pollution is not to go back to the time when so few people consumed luxuries that pollution was trivial but rather to learn to control the pollution that mass consumption tends to create.

It is only through further growth that the average citizen can enjoy consumption standards (of travel, culture, medical and health care, and so on) now available only to people in the top 25 percent of the income distribution—which includes the intellectuals who earn large royalties from the books they write in which they denounce growth. If you think that extra income confers little real benefit, just ask those in the top 25 percent to trade incomes with average citizens.

Ordinary citizens, do not be deceived by disguised elitist doctrines. Remember that the very rich and the elite have much to gain by stopping growth and even more by rolling it back, but you have everything to gain by letting it go forward.

Onward!

A. N. Optimist

---

are the primary means by which the gains from growth are distributed. For this reason, even in a growing economy, redistribution policies will be needed if poverty is to be reduced.

A rapid growth rate makes the alleviation of poverty easier politically. If existing income is to be redistributed, someone's standard of living will actually have to be lowered. However, when there is economic growth and when the *increment* in income is redistributed (through government intervention), it is possible to reduce income inequalities without actually having to lower anyone's income. It is much easier for a rapidly growing economy to be generous toward its less fortunate citizens—or neighbours—than it is for a static economy.

Costs of Growth

Other things being equal, most people would probably regard a high rate of growth as preferable to a low one. However, we know that other things are seldom equal. There are some important costs associated with economic growth.

APPLYING ECONOMIC CONCEPTS 32-2

An Open Letter from a Supporter of the "Growth Is Bad" School

Dear Ordinary Citizen:

You live in a world that is being despoiled by a mindless search for ever-higher levels of material consumption at the cost of all other values. Once upon a time, men and women knew how to enjoy creative work and to derive satisfaction from simple activities. Today, the ordinary worker is a mindless cog in an assembly line that turns out more and more goods that the advertisers must work overtime to persuade the worker to consume.

Statisticians count the increasing flow of material output as a triumph of modern civilization. You wake to the hum of your air conditioner, watch the shopping channel while you dress for work, brew your chemically treated decaffinated coffee, and eat your bread baked from superrefined flour; you climb into your car to sit in vast traffic jams on exhaust-polluted highways.

Television commercials tell you that by consuming more, you are happier, but happiness lies not in increasing consumption but in increasing the ratio of *satisfaction of wants* to *total wants*. Because the more you consume, the more the advertisers persuade you that you want to consume, you are almost certainly less happy than the average citizen in a small town in 1900, whom we can visualize sitting on the family porch, sipping lemonade, and enjoying the antics of the children as they jump rope using pieces of old clothesline.

Today, the landscape is dotted with endless factories that produce the plastic trivia of modern society. They drown you in a cloud of noise, air, and water pollution. The countryside is despoiled by strip mines, petroleum refineries, acid rain, and dangerous nuclear power plants, producing energy that is devoured insatiably by modern factories and motor vehicles. Worse, our precious heritage of natural resources is being rapidly depleted.

Now is the time to stop this madness. We must end this mad rush to produce more and more output, reduce pollution, conserve our natural resources, and seek justice through a more equitable distribution of existing total income.

Many years ago, Thomas Malthus taught us that if we do not limit population voluntarily, nature will do it for us in a cruel and savage manner. Today, the same is true of output: If we do not halt its growth voluntarily, the halt will be imposed on us by a disastrous increase in pollution and a rapid exhaustion of natural resources.

Citizens, awake! Shake off the worship of growth, learn to enjoy the bounty that is yours already, and reject the endless, self-defeating search for increased happiness through ever-increasing consumption.

Upward!

I. Realvalues

If economic growth just means more of the truly "unnecessary" things in life, is it really that worthwhile?

The Opportunity Cost of Growth

In a world of scarcity, almost nothing is free. Growth requires heavy investment of resources in capital goods, as well as in activities such as education. Often these investments yield no immediate return in terms of goods and services for consumption; thus, they imply that sacrifices have been made by the current generation of consumers.

Growth, which promises more goods tomorrow, is achieved by consuming fewer goods today. For the economy as a whole, this sacrifice of current consumption is the primary cost of growth.

An example will suggest the importance of this cost. Suppose that a hypothetical economy is operating at potential output and is experiencing growth in real GDP at the rate of 2 percent per year. Its citizens consume 85 percent of the GDP and invest 15 percent. But suppose that if they immediately decrease their consumption to 77 percent of GDP (and increase investment to 23 percent), they will produce more capital and thus shift at once to a 3 percent growth rate. The new rate can be maintained as long as they keep saving and investing 23 percent of real GDP. Should they do it?

Figure 32-1 illustrates the choice in terms of time paths of consumption. With the assumed figures, it takes ten years for the actual amount of consumption to catch up to what it would have been had no reallocation been made. In the intervening 10 years, a good deal of consumption is lost, and the cumulative losses in consumption must be made up before society can really be said to have broken even. It takes an *additional* 9 years before total consumption over the whole period is as large as it would have been if the economy had remained on the 2 percent path. [36]

Over a longer period, however, the payoff from the growth policy becomes enormous. Thirty years on, real GDP in the more rapidly growing economy is 21 percent higher than in the slower-growing economy. After fifty years, it is 48 percent higher.

Social Costs of Growth

A growing economy is also a changing economy. Part of growth is accounted for by existing firms expanding and producing more output, hiring more workers, and using more equipment and intermediate goods. But another part of growth is accounted for by

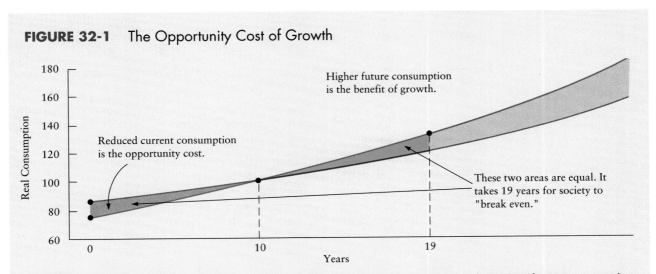

FIGURE 32-1   The Opportunity Cost of Growth

Higher future consumption is the benefit of growth.

Reduced current consumption is the opportunity cost.

These two areas are equal. It takes 19 years for society to "break even."

Transferring resources from consumption to investment lowers current consumption but raises future consumption. The example assumes that GDP in year 0 is 100 and that growth of 2 percent per year is possible when consumption equals 85 percent of GDP. It is further assumed that to achieve a 3 percent growth rate, consumption must fall to 77 percent of GDP. A shift from the red path to the blue path in year 0 decreases consumption for 10 years but increases it thereafter. By year 19 the gains in consumption have made up for the losses from the first 10 years.

existing firms' being overtaken and made obsolete by new firms, by old products' being made obsolete by new products, and by existing skills being made obsolete by new skills.

The process of economic growth renders some machines obsolete and also leaves some workers partly obsolete.

No matter how well-trained workers are at age 25, in another 25 years many will find that their skills are at least partly obsolete. A high growth rate usually requires rapid adjustments, which can cause much upset and misery to some of the people affected by it.

It is often argued that costs of this kind are a small price to pay for the great benefits that growth can bring. Even if this is true in the aggregate, these personal costs are borne very unevenly. Indeed, many of the people for whom growth is most costly (in terms of lost jobs or lowered incomes) share least in the fruits that growth brings.

Sources of Growth

We know that output is produced by combining the services of various factors of production such as labour, capital, and land. Furthermore, we know that the current state of our knowledge—or technology—limits our ability to get more and more output from a given set of factors of production. It follows, therefore, that we can account for growth in real GDP by increases in the *amount* of available factors of production, increases in the *quality* of the available factors of production, or increases in the state of *technology* that determines how much output we are able to get from a given set of factors of production.

The four fundamental determinants of growth of total output are:

1. *Growth in the labour force.* This may be caused by growth in population or by increases in the fraction of the population that chooses to participate in the labour force.

human capital   The capitalized value of productive investments in persons; usually refers to value derived from expenditures on education, training, and health improvements.

2. *Growth in human capital.* **Human capital** is the term economists use to refer to the set of skills that workers have. Human capital can increase through either formal education or on-the-job training.

3. *Growth in physical capital.* The stock of physical capital (such as factories, machines, transportation and communications facilities) increases only through the process of investment.

4. *Technological improvement.* This may be brought about by innovation that introduces new products, new ways of producing existing products, and new forms of business organization.

The various theories of economic growth that we explore in the remainder of this chapter can be viewed as theories of these different sources of growth. For example, some theories emphasize the role of increases in physical capital in explaining growth; others emphasize the role of increases in human capital; still others emphasize the importance of technological improvements. But all theories of economic growth take as a starting point these four fundamental determinants of growth.

Theories of Economic Growth

In this section we study some of the theories that economists use to understand economic growth. This is an exciting area. Ideas are changing rapidly as both theoretical and empirical research expands our knowledge. Our first step is to relate investment and saving, which we studied in detail in previous chapters, to economic growth.

Investment, Saving, and Growth

Both investment and saving affect the level and rate of growth of real GDP. To understand their influence, it is critical to distinguish between their short-run and long-run effects.

Short-Run and Long-Run Effects of Investment

The theory of output determination that we studied in Chapters 22 through 25 is a short-run theory. It takes potential output as constant and concentrates on the effects of shifts in aggregate demand brought about by changes in various types of desired expenditure, including investment. These shifts cause actual GDP to fluctuate around a given level of potential GDP. The short-term effects of changes in investment are shown by rightward shifts in the *AD* curve.

In the long run, by adding to the nation's capital stock, investment raises potential output. This effect is shown by rightward shifts in the *LRAS* curve.

The theory of economic growth is a long-run theory. It concentrates on the effects of investment in raising potential output and ignores short-run fluctuations of actual output around potential.

The contrast between the short- and long-run aspects of investment is worth emphasizing. In the short run, any activity that puts income into people's hands will raise aggregate demand. Thus, the short-run effect on real GDP is the same whether a firm spends by hiring workers to dig holes (and then hires more workers to refill them) or by building a new factory. But the long-run growth of potential GDP is affected only by the part of spending that *adds to a nation's productive capacity*—by the new factory but not by the refilled hole.

Similar observations hold for government purchases of goods and services. Any increase in purchases will add to aggregate demand and real GDP in the short run, but only some expenditures increase *potential* GDP and thus will increase GDP in the long run. Although public investment expenditure on such things as roads and health may increase potential GDP, expenditure that shores up a declining industry in order to create employment may have an adverse effect on potential GDP. The latter expenditure may prevent the reallocation of resources in response to shifts both in the pattern of world demand and in the country's comparative advantage. Thus, in the long run, the country's capacity to produce commodities that are demanded on world markets may be diminished.

Short-Run and Long-Run Effects of Saving

As we saw in Chapters 22 and 23, the short-run effect of an increase in saving is to reduce aggregate demand. If households or governments elect to save more, they must (by definition) decide to spend less. The resulting downward shift in the aggregate expenditure function lowers aggregate demand and thus lowers equilibrium real GDP.

Over the longer term, however, higher national saving is necessary for higher investment. Firms usually reinvest their own saving, and the saving of households passes to firms, either directly through the purchase of stocks and bonds or indirectly through financial intermediaries such as commercial banks and trust companies. In the long run, the higher the level of national saving, the higher the level of investment. And because of the accumulation of more and better capital equipment, the higher the level of investment, the higher the level of potential GDP.

In the long run, there is no paradox of thrift; societies with high rates of national saving have high investment rates and, other things being equal, high growth rates of real GDP.

Investment and Growth in Industrialized Countries

We said above that countries with high rates of investment are also countries with high rates of real GDP growth. To provide evidence in support of this claim, Figure 32-2 shows data from the most industrialized countries between 1970 and 1990. Each point in the figure corresponds to a single country and shows that country's annual average investment rate (as a percentage of GDP) plotted against the annual average growth rate in real per capita GDP. What is clear from the figure is a strong positive relationship between investment rates and growth rates, exactly as suggested by our discussion above.

Hong Kong is an example of an economy that has had very high rates of investment and also very high rates of real GDP growth.

Neoclassical Growth Theory

aggregate production function
The relation between the total amount of each factor of production employed in the nation and the nation's total GDP.

Recall the four fundamental sources of economic growth that we discussed at the beginning of this section. Much of what is referred to as *Neoclassical growth theory* is based on the idea that these four forces of economic growth can be connected by what is called the **aggregate production function**. This is an expression for the relation between the total amounts of labour (L) and physical capital (K) employed, the quality

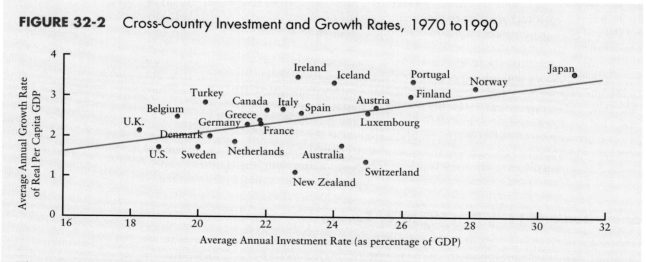

FIGURE 32-2   Cross-Country Investment and Growth Rates, 1970 to 1990

There is a strong positive relationship between a country's investment rate (as a percentage of GDP) and its growth rate of real per capita GDP. For each of the countries, the annual averages for investment rates and per capita GDP growth rates are computed between 1970 and 1990. Each point represents the average values of these variables for a single country over this 20-year period. The line is the "line of best fit" between the growth rates and the investment rates. Countries with high investment rates tend to be countries with high rates of economic growth.

(*Source:* International Monetary Fund)

of labour's human capital (H), the state of technology (T), and the nation's total level of output (GDP). The aggregate production function can be expressed as:

$$GDP = F_T(L, K, H)$$

It is an *aggregate* production function because it relates the economy's *total* output to the *total* amount of the factors that are used to produce that output.[1] (Those who have studied microeconomics will recall that a micro production function, such as is discussed in Chapters 7 and 8, relates the output of *one firm* to the factors of production employed by *that firm*.)

The production function above—indicated by F_T—tells us how much GDP will be produced for given amounts of labour and physical capital employed, given levels of human capital and a given state of technology. Using the notation F_T is a simple way of indicating that the function relating L, K and H to GDP depends on the state of technology. For a given state of technology (T), changes in either L, K or H will lead to changes in GDP. Similarly, for given values of L, K and H, changes in T will lead to changes in GDP. [37]

When discussing economic growth, we focus on the changes in potential output and ignore short-term fluctuations of output around potential. Hence we can interpret GDP in the aggregate production function as potential output.

Early Neoclassical growth theory dealt with economic growth when technological knowledge remained unchanged. There were no innovations: no new ways of making things and no new products. As a result, the relation between inputs and output, as shown by the aggregate production function, did not change. Since T was assumed to be constant, the aggregate production function could simply be written as

$$GDP = F(L, K, H)$$

indicating that growth in GDP was due only to changes in labour, physical capital, or human capital.

Properties of the Aggregate Production Function

The key aspects of the Neoclassical model are that the aggregate production function displays *diminishing returns* when either factor is increased on its own and *constant returns* when all factors are increased together (and in the same proportion).

To understand these important concepts, let us simplify things slightly by combining physical and human capital together so that we can think of a single factor called "capital." Now suppose that the labour force grows while the stock of capital remains constant. More and more people go to work using a fixed quantity of capital. The amount that each new unit of input adds to total output is called its *marginal product*. The operation of the **law of diminishing returns** tells us that the employment of additional units of labour will eventually add less to total output than the previous unit. In other words, each additional unit of labour will sooner or later produce a diminishing marginal product. This famous relation is referred to as *diminishing returns to a single factor*, and it is illustrated in Figure 32-3.

law of diminishing returns   The hypothesis that if increasing quantities of a variable factor are applied to a given quantity of fixed factors, the marginal product and average product of the variable factor will eventually decrease.

---

[1]Natural resources (including land, forests, mineral deposits, etc.) are also important inputs to the production process. We leave them out of this discussion only for simplicity.

FIGURE 32-3   Diminishing Returns to the Variable Factor

(1) Units of Variable Factor (Labour)	(2) Units of Total Output	(3) Average Product of Labour (2/1)	(4) Marginal Product of Labour ($\Delta 2/\Delta 1$)
1	12.0	12.0	
2	17.0	8.5	5.0
3	20.8	6.9	3.8
4	24.0	6.0	3.2
5	26.8	5.4	2.8
6	29.4	4.9	2.6
7	31.9	4.6	2.5
8	34.0	4.2	2.1
9	36.0	4.0	2.0
10	37.9	3.8	1.9

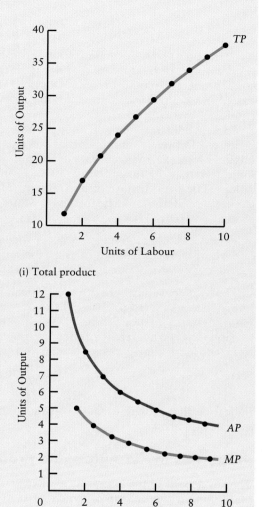

(i) Total product

(ii) Marginal and average product

With one input held constant, the marginal and average products of the variable factor eventually decline. We have assumed a hypothetical production function given by: output = $4\sqrt{KL}$; we have also assumed that K is constant and equal to 9. Column 2 shows total output as more of the variable factor, labour, is used with a fixed amount of capital. Total output is plotted in part (i) of the figure. Both the average product of labour and the marginal product of labour decline continuously. They are plotted in part (ii) of the figure.

The law of diminishing returns applies to any factor that is varied while the other factors are held constant. Hence, successive amounts of capital added to a fixed supply of labour will also eventually add less and less to GDP.

According to the law of diminishing returns, the increment to total production will eventually fall steadily whenever equal increases of a variable factor of production are combined with another factor of production whose quantity is fixed.

The other main property of the Neoclassical aggregate production function is called **constant returns to scale.** This says that if the amounts of labour and capital are both changed in equal proportion, total output will also change in that proportion. For ex-

constant returns to scale A situation in which output increases in proportion to the change in all inputs as the scale of production is increased.

ample, 10 percent increases in the amounts of both labour and capital will lead to a 10 percent increase in GDP. [38]

Sources of Growth in the Neoclassical Model

Now consider each of the sources of growth on the list at the beginning of this section. To begin, we let each source operate with the others held constant.

Labour-Force Growth.   Over the long term, we can associate labour-force growth with population growth (although in the short term, the labour force can grow if participation rates rise even though the population remains constant). As more labour is used, there will be more output produced. The law of diminishing returns tells us that sooner or later, each further unit of labour to be employed will cause smaller and smaller additions to GDP. Eventually, not only will the marginal product of labour be falling, but the average product will fall as well. Beyond that point, although economic growth continues in the sense that total output is growing, living standards are falling in the sense that average GDP *per person* is falling. If we are interested in growth in living standards, we are concerned with increasing real GDP per person.

In the Neoclassical growth model, whenever diminishing average returns applies, increases in population on their own are accompanied by increasing GDP but falling living standards.

Capital Accumulation.   Growth in physical capital occurs whenever there is enough investment to make up for the capital that wears out during the production process. But how does the stock of human capital increase?

Human capital has several aspects. One involves improvements in the health and longevity of the population. Of course, these are desired as ends in themselves, but they also have consequences for both the size and the productivity of the labour force. There is no doubt that improvements in the health of workers have increased productivity per worker-hour by cutting down on illness, accidents, and absenteeism.

A second aspect of human capital concerns technical training—from learning to operate a machine to learning how to be a scientist. This training depends on the current state of knowledge, and advances in knowledge allow us not only to build more productive physical capital but also to create more effective human capital. Also, the longer a person has been educated, the more adaptable and, hence, the more productive in the long run that person is in the face of new and changing challenges.

The accumulation of capital—either physical or human—affects GDP in a manner similar to population growth. Eventually, each successive unit of capital will add less to total output than each previous unit of capital.

There is, however, a major contrast with the case of labour-force growth because it is output *per person* that determines living standards, not output per unit of capital. Thus, as the amount of physical or human capital increases, living standards increase because output is rising while the population is constant. However, because the increases in capital are subject to diminishing returns, successive additions to the economy's capital stock bring smaller and smaller increases in per capita output.

In the Neoclassical model, the operation of diminishing returns means that capital accumulation on its own brings smaller and smaller increases in real per capita GDP.

Balanced Growth with Constant Technology.   Now consider what happens if labour and capital (both human and physical capital) grow at the same rate. In this case, the Neoclassical assumption of constant returns to scale means that GDP grows in proportion to the increases in inputs. As a result, per capita output remains constant. Thus, growth in labour and capital leads to growth in total GDP but unchanged per capita GDP.

This "balanced growth path" is not, however, the kind of growth that concerns people interested in explaining rising living standards. Since increases in living standards are determined largely by increases in *per capita* output, it is clear that this balanced growth path is unable to explain *rising* living standards.

If capital and labour grow at the same rate, GDP will increase. But in the Neoclassical growth model with constant returns to scale, this "balanced growth path" will not lead to improvements in living standards.

Technological Change

The Neoclassical model predicts that increases in the per capita stock of capital (physical or human) will improve living standards, but that such improvements will eventually stop due to diminishing returns. In contrast, if both capital and labour are growing at the same rate, the Neoclassical model predicts no improvements in living standards, as per capita GDP will be constant.

So how does the Neoclassical model explain the sort of ongoing long-term improvements in living standards that Canada and other countries have experienced over the past century or more? The answer is technological advance, including new knowledge and the improved technology contained within new plant and equipment.

New knowledge and inventions can contribute markedly to the growth of potential output, even without capital accumulation. To illustrate this point, suppose that the proportion of a society's resources devoted to the production of capital goods is just sufficient to replace capital as it wears out. If the old capital is merely replaced in the same form, the capital stock will be constant, and there will be no increase in the capacity to produce. However, if there is a growth of knowledge so that as old equipment wears out it is replaced by different and more productive equipment, then productive capacity will be growing.

embodied technical change Technical change that is intrinsic to the particular capital goods in use.

The increase in productive capacity created by installing new and better capital goods is called **embodied technical change**. Its historical importance is clear: The assembly line and automation transformed most manufacturing industries, the airplane revolutionized transportation, and electronic devices now dominate the information-technology industries. Innovations like these create new investment opportunities.

Less obvious but nonetheless important are technical changes that are embodied in *human* capital. These are changes that result from a better-educated, more experienced labour force; better management practices and techniques; improved design, marketing, and organization of business activities; and feedback from user experience leading to product improvement.

Many—perhaps most—innovations are embodied in either physical or human capital. These innovations cause continual changes in the techniques of production and in the nature of what is produced.

Looking back over the past century, firms produce very few products today in the same way that they did in the past, and much of what is produced and consumed is in the form of new or vastly improved products. Major innovations of the twentieth century include the development of such key products as telephones, radios, televisions, automobiles, airplanes, plastic, CD players, refrigerators, washing machines, coaxial cable, xerography, electron microscopes, telecommunications satellites, computers, transistors, and silicon chips. It is hard for us to imagine life without them.

We have been discussing the benefits of technological change in terms of raising overall living standards. Ever since the Industrial Revolution, however, some workers have feared the effects of technological change. Technological change, after all, is often responsible for workers' losing their jobs as employers replace less efficient labour with more efficient equipment. *Lessons from History 32-1* examines the relationship between technological progress and changes in employment. The main lesson we can learn is that technological change over the years has created far more jobs than it has destroyed.

Can We Measure Technological Change?

Technological change is obviously important. You need only look around you at the current products and production methods that did not exist a generation ago, or even ten years ago, to realize how the advance of technology changes our lives. The development of the Internet is an obvious example of such technological advance. But *how much* does technology change? Unfortunately, technology is not something that is easily measured and so it is very difficult to know just how important it is to the process of economic growth.

In 1957, Robert Solow, an economist at MIT who was awarded the Nobel prize 30 years later for his research on economic growth, attempted to measure the amount of technical change in the United States. He devised a way to infer from the data (under some assumptions about the aggregate production function) how much of the observed growth in real GDP was due to the growth in labour and capital, and how much was due to technical change. His method led to the creation of what is now called the "Solow residual." The Solow residual is the amount of growth in GDP that cannot be accounted for by growth in the labour force or by growth in the capital stock. Since Solow was thinking about changes in GDP as having only three possible sources—changes in capital, changes in labour, and changes in technology—the "residual" was naturally interpreted as a measure of technical change.

Today, economists do not view the Solow residual as a precise estimate of the amount of technical change. The main reason is that much technical change is known to be embodied in new physical and human capital. Thus, capital accumulation and technological change are inherently connected. For example, imagine a firm that replaces an old 286 PC with a new Pentium II PC. Both PCs might be considered one unit of capital, but clearly the Pentium embodies new technology that is completely absent in the old 286. In this case, even though the firm's total capital stock hasn't changed, the process of replacing the old capital with new capital also increased the firm's level of technology. Because capital accumulation and technological advance are so closely linked, Solow's method, which views the two processes as distinct, cannot provide a reliable estimate of technical change. Due to the amount of new technology embodied in new capital equipment, the Solow residual is, at best, an underestimate of the true amount of technical change.

Despite these problems, Solow's method of "growth accounting" and the Solow residual are still widely used by economists in universities and government. The Solow residual often goes by another name—the rate of growth of *total factor productivity (TFP)*.

See Chapter 32 of www.pearsoned.ca/lipsey for an interesting discussion of why the computer revolution has not yet appeared in measurements of productivity growth: Jeremy Leonard, "Computers and Productivity in the Information Economy," *World Economic Affairs.*

Endogenous Technological Change

In the Neoclassical model, innovation increases the amount of output producible from a given level of factor inputs. But this innovation is itself unexplained. The Neoclassical model thus views technological change as *exogenous*. It has profound effects on economic variables, such as GDP, but it is not itself influenced by economic causes. It just happens.

LESSONS FROM HISTORY 32-1

Should Workers Be Afraid of Technological Change?

From time immemorial people have observed that technological change destroys particular jobs and have worried that it will destroy jobs in general. Should they worry?

Technological change *does* destroy particular jobs. When water wheels were used to automate the fulling of cloth in 12th century Europe, there were riots and protests among the fullers who lost their jobs. A century ago, 50 percent of the labour force in North America and Europe was required to produce the required food. Today, less than 5 percent of the labour force is needed in the high-income countries to feed all their citizens. In other words, out of every 100 jobs that existed in 1900, 50 were in agriculture and 45 of those have been destroyed by technological progress over the course of the 20th century.

Just as technological change destroys some jobs, it also creates many new jobs. The displaced agricultural workers did not join the ranks of the permanently unemployed—although some of the older ones may have, their children did not. Instead they, and their children, took jobs in manufacturing and service industries and helped to produce the mass of new goods and services—such as automobiles, refrigerators, computers, and foreign travel—that have raised living standards over the century.

Worries that technological change will cause general unemployment have been recorded for at least 250 years but, so far at least, there is no sign that those displaced by technological change (or their children) are being forced into the ranks of the permanently unemployed. Over all

of recorded history, technological change has created more jobs than it has destroyed.

But how about today? Aren't there good reasons to be more afraid of technological change now than in the past? Modern technologies have two aspects that worry some observers. First, they tend to be *knowledge intensive*. A fairly high degree of literacy and numeracy, as well as familiarity with computers, is needed to work with many but not all of these new technologies. Second, through the process of globalization, unskilled workers in advanced countries have come into competition with unskilled workers everywhere in the world. Both of these forces are decreasing the relative demand for unskilled workers in developed countries and may lead to falling relative wages for unskilled workers in countries like Canada. If labour markets are insufficiently flexible, this change in relative demand may also lead to some structural unemployment.

For these reasons, some people blame the high unemployment rates in Europe (and to a lesser extent, in Canada) on the new technologies. This is hard to reconcile, however, with the fact that the lowest unemployment rates in the industrialized countries are currently being recorded in the United States, the most technologically dynamic of all countries. This suggests that the cause of high European unemployment rates may be not enough technological change and too much government interference rather than too much technological change.

Yet recent research by many scholars has established that technological change is responsive to such economic signals as prices and profits; in other words, it is *endogenous* to the economic system. Though much of the earliest work on this issue was done in Europe, the most influential overall single study was by an American, Nathan Rosenberg, whose trailblazing 1982 book *Inside the Black Box: Technology and Economics* argued this case in great detail.

Technological change stems from research and development and from innovating activities that put the results of R&D into practice. These are costly and highly risky activities, undertaken largely by firms and usually in pursuit of profit. It is not surprising, therefore, that these activities respond to economic incentives. If the price of some particular input such as petroleum or skilled labour goes up, R&D and innovating activities will be directed to altering the production function to economize on these inputs. This process is not simply a substitution of less expensive inputs for more expensive ones within the confines of known technologies; rather, it is the *development of new technologies* in response to changes in relative prices.

There are several important implications of this new understanding that, to a great extent, growth is achieved through costly, risky, innovative activity that often occurs in response to economic signals.

Learning by Doing

The pioneering theorist of innovation, Joseph Schumpeter (1883–1950), developed a model in which innovation flowed in one direction, from a pure discovery "upstream" to more applied R&D, then to working machines, and finally to output "downstream."

In contrast, modern research shows that innovation involves a large amount of "learning by doing" at all of its stages. (We discuss this kind of learning in more detail in Chapter 34.) What is learned downstream then modifies what must be done upstream. The best innovation-managing systems encourage such "feedback" from the more applied steps to the purer researchers and from users to designers.

This interaction is illustrated, for example, by the differences that existed for many years between the Japanese automobile manufacturers and their North American competitors in the handling of new models. North American design was traditionally centralized: Design production teams developed the overall design and then instructed their production sections what to do, as well as asking for bids from parts manufacturers to produce according to specified blueprints. As a result, defects in the original design were often not discovered until production was under way, causing many costly delays and rejection of parts already supplied. In contrast, Japanese firms involved their design and production departments and their parts manufacturers in all stages of the design process. Parts manufacturers were not given specific blueprints for production; instead, they were given general specifications and asked to develop their own detailed designs. As they did so, they learned. They then fed information about the problems they were encountering back to the main designers while the general outlines of the new model were not yet finalized. As a result, the Japanese were able to design a new product faster, at less cost, and with far fewer problems than were the North American firms. In recent years, however, the North American automotive firms have adopted many of these Japanese design and production methods.

Knowledge Transfer

The *diffusion* of technological knowledge from those who have it to those who want it is not costless (as it was assumed to be in Schumpeter's model). Firms need research capacity just to adopt the technologies developed by others. Some of the knowledge needed to use a new technology can be learned only through experience by plant managers, technicians, and operators. We often tend to think that once a production process is developed, it can easily be copied by others. In practice, however, the diffusion of new technological knowledge is not so simple.

For example, some economists argue that most industrial technologies require technology-specific organizational skills that cannot be "embodied" in the machines themselves, instruction books, or blueprints. The needed knowledge is *tacit* in the sense that it cannot be taught through books and can only be acquired by experience—much like driving a car or flying an airplane. Acquiring tacit knowledge requires a deliberate process of building up new skills, work practices, knowledge, and experience.

The fact that diffusion is a costly and time-consuming business explains why new technologies take considerable time to diffuse, first through the economy of the originating country and then through the rest of the world. If diffusion were simple and virtually costless, the puzzle would be why technological knowledge and best industrial practices did not diffuse very quickly. As it is, decades can pass before a new technological process is diffused everywhere that it could be employed.

Market Structure and Innovation

Because it is highly risky, innovation is encouraged by strong rivalry among firms and discouraged by monopoly practices. Competition among three or four large firms often produces much innovation, but a single firm, especially if it serves a secure home market protected by trade barriers, seems much less inclined to innovate. The reduction in trade barriers over the past several decades and the increasing globalization of markets as a result of falling transportation and communication costs have increased international competition. Whereas one firm in a national market might have had substantial monopoly power three or four decades ago, today it is more likely to be in intense competition with firms based in other countries.

Government interventions that are designed to encourage innovation often allow the firms in an industry to work together as one. Unless great care is exercised and unless sufficient foreign competition exists, the result may be a national monopoly that will discourage risk taking rather than encourage it, as is the intention of the policy.

Shocks and Innovation

One interesting consequence of endogenous technical change is that shocks that would be unambiguously adverse to an economy operating with fixed technology can sometimes provide a spur to innovation that proves a blessing in disguise. A sharp rise in the price of one input can raise costs and lower the value of output per person for some time. But it may lead to a wave of innovations that reduce the need for this expensive input and, as a side effect, greatly raise productivity.

Sometimes individual firms will respond differently to the same economic signal. Sometimes those that respond by altering technology will do better than those that concentrate their efforts on substituting within the confines of known technology. For example, in *The Competitive Advantage of Nations,* Harvard economist Michael Porter tells the story of the consumer electronics industry, in which U.S. firms moved their operations abroad to avoid high, rigid labour costs. They continued to use their existing technology and went where labour costs were low enough to make that technology pay. Their Japanese competitors, however, stayed at home. They innovated away most of their labour costs and then built factories in the United States to replace the factories of U.S. firms that had gone abroad!

Theories Based on Increasing Returns

We saw earlier that Neoclassical theories of economic growth assume that investment is always subject to diminishing returns. New growth theories emphasize the possibility of *historical increasing returns to investment:* As investment in some new area, product, or production technology proceeds through time, each new increment of investment is more productive than previous increments. Economists have noted a number of sources of increasing returns. These fall under the two general categories of *fixed costs* and *knowledge.*

Fixed Costs

There are three reasons why there may be an important fixed-cost component to the amount of investment undertaken in an industry or region.

1. Investment in the early stages of development of a country, province, or town may create new skills and attitudes in the workforce that are then available to all subsequent firms, whose costs are therefore lower than those encountered by the initial

firms. (For those who have studied microeconomics, the early firms are conferring a positive *externality* on those who follow them, as described in Chapter 16.)

2. Each new firm may find the environment more and more favourable to its investment because of the infrastructure that has been created by those who came before.

3. The first investment in a new product will encounter countless production problems that, once overcome, cause fewer problems to subsequent investors.

More generally, many investments require fixed costs, the advantages of which are then available to subsequent firms; hence, the investment costs for "followers" can be substantially less than the investment costs for "pioneers." In short, doing something really new is difficult, whereas making further variations on an accepted and developed new idea becomes progressively easier.

Another important issue concerns the behaviour of customers. When a new product is developed, customers will often resist adopting it, both because they may be conservative and because they know that new products usually have teething troubles. Customers also need time to learn how best to use the new product—they need to do what is called "learning by using."

Slow acceptance of new products by customers is not necessarily irrational. When a sophisticated new product comes on the market, no one is sure if it will be a success, and the first customers to buy it take the risk that the product may subsequently turn out to be a failure. They also incur the costs of learning how to use it effectively. Many potential users take the not unreasonable attitude of letting others try a new product, following only after the product's success has been demonstrated. This makes the early stages of innovation especially costly and risky.

Successive increments of investment associated with an innovation often yield a range of increasing returns as costs that are incurred in earlier investment expenditure provide publicly available knowledge and experience and as customer attitudes and abilities become more receptive to new products.

The implications of these ideas have been the subject of intense study ever since they were first embedded in modern growth models by Paul Romer of Stanford University and Maurice Scott of Oxford University.[2] Probably the most important contrast between these new theories and the Neoclassical theory concerns investment and income. In the Neoclassical model, diminishing returns to capital implies a limit to the possible increase of per capita GDP. In the new models, investment alone can hold an economy on a "sustained growth path" in which per capita GDP increases without limit, provided that the investment embodies the results of continual advances in technological knowledge.

Knowledge

An even more fundamental aspect of the new growth theories is the shift from the economics of goods to the economics of *ideas*. Physical goods, such as factories and machines, exist in one place at one time. This has two consequences. First, when physical goods are used by someone, they cannot be used by someone else. Second, if a given labour force is provided with more and more physical objects to use in production, sooner or later diminishing returns will be encountered.

A computer is an "ordinary" good because if I own it then you cannot also own it. But the knowledge required to build the computer is a public good. And knowledge, unlike traditional factors of production, is not necessarily subject to the law of diminishing returns.

---

[2]As with so many innovations, these new views have many historical antecedents, including a classic article in the 1960s by Nobel Prize winner Kenneth Arrow of Stanford University.

Ideas have different characteristics. Once someone develops ideas, they are available for use by everyone simultaneously. Ideas can be used by one person without reducing their use by others. For example, if one firm uses a truck, another firm cannot use it at the same time; but one firm's use of a revolutionary design for a new suspension on a truck does not prevent other firms from using that design as well. Ideas are often not subject to the same use restrictions as goods. (For those that have studied microeconomics, some knowledge has aspects that make it a *public good*, as we discussed in Chapter 16.)

Ideas are also not necessarily subject to diminishing returns. As our knowledge increases, each increment of new knowledge does not inevitably add less to our productive ability than each previous increment. A year spent improving the operation of semiconductors may be more productive than a year spent improving the operation of vacuum tubes (the technology used before semiconductors).

The evidence from modern research is that new technologies are usually *absolutely factor-saving*—in other words, they use less of all inputs per unit of output. Furthermore, there is no evidence that from decade to decade the factor saving associated with increments of new knowledge is diminishing.

Modern growth theories stress the importance of ideas in producing what is called *knowledge-driven growth*. New knowledge provides the input that allows investment to produce increasing rather than diminishing returns. Because there are no practical limits to human knowledge, there need be no immediate boundaries to finding new ways to produce more output using less of all inputs.

Neoclassical growth theories gave economics the name "the dismal science" by emphasizing diminishing returns under conditions of given technology. The modern growth theories are more optimistic because they emphasize the unlimited potential of knowledge-driven technological change.

Are There Limits to Growth?

Many opponents of growth argue that sustained world growth is undesirable; some argue that it is impossible. The idea that economic growth is limited by nature is not new. In the early 1970s, a group called the "Club of Rome" focused on the limits to growth arising from the finite supply of natural resources. Extrapolating from the oil shortages caused by the OPEC cartel, the Club of Rome concluded that industrialized countries faced an imminent absolute limit to growth. Do such limits really exist? We discuss the two issues of resource exhaustion and pollution.

Resource Exhaustion

The years since World War II have seen a rapid acceleration in the consumption of the world's resources, particularly fossil fuels and basic minerals. World population has increased from under 2.5 billion to over 6 billion in that period; this increase alone has intensified the demand for the world's resources. Furthermore, as people attain higher incomes, they consume more resources. Thus, not only are there more people in the world, but many of those people are consuming increasing quantities of resources.

The technology and resources available today could not possibly support all of the world's population at a standard of living equal to that of the average Canadian family. It is evident that resources and our present capacity to cope with pollution and environmental degradation are insufficient to accomplish this rise in living standards with present technology.

See the United Nations' website for international data on economic development: www.un.org. Click on "Economic and Social Development" and then go to "Statistics."

Most economists, however, agree that absolute limits to growth, based on the assumptions of constant technology and fixed resources, are not relevant. As modern growth theory stresses, technology changes continually, as do stocks of resources. For example, 40 years ago, few would have thought that the world could produce enough food to feed its present population of 6 billion people, let alone the 10 billion at which the population is projected to stabilize sometime in the twenty-first century. Yet this task now seems feasible.

The future is always uncertain, and it is instructive to recall how many things that we accept as commonplace today would have seemed miraculous a mere 25 years ago.

Yet there is surely cause for concern. Although many barriers can be overcome by technological advances, such achievements are not instantaneous and are certainly not automatic. There is a critical problem of timing: How soon can we discover and put into practice the knowledge required to solve the problems that are made ever more imminent by the growth in the population, the affluence of the rich nations, and the aspirations of the billions who now live in poverty? There is no guarantee that a whole generation will not be caught in transition between technologies, with enormous social and political consequences.

Pollution

A further problem is how to cope with pollution. Air, water, and soil are polluted by a variety of natural activities and, for billions of years, the environment has coped with these. The earth's natural processes had little trouble coping with the pollution generated by its 1 billion inhabitants in 1800. But the 6 billion people who now exist put demands on pollution abatement systems that threaten to become unsustainable. Smoke, sewage, chemical waste, hydrocarbon and greenhouse-gas emissions, spent nuclear fuel, and a host of other pollutants threaten to overwhelm the earth's natural regenerative processes.

Conscious management of pollution was unnecessary when the world's population was one billion people, but such management has now become a pressing matter.

Conclusion

The world faces many problems. Starvation and poverty are the common lot of citizens in many countries and are not unknown even in countries such as Canada and the United States, where average living standards are very high. Growth has raised the average citizens of advanced countries from poverty to plenty in the course of two centuries—a short time in terms of human history. Further growth is needed if people in developing countries are to escape material poverty, and further growth would help advanced countries to deal with many of their pressing economic problems.

Rising population and rising per capita consumption, however, put pressure on the world's natural ecosystems, especially through the many forms of pollution. Further growth must be *sustainable* growth, which must in turn be based on knowledge-driven technological change. Past experience suggests that new technologies will use less of all resources per unit of output. But if they are dramatically to reduce the demands placed on the earth's ecosystems, price and policy incentives will be needed to direct technological change in more "environmentally friendly" ways. Just as present technologies are much less polluting than the technologies of a century ago, the technologies of the twenty-first century must be made much less polluting than today's.

There is no guarantee that the world will solve the problems of sustainable growth, but there is nothing in modern growth theory and existing evidence to suggest that such an achievement is impossible.

SUMMARY

The Nature of Economic Growth   LO ① ② ③

- Sustained increases in real GDP are due mainly to economic growth, which continuously pushes the *LRAS* curve outward, thereby increasing potential output.
- Growth is frequently measured by using rates of change of potential real GDP per person. The cumulative effects of even small differences in growth rates become very large over periods of a decade or more.
- The most important benefit of growth lies in its contribution to the long-run struggle to raise living standards and to escape poverty. Growth also facilitates the redistribution of income among people.

- Growth, though often beneficial, is never costless. The opportunity cost of growth is the diversion of resources from current consumption to capital formation. For individuals who are left behind in a rapidly changing world, the costs are higher and more personal.
- There are four fundamental determinants of growth: increases in the labour force; increases in physical capital; increases in human capital; and improvements in technology.

Theories of Economic Growth   LO ④ ⑤

- Investment has short-term effects on real GDP through aggregate demand and long-term effects through growth in potential output. Saving reduces consumption and aggregate demand and therefore reduces real GDP in the short run, but in the long run, saving finances the investment that leads to growth in potential output.
- The Neoclassical theory of growth displays diminishing returns when one factor is increased on its own and constant returns when all factors are increased together. In a balanced growth path, the quantity of labour, the quantity of capital, and real GDP all increase at a constant rate. But since per capita output is constant, living standards are not rising.
- Changes in output that cannot be accounted for by changes in the levels of physical and human capital and in the size of the labour force are attributed to changes in what is called total factor productivity (TFP). Although it

is sometimes associated with technological change, TFP does not measure all of such change because much of it is embodied in new physical and human capital.
- In the Neoclassical growth model, technological change is assumed to be exogenous—unaffected by the size of the labour force, the size of the capital stock, or the level of economic activity.
- Recent growth theory treats technological change as an endogenous variable that responds to market signals. The diffusion of technology is also endogenous. It is costly and often proceeds at a relatively slow pace.
- Some modern growth theories display constant or increasing returns as investment increases on its own. This investment confers externalities such that successive increments of investment may add constant or even successively increasing amounts to total output.

Are There Limits to Growth?   LO ⑥

- The critical importance of increasing knowledge and new technology to the goal of sustaining growth is highlighted by the great drain on existing natural resources that has resulted from the explosive growth of population and output in recent decades. Without continuing technological change, the present needs and aspirations of the world's population cannot come anywhere close to being met.

- Rising population and rising real incomes place pressure on resources. Although not all resources will be exhausted, particular resources, such as petroleum, will be.
- The increase in population has similar effects on pollution: The earth's environment could cope naturally with much of human pollution 200 years ago, but the present population is so large that pollution has outstripped nature's coping mechanisms.

KEY CONCEPTS

The cumulative nature of growth
Benefits and costs of growth
Short-run and long-run effects of investment and saving
The aggregate production function

Diminishing marginal returns
Constant returns to scale
Balanced growth
Total factor productivity

Endogenous technical change
Increasing returns to investment
The economics of goods and of ideas
Resource depletion and pollution

STUDY EXERCISES

1. In the text we said that, over many years, small differences in growth rates can have large effects on the level of income. This question will help you understand this important point. Consider an initial value of real GDP equal to Y_0. If real GDP grows at a rate of g percent annually, then after N years real GDP will be equal to $Y_0(1+g)^N$. Now consider the following table. Let the initial level of GDP in all cases be 100.

| | Real GDP With Alternative Growth Rates | | | | | |
Year	(1) 1%	(2) 1.5%	(3) 2%	(4) 2.5%	(5) 3%	(6) 3.5%
0	100	100	100	100	100	100
1	—	—	—	—	—	—
3	—	—	—	—	—	—
5	—	—	—	—	—	—
10	—	—	—	—	—	—
20	—	—	—	—	—	—
30	—	—	—	—	—	—
50	—	—	—	—	—	—

a. Using the formula provided above, compute the level of real GDP in column 1 for each year. For example, in year 1, real GDP will equal $100(1+.01)^1 = 101$.

b. Now do the same for the rest of the columns.

c. In Year 20, how much larger (in percentage terms) is real GDP in the 3% growth case compared to the 1.5% growth case?

d. In Year 50, how much larger (in percentage terms) is real GDP in the 3% growth case compared to the 1.5% growth case?

2. The diagram below shows two paths for aggregate consumption. One grows at a rate of 3 percent per year; the other grows at 4 percent per year but begins at a lower level.

a. Suppose the economy jumps from Path 1 to Path 2 in year 0 because its rate of capital accumulation increases. What is the opportunity cost in this economy for this increase in capital accumulation?

b. Suppose the economy jumps from Path 1 to Path 2 in year 0 because its rate of R&D expenditures in-

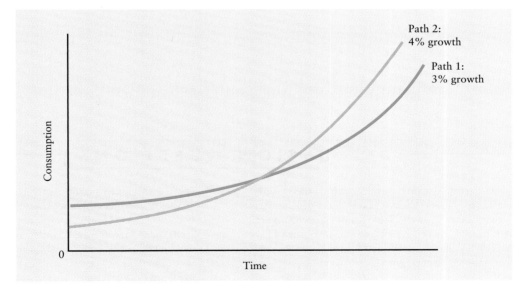

crease. The greater R&D leads to technological improvements that generate the higher growth rate. What is the opportunity cost to this economy for the increase in R&D expenditures?

c. Show in the figure the "breakeven" point for the economy after both of the changes described above. Explain.

3. In the text we discussed the short-run and the long-run effects of saving.

a. Explain why an increase in saving *reduces* real GDP in the short run.

b. Show the answer to part **a** in an *AD/SRAS* diagram.

c. Explain why an increase in saving *increases* real GDP in the long run.

d. Show the answer to part **c** in an *AD/SRAS* diagram.

4. The Neoclassical growth theory is based on the existence of an aggregate production function—showing the relationship between labour (*L*), capital (*K*), technology (*T*) and real GDP (*Y*). The table below shows various values for *L*, *K*, and *T*. In all cases, the aggregate production function is assumed to take the following form:

$$Y = T \times \sqrt{KL}$$

Labour (L)	Capital (K)	Technology (T)	Real GDP (Y)
10	20	1	—
15	20	1	—
20	20	1	—
25	20	1	—
10	20	1	—
15	30	1	—
20	40	1	—
25	50	1	—
20	20	1	—
20	20	3	—
20	20	4	—
20	20	5	—

a. Compute real GDP for each case and complete the table.

b. In the first part of the table, note that capital is constant but labour is increasing. What property of the production function is displayed? Explain.

c. In the second part of the table, note that capital and labour are increasing by the same proportion. What property of the production function is displayed? Explain.

d. What type of growth is being shown in the third part of the table?

5. In the early 1970s the Club of Rome, extrapolating from the rates of resource use at the time, predicted that the supply of natural resources (especially oil) would be used up within a few decades. Subsequent events appear to have proven them wrong.

a. What is predicted to happen to the price of oil (and other natural resources) as population and per capita incomes rise?

b. Given your answer to part **a**, what is the likely response by firms and consumers who use such resources?

c. Now explain why resource exhaustion should, through the workings of the price system, lead to technological developments that reduce the use of the resource.

DISCUSSION QUESTIONS

1. Economic growth is often studied in macroeconomic terms, but in a market economy, who makes the decisions that lead to growth? What kinds of decisions and what kinds of actions cause growth to occur? How might a detailed study of individual markets be relevant to understanding economic growth?

2. Discuss the following quote from a recent newspaper article: "Economics and the environment are not strange bedfellows. Environment-oriented tourism is one creative way to resolve the conflict between our desire for a higher standard of living and the realization that nature cannot absorb everything we throw at it. The growing demand for eco-tourism has placed a premium on

the remaining rain forests, undisturbed flora and fauna, and endangered species of the world."

3. "The case for economic growth is that it gives man greater control over his environment, and consequently increases his freedom." Explain why you agree or disagree with this statement by Nobel laureate W. Arthur Lewis.

4. Dr. David Suzuki, an opponent of further economic growth, has argued that despite the fact that "in the twentieth century the list of scientific and technological achievements has been absolutely dazzling, the costs of such progress are so large that negative economic growth may be right for the future." Policies to achieve this include "rigorous reduction of waste, a questioning and distrustful attitude toward technological progress, and braking demands on the globe's resources." Identify some of the benefits and costs of economic growth, and evaluate Suzuki's position. What government policies would be needed to achieve his ends?

5. In this chapter we discussed four fundamental determinants of growth in real output; increases in the labour force; increases in the stock of physical capital; increases in human capital; and improvements in technology. For each of the four, give an example of a government policy that is likely to increase growth. Discuss also the likely cost associated with each policy. Does one of your proposed policies appear better (in a cost-benefit sense) than the others?

6. The Solow residual has been called a "measure of our ignorance" of the causes of growth. Explain this viewpoint. Is the Solow residual a good measure of technical change?

CHAPTER 33

Challenges Facing the Developing Countries

🅛🅞 LEARNING OBJECTIVES

❶ Gain a general knowledge of the extent of world income inequality.

❷ Understand some of the main challenges facing developing countries.

❸ Understand the emergence of a new view of development, known as the "Washington consensus."

❹ Understand the current debates about development policies.

In the comfortable urban life of today's developed countries, most people have lost sight of the fact that a short time ago—very short in terms of the life span of the earth—people were nomadic food gatherers, garnering an existence as best they could from what nature threw their way. It has been only about 10 000 years since the Neolithic agricultural revolution, when people changed from food gatherers to food producers. Throughout most of subsequent human history, civilizations have been based on a comfortable life for a privileged minority and unremitting toil for the vast majority. Only within the past two centuries have ordinary people become able to expect leisure and high consumption standards—and then only in the world's economically developed countries.

In this chapter we review some of the challenges faced by the world's developing countries—those countries that have not yet been fortunate enough to achieve the living standards that we, in Canada, all too often take for granted.

developed countries
The higher-income countries of the world, including the United States, Canada, Western Europe, Japan, Australia, and South Africa.

developing countries
The lower-income countries of the world, most of which are in Africa, Asia, and Latin America.

newly industrialized countries (NICs)
Countries that have industrialized and grown rapidly over the past 40 years.

The Uneven Pattern of Development

Over 6 billion people are alive today, but the wealthy parts of the world contain no more than 20 percent of the world's population. Many of the rest struggle for subsistence. Many exist on a level at or below that endured by peasants in ancient Egypt or Babylon.

The richest countries with the highest per capita incomes are referred to by the United Nations as **developed countries.** These include the United States, Canada, most of the countries of Western Europe, South Africa, Australia, New Zealand, Japan, and a few others. The poorer states are referred to by the UN as the **developing countries** and include a diverse set of nations. Some, such as Vietnam, Argentina, and China, are growing very rapidly, while others, such as Haiti, Rwanda, and Sierra Leone are actually experiencing negative growth rates of real per capita income. Between these two is another group of nations, called the **newly industrialized countries (NICs).** They include South

Korea, Singapore, Taiwan, and Hong Kong. These countries grew rapidly in the three decades after 1960 and typically have per capita incomes close to 50 percent of those found in the developed nations. Several other countries in Southeast Asia are close behind the NICs. These include Indonesia, Malaysia, and Thailand. In 1997 and 1998, however, many of these NICs—especially Malaysia, Indonesia, Thailand, and South Korea—experienced sudden economic recessions brought on, to some extent, by the significant collapse in the external value of their currencies.

Viewing the problem of raising per capita income in a poorer country as one of economic *development* recognizes that the whole structure of its economy often needs to be altered to create economic growth. This is a complex task; many countries remain undeveloped today despite decades of effort by their governments (often assisted with aid from developed countries) to get them on a path of sustained growth.

Data on per capita incomes throughout the world (as shown in Table 33-1) cannot be accurate down to the last $100 because there are many problems in comparing national incomes across countries. For example, homegrown food is vitally important to living standards in developing countries, but it is excluded from or at best imperfectly included in the national income statistics of most countries. Nevertheless, the data reflect enormous real differences in living standards that no statistical inaccuracies can hide. The *development gap*—the discrepancy between the standards of living in countries at either end of the distribution—is real and large.

Figure 33-1 provides another way of looking at inequality. It shows the geographical distribution of per capita income. The map reveals why modern political discussions of income distribution often use the labels *North* and *South* to refer to the rich and the poor nations, respectively.

The consequences of low income levels can be severe. In rich countries like Canada and the United States, variations in rainfall are reflected in farm output and farm income. In poor countries, variations in rainfall are often reflected in the death rate. In these countries, many people live so close to a subsistence level that slight fluctuations in the food supply bring death by starvation to large numbers. Other, less dramatic characteristics of poverty include inadequate diet, poor health, short life expectancy, and illiteracy.

The North-South Institute is a Canadian research institute that focuses on economic development. See their website: www.nsi-ins.ca.

TABLE 33-1   Income and Population Differences Among Groups of Countries, 1996

GNP Per Capita (US$)	(1) Number of Countries	(2) GNP (US$ millions)	(3) Population (millions)	(4) GNP Per Capita (US$)	(5) Percentage of World Population	(6) Percentage of World GNP
Less than $785	63	1 596 837	3 236	493	56.2	5.4
$786 to $3115	63	1 962 719	1 125	1 745	19.6	6.6
$3116 to $9635	31	2 178 234	473	4 606	8.2	7.4
$9636 or more	53	23 771 825	919	25 867	16.0	80.6
World	210	29 509 615	5 754	5 129	100.0	100.0

There is considerable inequality in the distribution of world income. The unequal distribution of world income is shown in columns 5 and 6. The poorest half of the world's population earns just 5 percent of world income. The richest 16 percent earns over 80 percent of world income.

(*Source: World Bank Atlas*, 1998.)

FIGURE 33-1   Countries of the World, Classified by Per Capita GNP, 1996

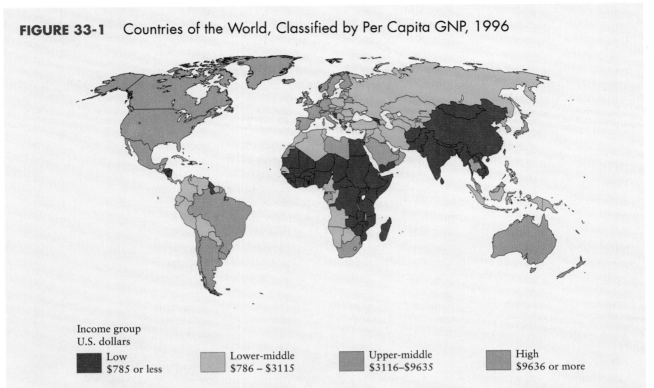

Income group
U.S. dollars

| | Low
$785 or less | | Lower-middle
$786 – $3115 | | Upper-middle
$3116–$9635 | | High
$9636 or more |

There is a sharp geographical division between "North" and "South" in the level of income per capita. The nations of the world are classified here according to four levels of measured per capita GNP, as shown in Table 33-1. The poorest group, shown in brown, represents 56 percent of the world's population and just over 5 percent of world GNP. The wealthiest group, shown in orange, includes North America, Europe, Japan, and Australia and represents 16 percent of the world's population and over 80 percent of world GNP.

For these reasons, reformers in developing countries feel a sense of urgency not felt by their counterparts in rich countries. Yet, as Table 33-2 shows, some of the poorest countries in the world are among those with very low or negative growth rates of per capita GDP, with the following consequence:

The development gap has been widening for the very poorest countries.

As we shall see, this is a problem of both output and population. It is also an international political problem. What are the causes of underdevelopment, and how may they be overcome?

| Impediments to Economic Development

Per capita income grows when aggregate income grows faster than population. Many forces can impede such growth. Here we study a number of possible impediments.

TABLE 33-2 The Relationship Between the Level and the Growth Rate of Per Capita Income, 1990–1996

Growth of GNP Per Capita, 1990–1996 (% per year)	Number of Countries	GNP (US$ million) 1996	Population (millions) 1996	GNP Per Capita (US$) 1996
Less than 0	69	2 152 165	832	2 587
0 to 0.9	21	6 037 894	342	17 655
1.0 to 1.9	25	15 772 567	1 043	15 122
2.0 to 2.9	20	1 399 561	488	2 868
3.0 or more	39	3 899 334	2 896	1 346

The very poorest countries spend much of their increase in income on a rising population. Hence, their increase in income per capita is less than half that of the countries that are already richer. The gap in income between rich and many of the very poor countries is not closing.

(*Source: World Bank Atlas*, 1998.)

Resources

A country's supply of natural resources is important. A country with infertile land and inadequate supplies of natural resources will find income growth more difficult to achieve than one that is richly endowed with such resources.

How these resources are managed also matters. When farmland is divided into many small parcels, it may be much more difficult to achieve the advantages of modern agricultural techniques than when the land is available in huge tracts for large-scale farming. Fragmented land holdings may result from a dowry or inheritance system or may be politically imposed. One of the populist policies following the Mexican Revolution early in the twentieth century was the redistribution of land from large landowners to ordinary peasants. Today, however, fragmented land ownership prevents Mexican agriculture from producing at costs low enough to compete in international markets. The Mexican government now faces an agonizing choice between allowing its populist land reforms to be reversed or continuing to protect a large agricultural sector whose inefficiency is increasing relative to competing suppliers.

Although abundant supplies of natural resources can assist growth, they are neither sufficient to ensure growth nor necessary for it. Some countries with large supplies of natural resources have poor growth performance because the economic structure encourages waste. Prime examples are the former Soviet Union, Argentina before the 1990s, and Uganda. In contrast, other countries have enjoyed rapid rates of economic growth based on human capital and entrepreneurial ability despite a dearth of natural resources. Prime examples are Switzerland in earlier centuries, Japan over the past 100 years (until its significant current economic malaise, beginning in the early 1990s), and Singapore, Hong Kong, and Taiwan since the end of World War II.

When we discuss inefficiency in resource use, it helps to distinguish between two kinds of economic inefficiency, which are studied in microeconomics. *Allocative inefficiency* occurs when factors of production are used to make an inefficient combination of goods. There are too many of some goods and too few of others, and thus the society is at the wrong point on its production possibility boundary. If resources are reallocated to produce less of some and more of other types of goods, some people can be made better off while no one is made worse off.

Productive inefficiency occurs when factors of production are used in inefficient combinations. Given the prices of capital and labour, some production processes use too much capital relative to labour, while others use too little. Productive inefficiency implies that the society is *inside* its production possibility boundary. If factor combinations are altered, more of all goods can be produced.

Monopolistic market structures, as well as taxes, tariffs, and subsidies, are some important sources of the distortions that lead to both allocative and productive inefficiencies.

A third kind of inefficiency, called *X-inefficiency*, occurs either when firms do not seek to maximize their profits or when owners of the factors of production do not seek to maximize their well-being. Like allocative and productive inefficiency, X-inefficiency also puts the economy inside its production possibility boundary.

Professor Harvey Liebenstein of the University of California, the economist who developed the concept, has studied X-inefficiency in developing countries. He cites psychological evidence to show that non-maximizing behaviour is typical of situations in which the pressure that has been placed on decision makers is either very low or very high. According to this evidence, if the customary living standard can be obtained with little effort, people are likely to follow customary behaviour and spend little time trying to make *optimal* decisions that would improve their well-being. When pressure builds up, so that making a reasonable income becomes more difficult, optimizing behaviour becomes more common. Under extreme pressure, however, such as very low living standards or a rapidly deteriorating environment, people become disoriented and once again do not adopt optimizing behaviour.

Human Capital

Numbers of people matter, and so do their training and experience. A well-developed entrepreneurial class, motivated and trained to organize resources for efficient production, is often missing in poor countries. The cause may be that managerial positions are awarded on the basis of family status or political patronage rather than merit, it may be the prevalence of economic or cultural attitudes that do not favour acquisition of wealth by organizing productive activities, or it may simply be an absence of the quantity or quality of education or training that is required.

In today's world, much production is knowledge-intensive, thus putting a premium on a well-educated workforce. The ability to read, do basic calculations, operate electronic equipment, and follow relatively complex instructions are important requirements for much modern labour. Failure to develop such essential labour skills can be an important cause of lack of growth.

Poor health is another source of inadequate human resources. When the labour force is healthy, less working time is lost, and more effective effort is expended.

Agriculture

A developing country whose labour force is mainly devoted to agriculture has little choice but to accept this basic allocation of resources. It can build up its industrial sector, and if its efforts are successful, the proportion of the population devoted to urban pursuits will rise. But the change will come slowly, leaving a large portion of the country's resources in rural pursuits for a long time to come.

It follows that policies to help the agriculture sector raise productivity are an important part of the development strategy in any agriculture-based poor country. These can fill the dual purposes of raising incomes of rural workers and reducing the cost of food for urban workers.

A developing country's government may choose to devote a major portion of its resources to stimulating agricultural production, say, by mechanizing farms, irrigating land, using new seeds and fertilizers, and promoting agricultural research and development. Modern developments of new crops and new growing techniques put a premium on agricultural research and development (R&D) so that a country can adopt, and usually adapt, other country's agricultural innovations. Also, nonfood agricultural and forest products are becoming increasingly important, and R&D expenditures are often needed if these are to become established products. If successful, the country will stave off starvation for its current population, and it may even develop an excess over current needs and thus have a crop available for export. A food surplus can earn foreign exchange to buy needed imports.

In many developing countries, the labour force is mainly devoted to agriculture. Increasing the efficiency of agriculture is an important part of a successful development strategy.

The gains from this strategy, while large at first, are subject to diminishing returns. Further gains in agricultural production have an ever-higher opportunity cost, measured in terms of the resources needed to irrigate land and to mechanize production. Critics of reliance on agricultural output argue that developing economies must start at once to develop other bases for economic growth.

Many developing countries (as well as many developed ones) suffer from misguided government intervention in the agriculture sector. In India, for example, the government—motivated by a desire to *diversify* agricultural production by increasing the number of crops under cultivation—has encouraged crops such as oilseeds and sugarcane, in which India has a comparative *dis*advantage, and discouraged crops such as rice, wheat, and cotton, in which India has a strong comparative advantage. It has subsidized food prices, thus giving large benefits to the urban population.

Population Growth

Population growth is one of the central problems of economic development. Some developing countries have population growth rates in excess of their GDP growth rates and therefore have *negative* growth rates of per capita GDP. Many developing countries have rates of population growth that are nearly as large as their rates of GDP growth. As a result, their standards of living are barely higher than they were 100 years ago. They have made appreciable gains in aggregate income, but most of the gains have been literally eaten up by the increasing population.

The critical importance of population growth to living standards was perceived early in the nineteenth century by Thomas Malthus (1766–1834). He asserted two relations concerning rates of increase. First, food production tends to increase in an *arithmetic* progression (e.g., 100, 103, 106, 109, 112, where the increments in this example are 3 *units* per period). Second, population tends to increase in a *geometric* progression (e.g., 100, 103, 106.09, 109.27, 112.55, where the increase in this example is 3 *percent* per period). Consequently, Malthus argued that under conditions of natural growth, population will always tend to outrun the growth in food supply. The difference in our example may not seem like much after only five periods. But after 20 periods, the arithmetic progression in food supply has increased it to 160, whereas the geometric progression in the population has increased it to 181.

Malthus's prediction helped to earn economics the label "the dismal science." And, in some poor areas of the world, the predictions ring all too true, even today. Where agricultural methods are fairly traditional so that food production increases only slowly, population tends to increase at more rapid rates. The result is subsistence living, with population held in check by low life expectancies and periodic famines.

Fortunately, over most of the world, Malthus's predictions have been proved false. Two reasons are paramount. First, Malthus underestimated the importance of technological

For a lot of good data about developing countries, see the UN's website: www.un.org. Click on "Economic and Social Development."

change, which has increased agricultural productivity at a *geometric* rate in many countries, a rate far higher than the rate at which the demand for food has been growing in most advanced countries. Second, he underestimated the extent of voluntary restrictions of population growth due both to the widespread use of birth control techniques and other changes in behaviour such as delayed marriages. As a result, population has grown more slowly than the production of food (and most other things) in developed countries. In these places, living standards have been rising rather than falling.

For the more advanced industrialized countries, Malthusian pressures are not a problem today. For many poor countries, where people subsist on what they grow for themselves, the tendency for the growth in population to outstrip the growth in the food supply makes Malthusian pressures a current threat.

Figure 33-2 illustrates actual and projected world population. By now, the population problem is almost completely limited to developing countries. About 97 percent of the expected growth in the world's population between now and 2050 will be in the developing countries of Africa, Asia, and Latin America.

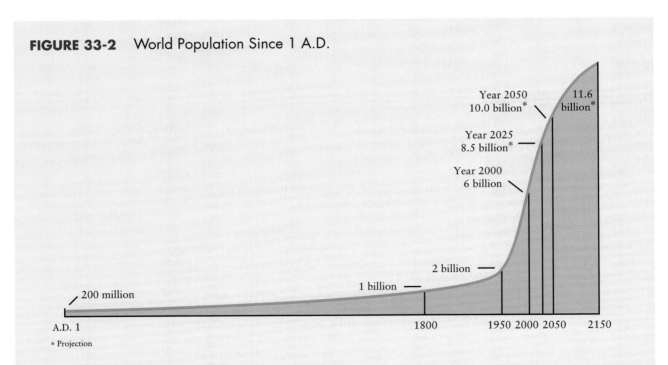

FIGURE 33-2   World Population Since 1 A.D.

World population was just over 6 billion in 2000 and is projected to rise to 10 billion by the middle of the 21st century. The population of industrialized countries has nearly stabilized. But, in developing countries, population is skyrocketing. Up to 97 percent of population growth between now and 2050 will occur in developing countries. By that time, total world population will have reached 10 billion. Birth and death rates among present populations allow estimates to be made up to about the middle of the next century with reasonable accuracy. The projection to 11.6 billion by 2150 is much more conjectural and highly uncertain.

(*Source:* United Nations Population Fund.)

Cultural Barriers

Traditions and habitual ways of doing business vary among societies, and not all are equally conducive to economic growth. In developing countries, cultural forces are often a source of inefficiency. Sometimes personal considerations of family, past favours, or traditional friendship or enmity are more important than market incentives in motivating behaviour. In a traditional society in which children are expected to stay in their parents' occupations, it is more difficult for the labour force to change its characteristics and to adapt to the requirements of growth than in a society in which upward mobility is a goal itself.

The fact that existing social, religious, or legal patterns may make growth more difficult does not imply that they are undesirable. Instead, it suggests that the benefits of these patterns must be weighed against the costs, of which the limitation on growth is one. When people derive satisfaction from a religion whose beliefs inhibit growth or when they value a society in which every household owns its own land and is more nearly self-sufficient than in another society, they may be quite willing to pay a price in terms of forgone growth opportunities.

Cultural traditions in developing countries often stand in the way of increases in efficiency and economic growth.

Many critics argue that development plans, particularly when imposed by economists coming from developed countries, pay too little attention to local cultural and religious values. Even when they are successful by the test of increasing GDP, such success may be at too great a cost in terms of social upheaval for the current generation.

A country that wants development must accept some alteration in traditional ways of doing things. However, a tradeoff between speed of development and amount of social upheaval can be made. The critics argue that such a tradeoff should be made by local governments and should not be imposed by outsiders who understand little of local customs and beliefs. An even more unfavourable possibility is that the social upheaval will occur without achieving even the expected benefits of GDP growth. If the development policy does not take local values into account, the local population may not respond as predicted by Western economic theories. In this case, the results of the development effort may be disappointingly small.

Domestic Saving

Although modern development strategies call in many instances for a large infusion of imported foreign capital, the rise of domestically owned firms, which will reap some of the externalities created by foreign technology, is one key to sustained development. This requires a supply of domestic saving to finance their growth.

If more domestic capital is to be created at home by a country's own efforts, resources must be diverted from the production of goods for current consumption. This reallocation of resources implies a reduction in *current* living standards. If living standards are already at or near the subsistence level, such a diversion will be difficult. At best, it will be possible to reallocate only a small proportion of resources to the production of capital goods.

Such a situation is often described as the *vicious circle of poverty:* Because a country has little capital per head, it is poor; because it is poor, it can devote few resources to creating new capital rather than to producing goods for consumption; because little new capital can be produced, capital per head remains low, and the country remains poor.

The vicious circle can be made to seem an absolute constraint on growth rates. Of course, it is not; if it were, we would all still be at the level of the early agricultural civilizations. The grain of truth in the vicious-circle argument is that some surplus must be available somewhere in the society to allow saving and investment. In a poor society with an even distribution of income, in which nearly everyone is at the subsistence level, saving may be very difficult. But this is not the common experience. Usually there is at least a small middle class that can save and invest if opportunities for the profitable use of funds arise.

Infrastructure

infrastructure   The basic installations and facilities (especially transportation and communications systems) on which the commerce of a community depends.

Key services, called **infrastructure**, such as transportation and a communications network, are necessary for efficient commerce. Roads, bridges, railways, and harbours are needed to transport people, materials, and finished goods. Phone and postal services, water supply, and sanitation are essential to economic development.

The absence of a dependable infrastructure can impose severe barriers to economic development.

Many governments feel that money spent on a new steel mill shows more impressive results than money spent on such infrastructure investments as automating the telephone system. Yet private, growth-creating entrepreneurial activity will be discouraged more by the absence of good telephone communications than by the lack of domestically produced steel.

Foreign Debt

The 1970s and early 1980s witnessed explosive growth in the external debt of many developing nations. Since the mid 1980s, most of these countries have experienced difficulties in making the payments required to service their debt. "Debt rescheduling"—putting off until the future payments that cannot be made today—has been common, and many observers feel that major defaults are inevitable unless ways of forgiving the debt can be found.

The trend toward increased debt started when OPEC quadrupled the world price of oil in 1973. Because many developing nations relied on imported oil, their trade balances moved sharply into deficit. At the same time, the OPEC countries developed massive trade surpluses. Commercial banks helped to recycle the deposits of their OPEC customers into loans to the developing nations. These loans financed some necessary adjustments and some worthwhile new investment projects. However, a large part of the funds were used unwisely; wasteful government spending and lavish consumption splurges occurred in many of the borrowing countries.

A doubling of energy prices in 1979 led to a further increase in the debt of developing nations. The severe world recession that began in 1981 reduced demand for the exports of many of these countries. As a result, they were unable to achieve many benefits from the adjustments and investment expenditures that they had made. Furthermore, sharp increases in real interest rates (caused in part by the widespread fight against inflation) led to increased debt-service payments; as a result, many countries could not make their payments.

The lending banks had little choice but to reschedule the debt—essentially lending the developing nations the money to make interest payments while adding to the principal of the existing loans. The International Monetary Fund (IMF) played a central role in arranging these reschedulings by making further loans and concessions conditional on appropriate policies of adjustment and restraint. These conditions were intended to limit wasteful government expenditure and consumption and thus to increase the likelihood that the loans would eventually be repaid. Critics of the IMF's role argued that much of the restraint resulted in reduced investment and hence that the IMF's conditions were counterproductive.

During the mid 1980s, the world economy recovered, inflation fell, and real interest rates fell. As a result, the developing countries' export earnings grew, their debt-service obligations stabilized, and the crisis subsided. A sharp fall in the price of oil, which started in late 1985, further eased the problems of the oil-importing nations, but it also created a new debt problem.

Throughout the period of rising energy prices in the 1970s, a number of oil-exporting developing nations—including Mexico, Venezuela, and Indonesia—saw in those high prices new opportunities for investment and growth. Based on their high oil revenues, their ability to borrow improved. Their external debt grew, and they were able to avoid many of the adjustments that the oil-importing developing nations had been forced to undertake. When oil prices fell in the 1980s and 1990s, however, these oil exporters found themselves in difficult positions.

By the late 1990s, attention had focused on the so-called highly indebted poor countries (HIPCs). Figure 33-3 shows for 1997 the ratios of external debt to GNP for the ten most indebted of the HIPCs. In 1999, a meeting of the most industrialized countries (the G8 countries) agreed in principal to accelerate debt relief for the HIPCs. But the details of this plan have not yet been worked out.

FIGURE 33-3   External Debt in the Highly Indebted Poor Countries, 1997

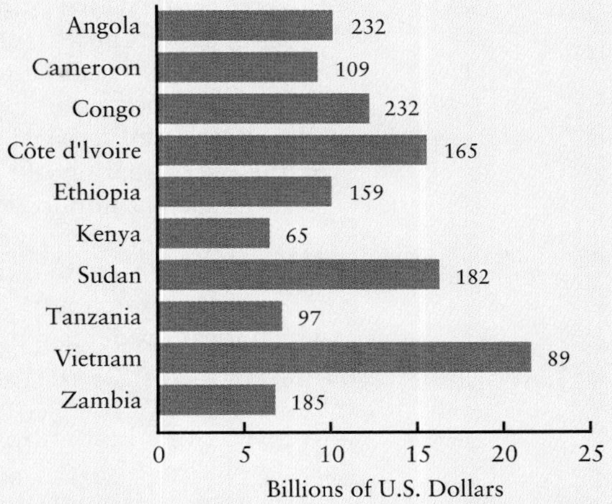

The **Highly Indebted Poor Countries (HIPCs) had external debts equal to $201 billion in 1997.** The data shown here are the external debts of the ten most indebted of the HIPCs. The numbers shown for each country are that country's external debt as a percentage of its GNP. Angola, for example, had just over $10 billion in external debt in 1997, which was 232 percent of its GNP.

(*Source*: These data are available on the World Bank's website: www.worldbank.org.)

Development Policies

The past two decades have seen a remarkable change in the views of appropriate policies for industrial development. The views that dominated development policies during the period from 1945 to the early 1980s have given way to a new set of views that reflect the experience of the earlier period.

The Older View

The dominant approaches toward development strategies from 1945 to the early 1980s were inward-looking and interventionist.

The policies were inward-looking in the sense that replacing imports was the primary goal of fostering local industries. These local industries were usually protected with very high tariffs and supported by large subsidies and favourable tax treatment. The exchange rate was almost always pegged, usually at a level which overvalued the currency (that is, the exchange rate was pegged *below* its free-market value). As we will explain in detail in Chapter 36, fixing the exchange rate below its free-market level raises the domestic currency prices of exports and lowers the prices of imports, which leads to an excess demand for foreign exchange. The argument for keeping export prices high was that foreign demand for traditional exports was inelastic so that (as we saw in Chapter 4) raising their prices would raise the amount received by their sellers. The excess demand for foreign exchange caused by the overvaluation of the currency led to a host of import restrictions and exchange controls such as import licences and quotas issued by government officials.

Many governments were hostile to foreign investment and made it difficult for multinational firms to locate in their countries. For example, many had local ownership rules requiring that any foreign firm wanting to invest there must set up a subsidiary in which local residents would own at least half of the shares. Much new investment was undertaken by government-owned industries, while subsidization of privately owned local industries was often heavy and indiscriminate. Industrial activity was often controlled, with a license being required to set up a firm or to purchase supplies of scarce commodities. Much investment was financed by local savings, which were sometimes made voluntarily and sometimes forced by the state.

This whole set of measures is often referred to as being *inward-looking* and based on *import substitution*. Strictly, import substitution refers to the attempt to build local industries behind protectionist walls to replace imports. Often, however, the term is used more generally to refer to the entire battery of related measures just described.

These interventionist measures gave great power to government officials and, not surprisingly, corruption was rife. Bribes were needed to obtain many things, including state subsidies, licences, and quotas. As a result, many resources were allocated to those who had the most political power and were willing to pay the highest bribes, rather than to those who could use the resources most efficiently.

Heavy subsidization of private firms and state investment in public firms required much money, and the tax structures of many poor countries could not provide sufficient funds. As a result, such expenditures were often financed by borrowing from the central bank which, as we saw in Chapters 28 and 29, ultimately leads to inflation. Persistent inflation was a major problem in many of these countries. Inflation was almost always in the double-digit range and quite often soared to several hundred percent per year.

Most of the economies where these policies were employed fell short of full central planning and full state ownership of resources. As a result, there was still some private initiative and some profit seeking through normal market means. But the overall policy thrust was inward-looking and interventionist.

The Rise of the New View

During the 1980s, four important events contributed to a reappraisal of this development model. First, developing countries that had followed these policies most faithfully had some of the poorest growth records. Second, the GDP growth rates of the more industrialized countries of Eastern Europe and the Soviet Union that had followed interventionist approaches to their own growth were visibly falling behind those of the market-based economies. Third, Taiwan, Singapore, South Korea, and Hong Kong, which had departed from the accepted model by adopting more market-based policies, were prospering and growing rapidly. Fourth, the globalization of the world's economy led to an understanding that countries could no longer play a full part in world economic growth without a substantial presence of multinational corporations within their boundaries. Given the size of developing countries, this meant the presence of foreign-owned multinationals. We now discuss each of these four events in more detail.

Experience of the Developing Countries

Highly interventionist economies fared poorly in the 1950s, 1960s, and 1970s. Economies as varied as Argentina, Myanmar (then Burma), Tanzania, Ethiopia, and Ghana were all interventionist and all grew slowly, if at all. In Ethiopia, the emperor was overthrown, and the new government adopted rigid Soviet-style policies. Attempts to collectivize agriculture led, as they had 50 years previously in the Soviet Union, to widespread famine. Some countries, such as Ghana, Nigeria, and Myanmar, started from relatively strong economic positions when they first gained their independence but later saw their GDPs and living standards shrink. Other countries, such as India and Kenya, sought a middle way between capitalism and socialism. They fared better than their more highly interventionist neighbours, but their development was still disappointingly slow.

Experience of the Socialist Countries

Earlier in this century, many observers were impressed by the apparent success of planned programs of "crash" development, of which the Soviet experience was the most remarkable and the Chinese the most recent. Not surprisingly, therefore, many of the early development policies of the poorer countries sought to copy the planning techniques that appeared to underlie these earlier socialist successes.

In recent decades, however, the more developed socialist countries began to discover the limitations of their planning techniques. Highly planned government intervention seems most successful in providing infrastructure and developing basic industries, such as electric power and steel, and in copying technologies developed in more market-oriented economies. However, it is now seen to be much less successful in providing the entrepreneurial activity, risk taking, and adaptivity to change that are key ingredients to *sustained* economic growth and technological change.

The discrediting of the Soviet approach to development was given added emphasis when the countries of Eastern Europe and the former Soviet Union abandoned their system *en masse* and took the difficult path of rapidly introducing market economies. Although China, the last major holdout, posted impressive growth figures in the 1990s, two "nonsocialist" reasons are important in explaining its performance. First, over 90 percent of the population is engaged in basically free-market agriculture—because that sector has long been free of the central-planning apparatus that so hampered agriculture in the former Soviet Union. Second, while the state-controlled industries suffer increasing inefficiencies, a major investment boom took place in China's Southeast coastal provinces. Here foreign investment, largely from Japan and the Asian NICs, introduced a rapidly growing and highly efficient industrialized market sector.

Experience of the NICs

South Korea, Taiwan, Hong Kong, and Singapore—the so-called Asian Tigers—have turned themselves from relative poverty to relatively high income in the course of less than 40 years.

During the early stages of their development, they used import restrictions to build up local industries and to develop labour forces with the requisite skills and experiences. In the 1950s and early 1960s, however, each of the four abandoned many of the

See Chapter 33 of www.pearsoned.ca/lipsey for a discussion of socialist Cuba's recent process of economic reform: Archibald Ritter, "Is Cuba's Economic Reform Process Paralyzed?" *World Economic Affairs.*

interventionist aspects of the older development model. They created market-oriented economies with less direct government intervention than other developing economies, who stuck with the accepted development model.

Korea and Singapore did not adopt a laissez faire stance. Instead, both followed quite strong policies that targeted specific areas for development and encouraged those areas with various economic incentives. In contrast, Hong Kong and Taiwan have had somewhat more laissez faire attitudes toward the direction of industrial development.

After local industries had been established, all four adopted outward-looking, market-based, export-oriented policies. This approach tested the success of various policies to encourage specific industries by their ability to compete in the international marketplace. With industries designed to serve a sheltered home market, it is all too easy to shelter inefficiency more or less indefinitely. With export-oriented policies *not based on subsidies,* the success of targeted firms and industries is tested in international markets, and unprofitable firms fail.

Not far behind the NICs is a second generation of Asian and Latin American countries that have also adopted more market-oriented policies and have seen substantial growth follow. Indonesia, Thailand, the Philippines, Mexico, Chile, and Argentina are examples. Even Vietnam and Laos are liberalizing their economies as communist governments come to accept that a market economy is a necessary condition for sustained economic growth.

Several Southeast Asian economies fell into significant recessions that began in late 1997 and continued throughout 1998 and early 1999. As of late 1999, however, it appears that these recessions, though very significant, will not lead to a return of interventionist policies in these countries. Of course, only time will tell.

Globalization

At the heart of globalization lies the rapid reduction in transportation costs and the revolution in information and communication technology that has characterized the past two decades. One consequence has been that the internal organization of firms is changing to become less hierarchical and rigid and more decentralized and fluid. Another consequence is that the strategies of transnational corporations (TNCs), which span national borders in their organizational structures, are driving globalization and much of economic development. Because most trade, and much investment, is undertaken by TNCs, no country can develop into an integrated part of today's world economy without a substantial presence of TNCs within its borders. The importance of TNCs is now recognized, and most aspiring developing countries generally put out a welcome mat for them.

Historically, only a few countries, notably Japan and Taiwan, have industrialized without major infusions of foreign direct investment (FDI). Moreover, these cases took place before the globalization of the world's economy. It is doubtful that many (or any) of today's poor countries could achieve sustained and rapid growth paths without a substantial amount of FDI brought in by foreign-owned transnationals. Without such FDI, both the transfer of technology and foreign networking would be difficult to achieve.

Developing countries have gradually come to accept the advantages of FDI. First, FDI often provides somewhat higher-paying jobs than might otherwise be available to local residents. Second, it provides investment that does not have to be financed by local saving. Third, it provides training in worker and management skills that come from working with large firms linked into the global market. Fourth, it can provide advanced technology that is not easily transferred outside of the firms that are already familiar with its use.

Today, virtually all developing economies encourage foreign TNCs to locate within their borders. Where governments used to worry that their countries had too much FDI, they now worry that there may be too little.

The Washington Consensus

As a result of these various experiences, a new consensus on development policy has emerged. The revised model calls for a more outward-looking, international-trade-oriented, and market-based route to development. It calls for accepting market prices as an instrument for the allocation of resources. This means abandoning both the heavy subsidization and the pervasive regulations that characterized the older approach. But it also calls for a careful use of government policy in providing basic infrastructure, public goods, and dealing with market failures.

This consensus is often referred to as the "Washington Consensus." It describes the conditions that are believed to be necessary for a poorer country to get itself on a path of sustained development. These views are accepted by a number of international agencies, including the World Bank, the IMF, and several UN organizations. The main elements of this consensus are as follows:

1. Government should adopt sound fiscal policies that avoid large budget deficits. In particular, persistent *structural* deficits should be avoided.

2. Government should adopt sound monetary policies, with the goal of maintaining low and stable inflation rates. Exchange rates should be determined by market forces rather than being pegged by central banks.

3. The tax base should be broad, and marginal tax rates should be moderate.

4. Markets should be allowed to determine prices and the allocation of resources. Trade liberalization is desirable, and import licencing, with its potential for corruption, should be avoided.

5. Targeted protection for specific industries and a moderate general tariff, say, 10 to 20 percent, may provide a bias toward widening the industrial base of a developing country. But such protection should be for a specified period that is not easily extended.

6. Industrial development should rely to an important extent on local firms and on attracting FDI and subjecting it to a minimum of local restrictions that discriminate between local and foreign firms. (Of course, restrictions will be required for such things as environmental policies, but these should apply to all firms, whether foreign-owned or locally owned.)

7. An export orientation (as long as exports do not rely on permanent subsidies) provides competitive incentives for the building of skills and technologies geared to world markets, permits realization of scale economies, and provides access to valuable information flows from buyers and competitors in advanced countries.

8. Education, health (especially for the disadvantaged), and infrastructure investment are desirable forms of public expenditure. Because future demands are hard to predict and subject to rapid change, a balance must be struck between training for specific skills and training for generalized and adaptive abilities.

Visit the World Bank's website at: www.worldbank.org.

Visit the IMF's website at:
www.imf.org.

9. Finally, emphasis needs to be placed on poverty reduction for at least two reasons. First, poverty can exert powerful antigrowth effects. People in poverty will not develop the skills to provide an attractive labour force, and they may not even respond to incentives when these are provided. Malnutrition in early childhood can affect a person's capacities for life. Second, although economic growth tends to reduce the incidence of poverty, it does not eliminate it.

Debate Beyond the Washington Consensus

The basic Washington consensus on outward-looking, market-oriented economic policies provides what many people believe are necessary conditions for a country to achieve a sustained growth path in today's world.

The policies suggested by the Washington consensus relate primarily to the behaviour of governments themselves.

Sufficient or Just Necessary?

There is substantial debate around one crucial issue: Are the conditions of the Washington consensus *sufficient* to encourage the kinds and volumes of both domestic and foreign investment needed to develop comparative advantages in higher-value-added industries, or are they merely *necessary?*

Some observers believe that these conditions are sufficient. In their view, all a country needs to do is to meet these conditions. Domestic saving will finance domestic investments, FDI will flow in, and a sustained growth path will be established. Other economists worry that many countries may have only limited ability to attract FDI, to benefit from it, and to create sufficient domestic investment, even after fulfilling the conditions of the Washington consensus. The latter set of economists point to the experience of some African countries where TNCs operated extractive industries that despoiled the countryside and produced little permanent benefit for the host country; they merely extracted the available resources and then left. Others point out that there is a major difference between pure extractive enterprises and manufacturing enterprises, the latter having more potential spillovers to the local economy than the former.

What does happen after the conditions of the consensus are fulfilled will depend in part on the existing endowments of the country in question. If large supplies of natural resources or cheap, well-educated labour are available, fulfilling these conditions may be sufficient. Commentators who call for policies beyond those of the Washington consensus argue that for some countries, a past history of nongrowth, plus the absence of positive externalities that go with a reasonably developed industrial sector, may require that the government adopt a more active set of *integrated* trade, technology-transfer, and innovation policies. This set of policies would be aimed at encouraging the development of human and technological capabilities.

Policies that go beyond the Washington consensus are directed at the interactions between governments and the private sector, particularly as represented by TNCs.

Implications of Modern Growth Theory

What is at issue in the debate just described is related to the newer views on economic growth that were discussed in Chapter 32. The key new view is that *endogenous* technological innovation is the mainspring of economic growth. Things emphasized by economists for centuries, such as aggregate saving and investment, are still essential, but technological change is now considered to lie at the core of the growth process.

As we saw in Chapter 32, technological change is a costly process that is undertaken mainly by firms in pursuit of profit. Research and development are by their nature risky and uncertain activities. The technological path followed by firms and industries is evolutionary in the sense that it develops as experiments and errors are made.

For developing countries, one of the most important of the many new insights stemming from research into the growth process is that adopting someone else's technology is often not a simple, costless task. Substantial R&D capacity is needed to adapt other people's technology to one's own purposes and to learn how to use it—except where the technology uses only very simple machines that can be operated by unskilled labour. For one reason, much of the knowledge required to use a technology is tacit; it can be obtained only from learning by doing and by using. This creates difficulties in imitating the knowledge, as well as uncertainty regarding which modifications will work in any new situation. It is true even when technology moves from one firm to another in the same industry and the same country. The problems are greater when technology moves across industrial or national borders. The difficulties of adopting new technologies also become more difficult the more complex and information-intensive the technology becomes.

It follows that all knowledge is not freely tradable. Neither a firm nor a government can go out and buy it ready-to-use. Acquiring *working* technological knowledge requires both investment and the experience that allows workers and management slowly to acquire the needed tacit knowledge.

Usable new knowledge comes to a developing country through a slow and costly diffusion process.

See Chapter 33 of www.pearsoned.ca/lipsey for an interview with Harvard's Jeffrey Sachs on the Asian crisis of 1997–98 and the need for reform of the IMF and World Bank: "The Devil's in the Details," *World Economic Affairs.*

What May Be Needed

The foregoing view of technological change suggests to some economists a major reason why active government policies that go beyond the Washington consensus may be needed.

Protection of the Domestic Market.   Such policies can work at the early stages by establishing a protected domestic market through tariffs and other import restrictions. Virtually every country that has moved to a sustained growth path in the past, including the United States, Canada, Japan, and all of the NICs, has used import substitution in its early stages of industrialization. A protected home market provides a possible solution to the problem of coping with the enormous externalities involved in building up an infrastructure of physical and human capital as well as the required tacit knowledge and abilities. Even if all the specific young industries that are protected by the import substitution policy do not grow into self-sufficient mature industries, the externalities may still be created and become available for a second generation of more profitable firms.

Protection of the home market from international competition can, however, pose serious problems unless it is selective and temporary. Investment may occur mainly in areas where comparative advantage never grows. High costs of protected industries may create a lack of competitiveness in other domestic industries whose inputs are the outputs of the protected industries. Some potential comparative advantages may not be exploited because of the distorting effects of existing tariffs, and—as always—consumers bear much of the cost in terms of high prices of protected outputs.

Innovation Policies.   Trade restrictions do not provide the only route to building industrial and R&D capacity by encouraging technological diffusion and creating structural competitiveness. Other methods include the much-needed public investment in infrastructure and in human capital and many other things such as the provision of adequate financial schemes to favour investment in physical and intangible assets, procurement and tax incentives, provision of technical and marketing information, consulting services for assisting firms in industrial restructuring and in the adoption of new technologies and organizational techniques, support services in design, quality assurance and standards, schemes for training and retraining personnel, and facilities for start-up companies.

Advocates of such a policy package stress the importance of having these incentives as part of a more general innovation and competition policy in order to encourage technological transfer to the local economy (such transfers are riddled with market failures arising from their externalities). Linkages among firms, and between firms and universities and research institutions, both within the country and with the rest of the world, are also important.

Policies that encourage the development of small- and medium-size enterprises are important to any development strategy. These tend to be locally owned and tend to be the vehicle by which know-how and best practices are transferred from TNCs to the local economy. They are also the sector most vulnerable to excessive red tape, rules and regulations, profit taxes, and other interferences that raise the cost of doing business.

A Cautionary Note.   There is no doubt that the governments of many poor countries have been highly interventionist—and some still are. Hence, a good first strategy is often to diminish the government's place in the economy. There is no point in adopting a new, relatively rational technology-promotion strategy if existing government interventions are irrational and heavy. The unproductive interventions must be cleared away first. This does not mean, however, that if a government were starting from scratch, the best objective would be to minimize its place in the economy.

Whatever methods are chosen, selective intervention is a delicate instrument, highly dangerous in inept hands; in fact, even when in practiced hands, much damage can be done.

The intervention needs to be carefully tailored to get specific results and to reduce the opportunities for small groups to gain at the expense of others. To meet these objectives, most assistance should, as a rule, be terminated after specified periods of time. It is also important to leave room for the market to generate, and support, unforeseen opportunities.

Conclusion

According to the World Bank, approximately 1.2 billion of the world's people subsist on less than one dollar (U.S.) per day. Despite the fact that one U.S. dollar buys much more in Addis Ababa than it does in New York, Toronto, or Paris, there is still a significant fraction of the world's population that is—by any reasonable standard—very poor.

What can be done? The World Bank's prescriptions fall into two broad categories:

1. Create new economic opportunities for the poor. Because the poor's main source of income is what they are paid for their labour, this means promoting labour-intensive economic growth.

2. Equip the poor to grasp these opportunities. This step calls for adequate provision of basic social services such as primary education, health, and family planning.

The World Bank also points out that one of the most damaging economic distortions in many developing countries is excessive taxation of farming. This hits the very part of the economy on which most of the poor depend for their livelihood.

The World Bank suggests that a major reduction in poverty is possible worldwide. What is needed is the acceptance of the new consensus on the importance of market determination and of reducing state control and state ownership of business activity. This, in addition to a large dose of enlightened policies to bring education, health, and jobs to ordinary people and improved technology to the nations' firms, could pay enormous dividends in reducing poverty and suffering. Only time will tell how much of that hopeful potential will be realized over the next decade or so.

S U M M A R Y

The Uneven Pattern of Development

- About one-quarter of the world's population still exists at a level of bare subsistence, and nearly three-quarters are poor by Canadian standards. Although some poorer societies have grown rapidly, the gap between the very richest and very poorest appears to be increasing.

Impediments to Economic Development

- Impediments to economic development include excessive population growth; resource limitations; inefficient use of resources; inadequate infrastructure; excessive government intervention; and institutional and cultural patterns that make economic growth difficult.

Development Policies

- The older model for development policies included heavy tariff barriers and a hostility to foreign direct investment (FDI) to protect the home market for local firms; many government controls over, and subsidization of, local activities; and exchange rates pegged at excessively low values (overvalued currencies) with imports regulated by licences.
- The new view is given in the Washington consensus, which calls for sound fiscal and monetary policies; broad-based taxes levied at moderate rates; market determination of prices and quantities; discriminating use of infant industry protection for moderate time periods; an acceptance of FDI and the presence of TNCs; active government provision of education, health care, and infrastructure; and antipoverty programs to help in human resource devel-

opment and to aid citizens who are left behind by the growth process.
- An active debate turns on whether the conditions of the Washington consensus are sufficient, or just necessary, to establish a country on a sustained growth path. Analysts who regard it as sufficient feel that once unleashed, natural market forces will create sustained growth.
- Analysts who regard the conditions of the Washington consensus as necessary but not sufficient point to substantial externalities and pervasive market failures in the diffusion of technological knowledge from developed to developing nations. These economists call for active government innovation policies to augment investment and to assist the transfer of technological know-how and practice to the local economy.

KEY CONCEPTS

The development gap
Impediments to economic development
The vicious circle of poverty

The NICs
TNCs and FDI
The Washington consensus

Externalities and market failures in the
diffusion of technology

STUDY EXERCISES

1. Go to the website for the United Nations (www.un.org). From the home page go to "Economic and Social Development." Then click on "Statistics" and search for "Social Indicators." Then answer the following questions.

   a. List the average rate of population growth for:
Albania	Canada	Iceland
Angola	Czech Republic	India
Bangladesh	Guatemala	Rwanda

   b. Explain why, *ceteris paribus*, high rates of population growth make it more difficult for a country to increase its average living standards. What role in your answer is played by the diminishing marginal returns to labour?

2. Go to the website for the United Nations (www.un.org). From the home page go to "Economic and Social Development." Then click on "Statistics" and search for "Social Indicators." Then answer the following questions.

   a. List the level of per capita GDP (US$) for the same group of countries as in Question 1, part a.

   b. Which country listed by the U.N. has the highest per capita GDP?

   c. Which country listed by the U.N. has the lowest per capita GDP?

3. Go to the World Bank's website (www.worldbank.org). Search for "Data" and then select "Data by Topic". Choose "Growth in Consumption and Investment" and then answer the following questions.

   a. List the amounts of gross saving and gross investment (as percentages of GDP) for:
Algeria	Côte d'Ivoire	Malaysia
Bolivia	Ecuador	Nigeria
Canada	Latvia	Tanzania

   b. On a scale diagram, with the investment rate on the horizontal axis and the saving rate on the vertical axis, plot the data for each of the chosen countries. Do you see any relationship?

   c. Based on what you have learned (perhaps especially from Chapter 32), explain why high investment rates are typically associated with high growth rates of GDP.

   d. In this chapter, we argued that some countries face a growth challenge because of their small pool of domestic saving. Based on your diagram from part a, explain the importance of domestic saving.

4. Go to the World Bank's website (www.worldbank.org). Search for "Data" and then select "Data by Topic." Choose "Agricultural Output and Productivity" and then answer the following questions.

   a. List the agricultural value added per worker for the following countries:
Australia	Dominican Republic	Netherlands
Botswana	Haiti	Niger
Chile	India	Paraguay

   b. Can you offer some possible explanations for the greater productivity in agriculture in the developed countries?

5. In the text we discussed that an adequate infrastructure is important to economic development. Go to the website for the United Nations (www.un.org). From the home page go to "Economic and Social Development." Then click on "Statistics" and search for "Social Indicators." Then answer the following questions.

   a. List the percentage of the population with access to safe water and to sanitation (both urban and rural populations) for:

Afghanistan	Norway
Bahrain	South Africa
Colombia	Thailand
Indonesia	

b. According to the "Washington Consensus," should the public or the private sector be providing water and sanitation in developing countries?

c. Can you provide a reason why public expenditures in sanitation (and health care, more generally) may lead to increases in long-run productivity?

DISCUSSION QUESTIONS

1. In his *Essay on the Principle of Population as it Affects the Future Improvement of Society,* first published in 1789, Thomas Malthus wrote:

   > This natural inequality of the two powers of population and of production in the earth ... [forms] the great difficulty that to me appears insurmountable in the way to perfectibility of society. All other arguments are of slight and subordinate consideration in comparison of this. I see no way by which man can escape from the weight of this law which pervades all animated nature. No fancied equality, no agrarian revolutions in their utmost extent, could remove the pressure of it even for a single century.

   Discuss Malthus's "insurmountable difficulty" in view of the events of the past 100 years.

2. To what extent does the vicious circle of poverty apply to poor families that are living in the richest developed countries? Consider carefully, for example, the similarities and differences facing a poor family living in Vancouver and one living in Ghana, where per capita income is less than $400 per year. Did it apply to Canadian immigrants who arrived at the turn of the century with $10 in their pockets?

3. Would removing all restrictions on immigration into the advanced countries help to improve living standards in the developing nations? How might such a policy affect living standards in the advanced countries?

4. "High coffee prices bring hope to impoverished Latin American peasants," reads the headline. Mexico, Kenya, and Burundi, among other developing countries, have the right combination of soil and climate to increase their coffee production greatly. Discuss the benefits and risks to them if they pursue coffee production as a major avenue of their development.

5. History has shown that rapid development of poor countries is often accompanied by some measure of devastation of the country's natural resources. Can you provide some examples? Must this outcome always occur? How can the developed countries help to stem the devastation? Why don't they help more than they do at present?

PART ELEVEN

International Economics

Does a country always benefit from free trade? If so, why do many people appear to believe the opposite? Can government policy influence a country's pattern of comparative advantage? Is there any connection between the government's budget deficit and the country's current account deficit? How is Canada's exchange rate determined? Should Canada maintain a flexible exchange rate or should it peg the value of its currency to the U.S. dollar? These are the sorts of questions you will be able to answer after reading the final three chapters of this book.*

Chapter 34 explores the gains from trade, and how these gains are based on the important concept of comparative advantage. We discuss the reasons why a country might have a comparative advantage in a particular product, and how some government policies can have the effect of changing a country's pattern of comparative advantage. We will also examine a country's terms of trade, the relative prices at which a country trades with the rest of the world.

In Chapter 35, the focus is on trade policy. We explore the case for free trade as well as the case for protection (we also examine some common but fallacious arguments for protection). We then discuss some methods of protection, such as tariffs, quotas, and nontariff barriers. The chapter then examines current trade policy in Canada, with an emphasis on the North American Free Trade Agreement.

Chapter 36 discusses the exchange rate and the balance of payments. We examine the foreign-exchange market and why the balance of payments accounts are always in balance. The important distinction between fixed exchange rates and flexible exchange rates will be discussed in detail, and we will explore the kinds of events that lead to an appreciation or a depreciation of the Canadian dollar. Finally, we explore three "hot" policy debates, including the cases for and against Canada's adopting a fixed exchange rate.

---

*Chapter 36 does not appear in *Microeconomics*.

CHAPTER 34

The Gains from International Trade

LEARNING OBJECTIVES

1. Understand why the gains from trade depend on comparative advantage and not on absolute advantage.

2. Explain the gains from trade due to economies of scale and learning-by-doing.

3. Understand how factor endowments and climate can influence a country's comparative advantage.

4. Explain the law of one price.

5. Explain why countries export some goods and import other goods.

6. Understand what is meant by a country's terms of trade.

Canadian consumers buy cars from Germany, Germans take holidays in Italy, Italians buy spices from Africa, Africans import oil from Kuwait, Kuwaitis buy Japanese cameras, and the Japanese buy Canadian lumber. *International trade* refers to the exchange of goods and services that takes place across international boundaries.

The founders of modern economics were concerned with foreign trade problems. The great eighteenth-century British philosopher and economist David Hume (1711–1776), one of the first to work out the theory of the price system as a control mechanism, developed his concepts mainly in terms of prices in foreign trade. Adam Smith (1723–1790) in his *Wealth of Nations* attacked government restriction of international trade. David Ricardo (1772–1823) developed the basic theory of the gains from trade that is studied in this chapter. The repeal of the Corn Laws—tariffs on the importation of grains into the United Kingdom—and the transformation of that country during the nineteenth century from a country of high tariffs to one of complete free trade were to some extent the result of agitation by economists whose theories of the gains from international trade led them to condemn tariffs.

International trade is becoming increasingly important, not just for Canada but for the world as a whole. As Figure 34-1 shows, the volume of world trade has grown much faster than has world real GDP over the past half-century. Since 1950, the world's real GDP has increased by six times, an average annual growth rate of 3.6 percent. Over the same period, however, the volume of world trade has increased by *seventeen* times, an average annual growth rate of 5.8 percent.

Figure 34-2 shows some data for Canadian trade in 1998. The figure shows the value of Canadian exports and imports in several broad industry groupings. There are three important points to note from the figure. First, international trade is very important for Canada. In 1998, Canada exported and imported over $300 billion in goods—if we added trade in services, the value would rise to over $360 billion. This amounts to over 40 percent of Canada's GDP. Second, exports and imports are roughly the same size, so that the *volume* of trade is much larger than the *balance* of trade—the value of exports equal minus the value of imports. Third, in most of the industry groupings there are significant amounts of both imports and exports. Such *intra-industry trade* will be discussed later in the chapter. Canada does not just export resource products and import manufactured goods; it also imports many resource products and exports many manufactured goods.

In this chapter, we inquire into the gains to living standards that result from such international trade. We find that the source of the gains from trade lies in differing cost conditions among geographical regions. World income is maximized when countries specialize in the products in which they have the lowest opportunity costs of production. These costs are partly determined by natural endowments (geographical and climatic conditions), partly by public policy, and partly by historical accident. We then go on to discuss the terms on which international trade takes place—this refers to the amount that must be exported to obtain a given amount of imports.

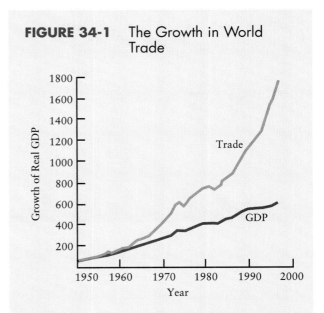

FIGURE 34-1   The Growth in World Trade

The volume of world trade has grown much faster than world GDP over the past fifty years. The figure shows the growth of real GDP and the volume of trade since 1950. Both are expressed as index numbers, set equal to 100 in 1950. Real world GDP has increased six times since 1950; world trade volume has increased seventeen times.

(*Source:* World Trade Organization.)

Sources of the Gains from Trade

An economy that engages in international trade is called an **open economy;** one that does not is called a **closed economy.** A situation in which a country does no foreign trade is called one of *autarky.*

The benefits of trade are easiest to visualize by considering the differences between a world with trade and a world without it. Although politicians often regard foreign trade differently from domestic trade, economists from Adam Smith on have argued that the causes and consequences of international trade are simply an extension of the principles governing domestic trade. What is the advantage of trade among individuals, among groups, among regions, or among countries?

For information on world trade, see the World Trade Organization's website: www.wto.org.

open economy   An economy that engages in international trade.

closed economy   An economy that has no foreign trade.

Interpersonal, Interregional, and International Trade

To begin, consider trade among individuals. Without trade, each person would have to be self-sufficient; each would have to produce all the food, clothing, shelter, medical services, entertainment, and luxuries that he or she consumed. A world of individual self-sufficiency would be a world with extremely low living standards.

Trade among individuals allows people to specialize in activities they can do well and to buy from others the goods and services they cannot easily produce. A good doctor who

FIGURE 34-2   Canadian Exports and Imports of Goods by Industry, 1998

Canada exports and imports large volumes of goods in most industries. The data show the value of goods exported and imported by industry in 1998 (trade in services is not shown). The total value of goods exported was $322.2 billion; the total value of goods imported was $303.4 billion.

(*Source:* These data are available on Statistics Canada's website: www.statcan.ca.)

is a bad carpenter can provide medical services not only for her own family but also for an excellent carpenter without the training or the ability to practice medicine. Thus, trade and specialization are intimately connected.

Without trade, everyone must be self-sufficient; with trade, people can specialize in what they do well and satisfy other needs by trading.

The same principle applies to regions. Without interregional trade, each region would be forced to be self-sufficient. With trade, each region can specialize in producing products for which it has some natural or acquired advantage. Plains regions can specialize in growing grain, mountain regions in mining and forest products, and regions with abundant power in manufacturing. Cool regions can produce wheat and other crops that thrive in temperate climates, and hot regions can grow such tropical crops as bananas, sugarcane, and coffee. The living standards of the inhabitants of all regions will be higher when each region specializes in products in which it has some natural or acquired advantage and obtains other products by trade than when all regions seek to be self-sufficient.

This same basic principle also applies to nations. A national boundary seldom delimits an area that is naturally self-sufficient. Nations, like regions and individuals, can gain from specialization. More of some goods are produced domestically than residents wish to consume, while residents would like to consume more of other goods than is produced domestically. International trade is necessary to achieve the gains that international specialization makes possible.

With trade, each individual, region, or nation is able to concentrate on producing goods and services that it produces efficiently while trading to obtain goods and services that it does not produce efficiently.

Specialization and trade go hand in hand because there is no motivation to achieve the gains from specialization without being able to trade the goods produced for goods desired. Economists use the term **gains from trade** to embrace the results of both.

gains from trade
The increased output due to the specialization according to comparative advantage that is made possible by trade.

We will examine two sources of the gains from trade. The first is differences among regions of the world in climate and resource endowment that lead to advantages in producing certain goods and disadvantages in producing others. These gains occur even though each country's costs of production are unchanged by the existence of trade. The second source is the reduction in each country's costs of production that results from the greater scale of production that specialization brings.

The Gains from Trade with Constant Costs

In order to focus on differences in countries' conditions of production, suppose that each country's average costs of production are constant. We will use an example below involving only two countries and two products, but the general principles apply as well to the case of many countries and many products.

Absolute Advantage

One region is said to have an **absolute advantage** over another in the production of good X when an equal quantity of resources can produce more X in the first region than in the second. Total production can be increased if each country specializes in producing the product for which it has an absolute advantage.

The gains from specialization make the gains from trade possible. If consumers in both countries are to get the goods they desire in the required proportions, each must export some of the commodity in which it specializes and import commodities in which other countries are specialized.

absolute advantage The situation that exists when a given amount of resources can produce more of some commodity in one country than in another.

Comparative Advantage

When each product has an absolute advantage over others in a product, the gains from trade are obvious. But what if one country can produce all commodities more efficiently than other countries? This was the question English economist David Ricardo (1722–1823) posed nearly 200 years ago. His answer underlies the theory of *comparative advantage* and is still accepted by economists today as a valid statement of the potential gains from trade.

The gains from specialization and trade depend on the pattern of comparative, not absolute, advantage.

An example will help to make the point. Let us assume that there are two countries, Canada and the European Union. Both countries produce the same two goods, wheat and cloth, but the opportunity costs of producing these two products differ between countries. Recall from Chapter 1 that the opportunity cost is given by the slope of the production-possibility curve, and it tells us how much of one good we have to give up in order to produce one more unit of the other. For the moment we assume that this opportunity cost is constant in each country at all combinations of outputs.

For the purposes of our example we assume that the opportunity cost of producing one kilogram of wheat is 0.60 metres of cloth in Canada, while in the European Union it is 2.0 metres of cloth. These data are summarized in Table 34-1. The second column of this table gives the same information again but expressed as the opportunity cost of one metre of cloth (so the numbers there are reciprocals of the numbers in the first column).

The sacrifice of cloth involved in producing wheat is much lower in Canada than it is in the EU. World wheat production can be increased if Canada rather than the EU produces it. Looking at cloth production, we can see that the loss of wheat involved in producing one unit of cloth is lower in the EU than in Canada. World cloth production can therefore be increased if the EU rather than Canada produces it. The gains from a Canadian shift towards wheat production and an EU shift towards cloth production are shown in Table 34-2.

TABLE 34-1 Opportunity Cost of Wheat and Cloth in Canada and the European Union (EU)

	Wheat (kg)	Cloth (m)
Canada	0.60 m of cloth	1.67 kg of wheat
EU	2.0 m of cloth	0.5 kg of wheat

Comparative advantages reflect opportunity costs that differ between countries. The first column expresses opportunity cost for a kilogram of wheat. The second column expresses the same information for a metre of cloth. Canada has a comparative advantage in wheat production, the EU in cloth.

TABLE 34-2 The Gains from Specialization

	Changes from each country producing one more unit of the product in which it has the lower opportunity cost	
	Wheat (kg)	Cloth (m)
Canada	+1.0	−0.6
EU	−0.5	+1.0
Total	+0.5	+0.4

Whenever opportunity costs differ between countries, specialization can increase the production of both products. These calculations show that there are gains from specialization given the opportunity costs of Table 34-1. To produce one more kilogram of wheat, Canada must sacrifice 0.6 m of cloth. To produce one more metre of cloth, the EU must sacrifice 0.5 kg of wheat. Making both changes increases world production of both wheat and cloth.

FIGURE 34-3   Gains from Trade with Constant Opportunity Costs

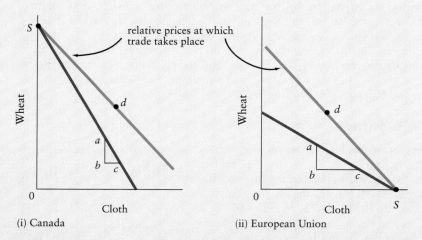

(i) Canada   (ii) European Union

International trade leads to specialization in production and increased consumption possibilities. The purple lines in parts (i) and (ii) represent the production possibility boundaries for Canada and the EU, respectively. In the absence of any international trade these also represent each country's consumption possibilities.

The difference in the slopes of the production possibility boundaries reflects differences in comparative advantage, as shown in Table 34-1. In each part the opportunity cost of increasing production of wheat by the same amount (measured by the distance *ba*) is the amount by which the production of cloth must be reduced (measured by the distance *bc*). The relatively steep production possibility boundary for Canada thus indicates that the opportunity cost of producing wheat in Canada is less than that in the European Union.

If trade is possible at some relative prices between the two countries' opportunity costs of production, each country will specialize in the production of the good in which it has a comparative advantage. In each part of the figure, production occurs at *S* (for specialization); Canada produces only wheat, and the EU produces only cloth.

Consumption possibilities are given by the green line that passes through *S* and has a slope equal to the with-trade relative prices. Consumption possibilities are increased in both countries; consumption may occur at some point such as *d* that involves a combination of wheat and cloth that was not obtainable in the absence of trade.

The gains from trade arise from differing opportunity costs in the two countries.

The slope of the production possibility boundary indicates the opportunity costs, and the existence of different opportunity costs implies comparative advantages that can lead to gains from trade. Figure 34-3 illustrates how two countries can both gain from trade when they have different opportunity costs in production and those opportunity costs are independent of the level of production. An alternative diagrammatic illustration of the gains from trade appears in *Extensions in Theory 34-1* where the production possibility boundary is concave (which means that the opportunity cost for each good is higher when more of that good is being produced).

The conclusions about the gains from trade arising from international differences in opportunity costs are summarized below.

1. Country A has a comparative advantage over Country B in producing a product when the opportunity cost of production in Country A is lower. This implies, however, that it has a comparative *dis*advantage in the other product.

2. Opportunity costs depend on the relative costs of producing two products, not on absolute costs.

3. When opportunity costs are the same in all countries, there is no comparative advantage and there is no possibility of gains from specialization and trade.

4. When opportunity costs differ in any two countries and both countries are producing both products, it is always possible to increase production of both products by a suitable reallocation of resources within each country.

The Gains from Trade with Variable Costs

So far, we have assumed that unit costs are the same whatever the scale of output, and we have seen that there are gains from specialization and trade as long as there are interregional differences in opportunity costs. If costs vary with the level of output, or as experience is acquired via specialization, *additional* gains are possible.

Scale and Imperfect Competition

Real production costs, measured in terms of resources used, generally fall as the scale of output increases. The larger the scale of operations, the more efficiently large-scale machinery can be used and the more a detailed division of tasks among workers is possible. Small countries, such as Switzerland, Belgium, and Israel, whose domestic markets are not large enough to exploit economies of scale would find it prohibitively expensive to become self-sufficient by producing a little bit of everything at very high cost.

Trade allows small countries to specialize and produce a few products at high enough levels of output to reap the available economies of scale.

Wine is a good example of an industry in which there is much intra-industry trade. Canada, for example, imports wine from many countries but also exports Canadian-made wine to the same countries.

Very large countries, such as the United States, have markets large enough to allow the production of most items at home at a scale of output great enough to obtain the available economies of scale. For them, the gains from trade arise mainly from specializing in products in which they have a comparative advantage. Yet, even for such countries, a broadening of their markets permits achieving scale economies in subproduct lines, such as specialty steels or certain lines of clothing.

One of the important lessons learned from patterns of world trade since World War II has concerned imperfect competition and product differentiation. Virtually all of today's manufactured consumer goods are produced in a vast array of differentiated product lines. In some industries, many firms produce this array; in others, only a few firms produce the entire array. In either case, they do not exhaust all available economies of scale. Thus, an increase in the size of the market, even in an economy as large as the United States, may allow the exploitation of some previously unexploited scale economies in individual product lines.

These possibilities were first dramatically illustrated when the European Common Market (now known as the European Union or EU) was set up in the late 1950s. Economists had expected that specialization would occur according to the theory of comparative advantage, with one country specializing in cars, another in refrigerators, another in fashion clothes, another in shoes, and so on. This is not the way it worked out. Instead, much of the vast growth of trade was in *intra-industry* trade—that is, trade of goods or services within the same broad industry. Today, one can buy French, English, Italian, and German fashion goods, cars, shoes, appliances, and a host of other products in London, Paris, Berlin, and Rome. Ships loaded with Swedish furniture bound for London pass ships loaded with English furniture bound for Stockholm, and so on.

EXTENSIONS IN THEORY 34-1

The Gains From Trade More Generally

Examining the gains from trade is relatively easy in the case where each country's production possibilities boundary is a straight line. What happens in the more realistic case where the production possibilities boundary is concave? As this box shows, the same basic principles of the gains from trade apply to this more complex case.

International trade leads to an expansion of the set of goods that can be consumed in the economy in two ways:

1. by allowing the bundle of goods consumed to differ from the bundle produced; and,

2. by permitting a profitable change in the pattern of production.

Without international trade, the bundle of goods produced is the bundle consumed. With international trade, the consumption and production bundles can be altered independently to reflect the relative values placed on goods by international markets.

Fixed Production

In each part of the figure, the purple curve is the economy's production possibility boundary. In the absence of interna-

tional trade, the economy must consume the same bundle of goods that it produces. Thus, the production possibility boundary is also the consumption possibility boundary. Suppose that the economy produces and consumes at point a, with x_1 of good X and y_1 of good Y, as in part (i) of the figure.

Next suppose that with production point a, good Y can be exchanged for good X internationally. The consumption possibilities are now shown by the line tt drawn through point a. The slope of tt indicates the quantity of Y that exchanges for a unit of X on the international market.

Although production is fixed at point a, consumption can now be anywhere on the line tt. For example, the consumption point could be at b. This could be achieved by exporting y_2y_1 units of Y and importing x_1x_2 units of X. Because point b (and all others on line tt to the right of a) lies outside the production possibility boundary, there are potential gains from trade. Consumers are no longer limited by their own country's production possibilities. Let us suppose that they prefer point b to point a. They have achieved a gain from trade by being allowed to exchange some of their production of good Y for some quantity of good X and thus to consume more of good X than is produced at home.

The same increase in intra-industry trade happened with Canada-U.S. trade over successive rounds of tariff cuts, the most recent being the 1989 Canada-U.S. Free Trade Agreement, and its 1994 expansion into the North American Free Trade Agreement that included Mexico. In several broad industrial groups, including automotive products, machinery, textiles, and forestry products, both imports and exports increased in each country.

What free trade in Europe and North America did was to allow a proliferation of differentiated products, with different countries each specializing in different subproduct lines. Consumers have shown by their expenditures that they value this enormous increase in the range of choice among differentiated products. As Asian countries have expanded into North American and European markets with textiles, cars, and electronic goods, North American and European manufacturers have increasingly specialized their production and now export textiles, cars, and electronic equipment to Asia even while importing similar but differentiated products from Asia.

Learning by Doing

The discussion so far has assumed that costs vary only with the *level* of output. But they may also vary with the *accumulated experience* in producing a product over time.

Variable Production

There is a further opportunity for the expansion of the country's consumption possibilities: With trade, the production bundle may be profitably altered in response to international prices. The country may produce the bundle of goods that is most valuable in world markets. That is represented by the bundle *d* in part (ii). The consumption possibility set is shifted to the line *t′t′* by changing production from *a* to *d* and thereby increasing the country's degree of specialization in good *Y*. For every point on the original consumption possibility set *tt*, there are points on the new set *t′t′* that allow

more consumption of both goods—for example, compare points *b* and *f*. Notice also that, except at the zero-trade point *d*, the new consumption possibility set lies *everywhere above the production possibility curve.*

The benefits of moving from a no-trade position, such as *a*, to a trading position such as *b* or *f* are the *gains from trade* to the country. When the production of good *Y* is increased and the production of good *X* decreased, the country is able to move to a point such as *f* by producing more of good *Y*, in which the country has a comparative advantage, and trading the additional production for good *X*.

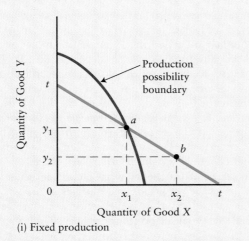

(i) Fixed production

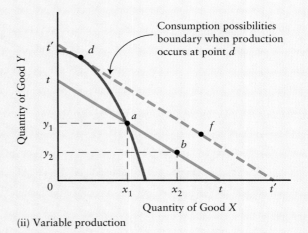

(ii) Variable production

Early economists placed great importance on a concept that is now called **learning by doing.** They believed that as countries gained experience in particular tasks, workers and managers would become more efficient in performing them. As people acquire expertise, costs tend to fall. There is substantial evidence that such learning by doing does occur. It is particularly important in many of today's knowledge-intensive high-tech industries.

The distinction between this phenomenon and the gains from economies of scale is illustrated in Figure 34-4. It is one more example of the difference between a movement along a curve and a shift of the curve.

Recognition of the opportunities for learning by doing leads to an important implication: Policymakers need not accept *current* comparative advantages as given. Through such means as education and tax incentives, they can seek to develop new comparative advantages.[1] Moreover, countries cannot complacently assume that their existing comparative advantages will persist. Misguided education policies, the wrong tax incentives, or policies that discourage risk taking can lead to the rapid erosion of a country's comparative advantage in particular products.

learning by doing
The increase in output per worker that often results as workers learn through repeatedly performing the same tasks. It causes a downward shift in the average cost curve.

---

[1]They can also foolishly use such policies to develop industries in which they do not have and will never achieve comparative advantages.

FIGURE 34-4 Gains from Trade Due to Scale and Learning Effects

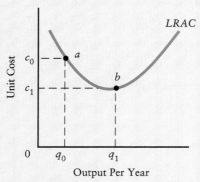

(i) Economies of scale

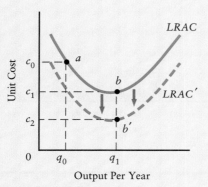

(ii) Learning by doing

Specialization may lead to gains from trade by permitting economies of larger-scale output, by leading to downward shifts of cost curves, or both. Consider a country that wishes to consume the quantity q_0. Suppose that it can produce that quantity at an average cost per unit of c_0. Suppose further that the country has a comparative advantage in producing this product and can export the quantity q_0q_1 if it produces q_1. This may lead to cost savings in two ways.

As shown in part (i), the increased level of production of q_1 compared to q_0 permits it to *move along* its cost curve from a to b, thereby reducing costs per unit to c_1. This is an economy of scale.

As shown in part (ii), as workers and management become more experienced, they may be able to produce at lower costs. This is learning by doing. The downward *shift,* shown by the arrows, lowers the cost of producing every unit of output. At output q_1, costs per unit fall to c_2. The movement from a to b' incorporates both economies of scale and learning by doing.

Sources of Comparative Advantage

We have seen that comparative advantage is the source of the gains from trade. But why do comparative advantages exist? Since a country's comparative advantage depends on its opportunity costs, we could also ask: Why do different countries have different opportunity costs?

Different Factor Endowments

The traditional answer to this question was provided early in the twentieth century by two Swedish economists, Eli Heckscher and Bertil Ohlin. Ohlin was subsequently awarded the Nobel Prize in economics for his work in the theory of international trade. Their explanation for international differences in opportunity costs is now incorporated in the Heckscher-Ohlin model. According to their theory, the international cost differences that form the basis for comparative advantage arise because factor endowments differ across countries. This is often called the *factor endowment theory of comparative advantage.*

To see how this theory works, consider the prices for various types of goods in countries *in the absence of trade.* A country that is well endowed with fertile land but has a small population (like Canada) will find that land is cheap but labour is expensive. It will therefore produce land-intensive agricultural goods cheaply and labour-intensive goods, such as machine tools, only at high cost. The reverse will be true for a second country that is small in size but possesses abundant and efficient labour (like Japan). As a result, the first country will have a comparative advantage in agricultural production and the second in goods that use much labour and little land.

According to the Heckscher-Ohlin theory, countries have comparative advantages in the production of goods that use intensively the factors of production with which they are abundantly endowed.

For example, Canada is abundantly endowed with forests relative to most other countries. According to the Hecksher-Ohlin theory, Canada has a comparative advantage in goods that use forest products intensively, such as newsprint, paper, raw lumber, and wooden furniture. In contrast, relative to most other countries, Canada is sparsely endowed with labour. Thus, Canada has a comparative disadvantage in goods that use labour intensively, such as cotton or many other textile products.

Different Climates

The factor endowment theory has considerable power to explain comparative advantage but it does not provide the whole explanation. One additional influence comes from all those natural factors that can be called *climate* in the broadest sense. If you combine land, labour, and capital in the same way in Nicaragua and in Iceland, you will not get the same output of most agricultural goods. Sunshine, rainfall, and average temperature also matter. If you seek to work with wool or cotton in dry climates, you will get different results than when you work in damp climates. (You can, of course, artificially create any climate you wish in a factory, but it costs money to create what is freely provided elsewhere.)

Canada is extremely well endowed with forests. It is no surprise, therefore, that it has a comparative advantage in a whole range of forestry products.

Climate affects comparative advantage.

Of course, if we consider "warm weather" a factor of production, then we could simply say that countries like Nicaragua are better endowed with that factor than countries like Iceland. In this sense, explanations of comparative advantage based on different climates are really just a special case of explanations based on factor endowments.

Acquired Comparative Advantage

Today it is clear that many comparative advantages are *acquired*. Further, they can change. Thus, comparative advantage should be viewed as being *dynamic* rather than static. New industries are seen to depend more on human capital than on fixed physical capital or natural resources. The skills of a computer designer, a videogame programmer, or a sound mix technician are acquired by education and on-the-job training. Natural endowments of energy and raw materials cannot account for Silicon Valley's leadership in computer technology, for Canada's prominence in communications technology or for Switzerland's prominence in private banking. When countries find their former dominance (based on comparative advantage) in such smokestack industries as cars and steel declining, their firms need not sit idly by. Instead, they can begin to adapt by developing new areas of comparative advantage.

Contrasts

This modern view is in sharp contrast with the traditional assumption that cost structures based largely on a country's natural endowments lead to a given pattern of international comparative advantage. The traditional view suggests that a government interested in maximizing its citizens' material standard of living should encourage specialization of production in goods where it currently has a comparative advantage. If all countries follow this advice, the theory predicts, each will be specialized in a relatively narrow range of distinct products. The British will produce engineering products, Canadians will be producers of resource-based primary products, Americans will be farmers and factory workers, Central Americans will be banana and coffee growers, and so on.

There are surely elements of truth in both extreme views. It would be unwise to neglect resource endowments, climate, culture, social patterns, and institutional arrangements. But it would also be unwise to assume that all of them were innate and immutable.

To some extent, these views are reconciled by the theory of human capital, which is a topic we discussed in *Microeconomics*. Comparative advantages that depend on human capital are consistent with traditional Heckscher-Ohlin theory. The difference is that this type of capital is acquired through conscious decisions relating to such matters as education and technical training.

The Determination of Trade Patterns

Comparative advantage has been the central concept in our discussion about the sources of the gains from trade. If Canada has a comparative advantage in lumber and Italy has a comparative advantage in shoes, then the total output of lumber and shoes could be increased if Canada specialized in the production of lumber and Italy specialized in the production of shoes. With such patterns of specialization, Canada would naturally export lumber to Italy and Italy would export shoes to Canada.

It is one thing to discuss the potential gains from trade if countries specialized in the production of particular goods and exported these to other countries. But do *actual* trade patterns occur along the lines of comparative advantage? In this section of the chapter we use a simple demand-and-supply model to examine why Canada exports some products and imports others. We will see that comparative advantage, whether natural or acquired, does indeed play a central role.

There are some products, such as coffee and mangos, that Canada does not produce (and will probably never produce). Any domestic consumption of these product must therefore be satisfied by imports from other countries. At the other extreme, there are some products, such as nickel or potash, where Canada is one of the world's major suppliers, and demand in the rest of the world must be satisfied partly by exports from Canada. There are also some products, such as houses, that are so expensive to transport that every country produces approximately what it consumes.

Our interest in this section is in the many intermediate cases in which Canada is only one of many producers of an internationally traded product, as with beef, oil, copper, wheat, lumber, and newsprint. Will Canada be an exporter or an importer of such products? And what is the role played by comparative advantage?

For data on Canadian trade by industry and by country, see Statistics Canada's website: www.statcan.ca. Go to "Canadian Statistics" and then "Trade."

The Law of One Price

Whether Canada imports or exports a product for which it is only one of many producers depends to a great extent on the product's price. This brings us to what economists call the *law of one price*.

The law of one price states that when a product which can be cheaply transported is traded throughout the entire world, it will tend to have a single worldwide price.

Many basic products, such as copper wire, steel pipe, iron ore, and computer RAM chips, fall within this category. The world price for each good is the price that equates the quantity demanded worldwide with the quantity supplied worldwide.

The world price of an internationally traded product may be influenced greatly, or only slightly, by the demand and supply coming from any one country. The extent of one country's influence will depend on how important its demands and supplies are in relation to the worldwide totals.

The simplest case for us to study arises when the country, which we will take to be Canada, accounts for only a small part of the total worldwide demand and supply. In this case, Canada does not itself produce enough to influence the world price significantly. Similarly, Canadian purchases are too small a proportion of worldwide demand to affect the world price in any significant way. Producers and consumers in Canada thus face a world price that they cannot influence by their own actions.

Notice that in this case, the price that rules in the Canadian market must be the world price (adjusted for the exchange rate between the Canadian dollar and the foreign currency). The law of one price says that this must be so. What would happen if the Canadian domestic price diverged from the world price? If the Canadian price were below the world price, no supplier would sell in the Canadian market because more money could be made by selling abroad. The absence of supply to the Canadian market would thus drive up the Canadian price. Conversely, if the Canadian domestic price were above the worldwide price, no buyers would buy from a Canadian seller because money could be saved by buying abroad. The absence of demand on the Canadian market would thus drive down the Canadian price.

The Pattern of Foreign Trade

Let us now see what determines the pattern of international trade in such circumstances.

An Exported Product

To determine the pattern of Canadian trade, we first show the Canadian domestic demand and supply curves for some product, say, lumber. This is done in Figure 34-5. The intersection of these two curves tells us what the price and quantity would be *if there were no foreign trade*. Now compare this no-trade price with the world price of that product.[2] If the world price is higher, the actual price in Canada will exceed the no-trade price. In this situation there will be an excess of Canadian supply over Canadian demand. Domestic producers want to sell q_2 units of lumber but domestic consumers want to buy only q_1 units. If Canada were a closed economy, such excess supply would drive the price down to p_d. But in an open economy with a world price of p_w, this excess supply gets exported to Canada's trading partners.

Countries export products whose world price exceeds the price that would exist domestically if there were no foreign trade.

What is the role of comparative advantage in this analysis? We have said that Canada will export lumber if the world price exceeds Canada's no-trade price. Note that in a competitive market the price of the product reflects the product's marginal cost, which in turn reflects the opportunity cost of producing the product. That Canada's no-trade price for lumber is lower than the world price reflects the fact that the opportunity cost of producing lumber in Canada is less than the opportunity cost of producing it in the rest of the world. Thus, by exporting goods which have a low no-trade price, Canada is exporting the goods in which it has a comparative advantage.

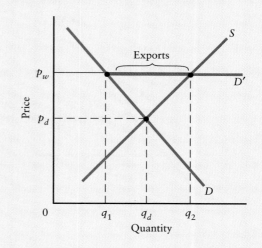

FIGURE 34-5   An Exported Good

Exports occur whenever there is excess supply domestically at the world price. The domestic demand and supply curves are D and S, respectively. The domestic price in the absence of foreign trade is p_d, with q_d produced and consumed domestically. The world price of p_w is higher than p_d. At p_w, q_1 is demanded while q_2 is supplied domestically. The excess of the domestic supply over the domestic demand is exported.

The Export Development Corporation is a crown corporation devoted to improving Canada's export prospects. For information about Canada's exports, check out its website: www. edc–see.ca.

---

[2]If the world price is stated in terms of some foreign currency (as it often is), then the price must be converted into Canadian dollars using the current exchange rate between the foreign currency and Canadian dollars.

FIGURE 34-6   An Imported Good

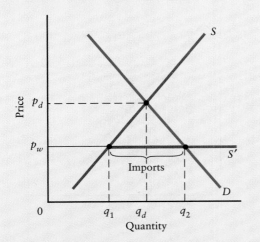

Imports occur whenever there is excess demand domestically at the world price. The domestic demand and supply curves are D and S, respectively. The domestic price in the absence of foreign trade is p_d, with q_d produced and consumed domestically. The world price of p_w is less than p_d. At the world price q_2 is demanded, whereas q_1 is supplied domestically. The excess of domestic demand over domestic supply is satisfied through imports.

Countries export the goods for which they are low-cost producers. That is, they export goods in which they have a comparative advantage.

An Imported Product

Now consider some other product—for example, computer RAM chips. Once again, look first at the domestic demand and supply curves, shown this time in Figure 34-6. The intersection of these curves determines the no-trade price that would rule if there were no foreign trade. The world price of RAM chips is below the Canadian no-trade price so that, at the price ruling in Canada, domestic demand is larger and domestic supply is smaller than if the no-trade price had ruled. The excess of domestic demand over domestic supply is met by imports.

Countries import products whose world price is less than the price that would exist domestically if there were no foreign trade.

Again, this analysis can be restated in terms of comparative advantage. The high Canadian no-trade price of RAM chips reflects the fact that RAM chips are more costly to produce in Canada than elsewhere in the world. This high cost means that Canada has a comparative disadvantage in RAM chips. So Canada imports goods for which it has a comparative disadvantage.

Countries import the goods for which they are high-cost producers. That is, they import goods for which they have a comparative disadvantage.

Is Comparative Advantage Obsolete?

In the debate preceding the signing of both the Canada-U.S. Free Trade Agreement and the North American Free Trade Agreement (NAFTA), some opponents argued that the agreements relied on an outdated view of the gains from trade based on comparative advantage. The theory of comparative advantage was said to be obsolete.

In spite of such assertions, comparative advantage remains an important economic concept. At any one time—because comparative advantage is reflected in international relative prices, and these relative prices determine what goods a country will import and what it will export—the operation of the price system will result in trade that follows the current pattern of comparative advantage. For example, if Canadian costs of producing steel are particularly low relative to other Canadian costs, Canada's price of steel will be low by international standards, and steel will be a Canadian export (which it is). If Canada's costs of producing textiles are particularly high relative to other Canadian costs, Canada's price of textiles will be high by international standards, and Canada will import textiles (which it does). Thus, there is no reason to change the view that Ricardo long ago expounded: *Current comparative advantage is a major determinant of trade under free-market conditions.*

What has changed, however, is economists' views about the *determinants* of comparative advantage. It now seems that current comparative advantage may be more open to change by private entrepreneurial activities and by government policy than used to be thought. Thus, what is obsolete is the belief that a country's current pattern of comparative advantage, and hence its current pattern of imports and exports, must be accepted as given and unchangeable.

The theory that comparative advantage determines trade flows is not obsolete, but the theory that comparative advantage is completely determined by forces beyond the reach of public policy has been discredited.

It is one thing to observe that it is *possible* for governments to influence a country's pattern of comparative advantage. It is quite another to conclude that it is *advisable* for them to try. The case in support of a specific government intervention requires that (1) there is scope for governments to improve on the results achieved by the free market, (2) the costs of the intervention be less than the value of the improvement to be achieved, and (3) governments will actually be able to carry out the required interventionist policies (without, for example, being sidetracked by considerations of electoral advantage).

The Terms of Trade

We have seen that world production can be increased when countries specialize in the production of the products in which they have a comparative advantage and then trade with one another. We now ask: How will these gains from specialization and trade be shared among countries? The division of the gain depends on what is called the **terms of trade,** which relate to the quantity of imported goods that can be obtained per unit of goods exported. They are measured by the ratio of the price of exports to the price of imports.

terms of trade The ratio of the average price of a country's exports to the average price of its imports, both averages usually being measured by index numbers.

A rise in the price of imported goods, with the price of exports unchanged, indicates a *fall in the terms of trade;* it will now take more exports to buy the same quantity of imports. Similarly, a rise in the price of exported goods, with the price of imports unchanged, indicates a *rise in the terms of trade;* it will now take fewer exports to buy the same quantity of imports. Thus, the ratio of these prices measures the amount of imports that can be obtained per unit of goods exported.

Because actual international trade involves many countries and many products, a country's terms of trade are computed as an index number:

$$\text{Terms of Trade} = \frac{\text{Index of Export Prices}}{\text{Index of Import Prices}} \times 100$$

A rise in the index is referred to as a *favourable* change in a country's terms of trade (sometimes called a terms of trade *improvement*). A favourable change means that fewer goods have to be exported per unit of goods imported than was previously the case. For example, if the export price index rises from 100 to 120 while the import price index rises from 100 to 110, the terms-of-trade index rises from 100 to 109. At the new terms of trade, a unit of imports will require approximately 9 percent fewer exports than at the old terms of trade.

A decrease in the index of the terms of trade, called an *unfavourable* change (or a terms of trade *deterioration*), means that the country can import less in return for any given amount of exports, or, equivalently, it must export more to pay for any given

FIGURE 34-7   Canada's Terms of Trade, 1970–1998

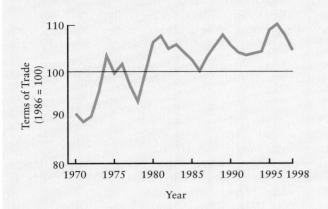

Canada's terms of trade have been quite variable over the past 30 years, but they have also displayed a long-term improvement. The data shown are Canada's terms of trade—the ratio of an index of Canadian export prices to an index of Canadian import prices. As the relative prices of lumber, oil, wheat, electronic equipment, textiles, fruit, and other products change, the terms of trade naturally change. Especially notable are the sharp increases in 1973 and 1980, caused by the OPEC oil shocks. The decline in the late 1990s is due to the reduction in world commodity prices following the Asian crisis in 1997-1998.

(Source: Economic Reference Tables, Department of Finance, and Bank of Canada.)

amount of imports. For example, the sharp rise in oil prices in the 1970s led to large unfavourable shifts in the terms of trade of oil-importing countries. When oil prices fell sharply in the mid 1980s, the terms of trade of oil-importing countries changed favourably. The converse was true for oil-exporting countries.

Canada's terms of trade since 1970 are shown in Figure 34-7. As is clear, the terms of trade are quite variable, reflecting frequent changes in the relative prices of different products. Also clear from the figure is that Canada's terms of trade have displayed a long-term improvement over the past 30 years.

Note the deterioration in Canada's terms of trade in the late 1990s. Deep recessions in several Southeast Asian countries contributed to a dramatic fall in world commodity prices between the middle of 1997 and the end of 1998. Many of these commodities—copper, gold, oil, newsprint, lumber, pork—are important Canadian exports. Thus, a decline in their price implies a deterioration in Canada's terms of trade.

S U M M A R Y

Sources of the Gains from Trade

- One country (or region or individual) has an absolute advantage over another country (or region or individual) in the production of a specific product when, with the same input of resources in each country, it can produce more of the product than can the other.
- Comparative advantage is the relative advantage one country enjoys over another in the production of various products. It occurs whenever countries have different

opportunity costs of producing particular goods. World production of all products can be increased if each country transfers resources into the production of the products in which it has a comparative advantage.

- The most important proposition in the theory of the gains from trade is that trade allows all countries to obtain the goods in which they do not have a comparative advantage at a lower opportunity cost than they would face if they were to produce all products for themselves; specialization and trade therefore allow all countries to have more of all products than they could have if they tried to be self-sufficient.

- As well as gaining the advantages of specialization arising from comparative advantage, a nation that engages in trade and specialization may realize the benefits of economies of large-scale production and of learning by doing.

- Classical theory regarded comparative advantage as largely determined by natural resource endowments that are difficult to change. Economists now believe that some comparative advantages can be acquired and consequently can be changed. A country may, in this view, influence its role in world production and trade. Successful intervention leads to a country's acquiring a comparative advantage; unsuccessful intervention fails to develop such an advantage.

The Determination of Trade Patterns

- The law of one price says that internationally traded goods that are inexpensive to transport must sell at the same price in all countries. Economists call this the world price.
- Countries will export a good when the world price exceeds the price that would exist in the country if there were no trade. The low no-trade price reflects a low opportunity cost and thus a comparative advantage in that

good. Thus, countries export goods for which they have a comparative advantage.
- Countries will import a good when the world price is less than the price that would exist in the country if there were no trade. The high no-trade price reflects a high opportunity cost and thus a comparative disadvantage in that good. Thus, countries import goods for which they have a comparative disadvantage.

The Terms of Trade

- The terms of trade refer to the ratio of the prices of goods exported to the prices of those imported. This determines the quantity of imports that can be obtained per unit of exports. The terms of trade determine how the gains from trade are shared.

- A favourable change in the terms of trade—a rise in export prices relative to import prices—means that a country can acquire more imports per unit of exports, and vice versa.

K E Y   C O N C E P T S

Interpersonal, interregional, and international specialization
Absolute advantage and comparative advantage

Opportunity cost and comparative advantage
The gains from trade: specialization, scale economies, and learning by doing

The sources of comparative advantage
Factor endowments
Acquired comparative advantage
The law of one price
The terms of trade

STUDY EXERCISES

1. The following diagram shows the production possibilities boundary for Arcticland, a country that produces two goods, ice and fish. Labour is the only factor of production.

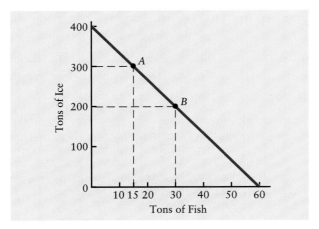

a. Beginning at any point on Arcticland's production possibilities boundary, what is the opportunity cost of producing 10 more tons of fish?
b. Beginning at any point on Arcticland's production possibilities boundary, what is the opportunity cost of producing 100 more tons of ice?

2. The following table shows the production of wheat and corn in Brazil and Mexico. Assume that both countries have one million acres of arable land.

	Brazil	Mexico
Wheat	90 bushels per acre	50 bushels per acre
Corn	30 bushels per acre	20 bushels per acre

a. Which country has the absolute advantage in wheat? In corn? Explain.
b. Which country has the comparative advantage in wheat? In corn? Explain.
c. Explain why one country can have an absolute advantage in both goods but cannot have a comparative advantage in both goods.
d. On a scale diagram with wheat on the horizontal axis and corn on the vertical axis, draw each country's production possibilities boundary.
e. What is shown by the slope of each country's production possibilities boundary? Be as precise as possible.

3. The following diagrams show the production possibilities boundaries for Canada and France, both of which produce two goods, wine and lumber.

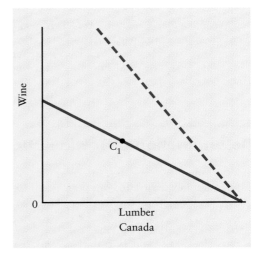

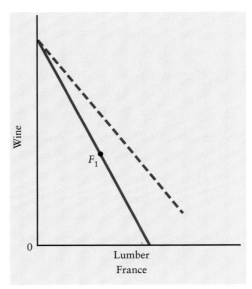

a. Which country has the comparative advantage in lumber? Explain.
b. Which country has the comparative advantage in wine? Explain.
c. Suppose that Canada and France are initially not trading with each other and are producing at points C_1 and F_1, respectively. Suppose when trade is introduced, the free-trade relative prices are shown by the dashed line. Which combination of goods will each country now produce?
d. In this case, what will be the pattern of trade for each country?

4. The diagrams below show the Canadian markets for newsprint and machinery, which we assume to be competitive.

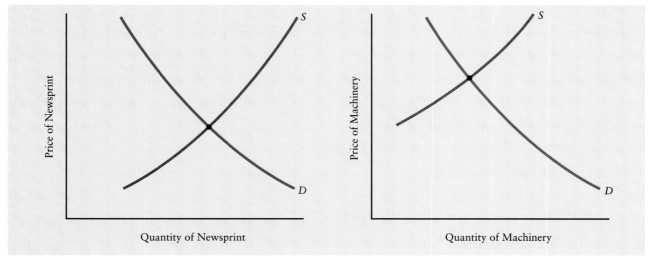

a. Suppose there is no international trade. What would be the equilibrium price and quantity in the Canadian newsprint and machinery markets?

b. Now suppose that Canada is open to trade with the rest of the world. If the world price of newsprint is *higher* than the price of newsprint from part **a**, what will happen to the levels of domestic production and consumption? Explain.

c. If the world price of machinery is lower than the price of machinery from part **a**, what happens to the levels of domestic consumption and production? Explain.

5. The table below shows indexes for the prices of imports and exports over several years for a hypothetical country.

Year	Import Prices	Export Prices	Terms of Trade
1996	90	110	—
1997	95	87	—
1998	98	83	—
1999	100	100	—
2000	102	105	—
2001	100	112	—
2002	103	118	—

a. Compute the terms of trade in each year for this country and fill in the table.

b. In which years does the terms of trade improve?

c. In which years does the terms of trade deteriorate?

d. Explain why a terms of trade "improvement" is good for the country.

6. For each of the following events, explain the likely effect on Canada's terms of trade. Your existing knowledge of Canada's imports and exports should be adequate to answer this question.

a. A hurricane damages much of Brazil's coffee crop.

b. OPEC countries succeed in significantly restricting the world supply of oil.

c. Several new large copper mines come into production in Chile.

d. A major recession in Southeast Asia reduces the world demand for pork.

DISCUSSION QUESTIONS

1. Adam Smith saw a close connection between the wealth of a nation and its willingness "freely to engage" in foreign trade. What is the connection?

2. One critic of the North American Free Trade Agreement argued that "it can't be in our interest to sign this deal; Mexico gains too much from it." What does the theory of the gains from trade have to say about that criticism?

3. One product innovation that appears imminent is the electric car. However, development costs are high and economies of scale and learning by doing are both likely to be operative. As a result, there will be a substantial competitive advantage for those who develop a marketable product early. What implications might this have for government policies toward North American automobile manufacturers' activities in this area? Should the Canadian or U.S. governments encourage joint efforts by Chrysler, Ford, and GM, even if this appears to lessen competition between them?

4. Studies of Canadian trade patterns have shown that industries with high wages are among the largest and fastest-growing export sectors. One example is the computer software industry. Does this finding contradict the principle of comparative advantage?

5. Predict what each of the following events would do to the terms of trade of the importing country and the exporting country, other things being equal.

   a. A blight destroys a large part of the coffee beans produced in the world.
   b. The Koreans cut the price of the steel they sell to Canada.
   c. General inflation of 4 percent occurs around the world.
   d. Violation of OPEC output quotas leads to a sharp fall in the price of oil.

6. Are there always benefits to specialization and trade? When are the benefits greatest? Under what situations are there *no* benefits from specialization and trade?

CHAPTER 35

Trade Policy

LEARNING OBJECTIVES

❶ Understand the various situations in which a country may rationally choose to protect some industries.

❷ Recognize the most common fallacious arguments in favour of protection.

❸ Explain the effects of placing a tariff or a quantity restriction on an imported good.

❹ Recognize that trade-remedy laws are sometimes just thinly disguised protection.

❺ Explain the difference between trade creation and trade diversion.

❻ Know the main features of the North American Free Trade Agreement.

Conducting business in a foreign country is not always easy. Differences in language, in local laws and customs, and in currency often complicate transactions. Our concern in this chapter, however, is not with these complications but with government policy toward international trade, which is called **trade policy.** At one extreme is a policy of free trade—that is, an absence of any form of government interference with the free flow of international trade. Any departure from free trade designed to protect domestic industries from foreign competition is called **protectionism.**

We begin by briefly restating the case for free trade and then go on to study various valid and invalid arguments that are commonly advanced for some degree of protection. We then explore some of the methods that are commonly used to restrict trade, such as tariffs and quotas. Finally, we examine the many modern institutions designed to foster freer trade on either a global or a regional basis. Of central importance to Canada is the North American Free Trade Agreement (NAFTA).

trade policy
A government's policy involving restrictions placed on international trade.

protectionism Any government policy that interferes with free trade in order to give some protection to domestic industries against foreign competition.

Free Trade or Protection?

Today, most governments accept the proposition that a relatively free flow of international trade is desirable for the health of their individual economies. But heated debates still occur over trade policy. Should a country permit the completely free flow of international trade, or should it sometimes seek to protect its local producers from foreign competition? If some protection is desired, should it be achieved by tariffs or by nontariff barriers? **Tariffs** are taxes designed to raise the price of foreign goods. **Nontariff barriers (NTBs)** are devices other than tariffs that are designed to reduce the flow of imports;

tariff A tax applied on imports of goods or services.
nontariff barriers (NTBs) Restrictions other than tariffs designed to reduce the flow of imported goods or services.

examples are quotas and customs procedures that are deliberately more cumbersome than necessary.

The Case for Free Trade

The case for free trade was presented in Chapter 34. Comparative advantages arise whenever countries have different opportunity costs. Free trade encourages all countries to specialize in producing products in which they have a comparative advantage. This in turn maximizes world production and hence maximizes average world living standards (as measured by the world's per capita GDP).

Free trade does not necessarily make *everyone* better off than they would be in its absence. For example, reducing an existing tariff often results in individual groups receiving a smaller share of a larger world output so that they lose even though the average person gains. If we ask whether it is *possible* for free trade to improve everyone's living standards, the answer is "yes." But, if we ask whether free trade always does so, the answer is "not necessarily."

Given that all countries can be better off by specializing in those goods in which they have a comparative advantage, it is puzzling that most countries of the world continue in some way to restrict the flow of trade. Why do tariffs and other barriers to trade continue to exist two centuries after Adam Smith and David Ricardo stated the case for free trade? Is there a valid case for some protection?

The Case for Protection

Two kinds of arguments for protection are commonly offered. The first concerns national objectives *other than* maximizing total income; the second concerns the desire to increase one country's national income, possibly at the expense of the national incomes of other countries.

Objectives Other than Maximizing National Income

It is possible to believe that a country's national income is maximized with free trade and yet rationally oppose free trade because of a concern with other policy objectives.

Noneconomic Advantages of Diversification.   Comparative advantage might dictate that a small country should specialize in producing a narrow range of products. However, there may be social advantages in a more diverse economy. Citizens would be given a wider range of occupations, and the social and psychological advantages of diversification may more than compensate for the reduction in per capita output.

Countries whose economies are based on the production of only a few goods face risks from fluctuations in world prices. For this reason, protection to promote diversification may be viewed as desirable.

Risks of Specialization.   For a very small country, specializing in the production of only a few products—though dictated by comparative advantage—might involve risks that the country does not wish to take. One such risk is that technological advances may render its basic product obsolete. Another risk, especially for countries specialized in producing a small range of agricultural products, is that swings in world prices lead to large swings in national income. Everyone understands these risks, but there is debate about what governments can do about it. The pro-tariff argument is that the government can encourage a more diversified economy by protecting industries that otherwise could not compete. Opponents argue that governments, being naturally influenced by political motives, are poor judges of which industries can be protected in order to produce diversification at a reasonable cost.

Protection of Specific Groups.   Although free trade—and specialization according to comparative advantage—will maximize per capita GDP over the whole economy, some specific groups may have higher incomes under protection than under free trade. Of particular interest in Canada and the United States has been the effect that greater international trade has on the incomes of unskilled workers.

Consider the ratio of skilled workers to unskilled workers. There are plenty of both types throughout the world. Compared to much of the rest of the world, however, Canada has more skilled and fewer unskilled people. When trade is expanded because of a reduction in tariffs, Canada will tend to export goods made by its abundant skilled workers and import goods made by unskilled workers. (This is the basic prediction of the *factor endowment theory* of comparative advantage that we discussed in Chapter 34.) Because Canada is now exporting more goods made by skilled labour, the domestic demand for such labour rises. Because Canada is now importing more goods made by unskilled labour, the domestic demand for such labour falls. This specialization according to comparative advantage raises average Canadian living standards, but it will also tend to raise the wages of skilled Canadian workers relative to the wages of unskilled Canadian workers.

If increasing trade has these effects, then reducing trade by raising trade barriers can have the opposite effects. Raising trade barriers may raise the incomes of unskilled Canadian workers, giving them a larger share of a smaller total GDP. The conclusion is that trade restrictions can improve the earnings of one group whenever the restrictions increase the demand for that group's services. This is done, however, at the expense of a reduction in *overall* national income and hence the country's average living standards.

This analysis is important because it reveals both the grain of truth and the dangers that lie behind the resistance to reductions in trade restrictions on the part of some labour groups and some organizations whose main concern is with the poor.

Social and distributional concerns may lead to the rational adoption of protectionist policies. But the cost of such protection is a reduction in the country's average living standards.

Economists cannot say that it is irrational for a society to sacrifice some income to achieve other goals. But economists can do three things when presented with such arguments for adopting protectionist measures. First, they can ask if the proposed measures really do achieve the ends suggested. Second, they can calculate the cost of the measures in terms of lowered living standards. Third, they can see if there are alternative means of achieving the stated goals at lower cost in terms of lost national income.

Maximizing One Country's National Income

Next we consider several arguments for the use of tariffs when the objective is to maximize a country's national income.

To Alter the Terms of Trade.   Tariffs can be used to change the terms of trade in favour of a country that makes up a large fraction of the world demand for some product that it imports. By restricting its demand for that product through a tariff, it can force down the price that foreign exporters receive for that product. The price paid by domestic consumers will probably rise but as long as the increase is less than the tariff, foreign suppliers will receive less per unit. For example, a 20 percent U.S. tariff on the import of

Canadian softwood lumber might raise the price paid by U.S. consumers by 12 percent and lower the price received by Canadian suppliers by 8 percent (the difference between the two prices being received by the U.S. treasury). This reduction in the price received by the foreign suppliers of a U.S. import is a terms-of-trade improvement for the United States (and a terms-of-trade deterioration for Canada).

To Protect Against "Unfair" Actions by Foreign Firms and Governments.

Tariffs are used to prevent foreign industries from harming domestic industries by employing predatory practices. Two common practices are subsidies paid by foreign governments to their exporters and price discrimination by foreign firms, which is called *dumping* when it is done across international borders. These practices are typically countered by levying tariffs called *countervailing duties* and *antidumping duties*. The circumstances under which dumping and foreign subsidization provide a valid argument for such tariffs are considered in detail later in this chapter.

To Protect Infant Industries.

infant industry argument The argument that new domestic industries with potential for economies of scale or learning by doing need to be protected from competition from established, low-cost foreign producers so that they can grow large enough to achieve costs as low as those of foreign producers.

The oldest valid argument for protection as a means of raising living standards concerns economies of scale. It is usually called the **infant industry argument.** An infant industry is nothing more than a new, small industry. If such an industry has large economies of scale, costs will be high when the industry is small but will fall as the industry grows. In such industries, the country first in the field has a tremendous advantage. A developing country may find that in the early stages of development, its industries are unable to compete with established foreign rivals. A trade restriction may protect these industries from foreign competition while they grow up. When they are large enough, they will be able to produce as cheaply as foreign rivals and thus be able to compete without protection.

Most of the now industrialized countries developed their industries initially under quite heavy tariff protection. (In Canada's case, the National Policy of 1876 established a high tariff wall behind which many Canadian industries developed and thrived for many years.) Once the industrial sector was well developed, these countries moved to reduce their levels of protection, thus moving a long way toward freer trade.

To Encourage Learning by Doing.

Learning by doing, which we discussed in Chapter 34, suggests that the pattern of comparative advantage can be changed. If a country learns enough by producing products for which it currently has a comparative *dis*advantage, it may gain in the long run by specializing in those products, developing a comparative advantage as the learning process lowers their costs.

Learning by doing is an example of what in Chapter 34 we called *dynamic* comparative advantage. The success over the past three decades of such newly industrializing countries (NICs) as Hong Kong, South Korea, Singapore, Taiwan, Indonesia, and Thailand seemed to many observers to be based on acquired skills and government policies that created favourable business conditions. These successes gave rise to the theory that comparative advantages can change and that they can be developed by suitable government policies, which can, however, take many forms other than restricting trade.

Some countries have succeeded in developing strong comparative advantages in targeted industries, but others have failed. One reason such policies sometimes fail is that protecting local industries from foreign competition may make the industries unadaptive and complacent. Another reason is the difficulty of identifying the industries that will be able to succeed in the long run. All too often, the protected infant grows up to be a weakling requiring permanent protection for its continued existence, or else the rate of learning is slower than for similar industries in countries that do not provide protection from the chill winds of international competition. In these instances, the anticipated comparative advantage never materializes. The NICs mentioned above avoided these problems by insisting that the protected industries serve the export market. If they could not succeed within a few years in the tough world of international competition, they lost their domestic support.

To Earn Pure Profits.   Another argument for tariffs or other trade restrictions is to help create an advantage in producing or marketing some new product that is expected to generate pure profits. To the extent that all lines of production earn normal profits, there is no reason to produce goods other than ones for which a country has a comparative advantage. Some goods, however, are produced in industries containing a few large firms where economies of scale provide a natural barrier to entry. Firms in these industries can earn high profits even over long periods of time. If protection of the domestic market can increase the chance that one of the protected domestic firms will become established and thus earn high profits, the protection may pay off. This is the general idea behind the concept of *strategic trade policy*.

Opponents of strategic trade policy argue that it is nothing more than a modern version of age-old and faulty justifications for tariff protection. Once all countries try to be strategic, they will all waste vast sums trying to break into industries in which there is no room for most of them. Domestic consumers would benefit most, they say, if their governments let other countries engage in this game. Consumers could then buy the cheap, subsidized foreign products and export traditional nonsubsidized products in return. The opponents of strategic trade policy also argue that democratic governments that enter the game of picking and backing winners are likely to make more bad choices than good ones. One bad choice, with all of its massive development costs written off, would require that many good choices also be made in order to make the equivalent in profits that would allow taxpayers to break even overall.

An ongoing dispute between Canada and Brazil illustrates how strategic trade policy is often difficult to distinguish from pure protection. The world's two major producers of regional jets are Bombardier, based in Montreal, and Embraer SA, based in Brazil. For several years, each company has accused their competitor's government of using illegal subsidies to help their domestic company sell jets in world markets. Brazil's Pro-Ex program provides Embraer's customers with low-interest loans with which to purchase Embraer's jets. The Canadian government's Technology Partnerships program is a $300 million annual fund that subsidizes research and development activities in high-tech aerospace and defence companies. As the leading Canadian aerospace company, Bombardier benefits significantly from this program.

See Chapter 35 of www.pearsoned.ca/lipsey for an interview with Bombardier's Laurent Beaudoin on the need for subsidies in the aerospace industry: "Trade and Subsidies in the Air," *World Economic Affairs.*

In 1999, the World Trade Organization (WTO) ruled that both the Brazilian and Canadian governments were using illegal subsidy programs to support their aerospace firms. Both countries, however, naturally view their respective programs as necessary responses to the other country's subsidization. Many economists believe that an agreement to eliminate both programs would leave a "level playing field" while saving Brazilian and Canadian taxpayers a considerable amount of money. By the end of 1999, the two countries had not reached an agreement involving reductions in their subsidy programs.

The Importance of Competition

In today's world, a country's products must stand up to international competition if they are to survive. Over time, this requirement demands that they hold their own in competition for successful innovations. Over even so short a period as a few years, firms that do not develop new products and new production methods fall seriously behind their competitors in many industries. Protection, by reducing competition from foreign firms, reduces the incentive for industries to fight to succeed internationally. If any one

For a list and discussion of many ongoing trade disputes, see the WTO's website: www.wto.org.

country adopts high tariffs unilaterally, its domestic industries will become less competitive. Secure in its home market because of the tariff wall, its protected industries are likely to become less and less competitive in the international market. As the gap between domestic and foreign industries widens, any tariff wall will provide less and less protection. Eventually, the domestic industries will succumb to the foreign competition. Meanwhile, domestic living standards will fall relative to foreign ones as an increasing productivity gap opens between domestic protected industries and foreign, internationally oriented ones.

Although restrictive trade policies have sometimes been pursued following a rational assessment of the approximate cost, such policies are often pursued for political objectives or on fallacious economic grounds, with little appreciation of the actual costs involved.

Fallacious Arguments for Protection

We have seen that there are generally gains from trade, although trade does not necessarily make everyone in a country better off. We have also seen that there are some situations in which there are valid arguments for restricting trade. For every valid argument, however, there are many fallacious arguments—many of these are based, directly or indirectly, on the misconception that in every transaction there is a winner and a loser. Here we review a few such arguments that are frequently advanced in political debates concerning international trade.

Keep the Money at Home

This argument says that if I buy a foreign good, I have the good and the foreigner has the money, whereas if I buy the same good locally, I have the good and our country has the money, too. This argument is based on a common misconception. It assumes that domestic money actually goes abroad physically when imports are purchased and that trade flows only in one direction. But when Canadian importers purchase Japanese goods, they do not send dollars abroad. They (or their financial agents) buy Japanese yen and use them to pay the Japanese manufacturers. They purchase the yen on the foreign-exchange market by giving up dollars to someone who wishes to use them for expenditure in Canada. Even if the money did go abroad physically—that is, if a Japanese firm accepted a shipload of Canadian $100 bills—it would be because that firm (or someone to whom it could sell the dollars) wanted them to spend in the only country where they are legal tender—Canada.

Canadian currency, or any other national currency, ultimately does no one any good except as purchasing power. It would be miraculous if Canadian money could be exported in return for real goods. After all, the Bank of Canada has the power to create as much new Canadian money as it wishes (at almost zero direct cost). It is only because Canadian money can buy Canadian products and Canadian assets that others want it.

Protect Against Low-Wage Foreign Labour

This argument says that the products of low-wage countries will drive Canadian products from the market, and the high Canadian standard of living will be dragged down to that of its poorer trading partners. Arguments of this sort have swayed many voters over the years.

As a prelude to considering this argument, think what the argument would imply if taken out of the international context and put into a local one, where the same principles govern the gains from trade. Is it really impossible for a rich person to gain by trading with a poor person? Would the local millionaire be better off if she did all her own typing, gardening, and cooking? No one believes that a rich person gains nothing by trading with those who are less rich.

Why, then, must a rich group of people lose when they trade with a poor group? "Well," some may say, "the poor group will price its goods too cheaply." Does anyone believe that consumers lose from buying in discount houses or supermarkets just because the prices are lower there than at the old-fashioned corner store? Consumers gain when they can buy the same goods at a lower price. If Mexican or Malaysian firms pay low wages and sell their goods cheaply, workers in those countries may suffer, but Canadians will gain by obtaining imports at a low cost in terms of the goods that must be exported in return. The cheaper our imports are, the better off we are in terms of the goods and services available for domestic consumption.

As we said earlier in this chapter, *some* Canadians may be better off if Canada places high tariffs on the import of Mexican goods. In particular, if the Mexican goods compete with goods made by unskilled Canadian workers, then those unskilled workers will be better off if a Canadian tariff protects their firms and thus their jobs. But Canadian income overall—that is, average per capita real income—will be higher when there is free trade.

See Chapter 35 of www.pearsoned.ca/lipsey for an interview with MIT's Paul Krugman, who explains why countries do not "compete" against each other: Paul Krugman, "Fresh Thoughts from a Saltwater Economist," *World Economic Affairs.*

Exports Are Good; Imports Are Bad

Exports create domestic income; imports create income for foreigners. Thus, other things being equal, exports tend to increase our total GDP, and imports tend to reduce it. Surely, then, it is desirable to encourage exports by subsidizing them and to discourage imports by taxing them. This is an appealing argument, but it is incorrect.

Exports raise GDP by adding to the value of domestic output, but they do not add to the value of domestic consumption. The standard of living in a country depends on the goods and services available for consumption, not on what is produced.

If exports really were "good" and imports really were "bad," then a fully employed economy that managed to increase exports without a corresponding increase in imports ought to be better off. Such a change, however, would result in a reduction in current standards of living because when more goods are sent abroad but no more are brought in from abroad, the total goods available for domestic consumption must fall.

The living standards of a country depend on the goods and services consumed in that country. The importance of exports is that they provide the resources required to purchase imports, either now or in the future.

Create Domestic Jobs

It is sometimes said that an economy with substantial unemployment, such as Canada during much of the 1990s, provides an exception to the case for freer trade. Suppose that tariffs or import quotas cut the imports of Japanese cars, Korean textiles, German kitchen equipment, and Polish vodka. Surely, the argument maintains, this will create more employment in Canadian industries producing similar products. This may be true but it will also *reduce* employment in other industries.

The Japanese, Koreans, Germans, and Poles can buy from Canada only if they earn Canadian dollars by selling their domestically produced goods and services to Canada (or by borrowing dollars from Canada).[1] The decline in their sales of cars, textiles,

---

[1]They can also get dollars by selling to other countries and then using their currencies to buy Canadian dollars. But this intermediate step only complicates the transaction; it does not change its fundamental nature. Other countries must have earned the dollars by selling goods to Canada or borrowing from Canada.

kitchen equipment, and vodka will decrease their purchases of Canadian lumber, cars, software, banking services, and holidays. Jobs will be lost in Canadian export industries and gained in industries that formerly faced competition from imports. The major long-term effect is that the same total employment will merely be redistributed among industries. In the process, living standards will be reduced because employment expands in inefficient import-competing industries and contracts in efficient exporting industries.

A country that imposes tariffs in an attempt to create domestic jobs risks starting a "trade war" with its trading partners. Such a trade war can easily leave every country worse off, as world output (and thus income) falls significantly. An income-reducing trade war followed the onset of the Great Depression in 1929 as many countries increased tariffs to protect their domestic industries in an attempt to stimulate domestic production and employment. Most economists agree that this trade war made the Great Depression worse than it otherwise would have been.

There are several fallacious arguments for protection that are often heard in political debate. These arguments suffer from a misunderstanding of the sources of gains from trade or from the misbelief that protection can increase total employment.

Methods of Protection

We now go on to explore the various tools that governments use to provide protection to domestic industries.

Two main types of protectionist policy are illustrated in Figure 35-1. Both cause the price of the imported good to rise and its quantity demanded to fall. They differ, however, in how they achieve these results. The caption to the figure analyses these two types of policy.

Policies that Directly Raise Prices

The first type of protectionist policy directly raises the price of the imported product. A tariff, also often called an *import duty*, is the most common policy of this type. Other such policies are any rules or regulations that fulfill three conditions: They are costly to comply with; they do not apply to competing, domestically produced products; and they are more than is required to meet any legitimate purpose other than restricting trade.

As shown in part (i) of Figure 35-1, tariffs affect both foreign and domestic producers, as well as domestic consumers. The initial effect is to raise the domestic price of the imported product above its world price by the amount of the tariff. Imports fall. As a result, foreign producers sell less and must transfer resources to other lines of production. The price received on domestically produced units rises, as does the quantity produced domestically. On both counts, domestic producers earn more. However, the cost of producing the extra production at home exceeds the price at which it could be purchased on the world market. Thus, the benefit to domestic producers comes at the expense of domestic consumers. Indeed, domestic consumers lose on two counts: First, they consume less of the product because its price rises, and second, they pay a higher price for the amount that they do consume. This extra spending ends up in two places: The extra that is paid on all units produced at home goes to domestic producers, and the extra that is paid on units still imported goes to the government as tariff revenue.

FIGURE 35-1   Tariffs and Quotas to Protect Domestic Producers

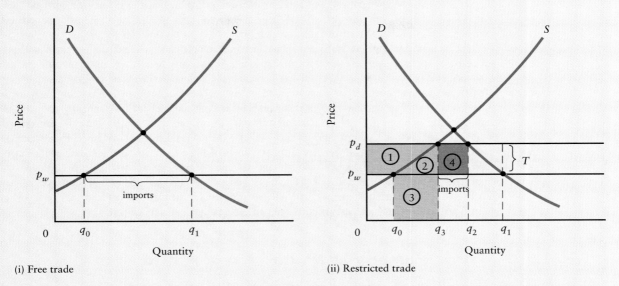

(i) Free trade

(ii) Restricted trade

The same reduction in imports and increase in domestic production can be achieved by using either a tariff or a quantity restriction. In both parts of the figure, D and S are the domestic demand and supply curves, respectively, and p_w is the world price of some product that is both produced at home and imported.

Part (i) of the figure shows the situation under free trade. Domestic consumption is q_1, domestic production is q_0, and imports are $q_0 q_1$.

Part (ii) shows what happens when protectionist policies restrict imports to the amount $q_3 q_2$. When this is done by levying a tariff of T per unit, the price in the domestic market rises by the full amount of the tariff to p_d. Consumers reduce consumption from q_1 to q_2 and pay an extra amount, shown by the shaded areas 1, 2, and 4, for the q_2 that they now purchase. Domestic production rises from q_0 to q_3. Because domestic producers receive the domestic price, their receipts rise by the three light-shaded areas, labelled 1, 2, and 3. Area 3 is revenue that was previously earned by foreign producers under free trade, while areas 1 and 2 are now paid by domestic consumers because of the higher prices they now face. Foreign suppliers of the imported good continue to receive the world price, so the government receives as tariff revenue the extra amount paid by consumers for the $q_3 \, q_2$ units that are still imported (shown by the dark shaded area, 4).

When the same result is accomplished by a quantity restriction, the government—through either a quota or a voluntary export restriction (VER)—reduces imports to $q_3 q_2$. This drives the domestic market price up to p_d and has the same effect on domestic producers and consumers as the tariff. Since the government has merely restricted the quantity of imports, both foreign and domestic suppliers get the higher price in the domestic market. Thus, foreign suppliers now receive the extra amount paid by domestic consumers (represented by the shaded area labelled 4) for the units that are still imported.

Policies that Directly Reduce Quantities

The second type of protectionist policy directly restricts the quantity of an imported product. A common example is the **import quota,** by which the importing country sets a maximum of the quantity of some product that may be imported each year. Another measure is the **voluntary export restriction (VER),** an agreement by an exporting country to limit the amount of a product that it sells to the importing country.

Figure 35-1 shows that a quantity restriction and a tariff have similar effects on domestic consumers and producers—they both raise domestic prices, increase domestic

import quota   A limit set by the government on the quantity of a foreign commodity that may be shipped into that country in a given time period.

voluntary export restriction (VER)   An agreement by an exporting country to limit the amount of a good exported to another country.

production, and reduce domestic consumption. But a quantity restriction is actually *worse* than a tariff for the importing country because the effect of the quantity restriction is to raise the price received by the foreign suppliers of the good. In contrast, a tariff leaves the foreign suppliers' price unchanged and instead generates tariff revenue for the government of the importing country.

Canada, the United States, and the European Union have used VERs extensively, and the EU makes frequent use of import quotas. Japan has been pressured into negotiating several VERs with Canada, the United States, and the EU in order to limit sales of some of the Japanese goods that have had the most success in international competition. For example, in 1983, the United States and Canada negotiated VERs whereby the Japanese government agreed to restrict total sales of Japanese cars to these two countries for three years. When the agreements ran out in 1986, the Japanese continued to restrict their automobile sales by unilateral voluntary action. Japan's readiness to restrict its exports to North America reflects the high profits that Japanese automobile producers were making under the system of VERs, as explained in Figure 35-1. In recent years, such VERs have become less important because Japan's major automobile producers, Honda and Toyota, both have established manufacturing plants in Canada.

Trade-Remedy Laws and Nontariff Barriers

As tariffs were lowered over the years since 1947, countries that wished to protect domestic industries began using, and often abusing, a series of trade restrictions that came to be known as nontariff barriers (NTBs). The original purpose of some of these barriers was to remedy certain legitimate problems that arise in international trade and, for this reason, they are often called *trade-remedy laws*. All too often, however, such laws are misused to become potent means of simple protection.

Dumping

dumping The practice of selling a commodity at a lower price in the export market than in the domestic market for reasons unrelated to differences in costs of servicing the two markets.

Selling a product in a foreign country at a lower price than in the domestic market is known as **dumping**. Dumping is a form of price discrimination studied in the theory of monopoly. Most governments have antidumping duties designed to protect their own industries against what is viewed as unfair foreign pricing practices.

Dumping, if it lasts indefinitely, can be a gift to the receiving country. Its consumers get goods from abroad at less than their full cost of production.

Dumping is more often a temporary measure, designed to get rid of unwanted surpluses, or a predatory attempt to drive competitors out of business. In either case, domestic producers complain about unfair foreign competition. In both cases, it is accepted international practice to levy antidumping duties on foreign imports. These duties are designed to eliminate the discriminatory elements in their prices.

Unfortunately, antidumping laws have been evolving over the past three decades in ways that allow antidumping duties to become barriers to trade and competition rather than to provide redress for unfair trading practices.

Several features of the antidumping system that is now in place in many countries make it highly protectionist. First, any price discrimination between national markets is classified as dumping and is subject to penalties. Thus prices in the producer's domestic market become, in effect, minimum prices below which no sales can be made in foreign markets, whatever the nature of demand in the domestic and foreign markets. Second, following a change in the U.S. law in the early 1970s, many countries' laws now calculate the "margin of dumping" as the difference between the price that is charged in that country's market and the foreign producer's average cost. Thus when there is a global slump in some industry so that the profit-maximizing price for all producers is below average cost, foreign producers can be convicted of dumping. This gives domestic producers enormous protection whenever the market price falls temporarily below average cost. Third, law in the United States (but not in all other countries) places the onus of proof on the accused. Facing a charge of dumping, a foreign producer must prove within the short time allowed for such a defence that the charge is unfounded. Fourth, U.S. antidumping duties are imposed with no time limit, so they often persist long after foreign firms have altered the prices that gave rise to them.

Governments have often been persuaded that low-price competition from foreign firms is "unfair" competition, and have levied antidumping duties on the imported goods. A recent example in Canada was an alleged case of dumping by Gerber, a U.S.-based producer of jarred baby food. In 1997, Heinz, the only Canadian producer, claimed that Gerber was pricing its products in Canada below costs, causing Heinz to lose sales. Heinz pushed for antidumping duties to be imposed on Gerber imports, and in April of 1998 the Canadian government agreed and imposed a 69 percent duty on Gerber imports. This duty was high enough to cause Gerber to reconsider the value of selling in the Canadian market. Later in the same year, however, consumer groups and the federal Competition Bureau argued that the very high duties on Gerber's products effectively left Heinz as a monopolist in the Canadian market. They urged a reluctant Canadian government to repeal the duty so that consumers could benefit from the competition between Gerber and Heinz.

Countervailing Duties

Countervailing duties, which are commonly used by the U.S. government but much less so elsewhere, provide another case in which a trade-remedy law can sometimes become a covert method of protection. The countervailing duty is designed to act, not as a tariff barrier, but rather as a means of creating a "level playing field" on which fair international competition can take place. Privately owned domestic firms rightly complain that they cannot compete against the seemingly bottomless purses of foreign governments. Subsidized foreign exports can be sold indefinitely at prices that would produce losses in the absence of the subsidy. The original object of countervailing duties was to counteract the effect on price of the presence of such foreign subsidies.

If a domestic firm suspects the existence of such a subsidy and registers a complaint, its government is required to make an investigation. For a countervailing duty to be levied, the investigation must determine, first, that the foreign subsidy to the specific industry in question does exist and, second, that it is large enough to cause significant injury to competing domestic firms.

There is no doubt that countervailing duties have sometimes been used to counteract the effects of unfair competition that are caused by foreign subsidies. Many governments complain, however, that countervailing duties are often used as thinly disguised protection. At the early stages of the development of countervailing duties, only subsidies whose prime effect was to distort trade were possible objects of countervailing duties. Even then, however, the existence of equivalent domestic subsidies was not taken into account when decisions were made to put countervailing duties on subsidized imports. Thus the United States levies some countervailing duties against foreign goods even though the foreign subsidy is less than the domestic subsidy. This does not create a level playing field.

Over time, the type of subsidy that is subject to countervailing duties has evolved until almost any government program that affects industry now risks becoming the object of a countervailing duty. Because all governments, including most U.S. state governments,

Canada's supply-management programs such as those in the dairy industry have been a perpetual source of friction in international trade negotiations.

have programs that provide direct or indirect assistance to industry, the potential for the use of countervailing duties as thinly disguised trade barriers is enormous.

Current Trade Policy

In the remainder of the chapter, we discuss trade policy in practice. We start with the many international agreements that govern current trade policies and then look in a little more detail at the NAFTA.

Before 1947, any country was free to impose tariffs on its imports. However, when one country increased its tariffs, the action often triggered retaliatory actions by its trading partners. The 1930s saw a high-water mark of world protectionism as each country sought to raise its employment and output by raising its tariffs. The end result was lowered efficiency, less trade, but no more employment or income. Since the end of World War II, much effort has been devoted to reducing tariff barriers, both on a multilateral and on a regional basis.

The GATT and the WTO

One of the most notable achievements of the post-World War II era was the creation of the General Agreement on Tariffs and Trade (GATT). The GATT has since been replaced by the World Trade Organization (WTO). The principle of the GATT was that each member country agreed not to make unilateral tariff increases. This prevented the outbreak of "tariff wars" in which countries raised tariffs to protect particular domestic industries and to retaliate against other countries' tariff increases.

The Uruguay Round—the final round of trade agreements under GATT—was completed in 1994 after years of negotiations. It reduced world tariffs by about 40 percent. But a significant failure of these talks was not getting a major liberalization of trade in agricultural goods. Such an agreement was resisted by the EU and Canada. The EU has a scheme called the Common Agricultural Policy (CAP) that provides general support for most of its agricultural products, many of which are exported. The EU's position as a subsidized net exporter causes major harm to agricultural producers in developing countries whose governments are too poor to compete with the EU in a subsidy war.

Canada, which has free trade in many agricultural commodities, was concerned to maintain its supply management over a number of industries including poultry, eggs, and dairy products. These schemes are administered by the provinces who restrict domestic production and thus push domestic prices well above world levels. The federal government made them possible by imposing quotas on imports of these products at the national level.

Canada, the EU, and a number of other countries that lavishly protect some or all of their domestic agricultural producers were finally forced to agree to a plan to end all import quotas on agricultural products. In a process called "tariffication," these quotas have been replaced by "tariff equivalents"—tariffs that restrict trade by the same amount as the quotas did. Canadian tariff equivalents are as high as several hundred percent in some products, showing just how restrictive the Canadian policy is. The hope among countries that are pushing for freer trade in agricultural commodities is that pressure will build to reduce these very high tariffs over the next few decades.

Despite the failure to achieve free trade in agricultural products, the Uruguay Round is generally viewed as a success. Perhaps its most significant achievement was the creation of the World Trade Organization (WTO) to replace the GATT. An important part of the WTO is its formal dispute-settlement mechanism. This mechanism allows countries to take cases of alleged trade violations—such as illegal subsidies or tariffs—to the WTO for a formal ruling, and also obliges member countries to follow the ruling. The WTO's dispute-settlement mechanism is thus a significant step toward a "rules based" global trading system.

The WTO, however, does have its opponents. In December 1999, trade ministers from the WTO member countries met in Seattle to set the agenda for a proposed new round of trade talks. (Not surprisingly, there were difficulties establishing the agenda—not least were the familiar problems in dealing with subsidies to agriculture.) The Seattle meetings were delayed and interrupted by massive protests from environmental and labour groups, among others, who argued that the WTO's process of negotiating trade agreements pays insufficient attention to environmental and labour standards, especially in the developing countries. Many WTO officials and trade ministers, including those from the developing countries, recognized the importance of environmental and labour issues but questioned the wisdom of formally including these concerns in trade agreements. Reaching agreement on trade issues among the 134 member countries of the WTO is difficult enough—it would be almost impossible if the issues were bundled with the even more contentious environmental and labour issues. The result would be an overall agreement that achieved very little in terms of either trade liberalization, environmental protection, or establishing labour standards. Instead, many trade officials argued that the existing International Labour Organization should be strengthened and a separate international organization like the WTO should be created to promote environmental issues. These organizations could then push ahead to achieve in their respective domains the same success that the GATT achieved over fifty years of negotiations.

For further progress to be made on trade liberalization, environmental and labour issues will probably have to be addressed. Either domestic political pressures will push individual member countries to insist that these issues be included within the WTO negotiations, or other organizations like the WTO will be developed and/or strengthened to address the concerns. Whatever approach is followed, it appears that these will surely continue to be hot policy issues into the 21st century.

Despite the obstacles, many economists and policy makers now see multilateral free trade in goods and services as an attainable goal. After notable success in liberalizing trade in goods and services, attention in recent years has swung toward accomplishing the same thing for foreign direct investment (FDI). *Applying Economic Concepts 35-1* discusses the attempt to negotiate a Multilateral Agreement on Investment (MAI), and the political difficulties that were encountered along the way.

For more information on the WTO, see its website at www.wto.org.

Regional Trade Agreements

Regional agreements seek to liberalize trade over a much smaller group of countries than the WTO membership. Three standard forms of regional trade-liberalizing agreements are *free trade areas, customs unions,* and *common markets.*

A **free trade area (FTA)** is the least comprehensive of the three. It allows for tariff-free trade among the member countries, but it leaves each member free to levy its own trade policy with respect to other countries. As a result, members must maintain customs points at their common borders to make sure that imports into the free trade area do not all enter through the member that is levying the lowest tariff on each item. They must also agree on *rules of origin* to establish when a good is made in a member country and hence is able to pass tariff-free across their borders and when it is imported from outside the FTA and hence is subject to tariffs when it crosses borders within the FTA.

free trade area (FTA) An agreement among two or more countries to abolish tariffs on all or most of the trade among themselves while each remains free to set its own tariffs against other countries.

APPLYING ECONOMIC CONCEPTS 35-1
The Multilateral Agreement on Investment

The view that free flows of foreign direct investment (FDI) are necessary to the efficient functioning of the world economy led governments of many developed countries to seek international rules on the treatment of foreign investment. In the absence of such rules, firms and investors face a great deal of uncertainty about how their foreign-located assets will be treated by the government in the host country, especially in regard to expropriation and discriminatory taxation. This kind of uncertainty leads firms to invest less than they otherwise would, thereby reducing the benefits that would otherwise accrue to both host and source countries.

Under the auspices of the Organization for Economic Cooperation and Development (OECD), Canada joined other countries in negotiations toward a Multilateral Agreement on Investment, popularly known as the MAI. The underlying principle of the MAI is that signatory governments would commit themselves to treat foreign-owned firms no differently from domestically owned firms. The proposed MAI also includes a mechanism for the settlement of disputes caused by alleged violations of the agreement.

By early in 1998, the MAI negotiations had stalled for two main reasons. First, many countries (including Canada and France) pushed strongly for some industries to be exempt from the agreement. These countries wanted the ability to discriminate against foreign firms in politically sensitive "cultural" industries, such as publishing and broadcasting. Many other countries argued that such exemptions defeat the purpose of the agreement and were reluctant to grant them. Further, exemptions greatly increase the complexity of the agreement, in part because it

becomes necessary to provide a precise industrial classification for every unit of foreign investment.

The second and probably more important difficulty encountered by the MAI was that many interest groups around the world began expressing their concerns about the MAI's impact on environmental standards and social programs. Environmental lobby groups argued that the MAI would weaken any country's ability to set environmental standards different from those of its trading partners. Grassroots citizens' movements expressed their concerns about a country's ability to continue providing generous social programs. Though these criticisms received considerable attention in the popular press, a careful examination of the proposed MAI suggests that many of the criticisms are baseless.

The text of the proposed MAI clearly specifies that a country party to the agreement is not restricted in its design and implementation of policies, provided the policies treat foreign and domestic firms equally. If Canada, for example, wished to toughen its environmental standards by requiring firms to install better scrubbers in smokestacks, this policy would not contravene the MAI as long as the new policy applied equally to foreign-owned and domestically owned firms.

By the summer of 1998, the member countries of the OECD decided to delay further negotiations of the MAI. But failure in this set of negotiations will not make the issue go away. With over $300 billion of FDI flowing *annually* between many countries of the world, foreign investment has become too important to be ignored. A widespread set of rules for FDI is surely in our future.

---

customs union
A group of countries who agree to have free trade among themselves and a common set of barriers against imports from the rest of the world.

A **customs union** is a free trade area in which the member countries agree to establish a common trade policy with the rest of the world. Because they have a common trade policy, the members need neither customs controls on goods moving among themselves nor rules of origin. Once a good has entered any member country it has met the common rules and regulations and paid the common tariff and so it may henceforth be treated the same as a good that is produced within the union. An example of a customs union is Mercosur, an agreement linking Argentina, Brazil, Paraguay, and Uruguay.

common market
A customs union with the added provision that factors of production can move freely among the members.

A **common market** is a customs union that also has free movement of labour and capital among its members. The European Union is by far the most successful example of a common market. Indeed, the EU is now moving toward a full *economic union* in which all economic policies in the member countries are harmonized. The adoption of the euro as the common currency of 11 EU countries in 1999 was a significant step in this direction.

Trade Creation and Trade Diversion

A major effect of regional trade liberalization is to reallocate resources. Economists divide these effects into two categories, *trade creation* and *trade diversion*. These concepts were first developed by Jacob Viner, a Canadian-born economist who taught at the University of Chicago and Princeton University and was a leading economic theorist in the first half of the 20th century.

Trade creation occurs when producers in one member country find that they can export to another member country as a result of the elimination of the tariffs. For example, when the North American Free Trade Agreement (NAFTA) eliminated most cross-border tariffs between Mexico, Canada, and the United States, some U.S. firms found that they could undersell their Canadian competitors in some product lines, and some Canadian firms found that they could undersell their U.S. competitors in other product lines. As a result, specialization occurred, and new international trade developed. This trade, which is based on (natural or acquired) comparative advantage, is illustrated in Table 35-1.

Trade creation represents efficient specialization according to comparative advantage.

Trade diversion occurs when exporters in one member country replace foreign exporters as suppliers to another member country. For example, trade diversion occurs when U.S. firms find that they can undersell competitors from the rest of the world in the Canadian market, not because they are the cheapest source of supply, but because their tariff-free prices under NAFTA are lower than the tariff-burdened prices of imports from other countries. This effect is a gain to U.S. firms and Canadian consumers of the product but a loss to Canada overall, which now has to export more goods for any given amount of imports than before the trade diversion occurred. Table 35-1 also illustrates trade diversion.

From the global perspective, trade diversion represents an inefficient use of resources.

The History of Free Trade Areas

The first important free trade area in the modern era was the European Free Trade Association (EFTA). It was formed in 1960 by a group of European countries that were unwilling to join the European Common Market (the forerunner of the European Union) because of its all-embracing character. Not wanting to be left out of the gains from trade, they formed an association whose sole purpose was tariff removal. First, they removed all tariffs on trade among themselves. Then each country signed a free-trade-area agreement with the EU. This made the EU-EFTA market the largest tariff-free market in the world (over 300 million people). In recent years almost all of the EFTA countries have entered the EU.

In 1989, a sweeping agreement between Canada and the United States instituted free trade on almost

trade creation
A consequence of reduced trade barriers among a set of countries whereby trade within the group is increased and trade with the rest of the world remains roughly constant.

trade diversion
A consequence of reduced trade barriers among a set of countries whereby trade within the group replaces trade that used to take place with countries outside the group.

TABLE 35-1 Trade Creation and Trade Diversion

Producing Country	Canadian Delivered Price Without Tariffs (dollars)	Canadian Delivered Price with a 10 Percent Tariff (dollars)
Trade creation		
Canada	40.00	40.00
United States	37.00	40.70
Trade diversion		
Taiwan	20.00	22.00
United States	21.50	23.65

Regional tariff reductions can cause trade creation and trade diversion. The table gives two cases. In the first case, a U.S. good, which could be sold for $37.00 in Canada, has its price increased to $40.70 by a 10 percent Canadian tariff. The Canadian industry, which can sell the good for $40.00 with or without a tariff on imports, is protected against the more efficient U.S. producer. When the tariff is removed by the NAFTA, the U.S. good wins the market by selling at $37.00. Trade is created between Canada and the United States by eliminating the inefficient Canadian production.

In the second case, Taiwan can undersell the U.S. in the Canadian market for another product when neither is subject to a tariff (column 1) and when both are subject to a 10 percent tariff (column 2). But after the NAFTA, the U.S. good enters Canada tariff-free and sells for $21.50, whereas the Taiwanese good, which is still subject to the Canadian tariff, continues to sell for $22.00. The U.S. good wins the market, and Canadian trade is diverted from Taiwan to the U.S. even though Taiwan is the lower-cost supplier (excluding the tariff).

all goods and most nongovernment services and covered what is the world's largest flow of international trade between any two countries. In 1994, this agreement was extended into the North American Free Trade Agreement (NAFTA) by renegotiating the Canada-U.S. agreement to include Mexico. Provision is made within the NAFTA for the accession of other countries with the hope that it may eventually evolve into an agreement linking all countries of the western hemisphere.

The possible expansion of NAFTA is being examined. Indeed, the first accession was to have been Chile. But the negotiations for its entry into NAFTA were held up by domestic political considerations in the United States. The first few years of the 21st century may well see a significant push for expansion of NAFTA.

Australia and New Zealand have also entered into an association that removes restrictions on trade in goods and services between their two countries. The countries of Latin America have been experimenting with free trade areas for many decades. Most earlier attempts failed but, in the past few years, more durable FTAs seem to have been formed, the most successful of which is Mercosur, which includes Argentina, Brazil, Uruguay, and Paraguay. Whether these will remain stand-alone agreements or evolve into a broader continental agreement remains to be seen.

In early 1998, the negotiations for the Free Trade Area of the Americas (FTAA) were formally launched in Santiago, Chile. These negotiations will take many years and will involve discussions of rules of origin, environmental concerns, the treatment of foreign direct investment, agricultural policy, and how best to integrate the many regional agreements into a single comprehensive agreement. Only time will reveal the eventual outcome of these negotiations.

The North American Free Trade Agreement

The NAFTA is an extension of the 1989 Canada-U.S. Free Trade Agreement (FTA) with some important improvements based on the experience of the earlier agreement. It is a free trade area and not a customs union; each country retains its own external trade policy, and rules of origin are needed to determine when a good is made within the NAFTA and thus allowed to move freely among the members.

National Treatment

The fundamental principle that guides the NAFTA is the principle of *national treatment*. The principle of national treatment means that countries are free to establish any laws they wish and that these can differ as much as desired among member countries, with the sole proviso that these laws must not discriminate on the basis of nationality. Canada can have tough environmental laws or standards for particular goods, but it must enforce these equally on Canadian, Mexican, and U.S. firms and on domestically produced and imported goods. The idea of national treatment is to allow a maximum of policy independence while preventing national policies from being used as barriers to trade and investment.

Other Major Provisions

There are several other major provisions in NAFTA. First, all tariffs on trade between the United States and Canada were eliminated by 1999. Canada-Mexico and Mexico-U.S. tariffs are to be phased out over a 15-year period that started in 1994. Also, a number of nontariff barriers are eliminated or circumscribed.

Second, the agreement guarantees national treatment to foreign investment once it enters a country while permitting each country to screen a substantial amount of inbound foreign investment before it enters.

Third, all existing measures that restrict trade and investment that are not explicitly removed by the agreement are "grandfathered," a term referring to the continuation of a practice that predates the agreement and would have been prohibited by the terms of the agreement were it not specifically exempted. This is probably the single most important departure from free trade under the NAFTA. Under it, a large collection of restrictive measures in each of the three countries are given indefinite life. An alternative would have been to "sunset" all of these provisions by negotiating dates at which each would be eliminated. From the point of view of long-term trade liberalization, even a 50-year extension would have been preferable to an indefinite exemption.

Fourth, a few goods remain subject to serious nontariff trade restrictions. In Canada, the main examples are supply-managed agricultural products, beer, textiles, and the cultural industries. Restrictions for the Canadian supply-managed agricultural products may be short-lived because of their tariffication under the Uruguay round of GATT. Textile restriction in both the United States and Canada comes under the Multifiber Agreement, which is being phased out over a 15-year period under the Uruguay round. In the United States, textiles, shipping between U.S. ports, and banking were shielded from free trade in good and services.

APPLYING ECONOMIC CONCEPTS 35-2

Canadian Wine: A Free-Trade Success Story

Before the Canada-U.S. FTA was signed in 1989, great fears were expressed over the fate of the Canadian wine industry, located mainly in Ontario and British Columbia. It was heavily tariff protected and, with a few notable exceptions, concentrated mainly on cheap, low-quality products. Contrary to most people's expectations, rather than being decimated, the industry now produces a wide variety of high-quality products, some of which have won international competitions in Europe.

Why did this surprising result occur? The high Canadian tariff was levied on a per unit rather than on an *ad valorem* basis. For example, the tariff was expressed as so many dollars per litre rather than as a specific percentage of the price. Charging a tariff by the litre gave most protection to the low quality wines with low value per litre. The higher the per-litre value of the wine, the lower the percentage tariff protection. For example, a $5-per-litre tariff would have the following effects. A low-quality imported wine valued at $5 per litre would have its price raised to $10, a 100 percent increase in price, whereas a higher quality imported wine valued at $25 per litre would have its price increased to $30, only a 20 percent increase in price.

Responding to these incentives, the Canadian industry concentrated on low-quality wines. The market for these wines was protected by the nearly prohibitive tariffs on competing low-quality imports, and also by the high prices charged for high-quality imports. In addition, protection was provided by many hidden charges that the various provincial governments' liquor monopolies levied in order to protect local producers.

When the tariff was removed, the incentives were to move up-market, producing much more value per acre of land. Fortunately, much of the Canadian wine-growing land in the Okanagan Valley in BC and the Niagara Peninsula in Ontario is well-suited for growing the grapes required for good wines. Within a very few years, and with some government transitional assistance, Canadian wines were competing effectively with imported products in the medium-quality range. BC and Ontario wines do not yet reach the quality of major French wines in the $40-$70 (per bottle) range but they compete very effectively in quality with wines in the $10-$25 range, and sometimes even higher up the quality scale.

The success of the wine industry is a fine example of how tariffs can distort incentives and push an industry into a structure that makes it dependent on the tariff. Looking at the pre-FTA industry, very few people suspected that it would be able to survive, let alone produce a world-class product.

APPLYING ECONOMIC CONCEPTS 35-3

Headline Trade Disputes Between Canada and the United States

The flow of goods and services across the Canada-U.S. border is the largest flow of trade between any two countries. In 1998, approximately $500 billion worth of goods and services crossed this border. Although more than 95 percent of this trade passes between the two countries without dispute or hindrance, some items have been beset by persistent disputes. Here is a brief discussion of three of the most contentious areas in U.S.-Canadian trade.

Softwood Lumber

Canada exports large amounts of softwood lumber to the United States. And U.S. producers have persistently claimed that Canadian provincial government policies provide a concealed subsidy that should be evened out with a countervailing duty. The main bone of contention is *stumpage*, which is the royalty that governments charge the logging companies for cutting timber on government-owned land. In the United States, stumpage fees are set by open auction. In Canada, the fees are set in private negotiations between logging companies and the government. U.S. critics argue that the much lower Canadian stumpage fees that emerge from this negotiation process are a subsidy from the government to the lumber industry. Canadians argue that the higher U.S.

stumpage fees reflect the higher services that U.S. governments provide for their lumber companies by way of infrastructure that Canadian lumber companies must provide for themselves.

Just before the Canada-U.S. FTA was finalized, the Canadian government imposed an export tax on lumber going to the United States, to forestall the imposition of a U.S. countervailing duty. When this tax expired, Canada did not renew it and the United States imposed a countervailing duty. Two dispute-settlement panels found in Canada's favour, but largely on the grounds of narrow technicalities. The United States then changed its laws to remove what they saw as the loopholes that the Canadians had used. In 1996, the Canada-U.S. Softwood Lumber Agreement was signed. This agreement restricts the volume of duty-free exports of Canadian softwood lumber to the United States until 2001, with the Canadian government imposing export taxes on any exports that exceed the limit.

Supply-Managed Agricultural Industries

Several of the Canadian provinces use supply-management systems to support farm incomes. Such systems typically involve issuing quotas to farmers to restrict output. The result

---

For information about NAFTA, go to the website for the NAFTA Secretariat: www.nafta-sec-alena.org.

Fifth, trade in most nongovernmental services is liberalized by giving service firms the right of establishment in all member countries and the privilege of national treatment. There is also a limited opening of the markets in financial services to entry from firms based in the NAFTA countries.

Finally, a significant minority of government procurement is opened to cross-border bids.

Dispute Settlement

From Canada's point of view, by far the biggest setback in the negotiations for the Canada-U.S. FTA was the failure to obtain agreement on a common regime for countervailing and antidumping duties. In view of that failure, no significant attempt was made to deal with this issue in the NAFTA negotiations. The U.S. Congress has been unwilling to abandon the unilateral use of these powerful weapons.

In the absence of such a multilateral regime, a dispute-settlement mechanism was put in place. Under it, the domestic determinations that are required for the levying of antidumping and countervailing duties are subject to review by a panel of Canadians, Americans, and Mexicans. This international review replaces appeal through the domestic courts. Panels are empowered to uphold the domestic determinations or refer the decision to the domestic authority—which in effect is a binding order for a new in-of such quotas is to substantially raise the prices paid by Canadian consumers. For years, the Canadian government had supported these policies by imposing import quotas on the managed products, without which their prices would be driven down to world levels. The Canadian government successfully negotiated exemptions for these quotas under the Canada-U.S. FTA. In the Uruguay round of GATT negotiations, despite spirited resistance, the Canadian government was forced to agree to "tariffication" of these quotas. The United States then took the position that although the quotas had been exempt under the FTA, their tariff equivalents were not. After all, the U.S. argued, all tariffs without exception are to be removed by 1999 under the FTA. At the time of writing, the debate continues without an obvious resolution.

Cultural Industries

Canada has always sought to support its magazines, book sellers, film distributors, and other cultural industries from U.S. competition. Although there was never any pressure to prevent governments on both sides of the border from subsidizing the performing arts, such as music and drama, protection of the cultural industries more widely defined was a serious bone of contention during the FTA negotiations. In the end, Canada got exemption for all of its broadly defined cultural industries.

In the mid 1990s, the Canadian government became concerned over the presence of Canadian editions of U.S. split-run magazines. These magazines, such as *Time* and *Sports Illustrated*, contain mostly U.S. content but also include a few pages of Canadian editorial content. Because the fixed costs of the magazine are covered by the U.S. sales of the magazine, the Canadian advertising rates can be lower than those of Canadian-based magazines. The Canadian government and Canadian magazine publishers argued that the presence of such split-run magazines would make it more difficult for Canadian magazines to sell advertising space, thus putting them in an untenable financial position. Failure of Canadian magazines would then damage an important part of Canadian culture. In 1995, the Canadian government imposed an 80 percent tax on advertising expenditures in the Canadian editions of U.S. split-run magazines.

The U.S. government and U.S. magazine publishers argued that the Canadian government's attempts to protect Canadian culture by protecting their magazines were nothing more than simple trade protection. On this basis, they saw no difference between aid to Canadian magazines and aid to textiles firms or the aerospace industry. The United States brought their complaint to the World Trade Organization and, in 1997, the WTO ruled against Canada—that is, it ruled that Canada's tax on split-run advertising contravened international trade agreements.

The Canadian government then attempted to write new legislation that would be consistent with WTO rules but would still have the effect of preventing the U.S. split-run magazines. This prompted the United States to threaten the imposition of duties on a whole range of Canadian exports if the Canadian government did not drop its attempts to prevent the split-runs. Finally, in 1999, the Canadian and U.S. governments reached an agreement to provide limited access to the Canadian market for the U.S.-based split-run magazines.

vestigation. The referral can be repeated until the panel is satisfied that the domestic laws have been correctly and fairly applied.

This is pathbreaking: For the first time in its history, the United States has agreed to submit the administration of its domestic laws to *binding* scrutiny by an international panel that often contains a majority of foreigners.

Results

The Canada-U.S. FTA aroused a great debate in Canada. Indeed, the Canadian federal election of 1988 was fought almost entirely on the issue of free trade. Supporters looked for major increases in the security of existing trade from U.S. protectionist attacks and for a growth of new trade. Detractors predicted a flight of firms to the U.S., the loss of Canadian competitiveness, and even the loss of Canada's political independence.

By and large, however, both the Canada-U.S. FTA and NAFTA agreements have worked out just about as expected by their supporters. Industry has clearly restructured in the direction of greater export orientation in all three countries, and trade creation has occurred. All three countries are importing more from and exporting more to each other. This trend is particularly true between Canada and the United States. As the theory of trade predicts, specialization has occurred in many areas, resulting in more U.S. imports of some product lines from Canada and more U.S. exports of other

See Chapter 35 of www.pearsoned.ca/lipsey for an interesting discussion of the results of FTA and NAFTA: Richard Lipsey, "Free Trade—Real Results Versus Unreal Expectations," *World Economic Affairs*.

See Chapter 35 of www.pearsoned.ca/lipsey for an interview with former Prime Minister Brian Mulroney on the political aspects of FTA and NAFTA: "Standing Firm on Free Trade," *World Economic Affairs*.

See the website for the Department of Foreign Affairs and International Trade for information on the dispute-settlement mechanism: www.dfait-maeic.gc.ca.

goods to Canada. In 1988, before the Canada-U.S. FTA took effect, Canada exported $85 billion in goods and services to the United States, and imported $74 billion from the United States. By 1998, the value of Canada-U.S. trade had almost quadrupled—Canadian exports to the United States had increased to $271 billion and imports from the United States had increased to $234 billion.

It is hard to say how much trade diversion there has been and will be in the future. The greatest potential for trade diversion is with Mexico, which competes in the U.S. and Canadian markets with a large number of products produced in other low-wage countries. South-East Asian exporters to the United States and Canada have been worried that Mexico would capture some of their markets by virtue of having tariff-free access denied to their goods. Most estimates predict, however, that trade creation will dominate over trade diversion.

Most transitional difficulties were initially felt in each country's import-competing industries, just as theory predicts. An agreement such as the NAFTA brings its advantages by encouraging a movement of resources out of protected but inefficient import-competing industries, which decline, and into efficient export industries, which expand because they have better access to the markets of other member countries. Southern Ontario and parts of Quebec had major problems as some traditional exports fell and resources had to be moved to sectors where trade was expanding. Eight years after the agreement, however, southern Ontario was booming again and its most profitable sectors were those that exported to the United States.

There were also some pleasant surprises resulting from free trade. Two Canadian industries that many economists expected to suffer from the FTA and NAFTA were wine-making and textiles. Yet both of these industries have prospered as Canadian firms have improved quality, productivity, and benefited from increased access to the huge U.S. market. *Applying Economic Concepts 35-2* discusses the success of the Canadian wine industry after the tariffs on wine were eliminated.

Finally, the dispute-settlement mechanism seems to have worked well. A large number of disputes have arisen and have been referred to panels. Panel members have usually reacted as professionals rather than as nationals. Most cases have been decided on their merits; allegations that decisions were reached on national rather than professional grounds have been rare.

With over $500 billion annually in two-way trade between Canada and the United States, however, it is inevitable that some disputes arise. *Applying Economic Concepts 35-3* discusses three of the most contentious trade disputes that still disturb the generally tranquil state of Canada-U.S. trade.

S U M M A R Y

Free Trade or Protection?   ⑩❶❷

- The case for free trade is that world output of all products can be higher under free trade than when protectionism restricts regional specialization.
- Protection for an individual country can be urged as a means to ends other than maximizing that country's living standards. Examples of such ends are to produce a

diversified economy, to reduce fluctuations in national income and to retain distinctive national traditions.
- Protection can also be urged on the grounds that it may lead to higher living standards for the protectionist country than would a policy of free trade. Such a result might come about by using a monopoly position to influence

the terms of trade or by developing a dynamic comparative advantage by allowing inexperienced or uneconomically small industries to become efficient enough to compete with foreign industries.

- Some fallacious protectionist arguments are that (a) mutually advantageous trade is impossible because one trader's gain must always be the other's loss; (b) buying abroad sends our money abroad, while buying at home keeps our money at home; (c) our high-paid workers must be protected against the competition from low-paid foreign workers; and (d) imports are to be discouraged because they lower national income and cause unemployment.

Methods of Protection   (LO)③④

- Trade can be restricted by policies that either directly raise prices, such as tariffs, or operate in the first instance on quantities, such as import quotas and voluntary export restrictions.
- As tariff barriers have been reduced over the years, they have been replaced in part by nontariff barriers. The two most important are antidumping and countervailing duties which, although providing legitimate restraints on unfair trading practices, are also used as serious nontariff barriers to trade.

Current Trade Policy   (LO)⑤⑥

- The General Agreement on Tariffs and Trade (GATT), under which countries agree to reduce trade barriers through multilateral negotiations and not to raise them unilaterally, has greatly reduced world tariffs since its inception in 1947.
- The World Trade Organization (WTO) was created in 1995 as the successor to GATT. It has 134 member countries and contains a formal dispute-settlement mechanism.
- Regional trade-liberalizing agreements such as free trade areas and common markets bring efficiency gains through trade creation and efficiency losses through trade diversion.

- The North American Free Trade Agreement (NAFTA) is the world's largest and most successful free trade area, and the European Union is the world's largest and most successful common market.
- NAFTA is based on the principle of "national treatment". This allows Canada, the United States, and Mexico to implement whatever social, economic, or environmental policies it chooses providing that such policies treat foreign and domestic firms (and their products) equally.

KEY CONCEPTS

Free trade and protectionism
Tariffs and import quotas
Voluntary export restrictions (VERs)
Countervailing and antidumping duties

The General Agreement on Tariffs and Trade (GATT)
The World Trade Organization (WTO)
Common markets, customs unions, and free trade areas

Trade creation and trade diversion
Nontariff barriers
The North American Free Trade Agreement (NAFTA)

STUDY EXERCISES

1. Canada produces steel domestically and also imports it from abroad. Assume that the world market for steel is competitive and that Canada is a small producer, unable to affect the world price. Since Canada imports steel, we know that in the absence of trade, the Canadian equilibrium price would exceed the world price.

    a. Draw a diagram showing the Canadian market for steel, with imports at the world price.
    b. Explain why the imposition of a tariff on imported steel will increase the price of *both* domestic and imported steel.
    c. Show the effects of such a tariff in the diagram.
    d. Who benefits and who is harmed by such a tariff?

2. The diagram below shows the Canadian market for leather shoes, which we assume to be competitive. The world price is p_w. If the Canadian government imposes a tariff of t dollars per unit, the domestic price then rises to $p_w + t$.

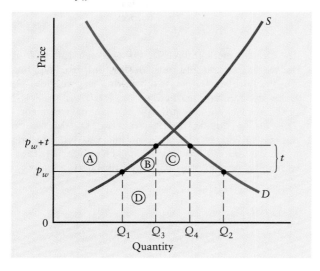

    a. What quantity of leather shoes is imported before the tariff is imposed? After the tariff?
    b. What is the effect of the tariff on the Canadian production of shoes? Which areas in the diagram show the increase in domestic producers' revenue?
    c. With the tariff in place, Canadian shoe producers are earning higher revenues. Which areas in the diagram show how much of this increased revenue is attributed to the higher price paid by Canadian consumers?
    d. The Canadian government earns tariff revenue on the imported shoes. Which area in the diagram shows this tariff revenue?

3. Use the diagram from Question 2 to analyse the effects of imposing an import quota instead of a tariff to protect domestic shoe producers. Draw the diagram as in Question 2 and answer the following questions.

    a. Explain why an import quota of Q_3Q_4 raises the domestic price to $p_w + t$.
    b. With import quotas, the Canadian government earns no tariff revenue. Who gets this money now?
    c. Is the import quota better or worse than the tariff for Canada as a whole? Explain.

4. Under pressure from the Canadian and U.S. governments in the early 1980s, Japanese automobile producers agreed to restrict their exports to the North American market. After the formal agreement ended, the Japanese producers decided unilaterally to continue restricting their exports. Carefully review Figure 35-1 and then answer the following questions.

    a. Explain why such Voluntary Export Restrictions (VERs) are "voluntary."
    b. Explain why an agreement to export only 100 000 cars to North America is better for the Japanese producers than a North American tariff that results in the same volume of Japanese exports.
    c. Who is paying for these benefits to the Japanese producers?

5. Go to Statistics Canada's website: www.statcan.ca. Find the data on "the economy" and then on "international trade," and answer the following questions.

    a. For the most recent year shown, what was the value of Canada's exports to the United States? To the European Union?
    b. For the same year, what was the value of Canada's imports from the United States? From the European Union?
    c. Compute what economists call the "volume of trade" (the sum of exports and imports) between Canada and the United States. How has the volume of trade grown over the past five years? Has trade grown faster than national income?

6. The table below shows the prices *in Canada* of cotton towels produced in the United States, Canada, and Malaysia. All cotton towels are identical.

Producing Country	Canadian Price (in $) without tariff	Canadian Price (in $) with 20% tariff
Canada	4.75	4.75
United States	4.50	5.40
Malaysia	4.00	4.80

a. Suppose Canada imposes a 20 percent tariff on imported towels from any country. Assuming that Canadians purchase only the lowest-price towels, from which country will Canada buy its towels?

b. Now suppose that Canada eliminates tariffs on towels from all countries. Which towels will Canada now buy?

c. Canada and the United States now negotiate a free-trade agreement that eliminates all tariffs between the two countries, but Canada maintains the 20 percent tariff on other countries. Which towels now get imported into Canada?

d. Which of the situations described above is called trade creation and which is called trade diversion?

DISCUSSION QUESTIONS

1. Some Canadians opposed Canada's entry into NAFTA on the grounds that Canadian firms could not compete with the goods produced by cheap Mexican labour. Comment on the following points in relation to the above worries:

   a. "Mexicans are the most expensive cheap labour I have ever encountered"—statement by the owner of a Canadian firm who is moving back from Mexico to Canada.

   b. The theory of the gains from trade says that a high-productivity, high-wage country can gain from trading with a low-wage, low-productivity country.

   c. Technological change is rapidly reducing labour costs as a proportion of total costs in many products; in many industries that use high-tech production methods this proportion is already well below 20 percent.

2. Should Canada and the United States trade with countries with poor human rights records? If trade with China is severely restricted because of its lack of respect for human rights, who will be the gainers and who the losers? Argue the cases that this policy will help, and that it will hinder, human rights progress in China.

3. Import quotas and voluntary export restrictions are often used instead of tariffs. What real difference, if any, is there between quotas, voluntary export restrictions (VERs), and tariffs? Explain why lobbyists for some import-competing industries (cheese, milk, shoes) support import quotas while lobbyists for others (pizza manufacturers, soft drink manufacturers, retail stores) oppose them. Would you expect labour unions to support or oppose quotas?

4. Over the past several years, many foreign automobile producers have built production and assembly facilities in Canada and in the United States. What are some advantages and disadvantages associated with shifting production from, for example, Japan to Canada? Will these cars still be considered "imports"? What is beginning to happen to the definitions of "foreign made" and "domestic made"?

5. Consider a mythical country called Forestland, which exports a large amount of lumber to a nearby country called Houseland. The lumber industry in Houseland has convinced its federal government that it is being harmed by the low prices being charged by the lumber producers in Forestland. You are an advisor to the government in Forestland. Explain who gains and who loses from each of the following policies.

   a. Houseland imposes a tariff on lumber imports from Forestland

   b. Forestland imposes a tax on each unit of lumber exported to Houseland

   c. Forestland agrees to restrict its exports of lumber to Houseland

   d. Which policy is likely to garner the most political support in Houseland? In Forestland?

6. In March 1999, the Canadian government imposed antidumping duties of up to 43 percent on hot-rolled steel imports from France, Russia, Slovakia, and Romania. The allegation was that these countries were dumping steel into the Canadian market.

   a. Who benefits from such alleged dumping? Who is harmed?

   b. Who benefits from the imposition of the antidumping duties? Who is harmed?

   c. Is Canada as a whole made better off by the imposition of the duties? Explain.

CHAPTER 36

Exchange Rates and the Balance of Payments

🔵 *LEARNING OBJECTIVES*

① Explain the various components of Canada's balance of payments.

② Understand why the balance of payments accounts always balance.

③ Understand the determinants of the demand for and the supply of foreign currency.

④ Explain the various factors that cause changes in the exchange rate.

⑤ Explain why a current account deficit is not necessarily undesirable.

⑥ Understand the theory of purchasing power parity, as well as its limitations.

⑦ Explain how flexible exchange rates can dampen the effects of terms-of-trade shocks on output and employment.

As we saw in Chapter 19, the external value of the Canadian dollar has fluctuated considerably over the past 25 years. It fell sharply between 1983 and 1988, and then increased until 1992 when it was back at the level of the early 1980s. Between 1992 and 1999, it fell again, by over 20 percent.

In this chapter, we ask what it means to speak of the "external value of the dollar," what causes this value to change, and the implications that such changes have for the economy. We examine the important difference between *flexible* and *fixed* exchange rates, and the Bank of Canada's role under each system. The discussion will bring together material on three topics studied elsewhere in this book: the theory of supply and demand (Chapter 3), the nature of money (Chapter 26), and international trade (Chapter 34).

We begin, however, by examining a country's balance of payments—the record of transactions in goods, services, and assets with the rest of the world. We examine what is meant by a balance of payments deficit or surplus, and what role the central bank plays in determining it.

balance-of-payments accounts A summary record of a country's transactions with the rest of the world, including the buying and selling of goods, services, and assets.

The Balance of Payments

To know what is happening to the course of international trade, government statistical agencies (like Statistics Canada) keep track of the transactions between countries. The record of such transactions is made in the **balance-of-payments accounts.** For computing Canada's balance of payments, each transaction, such as the exports or imports of

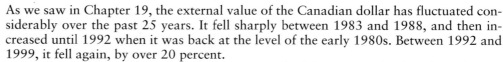

goods, or the purchase or sales of assets, is classified according to whether the transaction generates a *payment* or a *receipt* for Canada.

Table 36-1 shows the major items in the Canadian balance-of-payments accounts for 1998. Transactions that represent a receipt for Canada, such as the sale of a product or asset to foreigners, are recorded in the balance-of-payments accounts as a *credit* item. Transactions that represent a payment for Canada, such as the purchase of a product or asset from foreigners, are recorded as a *debit* item.

There are three main categories to the balance of payments: the *current account*, the *capital account*, and the *official financing account*. We examine each account in turn.

The Current Account

The **current account** records transactions arising from trade in goods and services. It also includes net investment income that residents of one country earn from assets issued to them by foreigners. The current account is divided into two main sections.

The first section, called either the **trade balance** or the *balance of trade*, records payments and receipts arising from the import and export of goods, such as computers and cars, and services, such as legal or architectural services. (Tourism constitutes a large part of the trade in services.) Canadian imports of goods and services require a payment to foreigners and thus are entered as debit items on the trade account; Canadian exports of goods and services generate a receipt to Canada and thus are recorded as credit items.

The second section, called **capital-service account**, records the payments and receipts that represent income on assets. When Canadians pay income to the foreign owners of Canadian-located assets, this requires a payment to foreigners and thus is entered as a debit item. Income Canadians receive that is earned from their assets located abroad is a receipt from foreigners and thus enters as a credit item.

As shown in Table 36-1, Canadian exports of goods and services were just under $370 billion in 1998, and Canadian imports of goods and services were just under $360 billion. The trade account had a surplus of $11 billion—in other words, in 1998 Canada sold $11 billion more worth of goods and services to the world than it bought from the world. But in terms of the capital-service account, things were the

TABLE 36-1   Canadian Balance of Payments, 1998 (billions of dollars)

CURRENT ACCOUNT	
Trade Account	
Merchandise exports	+323.4
Service exports	+43.7
Merchandise imports	−304.0
Service imports	−52.1
Trade balance	+11.0
Capital-Service Account	
Net investment income (including unilateral transfers)	−29.4
Current Account balance	−18.4
CAPITAL ACCOUNT	
Net change in Canadian investments abroad [capital outflow (−)]	−33.6
Net change in foreign investments in Canada [capital inflow (+)]	+52.1
Capital Account balance	+18.5
OFFICIAL FINANCING ACCOUNT	
Changes in reserves [increases (−)]	−7.4
Statistical Discrepancy	+7.3
Official Financing balance	−0.1
Balance of Payments	0.0

The overall balance of payments always balances, but the individual components do not have to. In 1998, Canada had an overall trade surplus (including trade in goods and services) of $11.0 billion. There was a deficit of $29.4 billion on the capital-service account. There was thus a $18.4 billion deficit on current account. There was also a surplus on the capital account because capital imports exceeded capital exports. The capital plus current account surplus is what is sometimes referred to as the balance of payments, and in 1998, there was an overall surplus of just $0.1 billion. This is exactly offset by the official financing balance plus the statistical discrepancy. The statistical discrepancy entry compensates for the inability to measure some items accurately.

(*Source: Bank of Canada Review,* Spring 1999.)

other way around. The table shows that Canadians paid $29.4 billion more to foreigners in investment income than they received from foreigners. The current account balance (the sum of the trade and capital-service accounts) thus had a deficit of $18.4 billion.

current account The part of the balance-of-payments accounts that records payments and receipts arising from trade in goods and services and from interest and dividends that are earned by capital owned in one country and invested in another.

trade balance The difference between the value of exports and the value of imports of goods and services.

capital-service account In the balance of payments, this account records the payments and receipts that represent income on assets (such as interest and dividends).

capital account The part of the balance-of-payments accounts that records payments and receipts arising from the import and export of long-term and short-term financial capital.

direct investment Nonresident investment in the form of a takeover or capital investment in a domestic branch plant or subsidiary corporation in which the investor has voting control. Also called foreign direct investment.

portfolio investment Foreign investment in bonds or a minority holding of shares that does not involve legal control.

The Capital Account

The second main division in the balance of payments is the **capital account,** which records international transactions in assets. The purchase of foreign assets by Canadians is treated just like the purchase of foreign goods. Since purchasing a foreign asset requires a payment from Canadians to foreigners, it is entered as a debit item in the Canadian capital account. Note that when Canadians purchase foreign assets, financial capital is leaving Canada and going abroad, and so this is called a *capital outflow.*

The sale of Canadian assets to foreigners is treated just like the sale of Canadian goods to foreigners. Since selling a Canadian asset abroad generates a receipt for Canada, it is entered as a credit item in the Canadian capital account. Note that when Canadians sell assets to foreigners, financial capital is entering Canada from abroad, and so this is called a *capital inflow.*

As shown in Table 36-1, in 1998, Canadians increased their holdings of assets abroad by $33.6 billion, resulting in a capital outflow of that amount. At the same time, foreigners increased their holdings of assets in Canada by $52.1 billion, resulting in a capital inflow of that amount. The net capital inflow resulted in a surplus in the capital account of $18.5 billion.

Though not shown in Table 36-1, the capital account is divided into direct investment and portfolio investment. **Direct investment** (also called *foreign direct investment*) relates to changes in foreign ownership of domestic firms and domestic ownership of foreign firms. One form of direct investment in Canada is capital investment in a branch plant or a subsidiary corporation in Canada in which the investor has voting control. Another form is a takeover, in which a controlling interest in a firm, previously controlled by residents, is acquired by foreigners. **Portfolio investment** is investment in bonds or a minority holding of shares that does not involve legal control.

The Official Financing Account

The final section in the balance of payments represents transactions in the official reserves that are held by the central bank and is called the *official financing account* or sometimes the *official settlements account.* The central banks of most countries, including Canada, hold financial reserves in the form of gold, foreign currencies, and bonds denominated in foreign currencies.

The Bank of Canada can intervene in the market for foreign currency to influence the Canadian dollar's exchange rate. For example, to prevent the external value of the dollar from falling, the Bank of Canada must purchase Canadian dollars and sell foreign currency. It can do so only if it holds reserves of foreign currency. When the Bank of Canada wishes to stop the value of the dollar from rising, it enters the market and sells dollars. In this case, the Bank purchases foreign currency, which it then adds to its reserves.

Since foreign currency is an asset for the Bank of Canada, it follows that when the Bank of Canada enters the foreign-exchange market to buy or sell foreign currency, it is simply buying or selling an asset. We deal with that transaction in the same way we deal with the other asset transactions in the capital account. Specifically, when the Bank purchases foreign currency (and sells Canadian dollars) this transaction represents the purchase of an asset from abroad, and thus it enters as a debit item in the balance of payments. Conversely, when the Bank sells foreign currency (and purchases Canadian dollars), this transaction represents the sale of an asset to foreigners, and thus it enters as a credit item in the balance of payments.

Table 36-1 shows that in 1998 the Bank of Canada *increased* its reserves of foreign exchange by $7.4 billion; it therefore purchased more foreign exchange during the year than it sold.

For balance of payments statistics for many countries, see the IMF's website: www.imf.org.

The Meaning of Payments Balances and Imbalances

We first examine why the overall balance of payments *always* balances. We then explore what is meant by the often-used terms "balance of payments deficit" or "balance of payments surplus."

The Balance of Payments Must Balance

The balance of payments accounts are based on the important idea of *double-entry bookkeeping*. Since any transaction involves something being sold and something being received, each transaction has two entries in the balance of payments. The value of the good or asset that is *sold* appears as a credit item in the balance of payments accounts. The value of the good or asset that is *received* in the transaction appears as a debit item in the balance of payments accounts. Since the dollar value of what is sold obviously equals the dollar value of what is received, these two entries clearly offset each other. Thus the balance of payments must always balance. In some cases, the different entries will appear on different accounts; in other cases both entries will appear on the same account. Some examples will help to illustrate how this works.

Suppose that a Canadian software company sells some computer software to a customer in Germany for $1 million. The sale of the software is an export of a good for Canada and thus enters as a credit item in Canada's current account. In return, the Canadian firm receives $1 million cash, which is clearly an asset. This is essentially a "purchase" of assets for Canada and appears as a debit item in Canada's capital account. Thus, as a result of this transaction, the $1 million credit on current account is offset by the $1 million debit on the capital account. The balance of payments, as always, is in balance.

Now consider a wealthy Canadian investor who sells a Canadian government bond to a Swiss citizen for $5 million. The sale of the bond appears as a credit item in Canada's capital account. In return, suppose that the Canadian investor receives the $5 million cash directly into his Swiss bank account. This is the accumulation of an asset for Canada and thus appears as a debit item in Canada's capital account. Thus, as a result of this transaction, the $5 million credit on capital account is offset by the $5 million debit on capital account. The current account is not affected by this transaction. And, as always, the balance of payments is in balance.

Double-entry bookkeeping in the balance of payments means that any transaction leads to both a credit item and an equal-value debit item. The balance of payments must therefore always balance.

This accounting result is important. It is not based on assumptions about behaviour or any other theoretical reasoning—it is an *accounting identity*. Many people nonetheless find the idea of double-entry bookkeeping confusing. *Applying Economic Concepts 36-1* discusses an individual student's balance of payments with the rest of the world, and illustrates why any individual's balance of payments must always balance.

The Relationships Among Various Balances

Two important implications follow directly from our observation that the overall payments must balance:

APPLYING ECONOMIC CONCEPTS 36-1

A Student's Balance of Payments with the Rest of the World

Many students find a country's balance of payments confusing, especially the idea that the balance of payments *must always* balance. Why, they often ask, can't Canada export more goods and services to the world than it imports, and at the same time have a net sale of assets to the rest of the world? The connection between the current-account transactions and the capital-account transactions is not always obvious.

Perhaps the easiest way to see this connection is to consider an individual's "balance of payments" with the rest of the world. Of course, most individuals would not normally compute their balance of payments, but by doing so we can recognize the everyday concepts involved and also see the necessary connection between any individual's "current account" and "capital account." The reason why Canada's balance of payments must always balance is exactly the same reason why an individual's balance of payments must always balance.

The table shows the balance of payments for Stefan, a university student. Stefan is fortunate in several respects. First, his parents are able to provide some of the funds needed to fi-

Stefan's Balance of Payments

Current Account (Income and Expenditure)	
Labour income ("exports")	+$10 000
Purchase of goods and services ("imports")	−$17 000
Interest income	+$ 500
Transfers (from his parents)	+$10 000
Current Account Balance	+ $3 500

Capital Account (Changes in Assets) (− denotes an increase)	
Financial Assets	
Purchase of Canada Savings Bonds	−$1 500
Change in Savings Account Deposits	−$2 000
Capital Account Balance	−$3 500
BALANCE OF PAYMENTS	$0

1. The terms *balance-of-payments deficit* and *balance-of-payments surplus* must refer to the balance on some part of the payments accounts. The terms make no sense if they are applied to the overall balance of payments.

2. A deficit on any one part of the accounts implies an offsetting surplus on the rest of the accounts.

We now consider two important applications of these statements. The first application concerns the balance on the official financing account and the combined balance on the current plus capital accounts; the second concerns the separate balances on current and capital accounts. Keep in mind that we use the word *overall* when referring to the balance of payments *including the official financing account.*

Official Financing and the Rest of the Accounts.   We know that the term "balance-of-payments deficit" does not strictly make sense since the balance of payments must always balance overall. But such a term is nonetheless often used in the

nance his education. Second, he has a summer job which pays well. Third, he was given some Canada Savings Bonds when he was born that provide him with some interest income every year.

The top part of the table shows Stefan's income and expenditures for a single year. This is his current account. The bottom part shows the change in Stefan's assets over the same year. This is his capital account. (Note that, for Stefan as well as for any country, the capital account does not show the overall stock of assets—it only shows the *changes* in the stock of assets during the year.)

Let's begin with his current account. Stefan has a good summer job that earns him $10 000 after taxes. This $10 000 represents Stefan's "exports" to the rest of the world—he earns this income by selling his labour services to a tree-planting company. Over the year, however, he spends $17 000 on tuition, books, clothes, beer, pizza, photocopying, and other goods and services. These are Stefan's "imports" from the rest of the world. Stefan clearly has a "trade deficit" equal to $7000—he "imports" more than he "exports."

There are two other sources of income shown in Stefan's current account. First, he earns $500 in interest income. Second, his parents give him $10 000 to help pay for his education—a *transfer* in the terminology of balance of payments accounting. The interest income and transfer together make up Stefan's "capital-service account"—Stefan has a surplus of $10 500.

Stefan's overall current account shows a surplus of $3500. This means he receives $3500 more in total income than he spends on goods and services. But where does this $3500 go?

Now let's consider Stefan's capital account, the bottom part of the table. The $3500 surplus on current account *must* end up as increases in Stefan's assets. He increases his holdings of Canada Savings Bonds by $1500 and increases his saving-account deposits by $2000. Note that since Stefan must make a "payment" to purchase these assets, they appear as a debit item in his capital account. Stefan's capital account balance is a deficit of $3500.

Finally, note that Stefan's current account and capital account *must* sum to zero. There is no way around this fact. Any surplus of income over expenditures (on current account) must show up as an increase in his assets (or a decrease in his debts) on capital account. Conversely, any excess of expenditures over income must be financed by reducing his assets (or by increasing his debts). Stefan's balance of payments *must* balance.

What is true for Stefan is true for any individual and also true for any accounting unit you choose to consider. Saskatoon's balance of payments with the rest of the world must balance. Saskatchewan's balance of payments with the rest of the world must balance. Western Canada's balance of payments with the rest of the world must balance. And so must Canada's, and any other country's.

press and even by some economists. What does this mean? Most often the term is used carelessly—a balance of payments deficit is mentioned when what is actually meant is a current account deficit. There are also occasions when people speak of a country as having a balance-of-payments deficit or surplus when they are actually referring to the balance of all accounts *excluding* official financing—that is, to the combined balance on current and capital accounts.

For example, consider a situation in which Canada has a current account deficit of $20 billion—Canada is buying $20 billion more in goods and services from the rest of the world than it is selling to the world. At the same time, suppose the capital account surplus is only $15 billion—Canada is selling $15 billion more in assets to the rest of the world than it is buying in return. In this case, some people would say that Canada has a "balance of payments deficit" of $5 billion. But what is really true is that the Bank of Canada, on the official financing account, is selling $5 billion of foreign currency reserves. The $5 billion surplus on the official financing account is exactly "financing" the "balance of payments deficit."

In the opposite situation, where the current account and capital account together are in surplus, some people would say there is a "balance of payments surplus." But the Bank of Canada is in this case purchasing foreign-currency reserves. The overall balance of payments balances.

A "balance of payments deficit" refers to a situation where the Bank of Canada is selling foreign currency. A "balance of payments surplus" refers to a situation where the Bank of Canada is buying foreign currency. In both cases, as always, the balance of payments is actually in balance.

What we have just said implies that the balance of payments can be in deficit or surplus *only if* the central bank changes its foreign-exchange reserves. If the central bank does not participate in the foreign-exchange market, however, its foreign currency reserves will be unchanged and so the official financing balance must be zero. In this case, there can be no deficit or surplus in the balance of payments.

The Current and Capital Account Balances.   Suppose that the Bank of Canada does not engage in any foreign-exchange transactions. The official financing account is thus zero. Now any deficit or surplus on the current account must be matched exactly by an equal and opposite surplus or deficit on the capital account.

For example, if Canada has a current account deficit of $10 billion, then there *must* be a capital account surplus of $10 billion. The intuition is straightforward. If Canada has a $10 billion deficit on current account, then it is importing more goods and services (including debt service) than it is exporting. But how does it finance these "extra" imports? Some individual or firm or government in Canada must sell some Canadian assets to (or borrow from) some individual or firm or government in the rest of the world—that is, Canada must have a capital account surplus.

Similarly, suppose Canada has a current account surplus of $10 billion, reflecting more earnings from exports than expenditures on imports. What does Canada do with the "extra" earnings? It must acquire some assets from the rest of the world—that is, Canada must have a capital account deficit.

If the central bank does not change its holdings of foreign-currency reserves, the current account and capital account must sum to zero.

This brings us to the end of our discussion of the balance of payments. Keep in mind that this is just an exercise in accounting. Though at times you may find it difficult to keep the various credits and debits in the various accounts straight in your mind, remember that the structure of the accounting system is quite simple. Here is a brief review:

1. The current account shows all transactions in goods and services between Canada and the rest of the world (including investment income and transfers).

2. The capital account shows all transactions in assets between Canada and the rest of the world.

3. The official financing account shows the change in the Bank of Canada's holding of foreign-currency reserves (including gold).

4. All transactions involving a payment from Canada appear as a debit item. All transactions involving a receipt to Canada appear as a credit item.

5. The balance of payments—the sum of the current account, capital account, and official financing account—must always be zero.

We now go on to explore how exchange rates are determined in the foreign-exchange market. We will see that a knowledge of the various categories in the balance of payments will help in our understanding of why changes in exchange rates occur.

The Bank of Canada holds millions of dollars worth of gold as part of its official reserves.

The Foreign-Exchange Market

Money is vital in any sophisticated economy that relies on specialization and trade. Yet money as we know it is a *national* matter. If you live in Argentina, you earn pesos and spend pesos; if you operate a business in Austria, you borrow schillings and pay your workers in schillings. The currency of a country is acceptable within the border of that country, but usually it will not be accepted by firms and households in another country. Just try buying your next pair of jeans in Canada with British pounds sterling or Japanese yen!

Trade between countries normally requires the exchange of the currency of one country for that of another.

The exchange of one currency for another is called a *foreign-exchange transaction*. The **exchange rate** is the rate at which one currency exchanges for another. In Canada's case, the exchange rate is the price of one unit of foreign currency in terms of Canadian dollars. Put another way, it is the Canadian-dollar price of one unit of foreign currency. For example, in August 1999, the price of one U.S. dollar was 1.52 Canadian dollars. Thus, the Canada-U.S. exchange rate was 1.52.

exchange rate The number of units of domestic currency required to purchase one unit of foreign currency.

We could just as easily define the exchange rate in the opposite way. We could define it as the number of units of foreign currency that could be purchased with one Canadian dollar. In our example from August 1999, the exchange rate between the Canadian and U.S. dollars would then be 1/1.52 = 0.657. One Canadian dollar would purchase 65.7 U.S. cents.

In this book, however, we *always* define the exchange rate in the way Canadian economists usually do—as the Canadian-dollar price of one unit of foreign currency. This definition makes it clear that foreign currency, like any good or service, has a price expressed in Canadian dollars. In this case, the price of the "good" has a special name—the exchange rate.

A rise in the external value of the Canadian dollar—an **appreciation** of the Canadian dollar—means that it takes fewer Canadian dollars to purchase one unit of foreign currency. For example, if the Canadian dollar appreciates against the U.S. dollar from 1.52 to 1.45, it takes 7 fewer Canadian cents to purchase one U.S. dollar. Thus, an appreciation of the Canadian dollar implies a *fall* in the exchange rate. Conversely, a decline in the external value of the Canadian dollar—a **depreciation** of the Canadian dollar—means that it takes more Canadian dollars to purchase one unit of foreign currency. Thus, a depreciation of the Canadian dollar means a *rise* in the exchange rate.

appreciation A rise in the external value of the domestic currency in terms of foreign currencies; a fall in the exchange rate.

depreciation A fall in the external value of domestic currency in terms of foreign currency; that is, a rise in the exchange rate.

The external value of a currency is the inverse of the exchange rate. Thus, an appreciation of the Canadian dollar is a fall in the exchange rate; a depreciation of the Canadian dollar is a rise in the exchange rate.

We now go on to build a simple model of the foreign-exchange market. This will allow us to analyse the determinants of the exchange rate. To keep things simple, we use an example involving trade between Canada and Europe, and thus we examine the determination of the exchange rate between the two currencies, the Canadian dollar and the euro. But, in this example, Europe is just a shorthand for "the rest of the world" and the euro is just a shorthand for "all other currencies." (It would be more natural to think in terms of Canada-U.S. trade since 80 percent of Canadian trade is with the United States, but this quickly becomes confusing because both country's currencies are called the dollar.)

Because dollars are traded for euros in the foreign-exchange market, it follows that a demand for euros implies a supply of dollars and that a supply of euros implies a demand for dollars.

For this reason, a theory of the exchange rate between dollars and euros can deal either with the demand and supply of dollars or with the demand and supply of euros; both need not be considered. We will concentrate on the demand, supply, and price of euros. Thus, the market we will be considering (in general terms) is the foreign-exchange market—the "product" is foreign exchange (euros in our case) and the "price" is the exchange rate (the Canadian-dollar price of euros).

We develop our example in terms of the demand and supply analysis first encountered in Chapter 3. To do so, we need only to recall that in the market for foreign exchange, transactions that generate a receipt for Canada in its balance of payments represent a *supply* of foreign exchange (foreign exchange is being supplied by the foreigners who purchase Canadian goods or assets). Conversely, transactions that are a payment from Canada in the balance of payments represent a *demand* for foreign exchange (foreign exchange is being demanded by the Canadians who are purchasing foreign goods or assets).

We begin by focusing only on the demand and supply of foreign exchange arising from the current and capital accounts. Later we turn to the important role of official financing by the Bank of Canada. But, for now, suppose that the Bank of Canada makes no transactions in the foreign-exchange market.

The Supply of Foreign Exchange

The supply of foreign exchange in the foreign-exchange market arises from all international transactions that represent a receipt in Canada's balance of payments.

Canadian Exports

One important source of supply of foreign exchange is foreigners who do not currently hold Canadian dollars but who wish to buy Canadian-made goods and services. A Japanese importer of lumber is such a purchaser; an Austrian couple planning a vacation in Canada is another; the Russian government seeking to buy Canadian steel is a third. All are sources of supply of foreign exchange, arising out of international trade. Each potential buyer wants to sell its own currency in exchange for Canadian dollars that it can then use to purchase Canadian goods and services.

Capital Inflows

A second source of supply of foreign exchange comes from foreigners who wish to purchase Canadian assets, such as government or corporate bonds, or plant and equipment currently located in Canada. To buy Canadian assets, holders of foreign currencies must first sell their foreign currency and buy Canadian dollars. In recent years, foreign households and firms have invested tens of billions of dollars in Canadian securities and real estate. This has required the conversion of foreign currencies into Canadian dollars. The resulting transactions are called *long-term capital flows*.

In Chapter 28 we discussed how the Bank of Canada's efforts to reduce inflation in the early 1990s pushed Canadian interest rates well above those in other countries. With the increase in Canadian rates, floods of "foreign money" came into Canada to buy short-term treasury bills and notes, certificates of deposit, and other securities. The buyers were seeking a high return on their liquid assets, but first these buyers had to convert their U.S. dollars, yen, guilder, marks, and francs into Canadian dollars in the foreign-exchange market. When people sell financial assets in one country for foreign exchange that they then use to buy short-term financial assets in another country, the transactions are called *short-term capital flows*.

Reserve Currency

Firms, banks, and governments often accumulate and hold foreign-exchange reserves, just as individuals maintain savings accounts. These reserves may be in several different currencies. For example, the government of Nigeria may decide to increase its reserve holdings of Canadian dollars and reduce its reserve holdings of euros; if it does so, it will be a supplier of euros (and a demander of Canadian dollars) in foreign-exchange markets.

The Total Supply of Foreign Exchange

The supply of foreign exchange (or the demand for Canadian dollars) by holders of foreign currencies is the sum of the supplies for all of the purposes just discussed—for purchases of Canadian exports, for capital inflow to Canada and for the purchase of Canadian dollars to add to currency reserves.

   Furthermore, because people, firms, and governments in all countries purchase goods and assets from many other countries, the demand for any one currency will be the aggregate demand of individuals, firms, and governments in a number of different countries. Thus, the total supply of foreign exchange (or the demand for Canadian dollars) may include Germans who are offering euros, Japanese who are offering yen, Argentinians who are offering pesos, and so on. For simplicity, however, we go back to our two-country example and use only Canada and Europe.

The Supply Curve for Foreign Exchange

The supply of foreign exchange on the foreign-exchange market is represented by a positively sloped curve, such

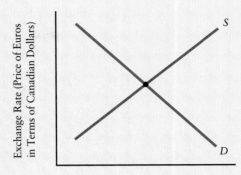

FIGURE 36-1 The Market for Foreign Exchange

Exchange Rate (Price of Euros in Terms of Canadian Dollars)

Quantity of Foreign Currency (Euros)

The demand for foreign exchange is negatively sloped, and the supply of foreign exchange is positively sloped, when plotted against the exchange rate, measured as the Canadian-dollar price of one unit of foreign currency. The demand for foreign exchange is given by the negatively sloped blue line *D*. It represents the sum of transactions on both current and capital accounts that require payments to foreigners.

   The supply of foreign exchange is given by the positively sloped red line *S*. It represents the sum of transactions on both current and capital accounts that represent receipts from foreigners.

   A depreciation of the Canadian dollar is a rise in the exchange rate (moving up the vertical axis); an appreciation of the dollar is a fall in the exchange rate (moving down the vertical axis).

as the one shown in Figure 36-1. This figure plots the Canadian-dollar price of euros (the exchange rate) on the vertical axis and the quantity of euros on the horizontal axis. Moving up the vertical scale, more dollars are needed to purchase one euro—the dollar is depreciating. Moving down the vertical scale, fewer dollars are needed to purchase one euro—the dollar is appreciating.

   Why is the supply curve for foreign exchange positively sloped? Consider the supply of foreign exchange derived from foreign purchases of Canadian exports. If the Canadian dollar depreciates, it takes fewer euros to purchase one Canadian dollar. Thus, for a given Canadian-dollar price of the product the euro price has fallen. European consumers will therefore buy more of the cheaper Canadian goods and will thus supply more foreign exchange for this purpose. In the opposite case, when the dollar appreciates, the euro price of Canadian exports rises. European consumers will buy fewer Canadian goods and thus supply less foreign exchange.[1]

---

[1]We have assumed here that the foreign price elasticity of demand for Canadian exports is greater than one, so that a price change leads to a proportionately larger change in quantity demanded. This is a common assumption in the analysis of international trade. In the case of Canada (and other small countries) it is common to go further and make the "small open economy" assumption—that the country faces *given world prices* for both its exports and imports. In this case, the foreign price elasticity of demand for exports is infinite.

Similar considerations affect other sources of supply of foreign exchange. When the Canadian dollar depreciates (a high exchange rate), Canadian assets and securities become attractive purchases, and the quantity purchased will rise. With this rise, the amount of foreign exchange supplied to pay for the purchases will increase.

The supply curve for foreign exchange is positively sloped when it is plotted against the exchange rate; a depreciation of the Canadian dollar (a rise in the exchange rate) increases the quantity of foreign exchange supplied.

The Demand for Foreign Exchange

The demand for foreign exchange arises from all international transactions that represent a payment in Canada's balance of payments. What sort of international transactions generate a demand for foreign exchange (and a supply of Canadian dollars)? Canadians seeking to purchase foreign products will be supplying Canadian dollars and demanding foreign exchange for this purpose. Holders of Canadian securities may decide to sell their Canadian holdings and shift them into foreign assets. If they do, they will supply Canadian dollars and demand foreign exchange. Similarly, a country with reserves of Canadian dollars may decide to sell them in order to demand some other currency.

The Demand Curve for Foreign Exchange

When the Canadian dollar depreciates, the Canadian-dollar price of European goods rises. Because it takes more dollars to buy the same European good, Canadians will buy fewer of the now more expensive European goods. The amount of foreign exchange being demanded by Canadians in order to pay for imported European goods will fall.[2] In the opposite case, when the Canadian dollar appreciates, European goods become cheaper, more are sold, and more dollars are spent on them. Thus, more foreign exchange will be demanded to pay for the extra imports. This same argument applies in exactly the same way to the purchases of foreign assets. Figure 36-1 shows the demand curve for foreign exchange.

The demand curve for foreign exchange is negatively sloped when it is plotted against the exchange rate; an appreciation of the Canadian dollar (a fall in the exchange rate) increases the quantity of foreign exchange demanded.

The Determination of Exchange Rates

The demand and supply curves in Figure 36-1 do not include official financing transactions (the demands or supplies for foreign exchange by the Bank of Canada). To complete our analysis, we must incorporate the role of official financing transactions. We need to consider three important cases:

---

[2]As long as the price elasticity of demand for imports is greater than one, the fall in the volume of imports will exceed the rise in price, and hence fewer dollars will be spent on them. This condition (and the one in the previous footnote) is related to a famous long-standing issue in international economics, called the *Marshall-Lerner condition*. In what follows, we take the standard approach of assuming that both the price elasticity of demand for imports and the price elasticity of the demand for Canadian exports exceeds one. This guarantees that the slopes of the curves are as shown in Figure 36-1.

1. When the central bank makes no transactions in the foreign-exchange market, the exchange rate is determined by the equality between the supply and demand for foreign exchange arising from the capital and current accounts. In this situation there is said to be a purely **flexible exchange rate.**

2. When the central bank intervenes in the foreign-exchange market to "fix" the exchange rate at a particular value, there is said to be a **fixed exchange rate** or *pegged exchange rate.*

3. Between these two "pure" systems are a variety of possible intermediate cases, including the *adjustable peg* and the *managed float.* In the **adjustable peg system,** governments set and attempt to fix specific values for their exchange rates, but they explicitly recognize that circumstances may arise in which they will change that value. In a **managed float,** the central bank seeks to have some stabilizing influence on the exchange rate but does not try to fix it at some publicly announced value.

Most countries today operate a mostly flexible exchange rate. It is mostly market determined but the central bank sometimes intervenes to offset short-run fluctuations. There are, however, some important exceptions. The countries of the European Union (EU), for example, had a system of fixed exchange rates (relative to each other's currencies) between 1979 and 1999. In 1999 the EU introduced a common currency—the euro—that was adopted by most of the EU member countries (an important exception being the United Kingdom). Thus, they now have fixed exchange rates relative to each other (since they have the same currency) but have a flexible exchange rate (with some short-term interventions) relative to countries outside the EU. The United States, Japan, the United Kingdom, Australia, and most other major industrialized countries have flexible exchange rates with relatively small amounts of foreign-exchange intervention by their central banks.

Canada used flexible exchange rates (with limited intervention) throughout most of the period following the Second World War. Even when most countries pegged their currencies to the U.S. dollar under the Bretton Woods system, Canada had a flexible exchange rate. Later in the chapter we examine the issues involved in choosing a flexible or fixed exchange-rate system. For now, let's explore how the various systems operate.

flexible exchange rate   An exchange rate that is left free to be determined by the forces of demand and supply on the free market, with no intervention by the monetary authorities.

fixed exchange rate   An exchange rate that is maintained within a small range around its publicly stated par value by the intervention in the foreign-exchange market by a country's central bank.

adjustable peg system   A system in which exchange rates are fixed in the short term but are occasionally changed in response to persistent payments imbalances.

managed float   A situation in which the central bank intervenes in the foreign exchange market to smooth out some of the large, short-term fluctuations in a country's exchange rate, while still leaving the market to determine the exchange rate in the longer term.

Flexible Exchange Rates

Consider an exchange rate that is set in a freely competitive market, with no intervention by the central bank. Like any competitive price, the exchange rate fluctuates according to the conditions of demand and supply.

Suppose the current exchange rate is so high (say, e_1 in Figure 36-2) that the quantity of foreign exchange supplied exceeds the quantity demanded. There is thus an abundance of foreign exchange and a shortage of Canadian dollars. This excess supply of foreign exchange, just as in our analysis in Chapter 3, will cause the price of foreign exchange (the exchange rate) to fall. As the exchange rate falls—an appreciation of the Canadian dollar—the euro price of Canadian goods rises, and this leads to a reduction in the quantity of foreign exchange supplied. Also, as the exchange rate falls, the Canadian-dollar price of European goods falls, and this fall leads to an increase in the quantity of foreign exchange demanded. Thus, the excess supply of foreign exchange leads to a fall in the exchange rate which in turn reduces the amount of excess supply. Where the two curves intersect, quantity demanded equals quantity supplied, and the exchange rate is at its equilibrium value.

In 1999, eleven countries of the European Union adopted a common currency—the euro. Early in 2000, the exchange rate was 1.05 euros per U.S. dollar, or 0.71 euros per Canadian dollar.

FIGURE 36-2   Fixed and Flexible Exchange Rates

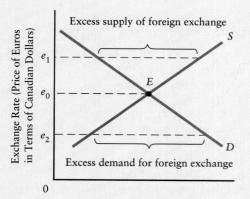

In the absence of official financing by the central bank, the exchange rate adjusts to clear the foreign-exchange market. The demand for and supply of foreign exchange are as in Figure 36-1. If official financing is zero, there is a flexible exchange rate. It will adjust to equate the demand and supply of foreign exchange; this occurs at E with an exchange rate of e_0.

If the exchange rate is higher than that, say at e_1, the supply of foreign exchange will exceed the demand. The exchange rate will fall (the dollar will appreciate) until it reaches e_0, where balance is achieved at E. If the exchange rate is below e_0, say at e_2, the demand for foreign exchange will exceed the supply. The exchange rate will rise (the dollar will depreciate) until it reaches e_0, where balance is achieved at E.

The central bank can fix the exchange rate by using its official financing transactions to meet the excess demands or supplies that arise at the fixed value of the exchange rate. For example, if it chooses to fix the exchange rate at e_1, there will be an excess supply of foreign exchange because receipts (on current and capital accounts) will exceed payments. The central bank will thus purchase foreign exchange (and sell dollars) to meet the excess supply. Alternatively, if the central bank chooses to fix the exchange rate at e_2, there will be an excess demand for foreign exchange because receipts (on current and capital accounts) will be less than payments. The central bank will thus sell foreign exchange (and buy dollars) to meet the excess demand.

What happens when the exchange rate is below its equilibrium value? The quantity of foreign exchange demanded will exceed the quantity supplied. With foreign exchange in excess demand, its price will naturally rise, and as it does the amount of excess demand will be reduced until equilibrium is re-established.

A foreign-exchange market is like other competitive markets in that the forces of demand and supply lead to an equilibrium price at which quantity demanded equals quantity supplied.

Recall that we have been assuming that there is no official financing by the central bank, so that demand and supply in the foreign-exchange market represent transactions only on the current or capital account. We now consider a system of fixed exchange rates in which official financing plays a central role in the analysis.

Fixed Exchange Rates

When official financing transactions are used to fix the exchange rate at a particular value, the current account and the capital account do not necessarily sum to zero. The balance on the official financing account has to be whatever is necessary to offset the excess demand or supply of foreign exchange that arises. This is also shown in Figure 36-2.

The gold standard that operated for much of the nineteenth century and the early part of the twentieth century was a fixed exchange-rate system. The Bretton Woods system, established by international agreement in 1944 and operated until the mid 1970s, was a fixed exchange-rate system that provided for circumstances under which the external value of the currency could be lowered (a *devaluation*) or raised (a *revaluation*). It was thus an adjustable peg system; the International Monetary Fund (IMF) has its origins in the Bretton Woods system, and one of its principal tasks was approving and monitoring exchange-rate changes. The European Exchange Rate Mechanism (ERM) of the early 1990s was also a fixed exchange-rate system for the countries in the European Union; their exchange rates were fixed to each other but floated as a block against the U.S. dollar and other currencies. As mentioned earlier, this system of separate currencies with fixed exchange rates was replaced in 1999 when most of the countries of the EU adopted a common currency—the euro.

Applying Economic Concepts 36-2 examines how a fixed exchange-rate system operates. It shows why a central bank that chooses to fix its exchange rate must give up some

For information on the new European Central Bank, see its website: www.ecb.int.

control of its foreign-exchange reserves. This presents some problems, as it did for Thailand in the summer of 1997, at the beginning of the 1997-1998 Asian Crisis.

We now go on to study the workings of a flexible exchange-rate system, the system used in Canada and most major countries.

Changes in Flexible Exchange Rates

What causes exchange rates to vary? The simplest answer to this question is changes in demand or supply in the foreign-exchange market. Anything that shifts the demand curve for foreign exchange to the right or the supply curve for foreign exchange to the left leads to a rise in the exchange rate—a depreciation of the Canadian dollar. Conversely, anything that shifts the demand curve for foreign exchange to the left or the supply curve for foreign exchange to the right leads to a fall in the exchange rate—an appreciation of the Canadian dollar. These points are nothing more than a restatement of the laws of supply and demand, applied now to the market for foreign exchange; they are illustrated in Figure 36-3.

What causes the shifts in demand and supply that lead to changes in exchange rates? There are many causes, some transitory and some persistent. We mention several of the most important ones.

FIGURE 36-3   Changes in Exchange Rates

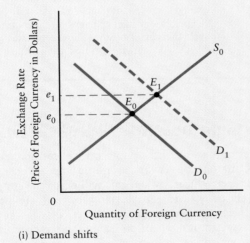
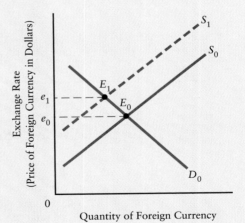

(i) Demand shifts   (ii) Supply shifts

An increase in the demand for foreign exchange or a decrease in the supply will cause the dollar to depreciate (the exchange rate to rise); a decrease in the demand or an increase in supply will cause the dollar to appreciate (the exchange rate to fall). The initial demand and supply curves D_0 and S_0 are as in Figures 36-1 and 36-2. Equilibrium is at E_0 with an exchange rate of e_0. An increase in the demand for foreign exchange as shown by a rightward shift in the demand curve from D_0 to D_1 in part (i), or a decrease in the supply of foreign exchange as shown by a leftward shift in the supply curve from S_0 to S_1 in part (ii), will cause the dollar to depreciate. In both parts, the new equilibrium is at E_1, and the dollar depreciation is shown by the rise in the exchange rate from e_0 to e_1. Conversely, a decrease in the demand for foreign exchange or an increase in the supply of foreign exchange will cause the dollar to appreciate.

APPLYING ECONOMIC CONCEPTS 36-2

Managing Fixed Exchange Rates

This box provides some details on how a central bank operates a regime of fixed exchange rates. Though Canada has a flexible exchange rate (with occasional foreign-exchange intervention by the Bank of Canada), we will imagine a situation where the Bank of Canada pegs the Canadian-U.S. exchange rate.

Suppose that the Bank of Canada fixed the exchange rate between the narrow limits of, say, C$1.47 to C$1.53 to the U.S. dollar. The Bank then stabilizes the exchange rate in the face of seasonal, cyclical, and other fluctuations in demand and supply, entering the market to prevent the rate from going outside the permitted band. At the price of $1.47, the Bank offers to buy any amount of U.S. dollars; at the price of $1.53, the Bank offers to sell any amount of U.S. dollars. When the Bank buys U.S. dollars, its exchange reserves rise; when it sells U.S. dollars, its reserves fall.

We make the following observations:

1. If the demand curve cuts the supply curve in the range 1.47 to 1.53, as D_0 does in the accompanying figure, then the Bank need not intervene in the market.

2. If the demand curve shifts to D_1, then the Bank must sell U.S. dollars from its reserves to the extent of q_4q_1

in order to prevent the price of U.S. dollars from rising above 1.53.

3. If the demand curve shifts to D_2, the Bank must buy U.S. dollars to the extent of q_2q_3 in order to prevent the price of U.S. dollars from falling below 1.47.

If, on average, the demand and supply curves intersect in the range 1.47 to 1.53, then the Bank's foreign-exchange reserves will be relatively stable, with the Bank buying U.S. dollars when the demand is abnormally low and selling them when the demand is abnormally high. Over a long period, the average level of reserves will then be fairly stable.

If conditions change, the Bank's foreign-exchange reserves will rise or fall more or less continuously. For example, suppose that the average level of demand becomes D_1, with fluctuations on either side of this level. The average drain on the Bank's foreign-exchange reserves will then be q_4q_1 *per period*. But this situation cannot continue indefinitely because the Bank only has a limited amount of foreign-exchange reserves. In this situation, the Bank has two alternatives: It can change the fixed exchange rate so that the band of permissible prices straddles the new equilibrium price, or it can try to shift the curves so that the intersection is in the band 1.47 to 1.53. To accomplish this goal, it must restrict demand for

A Supply-Side Increase in the Domestic Price of Exports

Suppose that some event on the supply side of the paper market results in an increase in the Canadian-dollar price of Canadian paper. For example, the government may impose a new pollution tax on paper producers. What this will do to the supply of foreign exchange depends on the price elasticity of foreign demand for the Canadian product. If the demand for Canadian paper is elastic, perhaps because other countries supply the same product in world markets, the total amount spent on Canadian paper will decrease and hence less foreign exchange will be supplied to purchase Canadian paper. Thus, the supply curve for foreign exchange will shift to the left and the Canadian dollar will depreciate. This is illustrated in part (ii) of Figure 36-3. If the demand is inelastic (say, because Canada is the only country that produces this particular kind of paper), then more will be spent, the supply of foreign exchange to pay the bigger bill will shift the supply curve to the right, and the Canadian dollar will appreciate.

A Rise in the Foreign Price of Imports

Suppose that the euro price of European automobiles increases sharply. Suppose also that Canadian consumers have an elastic demand for European cars because they can easily switch to Canadian-made substitutes. Consequently, they spend fewer euros for

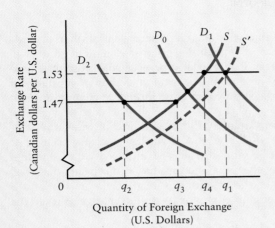

Exchange Rate
(Canadian dollars per U.S. dollar)

Quantity of Foreign Exchange
(U.S. Dollars)

the curve is shifted exactly to S' where it intersects D_1 at q_1 units of foreign exchange, the inflow of short-term capital just covers the potential shortfall, and the exchange reserves are not run down. Provided the Bank guessed correctly that the demand was abnormally high, the policy will work. If the demand now falls to produce a free-market rate within the permitted range, the Bank can lower interest rates, as it no longer needs to attract short-term capital to cover the excess demand for foreign exchange at the maximum permitted exchange rate.

Thailand in 1997 provides an example of an exchange rate fixed at a level that led to a persistent excess demand for foreign exchange. Thailand's central bank had fixed the value of its currency, the baht, to the U.S. dollar. When an excess demand for foreign currency developed in Thailand, the central bank began to deplete its stock of foreign-exchange reserves as it purchased the baht in an attempt to support its external value. By July of 1997, however, the central bank's stock of foreign-exchange reserves had been depleted to such an extent that it could no longer fix the exchange rate. With an excess demand for foreign exchange and a central bank that could no longer fix the exchange rate, depreciation was the natural result. The baht depreciated dramatically and Thailand then moved away from a fixed exchange-rate system. This event is generally viewed as the beginning of the 1997-1998 Asian Crisis during which several countries, including Malaysia, Indonesia, and South Korea, experienced similar declines in their foreign-exchange reserves and were forced to abandon their fixed exchange rates.

foreign exchange: It can impose import quotas and foreign-travel restrictions, or it can seek to increase the supply of U.S. dollars by encouraging Canadian exports.

The Bank can induce movements of short-term capital to assist in its policy of fixing the exchange rate in spite of fluctuations in the demand for and supply of foreign exchange. Suppose, for example, in the figure that the demand for U.S. dollars is D_1 and the supply S, so that there is a potential loss of reserves of q_4q_1 per period. The Bank of Canada can raise the short-term rate of interest and attract short-term capital, thus shifting the supply of U.S. dollars to the right. If

European automobiles than they did before and hence demand less foreign exchange. The demand curve for foreign exchange shifts to the left, and the Canadian dollar will appreciate. If the demand for European cars were inelastic, total spending on them would rise, and the demand for foreign exchange would shift to the right, leading to a depreciation of the Canadian dollar. This is illustrated in part (i) of Figure 36-3.

Changes in the Overall Price Levels

Suppose that instead of a change in the price of a specific export, such as cars or paper, there is a change in *all* prices because of a general inflation. We consider separate cases, each corresponding to a different pattern of Canadian relative to foreign inflation.

Equal Inflation in Both Countries.
Suppose that inflation is running at 5 percent in both Canada and Europe. In this case, the euro prices of European goods and the dollar prices of Canadian goods both rise by 5 percent. At the *existing* exchange rate, the dollar prices of European goods and the euro prices of Canadian goods will each rise by 5 percent, and hence the relative prices of imports and domestically produced goods will be unchanged in both countries. Since there is no reason to expect a change in either

country's demand for imports at the original exchange rate, the inflation in the two countries leaves the equilibrium exchange rate unchanged.

Inflation in Only One Country.

What will happen if there is inflation in Canada while the price level remains stable in Europe? The dollar price of Canadian goods will rise, and they will become more expensive in Europe. This increase will cause the quantity of Canadian exports, and therefore the amount of foreign exchange supplied by European importers, to decrease. Thus, the supply curve for foreign exchange shifts to the left.

At the same time, European goods in Canada will have an unchanged Canadian-dollar price, while the price of Canadian goods sold in Canada will increase because of the inflation. Thus, European goods will be more attractive compared with Canadian goods (because they have become relatively cheaper), and thus more European goods will be bought in Canada. At any exchange rate, the amount of foreign exchange demanded to purchase imports will rise. Thus, the demand curve for foreign exchange shifts to the right.

Canadian inflation that is unmatched in Europe will therefore cause the supply curve for foreign exchange to shift to the left and the demand curve for foreign exchange to shift to the right. As a result, the equilibrium exchange rate *must* rise—there is a depreciation of the Canadian dollar relative to the euro.

Inflation at Unequal Rates.

The two foregoing examples are, of course, just limiting cases of a more general situation in which the price levels change in both countries. The arguments can readily be extended when we realize that it is the *relative* size of the changes in prices in two countries that determines whether home goods or foreign goods look more or less attractive. If country A's inflation rate is higher than country B's, country A's exports are becoming relatively expensive in B's markets while imports from B are becoming relatively cheap in A's markets. This causes the price of A's currency to fall—A's currency depreciates relative to B's.

If the price level in one country is rising relative to that in another country, the equilibrium value of its currency will be falling relative to that of the other country.

Capital Movements

Capital flows can exert strong influences on exchange rates. For example, an increased desire by Canadians to purchase European assets (a capital export for Canada) will shift the demand curve for foreign exchange to the right, and the dollar will depreciate. This process is illustrated in part (i) of Figure 36-3.

A movement of financial capital has the effect of appreciating the currency of the capital-importing country and depreciating the currency of the capital-exporting country.

This statement is true for all capital movements, short-term or long-term. Because the motives that lead to large capital movements are likely to be different in the short and long terms, however, it is worth considering each separately.

Short-Term Capital Movements.

An important motive for short-term capital flows is a change in interest rates. International traders hold transactions balances just as do domestic traders. These balances are often lent out on a short-term basis rather than being left idle. Naturally, the holders of these balances will tend to lend them, other things being equal, in markets where interest rates are highest. Thus, if one country's short-term interest rate rises above the rates in other countries (say, because that country undertakes a contractionary monetary policy), there will tend to be a large inflow of short-term capital into that country in an effort to take advantage of the high rate. This inflow of financial capital will increase the demand for the domestic currency and cause it to appreciate. If the short-term interest rate should fall in one country (say, because of a monetary expansion in that country), there will tend to be a shift in capital away from that country and its currency will tend to depreciate.

A second motive for short-term capital movements is speculation about the *future value* of a country's exchange rate. If foreigners expect the Canadian dollar to appreciate in the near future, they will rush to buy assets that pay off in Canadian dollars, such as Canadian stocks or bonds; if they expect the Canadian dollar to depreciate in the near future, they will be reluctant to buy or to hold Canadian securities.

Long-Term Capital Movements.   Long-term capital movements are largely influenced by long-term expectations about another country's profit opportunities and the long-run value of its currency. A French firm would be more willing to purchase a Canadian factory if it expected that the dollar profits would buy more euros in future years than the profits from investment in a French factory. This could happen if the Canadian firm earned greater profits than the French firm, with exchange rates remaining unchanged. It could also happen if the profits were the same but the French firm expected the Canadian dollar to appreciate relative to the euro.

Structural Changes

An economy can undergo structural changes that alter the equilibrium exchange rate. *Structural change* is an all-purpose term for a change in cost structures, the invention of new products, changes in preferences between products, or anything else that affects the pattern of comparative advantage. Consider three examples.

Suppose that the reluctance of firms in one country to adopt technological innovations results in that country's products not improving as rapidly as those produced in other countries. Consumers' demand (at fixed prices) will shift slowly away from the first country's products and toward those of its foreign competitors. This shift will cause a gradual depreciation in the first country's currency because fewer people want to buy that country's goods and thus fewer people want to buy that country's currency.

A second example relates to the discovery of valuable mineral resources. Prominent examples are the development of natural gas in The Netherlands in the early 1960s, the development of North Sea oil in the United Kingdom in the 1970s, and the recent discovery of large diamond mines in the Northwest Territories. If firms in one country make such a discovery and begin selling these resources to the rest of the world, then the foreign purchasers must supply their foreign currency in order to purchase the currency of the exporting country. The result is an appreciation of the currency of the exporting country.

Anything that leads to changes in the pattern of trade, such as changes in costs or changes in demand, will generally lead to changes in exchange rates.

A final example relates to changes in demand for a country's exports. For many countries, including Canada, the prices of the goods that it sells to other countries are determined in world markets. Examples include commodities such as oil, copper, pulp, lumber, wheat, coffee, cocoa, zinc, tin, aluminum, and gold. Changes in the world demand or supply for these commodities typically have significant effects on exchange rates. For example, if there is a reduction in the world demand for these products there will be an accompanying reduction in demand for the currencies of those countries that export these products. Their currencies will depreciate. In 1997 and 1998, for example, there was a notable decline in many commodity prices, and the currencies of major commodity exporters such as Australia, New Zealand, Canada, and South Africa depreciated significantly.

The Volatility of Exchange Rates

We have discussed several variables that can lead to changes in the exchange rate, including changes in relative prices, changes in interest rates, and changes in the pattern of trade. Since these variables are changing at different times by different amounts and often in different directions, it should not be surprising that exchange rates are constantly changing. Indeed, exchange rates are one of the most volatile of all macroeconomic variables. One reason for this volatility that we have not yet discussed is that foreign-exchange traders, when they are deciding whether to buy or sell foreign currency, respond to all sorts of "news" that they think will influence economic conditions, both currently and in the future. Since such news is constantly becoming available, the exchange rate is continuously changing as this new information leads traders to change their demand and supply decisions. *Applying Economic Concepts 36-3* discusses in more detail how news affects the volatility of exchange rates.

Three Policy Issues

This chapter has so far been devoted to explaining how the balance of payments accounts are constructed and how exchange rates are determined. It is now time to use this knowledge to explore some important and interesting policy issues. We examine three policy issues that are commonly discussed in the popular press. As we will see, these discussions are not always as well-informed as they could be. We pose the three policy issues as questions:

1. Is a current account deficit bad for Canada?

2. Is there a "correct" value for the Canadian dollar?

3. Should Canada fix its exchange rate with the U.S. dollar?

Current Account Deficits

In recent years, Canada has had a current account deficit. Canada usually has a significant trade surplus since it exports more goods and services to the world than it imports. But because it makes more investment payments (both interest and dividends) to foreigners than it receives from foreigners, it has a deficit on the capital-service portion of the current account. The overall current account balance in recent years has been a deficit, usually between $15 billion and $25 billion.

As we have learned, Canada's balance of payments must always balance, so the current account deficit is matched by a capital account surplus of the same size (the balance on the official financing account is usually very small). This capital account surplus means that Canada sells more assets to the rest of the world—both bonds and equity—than it buys from the rest of the world.

Is it undesirable for Canada to have a current account deficit and, therefore, a capital account surplus? It is certainly common for TV anchors to report negatively upon a

APPLYING ECONOMIC CONCEPTS 36-3

News and the Exchange Rate

Foreign-exchange markets are different from markets for consumer goods in that the vast bulk of trading takes place between professional foreign-exchange traders working for banks, mutual-fund companies, and pension funds. These traders do not meet each other face to face. Rather, they do their transactions over the telephone, and the other party to the transaction could be anywhere in the world. The structure of this market has one interesting implication: exchange rates respond to news. Let's see why this is and what this means.

Deals done by the professional traders are all on a large scale, typically involving sums no smaller than $1 million and often very much larger. Each trader tends to specialize in trades between a small number of currencies, say the Canadian and the U.S. dollars, or the U.S. dollar and the Japanese yen. But the traders for all currencies for each bank sit close together in a trading room so they can hear what is going on in the other markets. When a big news event breaks, anywhere in the world, this will be shouted out simultaneously to all traders in the room.

Each trader is also faced with several computer screens and many buttons that connect him or her quickly by telephone to other traders. Speed of transaction can be very important if you are dealing with large amounts of money in a market that is continuously changing the prices quoted. The most recent price quotes from around the world appear on the screens. However, contracts are agreed over the telephone (and are recorded in case of a disagreement) and the paperwork follows within two days.

As exchange rates are closely related to expectations and to interest rates, the foreign-exchange traders have to keep an eye on all major news events affecting the economic environment. Since all the players in the foreign-

exchange markets are professionals, they are well-informed, not just about what has happened but also about forecasts of what is likely to happen. Accordingly, the exchange rate at any point in time reflects not just history but also current expectations of future events.

As soon as some future event comes to be expected—such as the central bank's plans to tighten monetary policy—it will be reflected in the current exchange rate. Events expected to happen soon will be given more weight than those events expected to happen in the more distant future. The fact that expectations of future events get incorporated quickly into the exchange rate has an interesting implication: the only component in today's news that will cause the exchange rate to change is what was *not expected* to happen. Economists attribute the unforecastable component of news to a random error. It is random in the sense that it has no detectable pattern and it is unrelated to the information available before it happened.

Some events are clearly unforecastable, like an earthquake in Japan or a head of state having a heart attack. Others are the production of economic statistics for which forecasts have generally been published. In the latter case it is the deviation of announced figures from their forecast value which tends to move exchange rates.

So, exchange rates are moved by news. And since news is random and unpredictable, changes in exchange rates will tend to be random. Some people, observing the volatility of exchange rates, conclude that foreign-exchange markets are inefficient. However, with well-informed professional traders who have forward-looking expectations, new information is rapidly transmitted into prices. The volatility of exchange rates, therefore, largely reflects the volatility of relevant, but unexpected, events around the world.

rise in the current account deficit and positively upon its decline. But are current account deficits really a problem? We address this issue in three parts.

Mercantilism

Many people argue that a current account deficit is undesirable because it means that Canada is buying more goods and services from the world than it is selling to the world. Central to this view is the belief that exports are "good" and imports are "bad." We discussed this belief, and argued why it was incorrect, in Chapter 35 when we explored some of the fallacious arguments for trade protection.

As a carryover from a long-discredited eighteenth-century doctrine called *mercantilism*, a current account surplus is sometimes called a "favourable balance," and a current account deficit is sometimes called an "unfavourable balance." Mercantilists, both ancient and modern, believe that a country's gains from trade arise only from having a "favourable" balance of trade—that is, by exporting more goods and services than it imports. But this belief misses the central point of comparative advantage that we explored in Chapter 34—that countries gain from trade because trade allows each country to specialize in the production of those products in which its opportunity costs are low. The gains from trade have *nothing* to do with whether there is a trade deficit or a trade surplus.

Lessons from History 36-1 discusses the doctrine of mercantilism. The lesson to be learned is that the gains from trade depend on the *volume* of trade (both imports and exports) rather than the *balance* of trade. There is nothing inherently bad about having a current account deficit.

International Borrowing

If Canada has a current account deficit, then it also has a capital account surplus. It is a net seller of assets to the rest of the world. These assets are either bonds, in which case Canadians are borrowing from foreigners, or they are shares in firms (equities) in which case Canadians are selling their capital stock to foreigners.

LESSONS FROM HISTORY 36-1
Mercantilism, Then and Now

Media commentators, politicians, and much of the general public often appear to believe that a nation should secure a current-account surplus. They believe that the benefits derived from international trade are measured by the size of that surplus.

This view is related to the *exploitation doctrine* of international trade: One country's surplus is another country's deficit. Hence, one country's gain, judged by its surplus, must be another country's loss, judged by its deficit.

People who hold such views today are echoing an ancient economic doctrine called *mercantilism*. The mercantilists were a group of economists who preceded Adam Smith. They judged the success of trade by the size of the trade balance. In many cases, this doctrine made sense in terms of their objective, which was to use international trade as a means of building up the political and military power of the state, rather than as a means of raising the living standards of its citizens. A current account surplus allowed the nation (then and now) to acquire assets. (In those days, the assets took the form of gold. Today, they are mostly claims on the currencies of other

countries.) These assets could then be used to pay armies, to purchase weapons from abroad, and to finance colonial expansions.

If the objective is to promote the welfare and living standards of ordinary citizens, however, the mercantilist focus on the balance of trade makes no sense. The principle of comparative advantage shows that average living standards are maximized by having individuals, regions, and countries specialize in the things that they can produce comparatively best and then trading to obtain the things that they can produce comparatively worst. The more specialization there is, the more trade occurs.

For the country as a whole, therefore, the gains from trade are to be judged by the *volume* of trade rather than by the *balance* of trade. A situation in which there is a large volume of trade even though each country has a zero balance of trade can thus be regarded as satisfactory. Furthermore, a change in policy that results in an equal increase in both exports and imports will generate gains because it allows for specialization according to comparative advantage, even though it causes no change in either country's trade balance.

It follows that the question "Should Canada have a current account deficit?" is the same as the question "Should Canadians be net sellers of assets to foreigners?" It is not immediately clear that the answer to this question should be: No. It is true that by selling bonds to foreigners, Canadians increase their indebtedness to foreigners and will eventually have to redeem the bonds as well as pay interest. And by selling income-earning equities to foreigners, Canadians give up a stream of income that they would otherwise have. But, in both cases, they get a lump-sum of funds that can be used for any type of consumption or investment. Is it obviously "better" to have a lower debt or a higher future income stream than to have a lump-sum of funds right now? If it were better, no family would ever borrow money to buy a house or a car, and no firm would ever borrow money to build a factory.

A country that has a current account deficit is either borrowing from the rest of the world or selling its ownership of some of its capital stock to the rest of the world. This is not necessarily undesirable.

To argue that it is undesirable for Canada to have a current account deficit is to argue that Canadians as a whole should not borrow from (or sell physical assets to) the rest of the world. But surely the wisdom of borrowing depends on *why* Canadians are borrowing. It is therefore important to know *why* there is a current account deficit.

Causes of Current Account Deficits

There are several possible causes of a current account deficit. This can be seen most clearly by recalling some national-income accounting from Chapter 20. Recall that GDP is equal to the sum of actual consumption, investment, government purchases and net exports,

$$GDP = C_a + I_a + G_a + NX_a$$

where the subscript "a" denotes *actual* expenditure rather than desired expenditure. Next, note that GNP is equal to GDP plus the net investment income received from abroad, which we call R.

$$GNP = GDP + R = C_a + I_a + G_a + NX_a + R$$

Note the current account balance is simply the trade balance, NX_a, plus the net investment income, R. We denote the actual current account balance CA_a. If CA_a is positive, there is a current account surplus; if CA_a is negative, there is a current account deficit. The equation now becomes

$$GNP = C_a + I_a + G_a + CA_a \tag{36-1}$$

Now consider how a given amount of GNP that accrues to households can be spent. There are only three ways to dispose of income. It can be consumed, saved, or paid in taxes. That is,

$$GNP = C_a + S_a + T_a \tag{36-2}$$

By equating Equations 36-1 and 36-2, and by omitting the "a" subscripts for simplicity, we derive an interesting relationship between national saving, investment, and the current account balance:

$$C + I + G + CA = C + S + T$$

$$\Rightarrow CA = S + (T-G) - I$$

This equation says that the current account balance in any year is exactly equal to the excess of national saving, $S + (T - G)$, over domestic investment. If Canadians (and their governments) decide to save more than is needed to finance the amount of domestic investment, where do the excess funds go? They are used to acquire foreign assets, and thus Canada has a current account surplus ($CA>0$). In contrast, if Canadians do not save enough to finance the amount of domestic investment, the balance must be financed by foreign funds. Thus, Canada has a current account deficit ($CA<0$). Finally, we can rearrange this equation very slightly to get

$$CA = (S - I) + (T - G) \tag{36-3}$$

which says that the current account balance is equal to the government budget surplus plus the excess of private saving over investment.

Equation 36-3 shows that there are three separate reasons for any given increase in the current account deficit (a fall in CA). First, a reduction in private saving, other things equal, will lead to a rise in the current account deficit. Second, a rise in domestic investment, other things equal, will increase the current account deficit. Finally, other things equal, a rise in the government's budget deficit (a fall in the budget surplus) will raise the current account deficit. This third case is often referred to as a situation of *twin deficits*. That is, a rise in the government's budget deficit will also have the effect (if S and I remain constant) of increasing the current account deficit.

An increase in the level of investment, a decrease in the level of saving, and an increase in the government's budget deficit are all possible causes of an increase in a country's current account deficit.

In the end, it makes little sense to discuss the desirability of a change in the current account deficit without first knowing the *cause* of the change. Knowing the cause is crucial to knowing whether the change in the current account deficit is undesirable. The following two examples illustrate this important point.

First, suppose that investment opportunities in Canada are very promising and, as a result, there is an increase in the level of investment. Most people would consider such an investment boom desirable because it would increase current output and employment and, by increasing the country's capital stock, it would also increase the level of potential output in the future. But as is clear from Equation 36-3, the immediate effect of the rise in Canadian investment is an increase in the Canadian current account deficit. In this case, it would be difficult to argue that Canada's current account deficit is undesirable.

For a second example, suppose the domestic economy begins to slow and households and firms are pessimistic about the future. In such a situation, we expect households to increase their saving and firms to reduce their investment, thus increasing the value of $(S - I)$. As the economy slows we would also expect the government's tax revenues to fall, thus decreasing the value of $(T - G)$. But it is easy to imagine a situation where the first effect dominates the second effect, thus leading to an increase in the current account surplus. Is the increase in Canada's current account surplus desirable? Most people would probably agree that the onset of a recession as described above is surely undesirable, involving a loss of output and employment.

A country's current account deficit can increase for a number of reasons. Whether the rise in the current account deficit is desirable depends on its underlying cause. A rise in the current account deficit may reflect a positive economic development; a decline in the current account deficit may reflect a negative economic development.

Is There a "Correct" Value for the Canadian Dollar?

From the summer of 1997 to the end of 1999, the external value of the Canadian dollar fell from about 72 to 65 U.S. cents. It was common to hear financial commentators discuss how the Canadian dollar was "undervalued." Opposite statements were heard a few years earlier in 1991 when, as a result of high Canadian interest rates caused by a significant monetary contraction, foreign financial capital flowed into Canada and the Canadian dollar appreciated enormously (its external value increased to about 90 U.S. cents). At that time many financial commentators argued that the Canadian dollar was "overvalued." In both cases, the observers appeared to believe that there was some "correct" value for the Canadian dollar. Is there?

As we saw in the previous section, a country that chooses to use a flexible exchange rate has its exchange rate determined by competitive forces in the foreign-exchange market. In Canada, and other countries as well, fluctuations in exchange rates have many causes. Some changes may be good for Canada, such as a world-wide shortage of wheat that drives up the world price of wheat, a major Canadian export. Others may be bad for Canada, such as the discovery of new copper mines in Chile that drives down the price of copper, also a major Canadian export. But the various supply and demand forces are coming together in the foreign-exchange market to determine the equilibrium value of the exchange rate. Changes in this value may reflect positive or negative events for Canada, but it makes little sense to think of this equilibrium value as being either too high or too low.

With a flexible exchange rate, the market determines the value of the exchange rate. With respect to the forces of demand and supply, the equilibrium exchange rate is the "correct" exchange rate.

In saying that the current equilibrium exchange rate is the "correct" rate in no way suggests that it will necessarily be the correct exchange rate in the future. Indeed, foreign-exchange markets are so large, with so many participants in so many countries, each responding to a slightly different set of events and expectations, that the equilibrium exchange rate is constantly changing. In other words, as various forces lead to frequent changes in the demand and supply for the Canadian dollar in foreign-exchange markets, the "correct" value of the Canadian exchange rate is constantly changing.

Some economists accept that the current exchange rate, as determined by the foreign-exchange market, is indeed the correct rate, but they make a distinction between the immediate value of the exchange rate and its long-run value. These economists argue that, whereas various shocks may cause the exchange rate to rise or fall in the short run, there does exist some "fundamental" level to which it will return. This brings us to the theory of *purchasing power parity*.

Purchasing Power Parity

The theory of **purchasing power parity (PPP)** holds that over the long term, the value of the exchange rate between two currencies depends on the two currencies' relative purchasing power. The theory holds that a currency will tend to have the same purchasing power when it is spent in its home country as it would have if it were converted to foreign exchange and spent in the foreign country. Another way to say the same thing is that the price of *identical baskets of goods* should be the same in the two countries when

purchasing power parity (PPP)   The theory that over the long term, the exchange rate between two currencies adjusts to reflect relative price levels (relative purchasing power).

the price is expressed in the same currency. If we let P_C and P_E be the price levels in Canada and Europe, respectively, and let e be the price of euros in terms of Canadian dollars (the exchange rate), then the theory of purchasing power parity can be expressed as

$$P_C = e \times P_E \qquad (36\text{-}4)$$

This equation simply says that if a basket of goods costs 1000 euros in Europe and the exchange rate is 1.2 (that is, 1.2 Canadian dollars per euro), then that same basket of goods should cost 1200 dollars in Canada (1.2 × 1000 = 1200).

According to the theory of purchasing power parity, the exchange rate between two country's currencies is determined by the relative price levels in the two countries.

For *The Economists'* Big Mac Index that uses the idea of PPP, see its website: www.economist.com.

The idea behind PPP is a simple one. Suppose that Equation 36-4 did *not* hold—specifically, suppose that P_C was greater than $e \times P_E$, so that Canadian-dollar prices in Canada exceed the Canadian-dollar prices of the same goods in Europe. In this case, people would increase their purchases of European goods and reduce their purchases of Canadian goods. These actions would have the effect of depreciating the Canadian dollar (a rise in e); and this would continue until the equality was reestablished.

The *PPP exchange rate* is the value of the exchange rate that makes Equation 36-4 hold. That is, the PPP exchange rate (between the Canadian dollar and the euro) is given by

$$e^{PPP} \equiv P_C/P_E \qquad (36\text{-}5)$$

Note that the PPP exchange rate is itself not constant. If inflation is higher in Canada than in Europe, for example, then P_C will be rising faster than P_E and so the PPP exchange rate will be rising. Conversely, if inflation is lower in Canada than in Europe, then P_C will be rising more slowly than P_E and the PPP exchange rate will be falling.

A Caveat About PPP

Should we expect the *actual* exchange rate to equal the PPP exchange rate? The theory of purchasing power parity predicts that if the actual exchange rate (e) does not equal the PPP exchange rate (e^{PPP}), then demands and supplies of Canadian and European goods will change until $e = e^{PPP}$. Thus, the theory of PPP predicts that the actual exchange rate will eventually equal the PPP exchange rate.

Recall from Equation 36-4 that P_C and P_E were defined as the prices of *identical baskets of goods* in Canada and Europe, respectively. Given that the goods are the same, the argument that the prices should (eventually) be equated across the two countries is sensible—if the prices are not equated across the two countries, then there would be an incentive to purchase in the cheaper country rather than in the more expensive country, and this would lead to changes in the exchange rate until Equation 36-4 *did* hold.

One problem, however, when we apply the theory of purchasing power parity to *national price indices,* such as the Consumer Price Index or the Implicit GDP Deflator, is that the two baskets of goods are typically *not* the same—for two reasons.

Different Countries Produce Different Goods.

Suppose we apply the theory of PPP to the Canada-Europe exchange rate and we use the GDP deflators from the two countries as the measures of prices. Recall from Chapter 20 that the GDP deflator is an index of prices *of the goods produced within the country.* But Canada and Europe clearly produce very different goods. The price of forest products will have a large weight in the Canadian GDP deflator, but less weight in the European GDP deflator; in contrast, the price of wine will have a much larger weight in the European GDP deflator than in the Canadian one.

The implication of these differences for the theory of PPP is important. As long as changes in the *relative* prices of goods occur, such as a change in the price of forest products relative to wine, then P_C (the Canadian GDP deflator) will change relative to P_E (the European GDP deflator) *even though the prices of individual goods might be equated across the two countries.* Thus, differences in the structure of the price indices between two countries mean that using a PPP exchange rate computed on the basis of Equation 36-5 will be misleading. In other words, in the presence of changing relative prices, there is no reason to expect the actual exchange rate to equal the PPP exchange rate as defined in Equation 36-5.

Nontraded Goods Are Important.   The previous discussion emphasized that the *baskets* of goods across two countries might differ even though the products in the baskets were the same. But even if Canada and Europe produced exactly the same range of goods, so that the various weights in the GDP deflators were the same, there is still a reason why the basket of goods in Canada differs from the basket of goods in Europe. Some of the goods produced in Canada are *nontraded goods,* such as haircuts and restaurant meals. Nontraded goods are also produced in Europe. But, since nontraded goods cannot be traded (by definition), there is nothing that will force their prices to be equal across the two countries. If haircuts are more expensive in Paris than in Toronto (as they are), we do not expect people to shift their consumption of haircuts away from Paris toward Toronto, and thus we should not expect the actual exchange rate to move to make Equation 36-4 hold.

The conclusion of this discussion is that we must be very careful in selecting the price indices we use when we apply the theory of purchasing power parity. We know that countries have different patterns of production and thus have different structures to their national price indices. Thus, in the presence of changes in relative prices of various products, the national price indices can change in ways that will not lead to changes in the exchange rate. Similarly, the presence of nontraded goods implies that some differences in prices across countries will not lead to changes in the location of demand and thus changes in the exchange rate.

Should Canada Have a Fixed Exchange Rate?

In recent years, some economists have suggested that Canada peg the value of its currency to the U.S. dollar. Advocates of a fixed Canadian exchange rate see this policy as a means of avoiding the significant fluctuations in the Canadian exchange rate that would otherwise occur—fluctuations such as the 15 percent appreciation that occurred between 1989 and 1991, and the 10 percent depreciation that occurred between 1997 and 1998. They argue that exchange-rate fluctuations generate uncertainty for importers and exporters and thus increase the costs associated with trade.

Others have gone further in suggesting that Canada actually abandon its currency altogether and simply adopt the U.S. dollar. They point to the European Union, which introduced the euro as its common currency in 1999. If a common currency is acceptable to most of Europe, why should Canada and the United States be any different? Note that if Canada and the United States were to share a common currency, the exchange rate between the two countries would, of course, be fixed.

These are contentious suggestions that have attracted a great deal of public attention in recent years. We examine this issue by comparing the main benefits of flexible and fixed exchange rates. Whereas flexible exchange rates dampen the effects on output and employment from shocks to a country's terms of trade, fixed exchange rates reduce the uncertainty faced by traders. The benefits and costs of having a common currency between two regions is examined in *Extensions in Theory 36-1*, which explains the theory of "optimal currency areas."

EXTENSIONS IN THEORY 36-1
Optimal Currency Areas

In 1961, Canadian economist Robert Mundell, now at Columbia University, developed the theory of "optimal currency areas." In 1999 he was awarded the Nobel Prize in economics, partly for this work. He examined the conditions under which it is optimal for two countries to have a common currency, and the conditions under which the countries would be better off maintaining separate currencies with a flexible exchange rate. Mundell's conclusions can be summarized as follows.

1. Other things equal, the more the two countries trade with one another, the larger are the benefits from having a common currency (and the lower are the benefits from having separate currencies with a flexible exchange rate).

2. Other things equal, the less correlated are the two countries' terms of trade, the smaller are the benefits from having a common currency (and the larger are the benefits from having separate currencies with a flexible exchange rate).

The Basic Theory

The accompanying diagram illustrates the situation that Mundell describes. Our example is that of Canada and the United States. The green arrows represent the trade of goods, services, and assets between the two countries. The red arrows represent the various shocks to each country's terms of trade. Mundell's central result is that, other things equal, the more important the green arrows are, the better it is to have a common currency. On the other hand, the "less similar" each country's red arrows are, the worse it is to have a com-

mon currency. By "less similar" we mean that the changes in one country's terms of trade are different, or occur at different times, than the changes in the other country's terms of trade.

To understand Mundell's arguments, we must understand how the green and red arrows relate to the costs and benefits of having a common currency (rather than separate currencies with a flexible exchange rate).

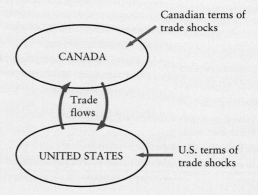

The main benefit of the two regions having a common currency is that importers and exporters in each country can save on the costs associated with having a flexible (and perhaps volatile) exchange rate. There are two types of costs. The first is the *uncertainty* that is generated by having a volatile exchange rate. The more uncertainty there is surrounding the price of foreign currency, the less likely are firms to enter contracts that involve foreign exchange. This reduc-

Flexible Exchange Rates as "Shock Absorbers"

See Chapter 36 of www.pearsoned.ca/lipsey for a debate on the appropriate exchange rate regime for Canada: Pierre Fortin, "What Can We Do About Exchange Rates that Move Too Much?" and Bill Robson, "Resisting the Lure of Fixed Exchange Rates," *World Economic Affairs*.

For most of the years following the Second World War, Canada has used a flexible exchange rate. Even when most other major countries chose to peg the value of their currencies to the U.S. dollar (and to gold) under the Bretton Woods system, Canada usually chose a flexible exchange rate (there were a few short periods in which Canada fixed its exchange rate). For all of its history Canada's economy has been dependent on the export of resource-based products, the prices of which are determined in world markets and are often highly variable from year to year. Changes in these prices constitute changes in Canada's terms of trade and, as we saw earlier in this chapter, changes in a country's terms of trade are an important reason why exchange rates are so variable.

tion in trade leads to a reduction in the gains from trade. The second cost is the *transaction cost* of converting one currency into another. If the two countries have separate currencies, then every time some good or service is traded between the two countries, someone (either the importer or the exporter) must spend the time and resources necessary to convert currencies. Given that such costs are incurred every time goods are traded, it follows that the greater is the volume of trade between the two regions, the greater are the benefits (that is, the costs avoided) from having a common currency.

The main benefit from each country's maintaining a separate currency with a flexible exchange rate is that the exchange rate can act as a "shock absorber," dampening the effects on the country's output and employment from shocks to its terms of trade. For example, consider what would happen if there were a reduction in the world price of copper. Copper is a major Canadian export but a U.S. import. When the price of copper falls due to a reduction in world copper demand, Canada's terms of trade deteriorate but the U.S. terms of trade improve. The fall in the price of copper leads to a contraction in the Canadian copper industry. If Canada shares a common currency with the United States, the result of the shock will simply be a reduction in output and employment in Canada's copper industry. The contraction in that sector will eventually reduce wages, and the economy will eventually return to potential output. But the adjustment may be long and painful.

In contrast, if Canada and the United States have separate currencies, then the reduction in the world price of copper will tend to depreciate the Canadian dollar relative to the U.S. dollar. The Canadian copper industry will still be in recession, for there has been a reduction in demand for its products, but the overall Canadian downturn will be dampened by the depreciation of the Canadian dollar. In other words, even though the copper industry is in recession, other sectors of the Canadian economy will actually *expand* as a result of the depreciation because their products are now more competitive in world markets. The overall result is that, with

a separate currency and flexible exchange rate, the deterioration in Canada's terms of trade leads to a less severe Canadian recession than if Canada shared a currency with the United States.

Mundell said that two countries constitute an *optimal currency area* if by adopting a common currency the two countries together save more in uncertainty and transactions costs than they incur by sacrificing the output-dampening effects of a flexible exchange rate.

What Is the Optimal Currency Area?

Some economists have recently advocated that Canada adopt the U.S. dollar as its currency. Do they believe that Canada and the United States constitute an optimal currency area? Probably not, but that is also not quite the right policy question. The provinces and territories of Canada already use a common currency even though they may not satisfy Mundell's condition for being an optimal currency area. Similarly, the U.S. states use a common currency and may not constitute an optimal currency area. Thus, the relevant policy question from Canada's perspective is whether Canada and the United States together form a *better* currency area than Canada by itself.

Some economists think this is probably true. They point to the massive and growing volume of trade between the two countries as the best reason for Canada and the United States to share a currency. Other economists stress the importance of exchange rates as shock absorbers. They point to the 1997-1998 decline in world commodity prices as an ideal example of a situation in which Canada benefited from having a flexible exchange rate. Canada's resource sector contracted sharply in response to this deterioration in Canada's terms of trade. Especially hard hit was British Columbia's forestry industry. But the depreciation of the Canadian dollar (by roughly 10 percent against the U.S. dollar) led to expansions in manufacturing industries in Ontario and Quebec that significantly reduced the overall effect of the terms of trade shock.

That the exchange rate adjusts in response to shocks is actually the main advantage of a flexible (rather than fixed) exchange rate. A flexible exchange rate acts as a "shock absorber", dampening the effects on the country's output and employment from shocks to its terms of trade. To understand how this happens, consider a simple example.

Suppose a reduction in world demand leads to a reduction in the world price of newsprint. Newsprint is a major Canadian export, and so when the world price of newsprint falls, Canada's terms of trade deteriorate. The fall in the price of newsprint leads to a leftward shift in the Canadian aggregate demand curve, as shown in part (i) of Figure 36-4. Canadian GDP declines, caused by the reduction in output in the newsprint industry. If Canada has a fixed exchange rate, that is pretty much the end of the story.

Canadian wages will eventually fall and output will eventually return to potential, but the recession may be slow and painful.

In contrast, if Canada has a flexible exchange rate, the deterioration in the terms of trade will lead to a reduction in the supply of foreign exchange and thus to a depreciation of the Canadian dollar. The aggregate demand curve will still shift to the left, reducing Canada's GDP. The newsprint industry will still be in recession, for there has been a reduction in demand for its products. But the overall Canadian downturn will be dampened by the depreciation of the Canadian dollar. Other sectors of the Canadian economy will actually *expand* as a result of the depreciation because their products are now more competitive in world markets. Thus, as shown in part (ii) of Figure 36-4, the leftward shift of the aggregate demand curve will not be as large as in the case of the fixed exchange rate. The overall result is that, with a flexible exchange rate, the deterioration in Canada's terms of trade leads to a less severe Canadian recession than if Canada had a fixed exchange rate.

One of the advantages of flexible exchange rates is that, in response to shocks to the terms of trade, the exchange rate can act as a shock absorber, dampening the effects of the shock on output and employment.

FIGURE 36-4   Flexible Exchange Rates as a Shock Absorber

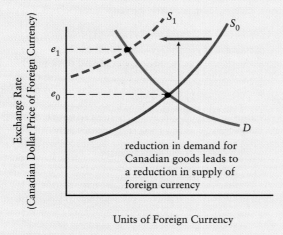

(i) Foreign-exchange market

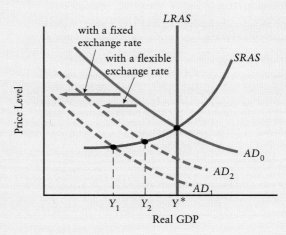

(ii) *AD* and *SRAS*

Flexible exchange rates adjust to terms of trade shocks and thus dampen the effect on output and employment. The economy begins with the exchange rate equal to e_0 in part (i) and GDP equal to Y^* in part (ii). A reduction in the world's demand for Canadian exports causes a reduction in the supply of foreign exchange, shifting S_0 to S_1 in part (i).

With a fixed exchange rate, the Bank of Canada maintains the exchange rate at e_0, satisfying the excess demand for foreign exchange by selling its foreign-currency reserves. The reduction in the demand for Canada's exports is a negative aggregate demand shock. AD_0 shifts to the left to AD_1 in part (ii), causing GDP to fall to Y_1. The recessionary gap eventually pushes wages down, the *SRAS* curve shifts to the right over time, and the economy moves along AD_1 to Y^*. The adjustment, however, may be protracted.

With a flexible exchange rate, the Bank of Canada allows the Canadian dollar to depreciate. The exchange rate rises to e_1 in part (i). The reduction in demand for Canadian exports still causes the *AD* curve to shift to the left in part (ii), but the shift is dampened by the depreciation of the dollar, which makes Canadian products more competitive in world markets. The *AD* curve shifts only to AD_2 and so GDP falls only to Y_2. There is a still a recession, but smaller than in the case with a fixed exchange rate.

The Asian crisis of 1997–1998 provides an excellent example of how Canada's flexible exchange rate dampened the effects of a negative terms of trade shock. When the Asian countries of Malaysia, Indonesia, Thailand, and South Korea experienced their large recessions in 1997 and 1998, their demand for many raw materials declined sharply. As they are major users of raw materials, the effect was felt on world markets. The average prices of raw materials fell by roughly 30 percent from the summer of 1997 to the end of 1998. Many of these raw materials, of course, are important exports for Canada, and so the decline in their world prices implied a terms of trade deterioration for Canada.

Especially hard hit was British Columbia's forestry sector, where output fell dramatically in many paper and lumber mills due to the lack of sales in Asia. As expected, there was also a significant depreciation of the Canadian dollar, just as described in Figure 36-4. But as the Canadian dollar depreciated, the Canadian manufacturing sector, concentrated mainly in Ontario and Quebec, was given a large boost. The 10 percent depreciation of the Canadian dollar meant that Canadian machinery, furniture, telecommunications equipment, and a whole range of other products were now more competitive in world markets. Thus, the boom in the central Canadian manufacturing sector offset to some extent the significant recession that was going on in British Columbia. If Canada had had a fixed exchange rate, the 10 percent depreciation would not have occurred. But the initial shock from the Asian crisis would still have taken place. The net result would have been lower output and higher unemployment than actually occurred.

For much analysis of the Asian Crisis, see Nouriel Roubini's website: www.stern.nyu.edu/~nroubini.

Note that having a fixed exchange rate does not prevent a country from being subjected to shocks. Many advocates of fixed exchange rates, however, seem to think that by fixing the value of a country's currency, the country is shielding itself from undesirable fluctuations. But shocks to a country's terms of trade will always occur. As long as there are changes in the demand and supply for various products around the world, there will also be changes in a country's terms of trade. What Figure 36-4 shows, however, is that by fixing the exchange rate and thus avoiding the fluctuations in the value of the currency, the effects of the shock merely show up as increased volatility in output and employment.

A country will always experience shocks in its terms of trade. A flexible exchange rate absorbs some of the shock, reducing the effect on output and employment. A fixed exchange rate simply redistributes the effect of the shock—the exchange rate is smoother but output and employment are more volatile.

Trade, Transactions Costs, and Uncertainty

Despite the benefits of international trade, there are costs involved in exporting and importing goods and services. The *transactions costs* of international trade involve the costs associated with converting one currency to another, as must be done either by the importer or the exporter of the product that is traded. For example, if you have an import-export business in Canada and want to import some bicycles from Japan, then you will probably have to purchase Japanese yen at a bank or foreign-exchange dealer and, with those yen, pay the Japanese seller for the bicycles. Even if the Japanese seller accepts Canadian dollars for the bicycles, and this often is the case, he will be required to convert those Canadian dollars into yen before he can use that money in Japan to pay his workers or pay for other costs of production.

See Chapter 36 of www.pearsoned.ca/lipsey for an interview with Milton Friedman on the desirability of flexible exchange rates: "Confirmed Convictions," *World Economic Affairs.*

The greater is the volume of trade between two countries, the higher are the aggregate transaction costs associated with international trade.

Note that such transactions costs exist even if trade takes place between two countries with fixed exchange rates. For example, if Canada pegged the value of the Canadian dollar to the U.S. dollar, any trade between the two countries would still require the costly conversion of one currency to the other. Thus, the existence of transactions costs cannot be used as an argument in favour of fixed exchange rates and against flexible exchange rates. As long as there are two currencies, the transactions costs must be borne by one party or the other. These transactions costs could only be avoided if the two countries shared a common currency. *Extensions in Theory 36-1* examines the theory of "optimal currency areas" in which these transactions costs play a central role.

Many economists believe, however, that the volatility of flexible exchange rates generates another type of cost for importers and exporters. Specifically, the unpredictability of the exchange rate leads to *uncertainty* in the profitability of any specific international transaction. Such uncertainty, given risk-averse firms, can be expected to lead to a smaller volume of international trade and thus to fewer benefits from such trade.

For example, suppose that a Canadian appliance manufacturer enters into a contract to purchase a specified amount of steel from a Japanese producer for a specified yen price in one year's time. In this case, the Japanese producer bears no *foreign-exchange risk* because the price is specified in yen. But the Canadian appliance manufacturer bears considerable risk. If the yen depreciates relative to the dollar over the coming year, fewer Canadian dollars will be required to pay for the steel. But if the yen appreciates relative to the dollar over the coming year, more Canadian dollars will be required to pay for the steel. The Canadian buyer therefore faces a risk in terms of the Canadian-dollar cost of the steel. If the firm is *risk averse*, meaning simply that it would be prepared to pay a cost to avoid the risk, then the presence of the risk may lead to fewer international transactions of this type. Perhaps to avoid the foreign-exchange risk, the Canadian buyer will decide instead to buy Canadian-made steel, even though it may be slightly more expensive or not quite the right type that is needed.

If the presence of foreign-exchange risk leads to less international trade, there will be a reduction in the gains from trade.

Many of the people who advocate Canada's move to a fixed exchange rate point to the avoidance of this foreign-exchange risk as the main benefit. They argue that if the Canadian dollar were pegged in value to the U.S. dollar, both importers and exporters would face less uncertainty on the most important part of their trade—that between Canada and the United States. With the greater certainty, they argue, would come greater trade flows and thus an increase in the overall gains from trade.

But many economists disagree. While accepting the basic argument regarding the risks created by flexible (and volatile) exchange rates, they note that importers and exporters already have the means to avoid this uncertainty. In particular, traders can participate in *forward markets* in which they can buy or sell foreign exchange *in the future* at prices specified today. For example, the Canadian appliance manufacturer could enter into a contract to purchase the required amount of yen in one year's time at a price of 100 yen per Canadian dollar. In this case, no matter what happened to the yen-dollar exchange rate in the intervening year, the uncertainty regarding the Canadian-dollar price of the steel would be entirely eliminated.

Summing Up

So, should Canada give up its flexible exchange rate and instead peg the value of the Canadian dollar to the U.S. dollar? Advocates of this policy emphasize the foreign-exchange risk faced by importers and exporters, and the gains from increased trade that would result from a fixed exchange rate. Opponents to the policy emphasize the shock-absorption benefits from a flexible exchange rate, and the greater volatility in output and employment that Canada would have if it were to fix its exchange rate.

This debate will surely go on for a while, partly because it is difficult to quantify the costs and benefits of a flexible exchange rate. Economists on both sides of the debate understand and accept the logic of the arguments from the other side. But researchers have so far been unable to determine how much of a shock is absorbed by a flexible exchange rate, and thus to estimate how much more volatile output and employment would be with a fixed exchange rate. Similarly, it is very difficult to estimate just how much more trade would take place if the foreign-exchange risk faced by traders was eliminated by means of a fixed exchange rate. Without convincing empirical evidence supporting the move to a fixed exchange rate, however, the status quo will probably remain. It is probably safe to assume that Canada will continue to have a flexible exchange rate, at least for the next several years.

S U M M A R Y

The Balance of Payments

- Actual transactions among the firms, households, and governments of various countries are reported in the balance-of-payments accounts. In these accounts, any transaction that represents a receipt for Canada (Canadians sell goods or assets to foreigners) is recorded as a credit item. Any transaction that represents a payment from Canada (Canadians purchase goods or assets from foreigners) is recorded as a debit item.
- If all transactions are recorded in the balance of payments, the sum of all credit items necessarily equals the sum of all debit items. Thus, the balance of payments must always balance.

- Major categories in the balance-of-payments accounts are the trade account, the capital-service account, the current account (which is equal to the trade account plus the capital-service account), the capital account, and the official financing account.
- When a country is said to have a "balance of payments deficit" (or surplus), what is usually meant is that the sum of current and capital accounts is a deficit (or surplus). That is, it excludes the transactions on the official financing account. If official financing is zero, a balance on current account must be matched by a balance on capital account of equal magnitude but opposite sign.

The Foreign-Exchange Market

- The exchange rate between the Canadian dollar and some foreign currency is defined to be the number of Canadian dollars required to purchase one unit of the foreign currency. A rise in the exchange rate is a depreciation of the Canadian dollar; a fall in the exchange rate is an appreciation of the Canadian dollar.
- The supply of foreign exchange (or the demand for Canadian dollars) arises from Canadian exports of goods and services, capital flows into Canada, and the desire of foreign banks, firms, and governments to use Canadian dollars as part of their reserves.

- The demand for foreign exchange (or the supply of Canadian dollars to purchase foreign currencies) arises from Canadian imports of goods and services, capital flows from Canada, and the desire of holders of Canadian dollars to decrease the size of their holdings.
- A depreciation of the Canadian dollar lowers the foreign price of Canadian exports and increases the amount of foreign exchange supplied (to purchase Canadian exports). Thus, the supply curve for foreign exchange is positively sloped when plotted against the exchange rate.

- A depreciation of the Canadian dollar raises the dollar price of imports from abroad and hence lowers the amount of foreign exchange demanded to purchase foreign goods. Thus, the demand curve for foreign exchange is negatively sloped when plotted against the exchange rate.

The Determination of Exchange Rates   ⓁⓄ④

- When the central bank does not intervene in the foreign exchange market, there is a flexible exchange rate. Under fixed exchange rates, the central bank intervenes in the foreign-exchange market to maintain the exchange rate at an announced value. To do this, the central bank must hold sufficient stocks of foreign-exchange reserves.
- Under a flexible, or floating, exchange rate, the exchange rate is determined by supply and demand for the currency.
- The Canadian dollar will appreciate in foreign-exchange markets if there is an increase in the supply of foreign exchange (an increase in demand for Canadian dollars) or if there is a reduction in demand for foreign exchange (a reduction in supply of Canadian dollars). The opposite changes will lead to a depreciation of the Canadian dollar.
- Changes in the exchange rate are caused by changes in such things as the rate of inflation in different countries, capital movements, structural conditions, and expectations about the future exchange rate.

Three Policy Issues   ⓁⓄ⑤⑥⑦

- The view that current account deficits are undesirable is usually based on the mercantilist notion that exports are "good" and imports are "bad." But the gains from trade have nothing to do with the balance of trade—they depend on the volume of trade.
- From national income accounting, the current account surplus is given by

$$CA = (S - I) + (T - G)$$

An increase in investment, a decrease in saving, and an increase in the government budget deficit can each be the cause of a rise in the current account deficit.

- With a flexible exchange rate, supply and demand in the foreign-exchange market determine the "correct" value of the exchange rate. But this "correct" value is constantly changing as market conditions vary.
- The theory of purchasing power parity (PPP) predicts that exchange rates will adjust so that the purchasing power of a given currency is the same in different countries. That is, the price of an identical basket of goods will be equated in different countries (when expressed in the same currency).

- If price indices from different countries are used as the basis for computing the PPP exchange rate, differences in the structure of price indices across countries, together with the presence of nontraded goods, can be responsible for persistent deviations of the actual exchange rate from this measure of the PPP exchange rate.
- An important benefit of a flexible exchange rate is that it acts as a shock absorber, dampening the effects on output and employment from shocks to a country's terms of trade.
- An important benefit of fixed exchange rates is that it reduces transactions costs and foreign-exchange risk faced by importers and exporters.

K E Y   C O N C E P T S

Balance-of-payments accounts
Current and capital accounts
Changes in official reserves
Foreign exchange and exchange rates
Appreciation and depreciation

Sources of the demand for and supply of foreign exchange
Fixed and flexible exchange rates
Mercantilist views on the balance of trade and volume of trade
Purchasing power parity

PPP exchange rate
PPP and nontraded goods
Exchange rate overshooting
Flexible exchange rates as shock absorbers
Foreign-exchange risk
Optimal currency areas

STUDY EXERCISES

1. The table below shows Deborah's financial details for 1999. Answer the following questions about her "balance of payments."

Deborah's Financial Details, 1999	
Income from babysitting	$2500
Income from newspaper route	$3500
Gift from grandparents	$1000
Interest from bank deposits	$ 150
Expenditure on coffee and pastry	$1000
Expenditure on tuition	$3500
Purchase of mutual funds	$1200
Bank balance at end of year	$3500
Increase in bank balance	$1450

   a. What is Deborah's "trade balance"? Explain.
   b. What is Deborah's overall current account balance? Explain.
   c. What is Deborah's capital account balance? Explain.
   d. There is one (and only one) piece of information shown above that is not needed to compute Deborah's balance of payments. What is it? Explain why it is not needed.

2. The diagram below shows the demand for foreign currency (the supply of Canadian dollars) and the supply of foreign currency (the demand for Canadian dollars). The equilibrium exchange rate is e^*. Assume that Canada has a flexible exchange rate.

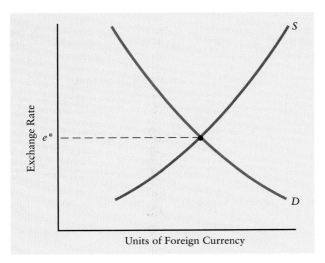

   a. Show in the diagram the effect of a general inflation in Canada (when there is no inflation in the rest of the world). Explain.
   b. Show what happens to the exchange rate if there is an increase in foreign demand for Canadian telecommunications equipment. Explain.
   c. Show the effect of an increase in Canadian investors' demand for Japanese government bonds. Explain.

3. The diagram below shows the demand for foreign currency (the supply of Canadian dollars) and the supply of foreign currency (the demand for Canadian dollars). The equilibrium exchange rate is e^*.

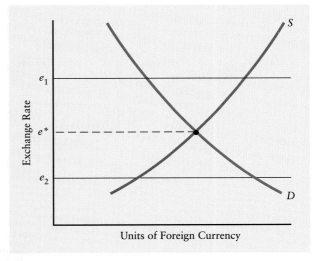

   a. Suppose the Bank of Canada decides to fix the exchange rate at e_1. What must the Bank do to accomplish its goal?
   b. In part **a**, do the current and capital accounts sum to zero? Explain.
   c. Now suppose the Bank of Canada decides to fix the exchange rate at e_2. What must the Bank do to accomplish this goal?
   d. With the exchange rate fixed at e_2, do the current and capital accounts sum to zero? Explain.

4. Suppose the Canadian economy is at potential output with a stable price level. There is then an upturn in the world demand for construction materials, especially lumber.

   a. Draw a diagram of the foreign-exchange market. Assuming that Canada has a flexible exchange rate, show the likely effect on the external value of the Canadian dollar.

b. Explain the Bank of Canada's participation in the foreign-exchange market if Canada has a fixed exchange rate.
c. Now draw an *AD/SRAS* diagram for the Canadian economy. What is the likely effect of the shock on Canadian GDP under the conditions in part **a**?
d. What would be the effect of the shock on Canadian GDP under the conditions of part **b**?
e. Explain how a flexible exchange rate acts as a shock absorber, insulating the economy from both positive and negative shocks.

5. Every few months, *The Economist* publishes its "Big Mac Index." Using the current exchange rates, it compares the U.S.-dollar price of Big Macs in several countries. It then concludes that countries in which the Big Mac is cheaper (in U.S. dollars) than in the United States have "undervalued" currencies. Similarly, countries with Big Macs more expensive than in the United States have "overvalued" currencies. The table below shows the domestic-currency prices of Big Macs in various countries. It also shows the exchange rate, expressed as the number of units of domestic currency needed to purchase one U.S. dollar.

Country	Domestic Currency Price	Current Exchange Rate	U.S. Dollar Price
Canada	$ 2.75 (Cdn.)	1.52	$ —
Australia	$ 3.50 (Aus.)	1.85	$ —
U.S.A.	$ 2.25	1.00	$ —
Japan	375 yen	125	$ —
France	3.6 euros	1.15	$ —
U.K.	1.50 pounds	0.80	$ —

a. For each country, use the exchange rate provided to convert the domestic-currency price to the U.S.-dollar price.
b. By the logic used in *The Economist*, which currencies are overvalued and which are undervalued relative to the U.S. dollar?
c. Are Big Macs traded goods? If not, does this present a problem for *The Economist*? Explain.
d. Which of the following goods do you think would be a better candidate for this exercise? Explain your choice.
   i) cement
   ii) diamonds
   iii) fresh fruit
   iv) computer RAM chips

6. A former Canadian Prime Minister once suggested that Canada should try to have balanced trade, industry by industry.

a. Do you think this makes sense? Explain.
b. How about the idea of balanced trade, country by country? Explain whether this makes sense.

DISCUSSION QUESTIONS

1. What is the probable effect of each of the following on the exchange rate of a country, other things being equal?

a. The quantity of oil imports is greatly decreased, but the value of imported oil is higher due to price increases.
b. The country's inflation rate falls well below that of its trading partners.
c. Rising labour costs of the country's manufacturers lead to a worsening ability to compete in world markets.
d. The government greatly expands its gifts of food and machinery to developing countries.

e. A major boom occurs with rising employment.
f. The central bank raises interest rates sharply.
g. More domestic oil is discovered and developed.

2. Canada's trade surplus with the United States (or the U.S. trade deficit with Canada) is the cause of considerable concern to some U.S. politicians. Many economists, however, argue that U.S. policy makers should not be concerned with reducing the U.S. trade deficit with Canada primarily because there is no reason to expect a balance between any two countries. Comment on the need for policies to address the U.S. trade deficit with Canada.

3. Outline the reasoning behind the following 1989 newspaper headline: "Loonie strengthens as Bank of Canada raises rates."

4. "Under a flexible exchange rate system, no country need suffer unemployment, for if its prices are low enough, there will be more than enough demand to keep its factories and farms fully occupied." The evidence suggests that flexible exchange rates have not generally eliminated unemployment. Can you explain why? Can changing exchange rates ever cure unemployment?

5. On November 27, 1995, a letter to *The Globe and Mail* said that "the economy of this once wonderful country is in the sewer and the politicians keep on tinkering, not knowing how to fix it." The letter proposed a 20 percent depreciation of the Canadian dollar, and argued that the immediate effects would be (among other things):

   - a dramatic rise in exports
   - a dramatic fall in imports
   - a large net inflow of new foreign investment

   What do you think of the proposal? What would the Bank of Canada have to do to achieve a 20 percent depreciation of the Canadian dollar? If such a depreciation were to take place, is it possible to have the effects claimed by the author of the letter? Explain.

6. Many commentators are perplexed when they observe a depreciation of the Canadian dollar but not a reduction in the Canadian current account deficit. Explain why there is not a precise relationship between the value of the dollar and the current account balance. Give one example of an event that would give rise to each of the following:

   a. appreciation of the Canadian dollar and a fall in Canada's current account surplus.
   b. depreciation of the Canadian dollar and a fall in Canada's current account surplus.

7. Every few months, *The Economist* publishes its "Big Mac Index." Using the current exchange rates, it compares the U.S.-dollar price of Big Macs in several countries. It then concludes that countries in which the Big Mac is cheaper (in U.S. dollars) than in the United States have "undervalued" currencies. Similarly, countries with Big Macs more expensive than in the United States have "overvalued" currencies.

   a. Explain how the logic of this approach is based on the "law of one price."
   b. Are Big Macs traded goods? If not, does this present a problem for *The Economist*? Explain.

MATHEMATICAL NOTES

1. Because one cannot divide by zero, the ratio $\Delta Y/\Delta X$ cannot be evaluated when $\Delta X = 0$. However, as ΔX *approaches* zero, the ratio $\Delta Y/\Delta X$ increases without limit:

$$\lim_{\Delta X \to 0} \frac{\Delta Y}{\Delta X} = \infty$$

Therefore, we say that the slope of a vertical line (when $\Delta X = 0$ for any ΔY) is equal to infinity.

2. Many variables affect the quantity demanded. Using functional notation, the argument of the next several pages of the text can be anticipated. Let Q^D represent the quantity of a commodity demanded and

$$T, \overline{Y}, N, \hat{Y}, p, p_j$$

represent, respectively, tastes, average household income, population, income distribution, the commodity's own price, and the price of the jth other commodity.

The demand function is

$$Q^D = D(T, \overline{Y}, N, \hat{Y}, p, p_j), \qquad j = 1, 2, \ldots, n$$

The demand schedule or curve is given by

$$Q^D = d(p) \,\Big|\, T, \overline{Y}, N, \hat{Y}, p_j$$

where the notation means that the variables to the right of the vertical line are held constant.

This function is correctly described as the demand function with respect to price, all other variables being held constant. This function, often written concisely as $q^d = d(p)$, shifts in response to changes in other variables. Consider average income: if, as is usually hypothesized, $\partial Q^D/\partial \overline{Y} > 0$, then increases in average income shift $q^d = d(p)$ rightward and decreases in average income shift $q^d = d(p)$ leftward. Changes in other variables likewise shift this function in the direction implied by the relationship of that variable to the quantity demanded.

3. Quantity demanded is a simple and straightforward but frequently misunderstood concept in everyday use, but it has a clear mathematical meaning. It refers to the dependent variable in the demand function from note 2:

$$Q^D = D(T, \overline{Y}, N, \hat{Y}, p, p_j)$$

It takes on a specific value whenever a specific value is assigned to each of the independent variables. The value of Q^D changes whenever the value of any independent variable is changed. Q^D could change, for example, as a result of a change in any one price, in average income, in the distribution of income, in tastes, or in population. It could also change as a result of the net effect of changes in all of the independent variables occurring at once.

Some textbooks reserve the term *change in quantity demanded* for a movement along a demand curve, that is, a change in Q^D as a result *only* of a change in p. They then use other words for a change in Q^D caused by a change in the other variables in the demand function. This usage is potentially confusing because it gives the single variable Q^D more than one name.

Our usage, which corresponds to that in more advanced treatments, avoids this confusion. We call Q^D *quantity demanded* and refer to any change in Q^D as a *change in quantity demanded*. In this usage it is correct to say that a movement along a demand curve is a change in quantity demanded, but it is incorrect to say that a change in quantity demanded can occur *only because of* a movement along a demand curve (because Q^D can change for other reasons, for example, a *ceteris paribus* change in average household income).

4. Similar to the way we treated quantity demanded in note 2, let Q^S represent the quantity of a commodity supplied and

$$C, X, p, w_i$$

represent, respectively, producers' goals, technology, the product's price, and the price of the ith input.

The supply function is

$$Q^S = S(C, X, p, w_i), \qquad i = 1, 2, \ldots, m$$

The supply schedule or curve is given by

$$Q^S = s(p) \,\Big|\, C, X, w_i$$

This is the supply function with respect to price, all other variables being held constant. This function, often written concisely as $q^s = s(p)$, shifts in response to changes in other variables.

5. Equilibrium occurs where $Q^D = Q^S$. For *specified values of all other variables,* this requires that

$$d(p) = s(p) \qquad [5.1]$$

Equation 5.1 defines an equilibrium value of *p;* hence, although *p* is an *independent* or *exogenous* variable in each of the supply and demand functions, it is an *endogenous* variable in the economic model that imposes the equilibrium condition expressed in Equation 5.1. Price is endogenous because it is assumed to adjust to bring about equality between quantity demanded and quantity supplied. Equilibrium quantity, also an endogenous variable, is determined by substituting the equilibrium price into either $d(p)$ or $s(p)$.

Graphically, Equation 5.1 is satisfied only at the point where the demand and supply curves intersect. Thus, supply and demand curves are said to determine the equilibrium values of the endogenous variables, price and quantity. A shift in any of the independent variables held constant in the *d* and *s* functions will shift the demand or supply curves and lead to different equilibrium values for price and quantity.

6. The definition in the text uses finite changes and is called *arc elasticity.* The parallel definition using derivatives is

$$\eta = \frac{dq}{dp} \cdot \frac{p}{q}$$

and is called *point elasticity.* Further discussion appears in the Appendix to Chapter 4.

7. The propositions in the text are proved as follows. Letting *TE* stand for total expenditure, we can write

$$TE = p \cdot q$$

It follows that the change in total expenditure is

$$dTE = q \cdot dp + p \cdot dq \qquad [7.1]$$

Multiplying and dividing both terms on the right-hand side of Equation 7.1 by $p \cdot q$ yields

$$dTE = \left[\frac{dp}{p} + \frac{dq}{q} \right] \cdot (p \cdot q)$$

Because *dp* and *dq* are opposite in sign as we move along the demand curve, *dTE* will have the same sign as the term in brackets on the right-hand side that dominates—that is, on which percentage change is largest.

A second way of arranging Equation 7.1 is to divide both sides by *dp* to get

$$\frac{dTE}{dp} = q + p \cdot \frac{dq}{dp} \qquad [7.2]$$

From the definition of point elasticity in note 6, however,

$$q \cdot \eta = p \cdot \frac{dq}{dp} \qquad [7.3]$$

which we can substitute into Equation 7.1 to obtain

$$\frac{dTE}{dp} = q + q \cdot \eta = q \cdot (1 + \eta) \qquad [7.4]$$

Because η is a negative number, the sign of the right-hand side of Equation 7.4 is negative if the absolute value of η exceeds unity (elastic demand) and positive if it is less than unity (inelastic demand).

Total expenditure is maximized when dTE/dp is equal to zero. As can be seen from Equation 7.4, this occurs when elasticity is equal to -1.

8. The axis reversal arose in the following way. Alfred Marshall (1842–1924) theorized in terms of "demand price" and "supply price," these being the prices that would lead to a given quantity being demanded or supplied. Thus,

$$p^d = d(q) \qquad [8.1]$$
$$p^s = s(q) \qquad [8.2]$$

and the condition of equilibrium is

$$d(q) = s(q)$$

When graphing the behavioural relationships expressed in Equations 8.1 and 8.2, Marshall naturally put the independent variable, *q*, on the horizontal axis.

Leon Walras (1834–1910), whose formulation of the working of a competitive market has become the accepted one, focused on quantity demanded and quantity supplied *at a given price.* Thus,

$$q^d = d(p)$$

$$q^s = s(p)$$

and the condition of equilibrium is

$$d(p) = s(p)$$

Walras did not use graphical representation. Had he done so, he would surely have placed p (his independent variable) on the horizontal axis.

Marshall, among his other influences on later generations of economists, was the great popularizer of graphical analysis in economics. Today, we use his graphs, even for Walras's analysis. The axis reversal is thus one of those historical accidents that seem odd to people who did not live through the "perfectly natural" sequence of steps that produced it.

9. The distinction made between an incremental change and a marginal change is the distinction for the function $Y = Y(X)$ between $\Delta Y/\Delta X$ and the derivative dY/dX. The latter is the limit of the former as ΔX approaches zero. We shall meet this distinction repeatedly—in this chapter in reference to marginal and incremental *utility* and in later chapters with respect to such concepts as marginal and incremental *product, cost,* and *revenue*. Where Y is a function of more than one variable—for example, $Y = f(X,Z)$—the marginal relationship between Y and X is the partial derivative $\partial Y/\partial X$ rather than the total derivative, dY/dX.

10. The hypothesis of diminishing marginal utility requires that we can measure utility of consumption by a function

$$U = U(X_1, X_2, \ldots, X_n)$$

where $X_1, \ldots, X_n$ are quantities of the n goods consumed by a household. It really embodies two utility hypotheses: first,

$$\partial U/\partial X_i > 0$$

which says that the consumer can get more utility by increasing consumption of the commodity; second,

$$\partial^2 U/\partial X_i^2 < 0$$

which says that the utility of *additional* consumption of some good declines as the amount of that good consumed increases.

11. Because the slope of the indifference curve is negative, it is the absolute value of the slope that de-

clines as one moves downward to the right along the curve. The algebraic value, of course, increases. The phrase *diminishing marginal rate of substitution* thus refers to the absolute, not the algebraic, value of the slope.

12. The relationship between the slope of the budget line and relative prices can be seen as follows. In the two-good example, a change in expenditure (ΔE) is given by the equation

$$\Delta E = p_C \cdot \Delta C + p_F \cdot \Delta F \qquad [12.1]$$

Expenditure is constant for all combinations of F and C that lie on the same budget line. Thus, along such a line we have $\Delta E = 0$. This implies

$$p_C \cdot \Delta C + p_F \cdot \Delta F = 0 \qquad [12.2]$$

and thus

$$-\Delta C/\Delta F = p_F/p_C \qquad [12.3]$$

The ratio $-\Delta C/\Delta F$ is the slope of the budget line. It is negative because, with a fixed budget, one must consume less C in order to consume more F. In other words, Equation 12.3 says that the negative of the slope of the budget line is the ratio of the absolute prices (i.e., the relative price). Although prices do not show directly in Figure 6A-3, they are implicit in the budget line: Its slope depends solely on the relative price, while its position, given a fixed money income, depends on the absolute prices of the two goods.

13. *Marginal product,* as defined in the text, is really *incremental* product. More advanced treatments distinguish between this notion and marginal product as the limit of the ratio as ΔL approaches zero. Marginal product thus measures the rate at which total product is changing as one factor is varied and is the partial derivative of the total product with respect to the variable factor. In symbols,

$$MP = \frac{\partial TP}{\partial L}$$

14. We have referred specifically both to diminishing *marginal* product and to diminishing *average* product. In most cases, eventually diminishing marginal product implies eventually diminishing average product. This is, however, not necessary, as the accompanying figure shows.

In this case, marginal product diminishes after v units of the variable factor are employed. Because marginal product falls toward, but never quite reaches, a value of m, average product rises continually toward, but never quite reaches, the same value.

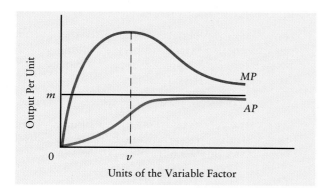

Units of the Variable Factor

15. Let q be the quantity of output and L the quantity of the variable factor. In the short run,

$$TP = q = f(L) \qquad [15.1]$$

We now define

$$AP = \frac{q}{L} = \frac{f(L)}{L} \qquad [15.2]$$

$$MP = \frac{dq}{dL} \qquad [15.3]$$

We are concerned with the relationship between these two. Where average product is rising, at a maximum, or falling is determined by its derivative with respect to L:

$$\frac{d(q/L)}{dL} = \frac{L \cdot (dq/dL) - q}{L^2} \qquad [15.4]$$

This may be rewritten

$$\frac{1}{L} \cdot \left[\frac{dq}{dL} - \frac{q}{L} \right] = \frac{1}{L} \cdot (MP - AP) \qquad [15.5]$$

Clearly, when MP is greater than AP, the expression in Equation 15.5 is positive and thus AP is rising. When MP is less than AP, AP is falling. When they are equal, AP is neither rising nor falling.

16. The text defines *incremental cost*. Strictly, marginal cost is the rate of change of total cost with respect to output, q. Thus,

$$MC = \frac{dTC}{dq}$$

From the definitions, $TC = TFC + TVC$. Fixed costs are not a function of output. Thus, we may write $TC = Z + f(q)$, where $f(q)$ is total variable costs and Z is a constant. From this we see that $MC = df(q)/dq$. MC is thus independent of the size of the fixed costs.

17. This point is easily seen if a little algebra is used:

$$AVC = \frac{TVC}{q}$$

but note that $TVC = L \cdot w$ and $q = AP \cdot L$, where L is the quantity of the variable factor used and w is its cost per unit. Therefore,

$$AVC = \frac{L \cdot w}{AP \cdot L} = \frac{w}{AP}$$

Because w is a constant, it follows that AVC and AP vary inversely with each other, and when AP is at its maximum value, AVC must be at its minimum value.

18. A little elementary calculus will prove the point:

$$MC = \frac{dTC}{dq} = \frac{dTVC}{dq} = \frac{d(L \cdot w)}{dq}$$

If w does not vary with output,

$$MC = \frac{dL}{dq} \cdot w$$

However, referring to note 15 (Equation 15.3), we see that

$$\frac{dL}{dq} = \frac{1}{MP}$$

Thus,

$$MC = \frac{w}{MP}$$

Because w is fixed, MC varies negatively with MP. When MP is at a maximum, MC is at a minimum.

19. Strictly speaking, the marginal rate of substitution refers to the slope of the tangent to the isoquant at a particular point, whereas the calculations in Table 8A-1 refer to the average rate of substitution between two distinct points on the isoquant. Assume a production function

$$Q = Q(K,L) \qquad [19.1]$$

Isoquants are given by the function

$$K = I(L,\overline{Q}) \qquad [19.2]$$

derived from Equation 19.1 by expressing K as an explicit function of L and Q. A single isoquant relates to a particular level of output, Q. Define Q_K and Q_L as an alternative, more compact notation for $\partial Q/\partial K$ and $\partial Q/\partial L$, the marginal products of capital and labour. Also, let Q_{KK} and Q_{LL} stand for $\partial^2 Q/\partial K^2$ and $\partial^2 Q/\partial L^2$, respectively. To obtain the slope of the isoquant, totally differentiate Equation 19.1 to obtain

$$dQ = Q_K \cdot dK + Q_L \cdot dL$$

Then, because we are moving along a single isoquant, set $dQ = 0$ to obtain

$$\frac{dK}{dL} = -\frac{Q_L}{Q_K} = MRS$$

Diminishing marginal productivity implies $Q_{LL} < 0$ and $Q_{KK} < 0$, and hence, as we move down the isoquant of Figure 8A-1, Q_K is rising and Q_L is falling, so the absolute value of MRS is diminishing. This is called the *hypothesis of a diminishing marginal rate of substitution*.

20. Formally, the problem is to maximize

$$Q = Q(K,L)$$

subject to the constraint

$$p_K \cdot K + p_L \cdot L = C$$

To do this, form the Lagrangean,

$$\mathcal{L} = Q(K, L) - \lambda(p_K \cdot K + p_L \cdot L - C)$$

The first-order conditions for this maximization problem are

$$Q_K = \lambda \cdot p_K \qquad [20.1]$$

$$Q_L = \lambda \cdot p_L \qquad [20.2]$$

$$p_K \cdot K + p_L \cdot L = C \qquad [20.3]$$

Dividing Equation 20.1 by Equation 20.2 yields

$$\frac{Q_K}{Q_L} = \frac{p_K}{p_L}$$

That is, the ratio of the marginal products, which is -1 times the MRS, is equal to the ratio of the factor prices, which is -1 times the slope of the isocost line.

21. Marginal revenue is mathematically the derivative of total revenue with respect to output, dTR/dq. Incremental revenue is $\Delta TR/\Delta q$. However, the term *marginal revenue* is used loosely to refer to both concepts.

22. For notes 22 through 24, it is helpful first to define some terms. Let

$$\pi_n = TR_n - TC_n$$

where π_n is the profit when n units are sold.

If the firm is maximizing its profits by producing n units, it is necessary that the profits at output q_n be at least as large as the profits at output zero. If the firm is maximizing its profits at output n, then

$$\pi_n \geq \pi_0 \qquad [22.1]$$

The condition says that profits from producing must be greater than profits from not producing. Condition 22.1 can be rewritten as

$$\begin{aligned} TR_n - TVC_n - TFC_n \\ \geq TR_0 - TVC_0 - TFC_0 \end{aligned} \qquad [22.2]$$

However, note that by definition

$$TR_0 = 0 \qquad [22.3]$$

$$TVC_0 = 0 \qquad [22.4]$$

$$TFC_n = TFC_0 = Z \qquad [22.5]$$

where Z is a constant. By substituting Equations 22.3, 22.4, and 22.5 into Condition 22.2, we get

$$TR_n - TVC_n \geq 0$$

from which we obtain

$$TR_n \geq TVC_n$$

This proves Rule 1.

On a per-unit basis, it becomes

$$\frac{TR_n}{q_n} \geq \frac{TVC_n}{q_n} \qquad [22.6]$$

where q_n is the number of units produced.

Because $TR_n = q_n \cdot p_n$, where p_n is the price when n units are sold, Condition 22.6 may be rewritten as

$$p_n \geq AVC_n$$

23. Using elementary calculus, we may prove Rule 2.

$$\pi_n = TR_n - TC_n$$

each of which is a function of output q. To maximize π, it is necessary that

$$\frac{d\pi}{dq} = 0 \qquad [23.1]$$

and that

$$\frac{d^2\pi}{dq^2} < 0 \qquad [23.2]$$

From the definitions,

$$\frac{d\pi}{dq} = \frac{dTR}{dq} - \frac{dTC}{dq} = MR - MC \quad [23.3]$$

From Equations 23.1 and 23.3, a necessary condition for attaining maximum π is $MR - MC = 0$, or $MR = MC$, as is required by Rule 2.

24. To prove that for a negatively sloped demand curve, marginal revenue is less than price, let $p = p(q)$. Then

$$TR = p \cdot q = p(q) \cdot q$$

$$MR = \frac{dTR}{dq} = q \cdot \frac{dp}{dq} + p$$

For a negatively sloped demand curve, dp/dq is negative, and thus MR is less than price for positive values of q.

25. The equation for a downward-sloping straight-line demand curve with price on the vertical axis is

$$p = a - b \cdot q$$

where $-b$ is the slope of the demand curve. Total revenue is price times quantity:

$$TR = p \cdot q = a \cdot q - b \cdot q^2$$

Marginal revenue is

$$MR = \frac{dTR}{dq} = a - 2 \cdot b \cdot q$$

Thus, the MR curve and the demand curve are both straight lines, and the (absolute value of the) slope of the MR curve ($2b$) is twice that of the demand curve (b).

26. The marginal revenue produced by the factor involves two elements: first, the additional output that an extra unit of the factor makes possible and, second, the change in price of the product that the extra output causes. Let Q be output, R revenue, and L the number of units of labour hired. The contribution to revenue of additional labour is $\partial R / \partial L$. This, in turn, depends on the contribution of the extra labour to output $\partial Q / \partial L$ (the marginal product of the factor) and $\partial R / \partial Q$ (the firm's marginal revenue from the extra output). Thus,

$$\frac{\partial R}{\partial L} = \frac{\partial Q}{\partial L} \cdot \frac{\partial R}{\partial Q}$$

We define the left-hand side as marginal revenue product, MRP. Thus,

$$MRP = MP \cdot MR$$

27. The proposition that the marginal labour cost is above the average labour cost when the average is rising is essentially the same proposition proved in note 15. Nevertheless, let us do it again, using elementary calculus.

The quantity of labour supplied depends on the wage rate: $L^s = f(w)$. Total labour cost along the supply curve is $w \cdot L^s$. The average cost of labour is $(w \cdot L^s) / L^s = w$. The marginal cost of labour is

$$\frac{d(w \cdot L^s)}{dL^s} = w + L^s \cdot \frac{dw}{dL^s}$$

Rewrite this as

$$MC = AC + L \cdot \frac{dw}{dL^s}$$

As long as the supply curve slopes upward, $dw/dL^s > 0$; therefore, $MC > AC$.

28. In general, for any growth rate per unit of time, g, and starting value, P_0, the price level at time t will be $P_0(1 + g)^t$. This is the formula for *compound growth* at rate g per unit of time. For small values of g, $(1 + g)^t$ will be very close to $(1 + tg)$. But as g gets larger, so does the difference. For example, if prices are growing at 2 percent per month, the annual growth will be $(1.02)^{12} = 1.268$, yielding a growth rate of 26.8 percent per year. This is considerably more than 24 percent, which is just the monthly rate times 12. Generally, annual rates of growth are calculated by compounding rates of growth that are measured over shorter or longer periods than one year.

29. In the text, we define *MPC* as an incremental ratio. For mathematical treatment, it is sometimes convenient to define all marginal concepts as derivatives: $MPC = dC/dY_D$, $MPS = dS/dY_D$, and so on.

30. The basic relationship is

$$Y_D = C + S$$

Dividing through by Y_D yields

$$\frac{Y_D}{Y_D} = \frac{C}{Y_D} + \frac{S}{Y_D}$$

and thus

$$1 = APC + APS$$

Next, take the first difference of the basic relationship to get

$$\Delta Y_D = \Delta C + \Delta S$$

Dividing through by ΔY_D gives

$$\frac{\Delta Y_D}{\Delta Y_D} = \frac{\Delta C}{\Delta Y_D} + \frac{\Delta S}{\Delta Y_D}$$

and thus

$$1 = MPC + MPS$$

31. The total expenditure over all rounds is the sum of an infinite series. If we let A stand for autonomous expenditure and z for the marginal propensity to spend, the change in autonomous expenditure is ΔA in the first round, $z \cdot \Delta A$ in the second, $z^2 \cdot \Delta A$ in the third, and so on. This can be written as

$$\Delta A \cdot (1 + z + z^2 + \ldots + z^n)$$

If z is less than 1, the series in parentheses converges to $1/(1 - z)$ as n approaches infinity. The total change in expenditure is thus $\Delta A/(1 - z)$. In the example in the box, $z = 0.80$; therefore, the change in total expenditure is five times ΔA.

32. This is easily proved. The banking system wants sufficient deposits (D) to establish the target ratio (v) of deposits to reserves (R). This gives $R/D = v$. Any change in D of size ΔD has to be accompanied by a change in R of ΔR of sufficient size to restore v. Thus, $\Delta R/\Delta D = v$, so $\Delta D = \Delta R/v$ and $\Delta D/\Delta R = 1/v$. This can be shown also in terms of the deposits created by the sequence in Table 26-7.

Let v be the reserve ratio and $e = 1 - v$ be the excess reserves per dollar of new deposits. If X dollars are initially deposited in the system, the successive rounds of new deposits will be X, eX, e^2X, $e^3X,\ldots$. The series

$$X + eX + e^2X + e^3X + \ldots$$
$$= X \cdot [1 + e + e^2 + e^3 + \ldots]$$

has a limit of $X \cdot \dfrac{1}{1 - e}$

$$= X \cdot \frac{1}{1 - (1 - v)} = \frac{X}{v}$$

This is the total new deposits created by an injection of \$$X$ of new reserves into the banking system. For example, when $v = 0.20$, an injection of \$100 into the system will lead to an overall increase in deposits of \$500.

33. Suppose that the public wishes to hold a fraction, c, of deposits in cash, C. Now suppose that X dollars are injected into the system. Ultimately, this money will be held either as reserves by the banking system or as cash by the public. Thus, we have

$$\Delta C + \Delta R = X$$

From the banking system's reserve behaviour, we have $\Delta R = v \cdot \Delta D$, and from the public's cash behaviour, we have $\Delta C = c \cdot \Delta D$. Substituting into the above equation, we get the result that

$$\Delta D = \frac{X}{v + c}$$

From this we can also relate the change in reserves and the change in cash holdings to the initial injection:

$$\Delta R = \frac{v}{v + c} \cdot X$$

$$\Delta C = \frac{c}{v + c} \cdot X$$

For example, when $v = 0.20$ and $c = 0.05$, an injection of \$100 will lead to an increase in reserves of \$80, an increase in cash in the hands of the public of \$20, and an increase in deposits of \$400.

34. Let $L(Y,r)$ give the real demand for money measured in purchasing power units. Let M be the

supply of money measured in nominal units and P the price level, so that M/P is the real supply of money. Now the equilibrium condition requiring equality between the demand for money and the supply of money can be expressed in real terms as

$$L(Y, r) = \frac{M}{P} \qquad [36.1]$$

or in nominal terms by multiplying through by P,

$$P \cdot L(Y, r) = M \qquad [36.2]$$

In Equation 36.1, a rise in P disturbs equilibrium by lowering M/P, and in Equation 36.2, it disturbs equilibrium by raising $P \cdot L(Y, r)$.

35. This is based on what is called the "rule of 72". Any sum growing at the rate of X percent per year will double in approximately $72/X$ years. For two sums growing at the rates of X percent and Y percent per year, the *difference* between the two sums will double in approximately $72/(X - Y)$ years.

36. The time taken to break even is a function of the *difference* in growth rates, not their *levels*. Thus, if 4 percent and 5 percent or 5 percent and 6 percent had been used in the example, it still would have taken the same number of years. To see this quickly, recognize that we are interested in the ratio of two growth paths:

$$\frac{e^{r_1 t}}{e^{r_2 t}} = e^{(r_1 - r_2)t}$$

37. A simple example of a production function is GDP $= z(LK)^{1/2}$. This equation says that to find the amount of GDP produced, multiply the amount of labour by the amount of capital, take the square root, and multiply the result by the constant z. This production function has positive but diminishing marginal returns to either factor. This can be seen by evaluating the first and second partial derivatives and showing the first derivatives to be positive and the second derivatives to be negative.

For example,

$$\frac{\partial \text{GDP}}{\partial K} = \frac{z \cdot L^{1/2}}{2 \cdot K^{1/2}} > 0$$

and

$$\frac{\partial^2 \text{GDP}}{\partial K^2} = -\frac{z \cdot L^{1/2}}{2 \cdot K^{3/2}} < 0$$

38. The production function GDP $= z(LK)^{1/2}$ displays contant returns to scale. To see this, multiply both L and K by the same constant, θ, and see that this multiplies the whole value of GDP by θ:

$$z(\theta L \cdot \theta K)^{1/2} = z(\theta^2 \cdot LK)^{1/2} = \theta z(LK)^{1/2} = \theta \cdot \text{GDP}$$

Time Line of Great Economists

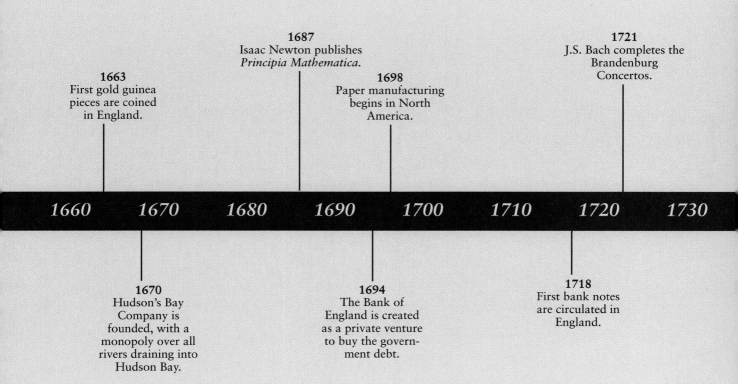

1663
First gold guinea
pieces are coined
in England.

1687
Isaac Newton publishes
Principia Mathematica.

1698
Paper manufacturing
begins in North
America.

1721
J.S. Bach completes the
Brandenburg
Concertos.

1660   1670   1680   1690   1700   1710   1720   1730

1670
Hudson's Bay
Company is
founded, with a
monopoly over all
rivers draining into
Hudson Bay.

1694
The Bank of
England is created
as a private venture
to buy the govern-
ment debt.

1718
First bank notes
are circulated in
England.

ADAM SMITH (1723–1790)

Adam Smith was born in 1723 in the small Scottish town of Kirkcaldy. He is perhaps the single most influential figure in the development of modern economics, and even those who have never studied economics know of his most famous work, *The Wealth of Nations*, and of the terms *laissez faire* and the *invisible hand,* both attributable to Smith. He was able to describe the workings of the capitalist market economy, the division of labor in production, the role of money, free trade, and the nature of economic growth. Even today, the breadth of his scholarship is considered astounding.

Smith was raised by his mother, as his father had died before his birth. His intellectual promise was discovered early, and at age 14 Smith was sent to study at Glasgow and then at Oxford. He then returned to an appointment as professor of moral philosophy at University of Glasgow, where he became one of the leading philosophers of his day. He lectured on natural theology, ethics, jurisprudence, and political economy to students who traveled from as far away as Russia to hear his lectures.

In 1759, Smith published *The Theory of Moral Sentiments*, in which he attempted to identify the origins of moral judgment. In this early work, Smith writes of the motivation of self-interest and of the morality that keeps it in check. After its publication, Smith left his post at the University of Glasgow to embark on a European tour as the tutor to a young aristocrat, the Duke of Buccleuch, with whom he traveled for two years. In exchange for this assignment Smith was provided with a salary for the remainder of his life. He returned to the small town of his birth and spent the next 10 years alone, writing his most famous work.

An Inquiry into the Nature and Causes of the Wealth of Nations was published in 1776. His contributions in this book (generally known as *The Wealth of Nations*) were revolutionary, and the text became the foundation of much of modern economics. It continues to be reprinted today. Smith rejected the notion that a country's supply of gold and silver was the measure of its wealth—rather, it was the real incomes of the people that determined national wealth. Growth in the real incomes of the country's citizens—that is, economic growth—would result from specialization in production, the division of labor, and the use of money to facilitate trade. Smith provided a framework for analyzing the questions of income growth, value, and distribution.

Smith's work marked the beginning of what is called the Classical period in economic thought, which continued for the next 75 years. This school of thought was centered on the principles of natural liberty (laissez faire) and the importance of economic growth as a means of bettering the conditions of human existence.

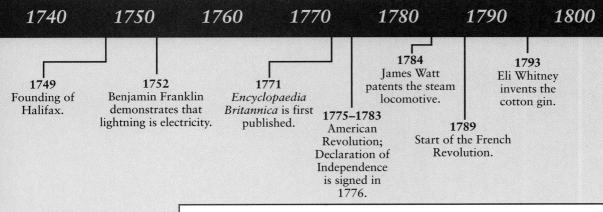

1740 1750 1760 1770 1780 1790 1800

1749 Founding of Halifax.

1752 Benjamin Franklin demonstrates that lightning is electricity.

1771 *Encyclopaedia Britannica* is first published.

1775–1783 American Revolution; Declaration of Independence is signed in 1776.

1784 James Watt patents the steam locomotive.

1789 Start of the French Revolution.

1793 Eli Whitney invents the cotton gin.

THOMAS MALTHUS (1766–1834)

Thomas Malthus was born into a reasonably well-to-do English family. He was educated at Cambridge and from 1805 until his death he held the first British professorship of political economy in the East India Company's college at Haileybury. In 1798 he published *An Essay on the Principle of Population as It Affects the Future Improvement of Society*, which was revised many times in subsequent years until finally he published *A Summary View of the Principle of Population* in 1830.

It is these essays on population for which Malthus is best known. His first proposition was that population, when unchecked, would increase in a geometric progression such that the population would double every 25 years. His second proposition was that the means of subsistence (i.e. the food supply) cannot possibly increase faster than in arithmetic progression (increasing by a given number of units every year). The result would be population growth eventually outstripping food production, and thus abject poverty and suffering for the majority of people in every society.

Malthus's population theory had tremendous intellectual influence at the time and became an integral part of the Classical theory of income distribution. However, it is no longer taken as a good description of current or past trends.

DAVID RICARDO *(1772–1823)*

David Ricardo was born in London to parents who had immigrated from the Netherlands. Ricardo's father was very successful in money markets, and Ricardo himself had earned enough money on the stock exchange that he was very wealthy before he was 30. He had little formal education, but after reading Adam Smith's *The Wealth of Nations* in 1799, he chose to divide his time between studying and writing about political economy and increasing his own personal wealth.

Ricardo's place in the history of economics was assured by his achievement in constructing an abstract model of how capitalism worked. He built an analytic "system" using deductive reasoning that characterizes economic theorizing to the present day. The three critical principles in Ricardo's system were (1) the theory of rent, (2) Thomas Malthus's population principle, and (3) the wages-fund doctrine. Ricardo published *The Principles of Political Economy and Taxation* in 1817, which dominated Classical economics for the following half-century.

Ricardo also contributed the concept of comparative advantage to the study of international trade. Ricardo's theories regarding the gains from trade had some influence on the repeal of the British Corn Laws in 1846—tariffs on the importation of grains into Great Britain—and the subsequent transformation of that country during the nineteenth century from a country of high tarrifs to one of completely free trade.

1814
British forces burn Washington, D.C., in the War of 1812.

1831
The first horse-drawn buses appear in New York.

1837
Victoria becomes Queen of England (until 1901). Rebellions in Upper and Lower Canada.

1800   **1810**   **1820**   **1830**

1805
Admiral Horatio Nelson's victory (and death) at Trafalgar.

1815
Napoleon defeated at Waterloo and exiled to St. Helena; Corn Laws passed in Britain.

1822
First textile mills are built in Lowell, Massachusetts.

JOHN STUART MILL *(1806–1873)*

John Stuart Mill, born in London, was the son of James Mill, a prominent British historian, economist, and philosopher. By age 12 he was acquainted with the major economics works of the day, and at 13 he was correcting the proofs of his father's book, *Elements of Political Economy*. J. S. Mill spent most of his life working at the East India Company—his extraordinarily prolific writing career was conducted entirely as an aside. In 1848 he published his *Principles of Political Economy*, which updated the principles found in Adam Smith's *The Wealth of Nations* and which remained the basic textbook for students of economics until the end of the nineteenth century. In *Principles*, Mill made an important contribution to the economics discipline by distinguishing between the economics of production and of distribution. He pointed out that economic laws had nothing to do with the distribution of wealth, which was a societal matter, but had everything to do with production.

Previous to Mill's *Principles* was his *System of Logic* (1843), which was the century's most influential text on logic and the theory of knowledge. His essays on ethics, contemporary culture, and freedom of speech, such as *Utilitarianism* and *On Liberty*, are still widely studied today.

KARL MARX *(1818–1883)*

Karl Marx was born in Trier, Germany (then part of Prussia), and studied law, history, and philosophy at the universities of Bonn, Berlin, and Jena. Marx traveled between Prussia, Paris, and Brussels, working at various jobs until finally settling in London in 1849, where he lived the remainder of his life. Most of his time was spent in the mainly unpaid pursuits of writing and studying economics in the library of the British Museum. Marx's contributions to economics are intricately bound to his views of history and society. *The Communist Manifesto* was published with Friedrich Engels in 1848, his *Critique of Political Economy* in 1859, and in 1867 the first volume of *Das Kapital*. (The remaining volumes, edited by Engels, were published after Marx's death.)

For Marx, capitalism was a stage in an evolutionary process from a primitive agricultural economy toward an inevitable elimination of private property and the class structure. Marx's "labor theory of value," whereby the quantity of labor used in the manufacture of a product determined its value, held the central place in his economic thought. He believed that the worker provided "surplus value" to the capitalist. The capitalist would then use the profit arising from this surplus value to reinvest in plant and machinery. Through time, more would be spent for plant and machinery than for wages, which would lead to lower profits (since profits arose only from the surplus value from labor) and a resulting squeeze in the real income of workers. Marx believed that in the capitalists' effort to maintain profits in this unstable system, there would emerge a "reserve army of the unemployed." The resulting class conflict would become increasingly acute until revolution by the workers would overthrow capitalism.

1846
Britain repeals
the Corn Laws.

1859
Charles
Darwin
publishes
*On the Origin
of Species.*

1867
British North America Act
establishes the Dominion of
Canada. Alfred Nobel
invents dynamite.

1840   **1850**   **1860**   **1870**

1844
Electric
telegraph
opens between
Washington
and Baltimore.

1861–1865
The U.S. Civil War;
Abraham Lincoln is
assassinated in
1865.

1869
Opening of the
Suez Canal.

1840
Act of Union
unites Upper
and Lower
Canada.

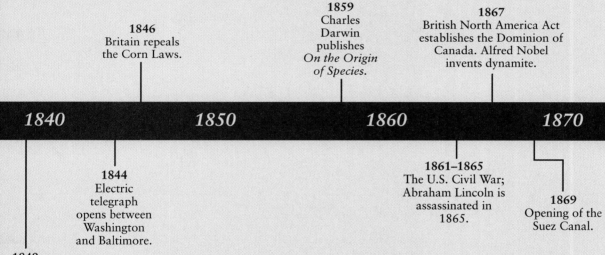

LEON WALRAS *(1834–1910)*

Leon Walras was born in France, the son of an economist. After being trained inauspiciously in engineering and performing poorly in mathematics, Walras spent some time pursuing other endeavors, such as novel writing and working for the railway. Eventually he promised his father he would study economics, and by 1870 he was given a professorship in economics in the Faculty of Law at the University of Lausanne in Switzerland. Once there, Walras began the feverish activity that eventually led to his important contributions to economic theory.

In the 1870s, Walras was one of three economists to put forward the marginal utility theory of value (simultaneously with William Stanley Jevons of England and Carl Menger of Austria). Further, he constructed a mathematical model of general equilibrium using a system of simultaneous equations that he used to argue that equilibrium prices and quantities are uniquely determined. Central to general equilibrium analysis is the notion that the prices and quantities of all commodities are determined simultaneously because the whole system is interdependent. Walras's most important work was *Elements of Pure Economics,* published in 1874. In addition to all of Walras's other accomplishments in economics (and despite his early poor performance in mathematics!), we today regard him as the founder of mathematical economics.

Leon Walras and Alfred Marshall are regarded by many economists to be the two most important economic theorists who ever lived. Much of the framework of economic theory studied today is either Walrasian or Marshallian in character.

CARL MENGER *(1840–1921)*

Carl Menger was born in Galicia (then part of Austria), and he came from a family of Austrian civil servants and army officers. After studying law in Prague and Vienna, he turned to economics and in 1871 published *Grundsatze der Volkswirtschaftslehre* (translated as *Principles of Economics*), for which he became famous. He held a professorship at the University of Vienna until 1903. Menger was the founder of a school of thought known as the "Austrian School," which effectively displaced the German historical method on the continent and which survives today as an alternative to mainstream Neoclassical economics.

Menger was one of three economists in the 1870s who independently put forward a theory of value based on marginal utility. Prior to what economists now call the "marginal revolution," value was thought to be derived solely from the inputs of labor and capital. Menger developed the marginal utility theory of value, in which the value of any good is determined by individuals' subjective evaluations of that good. According to Menger, a good has some value if it has the ability to satisfy some human want or desire, and *utility* is the capacity of the good to do so. Menger went on to develop the idea that the individual will maximize total utility at the point where the last unit of each good consumed provides equal utility—that is, where marginal utilities are equal.

Menger's emphasis on the marginal utility theory of value led him to focus on consumption rather than production as the determinant of price. Menger focused only on the demand for goods and largely ignored the supply. It would remain for Alfred Marshall and Leon Walras to combine demand and supply for a more complete picture of price determination.

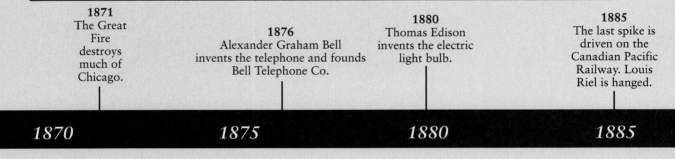

1871
The Great Fire destroys much of Chicago.

1876
Alexander Graham Bell invents the telephone and founds Bell Telephone Co.

1880
Thomas Edison invents the electric light bulb.

1885
The last spike is driven on the Canadian Pacific Railway. Louis Riel is hanged.

1870   *1875*   *1880*   *1885*

ALFRED MARSHALL *(1842–1924)*

Alfred Marshall was born in Clapham, England, the son of a bank cashier, and was descended from a long line of clerics. Marshall's father, despite intense effort, was unable to steer the young Marshall into the church. Instead, Marshall followed his passion for mathematics at Cambridge and chose economics as a field of study after reading J. S. Mill's *Principles of Political Economy*. His career was then spent mainly at Cambridge, where he taught economics to John Maynard Keynes, Arthur Pigou, Joan Robinson, and countless other British theorists in the "Cambridge tradition." His *Principles of Economics*, published in 1890, replaced Mill's *Principles* as the dominant economics textbook of English-speaking universities.

Marshall institutionalized modern marginal analysis, the basic concepts of supply and demand, and perhaps most importantly the notion of economic equilibrium resulting from the interaction of supply and demand. He also pioneered partial equilibrium analysis—examining the forces of supply and demand in a particular market provided that all other influences can be excluded, *ceteris paribus*.

Although many of the ideas had been put forward by previous writers, Marshall was able to synthesize the previous analyses of utility and cost and present a thorough and complete statement of the laws of demand and supply. Marshall refined and developed microeconomic theory to such a degree that much of what he wrote would be familiar to students of this textbook today.

It is also interesting to note that although Alfred Marshall and Leon Walras were simultaneously expanding the frontiers of economic theory, there was almost no communication between the two men. Though Marshall chose partial equilibrium analysis as the appropriate method for dealing with selected markets in a complex world, he did acknowledge the correctness of Walras's general equilibrium system. Walras, on the other hand, was adamant (and sometimes rude) in his opposition to the methods that Marshall was putting forward. History has shown that both the partial and the general equilibrium approaches to economic analysis are required for understanding the functioning of the economy.

THORSTEIN VEBLEN *(1857–1929)*

Thorstein Veblen was born on a farm in Wisconsin to Norwegian parents. He received his Ph.D. in philosophy from Yale University, after which he returned to his father's farm because he was unable to secure an academic position. For seven years he remained there, reading voraciously on economics and other social sciences. Eventually, he took academic positions at the University of Chicago, Stanford University, the University of Missouri, and the New School for Social Research (in New York). Veblen was the founder of "institutional economics," the only uniquely North American school of economic thought.

In 1899, Veblen published *The Theory of the Leisure Class,* in which he sought to apply Charles Darwin's evolutionism to the study of modern economic life. He examined problems in the social institutions of the day, and savagely criticized Classical and Neoclassical economic analysis. Although Veblen failed to shift the path of mainstream economic analysis, he did contribute the idea of the importance of long-run institutional studies as a useful complement to short-run price theory analysis. He also reminded the profession that economics is a *social* science, and not merely a branch of mathematics.

Veblen remains most famous today for his idea of "conspicuous consumption." He observed that some commodities were consumed not for their intrinsic qualities but because they carried snob appeal. He suggested that the more expensive such a commodity became, the greater might be its ability to confer status on its purchaser.

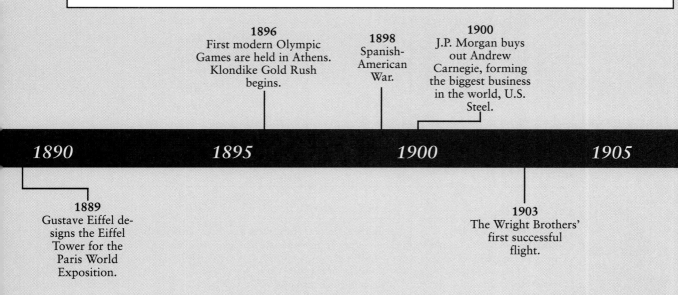

1896
First modern Olympic Games are held in Athens. Klondike Gold Rush begins.

1898
Spanish-American War.

1900
J.P. Morgan buys out Andrew Carnegie, forming the biggest business in the world, U.S. Steel.

1890   *1895*   *1900*   *1905*

1889
Gustave Eiffel designs the Eiffel Tower for the Paris World Exposition.

1903
The Wright Brothers' first successful flight.

VILFREDO PARETO *(1848–1923)*

Vilfredo Pareto was an Italian, born in Paris, and was trained to be an engineer. Though he actually practiced as an engineer, he would later succeed Leon Walras to the Chair of Economics in the Faculty of Law at the University of Lausanne.

Pareto built upon the system of general equilibrium that Walras had developed. In his *Cours d'économie politique* (1897) and his *Manuel d'économie politique* (1906) Pareto set forth the foundations of modern welfare economics. He showed that theories of consumer behavior and exchange could be constructed on assumptions of ordinal utility, rather than cardinal utility, eliminating the need to compare one person's utility with another's. Using the indifference curve analysis developed by F. Y. Edgeworth, Pareto was able to demonstrate that total welfare could be increased by an exchange if one person could be made better off without anyone else becoming worse off. Pareto applied this analysis to consumption and exchange, as well as to production. Pareto's contributions in this area are remembered in economists' references to *Pareto optimality* and *Pareto efficiency.*

JOSEPH SCHUMPETER (1883–1950)

Joseph Schumpeter was born in Triesch, Moravia (now in the Czech Republic). He was a university professor and later a Minister of Finance in Austria. In 1932, he emigrated to the United States to avoid the rise to power of Adolf Hitler. He spent his remaining years at Harvard University.

Schumpeter, a pioneering theorist of innovation, emphasized the role of the entrepreneur in economic development. The existence of the entrepreneur meant continuous innovation and waves of adaptation to changing technology. He is best known for his theory of "creative destruction," where the prospect of monopoly profits provides owners the incentive to finance inventions and innovations. One monopoly can replace another with superior technology or a superior product, thereby circumventing the entry barriers of a monopolized industry. He criticized mainstream economists for emphasizing the static (allocative) efficiency of perfect competition—a market structure that would, if it could ever be achieved, retard technological change and economic growth.

Schumpeter's best known works are *The Theory of Economic Development* (1911), *Business Cycles* (1939), and *Capitalism, Socialism and Democracy* (1943).

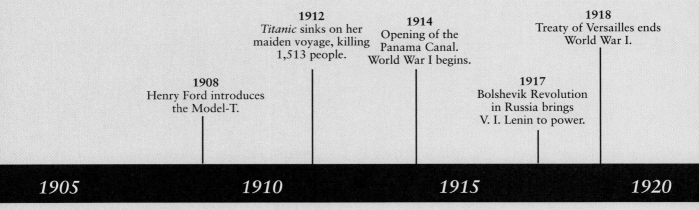

1912
Titanic sinks on her maiden voyage, killing 1,513 people.

1914
Opening of the Panama Canal. World War I begins.

1918
Treaty of Versailles ends World War I.

1908
Henry Ford introduces the Model-T.

1917
Bolshevik Revolution in Russia brings V. I. Lenin to power.

1905   *1910*   *1915*   *1920*

JOHN MAYNARD KEYNES (1883–1946)

John Maynard Keynes was born in Cambridge, England. His parents were both intellectuals, and his father, John Neville Keynes, was a famous logician and writer on economic methodology. The young Keynes was educated at Eton and then at Kings College, Cambridge, where he was a student of Alfred Marshall and Arthur Pigou. His career included appointments to the Treasury in Britain during both World Wars I and II, a leading role in the establishment of the International Monetary Fund (through discussions at Bretton Woods, New Hampshire, in 1944), and editorship of the *Economic Journal* from 1911 to 1945, all in addition to his academic position at Kings College.

Keynes published extensively during his life but his most influential work, *The General Theory of Employment, Interest, and Money,* appeared in 1936. This book was published in the midst of the Great Depression when the output of goods and services had fallen drastically, unemployment was intolerably high, and it had become clear to many that the market would not self-adjust to achieve potential output within an acceptable period of time. Fluctuations in economic activity were familiar at this point, but the failure of the economy to recover rapidly from this depression was unprecedented. Neoclassical economists held that during a downturn both wages and the interest rate would fall low enough to induce investment and employment and cause an expansion. They believed that the persistent unemployment during the 1930s was caused by inflexible wages and they recommended that workers be convinced to accept wage cuts.

Keynes believed that this policy, though perhaps correct for a single industry, was not correct for the entire economy. Widespread wage cuts would reduce the consumption portion of aggregate demand, which would offset any increase in employment. Keynes argued that unemployment could be cured only by manipulating aggregate demand, whereby increased demand (through government expenditure) would increase the price level, reduce real wages, and thereby stimulate employment.

Keynes's views found acceptance after the publication of his *General Theory* and had a profound effect on government policy around the world, particularly in the 1940s, 1950s, and 1960s. As we know from this textbook, Keynes's name is attached to much of macroeconomics, from much of the basic theory to the Keynesian short-run aggregate supply curve and the Keynesian consumption function. His contributions to economics go well beyond what can be mentioned in a few paragraphs—for, in effect, he laid the foundations for modern macroeconomics.

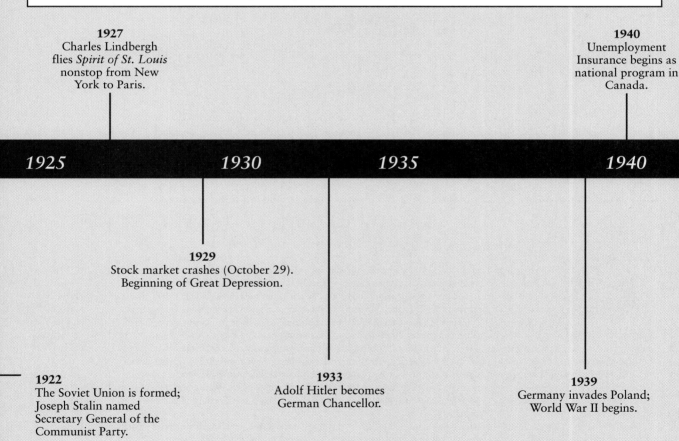

EDWARD CHAMBERLIN (1899–1967)

Edward Chamberlin was born in La Conner, Washington, and received his Ph.D. from Harvard University in 1927. He became a full professor at Harvard in 1937 and stayed there until his retirement in 1966. He published *The Theory of Monopolistic Competition* in 1933.

Before Chamberlin's book (which appeared more or less simultaneously with Joan Robinson's *The Economics of Imperfect Competition*), the models of perfect competition and monopoly had been fairly well worked out. Though economists were aware of a middle ground between these two market structures and some analysis of duopoly (two sellers) had been presented, it was Chamberlin and Robinson who closely examined this problem of imperfect markets.

Chamberlin's main contribution was explaining the importance of product differentiation for firms in market structures between perfect competition and monopoly. Chamberlin saw that though there may be a large number of firms in the market (the competitive element), each firm created for itself a unique product or advantage that gave it some control over price (the monopoly element). Specifically, he identified items such as copyrights, trademarks, brand names, and location as monopoly elements behind a product. Though Alfred Marshall regarded price as the only variable in question, Chamberlin saw both price and the product itself as variables under control of the firm in monopolistically competitive markets.

1927
Charles Lindbergh flies *Spirit of St. Louis* nonstop from New York to Paris.

1940
Unemployment Insurance begins as national program in Canada.

1925 **1930** **1935** **1940**

1929
Stock market crashes (October 29). Beginning of Great Depression.

1922
The Soviet Union is formed; Joseph Stalin named Secretary General of the Communist Party.

1933
Adolf Hitler becomes German Chancellor.

1939
Germany invades Poland; World War II begins.

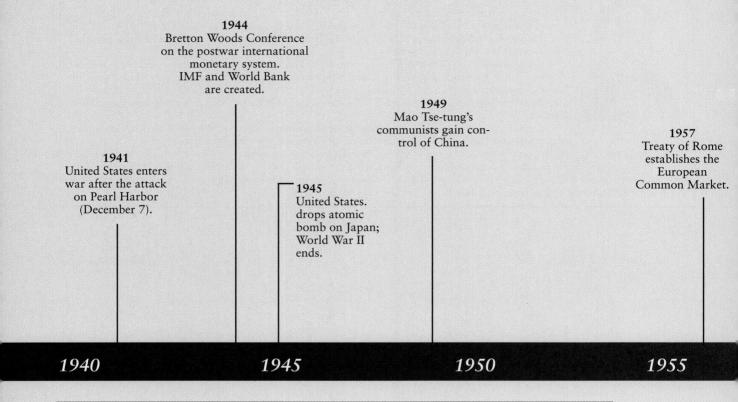

1944
Bretton Woods Conference
on the postwar international
monetary system.
IMF and World Bank
are created.

1949
Mao Tse-tung's
communists gain con-
trol of China.

1957
Treaty of Rome
establishes the
European
Common Market.

1941
United States enters
war after the attack
on Pearl Harbor
(December 7).

1945
United States.
drops atomic
bomb on Japan;
World War II
ends.

1940   *1945*   *1950*   *1955*

FRIEDRICH AUGUST VON HAYEK *(1899–1992)*

Friedrich von Hayek was born in Vienna and studied at the University of Vienna, where he was trained in the Austrian tradition of economics (a school of thought originating with Carl Menger). He held academic positions at the London School of Economics and the University of Chicago. He returned to Europe in 1962 to the University of Freiburg in what was then West Germany and the University of Salzburg in Austria. He was awarded the Nobel Prize in Economics in 1974.

Hayek contributed new ideas and theories in many different areas of economics, but he is perhaps best known for his general conception of economics as a "coordination problem." His observation of market economies suggested that the relative prices determined in free markets provided the signals that allowed the actions of all decision makers to mesh—even though there was no formal planning taking place to coordinate these actions. He emphasized this "spontaneous order" at work in the economy as the subject matter for economics. The role of knowledge and information in the market process became central to Hayek, an idea that has grown in importance to the economics profession over the years.

Hayek's theory of business cycles provided an example of the breakdown of this coordination. A monetary disturbance (e.g., an increase in the money supply) would distort the signals (relative prices) by artificially raising the return to certain types of economic activity. When the disturbance disappeared, the boom caused by these distorted signals would be followed by a slump. Although Hayek's business-cycle theory was eclipsed by the Keynesian revolution, his emphasis on economics as a coordination problem has had a major influence on contemporary economic thought.

Hayek was also prominent in advocating the virtues of free markets as contributing to human freedom in the broad sense as well as to economic efficiency in the narrow sense. His *The Road to Serfdom* (1944) sounded an alarm about the political and economic implications of the then-growing belief in the virtues of central planning. His *Constitution of Liberty* (1960) is a much deeper philosophical analysis of the forces, economic and otherwise, that contribute to the liberty of the individual.

1959
Fidel Castro
overthrows
Fulgencio Batista
in Cuba.

INDEX

The page on which a key term is defined is printed in boldface.